FLORIDA FORECLOSURE LAW

FLORIDA FORECLOSURE LAW

Michael Starks
Heidi Bassett
2020

Copyright © 2020 Fastcase. All Rights Reserved.

No part of this publication may be reproduced or transmitted in any form or by any means, electronic or mechanical, including photocopy, recording, or utilized by any information storage or retrieval system, without written permission from the publisher. For information about permissions or to request permissions online, visit us at www.fastcase.com, or a written request may be e-mailed to our permissions department at support@fastcase.com.

Printed in the United States of America

1 2 3 4 5 6 7 8 9 0

ISBN 978-1-949884-34-0

Summary of Contents

Table of Contents	vii
About This Book	xxi
Acknowledgments	xxiii
About the Authors	xxv

Chapter 1	THE LIFE OF A MORTGAGE FORECLOSURE IN FLORIDA	1
Chapter 2	DEFAULT AND ACCELERATION	11
Chapter 3	STATUTES OF LIMITATION AND REPOSE	27
Chapter 4	STANDING TO FORECLOSE	51
Chapter 5	TITLE CONSIDERATIONS IN MORTGAGE FORECLOSURE	63
Chapter 6	FORECLOSURE COMPLAINTS	77
Chapter 7	RESPONSES TO FORECLOSURE COMPLAINTS	103
Chapter 8	STATUTORY CLAIMS AND DEFENSES	115
Chapter 9	LITIGATING WITH ASSOCIATIONS IN THE FORECLOSURE CONTEXT	125
Chapter 10	LITIGATING WITH OTHER INTERESTS IN THE FORECLOSURE CONTEXT	161
Chapter 11	DISCOVERY	173
Chapter 12	MOTIONS FOR SUMMARY JUDGMENT IN FORECLOSURE CASES	191
Chapter 13	FORECLOSURE TRIALS AND EVIDENCE	219
Chapter 14	POST-JUDGMENT MOTION PRACTICE	233
Chapter 15	SANCTIONS	265
Chapter 16	ATTORNEY'S FEES IN FORECLOSURE ACTIONS	273
Chapter 17	BANKRUPTCY	287

Chapter 18 APPEALS **299**

Chapter 19 DEFICIENCY JUDGMENTS **311**

Appendix A—Forms and Samples 317
Table of Cases 411
Index 475

Table of Contents

About This Book xxi
Acknowledgments xxiii
About the Authors xxv

Chapter 1 THE LIFE OF A MORTGAGE FORECLOSURE IN FLORIDA 1

1-1	Introduction	1
	1-1:1 Elements of Foreclosure	1
	1-1:2 Title Reports/Discovery of Junior Liens	2
1-2	Initiation of a Foreclosure Action	3
1-3	Service of Process	3
	1-3:1 Methods of Service	3
	1-3:2 Motions to Quash Service of Process	4
1-4	Defaults	5
	1-4:1 Clerk Defaults	5
	1-4:2 Judicial Defaults	5
	1-4:3 Default Judgments	5
	1-4:4 Vacating Default	6
	1-4:4.1 Excusable Neglect	6
	1-4:4.2 Meritorious Defenses	6
	1-4:4.3 Due Diligence	7
1-5	Motions/Pleading Practice	7
1-6	Discovery	7
1-7	Summary Judgment	7
1-8	Trial	8
1-9	Final Judgment	8
1-10	Sale	8
	1-10:1 Scheduling of Foreclosure Sale	8
	1-10:2 Publication of Scheduled Sale	9
	1-10:3 Redemption and Reinstatement	9
	1-10:4 Auction and Bidding	10
	1-10:5 Objections to Sale	10
1-11	Title and Possession	10

TABLE OF CONTENTS

Chapter 2		**DEFAULT AND ACCELERATION**	**11**
2-1		Default	11
	2-1:1	Defined by Loan Documents	11
	2-1:2	Monetary Defaults	12
	2-1:3	Non-Monetary Defaults	13
		2-1:3.1 Non-Monetary Default by Act or Omission	13
		2-1:3.2 Non-Monetary Default Due to Existence of a Condition	14
	2-1:4	Grace Period	14
2-2		Notice of Default and Opportunity to Cure	15
	2-2:1	Notice as a Matter of Contract	15
	2-2:2	Notice as a Condition Precedent	15
	2-2:3	Notice in Standard Residential Mortgage	17
		2-2:3.1 Examples of Compliant Notices of Default	18
		2-2:3.2 Examples of Non-Compliant Notices of Default	19
	2-2:4	Opportunity to Cure as a Matter of Contract	19
	2-2:5	Opportunity to Cure in Standard Residential Mortgage	19
	2-2:6	"Face-to-Face Interview" Requirement in FHA Mortgage	20
2-3		Acceleration	21
	2-3:1	Contractual in Nature	21
	2-3:2	Automatic Versus Optional	21
	2-3:3	Effect of Pre-Acceleration Payments	22
	2-3:4	Standard Residential Mortgage	22
	2-3:5	Effect of Post-Acceleration Foreclosure, Dismissal and New Foreclosure	23
		2-3:5.1 Res Judicata	23
		2-3:5.2 Two-Dismissal Rule	24
		2-3:5.3 Statute of Limitations	25
Chapter 3		**STATUTES OF LIMITATION AND REPOSE**	**27**
3-1		Limitations Versus Repose	27
	3-1:1	Statute of Limitations in Brief	27
	3-1:2	Statute of Repose in Brief	28
	3-1:3	Comparison Table	29
3-2		Statute of Limitations	29
	3-2:1	Accrual	29
		3-2:1.1 The Default Theory of Accrual	30
		3-2:1.1a Effect of Conditions Precedent on Accrual	32
		3-2:1.1b Successive Accruals	33

		3-2:1.1c	Continuing State of Default—"All Subsequent Payments"	34
	3-2:1.2		The Acceleration Theory of Accrual	34
	3-2:1.3		Selected Accrual Examples	36
		3-2:1.3a	Where No Contractual Payment Date and No Maturity Date	36
		3-2:1.3b	Where No Contractual Payment Date But Maturity Date Specified	37
		3-2:1.3c	Where Accrual Is Triggered by Lender's Demand	37
		3-2:1.3d	Where Mortgage Debt Was Previously Discharged in Bankruptcy	37
	3-2:2		Successive Foreclosures	37
		3-2:2.1	*Bartram v. U.S. Bank, N.A.*	38
	3-2:3		Effect of Time Bar on Debt	41
		3-2:3.1	Effect on Past Due Installment Payments	41
		3-2:3.2	Effect on Foreclosure of Standard Residential Mortgage	41
		3-2:3.3	Effect When No Separate Obligation to Pay Full Debt	42
	3-2:4		Relation Back Doctrine	42
	3-2:5		Tolling	43
		3-2:5.1	Statutory Tolling	43
		3-2:5.2	Equitable Tolling	43
		3-2:5.3	Equitable Estoppel	44
	3-2:6		Counterclaim in Recoupment	44
	3-2:7		Deficiency Actions	44
3-3			Statute of Repose	45
	3-3:1		Terminates the Mortgage Lien	45
	3-3:2		Repose Time Periods	45
		3-3:2.1	Five Years After Maturity	45
		3-3:2.2	Twenty Years After Date of Mortgage	46
		3-3:2.3	Extension Agreements	47
		3-3:2.4	Incongruence Between Repose and Limitations	47
			3-3:2.4a Savings Clause for Mortgages With No Ascertainable Maturity	48
			3-3:2.4b Obligations Paid by Mortgagee	48
		3-3:2.5	No Tolling	48
		3-3:2.6	No Statute of Repose for Railroads, Public Utilities, or Construction Liens	49
3-4			Laches	49

Chapter 4	**STANDING TO FORECLOSE**	**51**
4-1	Overview of Standing to Foreclose	51
4-2	Surrender of the Original Note	52
4-3	Allonges to Promissory Notes	52
4-4	Proving Standing Through an Indorsement	54
4-5	Prima Facie Evidence of Standing	56
4-6	Constructive Possession of the Note	57
4-7	Standing as a Non-Holder in Possession	58
4-8	Standing to Enforce a Lost Note	60
4-9	Standing Where the Plaintiff Has Been Substituted	61
4-10	Standing to Foreclose a Line of Credit	62
Chapter 5	**TITLE CONSIDERATIONS IN MORTGAGE FORECLOSURE**	**63**
5-1	Overview	63
5-2	Typical Title Transfers in Foreclosure Litigation	63
	5-2:1 Certificate of Title Following a Foreclosure Sale	63
	5-2:1.1 Void Versus Voidable Certificates of Title	64
	5-2:1.2 Deeds in Lieu of Foreclosure	65
	5-2:1.3 Merger of Lien and Title	65
	5-2:2 Short-Sales and Short-Payoffs	66
5-3	Jurisdiction and Necessary Parties	66
5-4	Priority of Interests and Florida's Recording Act	67
	5-4:1 Recording Errors and Notice	68
	5-4:2 Equitable Subrogation	68
	5-4:2.1 Prejudice to the Prior Lienholder	69
5-5	The Lis Pendens	70
5-6	Final Judgment and Merger	71
5-7	Risks for Purchasers at Foreclosure Sales	72
5-8	Reforeclosure	74
5-9	Reformation	75
Chapter 6	**FORECLOSURE COMPLAINTS**	**77**
6-1	Introduction	77
	6-1:1 The Commencement of a Foreclosure Action	77
	6-1:2 Review of Title	77
	6-1:3 The Appropriate Venue and Forum for the Action	78
	6-1:4 The Filing and Recording of a Lis Pendens	79

TABLE OF CONTENTS

6-2		The Form of the Complaint	80
	6-2:1	Caption of the Complaint	80
	6-2:2	Verification of the Complaint	80
	6-2:3	Certification of Possession of the Promissory Note	81
	6-2:4	Attachments to the Complaint	82
	6-2:5	Minimizing the Filing of Sensitive Information in Exhibits	83
	6-2:6	Electronic Filing Required	84
6-3		The Parties	84
	6-3:1	The Plaintiff	84
	6-3:2	The Defendants	85
	6-3:3	The Borrowers	86
	6-3:4	Junior Lienholders	86
	6-3:5	Owners of the Property	87
	6-3:6	Tenants by the Entirety and Other Spousal Interests in the Property	87
	6-3:7	Lessees in Possession	88
	6-3:8	Condominiums and Homeowners' Associations	88
	6-3:9	Municipal, State, and Federal Lienholders	89
6-4		The Causes of Action and the Allegations	89
	6-4:1	A Claim for Mortgage Foreclosure	90
	6-4:2	The Agreement Between the Parties	90
	6-4:3	The Plaintiff's Standing	90
	6-4:4	The Plaintiff's Capacity to Sue	93
	6-4:5	The Superiority of the Plaintiff's Interest to Those of Other Defendants	93
	6-4:6	The Satisfaction of Conditions Precedent	93
	6-4:7	The Borrower's Default	94
	6-4:8	The Amount Due to the Plaintiff Resulting from the Borrower's Default	95
	6-4:9	Attorney's Fees	96
6-5		Additional Causes of Action	96
	6-5:1	A Claim Against a Guarantor	96
	6-5:2	Reestablishment: When the Note Has Been Lost	96
	6-5:3	Reformation: When the Mortgage or Deed Contains a Mistake	97
	6-5:4	Equitable Subrogation and Equitable Liens	98
	6-5:5	Seeking a Show Cause Order Under Section 702.10	99
	6-5:6	Injunctive Relief and Assignments of Rent Riders: When the Property Is Occupied by a Tenant	100
	6-5:7	Plea for a Deficiency Judgment: When the Sale of the Property May Fall Short of the Judgment Amount	101

Chapter 7 — RESPONSES TO FORECLOSURE COMPLAINTS — 103

7-1	Introduction	103
	7-1:1 Motions and Pleadings	103
7-2	Motions to Dismiss	103
	7-2:1 Introduction	103
	7-2:2 Common Grounds for Motions to Dismiss	104
7-3	Affirmative Defenses	106
	7-3:1 Introduction	106
	7-3:2 Lack of Standing	107
	7-3:3 Failure of Conditions Precedent	109
	7-3:4 Defenses Related to Payment	110
	7-3:5 Waiver	111
	7-3:6 Other Defenses to Foreclosure	111
	7-3:7 Motions to Strike Affirmative Defenses	112

Chapter 8 — STATUTORY CLAIMS AND DEFENSES — 115

8-1	Statutory Claims and Defenses	115
8-2	The Truth in Lending Act (TILA)	116
	8-2:1 The Home Ownership and Equity Protection Act (HOEPA)	116
	8-2:2 TILA Rescission	117
	8-2:3 TILA Damages	118
8-3	The Real Estate and Settlement Procedures Act (RESPA)	118
	8-3:1 RESPA Claims	120
8-4	FHA Home Loan Defenses	120
	8-4:1 HUD Counseling	122
8-5	Florida Consumer Collection Practices Act	123
8-6	The Florida Deceptive and Unfair Trade Practices Act (FDUTPA)	124

Chapter 9 — LITIGATING WITH ASSOCIATIONS IN THE FORECLOSURE CONTEXT — 125

9-1	Introduction	125
9-2	Pre-Foreclosure	125
9-3	During Foreclosure	127
9-4	Post-Foreclosure	132
	9-4:1 Anatomy of an Estoppel Dispute	132
	9-4:2 Foreclosing First Mortgagees Get Safe Harbor from Associations That Are Properly Named in the Foreclosure as Defendants	140

	9-4:3	The Declaration Trumps the Safe Harbor Statute	142
	9-4:4	Various Arguments Put Forth by Associations Seeking to Deny Safe Harbor	145
	9-4:5	Remedies Where Association Denies Safe Harbor or Otherwise Demands Improper Amounts	151
	9-4:6	Rule 1.540(b)(4) in the Context of Association Litigation	156

Chapter 10 LITIGATING WITH OTHER INTERESTS IN THE FORECLOSURE CONTEXT — 161

10-1	Necessary and Indispensable Parties		161
	10-1:1	Lis Pendens	161
10-2	Third-Party Purchasers		162
	10-2:1	Interest Subordinate to Prior Mortgage and Lis Pendens	162
	10-2:2	Intervention	164
	10-2:3	Right of Redemption	166
	10-2:4	Standing to Raise Defenses or Otherwise Participate	166
10-3	Tenants		169
	10-3:1	Tenancies Established Prior to Foreclosure	169
	10-3:2	Lessee Pendente Lite	171
	10-3:3	Writ of Possession	171
10-4	Governmental Entities		172
	10-4:1	Local Government Liens	172
	10-4:2	Internal Revenue Service	172

Chapter 11 DISCOVERY — 173

11-1	Introduction		173
11-2	Methods of Discovery		174
11-3	Requests to Produce (RTPs)		174
	11-3:1	Propounding RTPs	174
	11-3:2	Responding to RTPs	174
		11-3:2.1 Objections	175
		11-3:2.2 Production	176
	11-3:3	Inadvertent Production of Privileged Materials	176
	11-3:4	No Duty to Supplement Responses	176
11-4	Requests for Admissions (RFAs)		177
	11-4:1	Propounding RFAs	177
	11-4:2	Responding to RFAs	177
		11-4:2.1 Objections	178

		11-4:2.2	Admitting	178
		11-4:2.3	Denying	178
11-5	Interrogatories			178
	11-5:1	Propounding Interrogatories		179
	11-5:2	Responding to Interrogatories		179
		11-5:2.1	Objections	179
		11-5:2.2	Answering in Individual or Corporate Capacity	179
		11-5:2.3	Option to Produce Records	180
11-6	Depositions			180
	11-6:1	Preparing the Deponent for Deposition		181
		11-6:1.1	Party Deponent	181
		11-6:1.2	Non-Party Deponent	182
	11-6:2	Taking the Deposition		182
	11-6:3	Defending the Deposition of a Party-Deponent		183
11-7	Judicial Resolution of Discovery Disputes			183
	11-7:1	Motions to Compel		183
	11-7:2	Motions for Protective Orders		184
	11-7:3	Failure to Produce Discovery; Sanctions		185
11-8	Certiorari Review			186
11-9	Unique Considerations for Foreclosures			187
	11-9:1	Local Rules		187
	11-9:2	Discovery and Final Judgment		187
	11-9:3	A Foreclosure Plaintiff's Witness		188

Chapter 12	**MOTIONS FOR SUMMARY JUDGMENT IN FORECLOSURE CASES**			**191**
12-1	Introduction			191
	12-1:1	Overview of Summary Judgment in Florida		191
	12-1:2	Legal Standard		192
	12-1:3	Burden of Proof		192
		12-1:3.1	Burden of Proof as to Motions for Summary Judgment Made Before an Answer Is Filed	195
		12-1:3.2	Burden of Proof on a Plaintiff When a Defendant Raises Affirmative Defenses	195
	12-1:4	Contents of the Motion for Summary Judgment		198
		12-1:4.1	Identification of Summary Judgment Evidence in the Motion	199
	12-1:5	Summary Judgment Evidence		199
	12-1:6	Partial Summary Judgment		201

	12-1:7	Timing		202
	12-1:8	Continuances and Pending Discovery Issues		204
	12-1:9	Pending Counterclaims		207
	12-1:10	Summary Judgment in Foreclosure Lawsuits		208
		12-1:10.1	Summary Judgment of Foreclosure Claims	208
			12-1:10.1a Business Records	209
			12-1:10.1b Standing	211
			12-1:10.1c The Loan Agreement	213
			12-1:10.1d Default	214
			12-1:10.1e Conditions Precedent	214
			12-1:10.1f Pre-Acceleration Default Notice	216
			12-1:10.1g Amounts Due and Owing	217
			12-1:10.1h Non-Borrower Defendants' Affirmative Defenses	218

Chapter 13 FORECLOSURE TRIALS AND EVIDENCE 219

13-1	Introduction			219
13-2	Setting Trials			219
	13-2:1	Readiness for Trial		220
	13-2:2	Timing and Notice Requirements		220
13-3	Witnesses			221
	13-3:1	Fact Witnesses		222
	13-3:2	Expert Witnesses		222
	13-3:3	Subpoenas for Witness Testimony		223
13-4	Proof of Elements at Trial			223
	13-4:1	The Contract: Mortgage and Note		224
		13-4:1.1	Lost Note	225
		13-4:1.2	Right to Enforce Contract ("Standing")	226
		13-4:1.3	Additional Evidence of Standing	227
	13-4:2	Breach of Contract		228
	13-4:3	Conditions Precedent		229
	13-4:4	Damages		230
13-5	Burden of Proof			231
13-6	Motions for Involuntary Dismissal			231

Chapter 14 POST-JUDGMENT MOTION PRACTICE 233

14-1	Introduction	233
14-2	Rule 1.530 and Motions for Rehearing	233

	14-2:1	Appellate Considerations	234
	14-2:2	General Considerations	236
14-3	Rule 1.540 and Motions to Vacate Judgment		238
	14-3:1	Appellate Considerations	239
	14-3:2	Evidentiary Hearing	240
	14-3:3	One-Year Limitation Under Rule 1.540(b)(1) Through (3)	241
	14-3:4	Procedure Under Rule 1.540(b)(1); Mistake, Inadvertence, Surprise, or Excusable Neglect	243
	14-3:5	Procedure Under Rule 1.540(b)(2): Newly Discovered Evidence	244
	14-3:6	Procedure Under Rule 1.540(b)(3): Fraud, Misrepresentation, or Other Misconduct by a Party	245
	14-3:7	Procedure Under Rule 1.540(b)(4): Voidness	247
	14-3:8	Procedure Under Rule 1.540(b)(5): When a Judgment Has Been Satisfied, Released, Discharged, or It Is No Longer Equitable to Enforce It	253
	14-3:9	Uses of Rule 1.540(a) to Correct Clerical Errors	256
14-4	Post-Judgment Objections to Sale		257
14-5	Post-Judgment Claims for Surplus Funds		261

Chapter 15 SANCTIONS 265

15-1	Introduction		265
15-2	Courts' Inherent Authority to Sanction		266
	15-2:1	Courts' Authority to Sanction	266
	15-2:2	Differences Between Contempt and Sanctions	266
	15-2:3	Limitations on the Inherent Authority to Sanction	268
15-3	Sanctions Pursuant to Rule		269
	15-3:1	Introduction	269
	15-3:2	Sanctions for Discovery Violations	269
	15-3:3	Limitations on Sanctions for Discovery Violations	270
15-4	Sanctions Pursuant to Statute		271
	15-4:1	Sanctions for Frivolous Claims and Defenses, and Unreasonable Delay	271
	15-4:2	Safe Harbor from Sanctions	272

Chapter 16 ATTORNEY'S FEES IN FORECLOSURE ACTIONS 273

16-1	Introduction		273
	16-1:1	The "American Rule" on Attorney's Fees	273
16-2	The Note and Mortgage Contracts		273

TABLE OF CONTENTS

	16-2:1	The Terms of the Note and Mortgage Control	273
	16-2:2	Reciprocal Provisions of Fla. Stat. § 57.105(7) Apply to Foreclosure Actions	274
	16-2:3	No Contract, No Fees	274
16-3		Procedures to Recover Attorney's Fees	276
	16-3:1	Pleading Requirement	276
	16-3:2	Prevailing Party	276
	16-3:3	Time for Filing of Motion	277
	16-3:4	Burden of Proof and Evidence Required	278
	16-3:5	Must Prove Fees Are Reasonable	278
	16-3:6	Fees to Determine Party's Entitlement to Attorney's Fees, But Generally Not the Amount of Fees	279
	16-3:7	Contingency Fee Multipliers	280
	16-3:8	Recovery of Attorney's Fees Incurred in Bankruptcy	281
	16-3:9	Recovery of Attorney's Fees on Appeal	281
16-4		Attorney's Fees as a Sanction	282
	16-4:1	Court's Inherent Authority to Assess Attorney's Fees as a Sanction	282
	16-4:2	Attorney's Fees for Raising Unsupported Claim or Defense or for Unreasonable Delay Under Fla. Stat. § 57.105(1) & (2)	283
	16-4:3	Procedure to Obtain Attorney's Fees or Other Sanctions Under Fla. Stat. § 57.105(1) & (2)	284
16-5		Offers of Judgment and Proposals for Settlement	285
	16-5.1	Offer of Judgment and Demand for Judgment—Fla. Stat. § 768.79	285
	16-5.2	Procedural Rule Governing Offers of Judgment—Rule 1.442	285
16-6		Wrongful Act Doctrine	286
	16-6:1	The Doctrine	286

Chapter 17	**BANKRUPTCY**	**287**
17-1	Introduction	287
17-2	Mortgagee's Interest in Bankruptcy Proceedings	287
17-3	Automatic Stay	288
	17-3:1 Effect of the Automatic Stay	288
	17-3:2 Termination of the Automatic Stay	289
	17-3:3 Repeat Filers	290
17-4	Violations of Automatic Stay	291
17-5	Proofs of Claim	292
17-6	Strip Offs and Strip Downs	293

	17-6:1 A Matter of Equity	293
	17-6:2 Principal Residences	294
17-7	Discharge and Dischargeability	295
17-8	Statement of Intentions and Surrender	296
17-9	Dismissal	298

Chapter 18   APPEALS   299

18-1	Introduction	299
18-2	Initiating an Appeal	299
18-3	Preservation of Error	300
18-4	Types of Appeals Used in Foreclosure	301
	18-4:1 Final Appeal	301
	18-4:1.1 The Record on Final Appeal	302
	18-4:1.2 Supplementation of Record	303
	18-4:1.3 Timing of Briefs	303
	18-4:2 Non-Final Appeals	304
	18-4:2.1 The Record on Non-Final Appeal	304
	18-4:2.2 Timing of Briefs	304
	18-4:3 Interlocutory Appeals and Writs	304
	18-4:3.1 Certiorari	305
	18-4:3.2 Mandamus	305
	18-4:3.3 Prohibition	305
18-5	Stay of Action Pending Appeal	306
18-6	Standards of Review	306
	18-6:1 De Novo	307
	18-6:2 Abuse of Discretion	307
	18-6:3 Competent, Substantial Evidence	307
18-7	Oral Argument	308
18-8	Attorneys' Fees on Appeal	308
18-9	Rehearing and Clarification	309
18-10	Supreme Court Jurisdiction	309

Chapter 19   DEFICIENCY JUDGMENTS   311

19-1	Introduction	311
19-2	Jurisdiction	311
	19-2:1 In Personam Jurisdiction	311
	19-2:2 Rights of Assignees	312
	19-2:3 Where a Claim Can Be Brought	312
19-3	Calculation of Deficiency Amounts	313

		19-3:1	Burden of Proof	313
		19-3:2	Judge's Discretion	314
		19-3:3	Timing of Appraisals	314
		19-3:4	Defenses	315
19-4		Statute of Limitations		315
19-5		Deficiency Judgments Unavailable		316
		19-5:1	Waiver of Deficiency–Settlement	316
		19-5:2	Discharged in Bankruptcy	316

Appendix A   FORMS AND SAMPLES   317

1-001	Sample Complaint (Holders and Non-Holders in Possession)—Prepared by Sarah Weitz	319
1-002	Sample Complaint Lost Note—Prepared by Sarah Weitz	325
1-003	Sample Additional Claims—Prepared by Sarah Weitz	334
1-004	Sample Lis Pendens	340
1-005	Sample Answer and Affirmative Defenses	341
1-006	Sample Request for Production from Defendant to Plaintiff	344
1-007	Sample Request for Admissions from Defendant to Plaintiff	349
1-008	Sample Interrogatories from Defendant to Plaintiff	351
1-009	Sample Request for Production from Plaintiff to Defendant	356
1-010	Sample Request for Admissions from Plaintiff to Defendant	363
1-011	Sample Interrogatories from Plaintiff to Defendant	366
1-012	Sample Reference Chart: Evidentiary Basis for Introduction of Trial Exhibits—Prepared by Richard Bassett	372
1-013	Sample Final Judgment	374
1-014	Sample Final Judgment with Re-Establishment of Note	379
1-015	Sample Affidavit of Compliance	384
1-016	Form: Florida Standard Adjustable Rate Note	387
1-017	Form: Florida Standard Fixed Rate Note	391
1-018	Form: Standard Fannie Mae-Freddie Mac Mortgage	394

Table of Cases   411
Index   475

About This Book

Since the first publication of this book in 2016, foreclosure law in Florida has continued to evolve with incredible speed. Just when lawyers and litigants think they've identified all the issues to be resolved in foreclosures, new areas of discussion and disagreement arise. Such growth is reflected in this newest edition. We've added authors and chapters, and will continue to do so as the subject matter requires.

Like many areas of practice in Florida, this subject is far from settled. Even among the authors of this edition, intelligent minds may differ as to the appropriate arguments to make, motions to file, or strategies to employ in bringing a foreclosure case to conclusion. As we've always maintained, it must be noted that each of these chapters reflects the interpretation of Florida law as researched and understood by the respective author. Litigants and their attorneys are encouraged to review this information, conduct their own research, and craft their arguments according to the specific issues in each individual case. Finally, each author may describe the parties using different terminology. Mortgagor, borrower, and defendant are generally interchangeable, with the exception of defendants to a foreclosure action that are not the mortgagor/borrower. Mortgagee, lender and plaintiff are also generally interchangeable.

Acknowledgments

As a starting point, I should acknowledge my co-author, Heidi Bassett. When the original publisher contacted me to write a book on Florida foreclosure law, my initial response was, "No thanks, I'd like to stay married and have my kids recognize me." But I thought more about it and wanted to pursue it, so I naturally turned to Heidi, the firm colleague who, after I'd been taken to an emergency room on April 25, 2014, the last day of a firm retreat in Memphis, Tennessee, brought me an iPhone charger so I could call my wife and respond to e-mails congratulating me on the opinion that came out that morning, *U.S. Bank Nat. Ass'n v. Bartram*, 140 So. 3d 1007 (Fla. 5th DCA 2014), and then helped get my luggage from the hotel and me to the airport on time to fly home. She graciously agreed to co-author, and then, due to my need to focus on parental commitments with a third baby on the way, agreed to just handle the whole book while allowing me to write a single chapter, and the next year, two chapters. Ever persistent, Heidi asked me to co-author again. This time, I followed through. Heidi is to be commended for her tireless efforts, past and present, in working with the various chapter authors, editing and transferring the book from an idea to a concrete reality. I'd also like to acknowledge the many other lawyers in this field who have taught me so much over the past decade, many of which are the past and present chapter authors in this book. The rest of you, you know who you are. Last but not least, I thank God for this opportunity, and my beautiful and kind wife, Holly, and my three wonderful kids, Hayden, Kyle, and Addie, for the time to explore that opportunity.

Michael Starks

I have long been blessed with outstanding colleagues who humble me with their knowledge and generously share what they know for the benefit of the legal community and the public. The authors who contributed to this fifth edition are leaders in their field and I am grateful for all of their hard work. I'm particularly grateful to Mike Starks, who introduced me to this opportunity, and to my husband, Rick, for his ongoing love, support, and humor.

Heidi Bassett

About the Authors

Michael D. Starks is a senior attorney of Liebler, Gonzalez & Portuondo, and having practiced in the field exclusively since 2009, led the charge to clarify the law surrounding the foreclosure statute of limitations issue. He is a recognized voice in the consumer finance litigation, practice area. He has written and published two book chapters in this (and prior iterations of this) book, as well as two book chapters in two other treatises on the law of spoliation of evidence in Florida. Mr. Starks has lectured at Barry University's law school on various topics, including Florida constitutional law and legal ethics. He has been representing clients for 23 years in a wide array of legal areas, including foreclosure, consumer finance, general commercial litigation, products liability, construction, spoliation of evidence, and section 1983 actions defending law enforcement agencies.

Since 2012, Mr. Starks has received the Martindale-Hubbell® AV rating, and in 2016 and 2019 been recognized by Florida Trend Magazine as a legal elite honoree. In 2006, he received the Florida Bar *Journal* Excellence in Writing Award for best written article of that year, after which he served on The *Florida Bar Journal/News* Editorial Board until 2012. He is a proud member of the Christian Legal Society, the Federalist Society, and the Federal Bar Association, and now serves on the Legislation and Government Regulation of Lending Sub-Committee, and the Foreclosure and Debtor/Creditor Rights Sub-Committee of the Real Property Finance and Lending Committee, of the Real Property, Probate and Trust Law Section of The Florida Bar.

Mr. Starks received his J.D., *magna cum laude*, in 1996 from the Florida State University College of Law, where he was admitted to the Order of the Coif and served as both associate and legislative editor of the *Florida State University Law Review*. He received his B.S. in Advertising, *cum laude*, in 1990 from the University of Florida. He currently lives in Apopka, Florida with his beautiful wife, Holly, and three wonderful children, Hayden, Kyle, and Addie, who are the major source of his happiness.

Heidi Bassett has established herself as a leader in consumer finance litigation throughout Florida. She has also represented clients in more than two hundred appeals throughout Florida's appellate courts and testifies in Florida state courts regarding the reasonableness of attorney fees to prevailing parties. Ms. Bassett also represents clients in matters involving real estate, and business litigation.

In 2014, Ms. Bassett was named to the MReport's 35 Under 35 list of women poised to make significant strides in the housing industry, and for the past six consecutive years she has been named a Super Lawyers rising star. In 2017, Ms. Bassett was invited by the Litigation Counsel of America to become a fellow in the Trial Lawyer Honorary Society, an elite society comprised of less than one half of one percent of American lawyers. Ms. Bassett is rated AV Preeminent (starting in 2018) and AV Preeminent (Judicial Edition) (starting in 2019) by Martindale Hubbell.

Ms. Bassett obtained her J.D. from the University of St. Thomas School of Law in Minneapolis, Minnesota and her B.A. from the University of Minnesota Duluth. She is admitted to practice before all of the state courts of Minnesota and Florida, the United States District Courts for the Middle and Southern Districts of Florida, the United States Courts of Appeal for the Eighth and Eleventh Circuits and the United States Supreme Court. She is a litigator at the law firm of Hellmuth & Johnson, representing clients throughout Florida and Minnesota.

Contributing Authors

Jonathan Blackmore: Chapter 4

Jonathan Blackmore is a partner in the Florida office of Phelan Hallinan Diamond & Jones, PLLC, where he manages the litigation and trial departments. Jonathan received his J.D. from Nova Southeastern University and his Bachelor of Arts from Florida Southern College. He specializes in representing mortgage servicers and lenders in contested foreclosure and consumer finance litigation in state and federal court at the trial and appellate levels. Jonathan gives special thanks to his beautiful wife, Yvethe, and their sons, Samuel and Benjamin, for their love and support.

Ileen J. Cantor: Chapters 8, 12

Ileen J. Cantor has over 26 years of experience representing clients in public and private sectors throughout the state of Florida at both the state and federal levels. Ms. Cantor is rated AV Preeminent by Martindale-Hubbell. She received her B.A. degree in Political Science *summa cum laude* from the State University of New York at Stony Brook and her J.D. degree *cum laude* from Nova Southeastern University Law Center where she served as a staff member on the Nova Law Review and elected representative of the Student Bar Association.

Ms. Cantor is a lead litigation and appellate attorney in the Boca Raton office of the law firm of Shapiro, Fishman & Gaché, LLP, whose clients include mortgage lenders and mortgage loan servicers. Ms. Cantor maintains a broad practice, in recent years focusing primarily in the area of consumer finance litigation defense, title litigation and contested residential mortgage foreclosures in state and federal court at both the trial and appellate levels. Ms. Cantor serves as a member of a Legal and Compliance Committee that has the general responsibility to oversee implementation of compliance programs, policies and procedures for a national network of firms. She is also a member of the Subcommittee for the Real Property Finance and Lending Committee of the RPPTL Section of the Florida Bar.

Ms. Cantor has taught Law School for Administrators as an adjunct faculty member at the Abraham S. Fischler College of Education of Nova Southeastern University.

Ms. Cantor wishes to give special thanks to Michael Starks and Heidi Bassett for the opportunity to contribute to this book and to her son Noah, as well as her beloved parents.

Jennifer Chapkin: Chapters 1, 13

Jennifer Chapkin is the founder of Chapkin Law in Boca Raton, Florida. She handles a wide variety of civil and commercial litigation matters involving business, foreclosures, community associations, collections, contracts and real estate disputes. Jennifer has experience at both the trial and appellate levels and serves clients throughout

Florida, including Palm Beach, Broward and Miami-Dade counties. Her client base is diverse and consists of individuals, small businesses and large corporations. Ms. Chapkin has been licensed to practice law since 2009 and has handled more than 300 trials. She is admitted to practice in Florida and New York and before the United States District Courts for the Northern, Middle and Southern Districts of Florida and the United States Court of Appeals for the 11th Circuit. Jennifer earned a bachelor's degree in advertising and public relations from the University of Central Florida in 2003. She attained her law degree from Shepard Broad College of Law of Nova Southeastern University and received training in basic trial skills from the National Institute for Trial Advocacy. Since 2016, Jennifer has been named to the annual Florida Super Lawyers "Rising Stars" list, a rating earned by only 2.5 percent of attorneys in the state of Florida. Jennifer is involved in the legal community and maintains an active membership in the Broward County Bar Association. She is also a member of the appellate practice; real property, probate and trust law; business law; and trial lawyers sections of the Florida Bar.

Gaspar Forteza: Chapters 5, 11

Gaspar Forteza is a partner in the law firm of Blaxberg, Grayson, Kukoff & Forteza, P.A. and lives in Miami, Florida. He specializes in real estate, business and commercial litigation, with an emphasis in consumer and creditor rights. He was born in Argentina in 1980 and immigrated to the United States when he was 10 years old. Having come from a family comprised almost exclusively of doctors and other medical professionals, he naturally became a lawyer. Mr. Forteza received his Bachelor of Arts from University of Miami and Juris Doctorate from Florida International University School of Law. He owes the full sum of his happiness to his beautiful wife, Radia, and his two precocious daughters, Julia and Olivia.

Richard S. McIver: Chapter 16

Richard S. McIver is a shareholder of Kass Shuler, P.A. in Tampa, Florida, and has represented banks, mortgage companies and loan servicers in litigation matters in Florida for over 30 years. He is Board Certified by the Florida Bar as a specialist in Real Estate Law (2007-present), has an AV® Rating by Martindale-Hubbell, and has been recognized as a Super Lawyer®, from 2015 to the present. Richard is very active in the Florida Bar Real Property, Probate and Trust Law Section as chair of the Real Property Finance and Lending Committee. He is also a member of the Hillsborough County Bar Association, Mortgage Bankers Association, Bay Area Real Estate Council, and American Legal and Financial Network. Richard is a frequent author and lecturer, including as author of the "Mortgage Financing" chapter in Florida Real Property Sales Transactions, 5th through 8th Editions (Florida Bar, 2008-2015), as editor of: "Hotels, Motels, Restaurants, and Marinas" chapter in Florida Real Property Complex Transactions, 8th Edition (Florida Bar, 2016), "Navigating a Foreclosure Title Commitment" (RPPTL's Action Line, 2018), and as speaker: "Post Bartram—When is a Residential Mortgage Foreclosure Barred by the Statute of Limitations?" June 2017; Professionalism for the Real Property Litigator," November 2016; "Deutsche Bank v. Beauvais," October 2015; "When Is It Too Late to Foreclose a Mortgage?" April 2014; "Ethics Issues Concerning Short Sales, Defaults and Mortgage Foreclosures," November 2010. Richard was born in Texas, and received his J.D. in 1980 from Southern Methodist University, Dedman School of Law, Dallas, Texas, and his BBA from the SMU Edwin L. Cox School of Business. Richard has lived in Tampa, Florida, since

1985 with his wife, Lynda Scalf-McIver, Ph.D., and they are proud parents of their daughter, Caitlin, who lives in Brooklyn, New York.

Nicole Mariani Noel: Chapter 17

Nicole Mariani Noel is a shareholder at Kass Shuler, P.A., where she has been practicing in the fields of bankruptcy, creditor's rights and insolvency, real estate, group for the firm and handles cases throughout the state, including the Northern, Middle and Southern Districts. Her membership includes the American Bankruptcy Institute, the Florida State Alumni Real Estate Network, Tampa Bay Bankruptcy Bar Association, the Florida Bar, and the American Legal and Financial Network. Mrs. Noel is the co-chair of the Case Law Update Subcommittee for the Real Property Finance and Lending Committee of the RPPTL Section of the Florida Bar and co-chair of the Bankruptcy Practice Group for the American Legal and Financial Network (ALFN). Her published work includes *Was Brown a Rash Decision?* (The Cramdown, Summer 2014); *Incompatible Personalities: Investigating the Mutually Exclusive Nature of § 1322(b)(2), (5)* (ABI Journal, November 2012) and *Stripping Down Your Spouse: Tenancy by the Entirety Property Ownership under § 506* (ABI YLC Newsletter, September 2012). Ms. Noel is active in the community and frequently volunteers her time to speak at local universities on topics which include ethical concerns facing young attorneys, time management, and first year law practice pointers. Ms. Noel is an adjunct professor at St. Petersburg College teaching Bankruptcy and Civil Litigation. She participated in the 2016 Next Generation program held by the Bankruptcy Judges during the National Conference of Bankruptcy Judges (NCBJ). Ms. Noel was honored to become a Fellow for the Florida Bar Leadership Academy. She was also named one of ALFN's Junior Professionals and Executives Group (JPEG)'s standout young professionals to watch in 2016. She received her undergraduate degree from the Florida State University and her Juris Doctorate and Master of Business Administration degrees from Stetson University College of Law and Stetson University School of Business Administration. Ms. Noel would like to thank her husband and family for their unconditional support.

David Rodstein: Chapters 2, 3

David Rodstein represents national mortgage lenders, investors, and loan servicers, condominium owners, and pro bono clients. David litigates, lectures, and publishes on high-risk mortgage foreclosure issues that significantly impact the mortgage lending industry. He has represented clients at every trial and appellate level in the state and federal courts of Florida. His accredited legal education seminars include "When is it too late to foreclose a mortgage?" and "Evidence in Foreclosure Cases."

David has earned Martindale-Hubbell's prestigious AV Preeminent rating for attorneys. He is an active member of the Florida Bar's Appellate Law Section, Trial Lawyers Section, and the Real Property and Probate Law Section, in which he chairs the subcommittee on Legislation and Government Regulation of Lending, chairs the subcommittee on Stale Mortgages, and serves on the subcommittee on Partition Actions.

David is a graduate of the University of Pennsylvania with honors and the Washington & Lee University School of Law with distinction in trial advocacy. He served as law clerk to the Honorable Justice Lawrence L. Koontz, Jr. of the Supreme Court of

Virginia. David thanks the Almighty for his talents, for his wonderful wife, Rina, and for their four beautiful children.

Morgan Weinstein: Chapters 7, 15

Morgan Weinstein received his Juris Doctorate from the University of Florida Levin College of Law and his Bachelor of Arts *magna cum laude* from the University of Florida. He concentrates his practice on appellate law, as well as real property and commercial litigation. Mr. Weinstein is a member of the pro bono committee of the appellate practice section of the Florida Bar. Prior to establishing Weinstein Law, P.A., he was the managing attorney of the Miami, Florida office of Van Ness Law Firm, PLC. He thanks his wife, Shannon Weinstein, and gives special thanks to Frank P. Irizarry for his support and guidance over the years.

Sarah Weitz: Chapters 6, 10

Sarah Weitz is an attorney with the Fort Lauderdale law firm of Weitz & Schwartz, P.A., which focuses on real estate litigation. Ms. Weitz devotes her time to civil appellate matters and has handled more than 100 appeals across Florida's five district courts of appeal. She joined the Florida Bar's standing Appellate Court Rules Committee in 2018 and is an active member of the Florida Bar's Appellate Practice Section as well as the Broward County Bar Association's Appellate Practice Section.

Ms. Weitz graduated from Emory University School of Law in 2004. She obtained her B.A. in English from Boston College and spent her junior year studying literature at King's College London. She thanks her husband and colleague, Steven Weitz, for his encouragement and support, and their two wonderful children for their patience while she wrote her chapter. She also thanks Michael Starks and Heidi Bassett for the opportunity to contribute to this book.

Steven Weitz: Chapter 19

Steven Weitz is a partner with Weitz & Schwartz, P.A. Mr. Weitz focuses his practice on advising lenders, mortgage servicers and investors on issues related to consumer finance compliance and litigation, title litigation and other real estate related matters. Mr. Weitz graduated with a Bachelor of Arts from the University of Florida and a Juris Doctor degree from Emory University School of Law. He has earned Martindale-Hubbell's AV Pre-eminent rating for attorneys. He thanks his wife and colleague, Sarah Weitz, his amazing children, Julia and Joe, and his colleagues—past and present—at Weitz & Schwartz, P.A. without whom this would not have been possible. He also thanks Michael Starks and Heidi Bassett for the opportunity to contribute to this book.

CHAPTER 1

The Life of a Mortgage Foreclosure in Florida

Jennifer Chapkin

1-1 Introduction

Florida is one of the approximately 15 judicial foreclosure states that requires judicial intervention to foreclose a mortgage.[1] Mortgage foreclosures in Florida are governed by statutes and guided by local procedures. While each jurisdiction operates according to the available court resources and the volume of foreclosure filings, the law provides a blueprint which must be followed in every foreclosure action in Florida. Due to the high volume of foreclosure actions in the state of Florida and the associated litigation, this blueprint is constantly evolving. This book is a resource for those foreclosure actions which are litigated, but a basic understanding of the process provides the foundation upon which a case is built and defended. This first chapter is intended to provide the skeleton, but the chapters that follow will supply the muscle.

1-1:1 Elements of Foreclosure

Mortgage foreclosure is an action in equity.[2] The elements of a mortgage foreclosure action are consistent with those of any claim for breach of contract.[3] A mortgagee must first demonstrate the existence of a contract (the mortgage and corresponding promissory note) which was executed by the mortgagor.[4] Where the party attempting to foreclose is not the mortgagee named on the contract, the plaintiff must demonstrate

---

[1] *Deutsche Bank Tr. Co. Ams. v. Beauvais*, 188 So. 3d 938, 950-51 (Fla. 3d DCA 2016).
[2] Fla. Stat. § 702.01 (also requiring that counterclaims to foreclosure actions be severed, but this requirement was found unconstitutional by *Haven Federal Savings & Loan Ass'n v. Kirian*, 579 So. 2d 730 (Fla. 1991)).
[3] *AIB Mortgage Co. v. Sweeney*, 687 So. 2d 68, 69 (Fla. 3d DCA 1997) (citing *Miller v. Nifakos*, 655 So. 2d 192, 193 (Fla. 4th DCA 1995)) (To establish a breach of contract, a party must show the existence of a contract, a breach thereof, and damages.); *Bank of Am., N.A. v. Delgado*, 166 So. 3d 857, 859 (Fla. 3d DCA 2015) (To make a prima facie case, "[f]oreclosure plaintiffs must show: (1) an agreement; (2) a default; (3) an acceleration due to maturity; and (4) the amount due.").
[4] *Ginn v. Weiss*, 183 So. 2d 6 (Fla. 1st DCA 1966).

that it has 'standing' to foreclose.[5] For a complete discussion of standing, *see* Chapter 4: Standing to Foreclose.

Once the existence of a contract and the identity of the proper parties are established, the plaintiff must show that the mortgagor has breached the mortgage contract.[6] Finally, the plaintiff must demonstrate that it has suffered damages.[7] If the mortgage contract contains any conditions precedent to foreclosure, satisfaction of conditions precedent becomes an additional element necessary to proving entitlement to foreclose.[8] For a complete discussion of conditions precedent to foreclosure, *see* Chapter 2: Default and Acceleration.

1-1:2 Title Reports/Discovery of Junior Liens

Prior to the filing of a foreclosure action in Florida, the plaintiff must obtain and examine a title report to discover the existence of all junior lien holders and potential defects in title. Junior lienholders are necessary parties to the action and must be specifically identified in the lis pendens and final judgment, or their liens will be unaffected by the judgment.[9] For a complete discussion of title considerations in foreclosure, *see* Chapter 5: Title Considerations in Mortgage Foreclosure.

Liens held by community associations for outstanding assessments may also be foreclosed, except that the first mortgagee (or its successor) who acquires title at a foreclosure sale will only be responsible for a portion of the assessments.[10] For a

---

[5] *McLean v. JP Morgan Chase Bank, Nat'l Ass'n.*, 79 So. 3d 170 (Fla. 4th DCA 2012) (Standing may be established by either an assignment or an equitable transfer of the mortgage prior to the filing of the complaint.) (citing *WM Specialty Mortgage, LLC v. Salomon*, 874 So. 2d 680, 682-83 (Fla. 4th DCA 2004)). Florida Statute § 673.3011 provides a variety of ways which a party can demonstrate that they are entitled to enforce a promissory note.

[6] The most common breach is failure to make a required mortgage payment, which is considered a material breach of the contract. *David v. Sun Federal Savings & Loan Ass'n*, 461 So. 2d 93 (Fla. 1984). For a complete discussion of the various ways in which a mortgage contract may be breached, *see* Chapter 2: Default and Acceleration.

[7] *Sas v. Federal Nat. Mortg. Ass'n*, 112 So. 3d 778, 779-80 (Fla. 2d DCA 2013) (affirming in part and reversing and remanding trial court determination after foreclosure bench trial of amounts due and owing to mortgagee without admitting into evidence underlying records reviewed for testimony); *Terra Firma Holdings v. Fairwinds Credit Union*, 15 So. 3d 885, 886 (Fla. 2d DCA 2009) (reversing final summary judgment of foreclosure where failure to make a single payment was the only alleged default in the complaint and evidence supported the payment was actually made).

[8] *DiSalvo v. SunTrust Mortgage, Inc.*, 115 So. 3d 438 (Fla. 2d DCA 2013) ("[A] mortgagee's right to the security for a mortgage is dependent upon its compliance with the terms of the mortgage contract, and it cannot foreclose until it has proven compliance."); *David v. Sun Federal Savings & Loan Ass'n*, 461 So. 2d 93 (Fla. 1984) (The law does not require a mortgagee to notify a mortgagor of his intent to exercise his option to accelerate prior to instituting a foreclosure suit.).

[9] *Abdoney v. York*, 903 So. 2d 981, 983 (Fla. 2d DCA 2005) (When a junior mortgagee is omitted as a party to the foreclosure of a senior mortgage, the lien of the junior mortgagee is unaffected by the judgment).

[10] Fla. Stat. § 718.116(1)(b) (With respect to a condominium, liability is limited to unpaid common expenses and regular periodic assessments that accrued or came due within the six month period immediately preceding acquisition of title, or one percent of the original mortgage debt, whichever is less.); Fla. Stat. § 720.3085(2)(c) (With respect to property governed

1-2 Initiation of a Foreclosure Action

Every foreclosure action in Florida is initiated by preparing and filing a complaint with the clerk of court in the county where the mortgaged property is located.[11] At the same time, a Notice of Lis Pendens is recorded, providing constructive notice to the public that a legal claim to the property has been asserted. The recording of the Lis Pendens is necessary because it can be discovered by any potential parties who may obtain a subsequent interest in the property and will put them on notice that any interest they obtain will be subject to foreclosure.[12] For a complete discussion of foreclosure complaints and various counts which may be included in a complaint, see Chapter 6: Foreclosure Complaints.

1-3 Service of Process

Laws regarding service of process in Florida are strictly construed, and a mortgagee who intends to foreclose should be careful to follow service requirements exactly in order for the trial court to obtain jurisdiction over the defendants.[13]

1-3:1 Methods of Service

Upon the filing of a foreclosure Complaint and Lis Pendens, the clerk of court for the county with jurisdiction over the action will issue summonses to each named defendant.[14] As with any lawsuit filed in Florida, each defendant must be served with a summons within 120 days or the action may be dismissed without prejudice.[15] Service of Process on an individual in a mortgage foreclosure action may be effectuated by personal service, which requires delivering a copy of the summons, complaint and lis pendens at the usual place of abode of the intended recipient.[16] The documents may be left with any person residing therein who is at least 15 years old.[17] In lieu of

---

by a homeowner's association, liability is limited to unpaid common expenses and regular periodic assessments that accrued or came due within the 12-month period immediately preceding acquisition of title, or one percent of the original mortgage debt, whichever is less.).

[11] *Hudlett v. Sanderson*, 715 So. 2d 1050 (Fla. 4th DCA 1998); *see also Georgia Cas. Co. v. O'Donnell*, 147 So. 267, 268 (1933). If a mortgage encumbers property in two different counties, the foreclosure action may be brought in either county. Fla. Stat. § 702.04 (1995).

[12] Fla. Stat. § 48.23 (2019); *U.S. Bank Nat'l Ass'n. v. Quadomain Condominium Ass'n, Inc.*, 103 So. 3d 977, 978-79 (Fla. 4th DCA 2012). "One who purchases property subject to a *lis pendens* 'is bound by the judgment or decree rendered against the party from whom he makes the purchases as much so as though he had been a party to the judgment or decree himself.'" *Georgia Cas. Co. v. O'Donnell*, 147 So. 267, 109 Fla. 290, (1933) (citing *Greenwald v. Graham*, 100 Fla. 818, 130 So. 608, 611 (1930)).

[13] Fla. Stat. § 48.031(1)(a); *Baker v. Stearns Bank, N.A.*, 84 So. 3d 1122 (Fla. 2d DCA 2012); *Walton v. Walton*, 181 So. 2d 715, 717 (Fla. 2d DCA 1966); *Boca Stel 2, LLC v. Christiana Tr.*, 186 So. 3d 1117 (Fla. 4th DCA 2016).

[14] Fla. R. Civ. P. 1.070(a).

[15] Fla. R. Civ. P. 1.070(j).

[16] Fla. Stat. § 48.031(1)(a).

[17] Fla. Stat. § 48.031(1)(a).

personal service, substitute service may be made on the spouse of the person to be served at any place in the county, as long as the two reside together.[18] If personal or substitute service is not possible, the plaintiff may also be served by publication.[19] Florida Statutes also provide for service upon corporations and LLCs.[20]

1-3:2 Motions to Quash Service of Process

The party seeking to invoke the court's jurisdiction bears the initial burden of demonstrating that service was valid, but this is a relatively easy burden to meet because if the return of service is regular on its face, a presumption of proper service is achieved.[21] The burden then shifts to the served party to overcome that presumption.[22] The statutes that govern service of process are to be strictly construed, so any defect may result in service being quashed.[23]

A defendant wishing to challenge service of process must raise the issue at the first possible opportunity during the lawsuit—either by motion or by responsive pleading.[24] Service is most easily challenged by identifying a deficiency on the face of the service return, as this will shift the burden to the plaintiff to prove that service was proper.[25] Ineffective service of process may render a resulting judgment void, so it is critical that the plaintiff ensures perfect service.[26]

---

[18] Fla. Stat. § 48.031(2)(a).

[19] Service by publication is permitted upon filing of a sworn statement by the plaintiff, its agent or attorney, that a diligent search and inquiry to locate the defendant has been made, but the defendant could not be located. *See* Fla. Stat. § 49.031-49.071.

[20] Fla. Stat. § 48.061; Fla. Stat. § 48.062.

[21] *Koster v. Sullivan*, 103 So. 3d 882, 884 (Fla. 2d DCA 2012); *Re-Employment Services, Ltd. v. National Loan Acquisitions, Co.*, 969 So. 2d 467 (Fla. 5th DCA 2007).

[22] *Re-Employment Services, Ltd. v. National Loan Acquisitions, Co.*, 969 So. 2d 467 (Fla. 5th DCA 2007). *Williams v. Nuno*, 239 So. 3d 153 (Fla. 3d DCA 2018).

[23] *Romeo v. U.S. Bank Nat'l Assn.*, 144 So. 3d 585 (Fla. 4th DCA 2014); *Brown v. U.S. Bank Nat'l Assn.*, 117 So. 3d 823, 824 (Fla. 4th DCA 2013).

[24] Fla. R. Civ. P. 1.440; *Lennar Homes, Inc. v. Gabb Constr. Services*, 654 So. 2d 649, 651 (Fla. 3d 1995); *Re-Employment Services, Ltd. v. National Loan Acquisitions Co.*, 969 So. 2d 467 (Fla. 5th DCA 2007) ("The defense will be waived if it is not raised at the 'first opportunity.'") (internal citations omitted).

[25] *Gonzalez v. Totalbank*, 472 So. 2d 861, 864 (Fla. 3d DCA 1985) (burden to demonstrate valid service shifted to plaintiff when service return was not regular on its face, and service must be quashed where substitute service was made without confirming the person accepting substitute service was at least 15 years old); *Vives v. Wells Fargo Bank, N.A.*, 128 So. 3d 9, 15 (Fla. 3d DCA 2012) (return of service was not presumed valid where service was made on an unnamed person at defendant's residence. Service statutes required identification of person accepting service and confirmation that person actually resided at defendant's place of abode); *Shepheard v. Deutsche Bank Trust Co. Americas*, 922 So. 2d 340, 343 (Fla. 5th DCA 2006); *Sunseeker Int'l Ltd. v. Devers*, 50 So. 3d 715, 717 (Fla. 4th DCA 2010) (The party invoking the court's jurisdiction has the burden of proving proper service of process. To meet that burden, a plaintiff may produce evidence of a valid return of service. "If the return is regular on its face, then the service of process is presumed to be valid. . . . However, if the return is defective on its face, it cannot be relied upon as evidence that the service of process was valid.").

[26] *Reina v. Barnett Bank, N.A.*, 766 So. 2d 290, 292 (Fla. 4th DCA 2000) ("A judgment is void where service of process is so defective that it amounts to no notice of the proceedings.").

1-4 Defaults

Each defendant is afforded 20 days from the date on which they are served to respond to the Complaint.[27] When a defendant fails to timely respond, the legal remedy is entry of a default. When a default is entered (either by the clerk or by the court), all well-pled factual allegations in the complaint are deemed admitted.[28] Legal conclusions, however, are not admitted by a default.[29]

1-4:1 Clerk Defaults

If no paper of any kind is filed or served by a defendant within twenty (20) days of service, the clerk of court may enter a default against that party, and thereafter the court may enter a judgment at any time.[30] While it is proper for a clerk of court to enter a default as early as the twenty-first (21st) day following service of process, if a response is received before the twenty-sixth (26th) day, the default must be vacated.[31]

1-4:2 Judicial Defaults

When a defendant has filed any paper (including a request for extension of time or a notice of appearance by an attorney), the entry of a clerk's default is prevented. When this occurs, failure to plead or otherwise defend against the action is still subject to default, but now the plaintiff must petition the court for a judicial default.[32] In this case, the defendant is entitled to notice of the application for a default, but is not necessarily entitled to a hearing.[33]

1-4:3 Default Judgments

Default judgments may be entered following default without notice to a defendant only if all damages are liquidated, meaning they are readily ascertained from the pleadings, arithmetical calculations, or by application of definite rules of law.[34] If the action

---

[27] Fla. R. Civ. P. 1.500(a).

[28] *Fiera.com, Inc. v. DigiCast New Media Group, Inc.*, 837 So. 2d 451, 452 (Fla. 3d DCA 2002); *State Farm Mutual Auto Ins. Co. v. Horkheimer*, 814 So. 2d 1069, 1072 (Fla. 4th DCA 2001).

[29] *Days Inns Acquisition Corp. v. Hutchinson*, 707 So. 2d 747 (Fla. 4th 1997).

[30] Fla. R. Civ. P. 1.500(a); Fla. R. Civ. P. 1.500(e); *NCR Corp. v. Cannon & Wolfe Lumber Co., Inc.*, 501 So. 2d 157 (Fla. 1st DCA 1987) (even a letter sent by a defendant prevents the entry of a default without notice of application for default).

[31] *Nemeth v. Shore*, 511 So. 2d 1118, 1119 (Fla. 2d DCA 1987) ("We certainly cannot fault those clerks who insist on waiting until the twenty-sixth day before entering default, since they have been told by the courts and other sources that to do so earlier would be improper, erroneous, or premature. We also recognize that by allowing five days for mail delivery of a timely-served response, motions to set aside defaults would be reduced in number, thus avoiding a time-consuming and expensive process. Nonetheless, we believe that it is proper for the clerk to enter a default on the twenty-first day following personal service of process when his file reflects no timely response from the party required to respond, and that he should do so upon request.").

[32] Fla. R. Civ. P. 1.500(b).

[33] *EGF Tampa Associates v. Edgar V. Bohlen, G.F.G.M.A.G.*, 532 So. 2d 1318 (Fla. 2d DCA 1988).

[34] *Bowman v. Kingsland Development, Inc.*, 432 So. 2d 660, 662 (Fla. 5th DCA 1983). *Asian Imports, Inc. v. Pepe*, 633 So. 2d 551, 553 (Fla. 1st DCA 1994) (unpaid principal and interest constitute liquidated damages).

involves unliquidated damages, the defendant is entitled to notice prior to a final hearing or trial, even though they've been defaulted.[35]

1-4:4 Vacating Default

In certain circumstances, the Florida Rules of Civil Procedure provide for vacating a default.[36] The decision to set aside a default must be based on a finding that: (1) the failure to respond was the result of excusable neglect; (2) the defendant has meritorious defenses, and (3) the defendant demonstrated due diligence in acting upon the default when it was discovered.[37] A trial court's ruling on a request to vacate a default will not be disturbed on appeal unless the trial court abused its discretion.[38]

1-4:4.1 Excusable Neglect

Excusable neglect will be found when the failure to timely respond to a complaint results from clerical or secretarial errors, reasonable misunderstanding, an error in the system utilized by a party to track deadlines or assign tasks, or other human errors.[39] Misunderstanding of the law or the consequences of failing to defend do not constitute excusable neglect.[40] In order to demonstrate that excusable neglect caused the default, the circumstances must be set forth in an affidavit or sworn statement.[41]

1-4:4.2 Meritorious Defenses

A defendant seeking to vacate the default must file a motion attaching a proposed answer with affirmative defenses, demonstrating that if the default is vacated, the defendant will have meritorious defenses to assert.[42] The mere assertion that meritorious defenses exist is insufficient.[43]

---

[35] *Pierce v. Anglin*, 721 So. 2d 781, 783 (Fla. 1st DCA 1998); *Asian Imports, Inc. v. Pepe*, 633 So. 2d 551, 552 (Fla. 1st DCA 1994); *Lauxmont Farms, Inc. v. Flavin*, 514 So. 2d 1133, 1134 (Fla. 3d DCA 1987).

[36] Fla. R. Civ. P. 1.500(d) permits vacation of a default and any consequent judgment and directs parties to seek relief as provided under Florida Rule of Civil Procedure 1.540(b).

[37] *Elliott v. Aurora Loan Servs.*, LLC, 31 So. 3d 304, 307 (Fla. 4th DCA 2010); *Chetu, Inc. v. Franklin First Fin., Ltd.*, 4D18-2428, 2019 Fla. App. LEXIS 11309 (Fla. 4th DCA July 17, 2019).

[38] *George v. Radcliffe*, 753 So. 2d 573 (Fla. 4th DCA 1999).

[39] *Somero v. Hendry Gen. Hosp.*, 467 So. 2d 1103, 1106 (Fla. 4th DCA 1985); *Gables Club Marina, LLC v. Gables Condo & Club Ass'n, Inc.*, 948 So. 2d 21, 23-24 (Fla. 3d DCA 2006) ("Although ignorance of the law and failure to understand consequences are not viable excuses, 'a reasonable misunderstanding between attorneys regarding settlement negotiations does constitute excusable neglect sufficient to vacate a default.'").

[40] *Joe-Lin, Inc. v. LRG Restaurant Grp., Inc.*, 696 So. 2d 539, 541 (Fla. 5th DCA 1997) ("A defendant's failure to retain counsel or a defendant's failure to understand the legal consequences of his inaction is not excusable neglect.). *Szucs v. Qualico Development, Inc.*, 893 So. 2d 708, 710-11 (Fla. 2d DCA 2005) (Perceived indifference on the part of the plaintiff did not absolve the defendant from duty to answer.).

[41] *Geer v. Jacobsen*, 880 So. 2d 717, 720 (Fla. 2d DCA 2004); *Gibson Trust, Inc. v. Office of the Attorney General*, 883 So. 2d 379, 382 (Fla. 4th DCA 2004) (default vacated where defendant's affidavits were uncontroverted and established a misunderstanding between the parties).

[42] *Fortune Insurance Co. v. Sanchez*, 490 So. 2d 249 (Fla. 3d DCA 1996).

[43] *Church of Christ Written in Heaven of Georgia, Inc. v. Church of Christ Written in Heaven of Miami, Inc.*, 947 So. 2d 557, 559 (Fla. 3d DCA 2006).

1-4:4.3 Due Diligence

Due diligence requires a defendant to show that prompt action was taken to vacate the default upon its discovery.[44] An affidavit is also required to demonstrate due diligence, and the affidavit should be accompanied by evidence where possible.[45] While the law does not provide a set amount of time after discovery of a default in which a defendant can demonstrate due diligence, Florida appellate courts have found that six or seven weeks may be too long.[46] Because a clerk's default is entered when a defendant fails to plead or otherwise defend within twenty (20) days, a good rule of thumb is that a motion seeking to vacate the default should also be filed within twenty (20) days of discovery of the default.[47]

1-5 Motions/Pleading Practice

Defendants may avoid a default by responding to the Complaint (by way of pleading or motion) within 20 days from when they were served.[48] If 20 days have passed, but the plaintiff has not yet sought a default, a defendant may still respond to the Complaint at any time prior to the entry of a default.[49] A case that progresses beyond the default stage will proceed to pleadings and motions. For a complete discussion of available responses to foreclosure complaints, *see* Chapter 7: Responses to Foreclosure Complaints.

1-6 Discovery

Discovery is the process by which parties exchange information regarding the allegations in their pleadings. Any document or information which is relevant to the foreclosure action and is not privileged becomes discoverable during this process.[50] Generally, discovery is conducted through requests for admissions, requests for production of documents, interrogatories (or written questions), and depositions. It is important to be diligent in seeking discovery, because failure to submit timely requests will not stop the foreclosure action from proceeding.[51] For a complete discussion of discovery in a foreclosure action, *see* Chapter 11: Discovery.

1-7 Summary Judgment

Mortgage foreclosure actions are successful when they end with a final judgment. The judgment may be obtained by proceeding to trial, or the process may be abridged

---

[44] *Broward County v. Perdue*, 432 So. 2d 742 (Fla. 4th DCA 1983).
[45] *Cedar Mountain Estates, LLC v. Loan One, LLC*, 4 So. 3d 15, 17 (Fla. 5th DCA 2009).
[46] *Allstate Floridian Ins. Co. v. Ronco Inventions, LLC*, 890 So. 2d 300, 304 (Fla. 2d DCA 2004) (motion to vacate filed seven weeks after entry of default did not demonstrate due diligence); *Lazcar Intern., Inc. v. Caraballo*, 957 So. 2d 1191, 1192 (motion to vacate filed six weeks after entry of default did not demonstrate due diligence); *Hepburn v. All American General Const. Corp.*, 954 So. 2d 1250, 1252 (Fla. 4th DCA 2007) (four month delay was not an exercise of due diligence).
[47] *Techvend, Inc. v. Phoenix Network, Inc.*, 564 So. 2d 1145, 1146 (Fla. 3d DCA 1990).
[48] Fla. R. Civ. P. 1.140.
[49] *Lake Towers, Inc. v. Axelrod*, 216 So. 2d 86 (Fla. 4th DCA 1968).
[50] Fla. R. Civ. P. 1.280.
[51] *Congress Park Office Condos II, LLC v. First-Citizens Bank & Tr. Co.*, 105 So. 3d 602 (Fla. 4th DCA 2013) (trial court does not err in entering summary judgment while discovery is outstanding where party seeking discovery fails to act diligently).

when a judgment is sought through a Motion for Summary Judgment.[52] When ruling on a Motion for Summary Judgment, the court will examine whether all statutory requirements were met and whether plaintiff has shown that no genuine issue of material fact exists.[53] For a complete discussion of Motions for Summary Judgment as a tool for obtaining a foreclosure judgment, *see* Chapter 12: Motions for Summary Judgment.

1-8 Trial

When summary judgment is denied because of the existence of material factual issues, or when the parties do not attempt summary judgment, the action proceeds to non-jury trial. For a complete discussion of trial as a tool for obtaining a foreclosure judgment, *see* Chapter 13: Foreclosure Trials and Evidence.

1-9 Final Judgment

The enforcement of a mortgage lien requires that a Final Judgment of Foreclosure be entered.[54] A successful foreclosure action, either through summary judgment, consent, or trial, entitles the mortgagee to have the property sold and the proceeds applied against the judgment.[55] The form of every Final Judgment of Foreclosure in Florida substantially follows the form set out in Florida Rule of Civil Procedure 1.996(a), even though individual jurisdictions incorporate their own language regarding circuit-specific sale procedures.

1-10 Sale

Upon entry of a final judgment in a mortgage foreclosure action, Florida's judicial sales procedure governs.[56] The sale is necessary because the interest a foreclosure mortgagee can acquire (payment of the debt through sale, or in the alternative, possession of and title to the property) only occurs through judgment and sale.[57] Any remaining indebtedness after sale may be sought against the mortgagee personally through a deficiency judgment. For a complete discussion about deficiency judgments, *see* Chapter 19: Deficiency Judgments.

1-10:1 Scheduling of Foreclosure Sale

The clerk of court is tasked with holding foreclosure auctions, and the court is to direct the clerk to hold the sale on a specified date between 20 and 35 days from the entry of judgment.[58] If the plaintiff or its counsel agrees, a longer period of time may be permitted before the sale is held.[59] As a practical matter, many courts in Florida schedule foreclosure sales farther out, even over the objection of the plaintiff.

---

[52] Fla. R. Civ. P. 1.510.
[53] *OneWest Bank, FSB v. Jasinski*, 173 So. 3d 1009 (Fla. 2d DCA 2015).
[54] *Morris v. Osteen*, 948 So. 2d 821, 824 (Fla. 5th DCA 2007).
[55] *Bankers Trust Co. v. Edwards*, 849 So. 2d 1160, 1162 (Fla. 1st DCA 2003).
[56] Fla. Stat. § 45.031.
[57] *Martyn v. First Federal Savings & Loan Ass'n*, 257 So. 2d 576, 580 (Fla. 4th DCA 1971).
[58] Fla. Stat. § 45.031(1)(a).
[59] Fla. Stat. § 45.031(1)(a).

1-10:2 Publication of Scheduled Sale

A foreclosure judgment is served upon all parties, including the judgment debtor, but Florida also requires that a Notice of Sale be published once a week for two consecutive weeks in the county where the sale will be held, providing notice of certain details to the public.[60] Without proper publication of the Notice of Sale, the foreclosure sale cannot be confirmed.[61]

1-10:3 Redemption and Reinstatement

Mortgagors have a right of redemption throughout the foreclosure process, and this right may be exercised by the mortgagor or by the holder of any subordinate interest (such as a lessee or current owner of the property).[62] The right of redemption is the borrower's ongoing right to satisfy the indebtedness at any time prior to foreclosure.[63] Even after the judgment is entered, a mortgagor's right to redeem is not extinguished until the clerk issues a Certificate of Sale, or until a time specified within the final judgment, whichever occurs later.[64] If the judgment is redeemed, the foreclosure sale will be stopped and the borrower will not be divested of title.[65]

---

[60] Fla. Stat. § 45.031(2): Notice of Sale shall be published once a week for 2 consecutive weeks in a newspaper of general circulation, as defined in Chapter 50, published in the county where the sale is to be held. The second publication shall be at least 5 days before the sale. The notice shall contain:
  (a) A description of the property to be sold.
  (b) The time and place of sale.
  (c) A statement that the sale will be made pursuant to the order or final judgment.
  (d) The caption of the action.
  (e) The name of the clerk making the sale.
  (f) A statement that any person claiming an interest in the surplus from the sale, if any, other than the property owner as of the date of the lis pendens must file a claim within 60 days after the sale.

[61] *Castelo Development, LLC v. Aurora Loan Services LLC*, 85 So. 3d 515 (Fla. 4th DCA 2012).

[62] Fla. Stat. § 45.0315; *Dundee Naval Stores Co. v. McDowell*, 65 Fla. 15, 61 So. 108, 112 (1913); *Burns v. Bankamerica Nat'l Tr. Co.*, 719 So. 2d 999, 1001 (Fla. 5th DCA 1998); *Clay Cty. Land Tr. #08-04-25-0078-014-27, Orange Park Tr. Servs. v. JP Morgan Chase Bank, Nat'l Ass'n*, 152 So. 3d 83, 85 (Fla. 1st DCA 2014).

[63] Antonio Martinez, Jr., Geoffrey L. Travis, and Brad Redlein, Florida Real Property Litigation § 5.47 (4th ed. 2005).

"The phrase 'right of redemption' has a twofold meaning. When used with respect to a mortgagor, it refers to the right of a mortgagor, before being foreclosed from that right, to satisfy the mortgage indebtedness and thus clear the property from the encumbrance of the mortgage. When used with reference to a junior lienor, it refers to the right of the junior lienor, before being foreclosed from it, to satisfy a prior mortgage by payment of the debt secured by such prior mortgage, thereby becoming equitably subrogated to all rights of the prior mortgagee."

[64] Fla. Stat. § 45.0315.

[65] *Beauchamp v. The Bank of N.Y., Tr. Co., N.A.*, 150 So. 3d 827, 39 (Fla. 4th DCA 2014).

Mortgagors may also have the right to reinstate their loan at any time prior to the entry of a foreclosure judgment, but this right is controlled by the mortgage itself.[66]

1-10:4 Auction and Bidding

The public auction process is also governed by statute in mortgage foreclosure actions.[67] The final judgment must specify not only the date of the sale, but also the time and location of the sale (including a website if the sale is being held in an online format).[68] The winning bidder at the public auction is required to pay five percent of the final bid to the clerk of court, which is applied against the total sale price.[69] After the sale is complete, the clerk of court files a Certificate of Sale and serves it on all parties, confirming that the sale is complete.[70]

1-10:5 Objections to Sale

Once a foreclosure auction is concluded, there is a ten-day waiting period during which a defendant to a foreclosure action may file an objection to the sale.[71] For a complete discussion of objections to sale, *see* Chapter 14: Post-Judgment Motion Practice.

1-11 Title and Possession

If no objection to sale is filed during the ten day period following the sale, the clerk of court will issue a Certificate of Title, formally transferring title of the property to the winning bidder.[72] This confirms the sale, and the Certificate of Title is recorded with the county in which the property is located.[73] The clerk can then disburse the proceeds from the sale to be applied against the judgment.[74]

When title is transferred through a foreclosure action, the purchaser of the property is entitled to possession.[75] The Court will issue a writ of possession, placing any occupants in the property on notice that they must vacate, or they will be removed by the sheriff.[76]

---

[66] *Zimmerman v. Olympus Fidelity Trust, LLC*, 936 So. 2d 652 (Fla. 4th DCA 2006) (terms of reinstatement were controlled by each individual mortgage, so attempted reinstatement of first mortgage was not effective where second mortgage did not provide for reinstatement and borrower did not pay accelerated amount of second mortgage to cure that default).

[67] Fla. Stat. § 45.031.

[68] Fla. Stat. § 45.031(3).

[69] Fla. Stat. § 45.031(3).

[70] Fla. Stat. § 45.031(4).

[71] Fla. Stat. § 45.031(5).

[72] Fla. Stat. § 45.031(5).

[73] Fla. Stat. § 45.031(6).

[74] Fla. Stat. § 45.031(7).

[75] Fla. R. Civ. Pro. 1.580; *Redding v. Stockton, Whatley, Davin & Co.* 488 So. 2d 548 (Fla. 5th DCA 1986) ("[P]ossession, as well as title, is at issue in a foreclosure action in respect to all parties to the action.") (also citing *Ray v. Hocker*, 65 Fla. 265, 61 So. 500 (1913)); *Dundee Naval Stores Co. v. McDowell*, 65 Fla. 15, 61 So. 108 (1913); *Wilmott v. Equitable Building & Loan Ass'n.*, 44 Fla. 815, 33 So. 447 (1903).

[76] Fla. R. Civ. P. 1.580.

CHAPTER 2

Default and Acceleration

David W. Rodstein

2-1 Default

The failure to pay a debt or to perform a duty secured by the mortgage is a default under the mortgage[1] and is an element of the action to foreclose.[2] The default must exist at the time the foreclosure action is filed.[3]

2-1:1 Defined by Loan Documents

Since the mortgage is a contract,[4] the covenants of the mortgage are determined by the language in the mortgage, together with any other loan documents signed contemporaneously. In most cases, multiple documents[5] are executed together as part of a single transaction. "Where other instruments are executed contemporaneously with a mortgage and are part of the same transaction, the mortgage may be modified by these other instruments. All the documents should be read together to determine and give effect to the intention of the parties."[6]

---

[1] Default is defined as "the omission or failure to perform a legal or contractual duty . . . to observe a promise or discharge an obligation." *Reed v. Lincoln*, 731 So. 2d 104, 105 (Fla. 5th DCA 1999) (quoting Black's Law Dictionary 376 (6th Ed.1990)).

[2] *Bank of Am., N.A. v. Delgado*, 166 So. 3d 857, 859 (Fla. 3d DCA 2015) ("Foreclosure plaintiffs must show: (1) an agreement; (2) *a default*; (3) an acceleration of debt to maturity; and (4) the amount due.") (emphasis added); *cf. Rozanski v. Wells Fargo Bank, N.A.*, 250 So. 3d 747 (Fla. 2d DCA 2018) (affirming equitable lien based on satisfaction of prior mortgage but reversing foreclosure because no proof that prior mortgage was in default); *Bensman v. DeLuca*, 498 So. 2d 645 (Fla. 4th DCA 1986) (reversing judgment of foreclosure because late payment of taxes and failure to provide insurance certificate were mere technical breaches that did not impair mortgage holder's security).

[3] *Yelen v. Bankers Trust Co.*, 476 So. 2d 767, 769 (Fla. 3d DCA 1985) (reversing foreclosure because property owner had tendered amount necessary to bring loan current before plaintiff accelerated debt and filed foreclosure complaint).

[4] *Beach Cmty. Bank v. Spellman*, 206 So. 3d 843, 844 (Fla. 1st DCA 2016); *Pitts v. Pastore*, 561 So. 2d 297, 301 (Fla. 2d DCA 1990) (A mortgage "is an executory contract or agreement in which one generally promises to allow a future sale of real property if a debt is not paid."); *Glen Garron, LLC v. Buchwald*, 210 So. 3d 229, 234 (Fla. 5th DCA 2017).

[5] *E.g.*, promissory note, riders, affidavits, etc.

[6] *Sardon Found. v. New Horizons Serv. Dogs, Inc.*, 852 So. 2d 416, 419 (Fla. 5th DCA 2003).

There are no terms implied in a mortgage by law. As with contracts generally, the terms are only those that appear in the loan documents.[7]

The original loan terms may be modified by a subsequent agreement between the lender and the borrower. In such a case, default is determined by reference to the loan terms as modified.[8,9]

2-1:2 Monetary Defaults

Most foreclosures are predicated on a default in the payment of money—a monetary default. The borrower's monetary obligations, and by extension monetary defaults, are defined in the loan documents.

The loan documents in residential foreclosure cases are usually uniform documents, which all contain nearly identical terms and conditions.[10]

By contrast, non-standard residential loan documents and commercial loan documents vary widely in terms and conditions, including the payment terms. Such terms

---

[7] "The absence of a provision from a contract is evidence of an intention to exclude it rather than of an intention to include it." *Azalea Park Utilities, Inc. v. Knox-Florida Dev. Corp.*, 127 So. 2d 121, 123 (Fla. 2d DCA 1961); *see also Home Dev. Co. of St. Petersburg v. Bursani*, 178 So.2d 113, 117 (Fla. 1965) (citing *Azalea Park*).

[8] *Nowlin v. Nationstar Mortg., LLC*, 193 So. 3d 1043, 1044 (Fla. 2d DCA 2016); *Pijuan v. Bank of Am., N.A.*, 253 So. 3d 112, 115 (Fla. 3d DCA 2018); *Rouffe v. CitiMortgage, Inc.*, 241 So. 3d 870, 873 (Fla. 4th DCA 2018); *Kuehlman v. Bank of Am., N.A.*, 177 So. 3d 1282, 1283 (Fla. 5th DCA 2015).

[9] Regarding who bears the burden of pleading a loan modification agreement, *see* the following apparently conflicting cases: *Nowlin v. Nationstar Mortg., LLC*, 193 So. 3d 1043, 1044 (Fla. 2d DCA 2016) (reversing foreclosure judgment after trial because "[Plaintiff] could only foreclose by alleging and proving a breach of the modification agreement . . . neither of which was done"); *Bank of N.Y. Mellon v. Bloedel*, 236 So. 3d 1164, 1170 (Fla. 2d DCA 2018) (reversing involuntary dismissal after trial because "[Defendant] had the burden of pleading and proving the existence of a modification to the note that was the subject of the lawsuit" and failed to do so); *Pijuan v. Bank of Am., N.A.*, 253 So. 3d 112, 115 (Fla. 3d DCA 2018) (reversing foreclosure judgment after trial and remanding for involuntary dismissal, holding "lender can foreclose only by both pleading and proving a breach of the modification agreement," neither of which was done; *see* dissent by J. Logue arguing burden to plead modification was on defendant); *Kuehlman v. Bank of Am., N.A.*, 177 So. 3d 1282, 1283 (Fla. 5th DCA 2015) (reversing final judgment of foreclosure after trial because "lender can foreclose only by both pleading and proving a breach of the modification agreement," neither of which were done); *Rouffe v. CitiMortgage, Inc.*, 241 So. 3d 870, 873 (Fla. 4th DCA 2018) (affirming foreclosure judgment and following the 2d DCA's holding in *Bloedel* that "a modification to a legal agreement, to the extent it would constitute an avoidance of all or part of a defendant's liability under the agreement, is an affirmative defense that must be pled and proven by the defendant"); *Morales v. Fifth Third Bank*, 275 So. 3d 197 (Fla. 4th DCA 2019) (reversing final judgment of foreclosure after trial and remanding for involuntary dismissal because "borrowers were [] on notice through the pleadings to defend on the original note but then required at trial to defend against an entirely different instrument [a loan modification agreement]."). Reconciling these opinions, especially the apparent intra-district conflict between the 2d DCA's opinions in *Nowlin* and *Bloedel*, is beyond the scope of this chapter.

[10] *See* Appendix A, 1-018 Fannie Mae/Freddie Mac Uniform Instrument.

DEFAULT AND ACCELERATION

are limited only by the drafter's creativity and agreement of the parties.[11] Some examples include grace periods, credits, offsets, deferments, partial acceleration of payments, and method of payment. In all cases, the contractual language controls when a default occurs.

When a contractual default in payment occurs, it is a material breach of the mortgage contract and gives rise to a cause of action for foreclosure.[12]

2-1:3 Non-Monetary Defaults

2-1:3.1 Non-Monetary Default by Act or Omission

Nearly all mortgages contain ongoing non-monetary obligations in addition to payment obligations. Typical non-monetary obligations include: keeping the mortgaged property insured,[13] keeping the property taxes paid,[14] and paying the full loan balance upon a sale or transfer of the property.[15] Less common examples include: the borrower depositing cash other assets at the lending institution, the borrower submitting accounting statements to the lender and even the borrower following contractually mandated standards of business conduct.[16]

Non-monetary obligations are limited only by the drafter's creativity and agreement of the parties.[17] Default on a non-monetary obligation gives rise to a cause of

---

[11] "Contracts are voluntary undertakings, and contracting parties are free to bargain for—and specify—the terms and conditions of their agreement. That freedom is indeed a constitutionally protected right." *Okeechobee Resorts, L.L.C. v. E Z Cash Pawn, Inc.*, 145 So. 3d 989, 993 (Fla. 4th DCA 2014) (citing *Northwestern Nat'l Life Ins. Co. v. Riggs*, 203 U.S. 243, 252-53 (1906)).

[12] "Failure to pay goes to the heart of the agreement between the mortgagor and mortgagee, and is not a mere technical breach." *Smiley v. Manufactured Hous. Assocs. III Ltd. P'ship*, 679 So. 2d 1229, 1232 (Fla. 2d DCA 1996). Conceivably, the failure to pay a *de minimis* amount (*e.g.,* less than $1) would not be considered a material breach, despite the general rule that non-payment constitutes a material breach.

[13] *See* Appendix A, 1-018, section 5. *Delgado v. Strong*, 360 So. 2d 73 (Fla. 1978); *Pezzimenti v. Cirou*, 466 So. 2d 274, 277 (Fla. 2d DCA 1985).

[14] *Lunn Woods v. Lowery*, 577 So. 2d 705, 707 (Fla. 2d DCA 1991); *accord Heimer v. Albion Realty & Mortg. Inc.*, 300 So. 2d 31, 32 (Fla. 3d DCA 1974); *Siahpoosh v. Nor Properties, Inc.*, 666 So. 2d 988 (Fla. 4th DCA 1996).

[15] *See* Appendix A, 1-018, section 18. *Kaan v. Wells Fargo Bank, N.A.*, 981 F. Supp. 2d 1271, 1274 (S.D. Fla. 2013). However, in *Yellen v. Bankers Trust Co.*, the judicial sale of a property at the conclusion of a second mortgagee's foreclosure action was held not to constitute a sale that triggered the "due on sale" clause of the uniform residential mortgage. *Yelen v. Bankers Trust Co.*, 476 So. 2d 767 (Fla. 3d DCA 1985).

[16] *Broward County v. 8705 Hampshire Drive Condo., Inc.*, 127 So. 3d 853 (Fla. 4th DCA 2013); *Sardon Found. v. New Horizons Serv. Dogs, Inc.*, 852 So. 2d 416, 420 (Fla. 5th DCA 2003).

[17] "Contracts are voluntary undertakings, and contracting parties are free to bargain for—and specify—the terms and conditions of their agreement. That freedom is indeed a constitutionally protected right." *Okeechobee Resorts, L.L.C. v. E Z Cash Pawn, Inc.*, 145 So. 3d 989, 993 (Fla. 4th DCA 2014) (citing *Northwestern Nat'l Life Ins. Co. v. Riggs*, 203 U.S. 243, 252-53 (1906)).

action for foreclosure if the default puts the lender's security in jeopardy,[18] even if all payments are current.[19]

2-1:3.2 Non-Monetary Default Due to Existence of a Condition

The parties to a mortgage can define a default giving rise to foreclosure as the existence of conditions rather than the breach of a duty. Examples include the death of the mortgagor,[20] the mortgagor's insolvency or diminished ability to continue making payments,[21] a decline in the value of the mortgaged property, and the existence of a default under an unrelated loan.[22]

2-1:4 Grace Period

Some mortgages provide that payments and other obligations are not considered late until after the passage of additional time beyond the nominal due date. This additional time is commonly known as a "grace period." When the mortgage provides a grace period for specified obligations, there is no default of those obligations until after expiration of the grace period.[23] Whether a mortgage actually provides a grace period is a matter of contract interpretation and therefore depends on the exact contractual language employed in the loan documents.[24]

---

[18] Lapse in insurance on mortgaged property was sufficient to support foreclosure judgment even though trial court held it to be a "technical default" and even though mortgagor cured after case filed because default placed the lender's security in jeopardy. *Delgado v. Strong*, 360 So. 2d 73 (Fla. 1978); *Pezzimenti v. Cirou*, 466 So. 2d 274 (Fla. 2d DCA 1985) (fact that mortgagee purchased forced place insurance with retro-active date so that "property was never uninsured" did not cure mortgagor's breach which put the security in jeopardy). *But see Bensman v. DeLuca*, 498 So. 2d 645 (Fla. 4th DCA 1986) (reversing judgment of foreclosure because late payment of taxes and failure to provide insurance certificate were mere technical breaches that did not impair mortgage holder's security).

[19] "Thus, despite the court having found an improper application of payments, it was error to deny foreclosure on that basis since there was uncontradicted evidence of Thompson's breach of the covenant to pay real estate taxes and assessments." *Lunn Woods v. Lowery*, 577 So. 2d 705 (Fla. 2d DCA 1991). *Heimer v. Albion Realty & Mortg. Inc.*, 300 So. 2d 31 (Fla. 3d DCA 1974); *Siahpoosh v. Nor Properties, Inc.*, 666 So. 2d 988 (Fla. 4th DCA 1996).

[20] *See, e.g., BankAtlantic v. Estate of Glatzer*, 61 So. 3d 1222, 1223 (Fla. 3d DCA 2011); *and see Miller v. Estate of Baer*, 837 So. 2d 448, 450 (Fla. 4th DCA 2002).

[21] *See, e.g., CGI Fin., Inc. v. C & V Sportfishing, LLC*, 12-60857-CIV, 2012 WL 5077139, at *23-24 (S.D. Fla. Sept. 21, 2012) (enforcing provision in note in which borrower "agreed that he would be in default if 'the prospect of payment, performance or realization [was] significantly impaired.'").

[22] *Achva Vahava, LLC v. Anglo Irish Bank Corp. PLC*, 10-80649-CIV, 2011 WL 4389912, at *5 (S.D. Fla. 2011).

[23] *Banksville, N.V. v. McNeill*, 529 So. 2d 828, 829 (Fla. 5th DCA 1988) (reversing foreclosure judgment where all payments were made within the contractual grace period, making mortgagee's imposition of default interest rate contrary to the mortgage contract and negating contractual default).

[24] *See Genvest Gen. Investments v. Lake Nona Corp.*, 594 So. 2d 787, 789 (Fla. 5th DCA 1992) (distinguishing *Banksville, N.V. v. McNeill*, 529 So. 2d 828 (Fla. 5th DCA 1988) (based on "the pertinent language in the mortgage")).

2-2 Notice of Default and Opportunity to Cure

2-2:1 Notice as a Matter of Contract

The mortgage holder is not required by statute or by common law to notify the mortgagor of a default or allow the borrower an opportunity to cure a default.[25] Therefore, if the mortgage is silent as to notice, the mortgage holder can foreclose immediately upon default. If the mortgage clearly requires a notice of default, that notice requirement is interpreted and is enforceable in accordance with standard principles of contract interpretation.[26]

2-2:2 Notice as a Condition Precedent

When the mortgage requires a notice of default as a condition precedent to enforcement of the mortgage, or to acceleration of the amount due, the mortgage holder must comply with the condition.[27]

A foreclosure action filed before compliance with notice requirements is subject to dismissal,[28] provided the borrower suffered some prejudice from the mortgage holder's failure to comply.[29]

---

[25] "A mortgagee simply has no duty to give a mortgagor an opportunity to cure a default." *Millett v. Perez*, 418 So. 2d 1067, 1068 (Fla. 3d DCA 1982).

[26] *U.S. Bank Nat. Ass'n v. Busquets*, 135 So. 3d 488, 489-90 (Fla. 2d DCA 2014).

[27] *U.S. Bank Nat. Ass'n v. Busquets*, 135 So. 3d 488, 490 (Fla. 2d DCA 2014); *Samaroo v. Wells Fargo Bank*, 137 So. 3d 1127 (Fla. 5th DCA 2014), *reh'g denied* (May 1, 2014).

[28] *Holt v. Calchas, LLC*, 155 So. 3d 499, 507 (Fla. 4th DCA 2015).

[29] *Fed. Nat. Mortg. Ass'n v. Hawthorne*, 197 So. 3d 1237, 1240 (Fla. 4th DCA 2016) (holding notice of default sent to a valid alternate address of borrower's and not to property address as required by mortgage did not prejudice the defendant, and may have even benefitted him); *Gorel v. Bank of N.Y. Mellon*, 165 So.3d 44, 47 (Fla. 5th DCA 2015) (holding notice of default that set a date to cure default 29 days from date of letter instead of 30 days did not prejudice borrower because he made no attempt to cure the default); *see also Green Tree Servicing, LLC v. Milam*, 177 So. 3d 7, 13 n.2 (Fla. 2d DCA 2015) (noting 5th District's ruling in *Gorel* and in *Allstate Floridian Ins. Co. v. Farmer*, 104 So.3d 1242, 1248-49 (Fla. 5th DCA 2012), but leaving open the issue of "whether prejudice is required . . . outside the insurance context").

If the plaintiff intends to argue lack of prejudice to defeat an express allegation that it failed to comply with the pre-suit notice requirement, it should plead the lack of prejudice as an avoidance. Avoidances are pled under Fla. R. Civ. P. 1.110(d) in a reply to the affirmative defense. By pleading lack of prejudice in a reply, the plaintiff ensures that the issue is properly framed for trial. *Citigroup Mortg. Loan Tr. Inc. v. Scialabba*, 238 So. 3d 317, 323 (Fla. 4th DCA 2018) ("lack of prejudice is an avoidance which should be pleaded [by the plaintiff]"). Nevertheless, if the issue of prejudice is tried by consent of the parties, the plaintiff's failure to plead lack of prejudice will not prevent the court from finding that lack of prejudice defeated the affirmative defense. *Id.* Additionally, if the borrower puts prejudice at issue by alleging prejudice in his affirmative defense, then the issue of prejudice need not be raised again by the plaintiff in a reply to frame the issue for trial. *Denton v. HSBC Bank USA, N.A.*, 45 Fla. L. Weekly D270 (Fla. 4th DCA February 5, 2020) ("Homeowner's affirmative defense alleged that she was prejudiced, and thus Homeowner was required to prove her affirmative defense. Therefore, there was no requirement that Bank file a reply in avoidance.").

A defense based on failure of the condition precedent is personal to the borrower and cannot be raised by a subsequent owner of the property.[30] The borrower must plead the failure to comply with conditions precedent, including notice of default, with specificity. Failure to do so waives the issue for trial and appeal.[31] The defensive pleading must identify both the nature of the condition precedent and the nature of its alleged failing to present a valid defense.[32]

As with contractual conditions precedent generally, the mortgage holder's compliance is evaluated for "substantial compliance," not strict compliance.[33]

When moving for summary judgment, the plaintiff must prove substantial compliance with the default notice requirement if the borrower has challenged compliance, whether in the borrower's answer by specifically denying compliance in or in an affirmative defense alleging failure of compliance.[34]

At trial, the burden of proof depends on the pleadings. The plaintiff bears the burden to prove substantial compliance if the borrower alleges non-compliance as a specific denial.[35] The borrower bears the burden to prove non-compliance if he

---

[30] *Clay Cty. Land Tr. No. 08-04-25-0078-014-27, Orange Park Tr. Servs., LLC v. JP Morgan Chase Bank, Nat'l Ass'n*, 152 So. 3d 83, 84 (Fla. 1st DCA 2014) ("The borrower, Buckley, was the only party who could plead nonperformance of these [default notice] conditions precedent as required by Florida Rule of Civil Procedure 1.120(c)."); *accord LaFaille v. Nationstar Mortg., LLC*, 197 So. 3d 1246, 1247 (Fla. 3d DCA 2016) (non-borrower defendants "have no standing to assert this [default notice] defense."). *See* Section 10-2:4 for a full discussion of third parties' standing to raise other defenses.

[31] Fla. R. Civ. P. 1.120(c); *Bank of Am., Nat. Ass'n v. Asbury*, 165 So. 3d 808 (Fla. 2d DCA 2015).

[32] *Deutsche Bank Nat. Trust Co. v. Quinion*, 198 So. 3d 701, 703-04 (Fla. 2d DCA 2016).

[33] *Fed. Nat. Mortg. Ass'n v. Linares*, 202 So. 3d 886, 888 (Fla. 3d DCA 2016); *Ortiz v. PNC Bank, Nat. Ass'n*, 188 So. 3d 923, 925 (Fla. 4th DCA 2016); *Bayview Loan Servicing, LLC v. Heefner*, 198 So. 3d 918, 920 (Fla. 5th DCA 2016); *Green Tree Servicing, LLC v. Milam*, 177 So. 3d 7, 13 (Fla. 2d DCA 2015).

[34] *Bryson v. Branch Banking & Tr. Co.*, 75 So. 3d 783, 785 (Fla. 2d DCA 2011); *Roussell v. Bank of N.Y. Mellon*, 263 So. 3d 100, 103 (Fla. 4th DCA 2019). The plaintiffs in *Bryson* and *Roussell* both obtained summary judgments that were reversed because they failed to conclusively refute the borrowers' affirmative defenses of non-compliance with a contractual notice requirement. Where the borrower does not raise non-compliance as an affirmative defense but rather denies compliance in his answer (with the specificity required by Rule 1.120(c)), the plaintiff has the burden *at trial* of proving compliance, and so presumably has the same burden on summary judgment. *See, e.g., Palma v. JPMorgan Chase Bank, NA*, 208 So. 3d 771, 774 (Fla. 5th DCA 2016) (reversing final judgment and remanding for involuntary dismissal, where defendant alleged non-compliance in her answer and burden thus remained on plaintiff to prove compliance).

[35] For cases discussing burdens of proof at trial regarding conditions precedent, *see Chrzuszcz v. Wells Fargo Bank, N.A.*, 250 So. 3d 766, 770 (Fla. 1st DCA 2018) (reversing final judgment because "the specific denial did not amount to an affirmative defense," thus the burden remained on plaintiff to prove compliance); *Palma v. JPMorgan Chase Bank, NA*, 208 So. 3d 771, 774 (Fla. 5th DCA 2016) (reversing final judgment and remanding for involuntary dismissal, where defendant alleged non-compliance in her answer and burden thus remained on plaintiff to prove compliance); *McIntosh v. Wells Fargo Bank, N.A.*, 226 So. 3d 377, 379 (Fla. 5th DCA 2017) ("the burden rests with the plaintiff to prove compliance with conditions precedent if asserted in the complaint and denied in the answer, but with the defendant if raised instead as an affirmative defense in the answer.").

DEFAULT AND ACCELERATION

raised non-compliance as an affirmative defense only.[36] If the borrower raises non-compliance both as a specific denial and as an affirmative defense, the burden rests with the plaintiff.[37]

The notice requirement can be waived by agreement of the parties.[38] If non-compliance is pled as an affirmative defense, then waiver must be pled as an avoidance in the reply.[39]

2-2:3 Notice in Standard Residential Mortgage

The standard form of residential mortgage used in Florida is the Fannie Mae/Freddie Mac mortgage. The standard form is ubiquitous in Florida residential mortgages and can be found in its entirety in Appendix A.

Paragraph 22 of the standard mortgage requires the lender to send the borrower a notice of default at least 30 days prior to acceleration and/or an action to foreclose. Thus, when the mortgage at issue follows the standard residential mortgage form, sending the notice is a condition precedent to foreclosure. The mortgage holder must prove that the notice was sent by first class mail[40,41] to the "notice address" provided

---

[36] *McIntosh v. Wells Fargo Bank, N.A.*, 226 So. 3d 377, 379 (Fla. 5th DCA 2017) ("the burden rests with the plaintiff to prove compliance with conditions precedent if asserted in the complaint and denied in the answer, but with the defendant if raised instead as an affirmative defense in the answer.") This was only a dictum in *McIntosh,* but a dictum that follows the general rule that defendants bear the burden of proving affirmative defenses.

[37] *Derouin v. Universal Am. Mortg. Co., Ltd. Liab. Co.*, 254 So. 3d 595, 600 (Fla. 2d DCA 2018).

[38] *Hatadis v. Achieva Credit Union*, 159 So. 3d 256, 260 (Fla. 2d DCA 2015) ("the waiver of notice found in paragraph six of the forbearance agreement only applied during the six-month period of that agreement").

[39] *Derouin v. Universal Am. Mortg. Co., Ltd. Liab. Co.*, 254 So. 3d 595, 600 (Fla. 2d DCA 2018) (requiring plaintiff to raise waiver of condition precedent by way of reply in order to frame issue for trial).

[40] The standard form mortgage provides: "Any notice to Borrower in connection with this Security Instrument shall be deemed to have been given to Borrower when mailed by first class mail or when actually delivered to Borrower's notice address if sent by other means." *See* Appendix A, 1-018, Fannie Mae-Freddie Mac Form Mortgage, paragraph 15.

[41] The district courts of appeal have issued numerous opinions in recent years on what constitutes legally sufficient evidence that a notice was actually mailed. As a general matter, they all follow the Florida Supreme Court's holding that "proof of general office practice satisfies the requirement of showing due mailing." *Brown v. Giffen Indust., Inc.*, 281 So. 2d 897 (Fla. 1973).
Applying that general rule to the notice of default in foreclosure cases, the Second and Fourth Districts hold that "mailing must be proven by . . . proof of regular business practices, an affidavit swearing that the letter was mailed, or a return receipt." *Soule v. U.S. Bank Nat'l Ass'n*, 253 So. 3d 679, 681 (Fla. 2d DCA 2018) (reversing final judgment of foreclosure and remanding for involuntary dismissal); *Ensler v. Aurora Loan Servs.*, LLC, 178 So. 3d 95, 97 (Fla. 4th DCA 2015) (reversing foreclosure judgment for failure "to present any admissible evidence that the notice was actually sent"). In the Fifth District, testimony of a loan servicer's routine practice by an employee who had seen the routine practice first hand was held sufficient. *CitiMortgage, Inc. v. Hoskinson*, 200 So. 3d 191, 192 (Fla. 5th DCA 2016) (reversing involuntary dismissal after trial, where plaintiff's witness had personally seen the company's routine practice for mailing out default letters, which created a presumption of mailing, which went unrebutted). A mailing log and customer service notes

in the mortgage,[42] but need not prove that the mailed notice was actually delivered.[43] If the notice is not sent by first class mail, then the mortgage holder must prove that the notice was actually delivered.

The notice must (a) identify the default; (b) identify the action required to cure the default; (c) give a date by which the default must be cured; (d) state that failure to cure the default in time may result in acceleration, foreclosure and sale of the mortgaged property; (e) inform the borrower of the right to reinstate after acceleration; and (f) inform the borrower of his right to dispute the default and raise any other defense to acceleration and foreclosure.[44]

2-2:3.1 Examples of Compliant Notices of Default

A notice that says the borrower's failure to cure may result in "foreclosure proceedings" complies with the mortgage requirement of a notice that "judicial proceedings" may result. In Florida, "the only method for foreclosure is a judicial proceeding."[45]

A notice that says the borrower "may" have the right to reinstate the mortgage after acceleration complies with the requirement to "inform Borrower of the right to reinstate after acceleration."[46]

A notice that says the borrower has "the right to bring a court action" to assert defenses complies with the requirement to inform the borrower of the right to assert defenses to foreclosure.[47]

A notice that requires payment of amounts past due more than five years (the statute of limitations period) in order to cure the default complies with the requirement to inform the borrower of the action required to cure.[48]

A notice of default was held to be compliant with paragraph 22 of the standard form residential mortgage, even though it lacked the amount due to reinstate.[49]

---

    admitted in evidence carry the plaintiff's burden. *Stacknik v. U.S. Bank Nat'l Ass'n*, 283 So. 3d 981, 984 (Fla. 2d DCA 2019).

    In the summary judgment context, the same facts may be affirmatively proven by affidavit. *Rivera v. Bank of N.Y. Mellon*, 276 So. 3d 979 (Fla. 2d DCA 2019).

[42] *Blum v. Deutsche Bank Trust Co.*, 159 So. 3d 920, 920 (Fla. 4th DCA 2015).

[43] *JP Morgan Chase Bank, N.A. v. Ostrander*, 201 So. 3d 1281, 1283 (Fla. 2d DCA 2016) (reversing summary judgment for borrowers). Even in a case where the contract requires delivery—and not mere mailing as required in the standard form mortgage—delivery is presumed under the mailbox rule: "mail properly addressed, stamped, and mailed was received by the addressee." *Brown v. Giffen Indust., Inc.*, 281 So. 2d 897 (Fla. 1973) (citing 31A C.J.S. Evidence § 136a).

[44] *See* Appendix A, 1-018, section 22.

[45] *U.S. Bank Nat. Ass'n v. Busquets*, 135 So. 3d 488, 490 (Fla. 2d DCA 2014).

[46] *U.S. Bank Nat. Ass'n v. Busquets*, 135 So. 3d 488, 490 (Fla. 2d DCA 2014).

[47] *Bank of New York v. Mieses*, 187 So. 3d 919, 920 (Fla. 3d DCA 2016); *accord Ortiz v. PNC Bank, Nat. Ass'n*, 188 So. 3d 923, 925 (Fla. 4th DCA 2016); *see also Bayview Loan Servicing, LLC v. Heefner*, 198 So. 3d 918, 920 (Fla. 5th DCA 2016) ("you may bring an action" substantially complies).

[48] *U.S. Bank Nat. Ass'n v. Sturm*, 280 So. 3d 1124 (Fla. 2d DCA 2019).

[49] "Our review of the record reveals that Astoria is correct and that the notice that it provided to Kaufman was in compliance with paragraph 22." *Astoria Fed. Sav. & Loan Ass'n v. Kaufman*, 158 So. 3d 675 (Fla. 5th DCA 2015). However, the absence of the amount

2-2:3.2 Examples of Non-Compliant Notices of Default

A notice that fails to advise the borrower of the right to reinstate the mortgage after acceleration does not comply with paragraph 22 of the standard form residential mortgage.[50] A letter was held non-compliant in this regard where it advised the borrower: "acceptance of one or more payments for less than the amount required to cure the default shall not be deemed to reinstate your loan or waive any acceleration of the loan."[51]

A notice that fails to advise the borrower of the right to assert the non-existence of a default or other defenses does not comply.[52]

A notice that states acceleration has already occurred does not comply.[53]

2-2:4 Opportunity to Cure as a Matter of Contract

The purpose of the notice provision is to alert the borrower to the alleged default and to provide the borrower with an opportunity to either dispute the alleged default or cure the default.[54] However, an opportunity to cure is only required if the mortgage requires it.[55] If the mortgage requires notice but not an opportunity to cure, then the lender complies with the condition precedent by giving notice alone and can foreclose immediately thereafter. For the effect of a defendant tendering the required cure payment, see Sections 2-3:3 and 2-3:4.

2-2:5 Opportunity to Cure in Standard Residential Mortgage

Paragraph 22 of the standard Fannie Mae/Freddie Mac residential mortgage[56] requires the lender to give the borrower a period of at least 30 days to cure the default. The 30-day cure period begins to run when the lender gives the borrower notice of the default. A foreclosure action filed before expiration of the 30-day cure period must be

---

required to cure is not noted in the opinion. The opinion merely refers to the court's review of "the record." The record on appeal included a copy of the notice letter, which lacked the amount required to cure. Instead, it directed the borrower to call the lender to obtain that amount. Since that omission is only found in the record and not in the opinion itself, this case has limited precedential value. The inquisitive practitioner may find the entire text of the default letter in the lower court order, which was reversed, on Westlaw. *See Astoria v. Kafuman*, 2013 WL 10054283 (Fla. Cir. Ct Aug. 6, 2013) (order contains text of default letter).

[50] *Haberl v. 21st Mortg. Corp.*, 138 So. 3d 1192, 1193 n.1 (Fla. 5th DCA 2014).
[51] *Samaroo v. Wells Fargo Bank*, 137 So. 3d 1127, 1129 (Fla. 5th DCA 2014), *reh'g denied* (May 1, 2014).
[52] *Samaroo v. Wells Fargo Bank*, 137 So. 3d 1127, 1129 (Fla. 5th DCA 2014), *reh'g denied* (May 1, 2014).
[53] *Harper v. HSBC Bank USA, Nat. Ass'n*, 148 So. 3d 1285, 1287 (Fla. 1st DCA 2014); *Kurian v. Wells Fargo Bank, Nat. Ass'n*, 114 So. 3d 1052, 1055 (Fla. 4th DCA 2013), *reh'g denied* (June 5, 2013).
[54] *Green Tree Servicing, LLC v. Milam*, 177 So. 3d 7, 19 (Fla. 2d DCA 2015).
[55] "A mortgagee simply has no duty to give a mortgagor an opportunity to cure a default." *Millett v. Perez*, 418 So. 2d 1067, 1068 (Fla. 3d DCA 1982).
[56] *See* Appendix A, 1-018, section 22.

dismissed.⁵⁷ However, a notice that specifies a cure period less than 30 days may be deemed harmless if the lender actually filed the foreclosure complaint more than 30 days after giving the notice of default and the borrower made no attempt to reinstate the loan within 30 days.⁵⁸

2-2:6 "Face-to-Face Interview" Requirement in FHA Mortgage

Mortgages insured by the Federal Housing Administration (FHA) require the lender to comply with regulations promulgated by the Secretary of Housing and Urban Development (HUD).⁵⁹ Among HUD's regulations are a requirement that the lender attempt to conduct a face-to-face interview with the borrower before three full monthly installments are unpaid.⁶⁰ This requirement is a condition precedent that must be complied with before foreclosure may be initiated.⁶¹

The First and Fifth District Courts hold that a lender's alleged non-compliance with HUD's face-to-face interview requirement can be pled as a specific denial in the borrower's answer and need not be raised as an affirmative defense.⁶² The Second District has explicitly abstained from that pleading issue.⁶³ Nevertheless, the Sec-

---

⁵⁷ *Dixon v. Wells Fargo Bank, N.A.*, 207 So. 3d 899, 901 (Fla. 4th DCA 2017) (final judgment reversed with instructions to involuntarily dismiss case where complaint filed six days after date on notice); *see also Harper v. HSBC Bank USA, Nat. Ass'n*, 148 So. 3d 1285 (Fla. 1st DCA 2014) (reversing summary judgment for lender where complaint filed eight days after date on notice).

⁵⁸ *Gorel v. Bank of New York Mellon*, 165 So. 3d 47 (Fla. 5th DCA 2015); *Vasilevskiy v. Wachovia Bank, Nat. Ass'n*, 171 So. 3d 192 (Fla. 5th DCA 2015).

⁵⁹ The relevant language of FHA's form mortgage is quoted in *Palma v. JPMorgan Chase Bank, NA*, 208 So. 3d 771, 773 (Fla. 5th DCA 2016) as follows:

> If Borrower defaults by failing to pay in full any monthly payment, then Lender may, except as limited by regulations of the Secretary in the case of payment defaults, require immediate payment in full of the principal balance remaining due and all accrued interest. . . . This Note does not authorize acceleration when not permitted by HUD regulations. As used in this Note, "Secretary" means the Secretary of Housing and Urban Development or his or her designee.

⁶⁰ 24 C.F.R. § 203.604 (2019).

⁶¹ *Palma v. JPMorgan Chase Bank, NA*, 208 So. 3d 771, 775 (Fla. 5th DCA 2016).

⁶² The First and Fifth Districts hold that non-compliance with the face-to-face interview requirement is merely a denial of condition precedent, which under Rule 1.120(c) may be accomplished by a specific denial, i.e., the face-to-face interview did not occur, but need not be raised as an affirmative defense. *See Chrzuszcz v. Wells Fargo Bank, N.A.*, 250 So. 3d 766, 770 (Fla. 1st DCA 2018) (reversing final judgment because "the specific denial did not amount to an affirmative defense" and burden thus remained on plaintiff to prove compliance); *and see Palma v. JPMorgan Chase Bank, NA*, 208 So. 3d 771, 774 (Fla. 5th DCA 2016) (reversing final judgment and remanding for involuntary dismissal, where defendant alleged non-compliance and burden thus remained on plaintiff to prove compliance).

⁶³ *Derouin v. Universal Am. Mortg. Co., Ltd. Liab. Co.*, 254 So. 3d 595, 600 (Fla. 2d DCA 2018) suggests that the First and Fifth Districts disagree with each other and then explicitly abstains from the issue: "We need not weigh in on the conflict." The *Derouin* court perceived an inter-district conflict by contrasting *Palma v. JPMorgan Chase Bank, NA*, 208 So. 3d 771, 774 (Fla. 5th DCA 2016) with *Harris v. U.S. Bank Nat'l Ass'n*, 223 So. 3d 1030, 1032 (Fla. 1st DCA 2017). However, that comparison discounted the First District's 2018

ond District did hold that if the borrower raises the face-to-face interview issue as an affirmative defense, then the lender cannot argue the borrower waived the interview unless it does so by avoidance in a reply.[64]

2-3 Acceleration

2-3:1 Contractual in Nature

An acceleration clause is a provision in a mortgage, note, or other contract[65] that requires the obligor to pay part or all of the balance sooner than otherwise required upon the occurrence of an event or circumstance described in the contract.[66] Absent an acceleration provision, the loan balance cannot be accelerated.[67] Rather, the balance continues to be payable in installments according to the contract terms—even after the borrower defaults.[68]

As with any other contractual provision, acceleration clauses are "to be construed in accordance with the intention of the parties as disclosed by the ordinary meaning of the words used and the circumstances of the parties."[69]

2-3:2 Automatic Versus Optional

Acceleration clauses fall into two categories: automatic and optional.

An automatic, or self-executing, acceleration clause is triggered by the happening of the contingency stated in the acceleration clause, whether or not the holder of the instrument wants the acceleration to occur.[70]

An optional acceleration clause is one that expressly makes acceleration an option of the lender and is the type included in the uniform Fannie Mae/Freddie Mac residential mortgage. To exercise this option, "the holder or payee of the note must take some clear and equivocal [sic] action, indicating its intent to accelerate all payments under the note, and such action should apprise the maker of the fact that the option to accel-

---

Chrzuszcz v. Wells Fargo Bank, N.A. opinion, in which it explicitly stated that it agreed with *Palma* and distinguished its older *Harris* opinion. See *Chrzuszcz v. Wells Fargo Bank, N.A.*, 250 So. 3d 766, 770 (Fla. 1st DCA 2018).

[64] *Derouin v. Universal Am. Mortg. Co., Ltd. Liab. Co.*, 254 So. 3d 595, 600 (Fla. 2d DCA 2018) ("Once the [borrowers] raised noncompliance as an affirmative defense, [the lender] should have replied if it sought to avoid the defense.").

[65] Acceleration can theoretically apply to any obligation, requiring performance of even a non-payment obligation sooner than initially contemplated by the contract.

[66] *Reed v. Lincoln*, 731 So. 2d 104, 105 (Fla. 5th DCA 1999) (quoting Black's Law Dictionary 12 (6th Ed.1990)).

[67] *Reed v. Lincoln*, 731 So. 2d 104, 106 (Fla. 5th DCA 1999); *Miller v. Balcanoff*, 566 So. 2d 1340, 1342 (Fla. 1st DCA 1990) (citing *Bardill v. Holcomb*, 215 So. 2d 64 (Fla. 4th DCA 1968)).

[68] *Nat'l Educ. Centers, Inc. v. Kirkland*, 635 So. 2d 33, 34 (Fla. 4th DCA 1993).

[69] *Baader v. Walker*, 153 So. 2d 51, 54-55 (Fla. 2d DCA 1963); 59 C.J.S. Mortgages § 495(3) at 784.

[70] "The rule is also settled that when a mortgage in terms declares the entire indebtedness due upon default of certain of its provisions or within a reasonable time thereafter, the Statute of Limitations begins to run immediately the default takes place or the time intervenes." *Travis Co. v. Mayes*, 36 So. 2d 264, 265 (Fla. 1948); *Baader v. Walker*, 153 So. 2d 51, 54-55 (Fla. 2d DCA 1963) (quoting 59 C.J.S. Mortgages § 495(3) at 784); *Broward County v. 8705 Hampshire Drive Condo., Inc.*, 127 So. 3d 853 (Fla. 4th DCA 2013).

erate has been exercised."[71] Optional acceleration may be achieved by sending written notice to the debtor, by making an oral demand, by demanding acceleration in a court pleading, and the like.[72] Filing a foreclosure action constitutes an exercise of the option to accelerate.[73] Acceleration can be revoked by the same method used to exercise it.[74]

In the event of a note and mortgage that contain unambiguous but conflicting acceleration clauses, one automatic and the other optional, the optional clause controls.[75]

2-3:3 Effect of Pre-Acceleration Payments

Before acceleration, a borrower who pays all amounts then due under the note, the mortgage and other loan documents cures the default and prevents acceleration from occurring.[76] A borrower who pays part of the amounts due but leaves a balance owing generally cannot defeat acceleration.[77] Certain unique cases of partial payment may defeat acceleration if the particular facts and circumstances make acceleration unconscionable and the defendant pleads and proves those facts and circumstances.[78]

2-3:4 Standard Residential Mortgage

The acceleration provision of the standard Fannie Mae/Freddie Mac residential mortgage in Florida permits the lender to "require immediate payment in full of all sums secured" by the mortgage.[79] This is an optional acceleration provision.[80] Even after the

---

[71] *Cent. Home Trust. Co. of Elizabeth v. Lippincott*, 392 So. 2d 931, 933 (Fla. 5th DCA 1980) (quoting 11 Am.Jur.2d Bills and Notes § 296 (1963)).

[72] *Cent. Home Trust. Co. of Elizabeth v. Lippincott*, 392 So. 2d 931, 933 (Fla. 5th DCA 1980) (quoting 11 Am.Jur.2d Bills and Notes § 296 (1963)).

[73] *Gus' Baths v. Lightbown*, 101 Fla. 1211, 1213 (Fla. 1931) ("the institution of a suit for foreclosure is the exercise of the option of the mortgagee to declare the whole of the principal sum and interest secured by the mortgage due and payable."); *Campbell v. Werner*, 232 So. 2d 252, 254 n.1 (Fla. 3d DCA 1970) ("the filing of suit to foreclose operates as notice to the mortgagor of the election to accelerate, where the election to do so is declared in the complaint . . . or, in the absence of such declaration, where the complaint on its face shows that foreclosure for the entire mortgage indebtedness is sought therein."); *Fowler v. First Fed. Sav. & Loan Ass'n of Defuniak Springs*, 643 So. 2d 30, 34 (Fla. 1st DCA 1994).

[74] *Bartram v. U.S. Bank Nat'l Ass'n*, 211 So. 3d 1009, 1012 (Fla. 2016).

[75] *KRC Enters., Inc. v. Soderquist*, 553 So. 2d 760, 761 (Fla. 2d DCA 1989).

[76] "Until the holder of the mortgage exercised this option [to accelerate], though payments of interest and taxes were past due, the defendants had the right to make a tender of such payments, and if a proper tender was made and kept good the right of the complainant to declare the principal sum due and payable was thereby defeated and the suit to foreclose the mortgage was prematurely brought." *Kreiss Potassium Phosphate Co. v. Knight*, 124 So. 751, 754 (Fla. 1929).

[77] "Blackmon's first argument on appeal is that Jim Walter had no right to accelerate the mortgage because Blackmon mailed her payment after the default, but before Jim Walter gave notice of its election to accelerate. The 8 June 1992 check . . . did not bring Blackmon's account current. As Blackmon made only a partial tender of the arrearages, Jim Walter was not prevented from exercising its option to accelerate the mortgage." *Tompkins v. Jim Walter Homes, Inc.*, 656 So. 2d 963, 964 (Fla. 5th DCA 1995).

[78] *See Campbell v. Werner*, 232 So. 2d 252, 256 (Fla. 3d DCA 1970), and cases cited therein.

[79] *See* Appendix A, 1-018, section 22.

[80] *Bartram v. U.S. Bank Nat'l Ass'n*, 211 So. 3d 1009, 1013 (Fla. 2016).

DEFAULT AND ACCELERATION

lender elects to accelerate, the standard Fannie Mae/Freddie Mac mortgage allows the borrower to pay only those amounts that would be due absent acceleration, provided certain other conditions are met.[81] Payment of those amounts and fulfillment of the other conditions prevent foreclosure on an accelerated basis. This ability to prevent acceleration and foreclosure by paying less than the full debt is a peculiar contractual right created by the Fannie Mae/Freddie Mac mortgage and does not exist in the absence of a similar contractual provision.[82]

When the mortgagee exercises the option to accelerate by the filing of a foreclosure action, a dismissal of that action revokes the acceleration and returns the parties to their installment contract relationship.[83] The acceleration is revoked whether the dismissal is involuntary[84] or voluntary.[85]

2-3:5 Effect of Post-Acceleration Foreclosure, Dismissal and New Foreclosure

Many foreclosure cases in recent years have been successive foreclosures, meaning a second or third foreclosure on the same mortgage. This arises when a foreclosure action is filed, that action is dismissed, and a subsequent action is filed seeking to foreclose the mortgage again. This scenario gives rise to three ostensible defenses in the subsequent case. These are: (1) res judicata; (2) the two dismissal rule; and (3) the statute of limitations. All three ostensible defenses have been rejected.[86]

2-3:5.1 Res Judicata

When an action is adjudicated on the merits, the doctrine of res judicata will bar a subsequent action if the two actions share four identical traits, called the four "identities." The four identities are: (1) identity of the thing sued for; (2) identity of the cause of action; (3) identity of persons and parties; (4) identity of the quality or capacity of the

---

[81] *See* Appendix A, 1-018, section 19.

[82] *Old Republic Ins. Co. v. Lee*, 507 So. 2d 754, 754-55 (Fla. 5th DCA 1987) ("Once the mortgage holder has exercised his option to accelerate, the right of the mortgagor to tender only the arrears is terminated.").

[83] "[A]fter the dismissal, the parties are simply placed back in the same contractual relationship as before, where the residential mortgage remained an installment loan, and the acceleration of the residential mortgage declared in the unsuccessful foreclosure action is revoked." *Bartram v. U.S. Bank Nat'l Ass'n*, 211 So. 3d 1009, 1019 (Fla. 2016).

[84] "When a mortgage foreclosure action is involuntarily dismissed pursuant to Rule 1.420(b), either with or without prejudice, the effect of the involuntary dismissal is revocation of the acceleration, which then reinstates the mortgagor's right to continue to make payments on the note and the right of the mortgagee, to seek acceleration and foreclosure based on the mortgagor's subsequent defaults." *Bartram v. U.S. Bank Nat'l Ass'n*, 211 So. 3d 1009, 1012 (Fla. 2016).

[85] *Gomez v. Household Fin. Corp., III*, 688 Fed. Appx. 680, 684 (11th Cir. 2017) ("The analysis and express holdings of *Bartram* give no indication that this distinction [between involuntary dismissal and voluntary dismissal] is significant..."); *Deutsche Bank Tr. Co. Ams. v. Beauvais*, 188 So. 3d 938, 945 (Fla. 3d DCA 2016) ("Under *Singleton*, subsequent defaults allow for subsequent accelerations regardless of the nature of a prior dismissal.").

[86] *Singleton v. Greymar Associates*, 882 So. 2d 1004, 1005 (Fla. 2004) (res judicata); *Olympia Mortgage Corp. v. Pugh*, 774 So. 2d 863, 865-66 (Fla. 4th DCA 2000) (two dismissal rule); *Bartram v. U.S. Bank Nat'l Ass'n*, 211 So. 3d 1009, 1019 (Fla. 2016) (statute of limitations).

persons for or against whom the claim is made.[87] The dismissal of an action with prejudice is an adjudication on the merits for res judicata purposes, whether the dismissal is voluntary[88] or involuntary.[89]

Thus, a refiled foreclosure that has all four identities with a prior foreclosure will be subject to dismissal on res judicata grounds. However, the second identity requires the two actions be premised on the same alleged event(s) of default. When the first and second actions are premised on different events of default, there is no identity of the cause of action, and the second action is not barred.[90] Identity of the cause of action is lacking where additional payments have become delinquent between the first and second actions, such that res judicata will not bar the second action.[91]

A foreclosure that fails due to lack of fulfillment of condition precedent is not an adjudication on the merits for res judicata purposes.[92]

2-3:5.2 Two-Dismissal Rule

The two dismissal rule, Florida Rule of Civil Procedure 1.420(a), provides that "a notice of dismissal operates as an adjudication on the merits when served by a plaintiff who has once dismissed in any court an action based on or including the same claim." The rule applies where there is an identity of the causes of action.[93] The causes of action

---

[87] *State of Wis. on Behalf of N. v. Martorella*, 670 So. 2d 1161, 1162 (Fla. 4th DCA 1996).
[88] *Capital Bank v. Needle*, 596 So. 2d 1134, 1135 (Fla. 4th DCA 1992).
[89] *Singleton v. Greymar Associates*, 882 So. 2d 1004, 1005 (Fla. 2004).
[90] *Singleton v. Greymar Associates*, 882 So. 2d 1004, 1008 (Fla. 2004). In *Singleton*, the default alleged in the first case was "failure to make payments from September 1, 1999 onward." *Singleton v. Greymar Associates*, 840 So. 2d 356, 356 (Fla. 4th DCA 2003). The default alleged in the second case was "failure to make payments from April 1, 2000 onward." *Capital Bank v. Need e*, 596 So. 2d 1134 (Fla. 4th DCA 1992).
[91] "The actual number of individual monthly payments missed as of the filing date of each complaint differed due to the passage of time between the 2010 suit, the 2013 suit, and this 2014 complaint. It was undisputed that the first missed installment payment, and thus the first default on the note and mortgage, occurred December 1, 2008. It was also undisputed that no payments were made for each month thereafter. Accordingly, the actual defaults upon which the previous foreclosure actions were based did not include the additional defaults for the subsequent months at issue in this third action, even though the same language was used in each complaint to describe the period of default." *Forero v. Green Tree Servicing, LLC*, 223 So. 3d 440, 444 (Fla. 1st DCA 2017).

"In this case, both the first and second foreclosure actions sought foreclosure and an acceleration of the balance due on the note and mortgage. However, the facts at issue in each foreclosure action differed, because the possible dates of default differed." *Olympia Mortgage Corp. v. Pugh*, 774 So. 2d 863, 866 (Fla. 4th DCA 2000).
[92] *See State St. Bank & Tr. Co. v. Badra*, 765 So. 2d 251, 254 (Fla. 4th DCA 2000) ("The trial court, in the first action, held that State Street Bank relied upon notices of acceleration that were insufficient to satisfy its burden of proof with regard to the conditions precedent under the mortgage. Since the first and second actions involved different notices of acceleration and such letters were essential to the maintenance of each action, there existed essential facts between the two cases which differed. The Final Judgment in the first action was not an adjudication on the merits.").
[93] *Olympia Mortgage Corp. v. Pugh*, 774 So. 2d 863, 865-66 (Fla. 4th DCA 2000).

are identical if the defaults alleged in both cases are exactly identical.[94] However, if the foreclosure complaint alleges a different *range of dates*, then the causes of action are not identical.[95] Thus "the rule did not apply, even though both complaints alleged the same missed payment of April 1, 1995, because the second case alleged a longer span of missed monthly payments thereafter than the first case."[96]

2-3:5.3 Statute of Limitations

The statute of limitations does not bar subsequent foreclosure actions, provided the subsequent case alleges a default within the preceding five years.[97] This issue is discussed in detail in Chapter 3.

---

[94] *E.g., Collazo v. HSBC Bank USA, N.A.*, 213 So. 3d 1012, 1013 (Fla. 3d DCA 2016) ("The record in the present case discloses that HSBC asserted the same payment default date and basis for acceleration in both the 2008 and 2014 complaints . . . .").
[95] *Forero v. Green Tree Servicing, LLC*, 223 So. 3d 440 (Fla. 1st DCA 2017).
[96] *Olympia Mortgage Corp. v. Pugh*, 774 So. 2d 863, 865-66 (Fla. 4th DCA 2000).
[97] *Bartram v. U.S. Bank Nat'l Ass'n*, 211 So. 3d 1009, 1013 (Fla. 2016).

CHAPTER 3
Statutes of Limitation and Repose

David W. Rodstein

3-1 Limitations Versus Repose

The statute of limitations and the statute of repose are both affirmative defenses.[1] They are both waived if not pled, and the burden of proof rests with the party raising the affirmative defense.[2]

However, the two defenses differ in several fundamental respects, including: the length of the statutory time period, the event that triggers the time period to run, and the effect of the time period's expiration.

Some older appellate opinions conflate limitations with repose, in part because the repose statute is inaptly titled "Limitations."[3] This statutory confusion has been clarified by more recent appellate opinions, and today's practitioners and courts should be familiar with the difference.

3-1:1 Statute of Limitations in Brief

Foreclosure actions in Florida are subject to a five-year statute of limitations.[4] The five-year period begins when the cause of action accrues.[5] For a detailed discussion of accrual, see Section 3-2:1. When the five-year period expires, the claimant's ability to obtain relief is barred.[6]

However, statutes of limitation in Florida are *procedural*, and "their expiration does not affect the underlying substantive rights of the parties involved."[7] The statute of limitations does not eliminate a foreclosure claim; it "merely cuts off the right

---

[1] *Hess v. Philip Morris USA, Inc.*, 175 So. 3d 687, 694 (Fla. 2015); *Johnston v. Hudlett*, 32 So. 3d 700, 704 (Fla. 4th DCA 2010); *Doe v. Hillsborough County Hosp. Auth.*, 816 So. 2d 262, 264 (Fla. 2d DCA 2002); *Square D Co. v. State Farm Fire & Cas. Co.*, 610 So. 2d 522 (Fla. 3d DCA 1992).
[2] *Hess v. Philip Morris USA, Inc.*, 175 So. 3d 687, 694 (Fla. 2015).
[3] *Houck Corp. v. New River, Ltd., Pasco*, 900 So. 2d 601, 603 (Fla. 2d DCA 2005).
[4] Fla. Stat. § 95.11(2)(c).
[5] Fla. Stat. § 95.031; *Hess v. Philip Morris USA, Inc.*, 175 So. 3d 687, 695 (Fla. 2015).
[6] "Statutes of limitations 'bar actions by setting a time limit within which an action must be filed as measured from the accrual of the cause of action, after which time obtaining relief is barred.'" *Hess v. Philip Morris USA, Inc.*, 175 So. 3d 687, 695 (Fla. 2015).
[7] *Allie v. Ionata*, 503 So. 2d 1237, 1241-42 (Fla. 1987).

to file suit on that claim."[8] Therefore, the mortgage lien survives the time bar.[9] Additionally, the foreclosure claim may be viable as a counterclaim in recoupment. *See* Section 3-2:6.

3-1:2 Statute of Repose in Brief

In contrast to the statute of limitations, the statute of repose is *substantive*. When the repose time period expires, the lien of the mortgage terminates.[10]

The repose time period is calculated in either of two different ways, depending on whether the maturity date of the mortgage loan is "ascertainable"[11] from a search of the land records. If the maturity date is ascertainable from the recorded mortgage or its attachments, then the repose period is five years from that maturity date. If the maturity date is not ascertainable from the recorded mortgage or its attachments, then the repose period is twenty years from the "date of the mortgage." Both the length of time *and* the starting point differ, depending on whether the maturity date is ascertainable from the record.

If the maturity date is not ascertainable from the original recording of the mortgage (making the repose period twenty years from execution), then the holder of the mortgage has the option of recording additional documents described in the statute and thereby changing the repose period to five years from maturity.[12]

In the case of "obligations, including taxes, paid by the mortgagee," the repose period is five years from the date of the payment.[13]

After the applicable repose period expires, no cause of action for foreclosure can accrue because there is no lien to be foreclosed.[14] Even though the lien has terminated, the statute of repose is an affirmative defense which must be pled, or it is waived.[15]

---

[8] *Houck Corp. v. New River, Ltd., Pasco*, 900 So. 2d 601, 603 (Fla. 2d DCA 2005); and *see Allie v. Ionata*, 503 So. 2d 1237, 1241-42 (Fla. 1987).

[9] *Reverse Mortg. Sols., Inc. v. Unknown Heirs*, 207 So. 3d 917, 922 (Fla. 1st DCA 2016); *Countrywide Home Loans, Inc. v. Burnette*, 177 So. 3d 1032, 1034 (Fla. 1st DCA 2015); *Houck Corp. v. New River, Ltd., Pasco*, 900 So. 2d 601, 605 (Fla. 2d DCA 2005).

[10] Fla. Stat. § 95.281(1); *Hess v. Philip Morris USA, Inc.*, 175 So. 3d 687, 695 (Fla. 2015).

[11] Fla. Stat. 95.281(1)(a) and (1)(b) provide: "... if the final maturity of an obligation secured by a mortgage is ascertainable from the record of it." Whether the word "it" refers to the mortgage or to the obligation is debatable. However, as a practical matter, the test is whether the maturity date can be "ascertained" by reference to all the recorded documents.

[12] Fla. Stat. § 95.281(1)(b).

[13] Fla. Stat. § 95.281(1)(c).

[14] *Houck Corp. v. New River, Ltd., Pasco*, 900 So. 2d 601, 603 (Fla. 2d DCA 2005); *Am. Bankers Life Assur. Co. of Florida v. 2275 W. Corp.*, 905 So. 2d 189, 192 (Fla. 3d DCA 2005); *City of Riviera Beach v. Reed*, 987 So. 2d 168, 170 (Fla. 4th DCA 2008).

[15] *Hess v. Philip Morris USA, Inc.*, 175 So. 3d 687, 694 (Fla. 2015).

3-1:3 Comparison Table

Statute of limitation	Statute of repose
Florida Statutes § 95.11(2)(c)	Florida Statutes § 95.281
Procedural	Substantive
No effect on mortgage lien	Terminates mortgage lien
Bars cause of action	No cause of action can accrue
5 years from when cause of action accrues	5 years from maturity, or 20 years from execution

3-2 Statute of Limitations

Foreclosure actions are subject to a five-year statute of limitations.[16] Statutes of limitation are procedural, and "their expiration does not affect the underlying substantive rights of the parties involved."[17]

Once the procedural bar arises under a statute of limitation, the procedural bar itself is a constitutionally protected right.[18] Since the procedural bar is a constitutionally protected right, neither a subsequent court decision nor a subsequent statutory enactment can remove the bar once it has arisen against a particular cause of action.[19] Nevertheless, the statute of limitations is an affirmative defense which must be pled, or it is waived.[20]

3-2:1 Accrual

The five-year statute of limitations begins to run when a cause of action accrues.[21] Accrual is considered the "trigger" which starts the five-year time clock running.[22]

The triggering function of accrual and the definition of accrual are contained in Fla. Stat. § 95.031. That statute in awkward fashion describes accrual as the triggering function before it defines accrual: "[T]he time within which an action shall be begun

---

[16] Fla. Stat. § 95.11(2)(c).

[17] *Allie v. Ionata*, 503 So. 2d 1237, 1241-42 (Fla. 1987).

[18] *In re Estate of Smith*, 685 So. 2d 1206, 1209 (Fla. 1996). *Smith* was a statute of limitations case, but the opinion could easily be misunderstood because it utilized particularly repose-like language. The court in *Smith* stated that the plaintiff's cause of action was "extinguished" and "cannot be revived," both of which are terms that describe statutes of repose but not statutes of limitation. *In re Estate of Smith*, 685 So. 2d 1206, 1210. However, a careful reading of *Smith* reveals that these quoted terms were used to describe the constitutional dimension of the statute of limitations defense, not to undermine the general principle that the statute of limitations only raises a procedural bar and does not extinguish a cause of action.

[19] *In re Estate of Smith*, 685 So. 2d 1206, 1209 (Fla. 1996); *Wiley v. Roof*, 641 So. 2d 66, 68-69 (Fla. 1994).

[20] *Hess v. Philip Morris USA, Inc.*, 175 So. 3d 687, 694 (Fla. 2015). *See generally Hojan v. State*, 212 So. 3d 982, 995 (Fla. 2017) (holding constitutionally protected rights were "waived because *Hojan* has not raised them in the present appeal.")

[21] Fla. Stat. § 95.031; *Hess v. Philip Morris USA, Inc.*, 175 So. 3d 687, 694 (Fla. 2015).

[22] *See, e.g., U.S. Bank Nat. Ass'n v. Bartram*, 140 So. 3d 1007, 1010 (Fla. 5th DCA 2014), approved by *Bartram v. U.S. Bank Nat'l Ass'n*, 211 So. 3d 1009 (Fla. 2016).

under any statute of limitations runs from the time the cause of action accrues."[23] The statute then defines accrual: "A cause of action accrues when the last element constituting the cause of action occurs."[24]

Consistent with the statute,[25] the Florida Supreme Court has stated that "a cause of action cannot be said to have accrued, within the meaning of the statute of limitations, until an action may be brought."[26]

The language of Fla. Stat. § 95.031 is highly precise; it pinpoints accrual at the occurrence of the "last element" constituting the cause of action. Practitioners must be equally precise in analyzing when the last element occurred in order to correctly assess when the cause of action accrued and the statute of limitations began to run. An imprecise assessment of accrual can result in the limitations period seeming to begin—and thus expire—either earlier or later than it should based on the facts of the case.

Despite the vital importance of accrual for determining whether an action is barred, the law remains unclear on which event constitutes the "last element" of a foreclosure cause of action. The last event could be: the default, an event related to the default, or acceleration of the debt. Practitioners should be aware of these competing theories, explained in detail below, and consider the implications of measuring accrual from different events in a given case.

3-2:1.1 The Default Theory of Accrual

The default theory of accrual holds that the date of default, or a date related to the default, is when the cause of action for foreclosure accrues. This approach flows from general contract principles.

A mortgage is "an executory contract or agreement in which one generally promises to allow a future sale of real property if a debt is not paid."[27] Therefore, the last element constituting a cause of action to foreclose would appear to be the default in payment or the default in some other material covenant of the mortgage.[28]

Consistent with the default theory of accrual, the Florida Supreme Court stated in the 2016 case of *Bartram v. U.S. Bank National Association*: "with each subsequent default, the statute of limitations runs from the date of each new default. . . ."[29] Also consistent with the default theory, the Supreme Court held that the lender was not barred from filing a subsequent foreclosure action "based on payment defaults occurring subsequent to the dismissal of the first foreclosure action, as long as the alleged

---

[23] Fla. Stat. § 95.031.
[24] Fla. Stat. § 95.031(1).
[25] Fla. Stat. § 95.031.
[26] *State Farm Mut. Auto. Ins. Co. v. Lee*, 678 So. 2d 818, 821 (Fla. 1996).
[27] "Mortgages are themselves contracts." *Beach Cmty. Bank v. Spellman*, 206 So. 3d 843, 844 (Fla. 1st DCA 2016); *see also Pitts v. Pastore*, 561 So. 2d 297, 300 (Fla. 2d DCA 1990).
[28] *See, e.g., Sardon Found. v. New Horizons Serv. Dogs, Inc.*, 852 So. 2d 416, 419 (Fla. 5th DCA 2003) (holding agreement to provide statement of receipts and expenditures, executed as part of loan transaction, was material obligation enforceable by foreclosure of mortgage). For more on non-monetary defaults, *see* Chapter 2, § 2-1:3.
[29] *Bartram v. U.S. Bank Nat'l Ass'n*, 211 So. 3d 1009, 1019 (Fla. 2016).

subsequent *default occurred within five years of the subsequent foreclosure action.*"[30] These two dicta from *Bartram* indicate that the cause of action accrues on the date of default.

However, accrual was not the issue in *Bartram*.[31] The issue in *Bartram* was whether the acceleration of a mortgage irrevocably set the statute of limitations running on all possible defaults under that mortgage. The Court answered that question with a qualified "no," but its answer was based on factors that did not depend on accrual—or even refer to accrual. Thus, the above-quoted statements are obiter dicta and are not binding precedent on the question of accrual.

Several District Court of Appeal opinions have similarly implied in dicta that the default theory of accrual applies to mortgage foreclosures.[32] However, other District

---

[30] *Bartram v. U.S. Bank Nat'l Ass'n*, 211 So. 3d 1009, 1012 (Fla. 2016) (emphasis added). The italicized language implies that the statute of limitations *would* bar a subsequent foreclosure action based on a default occurring more than five years before the action was filed. Thus, the Florida Supreme Court appeared to hold that a foreclosure cause of action accrues, and the five year clock starts, upon default.

[31] The Florida Supreme Court in *Bartram* answered a certified question about the lender's ability to file a future foreclosure action more than five years after the lender had accelerated the debt in a prior case, which was dismissed. Multiple statements in the opinion support the default theory of accrual. However, accrual was inconsequential to the court's answer to the certified question.

[32] The following cases all say that the default alleged in the second action must have occurred "within" the statute of limitations period. Although these statements are all dicta and do not represent the holdings of the various cases, they are nevertheless strong indicators that these courts consider the date of default to be the date of accrual.

The statute of limitations "did not bar the action due to the inclusion within the allegations of at least some *defaulted installment payments within five years* of the date the complaint was filed." *Forero v. Green Tree Servicing, LLC*, 223 So. 3d 440 (Fla. 1st DCA 2017) (emphasis added).

"[A] foreclosure action must be based on *a default that occurred within the five-year statute of limitations period....*" *Bollettieri Resort Villas Condo. Ass'n, Inc. v. Bank of N.Y. Mellon*, 198 So. 3d 1140, 1142 (Fla. 2d DCA 2016) (emphasis added).

"We therefore conclude that dismissal of a foreclosure action accelerating payment on one default does not bar a subsequent foreclosure action on a later default *if the subsequent default occurred within five years of the subsequent action.*" *Deutsche Bank Trust Co. Ams. v. Beauvais*, 188 So. 3d 938, 944 (Fla. 3d DCA 2016) (emphasis added).

"Appellants argue that the foreclosure action was barred by the statute of limitations because it was filed over five years after the date of default alleged in a 2008 foreclosure action that was voluntarily dismissed. However, the present action, which was brought in February 2014, was based upon a different event of default—namely, the borrowers' failure to make the payment due on March 1, 2009. We have held that a voluntarily dismissed foreclosure action 'does not bar subsequent actions and acceleration based upon different events of default,' and '*any acts of default still within the statute of limitations* may be raised in a subsequent suit.'" *Solonenko v. Georgia Notes 18, LLC*, 182 So. 3d 876 (Fla. 4th DCA 2016) (emphasis added) (quoting *Evergrene Partners, Inc. v. Citibank, N.A.*, 143 So. 3d 954, 955-56 (Fla. 4th DCA 2014).

"[T]he suit must still be based on *an act of default within the five-year statute of limitations period.*" *Hicks v. Wells Fargo Bank, N.A.*, 178 So. 3d 957, 959 (Fla. 5th DCA 2015) (emphasis added).

While these quotes from all five of Florida's District Courts of Appeal are not conclusive—because accrual was not the controlling issue in these cases—they indicate a common

Court of Appeal opinions and one Justice of the Florida Supreme Court have espoused an acceleration theory of accrual for mortgage foreclosures. *See* Section 3-2:1.2. Accrual thus remains open to further appellate litigation, despite the persuasive majority of dicta favoring the default theory of accrual.

3-2:1.1a Effect of Conditions Precedent on Accrual

Under the default theory of accrual, a cause of action accrues based on the date of default. Several appellate opinions have implied that a cause of action for foreclosure accrues *immediately* on the day after a payment is missed.[33] However, those opinions did not analyze what was the "last element" constituting the cause of action (as prescribed by Fla. Stat. § 95.031) and did not consider the effect of conditions precedent on accrual.

If the mortgage being foreclosed requires conditions precedent to be fulfilled prior to bringing the foreclosure action, the foreclosure is premature until the conditions precedent have been fulfilled or have been waived.[34] Since "a cause of action cannot be said to have accrued, within the meaning of the statute of limitations, until an action may be brought,"[35] the last condition precedent to be fulfilled should be the "last element" which constitutes the cause of action, and starts the statute of limitations running.

For example, the uniform Fannie Mae/Freddie Mac mortgage[36] requires that a notice of default must be given and a 30-day cure period must pass before a foreclosure action may be brought. *See* Chapter 2, Section 2-2. A foreclosure action filed before the lender gives the notice of default is subject to dismissal.[37] Similarly, a foreclosure action filed before expiration of the 30-day cure period is subject to dismissal.[38]

Therefore, a foreclosure cause of action arguably does not accrue until the contractually required notice has been given and the 30-day cure period has expired.[39] This

---

judicial focus on whether the default occurred within the limitations period, with little or no regard for when acceleration occurred.

[33] *See Bartram v. U.S. Bank Nat'l Ass'n*, 211 So. 3d 1009, 1012 (Fla. 2016); *Deutsche Bank Trust Co. Ams. v. Beauvais*, 188 So. 3d 938, 944 (Fla. 3d DCA 2016); *Solonenko v. Georgia Notes 18, LLC*, 182 So. 3d 876 (Fla. 4th DCA 2016).

[34] *U.S. Bank Nat. Ass'n v. Busquets*, 135 So. 3d 488, 490 (Fla. 2d DCA 2014); *Samaroo v. Wells Fargo Bank*, 137 So. 3d 1127 (Fla. 5th DCA 2014), *reh'g denied* (May 1, 2014).

[35] *State Farm Mut. Auto. Ins. Co. v. Lee*, 678 So. 2d 818, 821 (Fla. 1996).

[36] *See* Appendix A, 1-018, section 22.

[37] *Holt v. Calchas, LLC*, 155 So. 3d 499, 507 (Fla. 4th DCA 2015); *cf. Ramos v. Sabadell United Bank, N.A.*, 137 So. 3d 557, 557 (Fla. 4th DCA 2014) (summary judgment in the borrower's favor).

[38] *Dixon v. Wells Fargo Bank, N.A.*, 207 So. 3d 899, 901 (Fla. 4th DCA 2017) (final judgment reversed with instructions to involuntarily dismiss case where complaint filed six days after date on notice); *see also Harper v. HSBC Bank USA, Nat. Ass'n*, 148 So. 3d 1285 (Fla. 1st DCA 2014) (reversing summary judgment for lender where complaint was filed eight days after date on notice).

[39] *But see Federal Nat. Mortg. Ass'n v. Hawthorne*, 197 So. 3d 1237, 1240 (Fla. 4th DCA 2016) (holding notice of default that failed to comply with mailing address requirement in mortgage did not warrant involuntary dismissal because it caused no prejudice to borrower; notice of default was sent to a valid alternate address which "may have even benefitted" the borrower); and *Gorel v. Bank of N.Y. Mellon*, 165 So. 3d 44, 47 (Fla. 5th DCA 2015) (holding notice of default that set a date to cure default 29 days from date of letter instead of 30 days

approach is consistent with the Florida Supreme Court's analysis and ruling in *State Farm Mutual Auto Insurance Co. v. Lee*, which held that a cause of action for certain insurance benefits did not arise until the statutory compliance period prescribed for payment of the benefits expired.[40]

In some cases, the amount of time needed for the lender to give the mandatory notice of default, plus the 30-day cure period required by the mortgage, could push accrual of the cause of action far enough into the future to defeat a statute of limitations defense. In such a case, the rule of *State Farm Mutual Auto Insurance Co. v. Lee* would dictate that the cause of action only accrued after the required cure period expired, making the start of the limitations period later. A later start of the limitations period means a later end of the period and a later date within which the foreclosure action would be considered timely.

3-2:1.1b Successive Accruals

One consequence of the default theory of accrual is that successive defaults result in successive accruals. As a general matter of contract law, the failure to make several installment payments constitutes a series of defaults.[41] When a series of defaults occurs under a contract, a breach of contract cause of action accrues for each default.[42]

Accordingly, per the default theory of accrual "the statute of limitations starts running against each payment as it becomes due."[43] Since each installment becomes due on a different date, several statute of limitations periods run concurrently against the several causes of action—each period beginning when the corresponding cause of action accrued and ending five years later.[44] The causes of action that accrue earlier will be barred by the statute of limitations earlier. The causes of action that accrue later will be barred later. "Installments due at different times under a note mature or accrue the day after each is due to be paid, and the statute of limitations may run on some and not others."[45]

---

as required by mortgage did not prejudice borrower because he made no attempt to cure the default; *reversed on other grounds*).

[40] *State Farm Mut. Auto. Ins. Co. v. Lee*, 678 So. 2d 818, 821 (Fla. 1996).

[41] *Isaacs v. Deutsch*, 80 So. 2d 657, 660 (Fla. 1955) (installment contract); *Hannett v. Bryan*, 640 So. 2d 203, 204 (Fla. 4th DCA 1994) (assignment of future syndication fees).

[42] *Isaacs v. Deutsch*, 80 So. 2d 657, 660 (Fla. 1955).

[43] *Isaacs v. Deutsch*, 80 So. 2d 657, 660 (Fla. 1955).

[44] *Isaacs v. Deutsch*, 80 So. 2d 657, 660 (Fla. 1955) ("We hold, then, that where an express contract requires the father to pay a definite sum at stated intervals for the support of his minor child, the statute of limitations starts running against each payment as it becomes due."); *Central Home Tr. Co. of Elizabeth v. Lippincott*, 392 So. 2d 931, 933 (Fla. 5th DCA 1980) ("Installments due at different times under a note mature or accrue the day after each is due to be paid, and the statute of limitations may run on some and not others.").

[45] *Central Home Tr. Co. v. Lippincott*, 392 So. 2d 931, 933 (Fla. 5th DCA 1980). As discussed above, the statute of limitations runs on causes of action—not on installment payments. Accordingly, the true import of this quote is that the statute of limitations may run on some *causes of action* for non-payment of installments and not on other causes of action for non-payment. The critical implication of this quote is that the cause of action for foreclosure accrues, and the statute of limitations begins running, each time an installment payment is missed—i.e., a default occurs.

3-2:1.1c Continuing State of Default—"All Subsequent Payments"

Under the default theory of accrual, the statute of limitations may run on causes of action for defaults older than five years, while causes of action for newer defaults remain viable.

Therefore, a case was *not* barred by the statute of limitations where the complaint alleged a default in the monthly payment due five years and four months in the past (time-barred) and also alleged defaults on "all subsequent payments."[46] The "all subsequent payments" allegation included default on all 59 monthly payments that came due within the five years prior to the date the case was filed. All five of Florida's district courts of appeal agree that the statute of limitations is not a viable defense when the plaintiff alleges and proves defaults on "all subsequent payments."[47] These courts' reliance on default of all subsequent payments suggests that they should all hold to the default theory of accrual.

Nevertheless, an alternative theory remains—that the cause of action for foreclosure accrues when the loan is accelerated. That theory is discussed below.

3-2:1.2 The Acceleration Theory of Accrual

The acceleration theory of accrual was cogently advanced in the concurring opinion of Florida Supreme Court Justice Lawson in the 2017 case *Bollettieri Resort Villas Condo. Ass'n, Inc. v. Bank of N.Y. Mellon.*[48]

In *Bollettieri*, Justice Lawson criticized the default theory of accrual as "a widespread and fundamental misunderstanding." His opinion was advisory only, as the Supreme Court dismissed the Bollettieri appeal and did not speak to the accrual issue. In his concurrence, Justice Lawson opined that "the cause of action on a thirty-year note does not accrue until thirty years after signing—when the full balance is due—unless the lender accelerates and declares the full balance due earlier."[49]

Although two District Courts of Appeal have praised and followed Justice Lawson's concurring opinion in *Bollettieri*, they did so on a different point. In addition

---

[46] *Dhanasar v. JP Morgan Chase Bank, N.A.*, 201 So. 3d 825, 826 (Fla. 3d DCA 2016) ("Because the bank's complaint specifically alleged that *Dhanasar* had failed to pay the April 2008 payment *and all subsequent payments,* and the action was filed within five years of a default payment, we agree with the trial court's conclusion that the action survived the asserted statute of limitations bar.").

[47] *Dhanasar v. JP Morgan Chase Bank, N.A.*, 201 So. 3d 825, 826 (Fla. 3d DCA 2016); *Depicciotto v. Nationstar Mortgage, LLC*, 225 So. 3d 390, 391 (Fla. 4th DCA 2017) ("Nationstar's foreclosure action was not barred by the statute of limitations where it alleged and proved separate and continuing defaults that fell within the five years preceding the filing of this suit."); *see also Forero v. Green Tree Servicing, LLC*, 223 So. 3d 440, 444 (Fla. 1st DCA 2017); *Klebanoff v. Bank of New York Mellon*, No. 5D16-1637, 2017 WL 2818078, at *2 (Fla. 5th DCA June 30, 2017) ("Because the Bank alleged and proved missed payments within the five years prior to the filing of its complaint, its action was not barred by the statute of limitations."); *Bollettieri Resort Villas Condo. Ass'n, Inc. v. Bank of N.Y. Mellon*, 198 So. 3d 1140, 1142 (Fla. 2d DCA 2016).

[48] *Bollettieri Resort Villas Condo. Ass'n, Inc. v. Bank of N.Y. Mellon*, 228 So. 3d 72, 73 (Fla. 2017), J. Lawson concurring.

[49] *Bollettieri Resort Villas Condo. Ass'n, Inc. v. Bank of N.Y. Mellon*, 228 So. 3d 72, 73 (Fla. 2017), J. Lawson concurring.

to espousing the acceleration theory of accrual, Justice Lawson also opined that the dollar amount of the foreclosure judgment is not affected by the statute of limitations even if some installment payments were defaulted on more than five years before the complaint date.[50] The Fourth and Fifth Districts followed Justice Lawson on that point. However, both courts applied the *default theory* of accrual in their opinions.[51]

The acceleration theory of accrual is ostensibly based on the premise that acceleration is the "last event" constituting the cause of action.[52] Indeed, many Florida courts list acceleration as an element of the foreclosure cause of action.[53] Since the other elements (a contract, a debt, and a default) must exist before acceleration can occur, the date of acceleration is logically the "last element" that would constitute the cause of action and thus give rise to accrual.

Under the acceleration theory of accrual, a lender may not be able to delay accrual by delaying its exercise of optional acceleration. Rather, a lender that delayed acceleration for an extended time may find that the court will impute a fiction that it actually accelerated a "reasonable time" after the default. Such an imputed acceleration would push accrual backward in time and could give rise to a statute of limitations defense that would not otherwise be apparent from the facts of the case.[54]

That said, the acceleration theory has been questioned more than once by Florida's Fifth District Court of Appeal.[55] While the acceleration theory of accrual has support

---

[50] *Bank of Am., N.A. v. Graybush*, 253 So. 3d 1188 (Fla. 4th DCA 2018); *Grant v. Citizens Bank, N.A.*, 263 So. 3d 156, 158 (Fla. 5th DCA 2018).

[51] "[W]e hold that based on the contractual provisions of the note, neglecting to sue for missed payments beyond five years did not waive the Bank's entitlement to all sums due on a later date, when that later date did not lie five years beyond *a monthly default*, or five years beyond the maturity date of the note." *Bank of Am., N.A. v. Graybush*, 253 So. 3d 1188, 1194 (Fla. 4th DCA 2018); "[T]he statute of limitations runs from the date of each new *default*." *Grant v. Citizens Bank, N.A.*, 263 So. 3d 156, 158 (Fla. 5th DCA 2018); *see also U.S. Bank Nat. Ass'n v. Bartram*, 140 So. 3d 1007, 1010 (Fla. 5th DCA 2014) ("*Bartram I*"), which expressly rejected the defendant's detailed acceleration-accrual argument.

[52] Fla. Stat. § 95.031.

[53] "Foreclosure plaintiffs must show: (1) an agreement; (2) a default; (3) *an acceleration of debt to maturity*; and (4) the amount due." *Bank of America v. Delgado*, 166 So. 3d 857, 859 (Fla. 3d DCA 2015) (emphasis added); *Black Point Assets, Inc. v. Federal National Mortgage Association*, 220 So. 3d 566 (Fla. 5th DCA 2017); accord *Liberty Home Equity Sols., Inc. v. Raulston*, 206 So. 3d 58, 60 (Fla. 4th DCA 2016); *Pealer v. Wilmington Tr. Nat'l Ass'n for MFRA Tr.*, 212 So. 3d 1137, 1139 (Fla. 2d DCA 2017).

[54] In other words, the plaintiff may not, by failing or refusing to perform the condition, toll the running of the statute and reserve the right to sue within the statutory period from such time as he decides to make a demand.

> Specifically, the guaranty has, as a condition precedent, a "demand" requirement. As a general rule of contract law, where the contract requires a demand as a condition to the right to sue, the statute of limitations does not commence until such a demand is made. Where the plaintiff's cause of action depends on an act that he himself must perform, as here, he may not suspend indefinitely the running of the statute of limitations by delaying performance of this act.

Greene v. Bursey, 733 So. 2d 1111, 1114 (Fla. 4th DCA 1999).

[55] In *U.S. Bank Nat. Ass'n v. Bartram*, 140 So. 3d 1007, 1010 (Fla. 5th DCA 2014) ("*Bartram I*"), the Fifth District rejected the acceleration theory of acceleration. In *Bartram*

in older District Court opinions and express support from a Florida Supreme Court Justice, it is undermined by dicta from the Florida Supreme Court in *Bartram II* [56] and by direct criticism from the Fifth District in *Bartram I*.[57] The trend for years has been to view the date of each default as when each cause of action accrues and the statute of limitations starts running.

3-2:1.3 Selected Accrual Examples

3-2:1.3a Where No Contractual Payment Date and No Maturity Date

If neither the mortgage nor the note specify a date when payments are due or a date when the debt matures, the cause of action to foreclose accrues when demand is made for payment. If no demand for payment is made, the filing of the complaint constitutes the demand and thus the accrual of the cause of action.[58]

I, the Fifth District noted and rejected the borrower's argument "that the cause of action for default of future installment payments accrued upon acceleration." *Id*. The defendant's argument was expressly based on *Locke v. State Farm Fire & Cas. Co.*, 509 So. 2d (Fla. 1st DCA 1987); *Monte v. Tipton*, 612 So. 2d 714 (5th DCA 1993); *Greene v. Bursey*, 733 So. 2d 1111, 1114-15 (Fla. 4th DCA 1999); *Reed v. Lincoln*, 731 So. 2d 104 (Fla. 5th DCA 1999); and most importantly *Conner v. Coggins*, 349 So. 2d 780 (Fla. 1st DCA 1977). Critically, the Fifth District rejected the borrower's argument because, as the bank "point[ed] out [ ] all cases cited to the trial court predated *Singleton* and, furthermore, the root of the holdings in these cases stems from 'pure' dicta in *Conner*." *U.S. Bank Nat. Ass'n v. Bartram*, 140 So. 3d at 1010 (citing *Singleton v. Greymar Associates*, 882 So. 2d 1004 (Fla. 2004)). The Fifth District was presumably pointing out that in *Conner* there was no acceleration *at all*, as the mortgage did not even contain an acceleration clause. The Fifth Districts *Bartram I* opinion was approved by the Florida Supreme Court in *Bartram v. U.S. Bank Nat'l Ass'n*, 211 So. 3d 1009 (Fla. 2016) ("*Bartram II*").

Again in *Hicks v. Wells Fargo Bank, N.A*, the Fifth District held the foreclosure action was barred by the statute of limitations based exclusively on the date of the default. The default at issue allegedly occurred on June 1, 2006, and the foreclosure action was filed on January 9, 2013—more than five years later. The bank exercised its acceleration option in the 2013 complaint. If the 2013 acceleration was the date of accrual, the action would have been timely. On the contrary, since "the suit must still be based on an act of default within the five-year statute of limitations period," it was barred by the statute of limitations. *Hicks v. Wells Fargo Bank, N.A.*, 178 So. 3d 957, 959 (Fla. 5th DCA 2015).

[56] *Bartram v. U.S. Bank Nat'l Ass'n*, 211 So. 3d 1009 (Fla. 2016).
[57] *U.S. Bank Nat. Ass'n v. Bartram*, 140 So. 3d 1007 (Fla. 5th DCA 2014).
[58] *Smith v. Branch*, 391 So. 2d 797 (Fla. 2d DCA 1980) (citing Fla. Stat. 95.11(2)(c) and 95.031(1)). The plaintiff in *Smith v. Branch* filed suit in 1979 to foreclose a 1962 mortgage. Neither the mortgage nor the note contained a date for payment or maturity, and the plaintiff made no demand for payment. The trial court entered judgment for the defendant on statute of limitations grounds. The Second District Court of Appeal reversed, holding that the foreclosure "cause of action did not accrue until the filing of the complaint herein."

3-2:1.3b Where No Contractual Payment Date But Maturity Date Specified

In *Houck Corp. v. New River, Ltd., Pasco*,[59] the borrower executed two non-recourse[60] promissory notes and a mortgage in 1984. The mortgage contained no date for payments and no maturity date. The notes did not require installment payments, but both contained a maturity date of October 30, 1991. The court held that the foreclosure cause of action accrued when the maturity date stated in the notes arrived and the borrower failed to pay. Therefore, the foreclosure cause of action was time barred on October 30, 1996.

3-2:1.3c Where Accrual Is Triggered by Lender's Demand

In *Broward County v. 8705 Hampshire Drive Condominium, Inc.*, there was no monetary default, but the borrower failed to report certain information it agreed to report. This was a non-monetary breach that the court held sufficient to give rise to a foreclosure cause of action. However, the mortgage did not create a cause of action merely upon the failure to report. "The mortgage contained a specific clause allowing acceleration based upon breach of the reporting covenants. It also required the county to notify the appellee if the county exercised its option to accelerate the note."[61] Holding that the foreclosure cause of action accrued when the mortgagee made a written demand for the reporting information, the 4th DCA affirmed summary judgment for the borrower based on the statute of limitations.

3-2:1.3d Where Mortgage Debt Was Previously Discharged in Bankruptcy

A bankruptcy discharge of the borrower's personal obligation to pay does not prevent payment defaults from occurring and giving rise to an in rem foreclosure action.[62] Similarly, the borrower's surrender of mortgaged property in bankruptcy does not result in acceleration of the payments.[63]

3-2:2 Successive Foreclosures

The term "successive foreclosure" refers to a foreclosure action filed after the dismissal of an earlier foreclosure action on the same mortgage. If the second action is

---

[59] *Houck Corp. v. New River, Ltd., Pasco*, 900 So. 2d 601, 603 (Fla. 2d DCA 2005).

[60] A non-recourse promissory note merely creates the debt which the mortgage then imposes on real property as a lien, but the makers of the note are not liable in the event of a default. The only "recourse" is against the property.

[61] *Broward Cnty. v. 8705 Hampshire Drive Condo., Inc.*, 127 So. 3d 853 (Fla. 4th DCA 2013).

[62] A "bankruptcy discharge extinguishes only one mode of enforcing a claim—namely, an action against the debtor *in personam*—while leaving intact another—namely, an action against the debtor *in rem*." *Can Fin., LLC v. Krazmien*, 253 So. 3d 8 (Fla. 4th DCA 2018) (quoting *Johnson v. Home State Bank*, 501 U.S. 78, 84 (1991)).

[63] The fact of surrender through the bankruptcy court does not begin the statute of limitations because the surrender does not have the effect of accelerating the debt. *BMG Realty Grp., LLC v. U.S. Bank Nat'l Ass'n*, 45 Fla. L. Weekly D298 (Fla. 2d DCA February 7, 2020).

filed more than five years after the first action, the statute of limitations may be implicated. However, in cases based on the standard Fannie Mae/Freddie Mac mortgage a successive foreclosure is not barred by the statute of limitations. This was the holding of the Florida Supreme Court in *Bartram v. U.S. Bank, N.A.*[64]

3-2:2.1 *Bartram v. U.S. Bank, N.A.*

Bartram v. U.S. Bank, N.A.[65] holds that a subsequent foreclosure case will not be barred where: (1) the complaint alleges that a default occurred after the dismissal of the first case, (2) the subsequent case is filed within five years of that alleged default, and (3) the mortgage to be foreclosed contains a reinstatement provision. Where one or more of these elements is missing, the result could differ from *Bartram*.

The precedential value of *Bartram* is limited in several ways. Understanding its limitations and contours requires a review of the facts.

U.S. Bank filed a foreclosure case in 2006, in which it accelerated the balance due on the mortgage. The 2006 case was dismissed in 2011 because U.S. Bank failed to appear at a case management conference.

In 2012—more than five years after the 2006 acceleration—Mr. Bartram filed a preemptive action to quiet title (i.e., to cancel the mortgage). Mr. Bartram's theory was that acceleration of the debt in 2006 irrevocably started the statute of limitations running on the full accelerated debt. Since five years had passed since the statute started running, he argued that any future foreclosure case would be time barred. Since any future foreclosure case would be time barred, he argued that the mortgage was unenforceable and was a cloud on his title to the property. The trial court agreed with Mr. Bartram and canceled the mortgage and the note.[66]

The intermediate Court of Appeals reversed and certified a question of great public importance to the Florida Supreme Court.[67]

The Florida Supreme Court accepted the case and answered the following highly specific (and slightly revised) certified question.

DOES ACCELERATION OF PAYMENTS DUE UNDER A RESIDENTIAL NOTE AND MORTGAGE WITH A REINSTATEMENT PROVISION IN A FORECLOSURE ACTION THAT WAS DISMISSED PURSUANT TO RULE 1.420(B), FLORIDA RULES OF CIVIL PROCEDURE, TRIGGER APPLICATION OF THE STATUTE OF LIMITATIONS TO PREVENT A SUBSEQUENT FORECLOSURE ACTION BY THE MORTGAGEE BASED ON PAYMENT DEFAULTS OCCURRING SUBSEQUENT TO DISMISSAL OF THE FIRST FORECLOSURE SUIT?[68]

---

[64] *Bartram v. U.S. Bank Nat'l Ass'n*, 211 So. 3d 1009 (Fla. 2016).
[65] *Bartram v. U.S. Bank Nat'l Ass'n*, 211 So. 3d 1009 (Fla. 2016).
[66] The statute of limitations on a case to enforce the note would also be five years and thus, arguably, barred on the same theory. Fla. Stat. § 95.11(2).
[67] *U.S. Bank Nat. Ass'n v. Bartram*, 140 So. 3d 1007 (Fla. 5th DCA 2014).
[68] *Bartram v. U.S. Bank Nat'l Ass'n*, 211 So. 3d 1009, 1012 (Fla. 2016).

The Court answered the certified question as follows.

> [W]e answer the rephrased certified question in the negative and hold, consistent with our reasoning in *Singleton*, that the mortgagee, also referred to as the lender, was not precluded by the statute of limitations from filing a subsequent foreclosure action based on payment defaults occurring subsequent to the dismissal of the first foreclosure action, as long as the alleged subsequent default occurred within five years of the subsequent foreclosure action.

The Court explained that its holding would be the same whether the first case was dismissed with or without prejudice.[69] However, the holding is limited to cases where the three factors mentioned at the beginning of this section are present: (1) the complaint alleges that a default occurred after the dismissal of the first case; (2) the subsequent case is filed within five years of that alleged default; and (3) the mortgage contains a certain type of reinstatement provision. If any of these factors is missing, the holding may not apply. A brief exposition of each factor follows.

(1) The holding of *Bartram* expressly applies where the second foreclosure action is "premised on a default occurring *subsequent* to the dismissal of the first foreclosure action."[70] That hypothetical fact[71] was stated in the certified question from the Fifth District Court of Appeal and was retained by the Supreme Court in its revised version of the question. By limiting its answer to cases where the second action was based on a post-dismissal default, the Court left open for a future case whether the holding would apply where the second case is premised on a default occurring before dismissal of the first case.[72] More than one District Court

---

[69] *Bartram v. U.S. Bank Nat'l Ass'n*, 211 So. 3d 1009, 1012 (Fla. 2016).
[70] *Bartram v. U.S. Bank Nat'l Ass'n*, 211 So. 3d 1009, 1020 (Fla. 2016).
[71] The fact was hypothetical because there was no second foreclosure case filed in *Bartram*. Therefore, in some ways the opinion as a whole—and particularly the question of whether the second case has to be premised on a post-dismissal default—resembles an advisory opinion.
[72] The Court expressly stated that a second case premised on the same default as the first case would not be barred, so long as the first dismissal was without prejudice and the second case was filed within five years of the default. "[A] dismissal without prejudice would allow a mortgagee to bring another foreclosure action premised on the same default [as the first case] *as long as the action was brought within five years of the default.*" *Bartram v. U.S. Bank Nat'l Ass'n*, 211 So. 3d 1009, 1020 (Fla. 2016) (emphasis added). Curiously, this statement came immediately on the heels of the Court stating that the distinction between dismissals with prejudice and without prejudice "is not material for purposes of the statute of limitations analysis." Perhaps the Court meant that distinction is not material where the second case is premised on a subsequent default but is material where the second case is based on the same or earlier default.
    Indeed, that seems to be the only explanation for the very next sentence of the opinion: "As the federal district court in *Dorta* reasoned, if the mortgagee's foreclosure action is unsuccessful *for whatever reason*, the mortgagee still has the right to file subsequent foreclosure actions—and to seek acceleration of the entire debt—so long as they are based on *separate defaults.*" *Bartram v. U.S. Bank Nat'l Ass'n*, 211 So. 3d 1009, 1020 (Fla. 2016) (emphasis in original) (quoting *Dorta v. Wilmington Trust Nat'l Assoc.*, 13–cv–185–OC–10PRL, 2014 WL 1152917, at *2-4 (M. D. Fla. Mar. 24, 2014)). Apparently, the distinction is not material where the second case is premised on a subsequent default but is material where the second case is based on the same (or presumably an earlier)

of Appeal has held that *Bartram* applies (i.e., no statute of limitations bar) where the complaint alleged a date of default before dismissal of the first case "and all subsequent payments."[73]

(2) The holding of *Bartram* expressly applies where the second case is filed within five years after the default alleged in the second case. What remains undecided by the Supreme Court is whether a complaint alleging a payment default older than five years "and all subsequent payments" would pass this second factual test.

---

default. At least one District Court has applied *Bartram* that way. *HSBC Bank United States v. Leone*, 271 So. 3d 172, 175 (Fla. 2d DCA 2019) (in challenge to notice of default, the Court held a second case based on the same default did not require a new notice of default to comply with the pre-acceleration notice requirement, relying on the preceding quote from *Bartram*).

Unfortunately, the entire discussion in *Bartram* of whether or not the second case is premised on a subsequent default has no explicit basis in the statute of limitations, Chapter 95, Fla. Stat. Neither does the with prejudice/without prejudice distinction find any mention in the limitations statute itself. Rather, both issues appear to have been inadvertently transferred by the Supreme Court from the res judicata analysis in *Singleton* to the statute of limitations context in *Bartram*.

The Supreme Court recognized in *Bartram* that a dismissal without prejudice would not prevent the subsequent case from alleging the same default as the first case. However, the Court did not attribute that distinction to the res judicata principles that it rests on. Rather, the Court implied that result is based on something inherent about the statute of limitations.

The author of this chapter respectfully submits that both issues—(1) the second case being premised on a default before or after dismissal, and (2) the prejudice/without prejudice distinction—are foreigners to the statute of limitations and should remain foreigners. The Florida Supreme Court should take the first opportunity that presents itself to so state. The judicial doctrine of res judicata and the legislative bar of the statute of limitations serve different purposes. Res judicata seeks to prevent multiple lawsuits, conserve judicial resources, and promote reliance on adjudications. *Allen v. McCurry*, 449 U.S. 90, 94 (1980). The statute of limitations seeks to protect defendants from unfair surprise and stale claims. *Major League Baseball v. Morsani*, 790 So. 2d 1071, 1074-75 (Fla. 2001). Based on their different purposes, the two defenses have different elements, and different exceptions apply to each. Accordingly, the analysis of each defense should be applied independently of the other. Keeping the analyses separate will encourage precise legal analysis, will promote reliability in the judicial process, and will help ensure correct outcomes in actual controversies based on their merits.

Moreover, the requirement of a post-dismissal default does not follow from the facts in *Singleton*, which undergirds *Bartram*. The second case in *Singleton* case was based on an April 1, 2004 default, which was a default occurring *before* the July 14, 2004 dismissal of the first suit. Thus, the *Bartram* rule would have led to the opposite result in *Singleton* if *Singleton* had been challenged on statute of limitations grounds instead of res judicata grounds. In other words, the statute of limitations rule that flows from *Singleton's* res judicata rationale would have caused the opposite result in *Singleton* if the statute of limitations had been raised.

For all these reasons, this author finds the subsequent default requirement to be better left in *Bartram's* dicta and not carried forward as law in cases where the factual scenario of a pre-dismissal default presents itself.

[73] *Desai v. Bank of N.Y. Mellon Tr. Co.*, 240 So. 3d 729, 730 (Fla. 4th DCA 2018) (dismissal in September, 2013—new case alleged default of payment due March 1, 2009, "and all subsequent payments"); *Wells Fargo Bank, NA v. BH-NV Invs. 1, LLC*, 230 So. 3d 60 (Fla. 3d DCA 2017) (dismissal on April 1, 2011—new case alleged default of August 1, 2010, "and all subsequent payments").

(3) Finally, the holding of *Bartram* expressly applies where there is a reinstatement provision that grants "the mortgagor the right to avoid foreclosure by paying only the past due defaults" after acceleration.[74] In a case with a different reinstatement provision, or no reinstatement provision, it is doubtful that the Court's holding would apply.[75]

Nevertheless, the guiding principle of *Singleton* that "the dismissal returned the parties back 'to the same contractual relationship with the same continuing obligations'" was reinforced and extended by *Bartram* and should provide the foundation for clarifications in future cases.[76]

3-2:3 Effect of Time Bar on Debt

3-2:3.1 Effect on Past Due Installment Payments

Statutes of limitation are procedural and do not affect the underlying substantive rights and obligations of the parties.[77] Repayment of the mortgage debt "goes to the heart of the agreement between a mortgagor and mortgagee."[78] Thus, the statute of limitations does not run against unpaid installments. It runs against the causes of action for failure to pay those installments.

Older judicial opinions suggested in dicta that the statute of limitations runs against the past due "installments," but after Bartram and its progeny, this is unmistakably wrong.[79]

3-2:3.2 Effect on Foreclosure of Standard Residential Mortgage

The statute of limitations has no effect on the dollar amount due to the lender in a foreclosure judgment, at least not under the standard Fannie Mae/Freddie Mac residen-

---

[74] *Bartram v. U.S. Bank Nat'l Ass'n*, 211 So. 3d 1009, 1018 (Fla. 2016).

[75] *But see Broward Cnty. v. 8705 Hampshire Drive Condo., Inc.*, 127 So. 3d 853, 854 (Fla. 4th DCA 2013) (suggesting subsequent foreclosure was possible with no discussion of reinstatement provisions) ("Nevertheless, the reporting requirements are continuing duties under the mortgage, and a subsequent breach of those duties could trigger another demand by the county to cure the default in accordance with the terms of the mortgage or face acceleration.").

[76] *Bartram v. U.S. Bank Nat'l Ass'n*, 211 So. 3d 1009, 1022 (Fla. 2016).

[77] *Allie v. Ionata*, 503 So. 2d 1237, 1241-42 (Fla. 1987); *BCML Holding LLC v. U.S. Bank Nat'l Ass'n (In re BCML Holding LLC)*, No. 18-11600-EPK, 2018 WL 2386814, 2018 Bankr. LEXIS 1530, at *5 (Bankr. S.D. Fla. May 24, 2018). ("In other words, the statute of limitations is a procedural bar only. Once a timely action is filed, the remedy is controlled by contract.")

[78] *David v. Sun Fed. Sav. & Loan Ass'n*, 461 So. 2d 93, 96 (Fla. 1984).

[79] "[T]he statute of limitations may run on some installments and not others." *U.S. Bank Nat. Ass'n v. Bartram*, 140 So. 3d 1007, 1010 (Fla. 5th DCA 2014), approved in *Bartram v. U.S. Bank Nat'l Ass'n*, 211 So. 3d 1009 (Fla. 2016); *see also Greene v. Bursey*, 733 So. 2d 1111, 1114 (Fla. 4th DCA 1999).

tial mortgage.[80] Under that standard mortgage, the lender is entitled to all amounts due as described in the contract.[81]

3-2:3.3 Effect When No Separate Obligation to Pay Full Debt

There are cases where the procedural bar of the statute of limitations will definitely reduce the amount due. This occurs when the contract between the parties contains no separate promise to pay a specified sum, as in *Isaacs v. Deutsch*.[82] The defendant in *Isaacs* promised to make a series of child support payments *without* separately promising to pay a specified sum. Therefore, when the cause of action for the first failure to pay became time barred, there was no other provision of the contract requiring the amount of that installment to be paid. As a result, only the installments due within five years preceding the lawsuit were collectible.

3-2:4 Relation Back Doctrine

Under the relation back doctrine, an amended foreclosure complaint can validly allege new facts and raise new theories[83] after the statute of limitations has run.

---

[80] The standard mortgage note contains several promises by the borrower to repay the full debt, including a separate promise to repay upon maturity. *See* Appendix A, 1-017, paragraphs 1, 2, 3.

The standard mortgage incorporates these provisions in paragraph 1 under Uniform Covenants: "Borrower shall pay when due the principal of, and interest on, the debt evidenced by the Note...." *See* Appendix A, 1-018, page 406.

Thus, a borrower who fails to pay the entire debt upon maturity breaches a contractual obligation separate from the one to make monthly installment payments. That separate breach gives rise to a separate cause of action to recover the full debt, without regard to when installment payments were first defaulted on. This provision may become important in the ongoing appellate development of this issue.

[81] *Bollettieri Resort Villas Condo. Ass'n, Inc. v. Bank of N.Y. Mellon*, 198 So. 3d 1140, 1142 (Fla. 2d DCA 2016) (review dismissed) ("*Bollettieri* alleges that the bank may not recover any of the installment payments that came due more than five years prior to the filing of the second complaint.... We disagree."); *Gonzalez v. Fed. Nat'l Mortgage Ass'n*, 276 So. 3d 332 (Fla. 3d DCA 2018) ("we conclude that Fannie Mae is *not* barred from seeking a final judgment that includes amounts due outside the five-year statute of limitations") (emphasis in original); *Bank of Am., N.A. v. Graybush*, 253 So. 3d 1188 (Fla. 4th DCA 2018) ("Bank was entitled to all sums alleged and proven due under the note and mortgage—even those sums due more than five years from the date of filing the complaint."); *Grant v. Citizens Bank, N.A.*, 263 So. 3d 156 (Fla. 5th DCA 2018); *In re BCML Holding LLC*, 65 Bankr. Ct. Dec. 193 (Bankr. S.D. Fla. May 24, 2018) ("When a lender seeks judgment on an accelerated debt, it makes no sense to suggest that any component of that accelerated obligation should be excluded from the judgment because it 'came due' more than five years prior. It did not come due more than five years prior. It came due upon acceleration.").

[82] *Isaacs v. Deutsch*, 80 So. 2d 657, 660 (Fla. 1955).

[83] "Although the two complaints allege slightly different facts or different theories of recovery, such differences do not preclude a finding of relation back." *Kopel v. Kopel*, 229 So. 3d 812 (Fla. 2017); *see also Flores v. Riscomp Indus., Inc.*, 35 So. 3d 146, 147 (Fla. 3d DCA 2010) ("Although additional allegations of fact were inserted into the complaint as it progressed through its steps, and the legal theories of recovery were supplemented and modified, the

"When the claim asserted in the amended [complaint] arose out of the conduct, transaction, or occurrence set forth or attempted to be set forth in the original [complaint], the amendment shall relate back to the date of the original pleading."[84]

3-2:5 Tolling

3-2:5.1 Statutory Tolling

Tolling has been consistently interpreted as a temporary suspension of the running of the statute of limitations time clock, which extends the period for filing a claim.[85] Fla. Stat. § 95.051 provides an exhaustive list of those conditions which toll statutes of limitation. That section abrogated the common law of tolling and "delineates an exclusive list of conditions that can 'toll' the running of the statute of limitations."[86]

While multiple subsections of § 95.051(1) could have application in a mortgage foreclosure, subsection (f) has the most pronounced impact. It provides for tolling based on "[t]he payment of any part of the principal or interest of any obligation or liability founded on a written instrument."

Contrary to the standard concept that tolling temporarily suspends the time clock, courts have consistently construed § 95.051(1)(f) as *restarting* the clock from zero. The rationale for this is that: "[b]y making partial payments on the debt, the debtor recognizes and signifies the intent to honor the obligation. It is not until the payee [sic] stops making payment that the creditor is placed on notice that the debtor is no longer willing or able to honor the underlying obligation."[87]

3-2:5.2 Equitable Tolling

Equitable tolling "has been applied when the plaintiff has been misled or lulled into inaction, [etc.]"[88] It can apply even where there has been "no misconduct on the part of the defendant."[89]

---

substantive factual situation remained the same as that found in the original complaint."); *Dailey v. Leshin*, 792 So. 2d 527, 532 (Fla. 4th DCA 2001) ("The proper relation back test is whether the amended claims arose out of the same conduct, transaction, or occurrence originally set forth, even if they raise a new legal theory.").

[84] Fla. R. Civ. P. 1.190.
[85] *Hankey v. Yarian*, 755 So. 2d 93, 96 (Fla. 2000).
[86] *Major League Baseball v. Morsani*, 790 So. 2d 1071, 1075 (Fla. 2001); *accord Larson & Larson, P.A. v. TSE Indus., Inc.*, 22 So. 3d 36 (Fla. 2009).
[87] *Cadle Co. v. McCartha*, 920 So. 2d 144, 146 (Fla. 5th DCA 2006); *accord Chaplin v. Cooke's Estate*, 432 So. 2d 778, 779 (Fla. 1st DCA 1983); *Hosp. Constructors Ltd. ex rel. Lifemark Hospitals of Florida, Inc. v. Lefor*, 749 So. 2d 546 (Fla. 2d DCA 2000); *see also Cuillo v. McCoy*, 810 So. 2d 1061 (Fla. 4th DCA 2002).
[88] *Machules v. Department of Admin.*, 523 So. 2d 1132, 1134 (Fla. 1988).
[89] *Major League Baseball v. Morsani*, 790 So. 2d 1071, 1077 n. 11 (Fla. 2001) (citing *Machules*).

3-2:5.3 Equitable Estoppel

Equitable estoppel is similar to equitable tolling but arises out of more directly culpable conduct of the defendant. It is said to apply where "the wrongdoer prevails upon the other to forego enforcing his right until the statutory period has lapsed."[90]

Any of these conditions—statutory tolling, equitable tolling, or equitable estoppel—can extend the five-year statute of limitations period. The statute of repose, however, cannot be tolled.

3-2:6 Counterclaim in Recoupment

"A civil defendant may assert a counterclaim in recoupment to recover an affirmative judgment even though the claim would be barred as an independent cause of action under the statute of limitation."[91] This rule applies to the collection of a time-barred debt, but it is questionable whether it extends to the equitable relief of foreclosure based upon that debt.[92]

3-2:7 Deficiency Actions

The statute of limitations on an action seeking a deficiency judgment is either one year or five years, depending on the character of the mortgaged property. If the mortgaged property is residential, then the one-year time period applies.[93] The one-year statute specifies that "[t]he limitations period shall commence on the day after the certificate is issued by the clerk of court or the day after the mortgagee accepts a deed in lieu of foreclosure."[94] If the mortgaged property is not residential, then the five-year time period applies.[95] For a full discussion of deficiencies, including the applicable statute of limitations, *see* Chapter 19.

---

[90] *Black Diamond Properties, Inc. v. Haines*, 69 So. 3d 1090, 1093 (Fla. 5th DCA 2011).

[91] *Regions Bank v. Cuny*, 118 So. 3d 329, 330 (Fla. 1st DCA 2013); s*ee also Maynard v. Household Fin. Corp. III*, 861 So. 2d 1204, 1207 (Fla. 2d DCA 2003) (citing *Allie v. Ionata*, 503 So. 2d 1237, 1238–39 (Fla. 1987)).

[92] *Rybovich Boat Works, Inc. v. Atkins*, 585 So. 2d 270, 272 (Fla. 1991).

[93] Fla. Stat. § 95.11(5)(h). This statute applies to mortgages on "residential property that is a one-family to four-family dwelling unit." The "one-family to four-family" limitation appears to exclude condominium units and cooperative housing units if the total number of units in the condominium or the cooperative is five or more, surprising as that may seem. That phrase is not defined in the Florida Statutes and the limitation has not been the subject of published appellate opinions thus far.

[94] Fla. Stat. § 95.11(5)(h). The "certificate" mentioned is vague because there are two different certificates.

[95] Fla. Stat. § 95.11(2)(b). The deficiency action is based upon the unpaid note or other contract calling for payment of the mortgage debt. Thus, the five year time period applicable to contracts generally is the time period applicable to deficiency actions. *See Barnes v. Escambia Cnty. Employees Credit Union*, 488 So. 2d 879, 881 (Fla. 1st DCA 1986) (five year time period applied to deficiency action before enactment of § 95.11(5)(h)). *See also Chrestensen v. Eurogest, Inc.*, 906 So. 2d 343, 346, n.1 (Fla. 4th DCA 2005) (parties agreed and court accepted that five year time period applied to deficiency action before enactment of § 95.11(5)(h)).

3-3 Statute of Repose

3-3:1 Terminates the Mortgage Lien

In contrast to the procedural nature of the statute of limitations, the statute of repose is substantive. "It provides a substantive right to be free from liability after the established time period."[96]

The statute of repose *terminates* the lien of the mortgage when the statutory period expires.[97] It "establishes an ultimate date when the lien of the mortgage terminates and is no longer enforceable."[98]

3-3:2 Repose Time Periods

The time period applicable to a mortgage lien varies, depending on the information "ascertainable from the record of it."[99] The applicable period is either five years after the date of *maturity* or twenty years after date of the *mortgage*.

3-3:2.1 Five Years After Maturity

If the maturity date is ascertainable from the record of the mortgage, then the repose period is five years after that maturity date.

> [B]y the time this action was commenced in March 2002, there was no valid lien to enforce. . . . The maturity date of the note secured by [plaintiff's] mortgage, which may be ascertained from the record, is September 15, 1993. Under section 95.281(1)(a), [plaintiff] had until September 15, 1998 to enforce its lien.[100]

This five-year time period applies even if the "maturity" date is not stated but is ascertainable only by calculating the date of final payment in a stream of installment payments.[101] A mathematical inconsistency in the mortgage document which leaves an

---

[96] *Am. Bankers Life Assur. Co. of Florida v. 2275 W. Corp.*, 905 So. 2d 189, 191 (Fla. 3d DCA 2005).

[97] Fla. Stat. § 95.281(1); *Am. Bankers Life Assur. Co. of Florida v. 2275 W. Corp.*, 905 So. 2d 189, 191 (Fla. 3d DCA 2005).

[98] *Houck Corp. v. New River, Ltd.*, 900 So. 2d 601, 603 (Fla. 2d DCA 2005).

[99] Fla. Stat. § 95.281(1)(a). The word "it" refers to the mortgage according to the doctrine of the last antecedent. According to the doctrine of the last antecedent, "relative and qualifying words, phrases and clauses are to be applied to the words or phrase immediately preceding, and are not to be construed as extending to, or including, others more remote. The last antecedent is the last word, phrase, or clause that can be made an antecedent without impairing the meaning of the sentence." *Penzer v. Transp. Ins. Co.*, 29 So. 3d 1000, 1007 (Fla. 2010). Whether the word "it" refers to the mortgage or to the obligation may still be debatable, but practically it makes no difference as long as the maturity date can be "ascertained" by reference to all the recorded documents. "[T]he maturity date must be ascertainable by one who reads the county records." *Layton v. Bay Lake Ltd. P'ship*, 818 So. 2d 552, 553 (Fla. 2d DCA 2002).

[100] *American Bankers Life Assur. Co. of Florida v. 2275 W. Corp.*, 905 So. 2d 189, 192 (Fla. 3d DCA 2005) (reversing final summary judgment of foreclosure).

[101] Fla. Stat. § 95.281(3).

unpaid balance at the end of the contractually fixed stream of payments does not render the maturity date unascertainable, at least where the inconsistency was not apparent.[102]

3-3:2.2 Twenty Years After Date of Mortgage

If the maturity date is not ascertainable, then the repose period is twenty years after the date of the mortgage[103] under subsection 95.281(1)(b). Note that when subsection (1)(b) applies, both the starting point and the length of time are different from subsection (1)(a) mortgages.

A clear example of this subsection's operation is *Houck Corp. v. New River Ltd., Pasco:*

> In this case, the mortgage was recorded on November 1, 1984. It secured non-recourse promissory notes that had a maturity date of October 30, 1991, but that date was not ascertainable from the recorded mortgage, and the notes were not recorded. . . . [Therefore] under section 95.281(1)(b), the mortgage lien was enforceable until November 1, 2004.[104]

A mortgage that bears no maturity date on its face does not have an "ascertainable" maturity date merely because it incorporates the terms of an unrecorded promissory

---

[102] "An unapparent mathematical error in the amount of some of the payments evinces no intent to extend the due date otherwise indicated by the recorded note and mortgage and does not alter the five year statute of limitation." *Irwin v. Grogan-Cole*, 590 So. 2d 1102, 1104 (Fla. 5th DCA 1991). The 5th DCA mistakenly referred to the five year Fla. Stat. § 95.281 time period as a "statute of limitation" rather than a statute of repose. This actually led to the wrong result in the case, but the quoted holding—that mathematical errors regarding payment amounts will not disturb an ascertainable maturity date—is not affected by the error and is good law.

The result in *Irwin* was wrong because based on the 5th DCA's analysis, the lien had been extinguished under Fla. Stat. § 95.281(a) in 1987—before the foreclosure action was filed. Because the 5th DCA determined that the maturity date was ascertainable, the applicable statute of repose period was five years from the date of maturity. The date of maturity was July 22, 1982 (after the seven annual payments recited in the mortgage had been made). Therefore, the five year repose period ran on July 22, 1987, and the mortgage lien was extinguished on that date. The foreclosure case was filed in 1990, after the mortgage lien had already expired. Therefore, the trial court reached the correct result in denying foreclosure, albeit for the wrong reason.

The Court erred by analyzing Fla. Stat. § 95.281 as a "statute of limitations." The statute of limitations can be tolled by payments, but the statute of repose cannot. "The time shall be extended only as provided in this law and shall not be extended by . . . part payment, operation of law, or any other method." Fla. Stat. § 95.281. Therefore, the 5th DCA's determination that the date of maturity was ascertainable (questionable but based in reason) meant that there was no mortgage lien to foreclose when the foreclosure case was filed.

[103] It is unclear whether "date of the mortgage" refers to the date of execution or the date of recording. This author reads it to be the date of execution, if for not other reason than a delay in recording of the mortgage should not extend the life of the mortgage. However, the *Houck Corp.* case cited below explicitly calculated the life of the lien based on the date of recording.

[104] *Houck Corp. v. New River, Ltd., Pasco*, 900 So. 2d 601, 605 (Fla. 2d DCA 2005).

note that has a stated maturity date.[105] Furthermore, a conflict between the maturity stated in the note and the mortgage renders the maturity "not ascertainable" and brings the case under the twenty year repose period of subsection (1)(b).[106]

When a mortgage secures two obligations, one of which has an ascertainable maturity date from the recorded mortgage and one of which does not, the twenty year statute applies.[107] Such arrangements are common in commercial loan arrangements. In *CCM Pathfinder Palm Harbor Management, LLC v. Unknown Heirs of Gendron*, one secured obligation had an ascertainable maturity, but the second secured obligation did not have an ascertainable maturity. The court held that the twenty year repose period applied.[108]

3-3:2.3 Extension Agreements

If an agreement extending the maturity date of the obligation is executed and recorded, the statutory repose time periods will run from the new date, as extended.[109] However, an unrecorded extension agreement will not extend the repose time period.[110]

3-3:2.4 Incongruence Between Repose and Limitations

Since the twenty year *repose* period (applicable when the maturity date is unascertainable) is measured from the date of the mortgage, and the five year *limitation* period is measured from the date of accrual, incongruent results can emerge.

A mortgage with no ascertainable maturity expires after twenty years, even if it secures a thirty year promissory note. In such a case, the borrower's default in year

---

[105] *Layton v. Bay Lake Ltd. P'ship*, 818 So. 2d 552, 553 (Fla. 2d DCA 2002).
[106] *Pitts v. Pastore*, 561 So. 2d 297, 299 (Fla. 2d DCA 1990).
[107] *CCM Pathfinder Palm Harbor Mgmt., LLC v. Unknown Heirs of Gendron*, 198 So. 3d 3, 5 (Fla. 2d DCA 2015).
[108] *CCM Pathfinder Palm Harbor Mgmt., LLC v. Unknown Heirs of Gendron*, 198 So. 3d 3, 5 (Fla. 2d DCA 2015).
[109] Fla. Stat. § 95.281(2).
[110] The requirement of recording is made plain in the statute and is enforced strictly by the courts. "*If an extension agreement* executed by the mortgagee or the mortgagee's successors in interest and the mortgagor or the mortgagor's successors in interest *is recorded*, the time shall be extended . . ." Fla. Stat. § 95.281(2) (emphasis added). "The time shall be extended only as provided in this law and *shall not be extended* by any other agreement . . . operation of law, or any other method." Fla. Stat. § 95.281(4) (emphasis added). These two subsections were read together in *Zlinkoff v. Von Aldenbruck* to defeat the lender's extension argument because the extension agreement was never recorded.

> An extension note with a maturity date of February 1993 was executed but not recorded. . . . Section 95.281(4) specifically states that anything other than a recorded agreement executed between the mortgagor and mortgagee (or their successors-in-interest) will not extend the time for pursuing a foreclosure action. Because the final maturity date of the mortgage was not made according to the provisions of section 95.281(2), the time to foreclose the mortgage terminated in February 1997 [five years after the date of maturity appearing on the recorded mortgage].

Zlinkoff v. Von Aldenbruck, 765 So. 2d 840, 842 (Fla. 4th DCA 2000).

21 would *not* give rise to a foreclosure cause of action because the mortgage lien would have already expired at the end of year 20.[111]

Conversely, a mortgage lien with no ascertainable maturity that secures a one year promissory note continues as a lien on the property for twenty years. This is so even though the five year statute of limitations bars a foreclosure for nonpayment of the underlying debt after six years. In such cases, the breach of a non-monetary covenant occurring more than five years but less than twenty years after maturity may give rise to a viable foreclosure cause of action and may in essence save the mortgage from the statute of limitations bar.[112]

3-3:2.4a Savings Clause for Mortgages With No Ascertainable Maturity

As described above in Section 3-3:2.2, if the maturity date of the mortgage is not ascertainable from the record, then the repose period is twenty years after the date of the mortgage.[113] However, subsection 95.281(1)(b) contains a savings clause that allows a lender whose mortgage contains no ascertainable maturity date to bring its mortgage into the repose period of five years from maturity. If the obligation (i.e., promissory note) contains a stated maturity date, the mortgage holder can, before the twenty year repose period expires: (1) rerecord the mortgage together with a copy of the obligation (i.e., promissory note);[114] or (2) record an affidavit identifying the mortgage, attaching a copy of the obligation, and certifying that the attached obligation is the one secured by the mortgage.[115] In either case, the expiration date of the mortgage will be converted to five years from the maturity date.

3-3:2.4b Obligations Paid by Mortgagee

When a mortgagee pays obligations of the property owner, including taxes, the repose period is five years from the date of payment.[116]

3-3:2.5 No Tolling

The statute of repose time periods cannot be extended by any of the tolling, equitable tolling, or equitable estoppel provisions applicable to the statute of limitations.[117]

---

[111] *Kush v. Lloyd*, 616 So. 2d 415, 421 (Fla. 1992) (affirming dismissal of medical malpractice case on grounds that the cause of action had been extinguished by the statute of repose before it even accrued, noting that dissenting Justice Kogan was "reluctan[t] to eliminate a cause of action before it has accrued. Yet, this is exactly what a statute of repose does.").

[112] *Houck Corp. v. New River, Ltd., Pasco*, 900 So. 2d 601, 605 (Fla. 2d DCA 2005).

[113] It is unclear whether "date of the mortgage" refers to the date of execution or the date of recording. This author reads it to be the date of execution, if for no other reason than a delay in recording of the mortgage should not extend the life of the mortgage. However, the *Houck Corp.* case cited above explicitly calculated the life of the lien based on the date of recording.

[114] Fla. Stat. § 95.281(1)(b)(1).

[115] Fla. Stat. § 95.281(1)(b)(2).

[116] Fla. Stat. § 95.281(1)(c).

[117] Fla. Stat. § 95.281(4); *American Bankers Life Assur. Co. of Florida v. 2275 W. Corp.*, 905 So. 2d 189, 192 (Fla. 3d DCA 2005).

3-3:2.6 No Statute of Repose for Railroads, Public Utilities, or Construction Liens

By its own terms, the statute of repose is inapplicable to mortgages given by railroads or public utility corporations. It is also inapplicable to the liens of Florida Statutes Chapter 713, which includes construction liens, certain labor liens, materialman's liens, mechanic's liens, professional liens, oil and gas liens, and other miscellaneous liens.[118]

3-4 Laches

"Laches is an omission to assert a right for an unreasonable and unexplained length of time, under circumstances prejudicial to the adverse party."[119] The required prejudice must manifest in the form of a legally cognizable loss or injury.[120] "Within the unique context of mortgage foreclosure law, any delay by the mortgagee in enforcing its rights generally acts to the property owner's benefit in permitting him or her to remain in the property and cannot amount to legal prejudice."[121]

---

[118] Fla. Stat. § 95.281(5).

[119] *Ticktin v. Kearin*, 807 So. 2d 659, 663 (Fla. 3d DCA 2001).

[120] *Avelo Mortg., LLC v. Vero Ventures, LLC*, 254 So. 3d 439 (Fla. 4th DCA 2018).

[121] *Avelo Mortg., LLC v. Vero Ventures, LLC*, 254 So. 3d 439 (Fla. 4th DCA 2018); *but see Travis Co. v. Mayes*, 36 So. 2d 264, 265-66 (Fla. 1948) (applying laches to prevent foreclosure where: defendant erroneously believed she owned the property through a tax deed that was eventually shown to be void; defendant immediately began paying the property taxes; true owner executed a mortgage on the property one year after defendant acquired the void tax deed; defendant continued paying property taxes for 25 more years; defendant took possession 10 years later and made substantial improvements, including: repairing the foundation, putting on a new roof, installing plumbing upstairs and down, and wiring the house for electricity; defendant continued in possession for 15 years continuously; and plaintiff took no action to enforce the mortgage until defendant's substantial investments in the property and other conditions "caused it to spiral in value").

CHAPTER 4

Standing to Foreclose

Jonathan L. Blackmore

4-1 Overview of Standing to Foreclose

Perhaps no issue in mortgage foreclosure has been the subject of more litigation than standing to foreclose.[1]

Standing to foreclose is examined by an analysis of whether the plaintiff is a "person entitled to enforce instrument" as defined by the Florida Uniform Commercial Code.[2] The "person entitled to enforce instrument" is defined as: (1) the holder of the instrument; (2) a non-holder in possession of the instrument who has the rights of a holder; or (3) a person not in possession of the instrument who is entitled to enforce the instrument pursuant to Fla. Stat. § 673.3091 or 673.4181(4).[3] A person may be a person entitled to enforce the instrument even though the person is not the owner of the instrument or is in wrongful possession of the instrument.[4] A "holder" is "[t]he person in possession of a negotiable instrument that is payable either to bearer or to an identified person that is the person in possession."[5]

Standing to foreclose must be proven as of the time the action is filed and at the time judgment is entered.[6] Lack of standing at the inception of the case is not a defect

---

[1] A LexisNexis search reveals 289 Florida District Court opinions that use the term "Standing to Foreclose."
[2] *Wells Fargo Bank, N.A. v. Morcom*, 125 So. 3d 320 (Fla. 5th DCA 2013) (Florida adopted the Uniform Commercial Code on January 1, 1967).
[3] Fla. Stat. § 673.3011.
[4] Fla. Stat. § 673.3011.
[5] Fla. Stat. § 671.201(21).
[6] *Corrigan v. Bank of Am., N.A.*, 189 So. 3d 187, 189 (Fla. 2d DCA 2016) (reversing final judgment for the bank where no evidence was presented at trial to show that the original plaintiff held the note indorsed in blank at the time the time the case was filed). The Second District issued its ruling *en banc* to recede from its decision in *AS Lily, LLC v. Morgan*, 164 So. 3d 124 (Fla. 2d DCA 2015) where it was suggested that standing may be established at the time an amended complaint is filed.

that can be cured after the case is filed.[7] Standing to foreclose must be proven by competent, substantial evidence.[8]

4-2 Surrender of the Original Note

Because a promissory note is a negotiable instrument, it is necessary to surrender the original note to the court to remove it from the stream of commerce and prevent the negotiation of the note to another person.[9] If the plaintiff is not in possession of the original note, it must reestablish the lost note pursuant to Fla. Stat. § 673.3091.[10] The mortgage follows the note as an incident to the debt.[11] Therefore, the plaintiff is not required to produce the original mortgage to foreclose.[12]

4-3 Allonges to Promissory Notes

An allonge is a piece of paper annexed to a promissory note, on which to write indorsements for which there is no room on the instrument itself.[13] An allonge is an elegant-sounding legal term for a supplemental attachment to a note in which indorsements to subsequent note holders may be identified.[14] An allonge may be executed prior to the

---

[7] *Kiefert v. Nationstar Mortgage, LLC*, 153 So. 3d 351, 353 (Fla. 1st DCA 2014) (reversing final judgment of foreclosure where the foreclosing plaintiff failed to present evidence that the original plaintiff was in possession of the original note indorsed in blank at the time the complaint was filed). The court cited *Focht v. Wells Fargo Bank, N.A.*, 124 So. 3d 308 (Fla. 2d DCA 2013), which reversed summary judgment in favor of the bank because the bank did not present summary judgment evidence establishing that it was in possession of the original note with the blank indorsement at the time it filed the complaint.

[8] *Phan v. Deutsche Bank Nat'l Trust Co.*, 198 So. 3d 744, 749 (Fla. 2d DCA 2016) (citing *Stone v. BankUnited*, 115 So. 3d 411, 413 (Fla. 2d DCA 2013)).

[9] *Heller v. Bank of Am., N.A.*, 209 So. 3d 641, 644 (Fla. 2d DCA 2017) (reversing final judgment and remanding for a new trial where the bank admitted a copy of the note instead of the original at trial, and the original note had not been filed with the court); *Deutsche Bank Nat'l Trust Co. v. Clarke*, 87 So. 3d 58, 61 (Fla. 4th DCA 2012) (holding that a plaintiff in a mortgage foreclosure must produce the original note or make a satisfactory explanation for failure to do so and the surrender of the note to the court file is one such "satisfactory explanation" for failing to produce the original at trial); *Perry v. Fairbanks Capital Corp.*, 888 So. 2d 725 (Fla. 5th DCA 2004) (holding that the original document that is generally required to be filed with the court in a mortgage foreclosure proceeding is the promissory note, not the mortgage).

[10] *Boumarate v. HSBC Bank USA, N.A.*, 172 So. 3d 535, 536 (Fla. 5th DCA 2015) (A plaintiff seeking to foreclose a mortgage must tender the original promissory note to the trial court or seek to re-establish the lost note pursuant to Fla. Stat § 673.3091.).

[11] *WM Specialty Mortg., LLC v. Salomon*, 874 So. 2d 680 (Fla. 4th DCA 2004) (quoting from *Johns v. Gillian*, 134 Fla. 575 (Fla. 1938)).

[12] *Perry v. Fairbanks Capital Corp.*, 888 So. 2d 725 (Fla. 5th DCA 2004).

[13] *Booker v. Sarasota, Inc.*, 707 So. 2d 886, 887 (Fla. 1st DCA 1998) (citing the *Black's Law Dictionary* definition of "allonge," which states that "[the allonge] must be so firmly affixed thereto as to become a part thereof").

[14] In *Wells Fargo Bank, N.A. v. Bohatka*, 112 So. 3d 596 (Fla. 1st DCA 2013), (the trial court dismissed the plaintiff's complaint with prejudice at a motion to dismiss hearing, where the bank's attorney appeared at the hearing with a copy of the allonge that he claimed would provide the plaintiff with standing to foreclose. The trial court *sua sponte* examined the original note filed with the court and determined that there was no evidence that an allonge

execution of the note so long as it is subsequently affixed to the note.[15] Florida's Uniform Commercial Code does not specifically mention an allonge, but notes that for the purpose of determining whether a signature is made on an instrument, a paper affixed to the instrument is part of the instrument.[16] The rationale underlying the affixation requirement is to protect subsequent purchasers from the risk that the present holder or a previous holder has negotiated the instrument to someone outside the apparent chain of title through a separate document.[17] Where an allonge contains evidence of a clear intent that the note and the allonge were to be physically attached to each other, such evidence of intent is sufficient to establish a valid indorsement under the UCC.[18] Evidence of an intent that the note and allonge were to be physically attached to each other exists where the note and allonge are imaged in the mortgage company's loan file together, the face of the allonge states that it is affixed to and is part of the original note, contains the borrower's name, loan number, loan amount, property address, and date of the note.[19] Because an allonge is essentially part of the note, the bank must file the original allonge together with the original note to prove standing to foreclose.[20]

---

had been affixed to the original note, and dismissed the complaint with prejudice. The First District reversed, holding that it was error for the court to dismiss the complaint without providing the plaintiff an opportunity to amend.).

[15] *Bank of N.Y. Mellon v. Fla. Kalanit 770 LLC,* 269 So. 3d 571, 573 (Fla. 4th DCA 2019) (The Fourth District reversed involuntary dismissal where trial court ruled that allonge could not be executed prior to execution of original note, noting that nothing in the UCC suggests that an allonge may not be executed prior to the note so long as it is subsequently attached to the note. Additionally, the UCC expressly states that "[a]n instrument may be antedated or postdated" §673.1131, Fla. Stat. (2018), and the After-acquired Title Doctrine recognizes that an entity may contract to sell property that it does not own at the time of contracting.).

[16] *Booker v. Sarasota, Inc.,* 707 So. 2d 886, 887 (Fla. 1st DCA 1998) (citing Fla. Stat. § 673.2041(1)).

[17] In *Purificato v. Nationstar Mortg., LLC,* 182 So. 3d 821 (Fla. 4th DCA 2016), the bank's witness testified that the note and allonge were imaged together prior to the filing of the complaint. Also, the allonge by its terms stated that it is affixed and is part of the original note, and contained the borrower's name, loan number, loan amount, property address, and date of the note. The Fourth District held that this constituted sufficient evidence that the allonge was sufficiently affixed to the note so as to become a part thereof and establish standing to foreclose. The Fourth District also noted that although previous versions of Florida's Uniform Commercial Code required the piece of paper to be *firmly affixed* to the instrument, the relevant version simply requires the paper to be *affixed* to the instrument.

[18] *Purificato v. Nationstar Mortg., LLC,* 182 So. 3d 821 (Fla. 4th DCA 2016).

[19] *Purificato v. Nationstar Mortg., LLC,* 182 So. 3d 821 (Fla. 4th DCA 2016).

[20] In *Mathis v. Nationstar Mortg., LLC,* 42 Fla. L. Weekly D 1190 (Fla. 4th DCA 2017), the Fourth District ruled that a copy of an allonge was not admissible into evidence under Florida's best evidence rule, and reversed final judgment of foreclosure. The *Mathis* court cited *Caballero v. U.S. Bank Nat'l Ass'n,* 189 So. 3d 1044 (Fla. 2d DCA 2016) in which the Second District reversed summary judgment for the bank where the bank filed the incorrect original allonge with the court, and therefore did not produce the original allonge it was relying upon for standing to foreclose. The *Caballero* court cited *Isaac v. Deutsche Bank Nat'l Trust Co.,* 74 So. 3d 495 (Fla. 4th DCA 2011), for the conclusion that "an allonge is essentially part of the note." In *U.S. Bank Nat'l Ass'n v. Kachik,* 222 So. 3d 592 (Fla. 4th DCA 2017), the Fourth District held that because the bank failed to produce the original allonge and did not plead a lost instrument count, the trial court was correct to enter judgment in favor of the homeowner.

4-4 Proving Standing Through an Indorsement

A plaintiff who is not the original payee of the note has standing to foreclose if the plaintiff, before filing the complaint, possesses the note and the note is indorsed to the plaintiff specifically or in blank.[21] An indorsement is a signature on the note for the purpose of negotiating the instrument.[22] An indorsement must be made by the holder of the note.[23] A plaintiff is not required to prove the validity of a signature on an indorsement unless the defendant presents evidence which would support a finding that the signature is forged or unauthorized.[24] Where the plaintiff seeks to prove standing through an indorsement, evidence should be submitted to demonstrate that the indorsement on the note was made prior to the filing of the action.[25] It is irrelevant exactly what day the indorsement is made so long as it is on the note at the time the action is filed.[26] If the note or allonge reflects on its face that the indorsement occurred before the filing of the action, this is sufficient to establish standing.[27] Testimony that the indorsement was effectuated before the filing of the action pursuant to the routine practice of an organization is sufficient to demonstrate that an indorsement was effectuated before the filing of the action.[28] Evidence that the bank advanced taxes and other fees associated with the mortgaged property prior to the filing of the complaint was a noteworthy factor in determining standing to foreclose, because financial institutions are not known to incur expenses on behalf of properties for which they do not hold an interest.[29] Evidence that a note was indorsed in blank and in possession of the plaintiff prior to the filing of the action pursuant to the terms of a pooling and servicing agreement and mortgage loan schedule is sufficient to demonstrate standing to foreclose.[30]

---

[21] *Bank of New York Mellon v. Heath*, 219 So. 3d 104 (Fla. 4th DCA 2017).
[22] Fla. Stat. § 673.2014(1).
[23] *PennyMac Corp. v. Frost*, 214 So. 3d 686, 688-89 (Fla. 4th DCA 2017).
[24] *PMT NPL Fin. 2015-1 v. Centurion Sys., LLC*, 2018 Fla. App. LEXIS 11956 (Fla. 5th DCA 2018).
[25] *McLean v. JP Morgan Chase Bank N.A.*, 79 So. 3d 170, 173 (Fla. 4th DCA 2012) (reversing summary judgment where the bank held a note with and undated special indorsement in its favor, but the summary judgment affidavit did not indicate when the indorsement was made, nor did the affidavit indicate the bank was the owner of the note before the complaint was filed).
[26] *JP Morgan Chase Bank Nat'l Ass'n v. Pierre*, 215 So. 3d 633 (Fla. 4th DCA 2017).
[27] *McClean v. JP Morgan Chase Bank N.A.*, 79 So. 3d 170, 173 (Fla. 4th DCA 2012).
[28] *Peuguero v. Bank of Am., N.A.*, 169 So. 3d 1198, 1202-03 (Fla. 4th DCA 2015) (holding that witness testimony as to the policy and procedure of the bank to have promissory notes indorsed before foreclosure complaints are filed was evidence of standing to foreclose).
[29] *Peuguero v. Bank of Am., N.A.*, 169 So. 3d 1198, 1202-03 (Fla. 4th DCA 2015).
[30] *Deutsche Bank Nat'l Trust Co. v. Marciano*, 190 So. 3d 166 (Fla. 5th DCA 2016) (finding the mortgage loan schedule demonstrated that the subject note became a trust asset of the plaintiff prior to the trust's closing, which predated the filing of the complaint, and section 2.01 of the pooling and servicing agreement stated that possession of the original note indorsed to the trustee or to blank has been delivered to the trustee).

In *Bolous v. U.S. Bank Nat'l Ass'n*, 210 So. 3d 691 (Fla. 4th DCA 2016), (The note attached to the bank's original complaint was not indorsed, the later-filed blank-indorsed allonge was undated, and the bank's witness did not known when the allonge was created. However, the pooling and servicing agreement and corresponding mortgage loan schedule showed that the loan was transferred to the bank's trust in 2005. Section 2.01 of the pooling and servicing agreement stated that loan was sold to the trust, and the original note with indorsement

In such cases, the plaintiff should demonstrate that the pooling and servicing agreement includes the note at issue.[31] The line of cases beginning with *Deutsche Bank National Trust Co. v. Marciano*[32] appears to represent a shift in the way the appellate courts have examined the relevance of a pooling and servicing agreement to the plaintiff's ability to demonstrate that a note was indorsed either in blank or to the plaintiff prior to the inception of the action.[33] While several previous cases held that evidence that the note was transferred into a trust was not sufficient to demonstrate standing to foreclose, those cases generally did not examine the specific provisions of the pooling and servicing agreements which discuss the delivery and indorsement of original promissory notes (usually section 2.01).[34] A plaintiff is not required to identify or prove the trust on whose behalf the plaintiff acts.[35] Therefore, it is not necessary that a specific indorsement to the plaintiff also specify the name of the trust on whose behalf the plaintiff is bringing the action, and even where the indorsement does not name the correct trust, it will not create a defect in the bank's standing to foreclose.[36]

Where the plaintiff has standing to foreclose through an indorsement, it is irrelevant that another party is the owner of the note.[37] This is because Florida's Uniform

---

has been delivered to the custodian for the benefit of the trust. The *Bolous* court specifically distinguished its holding in *Lewis v. U.S. Bank Nat'l Ass'n*, 188 So. 3d 46 (Fla. 4th DCA 2016), where it held that the bank's reliance on a pooling and servicing agreement was insufficient to prove standing at the inception of the case. The *Bolous* court stated that in *Lewis*, the plaintiff did not establish that the note was part of the trust, although the *Lewis* opinion itself did not make this point. *Bolous* was cited by the Fourth District in *Kronen v. Deutsche Bank Nat'l Trust Co.*, 267 So. 3d 447, n. 1 (Fla. 4th DCA 2019).

[31] *Bolous v. U.S. Bank Nat'l Ass'n*, 210 So. 3d 691 (Fla. 4th DCA 2016).

[32] *Deutsche Bank Nat'l Trust Co. v. Marciano*, 190 So. 3d 166 (Fla. 5th DCA 2016).

[33] *CitiBank, N.A. v. Manning*, 221 So. 3d 677 (Fla. 4th DCA 2017) (holding that a pooling and servicing agreement together with a mortgage loan schedule indicating that the indorsed note was delivered to the trustee prior to the date the complaint was filed, coupled with surrender of the original note indorsed in blank, is sufficient to demonstrate the bank's standing); *see also HSBC Bank USA, N.A. v. Alejandre*, 219 So. 3d 831 (Fla. 4th DCA 2017).

[34] *Jarvis v. Deutsche Bank Nat'l Trust Co.*, 169 So. 3d 194, 196 (Fla. 4th DCA 2015) (holding that evidence that the note was physically transferred into a trust prior to the bank filing its foreclosure complaint does not, by itself, establish standing); *Perez v. Deutsche Bank Nat'l Trust Co.*, 174 So. 3d 489, 491 (Fla. 4th DCA 2015) (finding testimony that the bank took ownership of the note prior to the filing of the complaint pursuant to a pooling and servicing agreement was insufficient where the document was not moved into evidence).

[35] In *Bank of New York Mellon Trust Co. v. Ginsberg*, 221 So. 3d 1196 (Fla. 4th DCA 2017) (The trial court entered summary judgment in favor of the borrower on the grounds that the special indorsement on the note attached to the plaintiff's complaint contained a slightly different trust name than the named plaintiff. The Fourth District reversed as the indorsement was made to the bank, and although the trust named in the indorsement was slightly different than the trust named in the complaint, it did not create a standing defect because the plaintiff is not required to identify or prove the trust on whose behalf the plaintiff acts.); *Wells Fargo Bank, N.A. v. Cook*, 2019 Fla. App. LEXIS 11785 (Fla. 2d DCA 2019) (which quoted *Ginsberg* and *Deutsche Bank Tr. Co. Ams. v. Harris,* 264 So. 3d 186, 190 (Fla. 4th DCA 2019) and held that even though the trust identified in the complaint is somewhat different than the trust identified in the special indorsement, the difference does not create a defect in standing).

[36] *Bank of New York Mellon Trust Co. v. Ginsberg*, 221 So. 3d 1196 (Fla. 4th DCA 2017).

[37] In *JPMorgan Chase Bank Nat'l Ass'n v. Pierre*, 215 So. 3d 633 (Fla. 4th DCA 2017), the trial court entered judgment in favor of defendants at trial in part on the basis that the witness

Commercial Code does not require a party to be both the holder of the note and the owner of the note to have standing to foreclose.[38] Accordingly, it is error for a court to require the bank to prove that it is both the owner and holder of the note.[39] An indorsement that is made by a person who is not the holder of the instrument is an anomalous indorsement.[40] An anomalous indorsement does not affect the manner in which the instrument may be negotiated.[41] Therefore, an anomalous indorsement is insufficient to provide a party with standing to foreclose.[42]

4-5 Prima Facie Evidence of Standing

Prima facie evidence of standing at the inception of the case exists, absent any testimony or evidence to the contrary, where the copy of the note attached to the plaintiff's initial complaint contains an indorsement that would provide the plaintiff with standing to foreclose and the original note in the same condition is later filed with the court.[43] This prima face evidence of standing exists where the loan numbers appear-

---

testified that an entity other than the plaintiff was the owner of the note. The Fourth District reversed the judgment because the plaintiff established that it was the holder of the note and whether another entity may be the owner of the note has no bearing on the plaintiff's status as a holder. The court cited *Tilus v. AS Michai, LLC*, 161 So. 3d 1284 (Fla. 4th DCA 2015), in which the court acknowledged the use of imprecise language in previous opinions in which where it suggested that a plaintiff was required to prove that it owned and held the note. Under Florida's Uniform Commercial Code, a plaintiff is not required be both the owner and holder in order to have standing to foreclose. The *Tilus* court cited *Wells Fargo Bank, N.A. v. Morcom*, 125 So. 3d 320, 322 (Fla. 5th DCA 2013), in which the court rejected the appellee's reliance upon case law stating that a bank must be both the owner and holder of a note to have standing to foreclose, because the case law pre-dated the enactment of Florida's Uniform Commercial Code. *See also HSBC Bank USA, Nat'l Ass'n v. Buset*, 241 So. 3d 882, 889 (Fla. 3d DCA 2018) ("[O]wnership is not relevant to standing so much as the question of who is the ultimate beneficial owner of the proceeds of the foreclosure, an issue not normally or necessarily part of a foreclosure case."); *Deutsche Bank Nat'l Trust Co. v. Viteri*, 264 So. 3d 963 (Fla. 4th DCA 2019) (following *Buset*).

[38] *JPMorgan Chase Bank Nat'l Ass'n v. Pierre*, 215 So. 3d 633 (Fla. 4th DCA 2017).

[39] In *One West Bank, F.S.B. v. Bauer*, 159 So. 3d 843 (Fla. 2d DCA 2014), the trial court dismissed the bank's case at trial where the bank did not present evidence that it owned the note after it pled that it owned and held the note. The Second District held that the trial court departed from the essential requirements of law by requiring the plaintiff to prove that it both owned and held the note by imposing a condition that is not required.

[40] Fla. Stat § 673.2051(4).

[41] Fla. Stat § 673.2051(4).

[42] *Buckingham v. Bank of Am., N.A.*, 230 So. 3d 923 (Fla. 2d DCA 2017); *Pennymac Corp. v. Frost*, 214 So. 3d 686 (Fla. 4th DCA 2017); *U.S. Bank v. Becker*, 211 So. 3d 142 (Fla. 4th DCA 2017).

[43] In *Ortiz v. PNC Bank, N.A.*, 188 So. 3d 923, 925 (Fla. 4th DCA 2016), the trial court entered judgment in favor of the defendant at trial in part because the bank's witness was unable to testify that the bank had physical possession of the note at the time the complaint was filed. The Fourth District reversed the judgment, holding that while the fact that a copy of a note is attached to a complaint does not conclusively or necessarily prove that the bank had actual possession of the note at the time the complaint was filed, if the bank later files with the court the original note in the same condition as the copy attached to the complaint, the combination of such evidence is sufficient to establish that the bank had actual possession of the note at the time the complaint was filed and, therefore, had standing to bring the

ing on the copy of the note attached to the plaintiff's initial complaint are redacted in accordance with Fla. R. Jud. Admin. 2.425(a)(4)(I), and there is an explanation of the difference between the copy and the original.[44]

4-6 Constructive Possession of the Note

A holder may possess the note directly or through an agent.[45] The agent who possesses the note on behalf of the holder may be a loan servicer[46] or law firm.[47] Constructive possession of a note exists where the holder has the power to exercise control over the note, such that he or she may deliver possession of the note possessed by the agent, if desired.[48] The existence of the agency relationship must be proved

---

foreclosure action, absent any testimony or evidence to the contrary. The *Ortiz* opinion followed *Clay Cty. Land Tr. #No. 08-04-25-0078-014-27, Orange Park Tr. Servs. v. JP Morgan Chase Bank, Nat'l Ass'n*, 152 So. 3d 83 (Fla. 1st DCA 2014), in which the First District held that where the bank attached to the complaint a copy of the note and an undated allonge to the note containing an indorsement in blank, this was sufficient to establish as a matter of law that the bank had standing to bring the foreclosure action. The *Ortiz* opinion has been cited in 39 Florida District Court Opinions.

[44] In *Kronen v. Deutsche Bank Nat'l Trust Co.*, 267 So. 3d 447 (Fla. 4th DCA 2019), the Fourth distinguished its opinion in *Friedle v. Bank of New York Mellon*, 226 So. 3d 976 (Fla. 4th DCA 2017), where there was no explanation of the differences between the copy of the note filed with the complaint and the original introduced at trial.

[45] UCC § 3-201 (2016) (The official comments explain that "[n]egotiation always requires a change in possession of the instrument because nobody can be a holder without possessing the instrument, either directly or through an agent."); *Phan v. Deutsche Bank Nat'l Trust Co.*, 198 So. 3d 744 (Fla. 2d DCA 2016) (holding that a plaintiff may demonstrate by competent, substantial evidence its standing to foreclose a mortgage under section 673.3011 where it has constructive possession of a mortgage note through its agent at the time it files a complaint for foreclosure); *Fannie Mae v. Rafaeli*, 225 So. 3d 264 (Fla. 4th DCA 2017) ("... although the note owner may have been able to initiate a foreclosure action as the holder with constructive possession of the note, the original servicer was also able to initiate the action as the holder with physical possession").

[46] In *Deutsche Bank Nat'l Trust Co. v. Applewhite*, 213 So. 3d 948 (Fla. 4th DCA 2017), the trial court dismissed the bank's case at trial on the grounds that a document was not produced showing the authority of the original loan servicer to file suit on behalf of the plaintiff. The Fourth District reversed the judgment, explaining that the bank was not required to prove its loan servicer's authority to file suit, because a loan-servicing agent is a proper representative to possess a mortgage note on behalf of the plaintiff, such that the plaintiff remains in constructive possession of the note as the holder sufficient to establish standing. *See also Bank of N.Y. Mellon v. Heath*, 219 So. 3d 104, 106 (Fla. 4th DCA 2017) ("... even though SPS physically possessed the note at the time the complaint was filed, Bank had standing because the testimony and evidence introduced at trial established that SPS, on behalf of Bank, was the servicer for Borrower's loan ... therefore, even without the PSA and mortgage loan schedule, Bank established standing.").

[47] *U.S. Bank, N.A. v. Angeloni*, 199 So. 3d 492, 493 (Fla. 4th DCA 2016) (reversing the trial court's involuntary dismissal of the bank's complaint at trial, where the bank's witness testified that the loan servicer sent the original note to its attorney prior to the filing of the complaint).

[48] In *Bank of N.Y. Mellon v. Heath*, 219 So. 3d 104, 106 (Fla. 4th DCA 2017), the trial court dismissed the bank's case at trial on the basis that the pooling and servicing agreement, which was not admitted into evidence, was the document that authorized the bank's loan servicer to act on its behalf. The Fourth District reversed the judgment, explaining that the

by competent, substantial evidence.[49] An agency relationship may be proven by the terms of a pooling and servicing agreement[50] or a power of attorney.[51] An attorney is the agent of the client in all matters concerning the prosecution or defense of a lawsuit.[52] The filing of the original note with the court by a previous noteholder is not by itself sufficient to establish constructive possession of the note by a new plaintiff that proceeds to file a subsequent foreclosure while the note remains filed with the court.[53] However, where the noteholder files the note with the clerk of court, and then proceeds to file a subsequent foreclosure while the note remains with the clerk of court, the noteholder has constructive possession necessary to establish standing in the later foreclosure action.[54] The clerk of court does not become the holder of the note when the noteholder files the note with the Court.[55]

4-7 Standing as a Non-Holder in Possession

Where a bank is seeking to enforce a note which is payable to another, the bank is a non-holder in possession.[56] A non-holder in possession may prove its right to enforce the note through evidence of an effective transfer, proof of purchase of the debt, or evidence of a valid assignment.[57] A non-holder in possession must prove the chain of transfers by which it acquired possession of the note, beginning with the first holder of the note.[58] If there are multiple prior transfers, the foreclosing plaintiff must prove

---

testimony and evidence admitted at trial, which included two limited powers of attorney between the loan servicer and the bank, one of which specifically provided the loan servicer the power to initiate foreclosures on the bank's behalf, established that the bank had constructive possession of the note.

[49] *Phan v. Deutsche Bank Nat'l Trust Co.*, 198 So. 3d 744, 749 (Fla. 2d DCA 2016). The court in *Phan* commented that ordinarily an agency relationship cannot be proven solely by the testimony of the purported agent. However, because the defendant in *Phan* did not object to the bank's witnesses' testimony that Wells Fargo was the servicer and agent for the bank, the court was satisfied that the record demonstrated the existence of an agency relationship between the loan servicer and the bank.

[50] *Caraccia v. U.S. Bank, N.A.*, 185 So. 3d 1277, 1279 (Fla. 4th DCA 2016). The *Caraccia* court distinguished its holding in *Tremblay v. U.S. Bank, N.A.*, 164 So. 3d 85 (Fla. 4th DCA 2015), in which it held that the bank's loan servicer was the proper party to initiate the action, rather than the bank, because the witness testified that the servicer was the holder of the note and the bank did not introduce the pooling and servicing agreement between the bank and the loan servicer into evidence.

[51] *Bank of New York Mellon v. Heath*, 219 So. 3d 104 (Fla. 4th DCA 2017); *U.S. Bank Nat'l Ass'n v. Cook*, 2019 Fla. App. LEXIS 11282 (Fla. 2d DCA 2019) (which quoted *McCabe v. Howard*, 281 So. 2d 362, 363 (Fla. 2d DCA 1973) for the proposition that "a power of attorney creates the relationship of principal and agent between the one who gives the power and the one who holds it" and was sufficient to prove an agency relationship between the bank and its servicer).

[52] Fla. R. Jud. Admin. 2.505(h).

[53] *Partridge v. Nationstar Mortg., LLC*, 224 So. 3d 839 (Fla. 2d DCA 2017).

[54] *Deutsche Bank Nat'l Trust Co. v. Noll*, 261 So. 3d 656, 658 (Fla. 2d DCA 2018).

[55] *Id.* at 659.

[56] *Bank of New York Mellon Trust Co., N.A. v. Conley*, 188 So. 3d 884 (Fla. 4th DCA 2016).

[57] *Bank of New York Mellon Trust Co., N.A. v. Conley*, 188 So. 3d 884 (Fla. 4th DCA 2016); *Wells Fargo Bank, N.A. v. Cook*, 2019 Fla. App. LEXIS 11785 (Fla. 2d DCA 2019).

[58] *Murray v. HSBC Bank USA*, 157 So. 3d 355, 358 (Fla. 4th DCA 2015). The *Murray* court cited *Anderson v. Burson*, 424 Md. 232, 35 A.3d 452 (Md. 2011), in which the court explained

each prior transfer.[59] Because its rights are purely derivative, a non-holder in possession must prove that the transferor of the note had the right to enforce the note.[60] Evidence that the foreclosing plaintiff acquired the original note through a pre-suit purchase and assumption agreement from the original lender[61] or a corporate merger between the original lender and the plaintiff is evidence of standing to foreclose.[62] Evidence of the purchase of the debt or effective transfer or valid assignment need not be documentary; witness testimony is sufficient.[63] In order to prove standing to foreclose based upon a merger, the surviving entity must prove that it acquired all of the absorbed entity's assets, including the note and mortgage, by virtue of the merger.[64] If there are multiple entities within the merger, the foreclosing plaintiff must establish and explain the relationship between the entities in the entire chain of mergers in order to establish standing.[65] However, notes can be sold or otherwise transferred even when the entire bank is not acquired.[66]

Standing to foreclose can be proven through a valid pre-suit assignment of note and mortgage.[67] An assignment of note and mortgage is not made defective because it is

---

the "shelter rule," which holds that because a non-holder in possession cannot rely on possession alone to enforce an instrument, the non-holder in possession must prove that the transferor from which it acquired the note had the right to enforce it. Therefore, if there were multiple prior transfers from the first holder, the non-holder in possession must prove each prior transfer.

[59] *Murray v. HSBC Bank USA*, 157 So. 3d 355, 358 (Fla. 4th DCA 2015).

[60] *PennyMac Corp. v. Frost*, 214 So. 3d 686, 689 (Fla. 4th DCA 2017).

[61] In *Stone v. BankUnited*, 115 So. 3d 411, 413 (Fla. 2d DCA 2013), the bank's witness testified that she worked for the original lender at the time that it seized and placed into a receivership, and that the foreclosing plaintiff acquired all of the assets of the original lender pursuant to a purchase and assumption agreement, which included the subject note and mortgage. The Second District held that this constituted competent, substantial evidence of standing to foreclose.

[62] *Amstone v. Bank of New York Mellon*, 182 So. 3d 804, 806-07 (Fla. 2d DCA 2016).

[63] *Certo v. Bank of N.Y. Mellon*, 268 So. 3d 901, 902-03 (Fla. 1st DCA 2019) (citing *Ham v. Nationstar Mortg., LLC*, 164 So. 3d 714 (Fla. 1st DCA 2015)).

[64] *Green v. Green Tree Servicing, LLC*, 230 So. 3d 989, 991 (Fla. 5th DCA 2017) (quoting *Vogel v. Wells Fargo Bank, N.A.*, 192 So. 3d 714, 716 (Fla. 4th DCA 2016) and *Fiorito v. JP Morgan Chase Bank, Nat'l Ass'n*, 174 So. 3d 519, 521 (Fla. 4th DCA 2015)); *Certo v. Bank of N.Y. Mellon*, 268 So. 3d 901, 902-03 (Fla. 1st DCA 2019).

[65] *Fielding v. PNC Bank Nat'l Ass'n*, 239 So. 3d 140, 143 (Fla. 5th DCA 2018).

[66] *U.S. Bank v. Glicken*, 228 So. 3d 1194, 1996 (Fla. 5th DCA 2017).

[67] In *Nationstar Mortg., LLC v. Kelly*, 199 So. 3d 1051 (Fla. 5th DCA 2016), the trial court dismissed the plaintiff's complaint for failure to prove standing at trial. The Fifth District reversed the judgment, holding that the plaintiff proved standing through an unbroken chain of assignments of note and mortgage from MERS as nominee for the original payee to the foreclosing plaintiff. The original plaintiff then assigned the note and mortgage to Nationstar, who was substituted as the party plaintiff. The court cited its holding in *Taylor v. Deutsche Bank Nat. Trust Co.*, 44 So. 3d 618, 623 (Fla. 5th DCA 2010); *Wells Fargo Bank, N.A. v. Cook*, 2019 Fla. App. LEXIS 11785 (Fla. 2d DCA 2019) (holding that trial court erred in granting involuntary dismissal at conclusion of trial for lack of standing where pre-suit assignment assigned and transferred all interest in the mortgage—together with the note—to the foreclosing plaintiff).

assigned by "MERS" as nominee for the assignor.[68] An assignment which only assigns the mortgage but does not also assign the note is insufficient to demonstrate standing to foreclose.[69] A post-complaint assignment of mortgage does not, standing alone, negate the plaintiff's ability to demonstrate standing to foreclose.[70] A holder of a note can enforce the note even where it has assigned the note to another party.[71] Where an assignment is made by a person as attorney-in-fact for the assignor, the plaintiff must establish that the person acting as attorney-in-fact was authorized to execute the assignment.[72]

4-8 Standing to Enforce a Lost Note

A lost instrument can be enforced if the person seeking to enforce the instrument was entitled to enforce it when the loss occurred or acquired ownership of it from someone entitled to enforce it when the loss occurred, the loss was not the result of a transfer or seizure, and the instrument cannot reasonably be obtained.[73] There is no requirement that the plaintiff prove exactly how possession was lost.[74] Proving the circumstances of the note's loss is necessary only if it is required to prove that the plaintiff was entitled to enforce it when the loss occurred.[75] A note may be assigned or transferred, even though it is lost.[76] The person seeking to enforce the instrument must prove the terms of the instrument and the right to enforce it, and then it is as if the person has produced the instrument.[77] The person may do so either through a lost note affidavit or by testimony from a person with knowledge.[78] Standing to enforce a lost note that has been reestablished must be proven in the same manner as an original note that had not been lost.[79] The fact that an original note is lost at the time the complaint is filed, and later found during the pendency of the case, does not negate the ability of the plaintiff to establish standing to foreclose, where the plaintiff pre-

---

[68] *Taylor v. Deutsche Bank Nat. Trust Co.*, 44 So. 3d 618, 623 (Fla. 5th DCA 2010) (holding that a pre-suit assignment of note and mortgage from MERS as nominee for the original payee established standing to foreclose).

[69] *Bristol v. Wells Fargo Bank, N.A.*, 137 So. 3d 1130, 1133 (Fla. 4th DCA 2014).

[70] *WM Specialty Mortg., LLC v. Salomon*, 874 So. 2d 680 (Fla. 4th DCA 2004).

[71] In *ALS-RVC, LLC v. Garvin*, 201 So. 3d 687 (Fla. 4th DCA 2016), the trial court dismissed the bank's case in part on the grounds that an assignment of note and mortgage had been executed in favor of an entity other than the plaintiff. The Fourth District reversed the judgment because the bank established standing to foreclose as the holder of the note at the time the complaint was filed.

[72] *Bonafide Props., LLC v. E-Trade Bank*, 208 So. 3d 1279 (Fla. 5th DCA 2017) (citing *Figueroa v. Federal Nat'l Mtg. Ass'n.*, 180 So. 3d 1110, 1115 (Fla. 5th DCA 2015)).

[73] Fla. Stat. § 673.3091 (2016); *Wisman v. Nationstar Mortg., LLC*, 239 So. 3d 726 (Fla. 5th DCA 2017).

[74] *Deakter v. Menendez*, 830 So. 2d 124, 129 (Fla. 3d DCA 2002).

[75] *Boumarate v. HSBC Bank USA, N.A.*, 172 So. 3d 535, 537 (Fla. 5th DCA 2015) (Reversing final judgment where the bank failed to prove that it was entitled to enforce the note at the time it was lost. The copy of the note was payable to another entity, contained no indorsements and there was no evidence of an assignment.).

[76] *Deakter v. Menendez*, 830 So. 2d 124, 129 (Fla. 3d DCA 2002).

[77] *Wisman v. Nationstar Mortg., LLC*, 239 So. 3d 726, 728 (Fla. 5th DCA 2017); *Mortgage Elect. Registration Sys. v. Badra*, 991 So. 2d 1037, 1039 (Fla. 4th DCA 2008).

[78] *Wisman v. Nationstar Mortg., LLC*, 239 So. 3d 726, 728 (Fla. 5th DCA 2017).

[79] *Boumarate v. HSBC Bank USA, N.A.*, 172 So. 3d 535, 537-38 (Fla. 5th DCA 2015).

sents evidence sufficient to establish the right to enforce the lost note at the time the suit was filed.[80]

4-9 Standing Where the Plaintiff Has Been Substituted

A substituted plaintiff acquires the standing of the original plaintiff.[81] The substituted plaintiff must prove the standing of the original plaintiff as of the filing of the complaint, as well as its own standing at the time of trial.[82] There is no requirement that the substituted plaintiff prove its standing as of the time of substitution.[83] The court is not permitted to dismiss the action solely because the plaintiff has transferred its interest during the pendency of the suit.[84] Two courts have ruled that a substituted plaintiff is unable to establish that it is the holder or non-holder in possession where the original note is filed with the court prior to substitution.[85] However, the Second District in 2018 held that where the substituted plaintiff obtains the original note from the Court file prior to trial and therefore physically possesses the note at the time of trial, this is sufficient to establish the substituted plaintiff's standing at the time of trial.[86] The Fourth District has distinguished the Second District's rulings and held that the transferred standing a substituted plaintiff acquires from the original plaintiff, coupled with the presentation of the original note indorsed in blank (despite the note being filed with the court at the time of trial), provides the substituted plaintiff standing to foreclose.[87] The Fifth District has also held that a substituted plaintiff establishes standing to foreclose where the original plaintiff files a note indorsed in blank with the court and the substituted plaintiff admits into evidence the original note, indorsed in blank, at the time of trial.[88]

---

[80] In *Wilmington Sav. Fund Soc'y, FSB v. Louissaint*, 212 So. 3d 473 (Fla. 5th DCA 2017), the bank filed its initial complaint with a lost note count and lost note affidavit. During the pendency of the case, it located the original note and filed it with the court. The trial court ruled for the defendant at trial on the grounds that the bank did not possess the original note at the time the complaint was filed. The Fifth District reversed the judgment, holding that the bank presented evidence establishing its right to enforce the lost note at the time it filed the complaint and established standing once the note was located by filing it with the court.

[81] *Brandenburg v. Residential Credit Solutions, Inc.*, 137 So. 3d 604 (Fla. 4th DCA 2014).

[82] *Ventures Trust 2013-I-H-R v. Asset Acquisitions & Holdings Trust*, 202 So. 3d 939, 943 (Fla. 2d DCA 2016); *Olivera v. Bank of Am., N.A.*, 141 So. 3d 770, 771-74 (Fla. 2d DCA 2014); *Wilmington Sav. Fund Soc'y, FSB v. Contreras*, 2019 Fla. App. LEXIS 11698 (Fla. 5th DCA 2019).

[83] *Ventures Trust 2013-I-H-R v. Asset Acquisitions & Holdings Trust*, 202 So. 3d 939, 944 (Fla. 2d DCA 2016); *Wilmington Trust v. Moon*, 238 So. 3d 425, 428 (Fla. 5th DCA 2018).

[84] *Miami Airlines v. Webb*, 114 So. 2d 361, 363 (Fla. 3d DCA 1959).

[85] *Creadon v. U.S. Bank N.A.*, 166 So. 3d 952 (Fla. 2d DCA 2015); *Geweye v. Ventures Trust 2013-I-H-R*, 189 So. 3d 231 (Fla. 2d DCA 2016).

[86] *Nationstar Mortg., LLC v. Johnson*, 2018 Fla. App. LEXIS 9266 (Fla. 2d DCA, June 29, 2018).

[87] *Spicer v. Ocwen Loan Servicing, LLC*, 238 So. 3d 275 (Fla. 4th DCA 2018).

[88] *Nationstar Mortg., LLC v. Bo Chan*, 226 So. 3d 330 (Fla. 5th DCA 2017); *PMT NPL Fin. 2015-1 v. Centurion Sys., LLC*, 2018 Fla. App. LEXIS 11956 (Fla. 5th DCA 2018).

4-10 Standing to Foreclose a Line of Credit

A line of credit which is not a fixed sum is not a negotiable instrument.[89] Standing to foreclose a line of credit can be established through assignment of the line of credit[90] or proof of ownership.[91]

---

[89] *Chuchian v. Situs Invs., LLC*, 219 So. 3d 992 (Fla. 5th DCA 2017); *Third Fed. Sav. & Loan Ass'n v. Koulouvaris*, 2018 Fla. App. LEXIS 6941 (Fla. 2d DCA 2018).

[90] *Chuchian v. Situs Invs., LLC*, 219 So. 3d 992 (Fla. 5th DCA 2017) (citing *Mason v. Flowers*, 91 Fla. 224, 107 So. 334, 335 (Fla. 1926); *Reddish v. Ritchie*, 17 Fla. 867, 870 (Fla. 1880)).

[91] *Compare: HSBC Bank USA, N.A. v. Buset*, 241 So. 3d 882, 889 (Fla. 3d DCA 2018) (A plaintiff proving standing to enforce a negotiable instrument as a holder does not need to prove ownership.).

CHAPTER 5

Title Considerations in Mortgage Foreclosure

Gaspar Forteza

5-1 Overview

There are no considerations or issues more fundamental to foreclosure litigation than those that concern the transfer of title. Indeed, a "security instrument" is no such thing without the means to effect a transfer of title to real property. This transfer is the very purpose for which the security instrument exists. Accordingly, any attorney seeking to enforce any mortgage or lien must base her entire litigation strategy with the goal of effecting clear and marketable title to the *res*.

While the complexity of foreclosure litigation has advanced in explosive measure over the last decade, these foundations remain much as they were more than 100 years ago. Because of this advanced complexity, however, many practitioners have adopted a high-volume and low-diligence approach to foreclosure litigation, particularly in the context of judicial title transfers. Ironically, this has greatly motivated the increased complexity of foreclosure litigation, which is the principal remedy crafted by the courts of appeal and Florida Supreme Court. The aim of this practical guide is to highlight the core title implications and principles encountered in mortgage foreclosure litigation.

Lastly, many of these core principles are applicable to all manner of lien foreclosures, such as construction liens, mechanic's liens, and even foreclosure of tax certificates. However, that is not the case for all, and the focus of this practical guide is to aid practitioners in the context of mortgage foreclosure litigation.

5-2 Typical Title Transfers in Foreclosure Litigation

5-2:1 Certificate of Title Following a Foreclosure Sale

Title is transferred by the clerk of court via Certificate of Title following the expiration of the post-sale objection period.[1] The foremost title concern to the titular owner of the property thereafter is the validity and insurability of her instrument. A Certificate of Title is a valid conveyance of title, provided that it is the product of a valid foreclosure

---

[1] Fla. Stat. § 45.031.

judgment and a valid foreclosure sale.[2] While that may appear to be obvious, a distinction must be made between *void* and *voidable* foreclosure judgments and foreclosure sales.

5-2:1.1 Void Versus Voidable Certificates of Title

Where a court order is so patently defective that substantive rights have been prejudiced, the order (as well as its operative effect) is invalid, as it is considered to never have had any effect.[3] On the other hand, where the order is the result of some procedural error that does not irrevocably violate some substantive right, the order (as well as its operative effect) is valid unless and until it is appropriately challenged and vacated.[4]

Accordingly, voidable judgments and voidable foreclosure sales do not necessarily result in invalid Certificates of Title.[5] Void judgments and void sales, however, do result in invalid Certificates of Title.[6] This is of particular importance to *bona fide* purchasers for value at the foreclosure sale, as void judgments or sales will result in an invalid conveyance, but this will not necessarily be the case when the defect or irregularity renders the judgment or sale merely voidable.

Appreciating this distinction is crucial when engaging in complaint drafting, service of process, or any other enterprise the defect of which deprives the trial court of jurisdiction *ab initio*. This distinction is not always immediately apparent. For example, mortgagors are often absent from the jurisdiction or cannot be located in order to effect service of process. Accordingly, it is common for foreclosing lenders to proceed with constructive service under section 49.021, Florida Statutes. Service by publication under this statute requires that the plaintiff have undertaken a "diligent search" for the defendant. The test for this diligence is "whether the complainant reasonably employed knowledge at his command, made diligent inquiry, and exerted an honest and conscientious effort appropriate to the circumstances, to acquire the information necessary to enable him to effect personal service on the defendant."[7] Diligence in searching for a defendant's whereabouts prior to proceeding with service of process by publication, therefore, is a bright-line rule. If the insufficiency of the diligence was evident from the record, the Certificate of Title is void.[8] However, if the insufficiency is not readily apparent from the record, then the foreclosure judgment is at most voidable, generally insulating a third-party purchaser's acquired title.[9]

---

[2] Fla. Stat. § 45.031.

[3] *Shepheard v. Deutsche Bank Trust Co. Americas*, 922 So. 2d 340 (Fla. 5th DCA 2006).

[4] *Sterling Factors Corp. v. U.S. Bank Nat. Ass'n*, 968 So. 2d 658, 665 (Fla. 2d DCA 2007); See also *Gans v. Heathgate-Sunflower Homeowners Ass'n, Inc.*, 593 So. 2d 549, 552-53 (Fla. 4th DCA 1992) ("Where the service by publication is void on its face a reversal of the order of sale will defeat the title of the non-party who purchases the property in good faith at the judicial sale.").

[5] *Southeast. & Assocs., Inc. v. Fox Run Homeowners Ass'n, Inc.*, 704 So. 2d 694, 696 (Fla. 4th DCA 1997).

[6] *Godsell v. United Guar. Residential Ins.*, 923 So. 2d 1209, 1211 (Fla. 5th DCA 2006).

[7] *Howard v. Gualt*, 259 So. 3d 119, 121 (Fla. 4th DCA 2018) (quoting *Green Emerald Homes, LLC v. Bank of N.Y. Mellon*, 204 So. 3d 512, 514 (Fla. 4th DCA 2016)).

[8] *Godsell v. United Guar. Residential Ins.*, 923 So. 2d 1209 (Fla. 5th DCA 2006).

[9] *Se. & Associates, Inc. v. Fox Run Homeowners Ass'n, Inc.*, 704 So. 2d 694 (Fla. 4th DCA 1997).

5-2:1.2 Deeds in Lieu of Foreclosure

For a variety of reasons, a "deed in lieu of foreclosure" may be preferable to judicial foreclosure for both mortgagor and mortgagee. For the mortgagee, the great benefit is avoiding the expense of litigation as well as the steep court clerk filing fees in Florida. For the mortgagor, a deed-in-lieu will also likely result in a less-adverse credit rating and generally preclude the issuance of a judgment against her.

A deed-in-lieu agreement is precisely what its name suggests—the mortgagor executes a deed in favor of the lender, and the lender agrees to forego foreclosure litigation against the borrower. The execution and acceptance of this deed, however, has significant and unique implications, the most important of which is merger.

5-2:1.3 Merger of Lien and Title

The doctrine of merger provides that a lien interest and a titular interest cannot exist in the same person. In other words, when the holder of a mortgage accepts a deed to the subject real property, its mortgage interest merges into the title, effectively extinguishing the mortgage and note.[10] This merger has two important consequences.

Firstly, because the deed conveyed by the mortgagor carries with it no greater rights than the mortgagor had upon conveying, the merger doctrine operates to elevate all junior liens above that of the former mortgagee.[11] To illustrate, if a first mortgagee accepts a deed-in-lieu of foreclosure, the merger doctrine would operate to elevate the second mortgage to first mortgage status, and the formerly first mortgagee would now be bound by the same.

Secondly, because the interests of title and equity have merged, the entire debt which was secured by the mortgage is similarly discharged.[12] This would naturally preclude any claim for a deficiency judgment or suit against guarantors of the debt.

However, as a result of the unjust result of the merger doctrine, Florida law uniformly holds that the intention of the parties will control whether the merger doctrine is implicated when the mortgagee accepts a deed-in-lieu.[13] Further, case law suggests that in the failure to make clear the parties' intent concerning the merger of the equitable and legal estates, the judge may presume that no merger has occurred.[14] Accordingly, a careful attorney will ensure merger language is included within the deed-in-lieu agreement and deed when the balance of the promissory note is waived, and conversely, non-merger language is included when it is not waived.

---

[10] *Floorcraft Distributors v. Horne-Wilson, Inc.*, 251 So. 2d 138 (Fla. 1st DCA 1971).
[11] *Gourley v. Wollam*, 348 So. 2d 1218 (Fla. 4th DCA 1977).
[12] *Prigal v. Kearn*, 557 So. 2d 647 (Fla. 4th DCA 1990).
[13] *Ennis v. Finanz und Kommerz-Union Establ.*, 565 So. 2d 374 (Fla. 2d DCA 1990); *Gourley v. Wollam*, 348 So. 2d 1218 (Fla. 4th DCA 1977); *Jackson v. Relf*, 26 Fla. 465 (1890).
[14] *Sanderson v. Hudlett*, 832 So. 2d 845, 848 (Fla. 4th DCA 2002) ("When there is no evidence of the intention of the owner in uniting the legal and equitable estates in himself, it is proper to presume that he intended that effect which is the most beneficial to him.") (quoting *Jackson v. Relf*, 26 Fla. 465, 8 So. 184, 185 (1890)); *Philippe v. Weiner*, 143 So. 3d 1086 (Fla. 3d DCA 2014); *Westbury Properties, Inc. v. Cardillo*, 638 So. 2d 519 (Fla. 2d DCA 1994).

5-2:2 Short-Sales and Short-Payoffs

Another form of title conveyance common in the context of mortgage foreclosure litigation is the short-sale. By very definition, it is the sale of the subject property for less than the total amount owed to the mortgagee. A short-sale is any sale whereby the mortgagee consents to release its mortgage lien in exchange for proceeds of the sale of the property to a third party. Similarly, in a short-payoff, the mortgagee consents to release its lien in exchange for an amount less than the total amount owed, irrespective of whether a sale of the property occurs.

As with a deed-in-lieu, both parties may benefit in agreeing to pursue a short-sale or short-payoff instead of a Certificate of Title following a foreclosure sale—it avoids a foreclosure judgment against the mortgagor and saves litigation costs for both sides. The mortgagee, moreover, avoids carrying and re-sale costs for the property. As the mortgagee never acquires title, it is generally not concerned with the existence of junior lienholders or marketability of the title. Instead, its concerns are typically limited to the amount it will receive as payoff and whether it will agree to waive the deficiency balance. To the mortgagor negotiating a short-sale, however, negotiating releases of liens by the various lienholders is often challenging. Accordingly, title transfer via short-sale to a third-party is more common in properties encumbered by only one or two inferior liens.

5-3 Jurisdiction and Necessary Parties

When initiating a suit for foreclosure, the practitioner should carefully examine the public records to determine the existence of all liens and interests of record encumbering the subject property. Most reputable title companies will provide a foreclosure commitment report, title abstract, or some similar title search report to assist in this review. Careful review of the public records prior to initiating suit is important for two reasons.

Firstly, a review of the public records will highlight which interests are inferior to those of the foreclosing litigant, and so, which parties should be joined to the foreclosure action. Failure to join inferior interest holders in a foreclosure action will result in a Certificate of Title subject to those pending interests. To the extent that inferior interest holders are not joined in the action, their interests remain intact and may not be prejudiced.[15] In most instances, this will require a re-foreclosure action to cure the inadvertent omission.[16]

Secondly, the practitioner's title review will highlight which interests appear to be *superior* to the interest being enforced. Superior interests are not joined.[17] In fact, a final judgment rendered against a superior interest holder is subject to being vacated as voidable, since any complaint seeking to foreclose a senior interest fails to state a cause of action.[18] It is not uncommon for a review of title to demonstrate the existence

---

[15] *Abdoney v. York*, 903 So. 2d 981 (Fla. 2d DCA 2005); *Posnansky v. Breckenridge Estates Corp.*, 621 So. 2d 736 (Fla. 4th DCA 1993).

[16] *See Quinn Plumbing Co. v. New Miami Shores Corp.*, 129 So. 690 (1930); *White v. Mid-State Federal Savings & Loan Ass'n*, 530 So. 2d 959 (Fla. 5th DCA 1988).

[17] *Poinciana Hotel of Miami Beach, Inc. v. Kasden*, 370 So. 2d 399 (Fla. 3d DCA 1979).

[18] *Bank of New York Mellon v. Condo. Ass'n of La Mer Estates, Inc.*, 175 So. 3d 282 (Fla. 2015); *Bank of Am., N.A. v. Kipps Colony II Condo. Ass'n*, 201 So. 3d 670, 675 (Fla. 2d DCA 2016).

of an apparently superior lien which the interest holder believed to have been satisfied or non-existent.[19] In such an event, the practitioner must determine the nature of the error and is advised to attempt to do so prior to the initiation of litigation.[20] Inclusion of these apparently senior parties within the foreclosure action may be necessary in order to adjudicate their interests inferior.[21]

5-4 Priority of Interests and Florida's Recording Act

Three statutes generally govern the priority of interest in real property. Florida is classified as a "notice" jurisdiction, which is established by Fla. Stat. § 695.01(1): "No conveyance, transfer, or mortgage of real property, or of any interest therein . . . shall be good and effectual in law or equity against creditors or subsequent purchasers for a valuable consideration and without notice, unless the same be recorded according to law."

Florida Statute § 28.222(2) requires the clerk of court to record instruments in the county's official records, including the date, time and description of the type of instrument. Section 695.11 further provides that the date and time of recording by the clerk determines the priority of recordation, and that "an instrument bearing the lower number in the then-current series of numbers shall have priority over any instrument bearing a higher number in the same series."

The recording of the interest provides constructive notice to the world.[22] Practically, this means that priority is not just determined by reviewing which interest was recorded first, but rather by whether the mortgagee had actual or constructive notice

---

[19] An illustration: Kira is the owner of a large tract of land located in the lush green hills of Bajor, and wants to refinance her existing mortgage loan. Quark, a savvy entrepreneur, jumps at the chance and lends Kira money to payoff an existing mortgage loan belonging to Rom, which is the only mortgage lien of record. Having paid off Rom's first mortgage, Quark takes a first mortgage from Kira. Kira defaults on the mortgage, and Quark prepares a foreclosure action. A review of title shows the Rom mortgage is still unsatisfied, which is a surprise to Quark. His closing documents clearly show the Rom mortgage was paid off with proceeds from his loan. No satisfaction of mortgage appears to have been recorded by Rom.

[20] In continuation of our illustration, the practitioner's task may be as simple as requesting and obtaining a satisfaction of the Rom mortgage (if he forgot to record a satisfaction), or it may be somewhat more complex. Consider this wrinkle: The Rom mortgage secured a revolving line of credit. A revolving line of credit is a loan that operates much like a credit card, whereby the borrower may draw on the credit line a certain sum, pay it down, and draw from it again in the future. These accounts are frequently paid down to zero, and the mortgage is typically not satisfied unless the borrower requests the account be closed. Closing documents from the Quark mortgage show the closing agent requested a payoff from Rom, but never instructed him to close the revolving line of credit and issue a satisfaction. Following the receipt of funds from the Quark mortgage closing, Kira continued to draw down on the Rom mortgage line of credit. In such a case, and in the absence of the application of equitable subrogation principles, the Quark mortgage may be relegated to second mortgagee status.

[21] *Mederos v. Selph (L.T.), Inc.*, 625 So. 2d 894 (Fla. 5th DCA 1993); *New York Life Ins. and Annuity Corp. v. Hammocks Community Ass'n, Inc.*, 622 So. 2d 1369 (Fla. 3d DCA 1993); *Blanchard v. Continental Mortg. Investors*, 217 So. 2d 586 (Fla. 1st DCA 1969).

[22] *Mayfield v. First City Bank of Florida*, 95 So. 3d 398, 399 (Fla. 1st DCA 2012).

of any other interests when taking its mortgage. The mortgagee's interest will be superior to any interest perfected subsequent to the recording of its own mortgage, but inferior to prior recorded mortgages and interests, as well as prior unrecorded mortgages and interests of which it had actual notice.

5-4:1 Recording Errors and Notice

If a properly recorded document provides constructive knowledge to the world of its existence and accordingly confers priority from the date of recording, what happens if the document is recorded *improperly*? Florida Statute § 695.03 provides that "[t]o entitle any instrument concerning real property to be recorded, the execution must be acknowledged by the party executing it, proved by a subscribing witness to it, or legalized or authenticated" as provided by the statute. The Statute further provides for notarial requirements for Florida Notaries, Notaries from other States, and authentications from foreign countries. Accordingly, a document that was recorded while not in compliance with the requirements of Fla. Stat. § 695.03 arguably does not confer constructive knowledge.[23]

The Florida Supreme Court has clarified, however, that absent a significant and substantive departure from Fla. Stat. § 695.03, the document provides constructive knowledge.[24] Errors of a technical nature will not defeat constructive knowledge.[25] Courts have instead interpreted departures from the statute to revoke constructive knowledge instead in circumstances where the document "is not within the contemplation of the recording statute (i.e. a forged deed, an uncertified copy of an agreement, or an unacknowledged contract)."[26]

5-4:2 Equitable Subrogation

The principle of equitable subrogation is recognized by Florida courts to elevate an apparently inferior mortgage to superior status in certain circumstances. Generally, the principle maintains that when proceeds from a loan are used to satisfy a prior

---

[23] *See Reed v. Fain*, 145 So.2d 858 (Fla.1961); *Lassiter v. Curtiss–Bright Co.*, 129 Fla. 728 (Fla.1937).

[24] *Edenfield v. Wingard*, 89 So. 2d 776, 778 (Fla. 1956) ("It is the established policy of the law to uphold certificates of acknowledgment and, wherever substance is found, obvious clerical errors and all technical omissions will be disregarded. Inartificialness [sic] in their execution will not be permitted to defeat them, if looking at them as a whole, either alone or in connection with the [instrument], we find that they reasonably and fairly indicate a compliance with the law. Clerical errors will not be permitted to defeat acknowledgments when they, considered either alone or in connection with the instrument acknowledged, and viewed in the light of the statute controlling them, fairly show a substantial compliance with the statute.").

[25] *House of Lyons v. Marcus*, 72 So. 2d 34, 36 (Fla. 1954) ("Clerical errors will not be permitted to defeat acknowledgments when they, considered either alone or in connection with the instrument acknowledged, and viewed in the light of the statute controlling them, fairly show a substantial compliance with the statute.").

[26] *In re Mead*, 374 B.R. 296, 310 (Bankr. M.D. Fla. 2007) (interpreting *Reed v. Fain*, 145 So. 2d 858 (Fla.1961) and *Lassiter v. Curtiss–Bright Co.*, 129 Fla. 728 (Fla.1937)); *See also In re Henry*, 200 B.R. 59 (Bankr. M.D. Fla. 1996) (same).

mortgage, the mortgagee "stands in the shoes" of that prior lienor.[27] In other words, when a mortgagee pays off a prior mortgage, that prior mortgage may be equitably subrogated to the paying mortgagee. Accordingly, a mortgage that appears to be inferior of record may be entitled to priority status in certain circumstances. This principle may be raised as both an affirmative claim or in defense.[28] There are, however, some important exceptions to its application.

5-4:2.1 Prejudice to the Prior Lienholder

Equitable subrogation is a principle grounded strictly in equity, and accordingly, it will only be applied when doing so will not prejudice innocent parties.[29] This is logical, of course, since the principle aims to prevent the second mortgagee from being unjustly enriched and receiving a windfall.

Accordingly, the principle may be applied to the entire amount secured by the lien, or to only a portion. For example, if the refinance mortgage exceeds the value of the mortgage being paid off, the mortgagee would be entitled to have its lien equitably subrogated only up to the value of the mortgage that was paid off.[30] Additionally, equitable subrogation may be rejected in instances where doing so would preclude an inferior lienholder from exercising its contractual rights, such as a due-on-sale clause.[31] As subrogation will be denied if it works any injustice to an innocent third party, its application is entirely case-specific.[32]

---

[27] See *Federal Land Bank of Columbia v. Godwin*, 107 Fla. 537 (1933); *Suntrust Bank v. Riverside Nat. Bank of Florida*, 792 So. 2d 1222 (Fla. 4th DCA 2001).

[28] *Aurora Loan Services LLC v. Senchuk*, 36 So. 3d 716 (Fla. 1st DCA 2010).

[29] *Federal Land Bank of Columbia v. Godwin*, 107 Fla. 537, 145 So. 883 (1933); *Suntrust Bank v. Riverside Nat. Bank of Florida*, 792 So. 2d 1222 (Fla. 4th DCA 2001); *Radison Properties v. Flamingo Groves*, 767 So. 2d 587 (Fla. 4th DCA 2000).

[30] An illustration: In January, Mr. Ender Wiggin gives a loan for $100,000.00 secured by a first mortgage on Utopia Planitia. That mortgage is recorded in January. In March, Mr. Montgomery Scott gives a loan for $50,000.00, taking a second mortgage on Utopia Planitia—again, recording the same in March. In November, a third individual Mr. Lazarus Long gives a loan for $130,000.00, paying off only Mr. Wiggin's first mortgage, and records it. The owners of Utopia Planitia pocket the remaining $30,000.00, and Mr. Scott is paid nothing.

Mr. Wiggin, being much too busy playing video games to remember to record a satisfaction of mortgage, fails to do so. A review of the record title would show the existence of three mortgages in the following order of priority: (1) the Wiggin mortgage; (2) the Scott mortgage; (3) the Long mortgage. In such a circumstance, Mr. Long could invoke the principle of equitable subrogation to elevate his mortgage to first position, eliminating the Wiggin mortgage altogether. However, Mr. Long would only be entitled to subrogation to the extent that it does not prejudice Mr. Scott's $50,000.00 second mortgage. Mr. Long's mortgage would be in first position up to $100,000.00 only, and in *third* position for the remaining $30,000.00.

Applying the principle of equitable subrogation here, the lien priorities would look like this: (1) the Long mortgage for $100,000.00; (2) the Scott mortgage for $50,000.00; (3) the Long mortgage for $30,000.00. *See Aurora Loan Services LLC v. Senchuk*, 36 So. 3d 716 (Fla. 1st DCA 2010).

[31] See *Velazquez v. Serrano*, 43 So. 3d 82 (Fla. 3d DCA 2010); *Sherman v. Deutsche Bank Nat. Trust Co.*, 100 So. 3d 95 (Fla. 3d DCA 2012).

[32] *National Union Fire Ins. Co. of Pittsburgh, Pa. v. KPMG Peat Marwick*, 742 So. 2d 328, 332 (Fla. 3d DCA 1999), *approved*, 765 So. 2d 36 (Fla. 2000) ("The right to recover from a third

5-5 The Lis Pendens

Latin for "suit pending," the *lis pendens* tool greatly avoids title issues during the pendency of litigation. Upon the filing of the complaint, the practitioner should immediately file and record in the public records of the county a *lis pendens*, identifying the property being foreclosed in conformity with the statute.[33] The *lis pendens* operates as constructive notice to the entire world of the pending litigation as well as the allegations of the complaint.[34] This means that any interest in the subject property acquired subsequent to the recording of the *lis pendens* will be subject and inferior to a valid judgment rendered thereon.[35]

From a practical perspective, the *lis pendens* protects the foreclosing mortgagee from intervening lienholders which would not otherwise be included as parties defendant. At the foreclosure sale, all such interests would be foreclosed, irrespective of whether they were expressly joined as parties in the complaint or not. The practitioner is well-advised to file suit and record the *lis pendens* as quickly as possible after obtaining her title abstract and reviewing title. Should too much time pass between the review of title and the recording of the *lis pendens*, intervening liens could result in a Certificate of Title subject to those liens.[36]

Additionally, the *lis pendens* forces the holders of unrecorded interests or liens to file a motion to intervene in the proceedings within 30 days of its recording, or else such interests and liens will be discharged at the foreclosure sale.[37] A corollary to this requirement is that the court wherein the *lis pendens* was recorded maintains exclusive jurisdiction to adjudicate any unrecorded intervening interest, and a separate suit on that unrecorded interest is inappropriate.[38] This requirement is substantive rather than procedural, and so not subject to constitutional challenge.[39] This provision does

---

person is conditional on whether or not the right of the one seeking subrogation is superior to the equities of those against whom the right is sought to be enforced.").

[33] Fla. Stat. § 48.23.

[34] *De Pass v. Chitty*, 105 So. 148 (1925); *See also Taylor v. Steckel*, 944 So. 2d 494 (Fla. 3d DCA 2006).

[35] See *Avalon Assocs. of Delaware Ltd. v. Avalon Park Assocs., Inc.*, 760 So. 2d 1132 (Fla. 5th DCA 2000).

[36] An illustration. Attorney Harvey Birdman reviews title on January 1, and determines that the necessary parties are A, B, and C. He files his complaint naming these individuals on February 15, and simultaneously records a *lis pendens*. Unknown to Mr. Birdman, his longtime nemesis, Myron Reducto, gave a large loan in return for a mortgage over the subject property on February 7. Since the *lis pendens* was recorded on February 15, Mr. Reducto is unaffected by the foreclosure proceedings, and the ensuing Certificate of Title will be subject to his mortgage.

[37] Fla. Stat. § 48.23.

[38] *U.S. Bank Nat. Ass'n v. Quadomain Condo. Ass'n, Inc.*, 103 So. 3d 977 (Fla. 4th DCA 2012). It must be highlighted that this jurisdictional preclusion is only applicable to *unrecorded* intervening interests, e.g., interests that arose after the recording of the *lis pendens* but before the rendition of final judgment, and were unrecorded. Holders of recorded intervening interests are not bound by the *lis pendens'* requirement to intervene or be extinguished, and may maintain separate suits for enforcement. *See CitiMortgage, Inc. v. Flowers*, 41 Fla. L. Weekly D916 (Fla. 4th DCA Apr. 13, 2016). Of course, irrespective of whether the intervening interest is recorded or not, the *lis pendens* will effectively discharge the interest at the foreclosure sale.

[39] *Adhin v. First Horizon Home Loans*, 44 So. 3d 1245 (Fla. 5th DCA 2010).

not affect the foreclosing plaintiff's right to amend its complaint, moreover, to include the omitted party as a defendant, effectively amending its *lis pendens*.[40]

The usage of the *lis pendens* remedy, however, must be measured. In foreclosure litigation, its usage is appropriate and necessary. The *lis pendens* has been described as a "harsh and oppressive remedy," since it has the operative effect of creating a cloud on title which prevents the owner of the subject property from selling or otherwise encumbering it.[41] Accordingly, those that engage in litigation which outcome will not impact the title to the subject property may not employ the usage of the *lis pendens*.[42]

The *lis pendens's* effect is only valid for one year from the commencement of the action when the pending pleading does not disclose that the relief sought is premised on a duly recorded instrument or on a lien claimed under Part 1 of Chapter 713.[43] Provided that the pending pleading does reflect that the relief sought is enforcement of a recorded mortgage, however, the *lis pendens* will be valid through the conclusion of the case. Effective June 7, 2019, section 84.23 was amended to clarify that in such cases, the *lis pendens* is valid "through the recording of any instrument transferring title to the property pursuant to the final judgment unless it expires, is withdrawn or is otherwise discharged." This addition to the statute clarifies the validity of the *lis pendens* post-judgment, in conformity with established jurisprudence.

5-6 Final Judgment and Merger

Upon the rendition, the promissory note, the mortgage, and the cause of action—all merge into the final judgment of foreclosure. Since the mortgage no longer exists, the mortgagee's status as lienholder is transformed from mortgagee to judgment creditor.[44] As a practical matter, this is of vital importance to foreclosure litigants seeking short-sales, short-payoffs, and loan modifications.

It is exceedingly common for foreclosure alternatives to be explored following the rendition of final judgment. Indeed, post-judgment, there is no loan to modify, as the note has merged into the final judgment.[45] If the litigants do agree to enter into a loan modification following the rendition of a final judgment, however, the judgment must be vacated and the note and mortgage revived. The proper procedural mechanism to use is Rule 1.540(b)(5), which provides that a court may relieve a party from a

---

[40] *Nikooie v. JP Morgan Chase Bank, N.A.*, 183 So. 3d 424, 432 (Fla. 3d DCA 2014).

[41] *Tetrault v. Calkins*, 79 So. 3d 213 (Fla. 2d DCA 2012) (citing *Avalon Associates of Delaware, Ltd. v. Avalon Park Associates, Inc.*, 760 So. 2d 1132 (Fla. 5th DCA 2000)).

[42] *DeGuzman v. Balsini*, 930 So. 2d 752 (Fla. 5th DCA 2006).

[43] Fla. Stat. § 48.23; *Rodriguez v. Banco Industrial de Venezuela, C.A.*, 576 So. 2d 870 (Fla. 3d DCA 1991).

[44] *Nack Holdings, LLC v. Kalb*, 13 So. 3d 92, 97 n.2 (Fla. 3d DCA 2009) ("The mortgage is merged into the judgment, is thereby extinguished, and 'loses its identity.'") (citing *Whitehurst v. Camp*, 699 So. 2d 679 (Fla.1997)).

[45] *Weston Orlando Park, Inc. v. Fairwinds Credit Union*, 86 So. 3d 1186 (Fla. 5th DCA 2012). See *One 79th Street Estates, Inc. v. American Investment Services*, 47 So. 3d 886, 889 n.4 (Fla. 3d DCA 2010) (" Ordinarily reinstatement occurs when the mortgagor tenders arrearages before acceleration. This 'results in a reinstatement of the mortgage loan to a current status. . . .' Kendall Coffey, *Foreclosures in Florida* 265 (2d ed. 2008). A reinstatement of a mortgage after acceleration and foreclosure can accomplish the intended result only if the foreclosure judgment is vacated.").

final judgment where "the judgment or decree has been satisfied, released, or discharged . . . or it is no longer equitable that the judgment should have prospective application."[46] A careful practitioner will always bear in mind the timeliness of a Rule 1.540 motion, as an untimely motion will be denied for want of jurisdiction.[47]

While Rule 1.540(b)(1)-(3) motions must be brought within one (1) year from the date of entry of the judgment, and no time limit applies to a void judgment under Rule 1.540(b)(4), a Rule 1.540(b)(5) motion must be made "within a reasonable time." Further, Rule 1.540(b)(5) was "designed to provide 'extraordinary relief' in exceptional circumstances, and is to be narrowly construed,"[48] and so it would behoove the litigant seeking vacatur to file the motion as soon as possible. Nonetheless, Florida's policy is to favor settlements, and in foreclosure contexts, specifically, the failure to vacate a foreclosure judgment after a loan modification has been executed by the parties is generally an abuse of discretion.[49]

In short-sales or short-payoffs, there is no need for vacatur of the judgment or reinstatement of the note and mortgage. The practitioner must take care, instead, to ensure that the short-sale or short-payoff agreement contemplates payment in return for a satisfaction of judgment, rather than a satisfaction of mortgage.

5-7 Risks for Purchasers at Foreclosure Sales

Bidding and purchasing real property at foreclosure sales can be a lucrative and rewarding endeavor, but it is fraught with pitfalls for the uninitiated—almost all relating to the title that is being acquired. As previously discussed, a Certificate of Title issued by the clerk of court only extinguishes the rights of defendants and lienholders that acquired the interest following the recording of the *lis pendens*. That is not to say that *all interests* are extinguished—particularly those of superior lienholders.

As part of her due diligence prior to bidding on real property up for auction, the prospective bidder must conduct a reliable title search. She must determine whether any lienholders were omitted from the foreclosure action. If so, taking title may not be advisable, as such will be subject to those omitted interests. She must also determine whether the property is subject to condominium or homeowner's association dues, since third-party purchasers at foreclosure are jointly and severally liable with the

---

[46] Fla. R. Civ. P. 1.540(b)(5).

[47] *Baker v. Baker*, 920 So. 2d 689, 692 (Fla. 2d DCA 2006) ("[U]pon rendition of a final judgment the trial court loses jurisdiction over the case except to enforce the judgment and except as provided by Florida Rule of Civil Procedure 1.540.").

[48] *See Pure H2O Biotechnologies, Inc. v. Mazziotti*, 937 So. 2d 242, 245 (Fla. 4th DCA 2006) (quoting *Dep't of Revenue ex rel. Stephens v. Boswell*, 915 So.2d 717, 721 (Fla. 5th DCA 2005)).

[49] *Wells Fargo Bank, N.A. v. Lupica*, 36 So. 3d 875, 876 (Fla. 5th DCA 2010); *Wells Fargo Bank, NA v. Giglio*, 123 So. 3d 60, 60-61 (Fla. 4th DCA 2013) (Vacating foreclosure sale but not judgment under Rule 1.540(b)(5) was abuse of discretion when parties had settled via loan modification.). *See also Sun Mircosystems of California, Inc. v. Engineering and Manufacturing. Systems, C.A.*, 682 So. 2d 219, 220 (Fla. 3d DCA 1996) ("The public policy of the State of Florida, as articulated in numerous court decisions, highly favors settlement agreements among parties and will seek to enforce them whenever possible.").

previous owner for all unpaid dues.[50] In short, a thorough title examination is prudent prior to bidding on real property at foreclosure.

A purchasing foreclosure bidder also must understand that by purchasing a property at foreclosure, they are also purchasing a lawsuit. Purchasing a property at a foreclosure sale is different from an ordinary purchase in a very big way: Time. When you buy a property directly from a seller, there is an inspection period and there are title contingencies—if the title insurance underwriter's report doesn't reflect that the title is clear, the buyer generally doesn't have to go forward with the purchase and can get their deposit back—no harm. In a foreclosure sale, title insurance doesn't generally protect the bidder.

A bidder will generally not take the time and expense of obtaining a title commitment from a title insurer before making her bid. Title insurance can be expensive, it takes time, and it is far from certain whether the bidder will be the ultimate and successful bidder on the property. Indeed, it is far from certain whether the sale will take place at all. The property owner could seek a sale cancellation, file for bankruptcy or obtain a loan modification—all common occurrences in foreclosures. This would completely frustrate the bidder's plan, making her investment in time and expense in buying a full title policy not practicable. Instead, the prudent bidder generally obtains a title report reflecting all the liens of record—there is no insurer guaranteeing title.

This is important because the bidder must understand that if she takes title to the property, there is a difference between what the uninsured title report shows and what a title company may willing to insure. Because a foreclosure bidder is also buying risky litigation, most underwriters will not consider approving title insurance before the expiration of any appellate periods, times for rehearing, nor insure the property if there are any "irregularities." These irregularities are subject to the insurer's interpretation.

Also, the bidder at a foreclosure sale is also required to be a legal expert at the risk of losing his title entirely. As noted in Section 5-2:1.1 above, title to the property following a foreclosure sale could be void or merely voidable, a distinction which hinges purely on the appreciation of the foreclosure documents. Consider, for example, a case where final judgment has been entered following constructive service of process (something common in foreclosure actions, as they are quasi-*in rem*). Florida Statute § 49.041 requires an affidavit of diligent search to be filed in order for constructive service to be effective. However, a bidder is required to carefully scrutinize that affidavit to ensure that it meets the requirements of the statute because when the affidavit is insufficient on its face, constructive notice is defective, personal jurisdiction doesn't attach, and the foreclosure judgment is void.[51] In such a case, the purchaser of a property at a foreclosure sale could theoretically have title and live in the property for some time, and thereafter have the prior owner challenge the sufficiency of the diligent search affidavit, thereby invalidating the purchaser's title altogether. This was the case in *Godsell v. United Guaranty Residential Ins.*,[52] where the Court invalidated a third-party bidder's title to a property because the diligent search affidavit "has a number of facial defects, such as whether the person is over or under eighteen, whether the address is unknown

---

[50] *See* Fla. Stat. § 720.3085 (for Homeowner Associations); *see* Fla. Stat. § 718.116 (for Condominium Associations).

[51] *See Godsell v. United Guar. Residential Ins.*, 923 So. 2d 1209 (Fla. 5th DCA 2006).

[52] *Godsell v. United Guar. Residential Ins.*, 923 So. 2d 1209 (Fla. 5th DCA 2006).

to the affiant, and it omits any reference to the important fact of defendant's Canadian residence." Conversely, even when constructive service of process is not appropriate, if the diligent search affidavit is sufficient on its face, the judgment is merely voidable and the title to the third-party bidder will not be nullified.[53]

Of course, reasonable minds may differ as to what is void, what is voidable, and (of course) what is insurable. This is a risk a purchaser at a foreclosure sale must take into consideration, and places a great impetus for every foreclosure sale bidder to review title and have the litigation documents thoroughly reviewed by an attorney in order to mitigate the possibility of such issues.

Fortunately, Florida law provides the buyer at a foreclosure sale with many tools with which to resolve her title issues. The first and greatest of which is seeking vacatur of the foreclosure sale altogether and refunding the purchase price.[54] This is generally available only in situations of justifiable and demonstrable mistakes. In cases where the foreclosing plaintiff inadvertently omitted lienholder or there are outstanding interests, however, the purchaser may have the right to seek a relief in reforeclosure.

5-8 Reforeclosure

A common-law suit for reforeclosure is a petition in equity seeking the discharge of the rights of inferior lienholders following the expiration of a reasonable period for redemption.[55] The right of reforeclosure belongs to the purchaser at the foreclosure sale or the mortgagee, and may be employed to remedy any irregularity in the foreclosure proceeding, including the addition of omitted parties.[56] It may be employed in a suit *de novo* by the purchaser,[57] or if the foreclosure judgment has reserved jurisdiction, the purchaser may seek a judgment of reforeclosure as a proceeding supplementary in the foreclosure action.[58]

As it concerns the foreclosing plaintiff, the right of reforeclosure is grounded on the equitable principle that seeks to avoid unjustly enriching one party as a result of the innocent error of the other. Likewise, reforeclosure actions, when brought by third-party purchasers, are premised on the equitable principle of subrogation. Upon purchasing the property at a foreclosure sale, the purchaser becomes the virtual assignee to the foreclosing plaintiff, and accordingly inherits its attending rights.[59]

---

[53] *Lewis v. Fifth Third Mortg. Co.*, 38 So. 3d 157 (Fla. 3d DCA 2010).

[54] *See U.S. Bank, N.A. v. Vogel*, 137 So. 3d 491, 494 (Fla. 4th DCA 2014) ("[A] judicial sale may be vacated on a showing of any equitable ground. One such equitable ground for vacating a judicial sale is mistake.").

[55] *Foster v. Foster*, 703 So.2d 1107 (Fla. 2d DCA 1997); *Nobani v. Barcelona Dev. Corp.*, 655 So. 2d 250 (Fla. 5 DCA 1995).

[56] *Trueman Fertilizer Co. v. Lester*, 155 Fla. 338, 20 So. 2d 349 (1944); *Edason v. Central Farmers' Trust Co.*, 100 Fla. 348, 129 So. 698 (1930).

[57] *Commercial Laundries of W. Florida, Inc. v. Tiffany Square Inv'rs Ltd. P'ship*, 605 So. 2d 116 (Fla. 5th DCA 1992).

[58] Traditionally, reforeclosure actions were a simple matter of filing the equitable petition as a supplement within the foreclosure court. More recently, however, Florida courts have highlighted that the trial court may only entertain these petitions if the final judgment expressly reserves jurisdiction to do so. *Ross v. Wells Fargo Bank*, 114 So. 3d 256 (Fla. 3d DCA 2013).

[59] *Crystal River Lumber Co. v. Knight Turpentine Co.*, 67 So. 974 (Fla. 1915).

It is not surprising that the principle of reforeclosure has over a hundred years of application and support from Florida courts. Doubtlessly, it was vital to ensure equity was done at a time where the review of title (no matter how diligent) frequently resulted in the inadvertent omission of parties at foreclosure. These circumstances are largely absent today, where anyone with an internet connection can review all of the public records of any Florida county. For this reason, the burden of diligence is high. The right of reforeclosure, while a helpful safety net for foreclosing plaintiffs and prospective foreclosure sale purchasers, each is nonetheless well advised to perform diligent title examinations prior to undertaking their endeavors.

5-9 Reformation

Often, the first time a mortgage loan receives scrutiny by an attorney is during the foreclosure process. Accordingly, it is not unusual for the careful practitioner to identify errors in the mortgage or subject deed. Florida law permits for the "reformation" of the mortgage, deed or other loan instruments, provided that the error was a mutual mistake.[60] Reformation should be pleaded in the complaint and the foreclosure judgment should reflect the correction to the instrument to be made. It is unfortunately common, however, for even the careful practitioner to fail to recognize the need for reformation until after the foreclosure judgment is entered.

As previously stated, when reviewing title documents in preparation for drafting a foreclosure complaint, the attorney is tasked with ensuring that the mortgage's description of the property matches the deed, and ensuring that any and all parties that could potentially claim an inferior interest to the property are included as parties' defendant. The attorney generally enlists the assistance of a title company to provide a title search and/or a foreclosure commitment report. However, if there were to be an error in the legal description of both the deed and mortgage (or if the title company did not recognize the error in the foreclosure commitment), it is possible for the error to not be recognized until after the foreclosure judgment is entered. In such a case, the foreclosure judgment, the foreclosure sale, and the Certificate of Title must be vacated.[61] This is because "the sale was premised upon the erroneous legal description and other potential bidders may have acted in reliance on that description."[62]

Such errors are often discovered only when a title company's underwriters are scrutinizing the documents in connection with providing title insurance and sale to a third party. This naturally occurs after the foreclosure sale, and so vacatur of the foreclosure judgment has been commonly sought pursuant to Rule 1.540(b). Foreclosure judgments which include such errors have been held to be *voidable* instead of *void*, and accordingly, the trial court's jurisdiction to vacate the judgment is limited to the one-year period immediately following the rendition of the foreclosure judgment.[63] Creative counselors have advanced the proposition that such errors could form the basis of vacatur pursuant to Rule 1.540(a), jurisdiction under which is not limited to

---

[60] For greater detail concerning the inclusion of a reformation count in a foreclosure action, refer to Chapter 6, Section 6-5:3: Reformation: When the Mortgage or Deed Contains a Mistake.
[61] *Federal Nat'l Mortg. Ass'n v. Sanchez*, 187 So. 3d 341, 343 (Fla. 4th DCA 2016).
[62] *Id.* (quoting *Wells Fargo Bank, N.A. v. Giesel*, 155 So. 3d 411, 413 (Fla. 1st DCA 2014)).
[63] *Epstein v. Bank of Am., Nat'l Ass'n*, 162 So. 3d 159 (Fla. 4th DCA 2015).

one year. Unfortunately, such clever attempts at correcting title defects have been rejected by appellate courts.[64]

Errors in the loan or title documents which were the result of the parties' mutual mistake must be corrected within one year of the rendition of the foreclosure judgment. Alternatively, the lender must file a new foreclosure and seek to reinvoke the court's jurisdiction to reform the instruments.

---

[64] *Cornelius v. Holzman*, 193 So. 3d 1029, 1031 (Fla. 4th DCA 2016) ("Here, the allegation must have been under subsection (1), because the lender argued that the legal description was incorrect. To move under subsection (1), the lender would have to move under rule 1.540(b) within one year of the final judgment.").

CHAPTER 6

Foreclosure Complaints

Sarah T. Weitz

6-1 Introduction

6-1:1 The Commencement of a Foreclosure Action

A mortgage foreclosure is an action in equity under Florida law.[1] A mortgage foreclosure action in Florida is conducted like other kinds of civil litigation, culminating in a judicial auction of the encumbered property to help satisfy the judgment.[2]

A plaintiff seeking to foreclose a mortgage in Florida initiates the action by filing a complaint with the clerk of court.[3] In additional to the equitable remedy of mortgage foreclosure, a complaint may also assert legal claims for money damages under the promissory note or other legal and equitable claims.[4] This chapter will discuss the considerations that a plaintiff should take when preparing a complaint in a mortgage foreclosure action.

6-1:2 Review of Title

As discussed in Chapter 5, the plaintiff should perform a title examination of the property to be foreclosed before filing its complaint. Doing so will identify parties whose interests in the property will need to be foreclosed for the plaintiff to obtain market-

---

[1] Fla. Stat. § 702.01; *see also Singleton v. Greymar Assocs.*, 882 So. 2d 1004, 1008 (Fla. 2004).
[2] Florida's judicial sales procedures are set forth in Fla. Stat. § 45.031. A mortgage is an executory contract "in which one generally promises to allow a future sale of real property if a debt is not paid" and a mortgage also constitutes "a specific lien on the property described in the mortgage." *Pitts v. Pastore*, 561 So. 2d 297, 301 (Fla. 2d DCA 1990). To the extent that a foreclosure sale falls short of satisfying a judgment amount, a plaintiff may be entitled to seek a deficiency judgment under Fla. Stat. § 702.06.
[3] Fla. R. Civ. P. 1.050 provides that "every action of a civil nature shall be deemed commenced when the complaint or petition is filed except that ancillary proceedings shall be deemed commenced when the writ is issued or the pleading setting forth the claim of the party initiating the action is filed." *See also* Fla. R. Civ. P. 1.110(b).
[4] Fla. R. Civ. P. 1.110(g) provides that a pleader may set up in the same action as many claims as the pleader has, including alternative claims. When a party alleges alternatives, the pleading is to be construed "so as to do substantial justice." Accordingly, the rule provides that when statements are made in the alternative and one of them would be sufficient on its own, the pleading is nevertheless adequately pled.

able title.[5] A title review also will confirm the priority of the plaintiff's mortgage on the property.[6] If a plaintiff fails to examine title before filing its foreclosure action, it may neglect to include necessary parties and its final judgment of foreclosure will not be effective as to those parties' interests.[7] The failure to examine title before filing a complaint also may result in a waiver of claims that could be made under an applicable title insurance policy. Accordingly, an examination of title is an important preliminary step in the preparation of the complaint.

6-1:3 The Appropriate Venue and Forum for the Action

A plaintiff must file its complaint in the correct venue to ensure that the circuit court can exercise subject matter jurisdiction over the action.[8] A circuit court generally cannot exercise in rem jurisdiction over property located outside the court's territorial boundaries.[9] Therefore, a plaintiff must file its mortgage foreclosure complaint in the county in which the encumbered property lies.[10] This is known as the "local action rule."[11]

There is an exception to the local action rule: when a mortgage encumbers two or more pieces of property located in different counties, the plaintiff may file its mortgage foreclosure complaint in any of the counties in which any of the properties lie.[12] The properties do not need to be contiguous for this exception to apply.[13]

In contrast, an action to enforce only a promissory note—without seeking the foreclosure of a mortgage—must be filed in the county in which the promissory note was signed by the maker, by one of the makers, or in which the maker or one of the makers resides.[14] Where the plaintiff files an action for mortgage foreclosure as well as to enforce a promissory note, and the plaintiff drops the mortgage foreclosure claim,

---

[5] Florida's recording statute is set forth in Fla. Stat. § 695.01.

[6] The relative priority of recorded liens is governed by Fla. Stat. § 695.11, which provides that the clerk of the circuit court shall affix the "consecutive official register numbers, required under s. 28.222 . . . [and that] an instrument bearing the lower number in the then-current series of numbers shall have priority over any instrument bearing a higher number in the same series."

[7] *Abdoney v. York*, 903 So. 2d 981, 983 (Fla. 2d DCA 2005); *see also Citibank, N.A. v. Villanueva*, 174 So. 3d 612, 613 (Fla. 4th DCA 2015) (holding that a final judgment of foreclosure was void where it omitted the record title owner of the property).

[8] *Frym v. Flagship Community Bank*, 96 So. 3d 452, 453 (Fla. 2d DCA 2012); *see also* Fla. R. Civ. P. 1.060(b).

[9] *Penton v. Intercredit Bank, N.A.*, 943 So. 2d 863, 864 (Fla. 3d DCA 2006).

[10] Fla. Stat. § 47.011; *see also Georgia Cas. Co. v. O'Donnell*, 147 So. 267, 268, 109 Fla. 290, 292 (1933).

[11] *Hudlett v. Sanderson*, 715 So. 2d 1050, 1052 (Fla. 4th DCA 1998); *Tavernier Towne Associates v. Eagle Nat'l Bank of Miami*, 593 So. 2d 306 (Fla. 3d DCA 1992).

[12] Fla. Stat. § 702.04; *Penton v. Intercredit Bank, N.A.*, 943 So. 2d 863, 864 (Fla. 3d DCA 2006).

[13] *Frym v. Flagship Community Bank*, 96 So. 3d 452, 453 (Fla. 2d DCA 2012) (where the promissory note was secured by two different mortgages on properties lying in two different counties, the plaintiff properly could file its action in either of those counties under Fla. Stat. § 702.04).

[14] Fla. Stat. § 47.061.

FORECLOSURE COMPLAINTS

the action may be subject to transfer if one of the defendants shows that venue is no longer proper in that county.[15]

As for the proper forum court, while the forum for most actions is determined by the amount in controversy, a lien foreclosure that falls within the county court's statutorily set threshold jurisdictional amount, which is set to increase in 2020 and 2023, may be filed in either the county court or circuit court.[16] Frequently, mortgage foreclosure actions are filed in the circuit court.

A plaintiff is not required to plead specific facts in support of its selection of venue in its complaint.[17] A general allegation that venue is appropriate in the county is sufficient. If one of the defendants believes that the foreclosure action was filed in the wrong county, he has the burden of showing that the venue is incorrect through a motion and proof.[18] If the defendant satisfies that burden, the proper remedy is a transfer of the action to that venue rather than a dismissal.[19]

6-1:4 The Filing and Recording of a Lis Pendens

With its complaint, a plaintiff should file a lis pendens and record it in the official records of the county in which the action is being filed.[20] If the mortgage encumbers more than one piece of property including properties lying outside of the county in which the action is filed, the plaintiff should also record its lis pendens in the official records of the county in which each property lies.

A lis pendens operates to put the world on notice of the pending litigation related to the property.[21] Any interests in the property that are acquired after the plaintiff

---

[15] Fla. Stat. § 47.061; *MML Development Corp. v. Eagle Nat. Bank of Miami*, 603 So. 2d 646 (Fla. 3d DCA 1992).

[16] *Alexdex Corp. v. Nachon Enterprises, Inc.*, 641 So. 2d 858, 862 (Fla. 1994) (holding that either the county court or the circuit court is an appropriate forum for the foreclosure of a lien on real property). Generally, a circuit court has original jurisdiction over any matters not subject to the jurisdiction of the county courts. *See* Fla. Stat. § 26.012 and Art V, § 5(b), Fla. Const. The county courts have jurisdiction over matters filed on or before December 31, 2019 with an amount in controversy that does not exceed $15,000. Fla. Stat. § 34.01. This jurisdictional amount increased to $30,000 for matters filed on or after January 1, 2020 and will increase to $50,000 for matters filed on or after January 1, 2023. Fla. Stat. § 34.01(1).

[17] *Searle v. Fortune Federal Sav. and Loan Ass'n*, 480 So. 2d 187, 188 (Fla. 2d DCA 1985).

[18] *Searle v. Fortune Federal Sav. and Loan Ass'n*, 480 So. 2d 187, 188 (Fla. 2d DCA 1985) (finding that in an action to enforce only a promissory note, the trial court erred in denying a defendant's motion to transfer venue because he had carried his burden of demonstrating that the venue was incorrect by filing an affidavit affirming that the note had been executed elsewhere and that he resided elsewhere); *Florida Gamco, Inc. v. Fontaine*, 68 So. 3d 923, 928 (Fla. 4th DCA 2011) (the defendant has the burden of proving that the plaintiff's venue selection was improper and of showing where proper venue is).

[19] *Florida Gamco, Inc. v. Fontaine*, 68 So. 3d 923, 928 (Fla. 4th DCA 2011).

[20] *See* Fla. Stat. § 48.23(1)(a) (providing that "an action in any of the state or federal courts in this state operates as a lis pendens on any real or personal property involved therein or to be affected thereby only if a notice of lis pendens is recorded in the official records of the county where the property is located and such notice has not expired pursuant to subsection (2) or been withdrawn or discharged").

[21] *De Pass v. Chitty*, 90 Fla. 77, 80 (Fla. 1925); *U.S. Bank Nat'l Ass'n v. Bevans*, 138 So. 3d 1185, 1189 (Fla. 3d DCA 2014).

records its lis pendens will be subject to the judgment in the plaintiff's foreclosure action.[22] The requisites of an effective lis pendens are dictated by statute.[23] For additional information regarding the formalities and the recording of a lis pendens, *see* Chapter 5.

6-2 The Form of the Complaint

The Florida Rules of Civil Procedure include two Florida Supreme Court-approved mortgage foreclosure complaint templates among its other forms.[24] While these forms provide reliable templates for the basic allegations, there are variables for a plaintiff to keep in mind when preparing its own complaint.[25]

6-2:1 Caption of the Complaint

Every complaint must include a caption containing the name of the court, a designation identifying the nature of the document, a space for the case number, and the full names of all the parties.[26]

6-2:2 Verification of the Complaint

Complaints to foreclose mortgages on residential properties must be verified under Rule 1.115(e) of the Florida Rules of Civil Procedure.[27] The rule provides that it is sufficient to include an oath, affirmation, or a statement that "under penalties of perjury, I declare that I have read the foregoing, and the facts alleged therein are true and correct to the best of my knowledge and belief."[28]

---

[22] Fla. Stat. § 48.23(2); *see also Adhin v. First Horizon Home Loans*, 44 So. 3d 1245, 1251 (Fla. 5th DCA 2010). In *Adhin,* the court found that the purpose of a common-law notice of lis pendens was to notify third parties "that whoever subsequently acquires an interest in the property will stand in the same position as the current owner/vendor, and take the property subject to whatever valid judgment may be rendered in the litigation." The court also noted that "a notice of lis pendens protects both the lis pendens proponent and third parties by alerting creditors, prospective purchasers and others to the fact that the title to a particular piece of real property is involved in litigation."

[23] Fla. Stat. § 48.23.

[24] *See* Fla. R. Civ. P. 1.944(a) and 1.944(b).

[25] Fla. R. Civ. P. 1.900 expressly states that the forms may be changed by the litigant to tailor them to the facts of a particular case, as do the 2014 comments to Forms 1.944(a) and 1.944(b). *See also Artime v. Brotman,* 838 So. 2d 691, 693 (Fla. 3d DCA 2003) (finding that language in a form does not supersede language of the rules of civil procedure and the existing case law).

[26] Fla. R. Civ. P. 1.100(c).

[27] Fla. R. Civ. P. 1.115(e); *see also Donato v. PennyMac Corp.*, 174 So. 3d 1041, 1043-44 (Fla. 4th DCA 2015) (reversing a final judgment and remanding the action for dismissal without prejudice where the complaint did not contain any of the required verification components under Fla. R. Civ. P. 1.115(e)). The rule was implemented in its current form on January 14, 2016 by the Florida Supreme Court in *In re Amendments to Florida Rules of Civil Procedure,* 190 So. 3d 999 (Fla. 2016).

[28] Fla. R. Civ. P. 1.115(e).

Courts have construed this requirement according to the plain language of the rule and have declined to add requirements not set forth in the rule.[29] Either the plaintiff or its agent, such as the servicer of the mortgage loan, may perform the verification.[30] Persons verifying the complaint are not required to attach evidence to the complaint reflecting their authority to verify the complaint on behalf of the plaintiff.[31] Signors are also not required to provide their title or position with their employer as part of the verification.[32]

The verification is not an element of a cause of action for the foreclosure of a mortgage on residential real property, but the plaintiff's failure to verify its complaint may result in a dismissal of the action without prejudice as a sanction for failure to comply with the rules.[33] Defendants who wish to challenge the verification, or the lack of verification, must raise the issue in their affirmative defenses.[34] Their failure to do so may result in a finding that they waived the challenge.[35]

6-2:3 Certification of Possession of the Promissory Note

If the plaintiff has possession of the original note, it is required by both the Florida Statutes and the Florida Rules of Civil Procedure to certify that it has possession of the original note when it files its complaint.[36] The certification is not a prerequisite to the cause of action, however.[37]

The certification must identify the location of the original note and include the time and date on which the location was verified.[38] Persons making the certification must identify themselves by name and title and identify the name of the person who personally verified that the plaintiff has possession of the original note.[39] Copies of the note and any allonge to the note must be attached to the certification.[40]

---

[29] *Deutsche Bank Nat. Trust Co. v. Plageman*, 133 So. 3d 1199, 1202 (Fla. 2d DCA 2014) (interpreting former rule 1.110(b), the requirements of which were deleted in 2014 and incorporated into the new rule 1.115).

[30] *Wells Fargo Del. Tr. Co., N.A. for Vericrest Opportunity Loan Tr. 201-NPL1 v. Petrov*, 230 So. 3d 575 (Fla. 2d DCA 2017) (reversing an order of dismissal and finding that servicing agents routinely verify complaints filed by noteholders); *see also Deutsche Bank Nat. Trust Co. v. Plageman*, 133 So. 3d 1199, 1202 (Fla. 2d DCA 2014) (reversing an order dismissing the complaint based on the plaintiff's failure to provide evidence showing that its servicer had the authority to verify the foreclosure complaint); *see also Deutsche Bank v. Prevratil*, 120 So. 3d 573, 576 (Fla. 2d DCA 2013) (granting a petition of certiorari and quashing an order dismissing an action where the servicer verified the complaint and showed that it was the plaintiff's agent).

[31] *Deutsche Bank Nat. Trust Co. v. Plageman*, 133 So. 3d 1199, 1202 (Fla. 2d DCA 2014).

[32] *U.S. Bank, N.A. v. Wanio–Moore*, 111 So. 3d 941, 941 (Fla. 5th DCA 2013) (reversing an order dismissing the complaint where the signor, an employee of the loan servicer, did not identify his position).

[33] *Beltway Capital, LLC v. Lucombe*, 211 So. 3d 328, 329 (Fla. 2d DCA 2017).

[34] *See, e.g., Beltway Capital, LLC v. Lucombe*, 211 So. 3d 328, 329 (Fla. 2d DCA 2017).

[35] *See, e.g., Beltway Capital, LLC v. Lucombe*, 211 So. 3d 328, 329 (Fla. 2d DCA 2017).

[36] Fla. R. Civ. P. 1.115(c) and Fla. Stat. § 702.015(4).

[37] In *Campbell v. Wells Fargo Bank, N.A.*, 204 So. 3d 476 (Fla. 4th DCA 2016), the court found that the certification requirement was not a mandatory prerequisite to the action, such that it could be enforced through mandamus relief.

[38] Fla. R. Civ. P. 1.115(c) and Fla. Stat. § 702.015(4).

[39] Fla. R. Civ. P. 1.115(c) and Fla. Stat. § 702.015(4).

[40] Fla. R. Civ. P. 1.115(c) and Fla. Stat. § 702.015(4).

A plaintiff's agent, such as its mortgage loan servicer or its attorney, may certify that it has possession of the original note on the plaintiff's behalf.[41] The certification does not need to be notarized.[42]

6-2:4 Attachments to the Complaint

Rule 1.130 of the Florida Rules of Civil Procedure requires a plaintiff to attach to its complaint a copy of the contract on which the action is based.[43] The rule is designed to help notify the defendant of "the nature and extent of the cause of action so that the defendant may plead with greater certainty."[44]

It generally is advisable for a plaintiff to attach a copy of the note, mortgage, and any other loan agreements on which it plans to rely to its complaint. A mortgage foreclosure complaint that does not attach an exhibit showing the existence of the agreement between the parties may be subject to dismissal without prejudice.[45] The plaintiff is not required to attach the entire agreement, but it must include the material portions.[46] In other words, the exhibits that the plaintiff attaches should be comprehensive enough to reflect the terms of the agreement and establish a cause of action for its breach.

For example, an appellate court has found that where the parties agreed to both a long-form mortgage and a short-form mortgage, and the plaintiff attached only the short-form mortgage to its complaint, the short-form mortgage was prima facie evi-

---

[41] *See Wells Fargo Bank N.A. v. Diz*, 253 So. 3d 705, 707 (Fla. 3d DCA 2018); *see also Deutsche Bank Nat. Trust Company v. Applewhite*, 213 So. 3d 948, 951 (Fla. 4th DCA 2017) (finding that "a loan servicing agent is a proper representative to possess a mortgage note on behalf of the plaintiff, such that the plaintiff remains in constructive possession of the note as the holder sufficient to establish standing"); *see also Bank of America, N.A. v. Leonard*, 212 So. 3d 417, 418 (Fla. 1st DCA 2016) (finding that "while section 702.015(4) requires the plaintiff to file a certification that the plaintiff is in possession of the original promissory note, it does not preclude the plaintiff's attorney from being the 'individual giving the certification' or 'the person who personally verified such possession'").

[42] Fla. Stat. § 702.015(4); *see also RBS Citizens N.A. v. Reynolds*, 231 So. 3d 591 (Fla. 2d DCA 2017).

[43] Fla. R. Civ. P. 1.130(a) provides that "all bonds, notes, bills of exchange, contracts, accounts, or documents on which action may be brought or defense made, or a copy thereof or a copy of the portions thereof material to the pleadings, must be incorporated in or attached to the pleading."

[44] *Amiker v. Mid-Century Ins. Co.*, 398 So. 2d 974, 976 (Fla. 1st DCA 1981).

[45] The same is true for an amended complaint. In *Hughes v. Home Savings of America, F.S.B.*, 675 So. 2d 649, 650 (Fla. 2d DCA 1996), the court found that the fact that the agreements on which the action was based were attached to the initial complaint but not the amended complaint did not "breathe life into the amended complaint." And courts have involuntarily dismissed complaints where the plaintiff failed to plead for relief under a loan modification agreement had been modified or attach a copy of that agreement to its complaint. *Morales v. Fifth Third Bank*, 275 So. 3d 197, 201 (Fla. 4th DCA 2019); *see also Tracey v. Wells Fargo, Nat'l Ass'n*, 264 So. 3d 1152, 1157 (Fla. 2d DCA 2019).

[46] *National Collegiate Student Loan Trust 2006-4 v. Meyer*, 265 So. 3d 715, 719-720 (Fla. 2d DCA 2019); *see also Glen Garron, LLC v. Buchwald*, 210 So. 3d 229 (Fla. 5th DCA 2017); *see also Amiker v. Mid-Century Ins. Co.*, 398 So. 2d 974, 976 (Fla. 1st DCA 1981) (finding that "Rule 1.130(a) does not require attachment of the entire contract, only attachment or incorporation of the contract's material provisions").

dence of the terms of the parties' agreement.[47] The short-form mortgage was introduced at trial and in combination with the promissory note, and it was sufficient to establish the terms of the parties' agreement and survive a motion to dismiss made at trial.

A plaintiff is not required under Rule 1.130 to attach a copy of the promissory note to the complaint in an action to foreclose a mortgage, though doing so will help the plaintiff establish its standing.[48] Where the plaintiff seeks to foreclose the mortgage and also brings a count for damages under the note, the plaintiff should attach documents sufficient to establish the material terms of the note. This may be the note itself or the relevant portions of the mortgage.[49]

6-2:5 Minimizing the Filing of Sensitive Information in Exhibits

By their nature, mortgage foreclosure actions may involve the filing of documents containing sensitive financial information. The parties to a mortgage foreclosure action are obligated to minimize the filing of such information like parties to any other form of civil litigation.

Although Rule 2.425 of the Florida Rules of Judicial Administration permits the filing of documents that contain an account number identifying the subject property, the rule also provides that no portion of certain kinds of account numbers are to be filed. These account numbers include: social security numbers, bank account numbers, credit card account numbers, charge account numbers, and debit account numbers.[50] The rule also requires certain account numbers to be restricted to the last four digits only, including taxpayer identification numbers (TIN), employee identification numbers, driver's license numbers, passport numbers, telephone numbers, financial account numbers (except for the kinds of account numbers mentioned above which the rule prohibits to be filed), brokerage account numbers, insurance policy account numbers, loan account numbers, customer account numbers, or patient or health care numbers.[51]

---

[47] *Khleif v. Bankers Trust Company of California, N.A. on behalf of Certificateholders Vendee Mortgage Trust 2001-1*, 215 So. 3d 619, 621 (Fla. 2d DCA 2017). It is worth noting that although the appellate court affirmed the final judgment, it observed that "the better practice is to attach to the pleading and introduce into evidence both the short and long-form mortgages."

[48] *Glen Garron, LLC v. Buchwald*, 210 So. 3d 229, 234 (Fla. 5th DCA 2017) (finding that in a mortgage foreclosure action, "the promissory note itself is not required to be attached to the complaint under Rule 1.130, as the object of a foreclosure action is to force the sale of the property through the plaintiff's contractual rights that were granted by the mortgage"). Meanwhile, in an action for payment under the promissory note, the plaintiff must attach a copy of the note to its complaint. *See Student Loan Mktg. Ass'n v. Morris*, 662 So. 2d 990, 991 (Fla. 2d DCA 1995). However, even where the complaint does not seek damages under the note, the plaintiff should attach a copy of the note to help it prove that it has standing, as discussed in Chapter 4.

[49] *Glen Garron, LLC v. Buchwald*, 210 So. 3d 229, 234 (Fla. 5th DCA 2017). The provisions of the note that are material to the action on the note may be incorporated into the mortgage and its riders, as the appellate court discusses in this case.

[50] Fla. R. Jud. Admin. 2.425(a)(3)(A)-(E).

[51] Fla. R. Jud. Admin. 2.425(a)(4)(A)-(K).

Before filing a complaint, a plaintiff should review the documents that it intends to attach as exhibits to its complaint for these kinds of numbers and redact accordingly in a way that makes it clear that the numbers were redacted affirmatively, such as black-out bars available in .pdf programs.[52] The use of whiteout or other kinds of redaction that simply appear to delete information are not recommended.

6-2:6 Electronic Filing Required

Florida requires the electronic filing of all pleadings, including complaints.[53] The filed documents must be accessible to persons with disabilities.[54] The procedure and format for electronic filing can be found in Rules 2.520 and 2.525 of the Florida Rules of Judicial Administration.

6-3 The Parties

As discussed previously, the parties must be identified by their full names in the caption of the complaint. However, the allegations in the body of the complaint ultimately will determine who is a party to the action.[55] The mere inclusion of a party's name in the caption, without allegations against that party in the body, generally is not enough to state a cause of action against that party.[56] Accordingly, care should be taken to adequately allege the facts relating to each party and the claims stated against each party in the complaint.

6-3:1 The Plaintiff

A plaintiff may foreclose any interest that is inferior to its own in a mortgage foreclosure action.[57] The plaintiff may be either the real party in interest—the person in

---

[52] As discussed in greater detail in the chapter related to standing, one way in which a plaintiff may establish its standing as the noteholder is by attaching a copy of the endorsed note to its complaint, then filing the original. If the original is in exactly the same condition as the copy attached to the complaint, the plaintiff is presumed to have been in possession of the original note when it filed the complaint. Therefore, redactions of sensitive information must be handled with care. *Kronen v. Deutsche Bank Nat'l Trust Co.*, 267 So. 3d 447, 448 (Fla. 4th DCA 2019) (during trial, the trial court reviewed redactions on the copy of the note that was filed with the complaint and determined that the loan number had been redacted, the copy and the original were substantially the same for purposes of determining whether the plaintiff had standing). Accordingly, it is advisable to make any redactions of account numbers discernable so that when the plaintiff surrenders the original note to the court later in the case, an explanation for the discrepancy will be possible under *Kronen*.

[53] Fla. R. Jud. Admin. 2.520(a).

[54] Fla. R. Jud. Admin. 2.526.

[55] *Altamonte Hitch and Trailor Services v. U-Haul Co. of Eastern Florida*, 498 So. 2d 1346, 1347 (Fla. 5th DCA 1986); *Beseau v. Bhalani*, 904 So. 2d 641, 642 (Fla. 5th DCA 2005).

[56] *Altamonte Hitch and Trailor Services v. U-Haul Co. of Eastern Florida*, 498 So. 2d 1346, 1347 (Fla. 5th DCA 1986); *Beseau v. Bhalani*, 904 So. 2d 641, 642 (Fla. 5th DCA 2005).

[57] *See U.S. Bank Nat'l Ass'n v. Bevans*, 138 So. 3d 1185, 1187 (Fla. 3d DCA 2014) (stating the general rule that a junior lienholder cannot normally name a superior lienholder as a defendant in a suit to foreclose a junior lien). A junior lienholder may not extinguish a senior lien, however. *Bank of America, N.A. v. Kipps Colony II Condominium Ass'n, Inc.*, 201 So. 3d 670, 675 (Fla. 2d DCA 2016).

whom the claim rests—or a party prosecuting the action on behalf of the real party in interest.[58] A personal representative, an administrator, a guardian, a trustee, a beneficiary of a contract, or a party expressly authorized by statute may sue in that person's own name without joining the real party in interest.[59] Known as Florida's "real party in interest" rule, the rule is permissive rather than mandatory.[60] Accordingly, a party that is acting on behalf of the real party in interest may—but is not obligated to—bring the action in its own name on behalf of the real party in interest.[61]

For example, a mortgage loan servicer may file a mortgage foreclosure complaint and maintain the action in its own name on behalf of the real party in interest.[62] In such a case, the question of the servicer's authority to act on behalf of the real party in interest will be an issue subject to proof at trial.[63]

Occasionally, the original plaintiff in an action will convey its interest in the note and mortgage to another entity while the action is pending. In this situation, the entity who acquires the interest in the note is not obligated to amend the complaint or move for an order deeming it the new plaintiff.[64] If it chooses to move for an order substituting it in the place of the original plaintiff, it acquires whatever standing the original plaintiff had based on the initial complaint.[65] The substituted plaintiff is not obligated to prove its standing at the time of the substitution, though; it inherits the standing of the original plaintiff.[66]

6-3:2 The Defendants

The complaint must name as a defendant any person with an interest in the property that is subordinate to the plaintiff's to ensure a successful foreclosure of the plaintiff's

---

[58] *See* Fla. R. Civ. P. 1.210(a) and Author's Comment to Rule 1.210(a) (1967); *see also Kumar Corp. v. Nopal Lines, Ltd.*, 462 So. 2d 1178, 1183 (Fla. 3d DCA 1985) (describing a real party in interest as "the person in whom rests, by substantive law, the claim sought to be enforced" and noting that the purpose of the rule is "to protect a defendant from facing a subsequent similar action brought by one not a party to the present proceeding and to ensure that any action taken to judgment will have its proper effect as res judicata").

[59] Fla. R. Civ. P. 1.210(a).

[60] Author's Comment to Fla. R. Civ. P. 1.210(a) (1967); *see also Kumar Corp. v. Nopal Lines, Ltd.*, 462 So. 2d 1178, 1183 (Fla. 3d DCA 1985).

[61] *See* Fla. R. Civ. P. 1.210(a); *see also Kumar Corp. v. Nopal Lines, Ltd.*, 462 So. 2d 1178, 1183 (Fla. 3d DCA 1985) ("Thus, where a plaintiff is either the real party in interest or is maintaining the action on behalf of the real party in interest, its action cannot be terminated on the ground that it lacks standing.").

[62] *Elston/Leetsdale, LLC v. CWCapital Asset Mgmt. LLC*, 87 So. 3d 14, 16-17 (Fla. 4th DCA 2012).

[63] *Phan v. Deutsche Bank Nat. Trust Co., ex rel. First Franklin Mortg. Loan Trust 2006-FF11*, 198 So. 3d 744, 749 (Fla. 2d DCA 2016).

[64] *See* Fla. R. Civ. P. 1.210(a); *see also* Fla. R. Civ. P. 1.260(c).

[65] *Assil v. Aurora Loan Servs., LLC*, 171 So. 3d 226, 227 (Fla. 4th DCA 2015); *see also Spicer v. Ocwen Loan Servicing, LLC*, 238 So. 3d 275, 276 (Fla. 4th DCA 2018) and *U.S. Bank, N.A. v. Glicken*, 228 So. 3d 1194 (Fla. 5th DCA 2017).

[66] *Wilmington Trust, Nat'l Ass'n v. Moon*, 238 So. 3d 425, 428 (Fla. 5th DCA 2018) (finding that there is no requirement that a substituted plaintiff must prove its standing at the time of the substitution); *Waters v. Wilmington Trust, N.A.*, 268 So. 3d 722, 723 (Fla. 4th DCA 2018).

mortgage.[67] Generally, the complaint should name any person materially interested, either legally or beneficially, in the subject matter of a suit.[68] Below is a discussion regarding the various kinds of subordinate interests that a plaintiff should identify and include in its complaint to ensure a successful foreclosure action.

6-3:3 The Borrowers

Borrowers (the note signors) and mortgagors (the persons who execute the mortgage) generally are indispensable parties to the mortgage foreclosure action.[69] Often, the borrowers and the mortgagors are the same people, but not always. The complaint must contain allegations to state a cause of action against each of the borrowers and the mortgagors.[70] The factual allegations should be detailed enough to identify the mortgage and note that is being foreclosed, since the borrowers may have executed second or third mortgages on the property as well.

The exception to the general rule requiring joinder of borrowers is when the original mortgagors, who are not obligated under the note, have conveyed away all of their interest in the property.[71] Otherwise, they must be named as parties.

6-3:4 Junior Lienholders

The plaintiff must also name any junior lienholders who have an interest in the property. Junior lienholders may include the holder of a life estate, the holder of a second or third mortgage recorded after the plaintiff's mortgage, the holder of a recorded final judgment against the property that post-dates the recording of the plaintiff's own mortgage, or a person who acquired an ownership interest in the property after the plaintiff's mortgage was recorded, among others.

The act of foreclosing a senior lien such as a first mortgage cuts off the right of redemption that any junior lienholders otherwise would have up until the issuance of a certificate of sale.[72] The foreclosure of a senior mortgage only extinguishes the liens of any junior mortgagees if the junior lienholders are listed in the final judgment.[73]

---

[67] *See Ezem v. Fed. Nat. Mort.*, 153 So. 3d 341, 345 (Fla. 1st DCA 2014) (finding that "all persons materially interested, either legally or beneficially, in the subject matter of a foreclosure suit, and who will be directly affected by an adjudication in such an action, are necessary parties to the suit"); *see also Abdoney v. York*, 903 So. 2d 981, 983 (Fla. 2d DCA 2005) (finding that "when a junior mortgagee is omitted as a party to the foreclosure of a senior mortgage, the lien of the junior mortgagee is unaffected by the judgment").

[68] *Oakland Properties Corp. v. Hogan*, 117 So. 846, 848 (1928).

[69] *Lambert v. Dracos*, 403 So. 2d 481, 484 (Fla. 1st DCA 1981) (finding that it was error for the trial court to deny a motion to dismiss for failure to join an indispensable party where the plaintiff did not name one of the co-obligors under the mortgage).

[70] *Lambert v. Dracos*, 403 So. 2d 481, 484 (Fla. 1st DCA 1981). There may be situations in which a borrower's spouse (for homestead property) or the co-owner of the property (with the note signor) may only sign the mortgage but not the note.

[71] *Mitchell v. Federal Nat. Mortg. Ass'n*, 763 So. 2d 358, 359 (Fla. 4th DCA 2005).

[72] Fla. Stat. § 45.0315; *Abdoney v. York*, 903 So. 2d 981, 983 (Fla. 2d DCA 2005); *AG Group Investments, LLC v. All Realty Alliance Corp.*, 106 So. 3d 950, 951 (Fla. 3d DCA 2013).

[73] *Abdoney v. York*, 903 So. 2d 981, 983 (Fla. 2d DCA 2005).

Accordingly, a foreclosure complaint must include allegations against any junior lienholders whose interests the plaintiff wishes to foreclose. The nature of those allegations will depend on the kind of junior lien being foreclosed. The sections below discuss the kinds of junior interests that may be connected with a property.

6-3:5 Owners of the Property

The mortgagor usually is the owner of the property, but sometimes the property changes hands before the plaintiff files its lis pendens.[74] Sometimes mortgagors convey their interest away. Sometimes, a plaintiff may find that a condominium association or homeowner's association has foreclosed its own lien and is now the owner through a certificate of title. Occasionally, the borrower surrenders the property to the bankruptcy trustee in a bankruptcy proceeding. Regardless of the circumstances, the owner of the property at the time the plaintiff files its foreclosure complaint is an indispensable party to the action.[75] A final judgment that fails to include the current owner is void, so it is imperative to name the owner in the complaint.[76]

The same is not true of a person who purchases the property after the plaintiff records its lis pendens. A purchaser who acquires its interest after the recording of a lis pendens is known as a purchaser pendente lite.[77] Purchasers pendente lite are deemed to have taken their interest subject to the pending foreclosure action and the plaintiff is not required to amend the complaint to add them as parties.[78]

6-3:6 Tenants by the Entirety and Other Spousal Interests in the Property

Another example of a title holder who generally is an indispensable party is the spouse of the borrower who holds title to a piece of homestead property as a tenant by the entirety.[79] Husbands and wives cannot convey interests in their homestead property without their spouse joining in the transaction, that is, without their spouse's signature

---

[74] In some situations, defendants may dispute the ownership of the property, raising questions regarding who is an indispensable party to the action. *See, e.g., Turkell-White v. Wells Fargo Bank N.A.*, 273 So. 3d 1021, 1023 (Fla. 4th DCA 2019).

[75] *Citibank, N.A. v. Villanueva*, 174 So. 3d 612, 613 (Fla. 4th DCA 2015); *see also Oakland Props. Corp. v. Hogan*, 117 So. 846, 848-49 (Fla. 1928).

[76] *FL Homes 1 LLC v. Kokolis Trustee of Toula Kokolis Revocable Trust*, 271 So. 3d 6, 9 (Fla. 4th DCA 2019); *Citibank, N.A. v. Villanueva*, 174 So. 3d 612, 613 (Fla. 4th DCA 2015).

[77] *Intermediary Fin. Corp. v. McKay*, 111 So. 531 (Fla. 1927) (finding that a purchaser pendente lite is not entitled to intervene).

[78] *See Bank of America, N.A. v. Mirabella Owners' Ass'n, Inc.*, 238 So. 3d 405, 407 (Fla. 1st DCA 2018); *Whitburn, LLC v. Wells Fargo Bank, N.A.*, 190 So. 3d 1087, 1091-92 (Fla. 2d DCA 2015); *see also Greenwald v. Graham*, 130 So. 608, 611 (Fla. 1930) (finding that a purchaser pendente lite "takes the risk of the result of the suit, and are concluded by the decree therein. It is not necessary that they should be made parties thereto"); *see also Trust No. 602W0 Dated 7/16/15, Dema Investments, LLC v. Wells Fargo Bank, N.A.*, 207 So. 3d 977, 978 (Fla. 5th DCA 2016) (finding that "the law is well settled that a purchaser pendente lite is not entitled to intervene or otherwise be made a party to the ongoing lawsuit").

[79] *Miller v. Washington Mut. Bank*, 184 So. 3d 558, 559 (Fla. 4th DCA 2016) (holding that property owned by a husband and wife as tenants by the entirety cannot satisfy the debt of one tenant alone); *Rocketrider Pictures, LLC v. BankUnited*, 138 So. 3d 1223 (Fla. 3d DCA 2014).

on the mortgage.[80] In a similar vein, a plaintiff cannot foreclose on homestead property without naming the spouse of a married borrower in the complaint, even if the spouse failed to execute the mortgage.[81] If the marital status of a borrower is unknown, it is advisable for the plaintiff to name the unknown spouse of the borrower as a party and attempt service on that individual when serving the borrower.[82]

6-3:7 Lessees in Possession

Lessees, also known as tenants, have a possessory interest in the property being foreclosed.[83] However, if a lessee holds an unrecorded lease for a term that is less than one year, they are not necessary parties to a foreclosure action. The benefit of naming tenants in a mortgage foreclosure complaint is to bring their interest within the jurisdiction of the trial court. Doing so enables the plaintiff to seek a writ of possession in the event that the tenants do not voluntarily relinquish the property.[84] A tenant's interest in the property stems from the borrower's interest and he has no independent right to redeem.[85]

6-3:8 Condominiums and Homeowners' Associations

A condominium association or a homeowners' association may have an interest in the property encumbered by the plaintiff's mortgage. Some properties are governed by more than one association, such as a master association in addition to a sub-association. All associations with an interest in the property should be named in the complaint.

An association's rights in the property arise from its recorded declaration of condominium or a declaration of homeowners' association, as well as from the Florida Statutes.[86] If the property owner has failed to pay the association's assessments, the associa-

---

[80] See Art. X, § 4, Fla. Const; see also Pitts v. Pastore, 561 So. 2d 297, 300 (Fla. 2d DCA 1990) (finding that Florida's Constitution does not prohibit the owner of homestead property from entering into contracts without the joinder of the spouse, but requires the owner's spouse to join in any alienation of homestead property).

[81] Chaudhry v. Pedersen, No. 5D18-709, 44 Fla. L. Weekly D405 (Fla. 5th DCA Feb. 8, 2019); Sudhoff v. Fed. Nat. Mortg. Ass'n., 942 So. 2d 425, 427-28 (Fla. 5th DCA 2005) (where an estranged spouse signed the mortgage as a title-holder, she was an indispensable party to the foreclosure action because her absence deprived her of her right of redemption).

[82] For example, the plaintiff in HSBC Bank USA, Nat. Ass'n v. Karzen, 157 So. 3d 1089, 1092-93 (Fla. 1st DCA 2015), named the borrower's unknown spouse in the complaint and served an individual who was later identified as the borrower's spouse. When the plaintiff amended the complaint to clarify his identity, the amended complaint was deemed to relate back to the original complaint. The court found that amending to clarify the spouse's identity did not give the spouse grounds to claim that he had no notice of the original action, was surprised by the amended complaint, or that he had no connection to the litigation prior to the amendment.

[83] See Redding v. Stockton, Whatley, Davin & Co., 488 So. 2d 548, 549 (Fla. 5th DCA 1986) (holding that a foreclosure action is the proper proceeding to terminate a tenant's possessory interest in a property).

[84] See Commercial Laundries, Inc. v. Golf Course Towers Associates, 568 So. 2d 501, 503 (Fla. 3d DCA 1990).

[85] See Sedra Family Ltd. Partnership v. 4750, LLC, 124 So. 3d 935, 936 (Fla. 4th DCA 2012).

[86] In Jallali v. Knightsbridge Village Homeowners Ass'n, Inc., 211 So. 3d 216, 220 (Fla. 4th DCA 2017), the Fourth District Court of Appeal found that a bank's lis pendens did not bar a con-

tion may have recorded a claim of lien for the unpaid assessments in the official records of the county.[87] The priority of first mortgagees in that case is determined by the statutes governing claims of lien for condominium associations and homeowners' associations.[88] If the mortgagee is a second or third mortgagee, it should examine the declaration of association and its related documentation to determine the priority of its rights.

6-3:9 Municipal, State, and Federal Lienholders

While an instrument recorded first in time generally has priority over subsequently recorded instruments,[89] Florida has established that certain liens have priority regardless of the date of recordation. This is known as "superpriority" and the plaintiff will be unable to foreclose such liens. For example, taxes imposed by the state of Florida constitute a first lien, superior to all other liens.[90]

Municipal code compliance liens, on the other hand, are subordinate to a previously recorded mortgage interest and the municipality should be named as a defendant in the plaintiff's mortgage foreclosure action.[91] Where the United States has a lien, it may be named as a party to a mortgage foreclosure action.[92] If the mortgage is inferior to the federal lien, the sale will be subject to the government's lien if it consents that the property may be sold free of its lien and the proceeds divided as the parties may be entitled.[93] There are special rules for service of initial process upon the United States in state court actions and unlike other defendants, the United States has 60 days in which to respond to the complaint after being served with initial process.[94]

6-4 The Causes of Action and the Allegations

The mortgage foreclosure complaint should include allegations identifying each party's interest in the property and state a cause of action against each defendant.[95] The

---

dominium association's action to foreclose its own lien for unpaid assessments because the condominium association's declaration of covenants, which gave it the right to lien and foreclose on the property, was a recorded "interest" at the time of the filing of lis pendens. *See also Bank of Am., N.A. v. Mirabella Owners' Ass'n, Inc.*, 238 So. 3d 405, 407 (Fla. 1st DCA 2018).

[87] A condominium association has the right to record a claim of lien and to foreclose its lien under Fla. Stat. § 718.116(5)(a). Homeowners' associations have the same right under Fla. Stat. § 720.3085(1).

[88] Fla. Stat. § 718.116(5)(a) and Fla. Stat. § 720.3085(1), respectively.

[89] The applicable rule governing priority of lien interests is "first in time is first in right." *Walter E. Heller & Co. Southeast, Inc. v. Williams*, 450 So. 2d 521, 532 (Fla. 3d DCA 1984), *review denied*, 462 So. 2d 1108 (Fla. 1985).

[90] *See* Fla. Stat. § 197.122; *see also Barton v. MetroJax Property Holdings, LLC*, 207 So. 3d 304, 306 (Fla. 3d DCA 2016) and *Miami-Dade Cty. Lansdowne Mortg., LLC*, 235 So. 3d 960, 961 (Fla. 3d DCA 2017).

[91] *City of Palm Bay v. Wells Fargo Bank, N.A.*, 114 So. 3d 924, 928-29 (Fla. 2013).

[92] 28 U.S.C. § 2410(a)(2).

[93] 28 U.S.C. § 2410(c).

[94] The procedures for service upon the United States can be found in 28 U.S.C. § 2410(b). The United States also has a special right of redemption following the judicial sale and unique procedures governing its redemption. Those rights are contained in 28 U.S.C. § 2410(c) and (d).

[95] *See* Fla. R. Civ. P. 1.110(b) (stating that a complaint "must state a cause of action and shall contain (1) a short and plain statement of the grounds upon which the court's jurisdiction

allegations should be designed to put the defendants on notice of the claims being asserted against them.[96]

6-4:1 A Claim for Mortgage Foreclosure

The elements of a prima facie claim for mortgage foreclosure are similar to other breach of contract claims. The complaint must assert: (1) that an agreement exists between the parties, (2) that the defendant borrower defaulted on his obligations under the agreement, (3) that the plaintiff is accelerating the debt to maturity, and (4) that there is a particular amount due to the plaintiff as the result of the defendant's default.[97] In addition to these basic allegations, the plaintiff must include allegations supporting its standing and setting forth the elements of any other claims in the complaint. It also should allege its superiority to any other inferior liens while identifying the nature of the inferior liens specifically.

6-4:2 The Agreement Between the Parties

The plaintiff should identify the agreements on which its foreclosure action is based in enough detail for the defendants to have notice of the subject of the foreclosure. As mentioned in Section 6-2:4 above, the allegations must be supported by evidence of the agreement between the parties as required under Rule 1.130(a) of the Florida Rules of Civil Procedure, including allegations sufficient to identify any loan modification agreements.[98] Additionally, as discussed in the next section, a complaint to foreclose a mortgage on residential property must include allegations to show that the plaintiff is entitled to enforce the note, referred to as a plaintiff's standing.

6-4:3 The Plaintiff's Standing

As discussed in detail in Chapter 4, the issue of a plaintiff's standing to bring a mortgage foreclosure action has been the topic of much litigation in Florida. Due to post-closing purchase and sales of mortgage loans accompanied by the delivery of the mortgage loan documents, the plaintiff may not be the original lender under the note

---

depends, unless the court already has jurisdiction and the claim needs no new grounds of jurisdiction to support it, (2) a short and plain statement of the ultimate facts showing that the pleader is entitled to relief, and (3) a demand for judgment for the relief to which the pleader deems himself or herself entitled. Relief in the alternative or of several different types may be demanded. Every complaint shall be considered to pray for general relief"). The 1967 Author's Comment to Fla. R. Civ. P. 1.110 adds that a pleading should "clearly and adequately inform the judge, the opposing party and the jury (in cases where the pleadings may be read to the jury) of the position of the pleader."

[96] *See* Fla. R. Civ. P. 1.110(b). Rule 1.110(g) also provides that a pleader may set up in the same action as many claims as the pleader has, including alternative claims.

[97] *Liberty Home Equity Solutions, Inc. v. Raulston*, 206 So. 3d 58, 60 (Fla. 4th DCA 2016).

[98] *Morales v. Fifth Third Bank*, 275 So. 3d 197, 199 (Fla. 4th DCA 2019) (reversing a final judgment where the complaint did not include allegations regarding a loan modification on which the plaintiff later relied at trial); *Tracey v. Wells Fargo Bank, N.A.*, 264 So. 3d 1152, 1157 (Fla. 2d DCA 2019); *Nowlin v. Nationstar Mortg., LLC*, 193 So. 3d 1043, 1046 (Fla. 2d DCA 2016) (finding that where the loan had been modified, the plaintiff "could only foreclose by alleging and proving a breach of the modification agreement and neither of which was done here").

and mortgage. The plaintiff must establish that it has standing to enforce those agreements at the outset of the action.[99] Lack of standing on the date that the plaintiff files its action cannot be cured.[100]

Florida law recognizes that a mortgage follows the promissory note that it secures.[101] Therefore, the logic goes, unless the parties otherwise agree, the right to enforce a mortgage follows the right to enforce the promissory note because the mortgage in equity passes as an incident to the debt.[102] Therefore, to assert standing, a plaintiff must show that it is entitled to enforce the promissory note secured by the mortgage. To do so, a person must be either (1) the holder of the promissory note; (2) a nonholder in possession of the promissory note who has the rights of a holder; or (3) a person not in possession of the promissory note instrument who is entitled to enforce it as a lost, destroyed, or stolen promissory note or under Fla. Stat. § 673.4181(4).[103]

When the plaintiff seeks to foreclose a mortgage on residential real property, the Florida Statutes and Rules of Civil Procedure now require a plaintiff to allege the basis for its standing in its complaint.[104] The failure to do so may expose the plaintiff to sanctions.[105]

A plaintiff who seeks to enforce a promissory note as its holder must allege that it is the holder of the promissory note in its complaint when the foreclosure action concerns residential real property.[106] Ultimately, the plaintiff must prove that it had the original note in its possession when it filed its foreclosure suit, or that it had constructive possession of a note in its agent's possession.[107] Its choice of attachments to the complaint can help prove later that it was the holder at the time that it filed its complaint. By attaching a copy of the endorsed note with its complaint, then later filing the original, endorsed note in the same condition with the trial court, the plaintiff can establish its standing as the holder in the absence of any evidence to the contrary.[108] Care should be taken to review the copy being attached to the complaint to

---

[99] *McLean v. JP Morgan Chase Bank N. A.*, 79 So. 3d 170, 173 (Fla. 4th DCA 2012); *Elsman v. HSBC Bank USA*, 182 So. 3d 770, 772 (Fla. 5th DCA 2015); *Seidler v. Wells Fargo Bank, N.A.*, 179 So. 3d 416, 419 (Fla. 1st DCA 2015); *Russell v. Aurora Loan Servs., LLC*, 163 So. 3d 639, 642 (Fla. 2d DCA 2015); *Nationstar Mortg., LLC v. Marquez*, 180 So. 3d 219, 221 (Fla. 3d DCA 2015).

[100] *McLean v. JP Morgan Chase Bank N. A.*, 79 So. 3d 170, 173 (Fla. 4th DCA 2012).

[101] *Johns v. Gillian*, 134 Fla. 575, 184 So. 140, 143 (1938).

[102] *Johns v. Gillian*, 134 Fla. 575, 184 So. 140, 143 (1938). A promissory note does not follow the mortgage, however, unless there is specific evidence that this is the case. *Peters v. Bank of New York Mellon*, 227 So. 3d 175, 179-80 (Fla. 2d DCA 2017).

[103] Fla. Stat. § 673.3011.

[104] Fla. Stat. § 702.015(2); *see also* Fla. R. Civ. P. 1.115 effective Jan. 14, 2016 (190 So. 3d 999).

[105] Fla. Stat. § 702.015(6).

[106] Fla. Stat. § 702.015(2); *see also* Fla. R. Civ. P. 1.115(a).

[107] *Ortiz v. PNC Bank, Nat'l Ass'n*, 188 So. 3d 923, 925 (Fla. 4th DCA 2016); *U.S. Bank Nat'l Ass'n v. Cook*, 276 So. 3d 472, 474 (Fla. 2d DCA 2019) (the evidence admitted at trial proved that the loan servicer possessed the original note on the noteholder's behalf as the noteholder's agent).

[108] *See Ortiz v. PNC Bank, Nat'l Ass'n*, 188 So. 3d 923, 925 (Fla. 4th DCA 2016) (recognizing that "the fact that a copy of a note is attached to a complaint does not conclusively or necessarily prove that the Bank had actual possession of the note at the time the complaint was filed" but holding that "if the Bank later files with the court the original note in the same condition as the copy attached to the complaint, then we agree that the combination

confirm that it is an exact copy of the original.[109] If there are discrepancies between the copy and the original, such as redactions of sensitive financial account numbers under Rule 2.425 of the Florida Rules of Judicial Administration, the discrepancies should be explained at summary judgment or trial.[110] For example, redactions should be done in a way that clearly reflects that the note was subject to redaction, not alteration, and that it therefore was an exact copy, and the plaintiff should evaluate whether testimony will be necessary to explain the discrepancy.

If the plaintiff seeks to enforce a lost, destroyed, or stolen promissory note in a foreclosure action related to residential real property, it should include allegations to reestablish the note as discussed in Section 6-5:2 below. The Florida Statutes and Florida Rules of Civil Procedure require the plaintiff to attach an affidavit to its complaint.[111] The affidavit must affirm, under penalty of perjury, the facts showing that the plaintiff is entitled to enforce the lost, destroyed, or stolen promissory note.[112] It also must describe the chain of all endorsements, transfers, or assignments of the promissory note.[113] Attached to the affidavit must be a copy of the promissory note and allonges to the note, audit reports showing receipt of the original note, or other evidence of the acquisition, ownership, and possession of the note that is available to the plaintiff.[114]

If a servicer or other party is filing the action on behalf of the real party in interest, the complaint must describe the authority that the plaintiff has been given.[115] It also must identify specifically the document that grants the plaintiff the authority to act on behalf of the real party in interest.[116] This may be a limited power of attorney although the rules do not require this specific kind of document.

---

of such evidence is sufficient to establish that the Bank had actual possession of the note at the time the complaint was filed and, therefore, had standing to bring the foreclosure action, absent any testimony or evidence to the contrary"); *see also Wilmington Sav. Fund Soc'y, FSB, v. Louissaint*, 212 So. 3d 473, 476 (Fla. 5th DCA 2017) (same); *see also Am. Home Mortg. Servicing, Inc. v. Bednarek*, 132 So. 3d 1222, 1223 (Fla. 2d DCA 2014) (holding that "because the note at issue is endorsed in blank, and because [the plaintiff] possessed the original note, its standing to foreclose is established from its status as the note holder"); *see also Clay Cty. Land Tr. #08-04-25-0078-014-27, Orange Park Tr. Servs., LLC v. JP Morgan Chase Bank*, 152 So. 3d 83, 85 (Fla. 1st DCA 2014) (holding that where the foreclosing plaintiff filed a copy of the note bearing an endorsement in blank at the time the complaint was filed, this was sufficient as a matter of law to establish its standing).

[109] *See Friedle v. Bank of N.Y. Mellon*, 226 So. 3d 976, 978-79 (Fla. 4th DCA 2017).
[110] *Kronen v. Deutsche Bank Nat'l Trust Co.*, 267 So. 3d 447, 448 (Fla. 4th DCA 2019).
[111] Fla. Stat. § 702.015(5)(a) and (b); *see also* Fla. R. Civ. P. 1.115(d). This chapter will discuss claims to enforce a lost note in Section 6-5:2.
[112] Fla. Stat. § 702.015(5)(a) and (b); *see also* Fla. R. Civ. P. 1.115(d).
[113] Fla. Stat. § 702.015(5)(a) and (b); *see also* Fla. R. Civ. P. 1.115(d). It is worth noting that Fla. Stat. § 673.3091, the part of Florida's enactment of the Uniform Commercial Code setting forth the requirements to enforce a lost, destroyed, or stolen instrument, does not require details of the chain of endorsements or the other various requirements now mandated by Fla. R. Civ. P. 1.115(d) and Fla. Stat. § 702.015(5).
[114] Fla. Stat. § 702.015(5)(c).
[115] Fla. Stat. § 702.015(3); *see also* Fla. R. Civ. P. 1.115(b).
[116] Fla. Stat. § 702.015(3); *see also* Fla. R. Civ. P. 1.115(b).

6-4:4 The Plaintiff's Capacity to Sue

A plaintiff is not obligated to allege its capacity to bring a mortgage foreclosure action in its complaint.[117] A defendant who wishes to challenge the plaintiff's capacity to bring suit must deny the plaintiff's ability to do so with particularity.[118]

Where the plaintiff is a trust that is qualified to do business under Chapter 609 of the Florida Statutes, it has the capacity to maintain a foreclosure action.[119] The individual trustees of such a trust are not indispensable parties to the foreclosure action.[120]

6-4:5 The Superiority of the Plaintiff's Interest to Those of Other Defendants

To state a prima facie cause of action for mortgage foreclosure, a plaintiff is not obligated to allege that its interest is superior to those of the defendants.[121] Parties that are included in a mortgage foreclosure complaint are put on notice that the plaintiff is asserting an interest superior to their own by virtue of being named in the complaint.[122]

6-4:6 The Satisfaction of Conditions Precedent

Many, but not all, notes and mortgages contain contractual conditions precedent to foreclosure or acceleration of all amounts due and owing under the loan. One example is a common contractual requirement that the plaintiff provide the borrower with

---

[117] Fla. R. Civ. P. 1.120(a) (stating that "it is not necessary to aver the capacity of a party to sue or be sued, the authority of a party to sue or be sued in a representative capacity, or the legal existence of an organized association of persons that is made a party, except to the extent required to show the jurisdiction of the court"); *Wilmington Savings Fund Society, FSB v. Contreras*, No. 5D18-2401, 44 Fla. L. Weekly D1925 (Fla. 5th DCA July 26, 2019).

[118] Fla. R. Civ. P. 1.120(a).

[119] *Tampa Properties, Inc. v. Great American Mortg. Investors*, 333 So. 2d 480, 481 (Fla. 2d DCA 1976).

[120] *Tampa Properties, Inc. v. Great American Mortg. Investors*, 333 So. 2d 480, 481 (Fla. 2d DCA 1976). Recently, the Fourth District Court of Appeal reversed a summary judgment in favor of a borrower, finding that "to prove standing, a plaintiff is not required to identify or prove the trust on whose behalf the plaintiff acts" and noting that the trust was not obligated to plead its capacity to sue. *Bank of New York Mellon Trust Company, National Association v. Ginsberg*, 221 So. 3d 1196, 1197 (Fla. 4th DCA 2017).

[121] *See Bank of N.Y. Mellon for Bear Stearns Arm Tr., Mortg. Pass-Through Certificates, Series 2003-7 v. Thompson*, 230 So. 3d 638 (Fla. 5th DCA 2017) (finding that it was error for the trial court to dismiss an action due to the plaintiff's failure to allege or prove the superiority of its lien); *see also Black Point Assets, Inc. v. Federal Nat'l Mortg. Ass'n*, 220 So. 3d 566, 568 (Fla. 5th DCA 2017). In *Black Point Assets, Inc.*, the court held that "because every complaint seeking foreclosure necessarily alleges that the plaintiff's interest in the property is superior to the parties' interests being foreclosed, we do not believe a complaint fails to state a claim simply because it does not explicitly state as much." The court further found that the defendants had notice of the relief sought through the plaintiff's request in its "wherefore" clause of the complaint, which requested that the court determine that the plaintiff's interest was "superior to any and all right, title or interest of the Defendants herein."

[122] *U.S. Bank Nat'l Ass'n v. Bevans*, 138 So. 3d 1185, 1187 (Fla. 3d DCA 2014).

a pre-suit notice of his default and permit him a certain amount of time to cure the default before the plaintiff files its foreclosure action. A plaintiff should review the note, mortgage, guaranty, and any other applicable agreements to determine whether it is obligated to fulfill any contractual pre-litigation conditions precedent to the foreclosure.

In its complaint, a plaintiff may allege in general terms that all conditions precedents to the action have been performed or have occurred.[123] It is not necessary to provide the particular facts showing the satisfaction of a condition precedent. The plaintiff should be aware that if other allegations or exhibits contradict its general assertion that all conditions precedent have been satisfied, its general assertion may not be enough.[124] Like the issue of the plaintiff's capacity, if a defendant wishes to challenge the plaintiff's satisfaction of a condition precedent, it will need to deny it with particularity.[125]

6-4:7 The Borrower's Default

The complaint must allege that the borrower has defaulted as an element of the mortgage foreclosure cause of action. Often, but not always, the default arises from the borrower's failure to make his regular payments. The default may be a non-monetary default such as an unauthorized conveyance of the property, the failure to maintain adequate insurance, or any other failure to satisfy the duties required under the note and mortgage. The plaintiff should describe the default in its complaint in enough detail to put the defendant on notice of the basis for the foreclosure action.

As discussed in Chapters 2 and 3, mortgage foreclosure actions are subject to a five-year statute of limitations from the date that the cause of action accrues.[126] The purpose of statutes of limitations is to "protect defendants from unusually long delays in the filing of lawsuits and to prevent prejudice to defendants from unexpected enforcement of stale claims."[127] Meanwhile, installment contracts such as mortgages obligate the borrower to make a payment every month, which in turn presents the possibility that there could be a missed payment—and therefore a fresh default—every month. Recognizing the unique nature of installment contracts, the Florida Supreme Court has held that after an initial default on payment "the statute of limitations runs from the date of each new default providing the mortgagee the right, but not the obligation, to accelerate all sums then due under the note and mortgage."[128]

With this in mind, a mortgage foreclosure complaint is timely when filed within five years of a missed payment. So, an action is timely when the plaintiff alleges that the borrower had missed a payment more than five years before the plaintiff filed its action *as well as all subsequent payments due after that*.[129] Furthermore, in a situation

---

[123] Fla. R. Civ. P. 1.120(c).
[124] *Wilmington Savings Fund Society, FSB v. Contreras*, No. 5D18-2401, 2019 WL 3366143 (Fla. 5th DCA July 26, 2019).
[125] Fla. R. Civ. P. 1.120(c).
[126] *See* Fla. Stat. § 95.11(2)(c) and Fla. Stat. § 95.031(1).
[127] *HSBC Bank USA, Nat. Ass'n v. Karzen*, 157 So. 3d 1089 (Fla. 1st DCA 2015) (citing *Caduceus Props., LLC v. Graney*, 137 So. 3d 987, 992 (Fla. 2014)).
[128] *Bartram v. U.S. Bank, Nat'l Ass'n*, 211 So. 3d 1009, 1119 (Fla. 2016).
[129] *See Bollettieri Resort Villas Condo. Ass'n v. Bank of N.Y. Mellon*, 198 So. 3d 1140, 1142 n.1 (Fla. 2d DCA 2016), *review dismissed*, 228 So. 3d 72 (Fla. Oct. 12, 2017) (an action was

FORECLOSURE COMPLAINTS

in which the action being filed is not the first foreclosure attempt, the lender may allege an initial default date on payment that occurred while the prior action was still pending.[130]

For purposes of drafting a complaint, where an initial default in payment is more than five years old and the borrowers have remained in a continuing state of default, the plaintiff should allege that the borrowers are in an ongoing state of default caused by their failure to make each monthly payment subsequent to their initial default.

Furthermore, where the note and mortgage contain optional acceleration clauses, the plaintiff should allege that it has opted to accelerate the debt pursuant to that clause with the filing of its complaint. The cause of action accrues when the last element takes place.[131] With a mortgage containing an optional acceleration clause, the last element—acceleration—occurs when the bank files its mortgage foreclosure complaint.[132]

6-4:8 The Amount Due to the Plaintiff Resulting from the Borrower's Default

Where the default is a monetary default, the plaintiff should allege the amount due and owing to it as the result of the default. While the failure to identify a specific amount is not a defect in the pleading, there are advantages in pleading a specific amount that may arise later in the litigation. For example, if the defendant fails to respond to the

---

timely where the complaint alleged an initial default on payments that occurred more than five years before the action was filed but also alleged that the borrowers had failed to make all subsequent payments due after the initial defaulted payment); *see also Desylvester v. Bank of New York*, 219 So.3d 1016, 1020 (Fla. 2d DCA 2017) (opinion on rehearing) (same); *Deutsche Bank Tr. Co. Ams. v. Beauvais*, 188 So. 3d 938, 945 (Fla. 3d DCA 2016) (en banc) (same, finding that "it is the fact that the bank alleged the failure to pay the October 1, 2006 installment payment 'and all subsequent payments' that makes the instant case fall within the rule as set out herein"); *see also Klebanoff v. Bank of New York Mellon*, 228 So. 3d 167, 169 (Fla. 5th DCA 2017) (same, finding that "because the Bank alleged and proved missed payments within the five years prior to the filing of its complaint, its action was not barred by the statute of limitations"); *see also Kebreau v. Bayview Loan Servicing, LLC*, 225 So. 3d 255 (Fla. 4th DCA 2017); *see also Forero v. Green Tree Servicing, LLC*, 223 So. 3d 440 (Fla. 1st DCA 2017); *but see Collazo v. HSBC Bank USA, N.A.*, 213 So. 3d 1012 (Fla. 3d DCA 2016) and *Hicks v. Wells Fargo Bank, N.A.*, 178 So. 3d 957, 959 (Fla. 5th DCA 2015) (because only one missed payment, outside the five-year statute of limitations was at issue in these cases, the plaintiffs' respective foreclosure claims were time barred). Both *Hicks* and *Collazo* have been distinguished on the grounds that they contained unique facts.

[130] *See PHH Mortg. Corp. v. Parish*, 244 So. 3d 338 (Fla. 2d DCA 2018); *HSBC Bank USA, N.A. v. Sanchez*, 245 So. 3d 784, 786 (Fla. 4th DCA 2018).

[131] *Locke v. State Farm Fire & Cas. Co.*, 509 So. 2d 1375, 1377 (Fla. 1st DCA 1987) (holding that because the lender had not exercised its optional right to accelerate until it filed its foreclosure complaint, the statute of limitations had not yet run).

[132] It is beyond the scope of this chapter to detail the evolution of statute of limitations law as applied to foreclosure claims. Although Fla. Stat. § 95.031 clearly states that the statute of limitations runs from the time the cause of action accrues, and acceleration is the last element of a foreclosure claim to accrue since it is exercised by the filing of the foreclosure complaint, it would be logical to assume that the statute of limitations would begin to run upon the filing of the complaint. Nonetheless, current case law emphasizes a default date within the five-year period before a complaint is filed.

complaint, the plaintiff may seek a default judgment against him. Once defaulted, a borrower may contest only unliquidated damages, and where the complaint identifies a specific amount due, the amount is deemed a liquidated damage that is deemed beyond dispute.[133]

Additionally, if the plaintiff is seeking pre-judgment interest among its damages, it should identify the date from which pre-judgment interest should be calculated. With a default on payments, this date usually will be the date of the last regular payment made. The plaintiff should review the terms of the note and mortgage to confirm their provisions on pre-judgment interest.

6-4:9 Attorney's Fees

If the plaintiff hopes to obtain an award of its attorney's fees incurred in the litigation, it should include an allegation that it is entitled to them in its complaint. A party's entitlement to its fees must be based in either a statute or a contract, so the plaintiff should review the note and mortgage before filing the complaint to determine whether the agreements provide for the award of attorney's fees, and under what circumstances.[134]

6-5 Additional Causes of Action

In addition to a claim to foreclose the note and mortgage, the plaintiff may assert other claims in its complaint necessitated by the facts of its situation. Below is a discussion of some of the more common claims brought in conjunction with a standard mortgage foreclosure claim.

6-5:1 A Claim Against a Guarantor

In addition to a note and mortgage, the borrower or another person may have signed a personal guaranty for payment of the debt. A guaranty may be absolute upon default or conditional on other events. A plaintiff may bring a count against the guarantor for money damages based on the guaranty in its mortgage foreclosure action.[135]

6-5:2 Reestablishment: When the Note Has Been Lost

Occasionally, an original promissory note is lost before the plaintiff files its action. Florida has enacted, among other things, those portions of the Uniform Commercial Code which permit enforcement of lost notes and which set forth the requirements for enforcing a lost, destroyed, or stolen note.[136]

To enforce a lost or destroyed promissory note, the plaintiff must show that it was entitled to enforce the note at the time that the note was lost, or that it directly or indirectly acquired ownership of the note from someone who was entitled to enforce the note when the note was lost.[137] The plaintiff also must show that the loss of pos-

---

[133] *See, e.g., Kotlyar v. Metropolitan Cas. Ins. Co.*, 192 So. 3d 562, 566 (Fla. 4th DCA 2016).

[134] *Bane v. Bane*, 775 So. 2d 938, 940 (Fla. 2000).

[135] Claims for damages under a guaranty are compatible with mortgage foreclosures. *Fort Plantation Investments, LLC v. Ironstone Bank*, 85 So. 3d 1169, 1171 (Fla. 5th DCA 2012).

[136] *See* Fla. Stat. § 673.3011 and Fla. Stat. § 673.3091, respectively.

[137] Fla. Stat. § 673.3091(1)(a).

session was not the result of a transfer by the person or a lawful seizure and that it cannot reasonably obtain possession of the instrument because the instrument was destroyed, its whereabouts cannot be determined, or it is in the wrongful possession of an unknown person or a person that cannot be found or is not amenable to service of process.[138] Additionally, the plaintiff must show, by reasonable means, that the borrower is adequately protected against potential claims by another person to enforce the instrument.[139] Finally, the plaintiff ultimately must prove the terms of the note.[140] The cause of action to enforce the lost note accrues upon the borrower's default, not when the note was lost.[141]

In its complaint, the plaintiff must attach an affidavit that (1) details a clear chain of all endorsements, transfers, or assignments of the note; (2) assert facts showing that the plaintiff is entitled to enforce the note; and (3) include as exhibits to the affidavit copies of the note and any allonges to the note, audit reports showing receipt of the original note, or other evidence of the acquisition, ownership, and possession of the note as may be available to the plaintiff.[142]

Although Fla. Stat. § 673.3091 does not provide for the re-establishment of the note, many foreclosure plaintiffs who have lost the note commonly bring a separate count to reestablish the lost note. On the other hand, Form 1.944(b) in the appendix to the Florida Rules of Civil Procedure provides a template for a complaint seeking to enforce a lost note without a second claim to re-establish the note and recent case law holds that the re-establishment of a lost note is not an independent cause of action.[143]

6-5:3 Reformation: When the Mortgage or Deed Contains a Mistake

A plaintiff may discover that the mortgage or the deed to the property contains a misspelling, an incorrect legal description, or similar typographical errors. While courts have deemed legal descriptions of properties sufficient despite minor mistakes where the description of the property could be determined from a review of the entire instrument, the plaintiff may need to reform the instrument to obtain marketable title.[144] To do so, the plaintiff should address these errors in its complaint.[145] A count for reformation of the document containing the mistake is appropriate in this situation.[146]

---

[138] Fla. Stat. § 673.3091(1)(b) and (c).

[139] Fla. Stat. § 673.3091(2).

[140] Fla. Stat. § 673.3091(2).

[141] *Mielke v. Deutsche Bank Nat'l Trust Co.*, 264 So. 3d 249, 253 (Fla. 1st DCA 2019).

[142] Fla. Stat. § 702.015(5)(a) and (b); *see also* Fla. R. Civ. P. 1.115(d).

[143] Form 1.944(b) of the Florida Rules of Civil Procedure and *Mielke v. Deutsche Bank Nat'l Trust Co.*, 264 So. 3d 249, 252-53 (Fla. 1st DCA 2019).

[144] *Salam v. U.S. Bank, Nat'l Ass'n*, 233 So. 3d 473, 475 (Fla. 4th DCA 2017). Reformation may be warranted when "the instrument's description of the property is patently ambiguous, and the instrument furnishes no other information from which the parties' intention can be gleaned, the attempted conveyance is void, and parol evidence may not be employed to cure the deficiency." *Mendelson v. Great Western Bank, F.S.B.*, 712 So. 2d 1194 (Fla. 2d DCA 1998).

[145] *Heartwood 2, LLC v. Dori*, 208 So. 3d 817, 822 (Fla. 3d DCA 2017).

[146] *Losner v. HSBC Bank USA, N.A.*, 190 So. 3d 160, 161 (Fla. 4th DCA 2016).

A claim for reformation of the mortgage is an equitable claim.[147] In reforming a written instrument, the court does not alter the agreement of the parties but only corrects the instrument so that it accurately reflects the true terms of the agreement actually reached.[148] Accordingly, the error being corrected must be the kind of error that arose from a mutual mistake between the parties.

In its allegations in support of this count, the plaintiff should identify the error specifically and allege that the error was the result of a mutual mistake between the parties.[149] The plaintiff should also allege the parties' actual, mutual intent. For example, if the legal description in the mortgage contains a typographical error, the plaintiff should provide the erroneous language and then provide the correct legal description, asking the court to reform the mortgage to reflect the corrected legal description. Ultimately, the plaintiff will be required to demonstrate the mutual mistake as well as the intentions of the parties through clear and convincing evidence.[150] Where the instrument being reformed is a deed, the original grantors and grantees involved in the mistake are necessary parties to the action, so the plaintiff should name them in the complaint.[151]

6-5:4 Equitable Subrogation and Equitable Liens

As discussed in Chapter 5, mortgages should be recorded in the official records of the county in which the property lies as soon as possible after their execution. Doing so ensures that the world has notice of the mortgage and establishes the mortgage's priority relative to other liens.[152] When a mortgage is not recorded, or where an owner of the property failed to sign the mortgage, its terms may still be enforceable, but it may be subject to other liens that were recorded after the mortgage's execution. The plaintiff should consider whether to include a claim for an equitable lien or for equitable subrogation in its complaint in such a case.

The plaintiff's pre-suit review of title should help identify the need for these causes of action. The plaintiff also should review the title insurance policy for the mortgage loan transaction and notify its title insurer before deciding whether to bring these claims. The failure to invoke the protections of the title insurance policy may result in a waiver of any potential title-related claims that otherwise might be covered.

As the terms indicate, both equitable subrogation and equitable liens are creatures of equity.[153] An equitable lien may arise where the conduct of the parties affected

---

[147] *Providence Square Ass'n, Inc. v. Biancardi*, 507 So. 2d 1366, 1369 (Fla. 1987).
[148] *Providence Square Ass'n, Inc. v. Biancardi*, 507 So. 2d 1366, 1369 (Fla. 1987).
[149] *Losner v. HSBC Bank USA, N.A.*, 190 So. 3d 160, 161 (Fla. 4th DCA 2016).
[150] *Losner v. HSBC Bank USA, N.A.*, 190 So. 3d 160, 161 (Fla. 4th DCA 2016).
[151] *Palm v. Taylor*, 929 So. 2d 566, 568 (Fla. 2d DCA 2006) (noting that the purpose of this policy is to discourage piecemeal litigation since "in a suit to reform a written instrument, all persons interested in the subject matter of the litigation, whether their interest be legal or equitable, should be made parties, so that the court may settle all rights at once thereby preventing a multiplicity of suits").
[152] *Argent Mortg. Co., LLC v. Wachovia Bank N.A.*, 52 So. 3d 796, 799 (Fla. 5th DCA 2010) (discussing Florida's notice recording statute and its effect on the priority of liens).
[153] Long ago, the Florida Supreme Court found that "the doctrine of equitable lien follows the doctrine of subrogation. They both come under the maxim, 'Equality is equity,' and are applied only in cases where the law fails to give relief and justice would suffer without them." *Jones v. Carpenter*, 106 So. 127, 129 (1925); *see also Suntrust Bank v. Riverside Nat.*

would entitle one party as a matter of equity to proceed against certain property.[154] The elements of an equitable lien count are similar to those of an unjust enrichment claim.[155] In its complaint, the plaintiff should allege the existence of the mortgage, that it provided the benefit of funding to the defendant under the terms of the mortgage, that the defendant accepted the funds, that the defendant defaulted under the obligations of the mortgage, and that it would be inequitable for the defendant to retain the property under the circumstances.

The plaintiff may also need to assert a claim for equitable subrogation. Equitable subrogation is "the placement of one party into the shoes of another so that the substituting party retains the rights, remedies, or securities that would otherwise belong to the original party."[156] Typically, it is applied when the proceeds from a mortgage loan are applied to satisfy a prior lien on the property but after the closing the prior lien is not satisfied of record. The mortgagee who paid the funds may be entitled to priority over the mortgagee whose interest would otherwise be superior. In this way, equitable subrogation is premised in the notion of doing justice to the parties and preventing the enrichment of one party as the result of another's loss.[157]

To state a cause of action for equitable subrogation, the plaintiff must allege facts showing that the plaintiff (1) made a payment to protect its own interest, (2) did not act as a volunteer, (3) was not primarily liable for the debt, (4) paid off the entire debt, and (5) works no injustice to the rights of a third party by its equitable subrogation claim.[158]

6-5:5 Seeking a Show Cause Order Under Section 702.10

The Florida Statutes provide a mechanism for an expedited foreclosure process where the plaintiff seeks in rem relief only. Fla. Stat. § 702.10(1) permits a plaintiff to request an order to show cause for the entry of final judgment in rem. This may be done by motion or in the plaintiff's complaint.

Bank of Florida, 792 So. 2d 1222, 1224 (Fla. 4th DCA 2001) (discussing the principle of equitable subrogation).

[154] *Tribeca Lending Corp. v. Real Estate Depot, Inc.*, 42 So. 3d 258, 262 (Fla. 4th DCA 2010); see also *Rozanski v. Wells Fargo Bank, Nat'l Ass'n*, 250 So. 3d 747, 750 (Fla. 2d DCA 2018) (imposing an equitable lien but denying a summary foreclosure judgment where the plaintiff had not shown that it was entitled to foreclosure at the time the circumstances giving rise to the lien existed).

[155] *Merritt v. Unkefer*, 223 So. 2d 723, 724 (Fla. 1969). An unjust enrichment claim requires a plaintiff to show that 1) the plaintiff conferred a benefit on the defendant; 2) the defendant had knowledge of the benefit; 3) the defendant accepted or retained the benefit conferred; and 4) the circumstances are such that it would be inequitable for the defendant to retain the benefit without paying fair value for it. *See also Della Ratta v. Della Ratta*, 927 So. 2d 1055, 1059 (Fla. 4th DCA 2006) (discussing the imposition of an equitable lien).

[156] *Aurora Loan Services LLC v. Senchuk*, 36 So. 3d 716, 718 (Fla. 1st DCA 2010) (citing Black's Law Dictionary 1440 (7th Ed. 1999)).

[157] *Suntrust Bank v. Riverside Nat. Bank of Florida*, 792 So. 2d 1222, 1224 (Fla. 4th DCA 2001). A party alleging entitlement to an equitable subrogation lien is not required to allege or prove fraud or misconduct, however. *Cone v. U.S. Bank Trust, N.A.*, 265 So. 3d 698, 699 (Fla. 5th DCA 2019).

[158] *See Tank Tech, Inc. v. Valley Tank Testing, LLC*, 244 So. 3d 383, 389 (Fla. 2d DCA 2018); *Columbia Bank v. Turbeville*, 143 So. 3d 964, 968 (Fla. 1st DCA 2014); see also *Sherman v. Deutsche Bank National Trust Company*, 100 So. 3d 95, 98 (Fla. 4th DCA 2012).

Once the plaintiff requests the entry of a show cause order under Fla. Stat. § 702.10(1), the court "shall immediately review the request and the court file in chambers and without a hearing."[159] If the court finds that the foreclosure complaint is verified and complies with statutory requirements, "the court shall promptly issue an order directed to the other parties named in the action to show cause why a final judgment of foreclosure should not be entered."[160] The defendant borrower may show cause by filing defenses in a motion or answer, or by filing an affidavit or other evidence which raises a legal defense to the foreclosure.[161] The failure to do so will result in the defendant's waiver of his defenses and the entry of an in rem foreclosure judgment.[162]

If the property is occupied by someone other than an owner, the plaintiff may include a count for the borrower to make payments during the foreclosure, or else an order to vacate the premises will be entered.[163] The plaintiff should allege that the property is not owner-occupied, that the borrower is in default, and that it is entitled to payments under the statute. As with subsection (1) of the statute, the court will then issue an order requiring the defendant to show cause why an order to make payments during the pendency of the foreclosure proceedings or an order to vacate the premises should not be entered.[164] The defendant must file a motion or a sworn or verified answer or appear at the hearing to avoid a finding that he has waived his defenses. At the hearing, the court considers the affidavits and other showings made by the parties appearing and determines the probable validity of the plaintiff's foreclosure claim and the borrower's defenses.[165] If the court determines that the plaintiff is likely to prevail on its claims, the court shall enter an order requiring the borrower to make the payment to the plaintiff.[166]

6-5:6 Injunctive Relief and Assignments of Rent Riders: When the Property Is Occupied by a Tenant

The Florida Statutes contemplate the ability of plaintiffs to obtain rents paid by tenants occupying the property as further security in the event of default by the borrower.[167] The parties to a mortgage may execute an assignment of rents rider, or the mortgage may contain an assignment of rents provision entitling the plaintiff to the rents collected in the event that the borrower defaults under the mortgage. This will operate as a lien

---

[159] Fla. Stat. § 702.10(1).

[160] The order must contain certain information set forth in the statute in subsection (1)(a). If the defendant has not yet been served with initial process, the order must be served along with the complaint and summons in accordance with the statutes governing service of process. See Fla. Stat. § 702.10(1)(a)(9)(b).

[161] The statute provides that the defendant must show through its filing that there is a genuine issue of material fact which would preclude entry of summary judgment or that otherwise constitutes a legal defense to foreclosure. Fla. Stat. § 702.10(1)(b).

[162] Fla. Stat. § 702.10(1)(b) and (d).

[163] Fla. Stat. § 702.10(2). Like an order entered under subsection (1) of the statute, an order entered under this subsection must contain certain information set forth in subsection (2)(a). If the defendant has not yet been served with initial process, the order must be served along with the complaint and summons in accordance with the statutes governing service of process. See Fla. Stat. § 702.10(2)(a)(5)(b).

[164] Fla. Stat. § 702.10(2).

[165] Fla. Stat. § 702.10(2)(d).

[166] Fla. Stat. § 702.10(2)(d).

[167] Fla. Stat. § 697.07(1).

and is enforceable by the plaintiff upon the borrower's default on the obligations of the mortgage.[168] The statute requires a written demand for the rents by the plaintiff to the borrower and contemplates that the borrower will turn over all rents in his possession at the time of the written demand or collected after that.[169] The plaintiff may allege a claim for rents in its complaint or move for the sequestration of the rents separately.

Where there is no assignment of rents rider to the mortgage and no other contractual provisions permitting the sequestration of rents during the pending foreclosure action, the plaintiff may consider asserting a claim for injunctive relief to obtain the rents generated by tenants.[170]

6-5:7 Plea for a Deficiency Judgment: When the Sale of the Property May Fall Short of the Judgment Amount

Due to market conditions in parts of the state, property values may not have rebounded from the recession of the late 2000s. The judicial sale of the property securing the plaintiff's mortgage and note may recover less than the amount of the judgment that eventually may be entered on the plaintiff's complaint. In that case, as discussed in the chapter regarding deficiency judgments, the plaintiff has the right to seek a judgment for the deficiency if the borrower has other assets that might be sufficient to satisfy the difference.[171]

The plaintiff may want to request the trial court to retain jurisdiction over the case to enter a deficiency judgment. The final judgment should address this request to ensure that jurisdiction is retained, and the plaintiff's right to a deficiency judgment will become ripe only after the judicial sale of the property. A plaintiff also may bring an independent action at law, even if the court reserved jurisdiction to entertain a motion for the deficiency in the foreclosure judgment, provided that the court has not yet entered a deficiency decree.[172] The plaintiff should evaluate whether to request a deficiency judgment as part of its requested relief in its complaint.

---

[168] Fla. Stat. § 697.07(2). The statute provides that "the mortgagee shall hold a lien on the rents, and the lien created by the assignment shall be perfected and effective against third parties upon recordation of the mortgage or separate instrument in the public records of the county in which the real property is located." Recently, the Second District Court of Appeal found that "while the statute creates a lien on rents which is effective against [the third-party appellant] by virtue of recordation of the mortgage ... the statute does not require that the third-party title owner assign to the mortgagee rents owed to it under a separate document not subject to the foreclosure action." *Green Emerald Homes, LLC v. Residential Credit Opportunities Tr.*, 256 So. 3d 211, 215 (Fla. 2d DCA 2018).

[169] Fla. Stat. § 697.07(3); *see also Ginsberg v. Lennar Florida Holdings, Inc.*, 645 So. 2d 490 (Fla. 3d DCA 1994).

[170] *See UV Cite III, LLC v. Deutsche Bank National Trust Co.*, 215 So. 3d 1280, 1282 (Fla. 3d DCA 2017).

[171] The right to a deficiency judgment arises under section 702.06 of the Florida Statutes. The statute provides that a deficiency judgment may be sought in the foreclosure action or in an entirely separate action after the sale. Fla. Stat. § 702.06. There is a one-year statute of limitations on actions for deficiency judgments. Fla. Stat. § 95.11(5)(h).

[172] *Dyck-O'Neal, Inc. v. Lanham*, 257 So. 3d 1, 2 (Fla. 2018) (finding that "the statute [section 702.06] plainly allows the foreclosure court to adjudicate the deficiency claim but also gives the complainant the right to sue at common law to recover such deficiency, unless the court in the foreclosure action has granted or denied a claim for a deficiency judgment").

CHAPTER 7

Responses to Foreclosure Complaints

Morgan Weinstein

7-1 Introduction

7-1:1 Motions and Pleadings

A defendant will typically respond to a foreclosure complaint by filing a motion to dismiss, followed by an answer and affirmative defenses in the event that the motion to dismiss is denied. Although defendants attempt to raise new and novel procedural and substantive arguments against foreclosure complaints at both the pre-answer and answer phase of litigation, there are a number of common allegations leveled against foreclosure complaints.

7-2 Motions to Dismiss

7-2:1 Introduction

A motion to dismiss should be filed to attack the form of a plaintiff's complaint. It is typically considered a pre-answer motion, meaning that it is not a pleading and further that a pleading need not be filed until after resolution of the motion to dismiss. A motion to dismiss, as a procedural mechanism, may be desirable for defendants, as it allows them additional time prior to filing a responsive pleading.

Motions to dismiss are designed to test whether a plaintiff has stated a cause of action within the four corners of the complaint.[1] If it is determined that the complaint states a cause of action, then the motion to dismiss should be denied.[2] The court is limited to review of the four corners of the complaint on a motion to dismiss, and is prohibited from considering extrinsic evidence.[3] However, the court may consider exhibits annexed to the complaint and may reconcile the face of such exhibits with the allegations raised in the complaint. The court may also consider

---

[1] *Lewis v. Barnett Bank of South Florida, N.A.*, 604 So. 2d 937, 938 (Fla. 3d DCA 1992).
[2] *Blue Supply v. Novos*, 990 So. 2d 1157, 1159 (Fla. 3d DCA 2008).
[3] *Hanft v. Phelan*, 488 So. 2d 531, 532 (Fla. 1986).

certain other grounds on a motion to dismiss, such as lack of jurisdiction.[4] Where a motion to dismiss raises multiple grounds, a trial court may nevertheless enter an unelaborated order denying the motion, which could render each ground of the motion subject to further review.[5]

7-2:2 Common Grounds for Motions to Dismiss

Motions to dismiss are an ill-developed area of case law, because an order denying a motion to dismiss is not a final appealable order.[6] However, the following arguments are frequently raised on motion to dismiss in foreclosure disputes. First, defendants will allege that a plaintiff has failed to comply with Rule 1.130(a), Florida Rules of Civil Procedure, by not incorporating certain documents in or attaching certain documents to the complaint.[7] Rule 1.130(a) prohibits the annexation of unnecessary papers to a complaint. Further, the limitation in Rule 1.130(a) regarding "documents upon which action may be brought" limit the class of documents in a foreclosure dispute to those which provide contractually-binding duties and remedies.[8] Even then, where an agreement, such as a short-form mortgage, refers to a part of itself which is recorded in the public records, only the short-form mortgage must be filed with the complaint.[9]

Additionally, motions to dismiss will often include arguments regarding whether a plaintiff has complied with conditions precedent or has failed to demonstrate its standing. Each of these issues presents an affirmative defense and should not be decided on a motion to dismiss.[10] However, there is authority suggesting that foreclosure cases contain standing as an element of the cause of action.[11] With regard to standing, defendants may attempt to allege that a plaintiff is not the owner of the note at issue in the case. The requirement is for the plaintiff to be the holder of the note, without regard to

---

[4] *See Brown v. BNB Inv. Holdings, LLC*, No. 3D-17-1993, 2018 Fla. App. LEXIS 10273 (Fla. 3d DCA July 25, 2018).

[5] *See Wilmington Sav. Fund Soc'y, FSB v. Contreras*, 2019 Fla. App. LEXIS 11698, 2019 WL 3366143, No. 5D18-2401 (Fla. 5th DCA July 26, 2019).

[6] *Williams v. Oken*, 62 So. 3d 1129, 1134 (Fla. 2011); *Alston v. Fla. Ins. Guar. Ass'n*, 842 So. 2d 842, 842 (Fla. 2003) (citing *Benton v. Moore*, 655 So. 2d 1272, 1273 (Fla. 1st DCA 1995)).

[7] *See* Fla. R. Civ. P. 1.130(a) (providing that "All . . . documents upon which action may be brought or defense made . . . shall be incorporated in or attached to the pleading"). *See also Glen Garron, LLC v. Buchwald*, 210 So. 3d 229, 233 (Fla. 5th DCA 2017).

[8] *See Samuels v. King Motor Co.*, 782 So. 2d 489, 500 (Fla. 4th DCA 2001) (holding that the "necessary exhibit in a case based upon a contract under Rule 1.130(a) is 'the instrument'"). *See also Glen Garron, LLC v. Buchwald*, 210 So. 3d 229, 233-34 (Fla. 5th DCA 2017) (holding that Rule 1.130 "does not require attachment of the entire contract, but only the attachment or the incorporation into the pleading of the material portions of the contract on which the action is based" and reasoning that, while the mortgage is required to be attached to a foreclosure complaint, a promissory note is not).

[9] *Khleif v. Bankers Trust Co. of California*, 215 So. 3d 619 (Fla. 2d DCA 2017).

[10] *Custer Med. Ctr. v. United Auto. Ins. Co.*, 62 So. 3d 1086, 1096-97 (Fla. 2010); *Krivanek v. Take Back Tampa Political Comm.*, 625 So. 2d 840, 842 (Fla. 1993), respectively.

[11] *U.S. Bank, N.A. v. Clarke*, 192 So. 3d 620, 622 (Fla. 4th DCA 2016) (holding that standing is a "crucial element" of a foreclosure proceeding).

ownership interest.[12] Unless the allegations of the complaint or its attachments negate a plaintiff's standing, a motion to dismiss on that ground should be denied.[13]

However, the following arguments are frequently raised on motion to dismiss in foreclosure disputes, and certain opinions have expressed a concern at trial as to whether a plaintiff owned the note.[14] Moreover, because it is permissive for a plaintiff to allege that it owns the note and proceed upon the theory that enforcement may be had based on an ownership interest, defendants may raise the allegation that the plaintiff does not own the note, to narrow this issue early on in the litigation.[15] With regard to allegations as to conditions precedent, a plaintiff is permitted to generally aver compliance and a defendant must then raise in the responsive pleading either a negative averment or an affirmative defense that plaintiff did not comply with a condition precedent.[16] This negative averment or defense must be raised specifically and with particularity.[17] Due to the fact that pleadings regarding compliance with conditions precedent fall under Florida's special pleading requirement, the averment by a defendant is treated as an affirmative defense, for which the defendant bears the burden of pleading and persuasion.[18] Defendants may also raise non-compliance with certain federal laws, such as the Fair Debt Collection Practices Act or the Real Estate Settlement Procedure Act. These arguments also point to affirmative defenses, to be raised in a responsive pleading.

Defendants will likewise attempt to delineate procedural defects in complaints and in the legal process in motions to dismiss. For instance, a motion to dismiss may claim that the plaintiff has not followed the strictures of former Rule 1.110(b), Florida Rules of Civil Procedure or Rule 1.115, Florida Rules of Civil Procedure, with regard to verification of the complaint. The verification does not need to comply with statutory verification requirements, such as a statement that the facts of the complaint, without limitation, are true.[19] The plaintiff need not be the entity that executes the verification. Instead, the plaintiff's agent or servicer may execute the verification.[20] Further,

---

[12] *MERS v. Azize*, 965 So. 2d 151, 153-54 (Fla. 2d DCA 2007); *Harvey v. Deutsche Bank Nat'l Trust Co.*, 69 So. 3d 300, 304 (Fla. 4th DCA 2011). *See also Aquasol Condo. Ass'n v. HSBC Bank USA, N.A.*, No. 3D17-352, 2018 Fla. App. LEXIS 11414 (Fla. 3d DCA Aug. 15, 2018).

[13] *Wilmington Sav. Fund Soc'y, FSB v. Contreras*, 2019 Fla. App. LEXIS 11698, 2019 WL 3366143, No. 5D18-2401 (Fla. 5th DCA July 26, 2019).

[14] *Law Offices of David J. Stern, P.A. v. Sec. Nat'l Servicing Corp.*, 969 So. 2d 962, 971 (Fla. 2007) (concurring opinion); *Joseph v. BAC Home Loans Servicing, LP*, 155 So. 3d 444, *passim* (Fla. 4th DCA Jan. 7, 2015); *Beltway Capital, LLC v. Greens Coa, Inc.*, 153 So. 3d 330 (Fla. 5th DCA 2014).

[15] *See Angelini v. HSBC Bank USA, N.A.*, 189 So. 3d 202, 203 (Fla. 4th DCA 2016) (holding that, "Because the Bank attempted to proceed as the holder of the note rather than as a non-holder in possession (a theory where the testimony regarding ownership may have been helpful to it), it was required to introduce evidence that it actually held the note at the time of filing").

[16] Fla. R. Civ. P. 1.120(c).

[17] Fla. R. Civ. P. 1.120(c); *Gardner v. Broward Cnty.*, 631 So. 2d 319, 320-21 (Fla. 4th DCA 1994); *Ashley v. Lamar*, 468 So. 2d 433, 434 (Fla. 5th DCA 1985).

[18] *Harris v. U.S. Bank, N.A.*, 223 So. 3d 1030, 1032-33 (Fla. 1st DCA 2017).

[19] *Trucap Grantor Trust 2010-1 v. Pelt*, 84 So. 3d 369, 372 (Fla. 2d DCA 2012). Florida Rule of Civil Procedure 1.115 replaces and expands upon former Florida Rule of Civil Procedure 1.110(b).

[20] *Deutsche Bank Nat'l Trust Co. v. Prevratil*, 120 So. 3d 573, 575 (Fla. 2d DCA 2013).

information regarding the positional authority of the signer is not required.[21] Finally, evidence of the agent's or servicer's authority to verify the complaint is not required.[22] Nevertheless, a failure to provide a verification in accordance with Rule 1.110(b) is grounds for dismissal of a foreclosure complaint on a motion to dismiss.[23]

Similarly, a defendant may attempt to claim that a plaintiff has failed to join an indispensable party to the dispute.[24] A motion to dismiss is the proper vehicle for raising the issue that an indispensable party is absent from the proceedings.[25] Such a motion must contain the facts demonstrating why the absent party or parties would be indispensable.[26]

Concurrently with allegations related to defects in the complaint, defendants may attempt in a motion to dismiss to challenge the court's jurisdiction or to attack the sufficiency of service of process. A defendant may raise service of process as an issue, independently, in an answer.[27] However, if the defendant files a pre-answer motion, rather than simply filing an answer, certain obligations arise. In particular, service of process must be asserted in a pre-answer motion, unless no pre-answer motion is filed.[28] If a party files a motion to dismiss, but does not raise service of process as an issue in that motion, then the defense is waived by the time the answer is filed.[29] As a result, a defendant who wishes to raise any deficiencies with regard to service of process must address those deficiencies in a pre-answer motion, should that defendant choose to file a pre-answer motion.

7-3 Affirmative Defenses

7-3:1 Introduction

An affirmative defense admits liability of the plaintiff's claim and seeks to avoid the claim by some other means.[30] There are numerous affirmative defenses to foreclosure, including lack of standing, failure of conditions precedent, and defenses related to payment and waiver. Other common law and statutory defenses are regularly asserted as well. These defenses must be pleaded with certainty and with sufficient ultimate facts to establish the necessary elements of the defense.[31]

---

[21] *Deutsche Bank Nat'l Trust Co. v. Plageman*, 133 So. 3d 1199, 1202 (Fla. 2d DCA 2014).
[22] *Deutsche Bank Nat'l Trust Co. v. Plageman*, 133 So. 3d 1199, 1202 (Fla. 2d DCA 2014).
[23] Fla. R. Civ. P. 1.110(b).
[24] *See Turkell-White v. Wells Fargo Bank, N.A.*, 273 So. 3d 1021, 1023-24 (Fla. 4th DCA 2019).
[25] *Turkell-White v. Wells Fargo Bank, N.A.*, 273 So. 3d 1021, 1023-24 (Fla. 4th DCA 2019).
[26] *Turkell-White v. Wells Fargo Bank, N.A.*, 273 So. 3d 1021, 1023-24 (Fla. 4th DCA 2019).
[27] *Chestnut v. Nationstar Mortg., LLC*, No. 3D17-1752, 2018 Fla. App. LEXIS 11406 (Fla. 3d DCA Aug. 15, 2018).
[28] *Chestnut v. Nationstar Mortg., LLC*, No. 3D17-1752, 2018 Fla. App. LEXIS 11406 (Fla. 3d DCA Aug. 15, 2018).
[29] *Chestnut v. Nationstar Mortg., LLC*, No. 3D17-1752, 2018 Fla. App. LEXIS 11406 (Fla. 3d DCA Aug. 15, 2018).
[30] *State Farm Auto. Ins. Co. v. Curran*, 135 So. 3d 1071, 1079 (Fla. 2014) (quoting *St. Paul Mercury Ins. Co. v. Coucher*, 837 So. 2d 483, 487 (Fla. 5th DCA 2002)).
[31] *Ellison v. City of Fort Lauderdale*, 175 So. 2d 198, 200 (Fla. 1965); *Cady v. Chevy Chase Sav. & Loan, Inc.*, 528 So. 2d 136, 137-38 (Fla. 4th DCA 1988); *Bliss v. Carmona*, 418 So. 2d 1017, 1019 (Fla. 3d DCA 1982).

7-3:2 Lack of Standing

Standing is an affirmative defense to be raised by a defendant in a responsive pleading.[32] Failure to raise standing as an affirmative defense may result in a waiver of the right to contest it.[33] Standing in a mortgage foreclosure case is broader than the question of ownership of the beneficial interest of a note.[34] Standing in a mortgage foreclosure case is also unique, inasmuch as it may also be an element of the plaintiff's claim.[35]

The party seeking to foreclose a mortgage must demonstrate that it has standing and must also demonstrate that the plaintiff that filed the case had standing at the time that the complaint was filed.[36] Because a mortgage promissory note is a negotiable instrument, standing may be determined by whether the plaintiff is the holder of the note or otherwise entitled to enforce the note, pursuant to Chapter 673, Florida Statutes.[37] A defendant asserting an affirmative defense to a plaintiff's standing must therefore allege that the plaintiff was not entitled to enforce the note and foreclose the mortgage. The defense must raise facts in support of this allegation without resorting to issues of whether a plaintiff has complied with the strictures of contractual arrangements to which the defendant was neither a party nor a third-party beneficiary.[38]

Under the statutes governing negotiable instruments, either a holder, a nonholder in possession who has the rights of a holder, or a person not in possession who is entitled to enforce the instrument may have standing in a foreclosure case.[39] A holder is the person in possession of a negotiable instrument that is payable either to the person in possession or to blank.[40] Where there is a trustee relationship regarding the note, an endorsement to a trustee is sufficient to establish standing, regardless of whether the identity of the trust is, itself, clear.[41] Under Florida law, the mortgage follows the note, meaning that the person or entity entitled to enforce the note is also entitled to foreclose the mortgage.[42]

Standing may be established in a number of ways. First, an assignment of mortgage or equitable transfer of the mortgage prior to the filing of the complaint may be proven.[43] Secondly, a special endorsement on the note in favor of plaintiff or a blank

---

[32] *Krivanek v. Take Back Tampa Political Comm.*, 625 So 2d 840, 842 (Fla. 1993).
[33] *Stratton v. 6000 Indian Creek, LLC*, 95 So. 3d 334, 336-37 (Fla. 3d DCA 2012).
[34] *Elston/Leetsdale, LLC v. CW Capital Asset Management, LLC*, 87 So. 3d 14, 16 (Fla. 4th DCA 2012).
[35] *Russell v. Bac Home Loans Servicing*, 239 So. 3d 98, 100 (Fla. 4th DCA 2018).
[36] *McLean v. JP Morgan Chase Bank N.A.*, 79 So. 3d 170, 172 (Fla. 4th DCA 2012). See also *AS Lily LLC v. Morgan*, 164 So. 3d 124 (Fla. 2d DCA 2015).
[37] See *Deutsche Bank Nat'l Trust Co. v. Clarke*, 87 So. 3d 58, 60-61 (Fla. 4th DCA 2012); *Taylor v. Deutsche Bank Nat'l Trust Co.*, 44 So. 3d 618, 622 (Fla. 5th DCA 2010).
[38] *Deutsche Bank Trust Co. Ams. v. Harris*, 264 So. 3d 186, 190-91 (Fla. 4th DCA 2019).
[39] Fla. Stat. § 673.3011; *Wells Fargo Bank, N.A. v. Morcom*, 125 So. 3d 320, 321-22 (Fla. 5th DCA 2013).
[40] *Olivera v. Bank of Am., N.A.*, 141 So. 3d 770, 773-74 (Fla. 2d DCA 2014).
[41] *Wells Fargo Bank, N.A. v. Cook*, 2019 Fla. App. LEXIS 11785, 2019 WL 3367299, No. 2D17-3913 (Fla. 2d DCA July 26, 2019).
[42] *Johns v. Gillian*, 184 So. 140, 143 (Fla. 1938); *WM Specialty Mtg., LLC v. Salomon*, 874 So. 2d 680, 682 (Fla. 4th DCA 2004).
[43] *McLean v. JP Morgan Chase Bank N.A.*, 79 So. 3d 170, 172-73 (Fla. 4th DCA 2012).

endorsement may be used to demonstrate standing.[44] Additionally, an assignment from the payee to the plaintiff or an affidavit of ownership may prove plaintiff's status as a holder of the note.[45] Alternatively, proof of mere delivery of the note and mortgage, with the intention to pass title based upon a proper consideration is sufficient to demonstrate standing.[46] A plaintiff may establish that the note is lost and that plaintiff is entitled to enforce the lost note pursuant to statute.[47] Moreover, the conduct of the parties may be used to determine whether a plaintiff has standing. If a plaintiff has been paying for upkeep of the property, in terms of paying for items such as taxes and insurance, then a court may use that fact to infer standing on the part of that plaintiff.[48] Ultimately, a plaintiff will need to demonstrate one or more of the following: evidence of a valid assignment; proof of the purchase of the debt; or evidence of an effective transfer.[49] A plaintiff may possess standing as the owner of the note, the holder of the note, or the agent of either.[50] The manner in which a plaintiff pleads its standing may determine the manner in which a defendant pleads its defense, because it controls the evidence necessary to prove or disprove standing, at trial.[51] Filing the note with the court establishes a clear presumption that the plaintiff has standing, at least as of the date that the note is filed.[52] Where the note filed with the court is endorsed either in blank or to plaintiff, and where the same endorsement appears on the copy of the note attached to the complaint, a plaintiff's standing as holder of the note is established.[53] The copy of the note attached to the complaint must be an exact copy of the original note introduced at trial, and redaction of information on the copy attached to the complaint may complicate a plaintiff's ability to establish standing.[54] Possession of the note may be actual or constructive.[55] Constructive possession occurs if a third party has physical possession of the note, but the plaintiff has the power to exercise control over the note.[56] A party that is substituted as plaintiff may acquire the status with regard to standing that the original plaintiff had at the time that suit was filed.[57]

---

[44] *McLean v. JP Morgan Chase Bank N.A.*, 79 So. 3d 170, 172-73 (Fla. 4th DCA 2012); *Riggs v. Aurora Loan Services, LLC*, 36 So. 3d 932, 933 (Fla. 4th DCA 2010).

[45] *McLean v. JP Morgan Chase Bank N.A.*, 79 So. 3d 170, 172-73 (Fla. 4th DCA 2012).

[46] Fla. Stat. § 673.2031; *McLean v. JP Morgan Chase Bank N.A.*, 79 So. 3d 170, 172-73 (Fla. 4th DCA 2012); *Isaac v. Deutsche Bank Nat'l Trust Co.*, 74 So. 3d 495, 495-96 (Fla. 4th DCA 2011).

[47] *Deutsche Bank Nat'l Trust Co. v. Smith*, 2019 Fla. App. LEXIS 11298, No. 4D18-2265 (Fla. 4th DCA July 17, 2019). *See also* Fla. Stat. § 673.3091.

[48] *Peuguero v. Bank of Am., N.A.*, 169 So. 3d 1198, 1202 (Fla. 4th DCA 2015) (reasoning that payment of taxes and fees "is a noteworthy factor in determining standing, as financial institutions are not known to incur expenses on behalf of properties for which they do not hold an interest").

[49] *Stone v. Bankunited*, 115 So. 3d 411, 412-13 (Fla. 2d DCA 2013).

[50] *Bank of New York Trust Co. v. Rodgers*, 79 So. 3d 108, 109 (Fla. 3d DCA 2012).

[51] *See Angelini v. HSBC Bank USA, N.A.*, 189 So. 3d 202, 203 (Fla. 4th DCA 2016).

[52] *McLean v. JP Morgan Chase Bank N.A.*, 79 So. 3d 170, 172 (Fla. 4th DCA 2012).

[53] *Ortiz v. PNC Bank, N.A.*, 188 So. 3d 923, 924-25 (Fla. 4th DCA 2016).

[54] *See Friedle v. Bank of New York Mellon*, 226 So. 3d 976, 978-79 (Fla. 4th DCA 2017) (taking issue with a note that was not in the "same condition" as the redacted copy attached to the complaint).

[55] *Caraccia v. U.S. Bank, N.A.*, 185 So. 3d 1277, 1279 (Fla. 4th DCA 2016).

[56] *Caraccia v. U.S. Bank, N.A.*, 185 So. 3d 1277, 1279 (Fla. 4th DCA 2016).

[57] *Spicer v. Ocwen Loan Servicing, LLC*, 238 So. 3d 275, 278 (Fla. 4th DCA 2018).

An endorsement may be on a separate sheet of paper, referred to as an "allonge."[58] The endorsement or the allonge need not be dated.[59] However, issues of fact arise when an endorsement is not dated, and the plaintiff will need to prove that the endorsement in blank or in favor of the original plaintiff occurred prior to the filing of the complaint.[60]

7-3:3 Failure of Conditions Precedent

The pleading and denial of conditions precedent are governed by Rule 1.120(c), Florida Rules of Civil Procedure. A plaintiff may simply plead that all conditions precedent have been performed or have occurred.[61] In denying the performance of conditions precedent, the defendant must make a denial specifically and with particularity.[62] An allegation that is subject to interpretation as to the manner of non-compliance is insufficient to meet the requirement that the allegation be made specifically and with particularity.[63] The failure to perform a condition precedent is an affirmative defense, and the defendant asserting it bears the burden of pleading and persuasion.[64] An element of this defense includes a demonstration of prejudice to the defending party.[65] Defendants in foreclosure actions typically raise two affirmative defenses alleging failures of conditions precedent: that the plaintiff failed to comply with paragraph 22 of the mortgage and that plaintiff failed to comply with statutory conditions that have been expressly incorporated into the loan documents.

Paragraph 22 of the form mortgage at issue in most foreclosure cases in Florida requires that the party seeking to foreclose provide a notice to the defendant. The notice specify that there has been a default, what the default is, what action is required to cure the default, a date not less than 30 days from the date the notice is given by which the default must be cured, and that failure to cure the default may result in acceleration of the debt, foreclosure by judicial proceeding, and sale of the property. The notice must further inform the defendant of the right to reinstate the loan and the right to assert defenses in the foreclosure proceeding.

A defendant may allege that the plaintiff has failed to send the notice of intent to accelerate or may allege that, although the notice was sent, it was non-compliant with the strictures of the mortgage. Defendants may attempt to allege that strict compliance with paragraph 22 of the mortgage is required or that, at least, compliance with each of the six requirements in paragraph 22 is required.[66] Plaintiffs will allege that,

---

[58] *Clay Cnty. Land Trust #08-04-25-0078-014-27, v. JP Morgan Chase Bank, N.A.*, 152 So. 3d 83, 84-85 (Fla. 1st DCA 2014).

[59] *Clay Cnty. Land Trust #08-04-25-0078-014-27, v. JP Morgan Chase Bank, N.A.*, 152 So. 3d 83, 84-85 (Fla. 1st DCA 2014).

[60] *Ham v. Nationstar Mortg., LLC*, 164 So. 3d 714 (Fla. 1st DCA 2015); *Olivera v. Bank of Am., N.A.*, 141 So. 3d 770, 773-74 (Fla. 2d DCA 2014); *Bristol v. Wells Fargo Bank, N.A.*, 137 So. 3d 1130, 1132 (Fla. 4th DCA 2014).

[61] Fla. R. Civ. P. 1.120(c).

[62] Fla. R. Civ. P. 1.120(c).

[63] *Deutsche Bank Nat'l Trust Co. v. Quinion*, 198 So. 3d 701, 704 (Fla. 2d DCA 2016).

[64] *Custer Med. Ctr. v. United Auto. Ins. Co.*, 62 So. 3d 1086, 1096-97 (Fla. 2010).

[65] *Ortiz v. PNC Bank, N.A.*, 188 So. 3d 923, 925 (Fla. 4th DCA 2016); *Bank of New York Mellon v. Johnson*, 185 So. 3d 594, 597 (Fla. 5th DCA 2016); *Gorel v. Bank of New York Mellon*, 165 So. 3d 44, 47 (Fla 5th DCA 2015).

[66] *Samaroo v. Wells Fargo Bank*, 137 So. 3d 1127, 1129 (Fla. 5th DCA 2014).

because the mortgage is a contract, the plaintiff is required to substantially comply with the terms of the mortgage.[67] Plaintiffs have been held to be required to substantially comply with conditions precedent found within the mortgage.[68] In either case, the doctrines of futility and anticipatory breach may operate to bar the defense.[69] This affirmative defense is successful where the notice was not given in the manner provided under the mortgage. This affirmative defense is also successful in circumstances in which the notice suffers from major deficiencies.

Where the loan documents specifically incorporate other statutory schemes, defendants will allege that conditions precedent in those statutes create contractual conditions precedent. There has been a recent trend toward agreement with this proposition. For instance, if a note or mortgage specifically incorporate the regulations of the federal Department of Housing and Urban Development regulations, such regulations are treated no differently than compliance with conditions precedent that are defined within the terms of the contract.[70] Following this reasoning, courts have held that federal Department of Veterans Affairs regulations may create contractual conditions precedent, provided that the contract expressly and specifically incorporates those regulations.[71] However, if the regulations are not specifically incorporated by the terms of the contract, then they do not constitute contractual conditions precedent.[72]

7-3:4 Defenses Related to Payment

Mortgage payments may be applied in different ways, depending on the loan documents at issue in the case. Generally, when a payment is made, a certain percentage or amount of the payment will be applied to principal, a certain percentage or amount will be applied to interest, and a certain percentage or amount will be applied to escrow. The amount of the application of payments to a particular category is important. The order in which payments are applied becomes important, as well, in the case of a payment that is for less than the full amount due.

A defendant in foreclosure may raise as an affirmative defense that the plaintiff has misapplied certain payments that were made.[73] Standing alone, a misapplication

---

[67] *Seaside Cmty. Dev. Corp. v. Edward*, 573 So. 2d 142, 145 (Fla. 1st DCA 1991); *Allstate Floridian Ins. Co. v. Farmer*, 104 So. 3d 1242, 1246 (Fla. 5th DCA 2012); *Samaroo v. Wells Fargo Bank*, 137 So. 3d 1127, 1129 (Fla. 5th DCA 2014), *U.S. Bank Nat'l Ass'n v. Busquets*, 135 So. 3d 488, 490 (Fla. 2d DCA 2014).

[68] *Ortiz v. PNC Bank, N.A.*, 188 So. 3d 923, 925 (Fla. 4th DCA 2016); *Green Tree Servicing, LLC v. Milam*, 177 So. 3d 7, 13-14 (Fla. 2d DCA 2015).

[69] *Alvarez v. Rendon*, 953 So. 2d 702, 708-09 (Fla. 5th DCA 2007).

[70] *Palma v. JP Morgan Chase Bank*, 208 So. 3d 771, 775 (Fla. 5th DCA 2016). *See also Derouin v. Universal Am. Mortg. Co., LLC*, No. 2D17-1002, 2018 WL 3999415, *passim* (Fla. 2d DCA Aug. 22, 2018).

[71] *DeLong v. Lakeview Loan Servicing, LLC*, 222 So. 3d 662 (Fla. 5th DCA 2017).

[72] *See Beacon Hill Homeowners Ass'n v. Colfin AH-Florida 7, LLC*, 221 So. 3d 710 (Fla. 3d DCA 2017).

[73] *Vargas v. Deutsche Bank Nat'l Trust Co.*, 104 So. 3d 1156, 1158 n.2 (Fla. 3d DCA 2012) (noting that misapplication of payments was raised as an affirmative defense in the trial court proceeding); *Pemco, Inc. v. American Gen. Home Equity*, 629 So. 2d 307, 308 (Fla. 2d DCA 1993) (holding that the question of misapplication of payments presented an issue of material fact sufficient to withstand a motion for summary judgment).

of payments should not be sufficient to deny foreclosure of a mortgage.[74] Moreover, where a default would exist notwithstanding any misapplication of payments, the misapplication is not a defense to foreclosure unless the ultimate facts establish that the defendant ceased making payments because of the alleged misapplication.[75] A tender of payment, on the other hand, when proper and timely, effects a satisfaction of the defendant's pending mortgage obligations.[76]

7-3:5 Waiver

Depending upon the facts, waiver may be a valid defense to foreclosure.[77] Waiver is the voluntary and intentional relinquishment of a known right.[78] The elements of the defense of waiver, therefore, are the existence of a right, actual or constructive knowledge of the right, and the intent to relinquish the right.[79] Proof of waiver may be express or implied.[80]

7-3:6 Other Defenses to Foreclosure

Defendants may raise any number of other defenses to foreclosure, with varying success rates. A defendant may argue that there is a failure of consideration for the note and/or mortgage, rendering same unenforceable.[81] However, under certain circumstances, a failure of consideration should be raised as a claim for damages.[82] A defendant may allege that the loan documents were procured by fraud, and may seek to affirm the agreement and claim money damages or claim rescission.[83] Estoppel is a valid defense to mortgage foreclosure.[84]

Further, mortgage foreclosure proceedings are equitable in nature.[85] Therefore, the defense of unclean hands may avoid an action for foreclosure of a mortgage.[86] The defense of unclean hands, like fraud, must be pleaded with precision.[87] A plaintiff's unclean hands may be based on inequitable conduct, but only if it impregnates the entire cause of action.[88]

---

[74] *Lunn Woods v. Lowery*, 577 So. 2d 705, 707 (Fla. 2d DCA 1991).
[75] *First Nat'l Bank v. Braun*, 474 So. 2d 386, 388 (Fla. 2d DCA 1985).
[76] *Paneson v. Paneson*, 825 So. 2d 523, 524 (Fla. 2d DCA 2002); *Wash. Mut. Bank, F.A. v. Shelton*, 892 So. 2d 547, 549-50 (Fla. 2d DCA 2005).
[77] *See Kimmick v. United States Bank Nat'l Ass'n*, 83 So. 3d 877, *passim* (Fla. 4th DCA 2012).
[78] *Raymond James Fin. Servs., Inc. v. Saldukas*, 896 So. 2d 707, 711 (Fla. 2005).
[79] *Bueno v. Workman*, 20 So. 3d 993, 998 (Fla. 4th DCA 2009).
[80] *Raymond James Fin. Servs., Inc. v. Saldukas*, 896 So. 2d 707, 711 (Fla. 2005).
[81] *Kresmer v. Tonokaboni*, 356 So. 2d 1331, 1332 (Fla. 3d DCA 1978).
[82] *Duncan Properties, Inc. v. Key Largo Ocean View, Inc.*, 360 So. 2d 471, 472-73 (Fla. 3d DCA 1978).
[83] *Meyerson v. Boyce*, 97 So. 2d 488, 489 (Fla. 3d DCA 1957).
[84] *Parker v. Dinsmore Co.*, 443 So. 2d 356, 358 (Fla. 1st DCA 1983); *Lambert v. Dracos*, 403 So. 2d 481, 482 (Fla. 1st DCA 1981).
[85] *Knight Energy Servs. v. Amoco Oil Co.*, 660 So. 2d 786, 788-89 (Fla. 4th DCA 1995).
[86] *Knight Energy Servs. v. Amoco Oil Co.*, 660 So. 2d 786, 788-89 (Fla. 4th DCA 1995).
[87] *Congress Park Office II, LLC v. First-Citizens Bank & Trust Co.*, 105 So. 3d 602, 609 (Fla. 4th DCA 2013).
[88] *Congress Park Office II, LLC v. First-Citizens Bank & Trust Co.*, 105 So. 3d 602, 609 (Fla. 4th DCA 2013).

A defendant may also allege that a plaintiff failed to pay the documentary stamp tax, pursuant to section 201.08, Florida Statutes. If a plaintiff does not pay the documentary stamp tax on all or part of the principal, then the note and mortgage at issue in a foreclosure action are not enforceable, until such taxes are paid.[89] This problem arises chiefly in cases in which a note is modified, the principal balance is increased, and the modification is not recorded, prior to trial. Although arguments regarding the documentary stamp tax may be framed as an affirmative defense, it is not necessary for defendants to so frame the issue, and the failure to pay the tax may be raised for the first time at trial, or even on appeal.[90]

Additionally, a defendant may raise purported violations of any of a number of federal or state statutory schemes relating to consumers or real property. Violations of the Fair Debt Collection Practices Act,[91] the Florida Consumer Collection Practices Act,[92] the Truth in Lending Act,[93] the Real Estate Settlement Procedures Act,[94] and many other statutory schemes may be alleged by a defendant as an avoidance of mortgage foreclosure. For a detailed discussion of the use of these defenses (or claims), please see Chapter 8: Statutory Claims and Defenses. As with the defense of failure of consideration, many of these defenses are more appropriately raised as counterclaims.[95] Moreover, certain routinely-attempted defenses, such as the claim that a plaintiff lacks capacity to sue, are required to be raised by specific negative averment, meaning a specific denial in the answer section of a defendant's pleading.[96] No list of defenses that may be pleaded in a foreclosure action will be completely exhaustive, and other defenses may have alleged or real application.

7-3:7 Motions to Strike Affirmative Defenses

Where an affirmative defense is not legally sufficient on its face or does not present a bona fide issue of fact, it is proper to strike the defense.[97] A motion to strike an affirmative defense tests the legal sufficiency of the defense.[98] The striking of pleadings is not favored.[99] A defense which lacks certainty or which states the pleader's conclusions, rather than the ultimate facts necessary to sustain the defense, is legally deficient.[100]

---

[89] *Nikooie v. JP Morgan Chase Bank, N.A.*, 183 So. 3d 424, *passim* (Fla. 3d DCA 2014).

[90] *Nikooie v. JP Morgan Chase Bank, N.A.*, 183 So. 3d 424, 430-31 (Fla. 3d DCA 2014). *See also Schroeder v. MTGLQ Investors, L.P.*, 4D18-3177 (Fla. 4th DCA 2019).

[91] 15 U.S.C. § 1692; *Kass Shuler, P.A. v. Barchard*, 120 So. 3d 165, 166-67 (Fla. 2d DCA 2013).

[92] Fla. Stat. § 559.72; *Kass Shuler, P.A. v. Barchard*, 120 So. 3d 165, 166-67 (Fla. 2d DCA 2013).

[93] 15 U.S.C. §§ 1602, 1640; *Beach v. Great Western Bank*, 692 So. 2d 146, *passim* (Fla. 1997).

[94] 12 U.S.C. §§ 2601-2617; *Good v. Deutsche Bank Nat'l Trust Co.*, 98 So. 3d 1255, 1256 (Fla. 4th DCA 2012).

[95] *See* Fla. R. Civ. P. 1.110(d); Fla. R. Civ. P. 1.170; *Block v. Orlando-Orange Cnty. Expressway Authority*, 313 So. 2d 75, 76-77 (Fla. 4th DCA 1975).

[96] *Wilmington Sav. Fund Soc'y, FSB v. Contreras*, 2019 Fla. App. LEXIS 11698, 2019 WL 3366143, No. 5D18-2401 (Fla. 5th DCA July 26, 2019).

[97] *Hulley v. Cape Kennedy Leasing Corp.*, 376 So. 2d 884, 885 (Fla. 5th DCA 1979).

[98] *Burns v. Equilease Corp.*, 357 So. 2d 786, 787 (Fla. 3d DCA 1978).

[99] *Hulley v. Cape Kennedy Leasing Corp.*, 376 So. 2d 884, 885 (Fla. 5th DCA 1979).

[100] *Ellison v. City of Fort Lauderdale*, 175 So. 2d 198, 200 (Fla. 1965); *Cady v. Chevy Chase Sav. & Loan, Inc.*, 528 So. 2d 136, 137-38 (Fla. 4th DCA 1988); *Bliss v. Carmona*, 418 So. 2d 1017, 1019 (Fla. 3d DCA 1982).

Additionally, a defense which merely denies a plaintiff's claim is improperly raised, as it does not seek to avoid the claim in the event that the claim is proven.[101]

As an alternative basis of moving to strike an affirmative defense, a plaintiff may successfully argue that defenses have been waived or that a defendant is judicially estopped from pursuing a defense. In foreclosure disputes, waiver or judicial estoppel may often occur due to a surrender in bankruptcy proceedings.[102] Where property has been surrendered, a trial court may take judicial notice of the bankruptcy proceedings, strike affirmative defenses, and hold that a defendant is estopped from defending against the foreclosure action.[103]

A plaintiff may move to strike affirmative defenses under either Rule 1.140(f), Florida Rules of Civil Procedure or Rule 1.150, Florida Rules of Civil Procedure. Rule 1.140(f) permits a motion to strike portions of a pleading which are redundant, immaterial, impertinent, or scandalous.[104] Rule 1.150 permits a motion to strike a pleading which is a sham. A sham pleading is one which is inherently false and clearly known to be false at the time the pleading was made.[105] A full evidentiary hearing is required under Rule 1.150.[106] A pleading may be stricken with or without leave to amend.[107]

---

[101] *State Farm Auto. Ins. Co. v. Curran*, 135 So. 3d 1071, 1079 (Fla. 2014) (quoting *St. Paul Mercury Ins. Co. v. Coucher*, 837 So. 2d 483, 487 (Fla. 5th DCA 2002)).
[102] *See Sayles v. Nationstar Mortg., LLC*, 268 So. 3d 723, 727 (Fla. 4th DCA 2018).
[103] *Sayles v. Nationstar Mortg., LLC*, 268 So. 3d 723, 727 (Fla. 4th DCA 2018).
[104] Fla. R. Civ. P. 1.140(f).
[105] *Cromer v. Mullally*, 861 So. 2d 523, 525 (Fla. 3d DCA 2003).
[106] *Reyes v. Roush*, 99 So. 3d 586, 590-91 (Fla. 2d DCA 2012).
[107] *See Easterly v. Wildman*, 99 So. 359, 361 (Fla. 1924).

CHAPTER 8
Statutory Claims and Defenses

Ileen J. Cantor

8-1 Statutory Claims and Defenses

Florida state courts routinely entertain federal and state statutory claims as counterclaims or affirmative defenses in state foreclosure actions.[1] Some provisions of these statutes provide for potential affirmative defenses to foreclosure, but they are few and far between. An affirmative defense is a defense which admits the cause of action, but avoids liability, in whole or in part, by alleging an excuse, justification, or other matter negating or limiting liability.[2] Hence, a statutory defense typically must admit the foreclosure plaintiff otherwise has a right to a foreclosure judgment but asserts that even so, a particular statute forbids the plaintiff's foreclosure claim. More often than not these statutory provisions are more effectively asserted as counterclaims.[3]

---

[1] *See Alejandre v. Deutsche Bank Trust Co. Amer.*, 44 So. 3d 1288, 1289 (Fla. 4th DCA 2010); *Dailey v. Leshin*, 792 So. 2d 527 (Fla. 4th DCA 2001); *Katline Realty Corp. v. Avedon*, 183 So. 3d 415, 417 (Fla. 3d DCA 2014); *Vidal v. Liquidation Props.*, 104 So. 3d 1274, 1278 (Fla. 4th DCA 2013).

[2] *St. Paul Mercury Ins. Co. v. Coucher*, 837 So. 2d 483 (Fla. 5th DCA 2002). *See Wiggins v. Portmay Corp.*, 430 So. 2d 541, 542 (Fla. 1st DCA 1983) ("Affirmative defenses do not simply deny the facts of the opposing party's claim. They raise some new matter which defeats an otherwise apparently valid claim.").

[3] It is beyond the scope of this chapter to discuss whether borrowers must assert certain statutory counterclaims in their foreclosure suits or risk waiving them pursuant to *res judicata* and the compulsory counterclaim rule. *See Iannucci v. Bank of Am., NA*, No. 2:14-cv-106-FtM-38DNF, 2014 U.S. Dist. LEXIS 74699, 2014 WL 2462978, at *3 (M.D. Fla. June 2, 2014) (noting the court's inclination to agree, although not deciding, that a TILA claim was a compulsory counterclaim to the state foreclosure action); *In re Tomasevic*, 275 B.R. 86, 101 (Bankr. M.D. Fla. 2001) (the debtor's claim under this section of the TILA was "clearly a compulsory counterclaim to the bank's claim for principal, interest, escrow advances, and late fees at issue and decided in the foreclosure action."); *Harper v. Chase Manhattan Bank*, 138 F. App'x 130, 133 (11th Cir. 2005) (mortgagor's federal statutory claims, including TILA and FDCPA claims, were barred under the *Rooker-Feldman* abstention doctrine because they were inextricably intertwined with an earlier foreclosure proceeding in state court and mortgagor could have raise these claims in the state court).

8-2 The Truth in Lending Act (TILA)

The Truth in Lending Act (TILA)[4] is a disclosure statute, the main purpose of which is to ensure borrowers are fully aware of the cost of credit.[5] TILA is an arduous statute with its own body of federal case law and lengthy federal regulations. The Dodd-Frank Wall Street Reform and Consumer Protection Act of 2010 (Dodd-Frank Act)[6] generally granted rulemaking authority under the TILA to the Consumer Financial Protection Bureau (CFPB).[7] Presently, borrowers rarely assert a TILA violation as an affirmative defense or a counterclaim to a foreclosure claim. Their attempts to do so in the past have, for the most part, proved unsuccessful.[8]

8-2:1 The Home Ownership and Equity Protection Act (HOEPA)

The Home Ownership and Equity Protection Act (HOEPA) was enacted in 1994 as an amendment to TILA to address abusive practices in refinances and closed-end home equity loans with high interest rates or high fees.[9] The purpose of both HOEPA and TILA is to provide up-front information to potential buyers so that they can assess the true cost of the loan they are about to take.[10] The law imposed new disclosure requirements and substantive limitations on certain closed-end mortgage loans bearing rates or fees above a certain percentage or amount, termed "high-cost mortgages."[11] Among other things, the statute provides that mortgage loans subject to HOEPA may not provide for an interest rate after default that is higher than the interest rate that applies before default[12] or contain terms imposing a prepayment penalty on a consumer for paying all or part of the principal before it is due.[13] The law also included new disclosure requirements to assist consumers in comparing the costs and other material considerations involved in a reverse mortgage transaction and authorized

---

[4] 15 U.S.C. § 1601 *et seq.* TILA was enacted on May 29, 1968, as title I of the Consumer Credit Protection Act (Pub. L. 90-321). The TILA, implemented by Regulation Z (12 C.F.R. § 1026), became effective July 1, 1969.

[5] 15 U.S.C. § 1601.

[6] Dodd-Frank Wall Street Reform and Consumer Protection Act, 12 U.S.C. §§ 5301*et seq.*

[7] The Consumer Financial Protection Bureau is the agency charged with interpreting the Truth in Lending Act (TILA) and promulgating rules to effectuate its purposes, 15 U.S.C.S. §§ 1602(b), 1604(a). The regulations implementing TILA are known as "Regulation Z," 12 C.F.R. pt. 1026.

[8] *See Monnot v. U.S. Bank, Nat'l Ass'n*, 188 So. 3d 896, 900 (Fla. 4th DCA 2016) (borrower unsuccessfully asserted affirmative defenses and a counterclaim which alleged a lack of compliance with TILA, Regulation Z, and untruthful disclosures in the TILA Statement, made by the original lender, as to the finance charges and APR on his mortgage loan); *Henderson v. Deutsche Bank Nat'l Tr. Co.*, 158 So. 3d 705, 705 (Fla. 4th DCA 2015) (trial court did not err in denying relief on the borrowers' counterclaim under TILA).

[9] *See* 15 U.S.C. §§ 1639 *et seq.*

[10] *Katline Realty Corp. v. Avedon*, 183 So. 3d 415, 420 (Fla. 3d DCA 2014).

[11] 15 U.S.C. § 1602(bb) currently defines "high-cost mortgages" by applying three different tests, any one of which will bring a mortgage loan within HOEPA's scope. Historically, these transactions have been referred to as "HOEPA loans" or as "Section 32 loans." The latter name is used because the HOEPA rules are found in Section 32 of Regulation Z (12 C.F.R. § 226.32), which prescribes the required disclosures for covered loans.

[12] 15 U.S.C. § 1639(d).

[13] 15 U.S.C. § 1639(c).

the Federal Reserve Board to prohibit specific acts and practices in connection with mortgage transactions.

Since HOEPA's enactment, refinances or home equity mortgage loans meeting any of HOEPA's three high-cost mortgage tests have been subject to special disclosure requirements and restrictions on loan terms. Consumers with high-cost mortgages have had enhanced remedies for violations of the law.[14]

In January 2013, after the passage of the Dodd-Frank Act,[15] the Consumer Financial Protection Bureau issued the *2013 HOEPA Rule*,[16] which amends TILA's Regulation Z to implement the Dodd-Frank Act's changes to HOEPA, which, among other things, expanded the scope of HOEPA coverage to include purchase money mortgages and home equity lines of credit. The new requirements in Regulation Z only apply to transactions that occurred on or after January 10, 2014.[17] In November 2018, the Bureau updated the Small Entity Compliance Guide regarding the HOEPA Rule to reflect changes made by the Economic Growth, Regulatory Relief, and Consumer Protection Act.[18]

A borrower alleging a HOEPA violation is entitled to actual and statutory damages as a defense of recoupment or setoff against an action for collection of the debt, even when a claim for rescission would be barred by TILA's statute of limitations.[19] Borrowers who assert TILA or HOEPA counterclaims for actual damages must establish they were harmed because of the statutory violation.[20]

Any mortgage containing a provision prohibited by HOEPA must be treated as a failure to deliver material disclosures under TILA, thereby subjecting the loan transaction to TILA remedies.[21] Those remedies include recovery of twice the amount of any finance charge made in connection with the transaction not to exceed $2,000 in the case of an individual action on a non-open-ended credit plan.[22]

8-2:2 TILA Rescission

Lenders originating refinance transactions and home equity transactions secured by a consumer's principal dwelling must include a notice to the borrower of the borrow-

---

[14] 2013 Home Ownership and Equity Protection Act (HOEPA) Rule Small Entity Compliance Guide found at http://business.cch.com/BANKD/HOEPA-Guide.pdf (last visited September 8, 2019).

[15] Dodd-Frank Wall Street Reform and Consumer Protection Act, 12 U.S.C. §§ 5301-641. The relevant Dodd-Frank amendments, however, were not effective until January 10, 2014. *See Berneike v. CitiMortgage, Inc.*, 708 F.3d 1141, 1145 n.3 (10th Cir. 2013).

[16] 12 C.F.R. § 1026.32.

[17] *See Berneike v. CitiMortgage*, 708 F.3d 1141, 1145 n.3 (10th Cir. 2013).

[18] Home Ownership and Equity Protection Act (HOEPA) Rule Small Entity Compliance Guide (Updated) found at https://files.consumerfinance.gov/f/documents/bcfp_hoepa_small-entity_compliance-guide.pdf (last visited September 8, 2019).

[19] *Martinec v. Early Bird Int'l, Inc.*, 126 So. 3d 1115, 1118 (Fla. 4th DCA 2012).

[20] 15 U.S.C. § 1640(a)(1).

[21] 15 U.S.C. § 1639(j).

[22] 15 U.S.C. § 1640(a)(2). The term "open-end credit plan" is defined as a plan "under which the creditor reasonably contemplates repeated transactions, which prescribes the terms of such transactions, and which provides for a finance charge that may be computed from time to time on the outstanding unpaid balance." 15 U.S.C. § 1602(j).

er's right to rescind the transaction within three business days.[23] If the lender fails to disclose that rescission right or fails to disclose a material cost of the transaction, the borrower has the right to rescind the contract within three *years* of the closing.[24] The three years is a statute of repose, not limitations, so the expiring of the time will be an absolute bar, whether or not the borrower was aware of the violation.[25] A consumer cannot rescind a purchase money mortgage or a construction loan mortgage.[26]

After the initiation of foreclosure on the consumer's principal dwelling, the consumer has the opportunity to rescind if: (i) A mortgage broker fee that should have been included in the finance charge was not included; or (ii) The creditor did not provide the properly completed appropriate model form in Appendix H of this part, or a substantially similar notice of rescission.[27]

Although rescission of a mortgage loan was a popular defense when the mortgage crisis began in 2008, foreclosure defendants rarely use it now. Rescission is a unique remedy which requires borrowers to return "the money or property to the creditor."[28] This is normally a sobering problem for borrowers in foreclosure, who lack enough funds to return the money borrowed and do not want to relinquish the property.

8-2:3 TILA Damages

A lender's TILA violations could give rise to a claim for actual damages,[29] statutory damages, and attorneys' fees.[30] Statutory damages are capped to twice the finance charge, but not less than $400 and not more than $4,000.[31]

A borrower may raise TILA non-compliance as a defense to a foreclosure through recoupment or a setoff regardless of the time limit applicable to TILA damages claims.[32]

8-3 The Real Estate and Settlement Procedures Act (RESPA)

The Real Estate Settlement Procedures Act of 1974 (RESPA)[33] requires lenders, mortgage brokers, or servicers of home loans to provide borrowers with pertinent and timely disclosures regarding the nature and costs of the real estate settlement pro-

---

[23] 12 C.F.R. § 226.23(a), (b).
[24] 15 U.S.C. §§ 1635(a), (f).
[25] *Beach v. Ocwen F.S.B.*, 523 U.S. 410, 417 (1998) (stating that the language in Section 1635(f) "talks not of a suit's commencement but of a right's duration, which it addresses in terms so straightforward as to render any limitation of the time for seeking a remedy superfluous").
[26] 12 C.F.R. § 226.23(f)(1) and 12 C.F.R. § 226.2(24).
[27] 12 C.F.R. § 226.23(h).
[28] 12 C.F.R. § 226.23(d)(3).
[29] Borrowers must prove the TILA violation *caused* the actual damages. 15 U.S.C. § 1640(a)(1) ("any actual damage sustained by such person *as a result of the failure*. . . .") (emphasis added).
[30] 15 U.S.C. § 1640.
[31] 15 U.S.C. § 1640(a)(2)(A)(i).
[32] 15 U.S.C. § 1640(k).
[33] 12 U.S.C. § 2601 *et seq.*

cess. RESPA also provides that those making or servicing mortgage loans must make certain disclosures relating to the servicing of the loan.[34]

The lender must disclose, at the time of application, whether the servicing of the loan may be assigned, sold, or transferred to any other person at any time while the loan is outstanding.[35] Further, the loan servicer must generally notify the borrower of any assignment, sale or transfer of the servicing of the loan within 15 days before the effective date of the transfer.[36] RESPA does not require notice when the underlying note or mortgage is transferred.[37]

In addition to these automatic disclosures, RESPA requires that a loan servicer respond to a *qualified written request* (QWR)[38] from borrowers and to written requests of "information relating to the servicing of such loan."[39] Servicing is defined as "receiving any scheduled periodic payments from a borrower pursuant to the terms of any loan . . . and making the payments of principal and interest and such other payments with respect to the amounts received from the borrower as may be required pursuant to the terms of the loan."[40] Courts have ruled that loan modifications do not relate to the servicing of mortgage loans so that loan servicers are not obligated to respond to QWRs related to a loan modification.[41] Similarly, courts have ruled that once a borrower defaults on a loan and the servicer is no longer accepting scheduled periodic payments, the *servicer* is no longer a "servicer" of the loan as defined by RESPA and is not obligated to respond to QWRs.[42]

---

[34] 12 U.S.C. §§ 2605(a), (b).
[35] 12 U.S.C. § 2605(a).
[36] 12 U.S.C. § 2605(b).
[37] *See generally* 12 U.S.C. § 2605.
[38] "Qualified written request" is a written correspondence that enables the servicer to identify the name and account of the borrower and contains a statement of the reasons for the borrower's belief that the account is in error, or provides sufficient detail to the servicer regarding other information sought by the borrower. 12 U.S.C. § 2605(e)(1)(B).
[39] 12 U.S.C. § 2605(e); *see also* 24 C.F.R. § 3500.21(e).
[40] 12 U.S.C. § 2605(i)(3).
[41] *See Beacham v. Bank of America, N.A.*, No. 3:12-CV-00801-G, 2012 U.S. Dist. LEXIS 86106, 2012 WL 2358299, at * 3 (N.D. Tex. May 25, 2012) (unpublished) ("Requesting information regarding loss mitigation review does not relate to 'servicing' of a loan as provided in 2605(i)(3)."); *Yakowicz v. BAC Home Loans Servicing, LP*, No. 12-1180, 2013 U.S. Dist. LEXIS 20586, 2013 WL 593902, at *5 (D. Minn. Feb. 15, 2013) (unpublished) (letters seeking loan modification "do not constitute QWRs"); *Van Egmond v. Wells Fargo Home Mortg.*, No. SACV 12-0112, 2012 U.S. Dist. LEXIS 42061, 2012 WL 1033281, at *4 (C.D. Cal. Mar. 21, 2012) (unpublished) (similar); *In re Salvador*, 456 B.R. 610, 623 (Bankr. M.D. Ga. 2011) (similar); *Williams v. Wells Fargo Bank, N.A.*, Inc., No. C 10-00399, 2010 U.S. Dist. LEXIS 36247, 2010 WL 1463521, at *3 (N.D. Cal. Apr. 13, 2010) (unpublished) (similar)).
[42] *Daw v. Peoples Bank & Trust Co.*, 5 Fed. Appx. 504, 505 (7th Cir. 2001) (concluding that once the plaintiff defaulted on the loan, the bank was no longer accepting scheduled periodic payments and was therefore not a "servicer" of the loan); *Sanchez v. OneWest Bank, FSB*, No. 11CV 6820, 2013 U.S. Dist. LEXIS 3861, 2013 WL 139870, at *3 (N.D. Ill. Jan. 10, 2013) (dismissing with prejudice RESPA and TILA claims because the judicial sale of the property had been approved and the bank therefore could not have been "servicing" the loan); *Toscione v. Wells Fargo*, No. 8:13-CV-02065-T-27AEP, 2013 U.S. Dist. LEXIS 189690, at *1 (M.D. Fla. Sept. 17, 2013) (unpublished) (after plaintiff's mortgage had been foreclosed and sold at judicial sale, servicer was not "servicing" the loan within the meaning of 12 U.S.C. § 2605(e)(1)(A)).

8-3:1 RESPA Claims

RESPA creates a private right of action for only three types of wrongful acts: (1) payment of a kickback and unearned fees for real estate settlement services,[43] (2) requiring a buyer to use a title insurer selected by the seller,[44] and (3) the failure by a loan servicer to give proper notice of a transfer of servicing rights or to respond to a QWR for information about a loan.[45] RESPA claims brought under 12 U.S.C. §§ 2607 or 2608 are subject to a one-year statute of limitation, while claims under 12 U.S.C. § 2605 are governed by a three-year statute of limitations, which begins running when the violation occurs.[46] Unlike TILA, RESPA does not contain a provision permitting its violations to be pled in a foreclosure proceeding as a setoff defense or a recoupment counterclaim.

8-4 FHA Home Loan Defenses

An FHA residential mortgage loan is insured by the federal government through the Federal Housing Administration (FHA).[47] This agency is part of the Department of Housing and Urban Development (HUD). The full name of this program is the HUD 203(b) Mortgage Insurance Program, commonly referred to as "FHA loans."[48]

Because HUD sets all the guidelines for this program, most FHA loans contain language that reference, in varying ways, HUD regulations. Typically, FHA (form) notes and mortgages contain language that a lender's option, upon a borrower's payment default, to require immediate payment in full and to foreclose, is not authorized if not permitted by HUD regulations.[49]

Based on such language, some Florida courts have ruled that an FHA loan's language referring generally to HUD regulations *incorporates* those regulations into the subject loans as *contractual* conditions precedent to foreclosure.[50] Nonetheless, fed-

---

[43] 12 U.S.C. §§ 2607(a), (b).

[44] 12 U.S.C. § 2608(b).

[45] 12 U.S.C. § 2605(f).

[46] 12 U.S.C. § 2614.

[47] The FHA was created with the passing of the National Housing Act in 1934. The FHA's original mission was to make home loans available to a larger number of Americans, primarily by giving lenders an added layer of protection and insurance.

[48] This program is authorized under Section 203, National Housing Act (12 U.S.C. 1709 (b), (i)). Program regulations are in 24 CFR Part 203.

[49] *See Chrzuszcz v. Wells Fargo Bank, N.A.*, 250 So. 3d 766, 767 (Fla. 1st DCA 2018); *Palma v. JPMorgan Chase Bank, NA*, 208 So. 3d 771, 773 (Fla. 5th DCA 2016).

[50] *Laws v. Wells Fargo Bank, N.A.*, 159 So. 3d 918, 919 (Fla. 1st DCA 2015) ("Because the note contains language specifically and expressly incorporating HUD regulations that require a written notice of acceleration, Laws was entitled to raise failure to comply with these regulations as a valid defense to foreclosure." *Id.*); *Palma v. JPMorgan Chase Bank, NA*, 208 So. 3d 771, 773 (Fla. 5th DCA 2016) (held the FHA note and mortgage clearly required compliance with HUD regulations); *Chrzuszcz v. Wells Fargo Bank, N.A.*, 250 So. 3d 766, 767 (Fla. 1st DCA 2018); *White v. Planet Home Lending, LLC*, 234 So. 3d 802 (Fla. 4th DCA 2018) (*per curiam*) (noting identical language in *Palma* mortgage contained in subject mortgage and approving of *Palma* court's finding such language incorporated the federal regulations as condition precedents). *But see Echeverria v. BAC Home Loans*, 2012 U.S. Dist. LEXIS 44487, 2012 WL 1081176 at *3 (M.D. Fla. Mar. 30, 2012) (court rejected the plaintiff's contention that compliance with HUD regulations was a precondition to foreclosure).

eral courts uniformly have rejected attempts by borrowers to bring affirmative causes of action under HUD's mortgage servicing regulations.[51]

FHA loan borrowers are asserting with increasing frequency either specific denials of lenders' general allegations of compliance with conditions precedent or affirmative defenses to foreclosure claiming non-compliance with a laundry list of various HUD regulations. The regulations applicable to federally insured mortgages are found in Part 203, Title 24, C.F.R. for Single-Family Mortgage Insurance.[52]

It is beyond the scope of this chapter to analyze each of the various regulations FHA foreclosure defendants are utilizing as a shield to foreclosure, but some are worth mentioning. Pursuant to the regulations, if the account is in default, the mortgagee is required to give notice to the mortgagor on a form approved by the Secretary no later than the end of the second month of any delinquency in payments.[53]

If the account is delinquent after the end of the second month, 24 C.F.R. § 203.604(b) requires a face-to-face interview with the mortgagor or a reasonable effort (defined as at least one letter by certified mail and at least one visit to the property) to arrange such a meeting, before three full monthly installments due on the loan are not paid. Some uncommon exceptions apply.[54] Strict compliance with 24 C.F.R. 203.604 means that mortgagees and their servicers have only one point in time when they can comply with this regulation—after the end of the second month but before the third month that an FHA borrower has not made his mortgage payment. Thus, a literal reading of this regulation would mean that if a servicer misses this one-time deadline, foreclo-

---

[51] *In re Miller*, 124 Fed. Appx. 152 (4th Cir. 2005) (no private right of action for failure to comply with NHA's loss mitigation requirements); *Hall v. BAC Home Loans*, 2013 U.S. Dist. LEXIS 71645, 2013 WL 2248253, at *4 (N.D. Ala. May 21, 2013) ("Federal courts throughout the country have repeatedly rejected . . . attempts by borrowers to bring claims under the [NHA] and its implementing regulations."); *Roberts v. Cameron-Brown Co.*, 556 F.2d 356, 360, 361 (5th Cir. 1977) (HUD regulations "deal only with the relations between the mortgagee and the government, and give the mortgagor no claim to duty owed nor remedy for failure to follow" and "No evidence exits demonstrating that Congress intended to create a private cause of action under the [NHA]."); *Bates v. JPMorgan Chase*, 768 F.3d 1126, 1130-31 (11th Cir. 2014) ("there is no express or implied statutory right of action for HUD violations") (citing *inter alia*, *Cornelius v. Bank of Am., N.A.*, 2012 U.S. Dist. LEXIS 139173, 2012 WL 4468746, at *16 (N.D. Ga. Sept. 27, 2012), and *Krell v. National Mortg. Corp.*, 214 Ga. App. 503, 504, 448 S.E. 2d 248, 249 (1994) ("holding violation of HUD regulations did not support a private cause of action")); *Coley v. Accredited Home Lenders*, 2011 U.S. Dist. LEXIS 38294, 2011 WL 1193072, at *2 (E.D. Ark. 2011) (lender's failure to advise of home ownership counseling is not actionable because "the National Housing Act 'govern[s]' relations between the mortgagee and the government"); *Mitchell v. Chase Home Fin. LLC*, 2008 U.S. Dist. LEXIS 17040, 2008 WL 623395 (N.D. Tex. 2008) (under the National Housing Act, there is no private right of action available to a mortgagor for a mortgagee's non-compliance); *Deubert v. Gulf Fed. Sav. Bank*, 820 F.2d 754, 758-59 (5th Cir. 1987) ("Our examination of the Cort factors leads us to conclude that no private cause of action can be implied from the National Housing Act."); *Brake v. Wells Fargo*, 2011 U.S. Dist. LEXIS 146875, 2011 WL 6719215, at *5 (M.D. Fla. Dec. 5, 2011).

[52] As noted in *Derouin v. Universal Am. Mortg. Co., Ltd. Liab. Co.*, 254 So. 3d 595, 599 (Fla. 2d DCA 2018), it is apparently unsettled as to whether non-compliance with the regulations must be raised as a defense or as a denial in an answer.

[53] 24 C.F.R. § 203.602.

[54] 24 C.F.R. § 203.604(c).

sure would be forever prohibited and would act as a forfeiture of the property. As at least one court has observed, it is implausible that an HUD regulation, promulgated with respect to the agency's role as an insurer of mortgages, was intended to create a permanent barrier to foreclosure of borrowers who stop making payments.[55]

Interestingly, to date, no Florida appellate court has yet had the opportunity to apply the standard of substantial compliance to these HUD regulation contractual condition precedent defenses. However, substantial compliance is the correct standard to any contractual condition precedent defense, particularly in a foreclosure suit.[56] Other state courts have similarly ruled that strict compliance with these HUD regulations is not required.[57]

Similarly, no Florida appellate court has yet addressed whether the HUD condition precedent defense fails absent prejudice to the borrowers. Likewise, the case law does not qualify the borrower's inability to raise a condition precedent defense due to lack of prejudice only to such defenses related to the default letter.[58]

8-4:1 HUD Counseling

The National Housing Act (NHA) elucidates the criteria of those mortgagors eligible for homeowner counseling: (1) their home must be their principal residence, (2) they are, or are expected to be, unable to make payments due to an involuntary loss of

---

[55] *U.S. Bank Natl. Assn. v. McMullin*, 55 Misc. 3d 1053, 47 N.Y.S.3d 882, 889 (N.Y. Sup. Ct. 2017). In *McMullin*, the court found that the lender substantially complied with the regulations because it made a good faith, reasonable effort over a multi-year period to negotiate a consensual resolution of the borrower's longstanding default before commencing foreclosure, including meeting with the borrower regarding the default (but not on the requisite deadline required by 24 C.F.R. § 203.604), sending numerous letters, offering assistance, considering applications for loan modifications, but ultimately these efforts did not culminate in a resolution.

[56] *Ortiz v. PNC Bank, Nat'l Ass'n*, 188 So. 3d 923, 925 (Fla. 4th DCA 2016) ("[S]ubstantial compliance with conditions precedent is all that is required in the foreclosure context."); Allstate Floridian Ins. Co. v. Farmer, 104 So. 3d 1242, 1246 (Fla. 5th DCA 2012) ("[c]ourts require there to be at least substantial compliance with conditions precedent in order to authorize performance of a contract"); Nationstar Mortgage, LLC v. Craig, 193 So. 3d 74 (Fla. 3d DCA 2016) (held pre-suit notice substantially complied with contractual requirement); Green Tree Servicing, LLC v. Milam, 177 So. 3d 7, 13 (Fla. 2d DCA 2015) ("In Florida, a party's adherence to contractual conditions precedent is evaluated for substantial compliance or substantial performance.").

[57] *See, e.g., Grimaldi v. U.S. Bank Nat'l Ass'n*, Civ. A. No. 16-519 WES, 2018 U.S. Dist. LEXIS 70927, 2018 WL 1997277, at *3 (D.R.I. Apr. 27, 2018) (holding that visiting property of defaulted borrower five years after default and leaving a letter because borrower was not home satisfied requirement of making a reasonable effort at arranging face-to-face meeting); *U.S. Bank Natl. Assn. v. McMullin*, 55 Misc. 3d 1053, 47 N.Y.S.3d 882, 889 (N.Y. Sup. Ct. 2017) (reasoning that § 203.604(b) should not be construed to command an impossibility where lender missed the deadline and could, therefore, never achieve "strict compliance"); *PNC Mortg. v. Garland*, 7th Dist. Mahoning No. 12 MA 222, 2014-Ohio-1173, ¶ 30 (7th Dist. Ohio Mar. 20, 2014) (describing the "specific time deadlines" set out in HUD regulations as "aspirational").

[58] *See Gorel v. Bank of New York Mellon*, 165 So. 3d 44, 47 (Fla. 5th DCA 2015) ("[a]bsent some prejudice, the breach of a condition precedent does not constitute a defense to the enforcement of an otherwise valid contract").

STATUTORY CLAIMS AND DEFENSES   123

income due to death, divorce, involuntary job loss, or (3) due to a significant increase in the basic expenses of the homeowner or an immediate family member of the homeowner.[59]

According to § 1701x of the NHA, a creditor[60] must provide notification of the availability of homeownership counseling no later than 45 days after the date on which the homeowner becomes delinquent.[61]

The Secretary of Housing and Urban Development is required to monitor compliance of creditors with the requirements of homeowner counseling notification and is required to submit a report to Congress at least annually regarding the extent of compliance.[62] The statute is ostensibly aimed at preventing preventable defaults and foreclosures so the government will not need to expend HUD insurance funds.[63]

8-5 Florida Consumer Collection Practices Act

The Florida Consumer Collection Practices Act (FCCPA) prohibits certain collection practices of consumer debt.[64] Such prohibitions apply to any "person," not only debt collectors.[65] The FCCPA lists 19 separate unlawful collection practices, many of which require intent.[66] Foreclosure defendants who assert FCCPA counterclaims may recover actual damages, statutory damages up to $1,000, and attorney's fees with court costs.[67]

One section of the FCCPA, § 559.715, requires the assignee of "the right to bill and collect a consumer debt" to give the debtor written notice of the assignment "as soon as practicable after the assignment is made."[68] Nevertheless, Fla. Stat. § 559.715 does not create a condition precedent to foreclosure.[69] Moreover, the Second District Court of Appeal takes a restrictive view of Fla. Stat. § 559.715 and holds that the statute

---

[59] 12 U.S.C. § 1701x(c)(4).
[60] It is worth noting that § 1701x(c) is directed to *creditors* and not *servicers*.
[61] 12 U.S.C. § 1701x(c)(5)(B).
[62] 12 U.S.C. § 1701x(c)(5)(D)(ii); 12 U.S.C. § 1701x(c)(5)(E).
[63] *See, e.g., Cronkhite v. Kemp*, 741 F. Supp. 822, 826 (E.D. Wash. 1989) (Mortgagor states facially valid claim that HUD did not perform its statutory duty under 12 U.S.C. § 1715u(d) to provide homeownership counseling to mortgagor in need of help and potential relief through HUD "assignment" program.).
[64] Fla. Stat. § 559.72; *Abby v. Paige*, 903 F. Supp. 2d 1330, 1334 (S.D. Fla. 2012).
[65] Fla. Stat. § 559.72.
[66] For example, the FCCPA prohibits communication with a debtor if the person *knows* the debtor has counsel, Fla. Stat. § 559.72(18), disclosure of information concerning a debt *known to be* reasonably disputed by a debtor, Fla. Stat. § 559.72(6), and disclosure to a person other than the debtor or his or her family information affecting the debtor's reputation, *with knowledge or reason to know* the other person does not have a legitimate business need for such information. Fla. Stat. § 559.72(5).
[67] Fla. Stat. § 559.77(2).
[68] Fla. Stat. § 559.715.
[69] *United States Bank N.A. v. Adams*, 219 So. 3d 211, 214 (Fla. 2d DCA 2017); *National Collegiate Student Loan Tr. 2007-1 v. Lipari*, 224 So. 3d 309, 311 (Fla. 5th DCA 2017); *McCall v. HSBC Bank USA, N.A.*, 186 So.3d 1134 (Fla. 1st DCA 2016); *Brindise v. U.S. Bank Nat. Ass'n*, 183 So. 3d 1215, 1221 (Fla. 2d DCA 2016); *Bank of Am., N.A. v. Siefker*, 201 So. 3d 811, 818 (Fla. 4th DCA 2016); *see Deutsche Bank v. Hagstrom*, 203 So. 3d 918, 922-24 (Fla. 2d DCA 2016); *Bank of N.Y. Mellon v. Welker*, 194 So. 3d 1078, 1079-80 (Fla. 2d DCA 2016).

"applies only to assignees of the right to bill and collect a consumer debt not to assignees of the debt itself."[70] "Neither is it an affirmative defense to foreclosure actions; it does not establish a condition precedent and in no other way avoids the claims to foreclose a mortgage and enforce a note."[71]

8-6 The Florida Deceptive and Unfair Trade Practices Act (FDUTPA)

The Florida Deceptive and Unfair Trade Practices Act (FDUTPA) prohibits "[u]nfair methods of competition, unconscionable acts or practices, and unfair or deceptive acts or practices in the conduct of any trade or commerce. . . ."[72] However, since loan servicing and debt collection activities do not fall within the "trade or commerce" requirement of FDUTPA,[73] the Act does not lend itself to a defense or counterclaim to foreclosure.

Nevertheless, FDUTPA violations may be asserted as an action for declaratory judgment. A successful declaratory judgment action can include an award of actual damages, as well as attorneys' fees and costs.[74] Conversely, if an action for purported violations of FDUTPA appears to be frivolous, void of merit, or brought for the purpose of harassment, the court may require the posting of a bond to indemnify the defendant in the event a motion seeking such relief is granted.[75]

FDUTPA claims cannot be based on oral representations which are in contradiction of the written terms of a contract.[76]

---

[70] *Deutsche Bank Nat. Tr. Co. v. Hagstrom*, 203 So. 3d 918, 921 (Fla. 2d DCA 2016).

[71] *Deutsche Bank Nat. Tr. Co. v. Hagstrom*, 203 So. 3d 918, 924 (Fla. 2d DCA 2016).

[72] Fla. Stat. § 501.204.

[73] *See Benjamin v. CitiMortgage, Inc.*, No. 12-62291-CIV, 2013 U.S. Dist. LEXIS 64515, 2013 WL 1891284, at *4 (S.D. Fla. May 6, 2013) ("[E]ven assuming the facts as pled establish that the defendant engaged in deceptive acts or unfair trade practices, the loan servicer's actions do not qualify as 'trade or commerce' under the Act."); *Acosta v. James A. Gustino, P.A.*, No. 6:11-cv-1266-Orl-31GJK (GAP), 2012 U.S. Dist. LEXIS 130656, 2012 WL 4052245, at *1 (M.D. Fla. Sept. 13, 2012) ("[T]he Defendants were not engaged in 'trade or commerce' when they sent demand letters and otherwise engaged in their debt collection efforts, and the Plaintiff has failed to state a claim for violation of FDUPTA."); *Trent v. Mortgage Electronic Registration Systems, Inc.*, 618 F.Supp.2d 1356, 1365 n. 12 (M.D. Fla. 2007) ("The MERS communicated pre-suit with plaintiffs that it was a 'creditor' or 'owned' the debt does not fall within the purview of 'trade or commerce.'"); *see also Acosta v. James A. Gustino, P.A.*, No. 6:11-cv-1266-Orl-31GHK, 2012 U.S. Dist. LEXIS 130656, 2012 WL 4052245, at *1 (M.D. Fla. Sept.13, 2012) (finding that the defendants were not engaged in "trade or commerce" because "attempt[ing] to collect a debt by exercising one's legal remedies does not constitute 'advertising, soliciting, providing, offering, or distributing' as those terms are used in Fla. Stat. § 501.203(8)"); *Economakis v. Butler & Hosch, P.A.*, No. 2:13-CV-832-FTM-38DN, 2014 U.S. Dist. LEXIS 26779, 2014 WL 820623, at *2-3 (M.D. Fla. Mar. 3, 2014) (citing *Begelfer v. Najarian*, 381 Mass. 177, 191, 409 N.E.2d 167 (1980)).

[74] Fla. Stat. § 501.211(1) and (2).

[75] Fla. Stat. § 501.211(3).

[76] *Mac-Gray Serv., Inc. v. DeGeorge*, 913 So. 2d 630, 634 (Fla. 4th DCA 2005).

CHAPTER 9

Litigating With Associations in the Foreclosure Context

Michael Starks

9-1 Introduction

This chapter deals only with homeowners and condominium associations in the context of foreclosure and post-foreclosure actions, and is not an attempt to analyze the whole of association law in Florida.[1] This chapter also does not address potential tort liability of associations or their counsel related to baseless lien recordations,[2] nor does it discuss litigation with receivers dealing with associations.[3] This chapter does, however, intend to analyze litigation that arises from association involvement in foreclosures, both during the foreclosure and after the foreclosure judgment and sale.[4]

9-2 Pre-Foreclosure

Before a foreclosure action is filed, the foreclosing lender should run a title report and be sure to name (and serve) any and all associations as defendants in the foreclosure. Care must be taken, for there is often more than one association *vis à vis* a given property. Joinder of the association is not required if, on the date the complaint is filed, the

---

[1] To the extent one desires such an analysis, Florida Community Association Litigation: Homeowners' Associations and Condominiums, by Ron M. Campbell, published by The ALM/Daily Business Review, is highly instructive.
[2] *See generally AGM Inv'rs, LLC v. Bus. Law Grp., P.A.*, 219 So. 3d 920 (Fla. 2d DCA 2017).
[3] *Fed. Nat'l Mortgage Ass'n v. JKM Services, LLC for Cedar Woods Homes Condo. Ass'n, Inc.*, 256 So. 3d 961, 967 (Fla. 3d DCA 2018) ("The Receiver's compensation, attorney's fees, and costs, are payable by the non-prevailing party if the receivership was commenced under subsection 718.116(6). . . . In the case of a common law receivership established for the preservation and protection of property involved in a pending lawsuit, the 'courts are generally vested with considerable discretion in determining who shall pay the cost and expenses of receiverships,' though '[r]eceivership fees, being a part of costs, follow the result of the suit.' . . . Under either of these scenarios and sources of authority, FNMA did not move for the Receiver's appointment and was not a party to the 2009 receivership lawsuit until its interests in intervention were asserted by motion. FNMA thus has no apparent obligation on this record to pay the Receiver and related receivership expenses.").
[4] "First mortgagee" is generally used herein as a shorthand for "first mortgagee, its successor or assignees."

association was dissolved or did not maintain an office or agent for service of process at a location that was known to or reasonably discoverable by the mortgagee.[5]

Failure to name an association results in the loss of the statutory "safe harbor" as to that association.[6] Safe harbor is discussed further below, but for introductory purposes, safe harbor is a statutory provision that benefits first mortgagees by tempering the general rule of joint and several liability for dues liability, both for homeowners associations ("HOAs") and condominium associations.[7] Under these safe harbor statutes, a first mortgagee or its successors or assigns is not responsible for any past due assessments for amounts over 12 months of dues, or 1 percent of the mortgage amount, whichever is less.[8]

However, in many cases an association's declaration provides something akin to, or even better than, the statutory safe harbor without the necessity of suing the association, but such may not remove the lien.[9] In any event, if that situation occurs, it is a happy accident,[10] but the wise foreclosure law firm will use wisdom as opposed to

---

[5] Fla. Stat. § 720.3085(2)(c) ("Joinder of the association is not required if, on the date the complaint is filed, the association was dissolved or did not maintain an office or agent for service of process at a location that was known to or reasonably discoverable by the mortgagee."); Fla. Stat. § 718.116(1)(b)1.b. ("Joinder of the association is not required if, on the date the complaint is filed, the association was dissolved or did not maintain an office or agent for service of process at a location which was known to or reasonably discoverable by the mortgagee.").

[6] First mortgagees only get the statutory safe harbor if the association is sued and served in the foreclosure. Fla. Stat. § 720.3085(2)(c) ("The limitations on first mortgagee liability provided by this paragraph apply only if the first mortgagee filed suit against the parcel owner and initially joined the association as a defendant in the mortgagee foreclosure action."); Fla. Stat. § 718.116(1)(b)1.b. ("The provisions of this paragraph apply only if the first mortgagee joined the association as a defendant in the foreclosure action.").

[7] Fla. Stat. § 720.3085(2)(c); Fla. Stat. § 718.116(1)(b).

[8] Fla. Stat. § 720.3085(2)(c); Fla. Stat. § 718.116(1)(b).

[9] *Willoughby Estates v. BankUnited*, 2015 WL 5472506 (Fla. Cir. Ct. Palm Beach June 23, 2015) (three-judge circuit court panel sitting in appellate capacity held that declaration provided safe harbor without requiring the association be sued, but held lien still intact). *But see, Ballantrae Homeowners Ass'n, Inc. v. Fed. Nat. Mortg. Ass'n*, 203 So. 3d 938, 941 (Fla. 2d DCA 2016) ("Fannie Mae points to *Willoughby Estates*. In that case, the declaration specifically provided that any institutional first mortgagee who obtains title to a lot pursuant to foreclosure or deed in lieu of foreclosure 'shall not be liable for any unpaid assessment or charges accrued against said Lot prior to the acquisition of title to said Lot by such Mortgagee.' *Willoughby Estates*, 2015 WL 5472506, at *1. The Fifteenth Judicial Circuit Court of Florida, sitting in its appellate capacity, held that BankUnited's failure to join the association as a defendant in a foreclosure proceeding did not preclude it from taking advantage of the provision absolving it from liability for unpaid assessments that accrued prior to BankUnited acquiring title. *Id*. at *2. The Declaration provision relied on by the trial court in the instant case, however, does not contain such a provision absolving Fannie Mae from liability for any unpaid assessments. Furthermore, the court in *Willoughby* noted that BankUnited's failure to include the association in its foreclosure left the association's lien intact as to the property. *Id*. at *2 (citing *Abdoney*, 903 So. 2d at 983).").

[10] *Ballantrae Homeowners Ass'n, Inc. v. Fed. Nat. Mortg. Ass'n*, 203 So. 3d 938, 940 (Fla. 2d DCA 2016) (Fannie Mae failed to name the association as a defendant, and the court held: "Here, the Declaration's subordination of lien provision relied on by Fannie Mae contains the first promise made in *Ecoventure,* subordinating the assessment lien to the first mort-

fortuity by ensuring that it has named and served all associations relevant to a given property.[11] With homeowners associations, as opposed to condominium associations, the association must be named *from the inception of the case* in order to obtain the statutory safe harbor, due to the word "initially" in Section 720.3082(2)(c).[12]

9-3 During Foreclosure

Normally, unless the association has already taken title from the borrower (and is thus likely renting out the property), the association usually doesn't actively attempt to thwart the mortgagee's foreclosure, as the association usually wants the non-paying borrower out of the property as much as the lender does.[13] Sometimes the associations will even attempt to hurry the mortgagee's foreclosure along, by various means. Sometimes this eagerness to oust the defaulted borrower will cause the association to admit the mortgagee's right to safe harbor in its answer (which it normally should in good faith anyway), prohibiting its ability to challenge safe harbor post-judgment and sale under a waiver doctrine.[14]

---

gage, but it does not contain language specifically limiting or eliminating a subsequent owner's liability for unpaid assessment.").

[11] Failure to name the association will require either paying the association all that it claims, or moving to compel redemption, or re-foreclosure; a declaratory relief action is not a proper mechanism for relief. *Ballantrae Homeowners Ass'n, Inc. v. Fed. Nat. Mortg. Ass'n*, 203 So. 3d 938, 941 (Fla. 2d DCA 2016) ("The only remedies available to the purchaser, here Fannie Mae, against the omitted junior lienor, the Association, are moving to compel redemption or filing a de novo action to re-foreclose."). However, no super-specificity is needed; merely naming the association presumes it is alleged to be a junior lienor. *See Black Point Assets, Inc. v. Fed. Nat'l Mortg. Ass'n (Fannie Mae)*, 220 So. 3d 566, 568-69 (Fla. 5th DCA 2017) ("Black Point provides no support for its argument that the plaintiff needs to allege the superiority of its interest in the property vis-à-vis named defendants. By naming a party in the complaint, the plaintiff provides notice to the named parties that the plaintiff is asserting a superior interest. . . . If the plaintiff succeeds on its claim, the foreclosure will extinguish the interests of parties having an inferior interest. . . . Because every complaint seeking foreclosure necessarily alleges that the plaintiff's interest in the property is superior to the parties' interests being foreclosed, we do not believe a complaint fails to state a claim simply because it does not explicitly state as much.").

[12] *Federal Nat. Mortg. Ass'n v. Mirabella at Mirasol Homeowners' Ass'n, Inc.*, 204 So. 3d 164 (Fla. 4th DCA 2016).

[13] *See U.S. Bank Nat. Ass'n v. Tadmore*, 23 So. 3d 822, 823 (Fla. 3d DCA 2009); *Deutsche Bank Nat'l Trust Co. v. Coral Key Condo. Ass'n*, 32 So. 3d 195 (Fla. 4th DCA 2010).

[14] *See Bank of Am., Nat. Ass'n v. Enclave at Richmond Place Condo. Ass'n*, 173 So. 3d 1095, 1097-98 (Fla. 2d DCA 2015) ("We conclude that the Association's affirmative plea of entitlement to only the lesser of six months' unpaid assessments or one percent of the mortgage debt was a waiver of any claim to a greater assessment figure."). However, judicial estoppel may not be applicable in this circumstance, because generally a party has to prevail on the prior inconsistent position, and additionally, the doctrine has been weakened somewhat in the case of *Anfriany v. Deutsche Bank Nat'l Tr. Co. for Registered Holders of Argent Secs., Inc., Asset-Backed Pass-Through Certificates, Series 2005-W4*, 232 So. 3d 425 (Fla. 4th DCA 2017). The *Anfriany* court also held that Florida law of judicial estoppel differs from federal law. *See id.* For general principles of waiver and judicial estoppel, *see Blumberg v. USAA Cas. Ins.*, 790 So. 2d 1061, 1067 (Fla. 2001) (the doctrine of judicial estoppel prevents parties from "making a mockery of justice by inconsistent pleadings" . . . and "playing fast and loose with the courts"); *DK Arena, Inc. v. EB Acquisitions I, LLC*, 112 So. 3d 85, 97-98

But any attempt by associations to obtain lien priority over a mortgagee as a sanction for delay in the foreclosure will fail,[15] and any attempt by the association to collect dues from the mortgagee before it takes title, due to alleged foreclosure delay, will fail.[16]

Where the association has taken title, and is thus renting the property or intends to do so, that association very well may challenge the foreclosure;[17] of course, the

---

(Fla. 2013) ("Waiver operates to estop one from asserting that upon which he otherwise might have relied...." (quoting *SourceTrack, LLC v. Ariba, Inc.*, 958 So. 2d 523, 527 (Fla. 2d DCA 2007))); *Barbe v. Villeneuve*, 505 So. 2d 1331, 1333 (Fla. 1987) ("A party will not be permitted to enforce wholly inconsistent demands respecting the same right[s]." (quoting *American Process Co. v. Fla. White Pressed Brick Co.*, 56 Fla. 116, 47 So. 942, 944 (1908))); *Tara Woods SPE, LLC v. Cashin*, 116 So. 3d 492, 501 (Fla. 2d DCA 2013) (discussing the elements of waiver and their application).

[15] *U.S. Bank Nat. Ass'n v. Farhood*, 153 So. 3d 955, 959 (Fla. 1st DCA 2014) ("Contrary to its assumption in the order imposing the sanction, the circuit court did not have 'equitable power and authority to give [the Association] first lien priority in this matter,' without regard to the statutes governing such lien priorities. The imposition of sanctions which contravene the recording and lien priority statutes, or the statutes establishing time and amount limits for a mortgagee's liability for condominium assessments, exceed a trial court's discretion and require reversal."). *See also PNC Bank, Nat. Ass'n v. Inlet Vill. Condo. Ass'n, Inc.*, 204 So. 3d 97, 100 (Fla. 4th DCA 2016) ("First, the involuntary dismissal of the Association from the foreclosure action did not render the assessment lien superior to the mortgage lien. The Association was involuntarily dismissed from PNC Bank's 2012 foreclosure action because it was involuntary dismissed from the 2008 foreclosure action as a sanction against the previous bank. This sanction could not, as a matter of law, render the Association's assessment lien superior to the first mortgage lien.... Second, even if the trial court had the authority to declare the Association's lien superior to the mortgage lien as a *sanction,* the fact remains that the issue of lien priority was never actually *litigated*.... Nor would it change the fact that PNC Bank, as the holder of the mortgage who obtained title to the subject property via foreclosure sale, qualified as a first mortgagee regardless of the fact that the Association's assessment lien survived the foreclosure..... Third, and aside from the fact that no recorded claim of lien appears in either record on appeal, the Association's assessment lien, if any, could not have been recorded prior to the recording of the first mortgage lien. This is because the record evidence establishes that the Association only sought unpaid assessments dating back to 2008, five years after the mortgage lien was recorded in 2003.") (emphasis in original), *rev. den. sub nom., 40 N.E. Plantation Rd. #306, LLC v. PNC Bank, Nat'l Ass'n,* No. SC17-65, 2017 WL 1279793 (Fla. Apr. 6, 2017).

[16] *U.S. Bank Nat. Ass'n v. Tadmore*, 23 So. 3d 822, 823 (Fla. 3d DCA 2009) ("The law is that a first mortgagee may be required to pay condominium maintenance fees *after it acquires title* and then only in a limited amount. Since equity follows the law, it cannot be utilized to impose this obligation without limitation before title is passed.") (emphasis in original); *Deutsche Bank Nat'l Trust Co. v. Coral Key Condo. Ass'n*, 32 So. 3d 195 (Fla. 4th DCA 2010) (same rule).

[17] *See Beacon Place of Coral Springs Condo. Ass'n, Inc. v. Nationstar Mortg., LLC*, 182 So. 3d 834 (Fla. 4th DCA 2016) (association that had taken title created fact issue as to mortgagee's standing, precluding summary judgment of foreclosure for the mortgagee); *Bank of New York Mellon v. Clark, Sanctuary at Redfish Condo. Ass'n, Inc., et al.*, 183 So. 3d 1271 (Fla. 1st DCA 2016) (in bank's foreclosure in case where association was defending as title owner, appellate court reversed trial court's dismissal of bank's foreclosure with prejudice as sanction for bank's alleged failure to respond to association's discovery, but solely for failure of trial court to consider the factors required by *Kozel v. Ostendorf*, 629 So. 2d 817 (Fla. 1993)).

association may challenge the foreclosure even if the association is just a lienor.[18] In their challenge, associations will often raise many of the same arguments and defenses raised by borrowers in foreclosures, sometimes successfully.[19] Older cases had allowed associations to challenge foreclosures, both as a lienor and a title holder, but without any analysis of their right to do so.[20]

There are now cases, increasing in number and vehemence, that hold that, third-party purchasers (which could be associations) with an interest in the underlying property have standing to contest a foreclosure action brought by a party claiming a superior interest.[21] In fact, the Third District's view is that there is no inter-district conflict such that all trial courts must follow its and the Fourth District's precedent on

---

[18] *See Country Place Community Ass'n, Inc. v. J.P. Morgan Mortg. Acquisition Corp.*, 51 So. 3d 1176 (Fla. 2d DCA 2010) (association defeated mortgagee's foreclosure on standing grounds and was awarded fees as a sanction under § 57.105(1) on appeal); *Hidden Ridge Condo. Homeowners Ass'n, Inc. v. OneWest Bank, N.A.*, 183 So. 3d 1266 (Fla. 5th DCA 2016) (upholding association's evidentiary objections, which was mere lienor, on business records issues).

[19] *Country Place Community Ass'n, Inc. v. J.P. Morgan Mortg. Acquisition Corp.*, 51 So. 3d 1176 (Fla. 2d DCA 2010) (association defeated mortgagee's foreclosure on standing grounds and was awarded fees as a sanction under § 57.105(1) on appeal); *Beacon Place of Coral Springs Condo. Ass'n, Inc. v. Nationstar Mortgage, LLC*, 182 So. 3d 834 (Fla. 4th DCA 2016) (association created fact issue as to mortgagee's standing, precluding summary judgment); *Hidden Ridge Condo. Homeowners Ass'n, Inc. v. OneWest Bank, N.A.*, 183 So. 3d 1266 (Fla. 5th DCA 2016) (upholding association's evidentiary objections on business records issues).

[20] *Beacon Place of Coral Springs Condo. Ass'n, Inc. v. Nationstar Mortg., LLC*, 182 So. 3d 834 (Fla. 4th DCA 2016); *Country Place Community Ass'n, Inc. v. J.P. Morgan Mortg. Acquisition Corp.*, 51 So. 3d 1176 (Fla. 2d DCA 2010); *Hidden Ridge Condo. Homeowners Ass'n, Inc. v. OneWest Bank, N.A.*, 183 So. 3d 1266 (Fla. 5th DCA 2016); *Fogarty v. Nationstar Mortg., LLC*, 224 So. 3d 313, 316 (Fla. 5th DCA 2017).

[21] *See 3709 N. Flagler Drive Prodigy Land Tr. v. Bank of Am., N.A.*, 226 So. 3d 1040, 1042 (Fla. 4th DCA 2017); *Green Emerald Homes, LLC v. 21st Mortgage Corp.*, 2D17-2192, 44 Fla. L. Weekly D1449, 2019 WL 2398015 (Fla. 2d DCA June 7, 2019); *Wilmington Tr., N.A. v. Alvarez*, 239 So. 3d 1265, 1266 n.1 (Fla. 3d DCA 2018) ("In so holding, we reject *Wilmington Trust's* claim that BCML lacks standing to raise the affirmative defense that the instant claim is barred by the statute of limitations."); *Benzrent 1, LLC v. Wilmington Sav. Fund Soc'y, FSB*, 273 So. 3d 107 (Fla. 3d DCA 2019); *Andrews v. Bayview Loan Servicing, LLC*, 175 So. 3d 316, 318 (Fla. 5th DCA 2015), *reh'g denied* (Sept. 18, 2015) ("Third persons whose rights or interests are adversely affected by a mortgage, such as junior mortgagees or creditors with an interest or lien in the underlying property, have standing to contest a foreclosure action brought by a party claiming a superior interest."). *But see Wells Fargo Del. Tr. Co., N.A. for Vericrest Opportunity Loan Tr. 201-NPL1 v. Petrov*, 230 So. 3d 575, 577 n.3 (Fla. 3d DCA 2017) ("We question whether FLIP had standing to raise any of these arguments. Although FLIP acquired its interest in the property before the filing of the lis pendens, there is no evidence that FLIP ever attempted to assume the mortgage or to cure the existing default when it purchased the property. Therefore, it does 'not stand in the shoes of the mortgagors and cannot participate in the bank's foreclosure as though [it] were a party to the mortgage.' . . . *Wells Fargo*, however, did not challenge FLIP's standing to participate in the foreclosure proceeding below and, in any event, does not raise this issue on appeal.") (dicta); *Pealer v. Wilmington Tr. Nat'l Ass'n for MFRA Tr.*, 212 So. 3d 1137, 1137-38 (Fla. 2d DCA 2017) (Sleet, J., specially concurring).

this issue.[22] However, while they no doubt must alert trial courts to this authority, first mortgagees may arguably attack the association's standing to raise certain defenses in light of contrary case law such as that cited below as well as that cited by Judge Sleet in his concurrence in *Pealer v. Wilmington Tr. Nat'l Ass'n for MFRA Tr.*, 212 So. 3d 1137, 1137-38 (Fla. 2d DCA 2017). Note however that the Second District has distinguished at length prior cases denying third-party purchaser standing to raise foreclosure defenses, in part on due process grounds.[23]

Still, there are several cases, still good law, preventing third parties from asserting such defenses. It has been held that alleged harm to the borrower caused in the loan origination is not harm to the association because the association is not a party to the mortgage.[24] It has been held that a third-party purchaser at an association's foreclosure sale cannot raise a forgery defense against a first mortgagee,[25] and it has been held that no one but the borrower can argue failure of a mortgage's condition precedent, like the breach letter.[26]

---

[22] *Benzrent 1, LLC v. Wilmington Sav. Fund Soc'y, FSB,* 273 So. 3d 107, 109-10 (Fla. 3d DCA 2019) ("Though it is somewhat unclear from the September 26, 2017 hearing transcript, when the predecessor judge struck Benzrent's pleading, it appears that the court was under the mistaken impression that *Pealer* was a majority opinion of the Second District; it was not. *Pealer* was a *per curiam* affirmance with a special concurring opinion that was not joined by the other panel members. Concurring opinions, of course, have no precedential value. . . . Absent a conflict, and because this Court had no binding precedent on this issue, the predecessor judge was duty bound to follow the Fourth District's decision in *3709 N. Flagler*. . . . The trial court's failure to follow *3709 N. Flagler* resulted in the erroneous striking of Benzrent's responsive pleading.") (citing *Pardo v. State,* 596 So. 2d 665, 666 (Fla. 1992) ("[I]n the absence of interdistrict conflict, district court decisions bind all Florida trial courts.")).

[23] *Green Emerald Homes, LLC v. 21st Mortgage Corp.*, 2D17-2192, 44 Fla. L. Weekly D1449, 2019 WL 2398015 (Fla. 2d DCA June 7, 2019). However, the reasoning of Judge Villanti in his *Green Emerald* concurrence/dissent seems solid, and his suggestion for legislative reform on the issue seems well-taken.

[24] *Henry v. Guaranteed Rates, Inc.*, 415 F. App'x 985, 985-86 (11th Cir. 2011) ("Munroe–Cooper lacked standing to complain about any alleged misconduct regarding a loan to which she was not a party. . . . Because Munroe–Cooper was not a party to the loan, she was not injured by any alleged misconduct of the defendants with respect to that loan. Munroe–Cooper also cannot complain about any alleged harm to Henry. . . . Munroe–Cooper lacks any authority to represent Henry.").

[25] *Wells Fargo Bank, N.A. v. Rutledge*, 230 So. 3d 550, 552 (Fla. 2d DCA 2017), *reh'g denied* (Nov. 28, 2017).

[26] *Clay Cty. Land Tr. No. 08-04-25-0078-014-27, Orange Park Tr. Servs., LLC v. JP Morgan Chase Bank, Nat. Ass'n*, 152 So. 3d 83, 84 (Fla. 1st DCA 2014) ("As to its first claim, appellant concedes it was not a party to the mortgage and was not entitled to a written notice of default or an opportunity to cure the default under the terms of the mortgage."); *LaFaille v. Nationstar Mortg., LLC*, 197 So. 3d 1246, 1247 (Fla. 3d DCA 2016) ("Appellants assert that Nationwide was required to prove compliance with the mortgage's notice provision and that its failure to do so requires reversal of the final judgment of foreclosure. However, even if the mortgage did require notice to the borrower upon his death (which it plainly did not), neither of the appellants was a party to, or a 'borrower' under, the mortgage or note, and thus, have no standing to assert this defense."); *Castillo v. Deutsche Bank Nat. Trust Co.*, 89 So. 3d 1069 (Fla. 3d DCA 2012) ("Because the appellant is neither a party to nor a third-party beneficiary of the trust, we find the appellant lacks standing to raise this issue

It has also been held that the association cannot raise a statute of limitations defense as to the mortgage, which defense is personal to the mortgagor,[27] unless, perhaps, the association has taken title from the borrower; some older authority distinguishes between the power of subsequent *owners* versus mere junior lienors to assert the statute of limitations defense.[28]

However, it is relatively clear an association can challenge the amount due on the note, when it owns the property since that affects its right of redemption.[29] The ambiguous status of third-party standing to raise foreclosure defenses needs to be addressed by the Florida Supreme Court or the Florida Legislature.

The wise foreclosure lawyer will also ensure that the foreclosing lender adduces evidence of past dues owed, lien priority[30] and safe harbor entitlement, and will ensure

---

and affirm the final judgment of foreclosure in favor of the appellee, as the holder of the original note and mortgage.").

[27] *Irwin v. Grogan-Cole*, 590 So. 2d 1102, 1104 (Fla. 5th DCA 1991) ("We agree with Irwin, however, that the court erred in denying foreclosure. Development took subject to (and did not assume) the mortgage and therefore may not assert the invalidity of the mortgage.... Although Development may assert that it does not dispute the original validity of the mortgage but merely contests its present enforceability because of the statute of limitations, we find the distinction unpersuasive in this case."); *Lindsey v. H.M. Raulerson, Jr., Memorial Hosp.*, 452 So. 2d 1087 (Fla. 4th DCA 1984). *See also Akin v. City of Miami*, 65 So. 2d 54 (Fla. 1953); *In re Estate of Rifkin*, 359 So. 2d 1197 (Fla. 3d DCA 1978); *Bollettieri Resort Villas Condo. Ass'n, Inc. v. Bank of N.Y.Mellon*, 198 So. 3d1140, 1142 n.1 (Fla. 2d DCA 2016) ("At no point in the proceedings below did the trial court address Bollettieri's standing to raise the statute of limitations issue, and neither party has placed that issue before us in the instant appeal."), *rev. dismissed*, 228 So. 3d 72 (Mem.) (Fla. Oct. 12, 2017).

[28] *Coe v. Finlayson*, 41 Fla. 169 (Fla. 1899). Any possible doubt whether the Florida Supreme Court intended in *Coe* to preclude junior mortgagees from asserting the statute of limitations against senior mortgagees (as distinct from subsequent owners) would be answered by looking at the United States Supreme Court case it cited, *Sanger v. Nightingale*, 122 U.S. 176, 185, 7 S. Ct. 1109, 1112 (1887). *But see, Wilmington Tr., N.A. v. Alvarez*, 239 So. 3d 1265, 1266 n.1 (Fla. 3d DCA 2018) ("In so holding, we reject *Wilmington Trust's* claim that BCML lacks standing to raise the affirmative defense that the instant claim is barred by the statute of limitations. *See 3709 N. Flagler Drive Prodigy Land Tr. v. Bank of Am., N.A.*, 226 So. 3d 1040 (Fla. 4th DCA 2017).").

[29] *Clay Cty. Land Tr. No. 08-04-25-0078-014-27, Orange Park Tr. Servs., LLC v. JP Morgan Chase Bank, Nat. Ass'n*, 152 So. 3d 83, 85 (Fla. 1st DCA 2014) ("As the current owner of the property, appellant had standing to challenge Klingelhofer's affidavit as to the amount of the debt owed because it related to appellant's right of redemption, i.e., how much appellant would have to pay under the judgment in order to exercise its right to stop the foreclosure sale."); *Beauchamp v. The Bank of N.Y., Tr. Co., N.A.*, 150 So. 3d 827 (Fla. 4th DCA 2014).

[30] *Hidden Ridge Condo. Homeowners Ass'n, Inc. v. OneWest Bank, N.A.*, 183 So. 3d 1266, 1270 n.4 (Fla. 5th DCA 2016) ("We also find neither party presented competent evidence to establish which one had a superior interest in the condo. Thus, on remand, either party may request an evidentiary hearing to resolve this issue."); *Fogarty v. Nationstar Mortgage, LLC*, 224 So. 3d 313, 316 (Fla. 5th DCA 2017) ("Nationstar argues the trial court improperly dismissed Seagrove as a superior lienholder to Nationstar. We reverse the dismissal and remand for the trial court to reinstate Seagrove as a party to this litigation. Because neither party presented competent evidence to establish which one had a superior interest, '[o]n remand, either party may request an evidentiary hearing to resolve this issue.'") (quoting *Hidden Ridge Condo. Homeowners v. Greentree Servicing, LLC*, 167 So. 3d 483 (Fla. 5th DCA 2015)).

that the final judgment specifically reserves jurisdiction for the circuit court to resolve post-judgment disputes over safe harbor and/or amounts owed to the association.[31]

9-4 Post-Foreclosure

9-4:1 Anatomy of an Estoppel Dispute

While associations may litigate with mortgagees over compliance with declarations, articles or bylaws regarding repairs, approval of prospective buyers, and other such mundane compliance issues, those issues are no different from issues an association may litigate with any other type of owner. The normal post-judgment issue, which is unique to a foreclosing lender and which arises with surprising frequency, is the amount of dues that a foreclosing first mortgagee owes to the association after it takes title after its foreclosure sale, and whether the foreclosing first mortgagee is entitled to "safe harbor." Without a proper estoppel, the foreclosing lender will find it difficult to find a buyer and the property may languish in REO status for months or years.

The issue arises because a borrower who does not pay his or her mortgage usually does not pay his or her association dues either. The general rule for condominiums and HOAs is one of joint and several liability, i.e., that a subsequent owner owes, as a "pre-title liability," with dues previously owed. For condominiums, Fla. Stat. § 718.116(1)(a) states that "a unit owner is jointly and severally liable with the previous owner for all unpaid assessments that came due up to the time of transfer of title." Similarly, for HOAs, Fla. Stat. § 720.3085(2)(b) states that "[a] parcel owner is jointly and severally liable with the previous parcel owner for all unpaid assessments that came due up to the time of transfer of title."

But the concept of safe harbor, which is a statutory provision that benefits first mortgagees, tempers the general rule of joint and several liability for dues liability, both for homeowners associations ("HOAs") and condominium associations.[32] Under these safe harbor statutes, a first mortgagee or its successors or assigns is not responsible for any past due assessments for amounts over 12 months of dues, or 1 percent of the mortgage amount, whichever is less.[33]

However, after a first mortgagee forecloses on that defaulting borrower and takes title, associations often attempt to refuse "safe harbor" to foreclosing first mortgagees, and seek instead, to use the first mortgagee as a deep pocket to pay for the failure of the borrower/prior unit owner to pay all of the unpaid dues, late fees, costs, interest and attorney's fees incurred by the borrower (or even prior owners) that the first mortgagee foreclosed on. If allowed, this is like the bank getting hit twice for the misconduct of the borrower. Alternatively, the association may seek to extract unpaid dues from the third-party purchaser who buys directly from the judicial sale following a foreclosure, or more importantly for present purposes, from the third-party pur-

---

[31] *See also Grand Cent. at Kennedy Condo. Ass'n, Inc. v. Space Coast Credit Union,* 173 So. 3d 1089, 1091 n.2 (Fla. 2d DCA 2015); *Montreux at Deerwood Lake Condo. Ass'n, Inc. v. Citibank, N.A.,* 153 So. 3d 961 (Fla. 1st DCA 2014); *Meadows on the Green Condo. Ass'n, Inc. v. Nationstar Mortg., LLC,* 188 So. 3d 883 (Mem), 2016 WL 72585 (Fla. 4th DCA 2016); *Central Park A Metrowest Condo. Ass'n., Inc. v. Amtrust REO I, LLC,* 169 So. 3d 1223 (Fla. 5th DCA 2015) (following *Montreux* and *Callahan*).

[32] Fla. Stat. § 720.3085(2)(c); Fla. Stat. § 718.116(1)(b).

[33] Fla. Stat. § 720.3085(2)(c); Fla. Stat. § 718.116(1)(b).

chaser who buys directly from the REO inventory of the foreclosing first mortgagee who took title after the sale.

As noted, there is almost never a dispute that the current owner owes the dues that come due while the current owner owns the home or unit, referred to herein as "post-title" dues. These post-title dues become owed by the current owner once title is obtained from the immediate prior owner.[34]

Instead, the dispute usually centers on "pre-title" dues and amounts, i.e., those amounts due as a "pre-title" liability that accrued *before* the current owner took title. Specifically, the litigated question is whether a third-party purchaser is liable *just* for the pre-title dues owed by *just* "the immediate-prior owner,"[35] or whether that third-party purchaser owes *all* unpaid dues owed by *all* prior owners who defaulted on their dues.

In *Aventura Management, LLC v. Spiaggia Ocean Condominium Association, Inc.* (*Spiaggia I*), the association obtained a foreclosure judgment and bought the condominium at the resulting foreclosure sale. Thereafter, the bank, the holder of the first mortgage on the condominium, foreclosed on the condominium and obtained a foreclosure judgment. A third party purchased the condominium at the foreclosure sale[36] following the bank's foreclosure action. The association therefore sought to recover from the third-party purchaser those condominium assessments that the original owner failed to pay pursuant to § 718.116(1)(a). In rebuttal, the third party argued that because the association was "an intervening owner" between the original owner and the third-party purchaser, the *association* was responsible for the original owner's assessments, not the third-party purchaser. The association argued, in so many words, that it was somehow exempt when it took title simply because it was "the association." The Third DCA rejected that position three times in three cases.[37] In that

---

[34] Fla. Stat. § 720.3085(2)(a) ("A parcel owner, regardless of how his or her title to property has been acquired, including by purchase at a foreclosure sale or by deed in lieu of foreclosure, is liable for all assessments that come due while he or she is the parcel owner."); Fla. Stat. § 718.116(1)(a) ("A unit owner, regardless of how his or her title has been acquired, including by purchase at a foreclosure sale or by deed in lieu of foreclosure, is liable for all assessments which come due while he or she is the unit owner."). These statutory sentences merely state that a unit or home owner is liable for whatever dues come due while it/he/she owns the unit, which are called "post-title" dues, referring to *post-the-current-owner's-title* dues.

[35] *Aventura Mgmt., LLC v. Spiaggia Ocean Condo. Ass'n., Inc.*, 149 So. 3d 690, 692 (Fla. 3d DCA 2014).

[36] Because the bank in the *Spiaggia* cases did not take title at the sale, there was no safe harbor available to the third-party purchaser. *Cf. Bay Holdings, Inc. v. 2000 Island Blvd. Condo. Ass'n*, 895 So. 2d 1197, 1197-98 (Fla. 3d DCA 2005).

[37] *Aventura Management, LLC v. Spiaggia Ocean Condo. Ass'n, Inc.*, 105 So. 3d 637 (Fla. 3d DCA 2013) (*Spiaggia I*) ("The Statute clearly provides that 'a unit owner is jointly and severally liable *with the previous owner* for all unpaid assessments that came due up to the time of transfer of title.' § 718.116(1)(a) (emphasis added). Appellee was the previous owner of the Unit. The plain language of the Statute does not state or suggest that an exception is to be made when the previous owner is the condominium association."); *Aventura Management, LLC v. Spiaggia Ocean Condo. Ass'n, Inc.*, 149 So. 3d 690, 692-93 (Fla. 3d DCA 2014) (*Spiaggia II*) ("While the majority could have been clearer that Aventura Management bore no liability, it specifically emphasized the singular definite article 'the' in the statute . . . , and noted that *Spiaggia* would have available to it the remedy of pursuing its lien against the

triumvirate of cases, the Third DCA explained that the singular definite article "the" in § 718.116(1)(a) (which by the way is identical to that in § 720.3085(2)(a)) meant that the association's taking of title made it "the immediate-prior owner" and that there was no statutory exception for an association when it took title.

After the Third District's *Spiaggia* line of cases discussed above,[38] the Florida Legislature legislated around those Third District cases in the sole instance when the association takes title.[39] Essentially, under the "*Spiaggia* Amendments" the association gets passed over as an "owner" for *Spiaggia* purposes, creating simultaneously a legal fiction and an exception to § 718.116(1)(a)'s and § 720.3085(2)(b)'s interpretation by the Third District that a subsequent owner is liable only for the unpaid dues of "the immediate-prior owner" (and none further back than that). If the HOA or condominium association took title before the relevant effective date, then the *Spiaggia* Amendment does not apply. The HOA *Spiaggia* Amendment was effective July 1, 2013, and the condominium *Spiaggia* Amendment was effective July 1, 2014.

In these *Spiaggia* Amendments, the Florida Legislature added two sentences. It amended Fla. Stat. § 720.3085(2)(b) by adding: "For the purposes of this paragraph, the term 'previous owner' shall not include an association that acquires title to a delinquent property through foreclosure or by deed in lieu of foreclosure. The present parcel owner's liability for unpaid assessments is limited to any unpaid assessments that accrued before the association acquired title to the delinquent property through foreclosure or by deed in lieu of foreclosure." And it amended Fla. Stat. § 718.116(1)(b) by adding: "For the purposes of this paragraph, the term 'previous owner' does not include an association that acquires title to a delinquent property through foreclosure or by deed in lieu of foreclosure. A present unit owner's liability for unpaid assessments is limited to any unpaid assessments that accrued before the association

---

original owner. . . . . Additionally, a recent decision from this Court has provided clarity to this issue. . . . Applying the same reasoning of *Park West* to the facts of this case, Aventura Management could only be responsible for unpaid assessments dating back to when Spiaggia took title at its own foreclosure sale; it cannot be held liable for the unpaid assessments of the original owner. The trial court therefore erred in holding Aventura Management jointly and severally liable with the prior two owners. We note, just as in *Spiaggia I*, that Spiaggia is free to pursue a direct action against the original owner for the unpaid fees."). See also *Bona Vista Condo. Ass'n, Inc. v. FNS6, LLC*, 194 So. 3d 490 (Fla. 3d DCA 2016).

[38] *Aventura Management, LLC v. Spiaggia Ocean Condo. Ass'n, Inc.*, 105 So. 3d 637 (Fla. 3d DCA 2013) (*Spiaggia I*); *Aventura Management, LLC v. Spiaggia Ocean Condo. Ass'n, Inc.*, 149 So. 3d 690, 692-93 (Fla. 3d DCA 2014) (*Spiaggia II*); *Park West Professional Center Condo. Ass'n v. Londono*, 130 So. 3d 711, 712 (Fla. 3d DCA 2013). See also *Bona Vista Condo. Ass'n, Inc. v. FNS6, LLC*, 194 So. 3d 490 (Fla. 3d DCA 2016).

[39] See Fla. Stat. § 720.3085(2)(b) ("For the purposes of this paragraph, the term 'previous owner' shall not include an association that acquires title to a delinquent property through foreclosure or by deed in lieu of foreclosure. The present parcel owner's liability for unpaid assessments is limited to any unpaid assessments that accrued before the association acquired title to the delinquent property through foreclosure or by deed in lieu of foreclosure.") (eff. 7/1/13); Fla. Stat. § 718.116(1)(b) ("For the purposes of this paragraph, the term 'previous owner' does not include an association that acquires title to a delinquent property through foreclosure or by deed in lieu of foreclosure. A present unit owner's liability for unpaid assessments is limited to any unpaid assessments that accrued before the association acquired title to the delinquent property through foreclosure or by deed in lieu of foreclosure.") (eff. 7/1/14).

acquired title to the delinquent property through foreclosure or by deed in lieu of foreclosure."

This "association-as-immediate-prior-owner" scenario was the only aspect of the *Spiaggia* rulings that was overruled by the Legislature's *Spiaggia* Amendments, in that the Legislature created a statutory exception for title-taking Associations,[40] that was previously non-existent, as noted by the Third DCA in these three cases.

How this issue can play out is demonstrated in a recent case from the Third District Court of Appeal, *Bona Vista Condominium Association, Inc. v. FNS6, LLC*, which was decided after the *Spiaggia* Amendments but decided on the prior version of the statute by agreement.[41] In *Bona Vista*, Guido Brito ("Brito") owned a condominium unit governed by the Bona Vista Condominium Association, Inc. (the "Association"). Sometime in or around 2009, Brito failed to make his monthly mortgage payment to Wells Fargo, and failed to make his monthly assessment payments to the Association. The Association filed a lien foreclosure in June 2009, and later obtained a Final Judgment of Foreclosure. The Association then became the successful purchaser at the resulting foreclosure sale, and took title to the condominium unit. Thereafter, Wells Fargo foreclosed its own first mortgage and obtained a final judgment. At the resulting foreclosure sale, the unit was sold to FNS6, LLC ("FNS6"). Following FNS6's acquisition of title, the Association demanded nearly $21,000 in unpaid assessments from FNS6, that came due during the time the Association held title to the unit. FNS6 then sought declaratory relief in the trial court, seeking a determination as to its obligations under Section 718.116(1)(a), Fla. Stat. (2013), to pay assessments that came due during the Association's ownership. The trial court ruled that FNS6 did not owe any assessments to the Association because even though Bona Vista and FNS6 were "jointly and severally [liable]" for these assessments, FNS6's right to recover any amounts it paid to or on behalf of Bona Vista made FNS6's obligation "basically a wash." The Association then appealed the final declaratory judgment. The *Bona Vista* Court agreed with the

---

[40] *Villagio at Estero Condo. Ass'n, Inc. v. Deutsche Bank Nat. Trust Co.*, 2016 WL 4580146, *3 (Fla. Cir. Ct. Lee County 2016) ("The Association attempts to argue that the *Spiaggia* Line of Opinions are not directly on point, due to factual dissimilarities, and that the *Spiaggia* Line of Opinions have been preempted by an amendment to § 718.116(1)(a). However, this Court finds those arguments unavailing. The third district determined that use of the singular definite article 'the' in § 718.116(1)(a), rather than 'a,' when referring to 'previous owner' was evidence of the legislature's intent to limit the amount of unpaid assessments a new owner could be held responsible for paying. *See Spiaggia II*, 149 So. 3d at 692; *Bona Vista*, 194 So. 3d at 492. Moreover, the mere fact that the applicable statute has been amended after the *Spiaggia* decisions does not undermine their legitimacy. *Heath v. State*, 532 So. 2d 9, 10 (Fla. 1st DCA 1988) ('Although legislative amendment of a statute may change law . . . it does not follow that court decisions interpreting a statute are rendered inapplicable by a subsequent amendment to the statute. Instead, the nature and effect of the court decisions and the statutory amendment must be examined to determine what law may be applicable after the amendment.'). Here, the amendment to the statute merely removed an intervening association who takes title to a unit from the definition of a 'previous owner.' *See* Fla. Stat. § 718.116(1)(a). However, as there is no intervening association in this case, the amendment is wholly irrelevant. Moreover, the third district has recently reiterated its stance in its decision in *Bona Vista*. 194 So. 3d at 490.")

[41] The Association and FNS6 agreed that the 2013 version of section 718.116(1)(a) controlled. *Id.* at n.2. This meant that the *Spiaggia* Amendment applicable to condominium associations was inapplicable.

trial court and affirmed the judgment. In so doing, the *Bona Vista* Court held that the liability of a purchaser of a condominium unit is limited to the assessments that accrued during the ownership of *the immediate-prior owner*.

> As this court's decisions in *Aventura Management, LLC v. Spiaggia Ocean Condominium Ass'n, Inc.*, 105 So. 3d 637, 638–39 (Fla. 3d DCA 2013) (*Spiaggia I*), *Aventura Management, LLC v. Spiaggia Ocean Condominium Ass'n, Inc.*, 149 So. 3d 690, 693 (Fla. 3d DCA 2014) (*Spiaggia II*), and *Park West Professional Center Condominium Ass'n, Inc. v. Londono*, 130 So. 3d 711, 712 (Fla. 3d DCA 2013) (quoting *Spiaggia I*, 105 So. 3d at 639) make clear, under the 2013 version of Section 718.116(1)(a) which applies here: . . . a third party which takes title from the condominium association upon foreclosure of a superior lien is not responsible for unpaid assessments of the "original owner," but is both solely responsible for all assessments that become due during its ownership and jointly and severally liable with the condominium association for assessments that came due during the condominium association's ownership.[42]

Applying its analysis of § 718.116(1)(a), Fla. Stat. (2013) to the facts before it, the *Bona Vista* Court correctly stated that "FNS6 (the current owner) is not liable for any unpaid assessments which came due while Brito (the original owner) held title." Thus, in analyzing the pre-2014 version of Section 718.116(1)(a), Fla. Stat. (i.e., before the effective date of the relevant *Spiaggia* Amendment), the *Bona Vista* Court confirmed that a third-party purchaser taking title from a lender or association who had foreclosed on the original owner, is jointly and severally liable with that foreclosing entity, but can never owe assessments which came due while the original owner held title.[43]

However, in *Coastal Creek Condo. Ass'n, Inc. v. Fla Tr. Services LLC*, the First District read the *Spiaggia* Amendments, added by the Florida Legislature to undo the Third District's cases[44] in the sole instance where the Association is "the immediate-prior owner,"[45] to evince a legislative intent to require third-party purchasers to be responsible for the dues of every defaulting owner of the property, not just "the immediate-prior owner," in all cases, not simply in situations where the Association is "the immediate-prior owner."

In *Coastal Creek*,[46] JPMorgan Chase Bank, NA, as mortgagee, obtained a final judgment of foreclosure against the mortgagors, and, at the ensuing judicial sale, Homes HQ, LLC ("the immediate prior owner") was the successful bidder and a certificate of title was issued to it on June 13, 2016. On July 26, 2016, Homes HQ quitclaimed the

---

[42] *Bona Vista Condo. Ass'n, Inc. v. FNS6, LLC*, 194 So. 3d 490, 492 (Fla. 3d DCA 2016).

[43] *Bona Vista Condo. Ass'n, Inc. v. FNS6, LLC*, 194 So. 3d 490 (Fla. 3d DCA 2016) (citing to *Spiaggia I*, *Spiaggia II* and *Londono*).

[44] *Aventura Management, LLC v. Spiaggia Ocean Condo. Ass'n, Inc.*, 105 So. 3d 637 (Fla. 3d DCA 2013) (*Spiaggia I*); *Aventura Management, LLC v. Spiaggia Ocean Condo. Ass'n, Inc.*, 149 So. 3d 690, 692-93 (Fla. 3d DCA 2014) (*Spiaggia II*); *Park West Professional Center Condo. Ass'n v. Londono*, 130 So. 3d 711, 712 (Fla. 3d DCA 2013); *Bona Vista Condo. Ass'n, Inc. v. FNS6, LLC*, 194 So. 3d 490 (Fla. 3d DCA 2016).

[45] *Aventura Mgmt., LLC v. Spiaggia Ocean Condo. Ass'n., Inc.*, 149 So. 3d 690, 692 (Fla. 3d DCA 2014).

[46] *Coastal Creek Condo. Ass'n, Inc. v. Fla Tr. Services LLC*, 275 So. 3d 836 (Fla. 1st DCA 2019).

property to FLA Trust (the current owner). The Association then recorded a claim of lien against the property for common expenses during the ownership of FLA Trust and any former owners with whom FLA Trust is jointly and severally liable pursuant to section 718.116, Florida Statutes, and sued FLA Trust for failure to pay. FLA Trust admitted that assessments had come due during its ownership, but asserted that pursuant to section 718.116(1)(a), Florida Statutes, and the Third District's *Spiaggia* line of cases, the present owner shares joint and several liability with only the immediate prior owner and not all prior owners. At the hearing on the parties' motions, the trial court explained that the disputed issue concerned the amount FLA Trust owed in assessments—all the prior unpaid assessments, as contended by the Association, or only the assessments that came due during its ownership and the immediate prior owner's ownership, as argued by FLA Trust—, and the parties agreed that the issue was dispositive. Much of the discussion at the hearing focused on the Third District's *Spiaggia* line of cases.

Unlike the Third District, the First District ruled that the current owner *was* liable for all unpaid dues of all prior owners and certified conflict with the Third District's four cases discussed above.[47]

An example might help explain the difference in effect between the First and Third District's approaches. Imagine a title transfer of a condo unit with the following owners represented by letters:

---

[47] *Coastal Creek Condo. Ass'n, Inc. v. Fla Tr. Services LLC*, 275 So. 3d 836 (Fla. 1st DCA 2019) ("Unlike the 2013 version of the statute that applied in the Third District cases, the version applicable in our case states that the term 'previous owner' does not include an association that acquires title and goes on to provide that '[a] present unit owner's liability for unpaid assessments is limited to any unpaid assessments that accrued before the association acquired title to the delinquent property through foreclosure or by deed in lieu of foreclosure.' There is only one reasonable interpretation of this provision: when the previous owner is the association, the present owner is liable only for unpaid assessments that accrued before the association acquired ownership; that is, during the original owner's ownership. This provision essentially skips the period of the association's ownership and absolves the present owner of liability for assessments unpaid during that time, while maintaining the present owner's liability for assessments unpaid during the original owner's ownership. In other words, it provides that the present owner is liable for unpaid assessments that came due during the ownership of the original owner, but not for unpaid assessments that came due during the ownership of the association as previous owner. When the statutory provisions are read together, the legislative intent is unambiguous: the present owner is jointly and severally liable with the previous owner for unpaid assessments that came due during the ownership of both the previous owner (unless it was the association) and the original owner. Therefore, FLA Trust is jointly and severally liable with Homes HQ for assessments that were unpaid by not only Homes HQ, but also the Original Owners. Accordingly, we reverse the final summary judgment. We certify conflict with the Third District's decisions in *Bona Vista Condominium Association, Inc. v. FNS6, LLC*, 194 So. 3d 490 (Fla. 3d DCA 2016), *Aventura Management, LLC v. Spiaggia Ocean Condominium Association, Inc.*, 149 So. 3d 690 (Fla. 3d DCA 2014), *Park West Professional Center Condominium Association, Inc. v. Londono*, 130 So. 3d 711 (Fla. 3d DCA 2013), and *Aventura Management, LLC v. Spiaggia cean Condominium Association, Inc.*, 105 So. 3d 637 (Fla. 3d DCA 2013), to the extent they limit the current owner's joint and several liability pursuant to section 718.116(1)(a) to unpaid assessments that came due during the ownership of the immediate prior owner, and not the original owner.").

A » B » C » D

Under the Third DCA's interpretation of Fla. Stat. § 718.116(1)(a) and § 720.3085(2)(b) in the *Spiaggia* line of cases, in the above "title transfer" chain, owner C owes (1) C's "post-title" dues that accrue after C took title and while C owns the unit, plus (2) the prior owner's, that is B's, "post-title" dues which accrued between the time B took title until the time C took title (which are C's "pre-title" liability but also B's "post-title" liability).[48] But C is not liable, under a "pre-title" theory, for A's "post-title" dues. But under the First District's approach in *Coastal Creek*, owner C owes *all* unpaid dues, that is, C owes C's own "post-title" dues, as well as both owner A's and B's post-title dues.

Again, under the Third District's *Spiaggia* approach, once owner D takes title to the condo unit from C, owner D owes (1) whatever dues accrue while D owns the unit (which are D's "post-title" dues), plus, (2) as D's "pre-title" liability, the dues that C owed to the association between the time C took title until the time D took title. But D does not owe whatever unpaid dues owner B owed before C took title. Owner B's dues were solely owner C's problem. B's dues do not become D's problem merely because neither B nor C paid them. However, under the First District's approach in *Coastal Creek*, owner D owes *all* unpaid dues, including its own "post-title" dues, as well as owner A's, B's, and C's "post-title" dues.

Coastal Creek should make any investor think twice before buying a property with unpaid association dues from a judicial sale following either an association or bank foreclosure (that is not located within the Third District) without negotiating with the association beforehand. First mortgagees have safe harbor, of course, and therefore are not affected directly by *Coastal Creek*, but since *Coastal Creek* did not involve a safe harbor issue (nor did the *Spiaggia* cases), it remains to be seen whether the First District would find the foreclosing first mortgagee benefits from safe harbor but that safe harbor does not benefit the purchaser from the first mortgagee (who would be on the hook for the balance of the unpaid dues). Some associations have for some time been issuing an estoppel that attempts to "bifurcate" what is owed by the bank under the safe harbor, but then states that whoever buys the property from the bank will be liable for the remaining unpaid dues. If this were the case, i.e., if associations are able to issue a "bifurcated estoppel," a bank's ability to sell foreclosed properties from its REO inventory will be greatly impacted. In essence, such a "bifurcated estoppel" from an association is, in effect, a denial of safe harbor because it tends to preclude what the foreclosing lender desires, insurable clear title and a sale. Such an estoppel is illusory because this threat must be disclosed to a potential buyer of the property and in many cases will result in the disappearance of said potential buyer.

This "bifurcated estoppel" method has been specifically rejected by at least one trial court,[49] although a number of courts have rejected the general theory behind the concept.[50] In fact, the Fourth District has decided a case applicable to such bifurcated

---

[48] In other words, C's "pre-title" dues and B's "post-title" dues are two titles for the same amount, depending on the point-of-view of whoever owes them.

[49] The court in *Villagio at Estero Condo. Ass'n, Inc. v. Deutsche Bank Nat. Trust Co.*, 2016 WL 4580146 (Fla. Cir. Ct. Lee Cnty. 2016) has specifically rejected the "bifurcated estoppel" concept.

[50] Other trial courts have also rejected the general argument that the association can pursue (for back dues owed by the borrower) a third-party purchaser that buys property from a foreclosing first mortgagee that took title. *See, e.g., Deutsche Bank v. Dofflevisnd*, 2009 WL

estoppels, when it stated that safe harbor was extended to a third-party purchaser who took title from a foreclosing first mortgagee who was entitled to safe harbor.[51] The Fourth District held that "although Fannie Mae was not 'a first mortgagee, or its successor or assignee as a subsequent holder of the first mortgage who acquire[d] title to a parcel by foreclosure or by deed in lieu of foreclosure' under § 720.3085(2)(c), Fannie Mae does *indirectly* benefit from the safe harbor provision because, under § 720.3085(2)(b), it is jointly and severally liable with the prior parcel owner, CitiMortgage, for all unpaid assessments due up to the time of transfer of title, and CitiMortgage did qualify for the safe harbor provision."[52]

The association may attempt to excuse the issuance of this "bifurcated" estoppel on the grounds of the *Spiaggia* Amendments, asserting that the *Spiaggia* Amendments basically overruled *Aventura Management, LLC v. Spiaggia Ocean Condominium Association, Inc. (Spiaggia I), Aventura Management, LLC v. Spiaggia Ocean Condominium Association, Inc.*, and *Park West Professional Center Condominium Association v. Londono*. This is, in fact, the implied holding of *Coastal Creek*. However, it appears more logical that the general rule in those Third District *Spiaggia* line of cases still stands, as noted by one trial court,[53] because the *Spiaggia* Amendments were solely designed to affect the limited situations where the association takes title.

8626512 (Fla. Cir. Ct. Palm Beach Cnty. 2009) ("The association may not seek to collect any other portions of unpaid assessments which other prior owners may have owed to the association from a new parcel owner acquiring title from the foreclosing first mortgagee who took title through a foreclosure action."); *U.S. Bank Nat. Ass'n v. Valdes*, 2011 WL 10725878 (Fla. Cir. Ct. Palm Beach Cnty. 2011) ("That the Defendant is not permitted to pursue any subsequent owners of the subject property for unpaid assessments that are capped or extinguished by Fla. Stat. § 718.116(1)(b)."); *U.S. Bank Nat. Ass'n v. The Stratford Winter Park Condo. Ass'n, Inc.*, 2012 WL 12869501 (Fla. Cir. Ct. Seminole Cnty. 2012) ("The Defendant is not permitted to pursue any subsequent title holder for the unpaid assessments, late fees, interest, or attorneys fees that fall within the 'Safe Harbor' exception of Fla. Stat. § 718.116(1)(b)."); *The Bank of New York Mellon v. Midport Place II Condo. Ass'n, Inc.*, 2012 WL 12869502 (Fla. Cir. Ct. St. Lucie Cnty. 2012) ("That the Defendant is not permitted to pursue any subsequent owners or title holder(s) of the subject condominium unit for unpaid assessments, late fees, interest, collection costs or attorney's fees which may have accrued prior to the time Plaintiff took title to the subject property and that they are capped or extinguished by Fla. Stat. § 718.116(1)(b) under the 'Safe Harbor' exception."); *Wells Fargo Bank, NA v. The Plaza Condo. Ass'n at Berkman Plaza*, 2013 WL 12096560 (Fla. Cir. Ct. Duval Cnty. 2013) ("That the Defendant is not permitted to pursue any subsequent owners or title holder(s) of the subject condominium unit for unpaid assessments, late fees, interest, collection costs or attorney's fees which may have accrued prior to the time Plaintiff took title to the subject property and that they are capped or extinguished by Fla. Stat. § 718.116(1)(b) under the 'Safe Harbor' exception."); *Aurora Loan Services, LLC v. Bravo*, 2011 WL 10959417 (Fla. Cir. Ct. Palm Beach Cnty. 2011) (same rule).

[51] *Villas of Windmill Point II Prop. Owners' Ass'n, Inc. v. Nationstar Mortg., LLC*, 229 So. 3d 822, 824 (Fla. 4th DCA 2017), *rev. den.*, No. SC18-36, 2018 WL 2059527 (Fla. May 2, 2018).

[52] *Villas of Windmill Point II Prop. Owners' Ass'n, Inc. v. Nationstar Mortg., LLC*, 229 So. 3d 822, 824 (Fla. 4th DCA 2017), *rev. den.*, No. SC18-36, 2018 WL 2059527 (Fla. May 2, 2018). In other words, there was no discussion in this case of Fannie Mae being the owner of the loan, or anything other than a third-party purchaser who was entitled to benefit from the safe harbor of the first mortgagee, who was the immediate-prior owner.

[53] *Villagio at Estero Condominium Ass'n, Inc. v. Deutsche Bank Nat. Trust Co.*, 2016 WL 4580146, *3 (Fla. Cir. Ct. Lee Cnty. 2016) ("The Association attempts to argue that the *Spiaggia* Line of Opinions are not directly on point, due to factual dissimilarities, and that

The issue depends in part on how one views safe harbor. It has been said that the foreclosure judgment wipes out the association's lien,[54] and the safe harbor provision merely creates a limited, monetary, pre-title statutory liability.[55] In other words, the safe harbor amount is not a partial resurrection of the association's lien,[56] but merely a monetary, statutory liability[57] Some associations' counsel call the safe harbor a "super-lien," implying the safe harbor portion is part of the association's lien that cannot be wiped out by foreclosure; the covert purpose behind this renaming of the safe harbor is most likely an attempt to portray the safe harbor as a floor, not a ceiling, but it is not an accurate description of safe harbor.

9-4:2 Foreclosing First Mortgagees Get Safe Harbor from Associations That Are Properly Named in the Foreclosure as Defendants

This general rule of joint and several liability is tempered in the case of foreclosing first mortgagees by application of a statutory "safe harbor," if the association is sued and served in the foreclosure.[58] There is a safe harbor statute both for homeowners associ-

---

the *Spiaggia* Line of Opinions have been preempted by an amendment to § 718.116(1)(a). However, this Court finds those arguments unavailing. The third district determined that use of the singular definite article 'the' in § 718.116(1)(a), rather than 'a,' when referring to 'previous owner' was evidence of the legislature's intent to limit the amount of unpaid assessments a new owner could be held responsible for paying. *See Spiaggia II*, 149 So. 3d at 692; *Bona Vista*, 194 So. 3d at 492. Moreover, the mere fact that the applicable statute has been amended after the *Spiaggia* decisions does not undermine their legitimacy. *Heath v. State*, 532 So. 2d 9, 10 (Fla. 1st DCA 1988) ('Although legislative amendment of a statute may change law . . . it does not follow that court decisions interpreting a statute are rendered inapplicable by a subsequent amendment to the statute. Instead, the nature and effect of the court decisions and the statutory amendment must be examined to determine what law may be applicable after the amendment.'). Here, the amendment to the statute merely removed an intervening association who takes title to a unit from the definition of a 'previous owner.' *See* Fla. Stat. § 718.116(1)(a). However, as there is no intervening association in this case, the amendment is wholly irrelevant. Moreover, the third district has recently reiterated its stance in its decision in *Bona Vista*. 194 So. 3d at 490.").

[54] All of a named association's liens recorded prior to the certificate of sale are foreclosed by the first mortgagee. *Ober v. Town of Lauderdale-by-the-Sea*, 218 So. 3d 952 (Fla. 4th 2017), *rev. den.*, No. SC17-748, 2017 WL 3883662 (Fla. Sept. 6, 2017).

[55] *In re Plummer*, 484 B.R. 882, 887, 890 (M.D. Fla. Bankr. Jan. 14, 2013).

[56] "[T]he lien in favor of the association was created by the statute itself." *Calendar v. Stonebridge Gardens Section III Condo. Ass'n, Inc.*, 234 So. 3d 18, 19-20 (Fla. 4th DCA 2017) ("We agree with this reasoning and we hold that the lien in favor of the association was created by the statute itself. Since there is no indication that a first mortgage was at issue in this case, the association was not required to file a claim to validate its lien.") (citing Fla. Stat. § 718.116(5)(a)).

[57] *In re Plummer*, 484 B.R. 882, 887, 890 (M.D. Fla. Bankr. Jan. 14, 2013).

[58] Fla. Stat. § 720.3085(2)(c) ("The limitations on first mortgagee liability provided by this paragraph apply only if the first mortgagee filed suit against the parcel owner and initially joined the association as a defendant in the mortgagee foreclosure action."); Fla. Stat. § 718.116(1)(b)1.b. ("The provisions of this paragraph apply only if the first mortgagee joined the association as a defendant in the foreclosure action.").

ations ("HOAs")[59] and condominium associations.[60] Under these safe harbor statutes, a first mortgagee is not responsible for any past due assessments for amounts over 12 months of dues, or 1 percent of the mortgage amount, whichever is less. The holder of the mortgage who takes title at the sale gets safe harbor.[61] Also, the owner (such as Fannie Mae and Freddie Mac) who owned the loan during the foreclosure, and who takes title at sale, even if not the plaintiff who took the judgment as holder of the loan, can also come into court, post-sale, prove its owner status, and get safe harbor.[62] In other words, both the holder and owner are entitled to safe harbor.[63] The benefits

---

[59] Fla. Stat. § 720.3085(2)(c) ("... the liability of a first mortgagee, or its successor or assignee as a subsequent holder of the first mortgage who acquires title to a parcel by foreclosure or by deed in lieu of foreclosure for the unpaid assessments that became due before the mortgagee's acquisition of title, shall be the lesser of:

1. The parcel's unpaid common expenses and regular periodic or special assessments that accrued or came due during the 12 months immediately preceding the acquisition of title and for which payment in full has not been received by the association; or

2. One percent of the original mortgage debt.")

[60] Fla. Stat. § 718.116(1)(b) ("1. The liability of a first mortgagee or its successor or assignees who acquire title to a unit by foreclosure or by deed in lieu of foreclosure for the unpaid assessments that became due before the mortgagee's acquisition of title is limited to the lesser of:

a. The unit's unpaid common expenses and regular periodic assessments which accrued or came due during the 12 months immediately preceding the acquisition of title and for which payment in full has not been received by the association; or

b. One percent of the original mortgage debt.").

[61] *Brittany's Place Condo. Ass'n, Inc. v. U.S. Bank, N.A.*, 205 So. 3d 794, 801 (Fla. 2d DCA 2016) ("Because we conclude that a successor or assignee of the first mortgage otherwise entitled to the limited liability of Section 718.116(1)(b) need not also be an owner of the note and mortgage at the time of foreclosure, we affirm the order granting final summary judgment."); *Vill. Square Condo. v. U.S. Bank Nat. Ass'n*, 206 So. 3d 806, (Mem)–807 (Fla. 5th DCA 2016) ("U.S. Bank argues that it was a first mortgagee because it was the holder of the note and mortgage. This issue was recently addressed by the Second District Court of Appeal in *Brittany's Place Condo. Ass'n, Inc. v. U.S. Bank, N.A.*, ... We agree with Judge Black's well-reasoned opinion, which concluded that ownership of the note and mortgage is not required in order for a foreclosing party to limit its liability pursuant to the safe harbor provisions of section 718.116(1)(b), Florida Statutes (2014)."); *San Matera the Gardens Condo. Ass'n, Inc. v. Fed. Home Loan Mortg. Corp.*, 207 So. 3d 1017, 1019 (Fla. 4th DCA 2017) ("Applying these principles to the instant case, we hold that *Bayview*, as the holder of the note, qualified for the safe harbor provision as the first mortgagee. Additionally, Freddie Mac, as an assignee of the first mortgagee, also qualified for the safe harbor provision."). *See also Bay Holdings, Inc. v. 2000 Island Blvd. Condo. Ass'n*, 895 So. 2d 1197, 1197-98 (Fla. 3d DCA 2005).

[62] *Beltway Capital, LLC v. Greens COA, Inc.*, 153 So. 3d 330 (Fla. 5th DCA 2014); *Hemingway Villa Condo. Owners Ass'n, Inc. v. Wells Fargo Bank, N.A.*, 240 So. 3d 104, 106-07 (Fla. 3d DCA 2018); *Citation Way Condominium Association, Inc. v. Wells Fargo Bank, N.A.*, 172 So. 3d 558 (Fla. 4th DCA 2015) (Wells Fargo obtained judgment as holder, but Fannie Mae was still entitled to safe harbor as mortgage owner and purchaser at sale).

[63] *San Matera the Gardens Condo. Ass'n, Inc. v. Fed. Home Loan Mortg. Corp.*, 207 So. 3d 1017, 1019 (Fla. 4th DCA 2017) ("Applying these principles to the instant case, we hold that Bayview, as the holder of the note, qualified for the safe harbor provision as the first mortgagee.

of safe harbor have even been extended beyond a holder and owner of the loan, even to a third-party purchaser who takes title from a foreclosing first mortgagee who is entitled to safe harbor.[64]

But it is highly recommended that the named plaintiff for whom a foreclosure judgment is entered also be the named bidder at the foreclosure sale, as this will avoid unnecessary litigation with opportunistic associations. A post-certificate-of-title quitclaim deed from holder to owner can always be used in place of an assignment of bid to avoid this issue.[65]

9-4:3 The Declaration Trumps the Safe Harbor Statute

The declaration in effect when the mortgage was issued trumps a later-enacted safe harbor statute, procedurally and substantively, if it does not include language incorporating later amendments, sometimes called "*Kaufman* language."[66] Such language in the association's relevant declaration would adopt later changes to the association chapter "as amended from time to time."[67]

Additionally, Freddie Mac, as an assignee of the first mortgagee, also qualified for the safe harbor provision.").

[64] *Villas of Windmill Point II Prop. Owners' Ass'n, Inc. v. Nationstar Mortg., LLC,* 229 So. 3d 822, 824 (Fla. 4th DCA 2017), *rev. den.*, No. SC18-36, 2018 WL 2059527 (Fla. May 2, 2018).

[65] *See Villas of Windmill Point II Prop. Owners' Ass'n, Inc. v. Nationstar Mortg., LLC,* 229 So. 3d 822, 824 (Fla. 4th DCA 2017), *rev. den.*, No. SC18-36, 2018 WL 2059527 (Fla. May 2, 2018).

[66] *Dimitri v. Commercial Ctr. of Miami Master Ass'n, Inc.*, 253 So. 3d 715, 719 n.2 (Fla. 3d DCA 2018) ("As the trial court correctly noted, later amendments to chapter 718 may alter the rights and duties of the parties to an existing declaration if the declaration specifically incorporates these amendments.") (citing *Kaufman v. Shere*, 347 So. 2d 627, 628 (Fla. 3d DCA 1977) ("[T]he provisions of the Condominium Act as presently existing, or as it may be amended from time to time, including the definitions therein contained, are adopted and included herein by express reference")).

[67] *See Angora Enters., Inc. v. Cole*, 439 So. 2d 832, 833 (Fla.1983); *Cohn v. Grand Condo. Ass'n, Inc.*, 62 So. 3d 1120, 1121 (Fla. 2011); *Sans Souci v. Div. of Fla. Land Sales & Condos., Dep't of Bus. Regulation,* 421 So. 2d 623, 628-29 (Fla. 1st DCA 1982) ("Although, as stated, the date of filing of the declaration of condominium and the master sublease fixes the rights and obligations of the parties and will many times determine which statutes are applicable to a given cause, . . . our research reveals that it has been routine for many developers to include a clause in their declarations of condominium incorporating the provisions of the Condominium Act by the reference 'as the same may be amended from time to time.' Known as the 'automatic amendment theory,' the legal effect of such a clause is to apply all subsequent amendments of the Condominium Act to the declaration, as if expressed therein.") (footnotes omitted). *Cf. Ecoventure WGV, Ltd. v. Saint Johns Northwest Residential Ass'n, Inc.*, 56 So. 3d 126, 128 (Fla. 5th DCA 2011) ("The Association could have incorporated the subsequent enactment of Section 720.3085 into the Declaration by including language expressly incorporating by reference the provisions of Chapter 720. . . . However, no such language was in the Declaration."); *Tropicana Condo. Ass'n, Inc. v. Tropical Condo., LLC,* 208 So. 3d 755, 758 (Fla. 3d DCA 2016) ("It bears noting that, in 1983, the drafters of Tropicana's Declaration had the benefit of our 1977 *Kaufman* decision and could have chosen to qualify the Declaration to include any subsequent revisions to Florida's Condominium Act enacted by the Florida Legislature. The drafters chose not to include such *Kaufman* language.") (citing *Kaufman v. Shere*, 347 So. 2d 627 (Fla. 3d DCA 1977)). *Absent Kaufman* language, an amendment to the Condominium Act will not have retroactive application to a condominium's Declaration if it impairs contractual obligations, but some level

This can be a good thing or a bad thing for a first mortgagee.[68] For instance, sometimes the foreclosure firm will have neglected to name one or more associations or country clubs, sometimes because the title company missed them. But it may be that the relevant declaration will give safe harbor (or better) without a specific requirement that the association be named and sued as a defendant in the foreclosure.[69] To find out what declaration and safe harbor statute applies, one needs to know when the subject mortgage was executed and when the declaration and amendments thereto were recorded.[70]

The declaration and amendments in effect when the mortgage was executed procedurally trumps the statutory safe harbor statute (if any), unless the declaration contains specific language incorporating the relevant association act and subsequent statutory amendments.[71]

---

of impairment is tolerable. *See Tropicana Condo. Ass'n, Inc. v. Tropical Condo., LLC,* 208 So. 3d 755, 758-60 (Fla. 3d DCA 2016). The Florida Supreme Court in *Pomponio v. Claridge of Pompano Condo., Inc.,* 378 So. 2d 774 (Fla.1979) adopted a three-pronged balancing test to determine whether a statutory change in the Condominium Act can be applied retroactively without running afoul of Florida's Constitution. *Id.* at 779. Additionally, if the Declaration gives complete discretion to the association on whether to give safe harbor, that provision is "illusory" and therefore unenforceable; thus, retroactive application of the statute does not unconstitutionally impair that provision by overriding it, even without *Kaufman* language in the Declaration. *The Plantation at Ponte Vedra, Inc. v. Wells Fargo Bank, N.A.,* 2016 WL 6127570 (Fla. Cir. Ct. St. Johns Feb. 25, 2016), *per curiam aff'd,* Nos. 5D16-2161, 5D16-2675 (Fla. 5th DCA July 25, 2017).

[68] *But see, The Plantation at Ponte Vedra, Inc. v. U.S. Bank, N.A.,* No. CA13–1072, 2014 WL 786346 (Fla. Cir. Ct. St. Johns Feb. 5, 2014). If the declaration contains specific language that its association liens relate back to the date the declaration was recorded and are thus superior to intervening mortgages, and no safe harbor statute applies, then the association's lien may be superior. *See Holly Lakes Ass'n v. Fed. Nat'l Mortgage Ass'n,* 660 So. 2d 266 (Fla.1995); *Ass'n of Poinciana Villages v. Avatar Props., Inc.,* 724 So. 2d 585 (Fla. 5th DCA 1998); *U.S. Bank Nat. Ass'n v. Grant,* 180 So. 3d 1092 (Fla. 4th DCA 2015) (declaration contained no language that liens relate back to recording of declaration so prior recorded mortgages are superior to subsequently recorded association liens); *In re Plummer,* 484 B.R. 882, 885-86 (M.D. Fla. Bankr. Jan. 14, 2013) (discussing the relevance of a declaration's language).

[69] *Willoughby Estates v. BankUnited,* 2015 WL 5472506 (Fla. Cir. Ct. Palm Beach June 23, 2015) (declaration provided safe harbor without requiring the association be sued).

[70] It seems that lenders in Florida, before closing, might want to study the declarations in associations so as to see how the lender will be treated, after foreclosure, if the borrower does not pay. Associations who do not provide safe harbor by declaration might feel the heat—when only the cash-wealthy can buy in their associations because lenders will not lend—and thereafter see the light.

[71] *See Angora Enters., Inc. v. Cole,* 439 So. 2d 832, 833 (Fla.1983); *Ecoventure WGV, Ltd. v. Saint Johns Northwest Residential Ass'n, Inc.,* 56 So. 3d 126, 128 n.1 (Fla. 5th DCA 2011) ("The Association could have incorporated the subsequent enactment of Section 720.3085 into the Declaration by including language expressly incorporating by reference the provisions of Chapter 720. . . . However, no such language was in the Declaration."); *Sans Souci v. Div. of Florida Land Sales & Condominiums, Dep't of Bus. Regulation,* 421 So. 2d 623, 628-29 (Fla. 1st DCA 1982) ("Although, as stated, the date of filing of the declaration of condominium and the master sublease fixes the rights and obligations of the parties and will many times determine which statutes are applicable to a given cause, . . . our research reveals that it has been routine for many developers to include a clause in their declarations

Substantively, too, sometimes the declaration will be more favorable than the relevant "safe harbor" statute. For instance, sometimes the declaration will state that a first mortgagee owes no dues at all while the first mortgagee owns it, or only owes "post-title" dues (meaning the first mortgagee owes no "safe harbor" amount, which is a "pre-title" statutory liability).[72] Sometimes, the declaration will provide that the first mortgagee only owes six months of pre-title dues (as opposed to 12 months, as in the safe harbor statutes) or 1 percent of the mortgage's face amount (whichever is less). Sometimes, the declaration will provide that the first mortgagee only owes a *pro rata* share, along with the other owners of homes or units, of pre-title dues. Sometimes, the declaration will even extend safe harbor, or better than safe harbor, beyond first mortgagees, to second or even more junior mortgagees or lienors.

Pursuant to Florida law, the first mortgagee's rights under the declaration vest when the declaration was relied upon, that is, at the time the mortgage was executed.[73] Moreover, Florida courts have held that an association may not unilaterally void

---

of condominium incorporating the provisions of the Condominium Act by the reference 'as the same may be amended from time to time.' Known as the 'automatic amendment theory,' the legal effect of such a clause is to apply all subsequent amendments of the Condominium Act to the declaration, as if expressed therein.") (footnotes omitted).

[72] However, if the investor does not appeal or argue this more favorable Declaration, or file the relevant Declaration in the trial court, the issue cannot be raised on appeal. *Catalina West Homeowners Ass'n v. Federal National Mortg. Ass'n*, 188 So. 3d 76, 79 n.3 (Fla. 3d DCA 2016).

[73] *See Ecoventure WGV, Ltd. v. Saint Johns N.W. Residential Ass'n, Inc.*, 56 So. 3d 126, 127 (Fla. 5th DCA 2011); *Coral Lakes Community Ass'n, Inc. v. Busey Bank, N.A.*, 30 So. 3d 579, 583-84 (Fla. 2d DCA 2010); *Pudlit 2 Joint Venture, LLP v. Westwood Gardens Homeowners Association, Inc.*, 169 So. 3d 145 (Fla. 4th DCA 2015); *Genesis Re Holdings, LLC v, Woodside Estates Homeowners Association, Inc.*, 2015 WL 5511558 (Fla. Cir. Ct. Broward May 8, 2015) (three judge circuit court panel in appellate capacity over county court judge); *Ero Properties, Inc. v. Cone*, 418 So. 2d 434, 435 (Fla. 3d DCA 1982); *Tradewinds of Pompano Ass'n, Inc. v. Rosenthal*, 407 So. 2d 976, 977 (Fla. 4th DCA 1981). *See also, Beacon Hill Homeowners Ass'n, Inc. v. Colfin Ah-Florida 7, LLC*, 221 So. 3d 710, 713 (Fla. 3d DCA 2017) ("The joint and several liability of section 720.3085(2)(b) was not incorporated into the terms of the Associations' Declarations. Accordingly, under the language adopted by the Associations in their Declarations, Colfin was not liable for any past due assessments, attorney's fees, or costs of the prior owner when it purchased the property in question at the foreclosure sale, for the reasons set forth in *Pudlit*.").

With regard to Florida associations, a federal judge has stated that, "an honest man's word is as good as his bond" and "[o]ne would think this doubly true of a corporate entity that published its charter so that purchasers and lenders could rely upon it." *United States of America v. Forest Hill Gardens E. Condo. Ass'n, Inc.*, 2014 WL 28723, *3 (S.D. Fla. Jan. 3, 2014). *But see, Ballantrae Homeowners Ass'n, Inc. v. Fed. Nat. Mortg. Ass'n*, 203 So. 3d 938, 940 (Fla. 2d DCA 2016) ("Here, the Declaration's subordination of lien provision relied on by Fannie Mae contains the first promise made in *Ecoventure*, subordinating the assessment lien to the first mortgage, but it does not contain language specifically limiting or eliminating a subsequent owner's liability for unpaid assessment. *See id.; see also Coral Lakes*, 30 So. 3d at 582; *Pudlit 2 Joint Venture, LLP v. Westwood Gardens Homeowners Ass'n*, 169 So. 3d 145, 148 (Fla. 4th DCA 2015) (quoting declaration provision expressly limiting subsequent owner's personal liability for delinquent assessments). Second, *Coral Lakes* and *Ecoventure* are distinguishable in that they do not address a subsequent owner's liability for assessments following a foreclosure that failed to include the association.").

provisions of a declaration unless the provisions violate public policy, are wholly arbitrary in their application, or violate fundamental constitutional rights.[74]

9-4:4 Various Arguments Put Forth by Associations Seeking to Deny Safe Harbor

Sometimes, even when the association was properly named and sued in the foreclosure, the association will (post-judgment and post-title) challenge the first mortgagee's right to safe harbor. In such instances, the association can be informed that the issue was already litigated in the foreclosure. For instance, foreclosure judgment form 1.966(a) states in essence that the plaintiff holds a mortgage lien and that on filing the certificate of sale, all persons claiming under or against the defendants since the lis pendens shall be foreclosed of all estate or claim in the property, except as to claims or rights under Chapter 718 or Chapter 720, Florida Statutes, if any. When the Court enters such a final judgment, it finds that first mortgagee had standing to foreclose as holder. This, of course, is because first mortgagee holds the note; and because the mortgage follows the note as a matter of Florida law.[75] The association arguably should be estopped by the doctrines of *res judicata* and collateral estoppel from denying first mortgagee, who foreclosed as holder, the right to the statutory safe harbor.[76]

However, there are cases that state that the form foreclosure judgment is not *res judicata* on the issue of safe harbor and past due assessments.[77] Still, this seems questionable, because, otherwise, why do the safe harbor statutes require that the association be named, if not to deal with the association-related issues in one case?[78]

---

[74] *See Grove Isle Ass'n, Inc. v. Grove Isle Assocs., LLLP*, 137 So. 3d 1081, 1090-91 (Fla. 3d DCA 2014); *see also Aquarian Foundation, Inc. v. Sholom House, Inc.*, 448 So. 2d 1166, 1167 (Fla. 3d DCA 1984) (reasoning that "strict enforcement of the restrictions of an association's private constitution, that is, its declaration of condominium, protects the members' reliance interests in a document which they have knowingly accepted. . . .").

[75] *Cf. Lamb v. Nationstar Mortg., LLC*, 174 So. 3d 1039, 1041 (Fla. 4th DCA 2015) ("Nationstar did not prove its standing to enforce the note through evidence of an assignment because the assignment at bar assigns *only the mortgage*. . . . A bank does not have standing to foreclose where it relies on an assignment of the mortgage only.") (emphasis in original); *Tilus v. AS Michai LLC*, 161 So. 3d 1284, 1286 (Fla. 4th DCA 2015) ("The mortgage follows the assignment of the promissory note, but an assignment of the mortgage without an assignment of the debt creates no right in the assignee.")).

[76] *See United States v. Bridgewater Community Ass'n, Inc.*, 2013 WL 3285399 (M.D. Fla. 2013). *See also Delcher Bros. Storage Co. v. Carter*, 132 So. 2d 593, 595 (Fla. 1965); *Donaldson Engineering, Inc. v. City of Plantation*, 326 So. 2d 209, 210 (Fla. 4th DCA 1976) (noting that, "[i]f the City had felt that such factual finding was erroneous, it should have sought a rehearing or sought a reversal upon appeal").

[77] *Montreux at Deerwood Lake Condo. Ass'n, Inc. v. Citibank, N.A.*, 153 So. 3d 961 (Fla. 1st DCA 2014); *Meadows on the Green Condo. Ass'n, Inc. v. Nationstar Mortg., LLC*, 188 So. 3d 883 (Mem), 2016 WL 72585 (Fla. 4th DCA 2016); *Central Park A Metrowest Condo. Ass'n, Inc. v. Amtrust REO I, LLC*, 169 So. 3d 1223 (Fla. 5th DCA 2015) (following *Montreux* and *Callahan*).

[78] *Cf. Citation Way Condo. Ass'n, Inc. v. Wells Fargo Bank, N.A.*, 172 So. 3d 558 (Fla. 4th DCA 2015).

But the issue is easily resolved by the bank putting on evidence of the association issue and inserting a ruling into the form foreclosure judgment, as well as a reservation of specific jurisdiction on the issue of subsequent disputes with the association.[79]

Similarly, when the Association in its answer and affirmative defenses in the lender's foreclosure action affirmatively pleads that lender is a first mortgagee entitled to safe harbor, it is arguably judicially estopped from arguing otherwise in a later dispute, or alternatively, has waived the issue.[80] An association should not be able to, post-judgment, argue exactly the opposite of what it earlier pled, just because the defaulting borrower is now out of title and the deep-pocket bank is in title.[81] Merely because the association's interests have changed, the salient facts have not. In such cases, the association has waived the argument that the first mortgagee is not entitled to safe harbor.[82]

---

[79] *See Grand Cent. at Kennedy Condo. Ass'n v. Space Coast Credit Union*, 173 So. 3d 1089, 1091 n.2 (Fla. 2d DCA 2015); *Hidden Ridge Condo. Homeowners Ass'n, Inc. v. OneWest Bank, N.A.*, 183 So. 3d 1266, 1270 n.4 (Fla. 5th DCA 2016) ("We also find neither party presented competent evidence to establish which one had a superior interest in the condo. Thus, on remand, either party may request an evidentiary hearing to resolve this issue."); *Fogarty v. Nationstar Mortg., LLC*, 224 So. 3d 313, 316 (Fla. 5th DCA 2017) ("Nationstar argues the trial court improperly dismissed Seagrove as a superior lienholder to Nationstar. We reverse the dismissal and remand for the trial court to reinstate Seagrove as a party to this litigation. Because neither party presented competent evidence to establish which one had a superior interest, '[o]n remand, either party may request an evidentiary hearing to resolve this issue.'") (quoting *Hidden Ridge Condo. Homeowners v. Greentree Servicing, LLC*, 167 So. 3d 483 (Fla. 5th DCA 2015)).

[80] *Bank of Am., Nat. Ass'n v. Enclave at Richmond Place Condo. Ass'n*, 173 So. 3d 1095, 1097-98 (Fla. 2d DCA 2015) ("We conclude that the Association's affirmative plea of entitlement to only the lesser of six months' unpaid assessments or one percent of the mortgage debt was a waiver of any claim to a greater assessment figure.").

[81] However, judicial estoppel may not be applicable in this circumstance, because generally a party has to prevail on the prior inconsistent position, and additionally, the doctrine has been weakened somewhat in the case of *Anfriany v. Deutsche Bank Nat'l Tr. Co. for Registered Holders of Argent Secs., Inc., Asset-Backed Pass-Through Certificates, Series 2005-W4*, 232 So. 3d 425 (Fla. 4th DCA 2017). The *Anfriany* court also held that Florida law of judicial estoppel differs from federal law. *See id.* For general principles of waiver and judicial estoppel, *see Blumberg v. USAA Cas. Ins.*, 790 So. 2d 1061, 1067 (Fla. 2001) (the doctrine of judicial estoppel prevents parties from "making a mockery of justice by inconsistent pleadings" . . . and "playing fast and loose with the courts"); *DK Arena, Inc. v. EB Acquisitions I, LLC*, 112 So. 3d 85, 97-98 (Fla. 2013) ("Waiver operates to estop one from asserting that upon which he otherwise might have relied. . . ." (quoting *Source-Track, LLC v. Ariba, Inc.*, 958 So. 2d 523, 527 (Fla. 2d DCA 2007))); *Barbe v. Villeneuve*, 505 So. 2d 1331, 1333 (Fla. 1987) ("A party will not be permitted to enforce wholly inconsistent demands respecting the same right[s]." (quoting *American Process Co. v. Fla. White Pressed Brick Co.*, 56 Fla. 116, 47 So. 942, 944 (1908))); *Tara Woods SPE, LLC v. Cashin*, 116 So. 3d 492, 501 (Fla. 2d DCA 2013) (discussing the elements of waiver and their application).

[82] *Bank of Am., Nat. Ass'n v. Enclave at Richmond Place Condo. Ass'n*, 173 So. 3d 1095, 1097-98 (Fla. 2d DCA 2015) ("We conclude that the Association's affirmative plea of entitlement to only the lesser of six months' unpaid assessments or one percent of the mortgage debt was a waiver of any claim to a greater assessment figure."). *See also DK Arena, Inc. v. EB Acquisitions I, LLC*, 112 So. 3d 85, 97–98 (Fla. 2013) ("Waiver operates to estop one from

Sometimes the association will attempt to argue that the foreclosing lender may have *held the note* and thus had standing to foreclose, but did not *own the mortgage* and thus was not a "first mortgagee" or its "successor or assignee" and therefore not entitled to the "narrower" safe harbor. But there is directly *contrary* authority.[83] The first mortgagee is *first* mortgagee because it holds the note secured by a mortgage that is *first* in position[84] Therefore, by this simple fact, the first mortgagee or its assignee is entitled to the statutory safe harbor.[85]

A first mortgagee can also be the "successor or assignee" to the originating lender for safe harbor purposes. For instance, the condominium safe harbor statute defines the term "successor or assignee" of the "first mortgagee" in Fla. Stat. § 718.116(1) (g), which provides:

> ... the term "successor or assignee" as used with respect to a first mortgagee includes only **a subsequent holder of the first mortgage.**

Fla. Stat. § 718.116(1)(g) (emphasis supplied).

Notably, the word "owner" of the mortgage is not mentioned in this definition. However, the word "holder" is used, but unlike a note, a mortgage is not a negotiable instrument to which Florida's Uniform Commercial Code (UCC) applies. In this regard, the definition of a first mortgagee's successor or assignee as "a subsequent holder of the first mortgage" is "not entirely unambiguous."[86] Looking to the dictionary definition of "holder," the Second DCA held that "a holder of a non-negotiable instrument may be an owner or a possessor of the instrument," but it reached "the same conclusion applying the UCC definition of holder."[87] Holding the note, and therefore the right to enforce the mortgage, renders theoretical "ownership" of the note

---

asserting that upon which he otherwise might have relied. . . ." (quoting *SourceTrack, LLC v. Ariba, Inc.*, 958 So. 2d 523, 527 (Fla. 2d DCA 2007))); *Barbe v. Villeneuve,* 505 So. 2d 1331, 1333 (Fla. 1987) ("A party will not be permitted to enforce wholly inconsistent demands respecting the same right[s]." (quoting *Am. Process Co. v. Fla. White Pressed Brick Co.*, 56 Fla. 116, 47 So. 942, 944 (1908))); *Tara Woods SPE, LLC v. Cashin*, 116 So. 3d 492, 501 (Fla. 2d DCA 2013) (discussing the elements of waiver and their application).

[83] *Brittany's Place Condo. Ass'n, Inc. v. U.S. Bank, N.A.*, 205 So. 3d 794 (Fla. 2d DCA 2016).
[84] *See Beltway Capital, LLC v. Greens COA, Inc.*, 153 So. 3d 330 (Fla. 5th DCA 2014); *Hemingway Villa Condo. Owners Ass'n, Inc. v. Wells Fargo Bank, N.A.*, 240 So. 3d 104, 106-07 (Fla. 3d DCA 2018); *Citation Way Condo. Ass'n, Inc. v. Wells Fargo Bank, N.A.*, 172 So. 3d 558 (Fla. 4th DCA 2015); *Brittany's Place Condo. Ass'n, Inc. v. U.S. Bank, N.A.*, 205 So. 3d 794, 798 (Fla. 2d DCA 2016) ("Thus a first mortgagee is the holder of the mortgage lien with priority over all other mortgages.").
[85] *San Matera the Gardens Condo. Ass'n, Inc. v. Fed. Home Loan Mortg. Corp.*, 207 So. 3d 1017, 1019 (Fla. 4th DCA 2017) ("Additionally, Freddie Mac, as an assignee of the first mortgagee, also qualified for the safe harbor provision.").
[86] *Brittany's Place Condo. Ass'n, Inc. v. U.S. Bank, N.A.*, 205 So. 3d 794, 799 (Fla. 2d DCA 2016)
[87] *Brittany's Place Condo. Ass'n, Inc. v. U.S. Bank, N.A.*, 205 So. 3d 794, 799-800 (Fla. 2d DCA 2016). *See also Everhome Mortg. Co. v. Janssen*, 100 So. 3d 1239, 1240 (Fla. 2d DCA 2012) ("We are compelled to point out that possession of the note determines standing to foreclose."); *Mortgage Electronic Registration Sys., Inc. v. Azize,* 965 So. 2d 151, 153 (Fla. 2d DCA 2007) ("The holder of a note has standing to seek enforcement of the note.").

and mortgage unnecessary for safe harbor.[88] Even when dealing with an HOA under Chapter 720, which does not define "successor or assignee," § 718.116(1)(g) may still be instructive.

To the extent that the association argues that an assignment of mortgage ("AOM") deprived the holder of the note of standing to get safe harbor (as opposed to foreclosing), this argument is belied by the existence of the aforementioned Form 1.966(a) final judgment, which the association presumably did not (at least successfully) appeal, which mentions the safe harbor statutes. Additionally, the assignment of mortgage statute itself states:

Notwithstanding subsections (1), (2), and (3) governing the assignment of mortgages, chapters 670-680 of the Uniform Commercial Code of this state govern the attachment and perfection of a security interest in a mortgage upon real

---

[88] *Brittany's Place Condo. Ass'n, Inc. v. U.S. Bank, N.A.*, 205 So. 3d 794, 799-801 (Fla. 2d DCA 2016); *Vill. Square Condo. v. U.S. Bank Nat. Ass'n*, 206 So. 3d 806, (Mem)–807 (Fla. 5th DCA 2016) ("U.S. Bank argues that it was a first mortgagee because it was the holder of the note and mortgage. This issue was recently addressed by the Second District Court of Appeal in *Brittany's Place Condominium Association, Inc. v. U.S. Bank, N.A.*, . . . We agree with Judge Black's well-reasoned opinion, which concluded that ownership of the note and mortgage is not required in order for a foreclosing party to limit its liability pursuant to the safe harbor provisions of section 718.116(1)(b), Florida Statutes (2014)."); *San Matera the Gardens Condo. Ass'n, Inc. v. Fed. Home Loan Mortg. Corp.*, 207 So. 3d 1017, 1019 (Fla. 4th DCA 2017) ("Applying these principles to the instant case, we hold that Bayview, as the holder of the note, qualified for the safe harbor provision as the first mortgagee. Additionally, Freddie Mac, as an assignee of the first mortgagee, also qualified for the safe harbor provision."). *See also Rodriguez v. Wells Fargo Bank*, 178 So. 3d 62, 64-67 (Fla. 4th DCA Oct. 14, 2015) (Conner, J., concurring) ("As can be seen from the statutory framework, *ownership* (or history of transfer) of the note is not the issue, with regards to standing, unless the note is not in bearer form or is payable to someone or some entity other than the plaintiff filing suit. In such case, documentation or evidence regarding ownership, assignment, or transfer of the note must prove the plaintiff has the rights of a holder. . . . Stated another way, ownership, assignment, or transfer of the note is important to the analysis of standing only when the plaintiff is a nonholder in possession of the note with the rights of a holder.") (emphasis in original); *Wells Fargo Bank, N.A. v. Morcom*, 125 So. 3d 320, 321-22 (Fla. 5th DCA 2013) ("The Florida UCC and recent cases from this court stand for the proposition that a plaintiff has standing to bring a foreclosure action if the plaintiff is the holder of a promissory note, endorsed in blank, secured by a mortgage. . . . Appellees cite Florida Supreme Court precedent dating back to the late 1800s to suggest Appellant must both hold and own the note and mortgage to satisfy the standing requirement for a foreclosure action. The cases Appellees cite are not persuasive because the supreme court decided the cases prior to the adoption of the now-instructive and binding Florida UCC."); *One West Bank, F.S.B. v. Bauer*, 159 So. 3d 843, 845 (Fla. 2d DCA 2014) ("Although One West Bank incorrectly pleaded that it held *and* owned the Bauers' note and mortgage, there is no dispute that One West Bank was in possession of the note at the time the foreclosure complaint was filed. In requiring One West Bank to prove ownership of the loan documents to establish its standing to foreclose, we conclude the trial court departed from the essential requirements of law by imposing a condition that is not required resulting in irreparable harm.") (emphasis in original); *HSBC Bank USA, NA v. Perez*, 165 So. 3d 696 (Fla. 4th DCA 2015) (interpreting Fla. Stat. § 701.02(4)).

property and in a promissory note or other right to payment or performance secured by that mortgage.

Fla. Stat. § 701.02(4).

In other words, the mortgage could be "assigned" to John Doe, but because the assignment statute in § 701.02(4) explicitly bows before the UCC, such an assignment could not be effective unless the note secured by the mortgage was also transferred to Mr. Doe.[89] As a matter of Florida law, whoever holds the note specifically indorsed or indorsed in blank holds the mortgage, regardless of any assignments.[90]

Sometimes associations will give safe harbor but tack on improper amounts, such as post-title amounts of dues that accrued while the association owned the property, which is not lawful if the association took title after the effective date of the relevant *Spiaggia* Amendment.[91]

---

[89] *HSBC Bank USA, NA v. Perez*, 165 So. 3d 696 (Fla. 4th DCA 2015) (interpreting Fla. Stat. § 701.02(4)). *See* Fla. Stat. § 671.201(21)(a); § 671.201(5).

[90] *See Wells Fargo Bank, N.A. v. Russell*, 194 So. 3d 1094, 1096-97 (Fla. 3d DCA 2016) ("The special magistrate and trial judge apparently concluded that the more complicated provenance of the mortgage—from Gateway Funding, with Mortgage Electronic Registration Systems, Inc. (MERS), as a nominee for Gateway and its successors (when the loan was closed in 2003), to Wells Fargo (in October 2011)—should control the standing analysis. It does not. Wells Fargo's obligation to demonstrate standing, whether in its own motion for summary judgment or at trial on remand, is to prove the allegations in its complaint: it is the holder of the note and is entitled to enforce the security instrument which secures repayment of that note. . . . On the face of the summary judgment evidence in this case, Wells Fargo possessed the original note, endorsed in blank, in 2007 as the case was filed. The Russells were not entitled to a summary judgment on their affirmative defense alleging lack of standing."); *ALS-RVC, LLC v. Garvin*, 201 So. 3d 687, 690-92 (Fla. 4th DCA 2016) ("Notwithstanding the confusing assignments, this evidence established the bank's standing. The trial court erred in granting the borrower's motion for involuntary dismissal. Nevertheless, the borrower argues the three assignments of mortgage, one of which assigned the note and mortgage to [third party] Maxim, show the bank lacked standing. This argument is without merit. Even though the bank assigned the note and mortgage to Maxim, the bank met the holder requirements under Section 673.3011(1), Florida Statutes. 'A person may be a person entitled to enforce the instrument even though the person is not the owner of the instrument or is in wrongful possession of the instrument.' § 673.3011, Fla. Stat. (2015).").

[91] *See* Fla. Stat. § 720.3085(2)(b) ("For the purposes of this paragraph, the term 'previous owner' shall not include an association that acquires title to a delinquent property through foreclosure or by deed in lieu of foreclosure. The present parcel owner's liability for unpaid assessments is limited to any unpaid assessments that accrued before the association acquired title to the delinquent property through foreclosure or by deed in lieu of foreclosure.") (eff. 7/1/13); Fla. Stat. § 718.116(1)(b) ("For the purposes of this paragraph, the term 'previous owner' does not include an association that acquires title to a delinquent property through foreclosure or by deed in lieu of foreclosure. A present unit owner's liability for unpaid assessments is limited to any unpaid assessments that accrued before the association acquired title to the delinquent property through foreclosure or by deed in lieu of foreclosure.") (eff. 7/1/14).

Similarly, under the safe harbor statutes, the first mortgagee is not responsible for any *pre-title* late fees, interest, collection costs, or attorney's fees.[92] The first mortgagee is, however, liable for such post-title amounts.[93]

One would think that a first mortgagee should be able to oppose interest, costs and attorney's fees that have accrued *post-title*, as not being recoverable by the association, based on equitable principles—namely, because they were incurred solely because the association refused to provide a timely, lawful estoppel letter and instead chose protracted litigation, at least as to interest. But this has been held to be improper as to interest because the Legislature has expressly provided for entitlement to interest— for a specified duration and at a specified rate—in claims for unpaid condominium assessments[94] One federal court made a similar finding as to "interest, late fees, and other costs that are authorized by statute the appropriate declarations, and their by-laws," albeit without analyzing the equities.[95]

However, even post-title *assessments* are not recoverable under § 718.303(1) (for condominiums) or § 720.305(1) (for HOAs) to the extent a court determines these amounts to be necessary to reimburse a first mortgagee for its share of assessments levied by the association to fund the expenses of the litigation against a first mortgagee. *Ipso facto*, late fees and interest cannot be assessed on such disgorgable post-title dues. In fact, even if a case is otherwise moot, the issue of potential dues disgorgement can keep a case against an association alive.[96]

---

[92] *Catalina West Homeowners Ass'n v. Federal National Mortg. Ass'n*, 188 So. 3d 76 (Fla. 3d DCA 2016) (analyzing *United States of America v. Forest Hill Gardens E. Condo. Ass'n, Inc.*, 2014 WL 28723, *3 (S.D. Fla. Jan. 3, 2014) (interpreting both Fla. Stat. § 720.3085(2)(c) and Fla. Stat. § 718.116(1)(b) as allowing only collection of pre-title dues, and excluding fees, interest, and late charges from the definition of "common expenses" and "regular periodic assessments"); *Emerald Estates Cmty. Ass'n v. U.S. Bank Nat'l Ass'n*, 242 So. 3d 429, 430 (Fla. 4th DCA 2018) ("We agree that based on Section 720.3085(2)(c) *Emerald Estates* was not entitled to costs and attorney's fees that accrued prior to *U.S. Bank* acquiring title.").

[93] *Emerald Estates Cmty. Ass'n v. U.S. Bank Nat'l Ass'n*, 242 So. 3d 429, 430 (Fla. 4th DCA 2018); *See United States of America v. Forest Hill Gardens E. Condo. Ass'n, Inc.*, 2014 WL 28723, at *3 (S.D. Fla. Jan. 3, 2014).

[94] *First Equitable Realty III, Ltd. v. Grandview Palace Condo. Ass'n, Inc.*, 246 So. 3d 445, 446-47 (Fla. 3d DCA 2018) ("While apparently acknowledging that the Association had calculated interest correctly at $50,007.64, the trial court nevertheless decreased the amount of interest due to the Association for 'equitable considerations.' Specifically, upon determining that the Association was responsible for protracted litigation giving rise to the Association's right to pursue the unpaid condominium assessments, and that the Association had somehow failed to mitigate its damages in this case, the trial court awarded the Association just $14,497.32 in interest. We conclude that the trial court erred when—for 'equitable considerations'—it decreased the amount of interest due to the Association in this case.").

[95] *United States v. Forest Hill Gardens E. Condo. Ass'n, Inc.*, 990 F. Supp. 2d 1344, 1351 (S.D. Fla. 2014) (footnote omitted).

[96] *Smulders for 129-31 Harrison St., LLC v. Thirty-Three Sixty Condo. Ass'n, Inc.*, 245 So. 3d 802, 805 (Fla. 4th DCA 2018) ("As appellants' counsel argued below, the case is not moot because there remains the issue of appellants' entitlement to reimbursement of the assessment they paid if they prove a violation of the declaration of condominium. Although not directly relevant on the issue of mootness, if appellants prevail below, there is the issue of their entitlement to recover such 'additional amounts as determined by the court to be necessary to reimburse [appellants] for his or her share of assessments levied by the asso-

Moreover, a condominium (unlike an HOA) is not entitled to collect pre-title "special assessments" levied against the property prior to a first mortgagee taking title. Pursuant to Fla. Stat. § 718.116(1)(b), safe harbor limits liability to 12 months of "unpaid common expenses and regular periodic assessments," nothing more. It is deducible that special assessments of any kind are excluded from safe harbor amounts owed to a condominium (as opposed to an HOA), and has been so held by one federal judge,[97] because, rather specifically in § 720.3085(2)(c), Florida Statutes, the Legislature *included* "special assessments" in the safe harbor amount provided pursuant to the Homeowners Association Act while not mentioning them in the Condominium Act. Thus, principles of statutory construction indicate the Florida Legislature intentionally chose to *exclude* special assessments from the safe harbor amount listed in the Condominium Act. Accordingly, due to this choice, it appears clear that a first mortgagee is not liable for any special assessment levied by a condominium against the property prior to it taking title.

If the association is claiming entitlement for the cost of repairs it made to the property during the period of time in which it owned it, it is unequivocally established under Florida law that the compensation owed to one making improvements to the land of another is measured by the amount to which the improvements have enhanced the value of the property, not by the cost (evidenced by receipts) of the actual improvements made.[98] Thus, an evidentiary hearing from appraisers who will testify to the improvement in market value solely attributable to the repairs themselves (and not from the passage of time with its concomitant up and down in land and home values) would be required to ascertain the amount that the association would be entitled to *vis a vis* the repairs and upgrades.

9-4:5 Remedies Where Association Denies Safe Harbor or Otherwise Demands Improper Amounts

Before legal action can be taken, a proper estoppel letter should be requested from the association, to be provided within 15 days under § 720.30851 or § 718.116(8), Florida Statutes, or the declaration, if it has a similar provision. If a proper estoppel is not timely received, there are three options for a pre-suit demand letter.

One approach is to explain to the association the reasons why the inflated estoppel amount is not owed, but to tender anyway the inflated amount demanded by the association, but also noting that the first mortgagee is paying the inflated amount "under protest" (the check should also state "paid under protest"), with a reservation of rights.[99] The main reason for this approach is so that the first mortgagee can quickly

---

ciation to fund its expenses of the litigation;' and there is also the issue of attorney's fees to the 'prevailing party.' § 718.303(1), Fla. Stat. (2017).").

[97] *See United States v. Forest Hill Gardens East Condo. Ass'n, Inc.*, 990 F.Supp.2d 1344 (S.D. Fla. 2014) (finding, among other things, that special assessments are excluded from "safe harbor" under the Condominium Act).

[98] *Arey v. Williams*, 81 So. 2d 525 (Fla. 1955); *Levine v. Fieni McFarlane, Inc.*, 690 So. 2d 712 (Fla. 4th DCA 1997); *601 West 26 Corp. v. Equity Capital Co.*, 178 So. 2d 894 (Fla. 3d DCA 1965).

[99] *Hemingway Villa Condo. Owners Ass'n, Inc. v. Wells Fargo Bank, N.A.*, 240 So. 3d 104, 106 (Fla. 3d DCA 2018) ("When the Association refused to revise the estoppel certificate, Wells Fargo paid the assessment amounts under protest with a reservation of all rights, later

sell the property despite the estoppel dispute. Tendering the full amount owed, with interest and fees owed up to that point, before suit is filed by either party, also cuts off liability for future interest and attorney's fees and may help determine who the prevailing party is in a suit between the association and the first mortgagee.[100] This situation might be necessary if the prospective third-party purchaser's offer is particularly attractive or if the prospective purchaser is particularly persistent or hostile. Under this approach, the demand letter should state that the association will be sued for a return of the unlawfully demanded amounts, that the inflated amount is being paid under protest so that the property can be sold and damages thus mitigated, and that the first mortgagee will seek disgorgement of the unlawful amount, pre-judgment interest on the unlawful amount (set forth exactly what the amount in excess of safe harbor is), as well as costs, attorney's fees, injunctive relief, and damages, pursuant to the declaration (if applicable), and Fla. Stat. § 718.303 or § 720.305(1), as applicable. The danger, though unlikely, is that a court may find that, by doing so, the first mortgagee waived its rights to dispute the amount owed. In this demand letter, the first mortgagee should also ask for a W-9, a ledger showing the monthly dues amount, and the date of the month that the dues going forward are due, so that they can be paid on a prospective basis.

When confronted by an inflated estoppel, a second option is not to pay the inflated amount, but to tender only the amount first mortgagee feels is actually due under the safe harbor statute, declaration, or otherwise. In the transmittal letter accompanying the check, the first mortgagee should demand a proper estoppel within 15 days under § 720.30851 or § 718.116(8), Florida Statutes, or the declaration, that equals that requested amount being tendered, failing which suit will be filed in order to obtain a proper estoppel, as well as damages, injunctive relief, costs and attorney's fees. Again, the first mortgagee should ask for a W-9, a ledger showing the monthly dues amount, and the date the dues going forward are due, so that they can be paid on a going-forward basis. This approach reflects the existence of good faith. Additionally, as with the first option above, tendering the amount actually believed to be owed, with interest and fees believed to be owed up to that point, may also cut off future liability for interest and attorneys' fees (if the court agrees with the amount tendered) and help determine who the prevailing party is in a suit between the association and the mortgagee.[101]

The third and most commonly used option, is to send a demand letter with no check, but asking for a proper estoppel within 15 days under § 720.30851 or § 718.116(8), Florida Statutes, or the declaration, that is proper under the safe harbor statute or dec-

---

determining that the payment was in excess of the assessments it was required to pay pursuant to the Safe Harbor provisions.").

[100] For some general cases on the legal effect of tender, *see, e.g., All-Brite Aluminum, Inc. v. Desrosiers,* 626 So. 2d 1020 (Fla. 2d DCA 1993); *Aetna Casualty & Surety Co. v. Protective Nat'l Ins. Co.,* 631 So. 2d 305 (Fla. 3d DCA 1994); *Rissman on Behalf of Rissman Inv. Co. v. Kilbourne,* 643 So. 2d 1136, 1140-41 (Fla. 1st DCA 1994); *Morton v. Ansin,* 129 So. 2d 177, 182 (Fla. 3d DCA 1961).

[101] For some general cases on the legal effect of tender, *see, e.g., All-Brite Aluminum, Inc. v. Desrosiers,* 626 So. 2d 1020 (Fla. 2d DCA 1993); *Aetna Casualty & Surety Co. v. Protective Nat'l Ins. Co.,* 631 So. 2d 305 (Fla. 3d DCA 1994); *Rissman on Behalf of Rissman Inv. Co. v. Kilbourne,* 643 So. 2d 1136, 1140-41 (Fla. 1st DCA 1994); *Morton v. Ansin,* 129 So. 2d 177, 182 (Fla. 3d DCA 1961).

laration, failing which suit will be filed to obtain a proper estoppel, as well as damages, injunctive relief, costs and attorney's fees. Again, the first mortgagee should request a W-9, a ledger showing the monthly dues amount, and the date the dues going forward are due, so that they can be paid on a going-forward basis. This approach can be used when a sale is not urgent, but this approach is not an actual tender.[102]

But in many cases, a demand letter will not resolve the stalemate and litigation will be necessary to obtain a proper estoppel. It used to be, when an association denied safe harbor, that the first mortgagee, or its successor or assign, could move to enforce the final judgment of foreclosure against the association.[103] This is no longer available except in cases where the foreclosing lender had the foresight to insert the proper specific jurisdictional language in the bank's foreclosure judgment. Still, while more time consuming, an independent action can also be very effective.[104] The declaration

---

[102] *Bowe v. US Bank Nat'l Ass'n*, 260 So. 3d 1189, 1190 (Fla. 5th DCA 2019) ("Bowe's oral representations of her ability and willingness to bring the mortgage current (made in early January 2010) did not constitute a legal tender of payment.").

[103] *See, e.g., Ocean Bank v. Caribbean Towers Condo. Assoc., Inc.*, 121 So. 3d 1087 (Fla. 3d DCA 2013); *HSBC Bank USA, N.A., as Trustee on Behalf of Ace Securities Corp. Home Equity Loan Trust and for the Registered Holders of Ace Securities Corp. Home Equity Loan Trust, Series 2006-ASAP5, Asset Backed Pass-Through Certificates v. Miguel Abreu*, 2014 WL 708904 (Fla. Cir. Ct. Duval Feb. 24, 2014); *The Bank of New York Mellon Trust Company, N.A., F/K/A/ The Bank of New York Trust Company, N.A., Successors To JP Morgan Chase Bank, N.A., RAMP 2006-RS3, v. Palmy Del Rosario, Merrill Pines Condo. Ass'n, et al.*, 2014 WL 1052431 (Fla. Cir. Ct. Duval March 5, 2014); *Deutsche Bank Nat'l Trust Co., as Trustee of the Indymac Indx Mortgage Loan Trust 2006-AR15, Mortgage Pass-Through Certificates, Series 2006-AR15 Under the Pooling and Servicing Agreement Dated May 1, 2006 v. Labarile*, 2014 WL 624401 (Fla. Cir. Ct. Pinellas January 16, 2014); *USA Residential Properties, LLC v. Ventzlislav Slavov, Ocean Grande Condo. Ass'n, Inc.*, 2013 WL 5462324 (Fla. Cir. Ct. St. Johns Sept. 26, 2013); *Deutsche Bank National Trust Company, as Trustee for the Registered Holders of Morgan Stanley ABS Capital I Inc. Trust 2007-NC3 Mortgage Pass-Through Certificates, Series 2007-NC3 v. Jill S. Nickens*, 2014 WL 519354 (Fla. 9th Jud. Cir. Orange Feb. 6, 2014) (Eaton, O.H., J.); *Aspen Shackleton II LLC v. Graham*, 2013 WL 1874305 (Fla. Cir. Ct. Brevard Apr. 25, 2013) (Eaton, O.H., J.); *U.S. Bank Nat'l Assoc., as Tr. for the BNC Mortgage Loan Trust 2006-1 v. Valdes*, 2011 WL 10725878 (Fla. Cir. Ct. Palm Beach 2011) (Hoy, John J., J.); *The Bank of New York as Tr. for the Certificate Holders CWABS, Inc. Asset-Backed Certificates, Series 2006-23 v. Colombine*, 2011 WL 10725888 (Fla. Cir. Ct. Palm Beach 2011) (Cotton, Roger B., J.); *U.S. Bank v. Mateiola and Summit Place*, 2010 WL 8742249 (Fla. Cir. Ct. Palm Beach 2010); *Fremont Investment and Loan v. Earl Winston Roache, et al*, 2009 WL 8626511 (Fla. Cir. Ct. Miami-Dade 2009) (Leesfield, Ellen L., J.); *Wells Fargo Bank, N.A., As Trustee for Carrington Mortgage Loan Trust, Series 2006-RFC1, Asset Backed Passed Through Certificates v. Debesa*, 2011 WL 8151877 (Fla. Cir. Ct. Miami-Dade 2011) (Schlesinger, John, J.); *As Lily, LLC v. Brisell Vazquez, Blue Bay Tower Condo. Assoc., Inc., et al*, 2013 WL 4519352 (Fla. Cir. Ct. Miami-Dade 2013) (Thornton, John W., J.).

[104] *See, e.g., Fed. Nat'l Mortgage Assoc. v. Countryside Master Assoc., Inc.*, 2012 WL 6916812 (Fla. Cir. Ct. Collier 2012) (Brode, Lauren L., J.); *The Bank of New York, as Tr. for the Certificate Holders CWALT, Inc., Alternative Loan Trust 2006-19CB, Mortgage Pass-Through Certificates, Series 2006-19CB v. River Walk Townhomes Assoc., Inc.*, 2012 WL 8015562 (Fla. Cir. Ct. Hillsborough 2012) (Levens, William P., J.); *Bank of America, N.A., Successor by Merger to BAC Home Loans Servicing, LP v. Colonnade at the Forum Homeowners Assoc., Inc.*, 2012 WL 8015567 (Fla. Cir. Ct. Lee 2012); *Fed. Nat'l Mortgage Assoc. v. The Cove at Pearl Lake Condo. Assoc., Inc.*, 2013 WL 1889432 (Fla. Cir. Ct. Seminole March 11, 2013) (Nelson,

should be attached to the complaint.[105] However, if the mortgagee seeks to litigate post-title assessments as well as safe harbor, evidence of post-title assessments must be presented.[106]

Debra, J.); *The Bank of New York, as Tr. for the Benefit of the Certificate-Holders CWALT, Inc., Alternative Loan Trust 2007-OA10, Mortgage Pass-Through Certificates, Series 2007-OA10 v. The Sterling Villages of Palm Beach Lakes Condo. Assoc., Inc.*, 2012 WL 8015574 (Fla. Cir. Ct. Palm Beach 2012) (Brown, Lucy Chernow, J.); *United States of America v. Forest Hill Gardens East Condo. Assoc., Inc.*, 2014 WL 28723 (S.D. Fla. Jan. 3, 2014) (Hurley, J.); *Fed. Nat'l Mortgage Assoc. v. The Quarter at Ybor Condo. Assoc., Inc.*, 2013 WL 1889465 (Fla. Cir. Ct. Hillsborough March 5, 2013) (Pendino, Sam D., J.); *Fed. Nat'l Mortgage Assoc. v. Cordoba at Beach Park Condo. Assoc., Inc.*, 2012 WL 6916814 (Fla. Cir. Ct. Hillsborough 2012); *HSBC Bank USA, Nat'l Assoc., as Trustee for Nomura Asset Acceptance Corp. Mortgage Pass-Through Certificates, Series 2006-AR4 v. The Villas Condo. Assoc., Inc.*, 2011 WL 9919180 (Fla. Cir. Ct. Hillsborough 2011) (Foster, Robert A., J.); *HSBC BANK USA, Nat'l Assoc. as Trustee for Nomura Asset Acceptance Corp. Mortgage Pass-Through Certificate Series 2006-AFI v. Renaissance Villas Condo Assoc., Inc.*, 2011 WL 9919181 (Fla. Cir. Ct. Hillsborough 2011) (Arnold, James D., J.); *Residential Funding Co., LLC v. Lincoln Place Residences Condo. Assoc., Inc.*, 2012 WL 8015558 (Fla. Cir. Ct. Miami-Dade 2012) (Schwabedissen, Elizabeth, J.); *Residential Funding Co., LLC v. Lincoln Place Residences Condo. Assoc., Inc.*, 2013 WL 1889386 (Fla. Cir. Ct. Miami-Dade Feb. 27, 2013) (Zabel, Sarah, J.); *Deutsche Bank Nat'l Trust Co., as Trustee Under the Pooling and Servicing Agreement Relating to Impac Secured Assets Corp., Mortgage Pass Through Certificates, Series 2007-3 v. Tuscany No. 3 Condo. Assoc., Inc.*, 2012 WL 8255399 (Fla. Cir. Ct. Broward 2012) (Gates, Michael, J.); *The Bank of New York as Tr. for the Certificate Holders CWALT, Inc., Alternative Loan Trust 2005-62 Mortgage Pass Through Certificates, Series 2005-62 v. Serenade on Palmer Ranch Condo. Assoc., Inc.*, 2013 WL 1889451 (Fla. Cir. Ct. Sarasota Feb. 19, 2013) (Defuria, Rick, J.); *Bank of New York v. Mirador 1200 Condo. Assoc., Inc.*, 2012 WL 6916808 (Fla. Cir. Ct. Miami-Dade 2012) (Baglev, Jerald, J.); *BAC Home Loans Servicing, L.P. v. The Plaza Condo. Assoc., Inc.*, 2012 WL 8015571 (Fla. Cir. Ct. Orange 2012) (Kirkwood, Lawrence R., J.); *The Bank of New York as Tr. for the Benefit of the Certificate Holders, CWALT, Inc., Alternative Loan Trust 2007-OA8 Mortgage Pass-Through Certificates v. The Greens COA, Inc.*, 2013 WL 1889448 (Fla. Cir. Ct. Orange March 11, 2013) (Doherty, J.); *Fed. Nat'l Mortg. Assoc. v. Mirabella At World Gateway Condo. Assoc., Inc.*, 2012 WL 8015568 (Fla. Cir. Ct. Orange 2012) (McGinnis, Adam, J.); *The Bank of New York Mellon v. The Plaza Condo. Assoc., Inc.*, 2013 WL 1889419 (Fla. Cir. Ct. Orange February 7, 2013) (Blackwell, Alice, J.); *U.S. Bank National Association as Trustee for Ramp 2005-EFC2 v. Pine Rush Villas Condo. Ass'n, Inc.*, 2013 WL 6991983 (Fla. Cir. Ct. Pinellas Aug. 27, 2013) (Schaefer, John, J.); *The Bank of New York for the Benefit of the CWABS, Inc. v. The Sterling Villages of Palm Beach Lakes Condo. Assoc., Inc.*, 2012 WL 8255393 (Fla. Cir. Ct. Palm Beach 2012).

[105] *Fed. Nat. Mortg. Ass'n v. Legacy Parc Condo. Ass'n, Inc.*, 177 So. 3d 92, 94 (Fla. 5th DCA 2015) ("It was error for the trial court to require Fannie Mae to attach more documents to survive the motion to dismiss. Its cause of action was based not upon the underlying foreclosure suit but upon section 718.116 and the Declaration. Fannie Mae properly attached the Declaration to its complaint. . . . Furthermore, Fannie Mae was not obligated to attach evidence proving its status as first mortgagee in its pleadings.").

[106] *Villas of Windmill Point II Prop. Owners' Ass'n, Inc. v. Bank of N.Y. Mellon*, 197 So. 3d 1288, 1289 (Fla. 4th DCA 2016) ("We affirm the trial court's entry of summary judgment for BONY, because BONY's affidavit established all the requirements of Section 720.3085(2)(c), and the trial court properly found that the Villas' affirmative defenses were legally insufficient to defeat BONY's cause of action. However, the final judgment not only includes a calculation of the amount due in accordance with the safe harbor provision, but also includes a calculation of the amount due from BONY to Villas for assessments that accrued since BONY took title to the parcel. Because BONY failed to present any evidence

An independent action can also be filed as a counterclaim in the almost inevitable foreclosure action that will be filed by the association if an inflated estoppel is not paid by the first mortgagee after it obtains title. But whether framed as an affirmative complaint or a counterclaim, various theories that the first mortgagee can assert are declaratory relief, breach of contract/declaration, or an action for violation of the relevant safe harbor statute. The first mortgagee can seek both injunctive relief and damages under Fla. Stat. § 718.303 or § 720.305(1). Statutory injunctions under Fla. Stat. § 718.303 or § 720.305(1) don't require proof of irreparable harm beyond demonstrating that the association has violated the relevant statute.[107]

However, merely moving to enforce a final judgment is no longer available,[108] unless the foreclosure judgment in the foreclosure action specifically reserved jurisdiction on safe harbor or dues issues.[109] Therefore, if there is a dispute, a new lawsuit must

---

to support the post-Certificate of Title assessment amount listed in the final judgment, we reverse and remand for the trial court to delete that calculation from the final judgment. On remand, the trial court may either: (1) take evidence and determine the correct post-Certificate of Title assessment amount due to Villas; or (2) if the parties agree, simply state in the final judgment that BONY is liable for all assessments that accrued since BONY received the Certificate of Title, without stating a specific dollar amount.").

[107] *Amelio v. Marilyn Pines Unit II Condo. Ass'n, Inc.*, 173 So. 3d 1037, 1040 (Fla. 2d DCA 2015) ("Under Section 718.303(1), the requirement of irreparable harm is satisfied when a violation of chapter 718 is shown."); *Hollywood Towers Condo. Ass'n, Inc. v. Hampton*, 40 So. 3d 784, 788 (Fla. 4th DCA 2010); *Mitchell v. Beach Club of Hallandale Condo. Ass'n, Inc.*, 17 So. 3d 1265, 1267 (Fla. 4th DCA 2009); *Hobbs v. Weinkauf*, 940 So. 2d 1151, 1153 (Fla. 2d DCA 2006) ("We reject Grenelefe's argument that the trial court's ruling on this claim should be upheld because 'no harm occurred as a result of how [the accounting records] were kept.' A violation of the requirements of chapter 718 is itself a harm for which Section 718.303 authorizes injunctive relief. The statute requires no additional showing of harm."). But at least one other case, without any analysis on this issue, applied the three prongs to a statutory injunction. *See Coconut Key Homeowner's Ass'n, Inc. v. Gonzalez*, 246 So. 3d 428 (Fla. 4th DCA 2018).

[108] *Central Mortgage Co. v. Callahan*, 155 So. 3d 373 (Fla. 3d DCA 2014); *Central Park A Metrowest Condominium Assoc., Inc. v. Amtrust REO I, LLC*, 169 So. 3d 1223 (Fla. 5th DCA 2015); *Grand Cent. at Kennedy Condo. Ass'n v. Space Coast Credit Union*, 173 So. 3d 1089 (Fla. 2d DCA 2015); *Montreux at Deerwood Lake Condominium Association, Inc. v. Citibank, N.A.*, 153 So. 3d 961 (Fla. 1st DCA 2014); *PLCA Condominium Association v. Amtrust-NP SFR Venture, LLC*, 182 So. 3d 668 (Fla. 4th DCA 2015); *Meadows on the Green Condominium Ass'n, Inc. v. Nationstar Mortgage, LLC*, 188 So. 3d 883 (Fla. 4th DCA 2016). But see, *Citation Way Condominium Association, Inc. v. Wells Fargo Bank, N.A.*, 172 So. 3d 558 (Fla. 4th DCA 2015). The 4th DCA in *PLCA Condominium Association* attempted to distinguish *Citation Way* based on the final judgment in *Citation Way*, stating in a parenthetical to the opinion, "finding that the trial court had jurisdiction to consider a motion to determine amounts due to the association where '[t]he issue of unpaid assessments was raised in the underlying foreclosure action')." Arguably, that should be the case in every foreclosure where the association is named as a defendant for safe harbor purposes. And one need only look at the *Citation Way* final judgment of foreclosure, recorded at Broward County Official Records Book 50087 Page 1573, to see the Fourth DCA's effort at distinguishing the prior holding is not persuasive, because the *Citation Way* judgment simply used the normal form foreclosure judgment language.

[109] Because safe harbor disputes are so common, the Second DCA suggested that circuit courts ought to specifically reserve such post-judgment jurisdiction. *Grand Cent. at*

generally be filed; unless the lender wants to wait for the association to foreclose its lien in order to assert counterclaims.

Of course, there are various defenses to an association's foreclosure action, other than those discussed in this chapter on the merits of safe harbor. One developing defense is federal preemption where the holder of the loan or property is a federal entity and the association has not obtained federal consent to foreclose.[110] For instance, unless the association obtains permission from the FHFA to foreclose on a Fannie Mae or Freddie Mac loan, both of which were placed into conservatorship with the FHFA on September 6, 2008, then the association cannot foreclose because 12 U.S.C. Section 4617(j)(3) preempts chapters 718 and 720.[111]

9-4:6 Rule 1.540(b)(4) in the Context of Association Litigation

Rule 1.540(b)(4) has application in a number of different association-related scenarios.

For instance, sometimes an association may attempt to foreclose out a first mortgagee[112] before it takes title, and is still only a first mortgagee. This is inappropriate, and any such judgment is a "nullity," "void," and not *res judicata* against the senior lienholder.[113] The Florida Supreme Court has held that "the law is pretty well settled that a first or senior mortgagee is not a proper party to foreclosure proceedings brought by a second or junior mortgagee."[114] That is, "persons holding mortgages or liens prior to the mortgage under foreclosure are neither necessary or proper parties to the action."[115] It is "not proper in foreclosure proceedings to try a claim of title superior or paramount to that of the mortgagor, and even if a party having title is made a party and judgment entered after a hearing, it will not bind his interest."[116] A judgment

---

Kennedy Condo. Ass'n v. Space Coast Credit Union, 173 So. 3d 1089, 1091 at n.2 (Fla. 2d DCA 2015).

[110] *See Saticoy Bay, LLC, Series 2714 Snapdragon v. Flagstar Bank, FSB*, 2016 WL 1064463, *3-4 (D. Nev. Mar. 17, 2016) ("Because the evidence supports a finding that the property was federally owned at the time of the HOA foreclosure sale, the court concludes that the HOA foreclosure sale at issue was invalid.").

[111] *Skylights LLC v. Fannie Mae*, 2015 WL 3887061 (D. Nev. June 24, 2015); *Premier Holdings, Inc. v. Federal Nation Mortg. Ass'n*, 2015 WL 4276169 (D. Nev. July 13, 2015).

[112] Sometimes the association's declaration may protect even more junior mortgagees and lienors, in which case the same analysis would apply.

[113] *Wells Fargo Bank, N.A. v. Rutledge*, 148 So. 3d 533 (Fla. 2d DCA 2014) ("Wells Fargo, as the superior lien holder, was not a proper party to Harbor Towers' foreclosure action. . . . Because it was not required to participate in the county court foreclosure action, Wells Fargo's failure to participate cannot form the basis of a laches argument."); *U.S. Bank Nat'l Ass'n v. Bevans*, 138 So. 3d 1185, 1187 (Fla. 3d DCA 2014) (explaining that "the final judgment of foreclosure entered in favor of the Association in the Association's foreclosure action did not eliminate the Bank's senior mortgage interest because '[f]oreclosure does not terminate interests in the foreclosed real estate that are senior to the mortgage being foreclosed'" (quoting *Garcia v. Stewart*, 906 So. 2d 1117, 1120 (Fla. 4th DCA 2005))); *Citi-Mortgage, Inc. v. Wachovia Bank*, 24 So. 3d 641, 642-43 (Fla. 2d DCA 2009); *Bank of Am., N.A. v. Kipps Colony II Condo. Ass'n, Inc.*, 201 So. 3d 670 (Fla. 2d DCA 2016).

[114] *Cone Bros. Constr. Co. v. Moore*, 141 Fla. 420, 426 (1940).

[115] *Cone Bros. Constr. Co. v. Moore*, 141 Fla. 420, 426 (1940).

[116] *Cone Bros. Constr. Co. v. Moore*, 141 Fla. 420, 426 (1940).

in a foreclosure action that favors a junior lienor is a "nullity" and does not bind the primary lienor;[117] thus arguably it is void and the foreclosure and resulting foreclosure judgment could be ignored, but this is most certainly not recommended. The risk-averse lender should defend any such foreclosure, and most certainly any declaratory relief or quiet title action, targeting its senior lien interest. This is particularly true because a recent Florida Supreme Court case seems to suggest, despite (but not citing in any way) earlier precedent,[118] that a bank is not free to ignore an attack on its mortgage, and has only one year to move to vacate because the judgment for failure to state a cause of action on these facts merely renders the judgment voidable, not void.[119] It should be pointed out, however, that the Second DCA has held that even a quiet title action in which a judgment has been obtained, stating that a senior lien was foreclosed by an earlier foreclosure, may not be dispositive of the issue.[120]

Another scenario where Rule 1.540(b)(4) becomes relevant is when an association records its own lien and files its own foreclosure after an investor has already recorded its own lis pendens.[121] In such a situation, any judgment or title obtained in

---

[117] *CitiMortgage, Inc. v. Wachovia Bank*, 24 So. 3d 641, 642-43 (Fla. 2d DCA 2009).

[118] *Cone Bros. Constr. Co. v. Moore*, 141 Fla. 420, 426 (1940). However, *Cone Bros.* is still good law and seems to suggest that the reason the judgment naming a senior lienor is void is a question of judicial power, not of pleading. *See also Puryear v. State*, 810 So. 2d 901, 905 (Fla. 2002) ("We take this opportunity to expressly state that this Court does not intentionally overrule itself sub silentio. Where a court encounters an express holding from this Court on a specific issue and a subsequent contrary dicta statement on the same specific issue, the court is to apply our express holding in the former decision until such time as this Court recedes from the express holding.").

[119] *The Bank of New York v. Condominium Association of La Mer Estates, Inc.*, 175 So. 3d 282 (Fla. 2015), approving *Condominium Ass'n of La Mer Estates, Inc. v. Bank of New York Mellon Corp.*, 137 So. 3d 396, 400-01 (Fla. 4th DCA 2014) (en banc). *See also Sterling Factors Corp. v. U.S. Bank Nat. Ass'n*, 968 So. 2d 658, 667 (Fla. 2d DCA 2007)).

[120] *Bank of Am., N.A. v. Kipps Colony II Condo. Ass'n, Inc.*, 201 So. 3d 670, 676 (Fla. 2d DCA 2016) ("Moreover, the quiet title judgment did not resolve this issue. Rule 1.540(b)(5) provides that the court may relieve a party from a final judgment where 'a prior judgment or decree upon which [the challenged judgment] is based has been reversed or otherwise vacated.' The rule also 'does not limit the power of a court to entertain an independent action to relieve a party from a judgment, decree, order, or proceeding or to set aside a judgment or decree for fraud upon the court.'").

[121] Section 48.23(1)(d), Florida Statutes, specifically provides that "the recording of [a] notice of lis pendens . . . *constitutes a bar to the enforcement against the property described in the notice of all interests and liens . . . unrecorded at the time of recording the notice* unless the holder of any such unrecorded interest or lien intervenes in such proceedings within 30 days after the recording of the notice." Fla. Stat. § 48.23(1)(d) (emphasis added).

However, the flip side is not true; banks with mortgages recorded prior to the association's lis pendens need not litigate in the association's foreclosure in order to have a valid judgment. *See CitiMortgage, Inc. v. Flowers*, 189 So. 3d 1032 (Fla. 4th DCA 2016). *Quadomain* only applies to interests which were unrecorded at the time of the initial lis pendens. *Id. See also Ditech Fin. LLC v. White*, 222 So. 3d 603, 605 (Fla. 4th DCA 2017) ("The lower court's ruling was based upon a misinterpretation of section 48.23(1)(d), Florida Statutes. Section 48.23(1)(d), Florida Statutes, only acts to preclude enforcement of liens unrecorded at the time a lis pendens is recorded. It is undisputed that the Bank recorded its interest in the subject property years *prior* to the Association's lis pendens filing/lien foreclosure action. The Bank was free to separately file the Foreclosure Action. The trial court did not lack subject matter jurisdiction.") (emphasis in original).

the association's action is arguably void under *Quadomain* and Rule 1.540(b)(4) for lack of subject matter jurisdiction.[122] In other words, the association must litigate in the prior action with the prior lis pendens, if at all.[123] If the association does not, and forecloses and a third party buys at the association's foreclosure sale, the buyer likely will not be allowed to intervene into the bank's foreclosure,[124] but if the buyer does successfully intervene, it will be subject to the proceedings as they stand.[125] However, if the bank does not record a lis pendens before the association files its foreclosure, the association is free to file its own action.[126] It must be stated that the efficacy of *Quadomain* has been largely gutted by the Fourth District, by its construing of an association's declaration as a "recorded interest" under § 48.23, Fla. Stat.[127] although

---

[122] *U.S. Bank Nat'l Ass'n v. Quadomain Condo. Ass'n, Inc.*, 103 So. 3d 977, 978-80 (Fla. 4th DCA 2012); *Bank of Am., N.A. v. Kipps Colony II Condo. Ass'n, Inc.*, 201 So. 3d 670, 676 (Fla. 2d DCA 2016). *Cf. CitiMortgage, Inc. v. Flowers*, 189 So. 3d 1032 (Fla. 4th DCA 2016). An order entered without personal jurisdiction is void. *Cesaire v. State*, 811 So. 2d 816, 817 (Fla. 4th DCA 2002).

[123] *See Baron v. Aiello*, 319 So. 2d 198, 200 (Fla. 3d DCA 1975) (holding that a judgment lien holder's attempt to foreclose said lien came too late when the action was commenced after the first mortgagee recorded a lis pendens). *Cf. CitiMortgage, Inc. v. Flowers*, 189 So. 3d 1032 (Fla. 4th DCA 2016).

[124] *See Bonafide Properties, As Trustee Only Under 14329 Village View Dr Land trust v. Wells Fargo Bank, N.A., as Trustee for the Certificate-holders of Banc of America Alternative Loan Trust 2006-5, Mortgage Pass-Through Certificates*, Series 2006-5, 198 So. 3d 694 (Fla. 2d DCA 2016); *Investor Tr. Servs., LLC v. DLJ Mortg. Capital, Inc.*, 225 So. 3d 833, 833 (Fla. 5th DCA 2017) ("Whoever purchases property that is the subject of a foreclosure lawsuit in which a mortgagee has previously filed a lis pendens is a purchaser pendente lite. . . . The law is well settled that a purchaser pendente lite is not entitled to intervene or otherwise be made a party to the ongoing lawsuit. . . ."); *Tikhomirov v. Bank of N.Y. Mellon*, 223 So. 3d 1112 (Fla. 3d DCA 2017) ("It is well established that a purchaser of property that is the subject of a pending foreclosure action is not entitled to intervene in the foreclosure action where a notice of lis pendens has been recorded.").

[125] *State Trust Realty, LLC v. Deutsche Bank Nat. Trust Co. Americas*, 207 So. 3d 923, 926-27 (Fla. 4th DCA 2016).

[126] *U.S. Bank Nat. Ass'n v. Bevans*, 138 So. 3d 1185, 1189 (Fla. 3d DCA 2014).

[127] *Jallali v. Knightsbridge Vill. Homeowners Ass'n, Inc.*, 211 So. 3d 216, 219-20 (Fla. 4th DCA 2017) ("*Quadomain* is factually distinguishable from this case. First, in *Quadomain*, the association was attempting to foreclose its lien against the bank, a first mortgagee, and not the homeowner. Second, *Quadomain* did not address the effect of the association's declaration of covenants, which constitute a recorded interest and thus take the case out of the purview of section 48.23, Florida Statutes. The Association's lien in the present case was imposed under the Association's Declaration of Covenants, recorded before the Lender recorded its notice of lis pendens. Therefore, because the Declaration provided for the imposition of a lien which related back to the filing of the Declarations, it was not an 'interest . . . unrecorded at the time of recording the notice' of lis pendens within the meaning of section 48.23(1)(d), Florida Statutes. We hold that an association's declaration of covenants (or of condominium) constitutes an 'interest' in property under section 48.23(1)(d), Florida Statutes. Therefore, declarations which are recorded not only prior to the filing of a notice of lis pendens by a first mortgagee, but prior to the mortgage itself, may constitute a prior recorded interest under section 48.23(1)(d), Florida Statutes. The filing of a lis pendens does not automatically preclude an association from foreclosing on a lien imposed under the declaration against parties other than a first mortgagee, although the association's foreclosure may be subordinate to the foreclosure of a first mortgage."), *rev. denied*, No. SC17-409, 2017 WL 2559143 (Fla. June 13, 2017).

it attempted to distinguish *Quadomain* as being a case where the association was attempting to take title from the bank and not merely a delinquent homeowner.[128] In reality, an association's declaration will almost always predate the subject mortgage and the foreclosure actions' lis pendens related to that mortgage, so that, practically speaking, *Quadomain* is of doubtful ongoing vitality.

Or, sometimes an association will not serve the bank properly with process, but the clerk will default the bank anyway.[129] Such title obtained without proper service of process can be vacated under Rule 1.540(b)(4) because process was not perfected and the trial court lacked personal jurisdiction.[130]

An association can risk sanctions by obtaining a void order.[131] Rule 1.540(b) applies to final orders as well as judgments.[132]

---

[128] *Jallali v. Knightsbridge Vill. Homeowners Ass'n, Inc.*, 211 So. 3d 216, 221 (Fla. 4th DCA 2017), ("Here, not only does the Association have a prior recorded interest through its Declaration of Covenants, its action was only **against the delinquent homeowner.** Unlike *Quadomain,* the Association's suit did not involve the Lender.") (emphasis in original), *rev. denied*, No. SC17-409, 2017 WL 2559143 (Fla. June 13, 2017).

[129] *HSBC Bank USA, National Ass'n v. Centre Court Ridge Condo. Ass'n, Inc.*, 147 So. 3d 593, 594 (Fla. 5th DCA 2014). *See Toscana at Vasari Village Ass'n, Inc., v. Deutsche Bank National Trust Company as Indentured Trustee for American Home Mortgage Investment Trust 2005-2, et al*, 2014 WL 1102739 (Fla. Cir. Ct. Lee March 14, 2014) (Kyle, Keith, J.); *Bahia at Delray Homeowners' Ass'n Inc. v. U.S. Bank National Association as Trustee for the Holders of Mastr Adjustable Rate Mortgages Trust 2006-OA1, et al.*, 2014 WL 4411579 (Fla. Cir. Ct. Palm Beach June 23, 2014).

[130] *HSBC Bank USA, National Association v. Centre Court Ridge Condominium Association, Inc.*, 147 So. 3d 593, 594 (Fla. 5th DCA 2014). *See Toscana at Vasari Village Association, Inc., v. Deutsche Bank National Trust Company as Indentured Trustee for American Home Mortgage Investment Trust 2005-2, et al*, 2014 WL 1102739 (Fla. Cir. Ct. Lee March 14, 2014) (Kyle, Keith, J.); *Bahia at Delray Homeowners' Ass'n Inc. v. U.S. Bank National Association as Trustee for the Holders of Mastr Adjustable Rate Mortgages Trust 2006-OA1, et al.*, 2014 WL 4411579 (Fla. Cir. Ct. Palm Beach June 23, 2014). *See Pelycado Onroerend Goed B.V. v. Ruthenberg*, 635 So. 2d 1001, 1005 (Fla. 5th DCA 1994) (holding a trial court lacks jurisdiction when a party fails to strictly comply with the statutes regarding service).

[131] *HSBC Bank USA, N.A. v. Biscayne Point Condo. Ass'n*, 184 So. 3d 606 (Fla. 3d DCA 2016).

[132] *De La Osa v. Wells Fargo Bank, N.A.*, 208 So. 3d 259, 261 (Fla. 3d DCA 2016) (on rehearing en banc). *See also Courtney v. Catalina, Ltd.*, 130 So. 3d 739, 740 (Fla. 3d DCA 2014) ("Courtney's attorney filed a verified motion to vacate the order of dismissal [for failure to prosecute] pursuant to Florida Rule of Civil Procedure 1.540(b)(4), which authorizes a trial court to afford relief to a party when '[a] judgment or decree is void.'"); *Deutsche Bank Nat. Trust Co. v. Basanta*, 88 So. 3d 216, 218 (Fla. 3d DCA 2011); *Boosinger v. Davis*, 46 So. 3d 152, 154 (Fla. 2d DCA 2010) (same). *Cf. State Department of Revenue v. Haughton*, 188 So. 3d 32 (Fla. 3d DCA 2016) (reversing trial court order denying Rule 1.540(b)(4) motion; holding that pursuant to Rule 1.540(b)(b)(4), trial court should have set aside "order" entered without notice as void).

CHAPTER 10

Litigating With Other Interests in the Foreclosure Context

Sarah T. Weitz[1]

10-1 Necessary and Indispensable Parties

Not infrequently, foreclosure proceedings also involve the holders of second mortgages, junior liens, and other encumbrances recorded against the subject property, as well as intervening title owners and tenants in possession of the subject property. When drafting the complaint, an attorney must conduct and review a title search or abstract in order to ascertain these other interests to be named as parties in the foreclosure action. Indispensable parties are necessary parties so essential to a suit that no final decision can be rendered without their joinder.[2] This is in contrast to other necessary parties, who have an interest in a suit and ought to be made parties, but who do not have to be joined before a final decision may be rendered.[3] A final decision will bind those parties joined in the suit, but will have no effect on the rights of necessary but unnamed parties.[4]

The preparation of the foreclosure complaint is discussed at length in Chapter 6. Litigating with condominium and homeowner associations is discussed at length in Chapter 9. Post-judgment disputes with junior lienholders over judicial sale surplus funds are discussed at length in Chapter 14.

10-1:1 Lis Pendens

The lis pendens recorded in conjunction with the filing of a foreclosure action notifies third parties "that whoever subsequently acquires an interest in the property will

---

[1] Ms. Weitz has provided updates to this chapter, which originally was written by Justin S. Swartz.
[2] *Sudhoff v. Fed. Nat. Mortg. Ass'n*, 942 So. 2d 425, 427 (Fla. 5th DCA 2006); *see also English v. Bankers Trust Co. of California*, 895 So. 2d 1120, 1121 (Fla. 4th DCA 2005) ("[A] foreclosure proceeding resulting in a final decree and a sale of the mortgaged property, without the holder of the legal title being before the court will have no effect to transfer his title to the purchaser at said sale.").
[3] *Sudhoff v. Fed. Nat. Mortg. Ass'n*, 942 So. 2d 425, 427 (Fla. 5th DCA 2006).
[4] *Alger v. Peters*, 88 So. 2d 903, 908 (Fla. 1956); *Abdoney v. York*, 903 So. 2d 981, 983 (Fla. 2d DCA 2005) ("When a junior mortgagee is omitted as a party to the foreclosure of a senior mortgage, the lien of the junior mortgagee is unaffected by the judgment.").

stand in the same position as the current owner/vendor, and take the property subject to whatever valid judgment may be rendered in the litigation."[5] "Lis pendens" literally means a pending lawsuit, and is defined as the jurisdiction, power, or control that courts acquire over property involved in a pending suit.[6] At common law the lis pendens was intended to warn all interests that the particular property was the subject of litigation, and that any interests acquired during the pendency of the suit were subject to its outcome.[7] A lis pendens serves as constructive notice of the claims asserted against the property in the pending litigation with respect to one acquiring an interest in the property after the lis pendens is filed.[8]

A notice of lis pendens also operates to protect its proponent by preventing intervening liens that could impair or extinguish claimed property rights.[9] A notice of lis pendens therefore protects both its proponent and third parties by alerting creditors, prospective purchasers and others to the fact that the title to a particular piece of real property is involved in litigation.[10]

A sample form of the lis pendens can be found in Appendix A, 1-004.

10-2 Third-Party Purchasers

10-2:1 Interest Subordinate to Prior Mortgage and Lis Pendens

A party who purchases the subject property after recording of a mortgage takes the property subject to that superior mortgage based on Florida's principle of constructive notice.[11] Such a party who purchases the subject property and holds recorded

---

[5] *Avalon Assocs. of Delaware Ltd. v. Avalon Park Assocs., Inc.*, 760 So. 2d 1132, 1134 (Fla. 5th DCA 2000) (citing *DePass v. Chitty*, 90 Fla. 77, 105 So. 148, 149 (1925); *Taylor v. Steckel*, 944 So. 2d 494, 497 (Fla. 3d DCA 2006); *Whitburn, LLC v. Wells Fargo Bank, N.A.*, 190 So. 3d 1087, 1090 (Fla. 2d DCA 2015) ("Because Whitburn purchased the property in June 2013 after Wells Fargo filed its notice of lis pendens in December 2012, Whitburn took the property subject to the outcome of the litigation in Wells Fargo's case, including the foreclosure sale to which Wells Fargo was entitled as a result of the judgment entered in its favor.").

[6] *De Pass v. Chitty*, 105 So. 148, 149 (Fla. 1925).

[7] Black's Law Dictionary, 942-43 (7th Ed. 1999).

[8] *U.S. Bank Nat'l Ass'n v. Bevans*, 138 So. 3d 1185, 1189 (Fla. 3d DCA 2014) (quoting *Westburne Supply, Inc. v. Cmty. Villas Partners, Ltd.*, 508 So. 2d 431, 434 (Fla. 1st DCA 1987)).

[9] *Adhin v. First Horizon Home Loans*, 44 So. 3d 1245, 1251 (Fla. 5th DCA 2010); *Chiusolo v. Kennedy*, 614 So. 2d 491, 492 (Fla. 1993).

[10] *S & T Builders v. Globe Props., Inc.*, 944 So. 2d 302, 303 n.1 (Fla. 2006) (quoting *Am. Legion Cmty. Club v. Diamond*, 561 So. 2d 268, 269 n.2 (Fla. 1990)); *State Trust Realty, LLC v. Deutsche Bank Nat. Trust Co. Americas*, 207 So. 3d 923, 926 (Fla. 4th DCA 2016).

[11] See § 695.01, Fla. Stat. (2013) and § 695.11, Fla. Stat. (1997); *Lesnoff v. Becker*, 135 So. 146, 147 (Fla. 1931) ("Under our recording statutes, subsequent purchasers, acquiring title without notice of a prior unrecorded deed, mortgage, or transfer of real property, or any interest therein, will be protected against such unrecorded instrument, unless the party claiming thereunder can show that such subsequent purchaser acquired the title with actual notice of such unrecorded conveyance or mortgage; and the burden of showing such notice is upon the party claiming under such unrecorded instrument, the presumption in such case being that such subsequent purchaser acquired his title in good faith and without notice of the prior unrecorded conveyance.") (quoting *Rambo v. Dickenson*, 110 So. 352, 353 (Fla.

legal title *prior to* the filing of a foreclosure action and recording of a lis pendens is an indispensable party to the foreclosure action as owners at the time of filing of the foreclosure suit are always indispensable parties.[12] Thus, the failure to include the sole title owner in a mortgage foreclosure action results in a void final judgment.[13] However, if there are multiple title owners and at least one is named, the resulting judgment is merely voidable by the unnamed owners.[14] Thus, in cases where there are multiple owners of property, but one or more of the property owners is omitted, "a foreclosure suit may be maintained even though the holder of the legal title to the property is not a party to the foreclosure, but . . . the decree only establishes the rights of persons who are parties."[15]

It is increasingly common for title to a property to be transferred while the property is subject of a foreclosure action and lis pendens.[16] A party who purchases the subject property *after* the filing of a foreclosure action and recording of a lis pendens is a "purchaser pendente lite"[17] and generally not a necessary party to, nor entitled to participate in, a foreclosure action.[18] In fact, one who purchases property subject

---

1926)); *Argent Mortg. Co., LLC v. Wachovia Bank N.A.*, 52 So. 3d 796, 800 (Fla. 5th DCA 2010).

[12] *Oakland Props. Corp. v. Hogan*, 117 So. 846, 848 (Fla. 1928) ("One who holds the legal title to mortgaged property is not only necessary, but is an indispensable, party defendant in a suit to foreclose a mortgage."); *English v. Bankers Trust Co. of California*, 895 So. 2d 1120 (Fla. 4th DCA 2005); *Citibank, N.A. v. Villanueva*, 174 So. 3d 612 (Fla. 4th DCA 2015); *CCM Pathfinder Palm Harbor Mgmt., LLC v. Unknown Heirs of Gendron*, 198 So. 3d 3, 7 (Fla. 2d DCA 2015) ("[I]f a recorded mortgage is valid on its face, a subsequent purchaser 'is assumed to have recognized it as a valid lien against the property which he is buying.'") (quoting *Spinney v. Winter Park Bldg. & Loan Ass'n,*, 162 So. 899, 904 (Fla. 1935)); *Bank of N.Y. Mellon v. Burgiel*, 248 So. 3d 237, 238 n.1 (Fla. 5th DCA 2018) ("The trial court did not err by allowing Boca Stel to participate in the proceedings. Boca Stel took title to the property before Bank filed the foreclosure action. Thus, Boca Stel was an indispensable party.").

[13] *FL Homes 1 LLC v. Kokolis Tr. of Toula Kokolis Revocable Tr.*, 271 So. 3d 6, 9 (Fla. 4th DCA 2019).

[14] *FL Homes 1 LLC v. Kokolis Tr. of Toula Kokolis Revocable Tr.*, 271 So. 3d 6, 10 (Fla. 4th DCA 2019); *R.W. Holding Corp. v. R.I.W. Waterproofing & Decorating Co., Inc.*, 131 Fla. 424, 179 So. 753 (Fla. 1938) (title owners for two of three parcels of land named in foreclosure action, but title owner of third parcel omitted); *Key West Wharf & Coal Co. v. Porter*, 63 Fla. 448, 58 So. 599 (Fla. 1912) (mortgagor named in foreclosure action, but not others whom the mortgagor had conveyed portions of the premises to); *Sudhoff v. Fed. Nat'l Mortg. Ass'n*, 942 So. 2d 425 (Fla. 5th DCA 2006) (husband named in foreclosure lawsuit, but not wife).

[15] *Pan Am. Bank of Miami v. City of Miami Beach*, 198 So. 2d 45, 47 (Fla. 3d DCA 1967).

[16] *YHT & Assocs., Inc. v. Nationstar Mortg. LLC*, 177 So. 3d 641, 642 (Fla. 2d DCA 2015).

[17] *Intermediary Finance Corporation v. McKay*, 93 Fla. 101 111 So. 531 (Fla. 1927); *Dema Invs., LLC v. Wells Fargo Bank, N.A.*, 207 So. 3d 977, 978 (Fla. 5th DCA 2016); *Investor Tr. Servs., LLC v. DLJ Mortg. Capital, Inc.*, 225 So. 3d 833 (Fla. 5th DCA 2017).

[18] *Andresix Corp. v. Peoples Downtown Nat. Bank*, 419 So. 2d 1107 (Fla. 3d DCA 1982); *Harrod v. Union Fin. Co.*, 420 So. 2d 108 (Fla. 3d DCA 1982); *SADCO, Inc. v. Countrywide Funding, Inc.*, 680 So. 2d 1072 (Fla. 3d DCA 1996); *Timucuan Props. v. Bank of New York Mellon*, 135 So. 3d 524, 524 (Fla. 5th DCA 2014) ("This court is committed to the doctrine that a purchaser pendente lite is not entitled to intervene.") (quoting *Intermediary Fin. Corp. v. McKay*, 111 So. 531, 531 (Fla. 1927)); *Bymel v. Bank of Am., N.A.*, 159 So. 3d 345 (Fla. 3d DCA 2015); *De Sousa v. JP Morgan Chase, N.A.*, 170 So. 3d 928, 930 (Fla. 4th DCA 2015); *Market Tampa Invs., LLC v. Stobaugh*, 177 So. 3d 31, 32 at n.1 (Fla. 2d DCA 2015); *Whitburn, LLC v. Wells Fargo Bank, N.A.*, 190 So. 3d 1087 (Fla. 2d DCA 2015); *Bonafide Properties v.*

to a lis pendens is bound by the judgment or decree rendered against the party from whom he made the purchase as much so as though he had been a party to the judgment or decree himself.[19]

10-2:2 Intervention

Although Florida Rule of Civil Procedure 1.230 provides that anyone claiming an interest in pending litigation may be permitted to assert a right by intervention, intervention under Rule 1.230 is permissive, not mandatory.[20] The rule further provides that the intervention shall be in subordination to, and in recognition of, the propriety of the main proceeding, unless otherwise ordered by the court in its discretion.[21]

The purchaser of property that is the subject of a pending foreclosure action is not entitled to intervene in the foreclosure action where a notice of lis pendens has been recorded.[22] Indeed, if such buyers purchase the property, they do so at their

---

Wells Fargo Bank, N.A., 198 So. 3d 694, 695 (Fla. 2d DCA 2016); *Dema Invs., LLC v. Wells Fargo Bank, N.A.*, 207 So. 3d 977, 978 (Fla. 5th DCA 2016); *Investor Tr. Servs., LLC v. DLJ Mortg. Capital, Inc.*, 225 So. 3d 833, at n. 1 (Fla. 5th DCA 2017) ("The law is well settled that a purchaser pendente lite is not entitled to intervene or otherwise be made a party to the ongoing lawsuit."); *Carlisle v. U.S. Bank, Nat'l Ass'n for Harborview 2005-10 Tr. Fund*, 225 So. 3d 893, 895-96 (Fla. 3d DCA 2017); *Tikhomirov v. Bank of N.Y. Mellon*, 223 So. 3d 1112, 1115 (Fla. 3d DCA 2017); *Rouffe v. CitiMortgage, Inc.*, 241 So. 3d 870, 872-73 (Fla. 4th DCA 2018); *Bank of N.Y. Mellon for Certificateholders CWALT, Inc. v. HOA Rescue Fund, LLC*, 249 So. 3d 731, 734 (Fla. 2d DCA 2018); *Bank of Am., N.A. v. Mirabella Owners' Ass'n, Inc.*, 238 So. 3d 405, 407 (Fla. 1st DCA 2018).

[19] *U.S. Bank Nat. Ass'n v. Bevans*, 138 So. 3d 1185, 1189 (Fla. 3d DCA 2014) (quoting *U.S. Bank Nat'l Ass'n v. Quadomain Condo. Ass'n*, 103 So. 3d 977, 979 (Fla. 4th DCA 2012); *see also Howard Cole & Co. v. Williams*, 27 So. 2d 352, 355 (Fla. 1946) ("A purchaser or lessee pendente lite from one who is a party to action which involves the property leased is bound by the judgment in the action to which his landlord is a party.").

[20] Fla. R. Civ. P. 1.230.

[21] Fla. R. Civ. P. 1.230; *De Sousa v. JP Morgan Chase, N.A.*, 170 So. 3d 928, 929 (Fla. 4th DCA 2015) (citing *Union Cent. Life Ins. Co. v. Carlisle*, 593 So. 2d 505, 507 (Fla. 1992) ("[I]ntervention pursuant to rule 1.230 is a matter of discretion.")).

[22] *Andresix Corp. v. Peoples Downtown Nat. Bank*, 419 So. 2d 1107 (Fla. 3d DCA 1982); *Harrod v. Union Fin. Co.*, 420 So. 2d 108 (Fla. 3d DCA 1982); *SADCO, Inc. v. Countrywide Funding, Inc.*, 680 So. 2d 1072 (Fla. 3d DCA 1996); *Timucuan Props. v. Bank of New York Mellon*, 135 So. 3d 524, 524 (Fla. 5th DCA 2014) ("This court is committed to the doctrine that a purchaser pendente lite is not entitled to intervene.") (quoting *Intermediary Fin. Corp. v. McKay*, 111 So. 531, 531 (Fla. 1927)); *Bymel v. Bank of Am., N.A.*, 159 So. 3d 345 (Fla. 3d DCA 2015); *De Sousa v. JP Morgan Chase, N.A.*, 170 So. 3d 928 (Fla. 4th DCA 2015); *Market Tampa Invs., LLC v. Stobaugh*, 177 So. 3d 31, 32 n.1 (Fla. 2d DCA 2015); *Whitburn, LLC v. Wells Fargo Bank, N.A.*, 190 So. 3d 1087 (Fla. 2d DCA 2015), reh'g denied (Apr. 29, 2016), review denied, No. SC16-945, 2016 WL 6998444 (Fla. Nov. 30, 2016); *Bonafide Properties v. Wells Fargo Bank, N.A.*, 198 So. 3d 694 (Fla. 2d DCA 2016); *Dema Invs., LLC v. Wells Fargo Bank, N.A.*, 207 So. 3d 977 (Fla. 5th DCA 2016); *Investor Tr. Servs., LLC v. DLJ Mortg. Capital, Inc.*, 225 So.3d 833 (Fla. 5th DCA 2017) ("The law is well settled that a purchaser pendente lite is not entitled to intervene or otherwise be made a party to the ongoing lawsuit."); *Carlisle v. U.S. Bank, Nat'l Ass'n for Harborview 2005-10 Tr. Fund*, 225 So. 3d 893, 895-96 (Fla. 3d DCA 2017); *Tikhomirov v. Bank of N.Y. Mellon*, 223 So. 3d 1112 (Fla. 3d DCA 2017); *Rouffe v. CitiMortgage, Inc.*, 241 So. 3d 870, 872-73 (Fla. 4th DCA 2018); *Bank of N.Y. Mellon for Certificateholders CWALT, Inc. v. HOA Rescue Fund, LLC*, 249 So. 3d 731 (Fla. 2d

own risk because they are on notice that the property is subject to the foreclosure action.[23] This rule stems from the purpose of a notice of lis pendens, which is to notify third parties of pending litigation and protect its proponents from intervening liens that could impair or extinguish claimed property rights.[24] An additional concern is that to allow third-party purchasers to intervene would unnecessarily protract litigation.[25]

Creative attempts by third-party purchasers to participate in the proceedings above and beyond a motion to intervene will similarly not be entertained.[26] The manner in which the third-party purchaser derived title to the subject property (e.g. lien foreclosure sale or deed from former owner) generally is not a determinative factor.[27] However, if the third-party purchaser derives title to the subject property by way of a short sale transaction with the foreclosing mortgagee, then they may be entitled to intervene in the foreclosure action.[28]

Third-party purchasers are not without a remedy. They may exercise their statutory right of redemption under Fla. Stat. § 45.0315.[29]

DCA 2018); *Bank of Am., N.A. v. Mirabella Owners' Ass'n, Inc.*, 238 So. 3d 405 (Fla. 1st DCA 2018).

[23] *Space Coast Credit Union v. Goldman*, 262 So. 3d 836, 838 (Fla. 3d DCA 2018); *Bymel v. Bank of America, N.A.*, 159 So. 3d 345, 347 (Fla. 3d DCA 2015) (citing *Centerstate Bank Cent. Fla., N.A. v. Krause*, 87 So. 3d 25, 28 (Fla. 5th DCA 2012) ("[T]he purpose of a notice of lis pendens is to notify third parties of pending litigation and protect its proponents from intervening liens that could impair or extinguish claimed property rights.")).

[24] *Centerstate Bank Cent. Fla., N.A. v. Krause*, 87 So. 3d 25, 28 (Fla. 5th DCA 2012); *SADCO, Inc. v. Countrywide Funding, Inc.*, 680 So. 2d 1072, 1072 (Fla. 3d DCA 1996); *Whitburn, LLC v. Wells Fargo Bank, N.A.*, 190 So. 3d 1087, 1089 (Fla. 2d DCA 2015).

[25] *Harrod v. Union Fin. Co.*, 420 So. 2d 108, 109 (Fla. 3d DCA 1982) (citing *Peninsular Naval Stores Company v. Cox*, 49 So. 191 (Fla. 1909)).

[26] *Bonafide Properties v. Wells Fargo Bank, N.A.*, 198 So. 3d 694, 695 (Fla. 2d DCA 2016) (affirming denial of third-party purchaser's motion to join or substitute as real party in interest).

[27] *Market Tampa Investments, LLC v. Stobaugh*, 177 So. 3d 31, 32 (Fla. 2d DCA 2015) (third-party purchaser who took title via a quitclaim deed from prior owner was not entitled to intervene); *Whitburn, LLC v. Wells Fargo Bank, N.A.*, 190 So. 3d 1087, 1090 (Fla. 2d DCA 2015) (third-party purchaser who took title via an association's lien foreclosure was not entitled to intervene).

[28] *Bymel v. Bank of Am., N.A.*, 159 So. 3d 345, 347 (Fla. 3d DCA 2015) (reversing the denial of third-party purchaser's motion to intervene who acquired property by way of a short sale transaction with the foreclosing mortgagee where the third-party purchaser and mortgagee and had entered into short sale agreement). *See Bymel*, 159 So. 3d at 347 ("[T]his is not a situation where Bymel believed that he was purchasing the property subject to the pending foreclosure action and the lis pendens. Instead, Bymel reasonably believed that following the short sale, Bank of America would dismiss its foreclosure action against the [borrowers], discharge its notice of lis pendens, and record a satisfaction of its mortgage, thereby clearing title to the real property.").

[29] *Tikhomirov v. Bank of N.Y. Mellon*, 223 So. 3d 1112, 1115 (Fla. 3d DCA 2017) (citing *De Sousa v. JP Morgan Chase, N.A.*, 170 So. 3d 928, 931 (Fla. 4th DCA 2015)); *AG Group Investments, LLC v. All Realty Alliance Corp.*, 106 So. 3d 950, 951-52 (Fla. 3d DCA 2013).

10-2:3 Right of Redemption

The statutory right of redemption allows the mortgagor or the holder of a subordinate interest in the subject property to cure the indebtedness (i.e., pay off the amounts set forth in the final judgment of foreclosure) and prevent a foreclosure sale up until the time of the filing of a certificate of sale by the clerk of the court or the time specified in the foreclosure judgment.[30] This right may be exercised prior to the entry of a foreclosure judgment by tendering the performance due under the security agreement, including any amounts due because of the exercise of a right to accelerate, plus the reasonable expenses of proceeding to foreclosure incurred to the time of tender, including reasonable attorney's fees of the creditor.[31]

The only parties entitled to this right of redemption are the (1) mortgagor or (2) the holder of a subordinate interest in the subject property.[32] Tenants can only redeem the property under or through the mortgagor's rights, and have no independent right of redemption.[33] The right of redemption is assignable.[34] Once the clerk issues the certificate of sale, redemption is precluded, even if parties asserting their rights were not made party to the foreclosure proceedings.[35] To that end, an omitted junior mortgagee cannot independently exercise the right to redeem in the original senior foreclosure action after the certificate of sale has been filed.[36] The trial court in the foreclosure action may extend the post-judgment time period to exercise the statutory right of redemption if a later time is set forth in the final judgment, order, or decree of foreclosure.[37]

10-2:4 Standing to Raise Defenses or Otherwise Participate

Third-party purchasers, also known as current owners or subsequent title holders, may participate in a foreclosure action.[38] This right to participate includes challenging

---

[30] Fla. Stat. § 45.0315; *Deluxe Motel, Inc. v. Patel*, 770 So. 2d 283, 284 (Fla. 5th DCA 2000); *De Sousa v. JP Morgan Chase, N.A.*, 170 So. 3d 928, 931 (Fla. 4th DCA 2015); *Rouffe v. CitiMortgage, Inc.*, 241 So. 3d 870, 873 (Fla. 4th DCA 2018).

[31] *See* Fla. Stat. § 45.0315.

[32] Fla. Stat. § 45.0315 ("Otherwise, there is no right of redemption.").

[33] *Sedra Family Ltd. P'ship v. 4750, LLC*, 124 So. 3d 935, 936 (Fla. 4th DCA 2012).

[34] *Sudhoff v. Fed. Nat. Mortg. Ass'n*, 942 So. 2d 425, 429 n.1 (Fla. 5th DCA 2006) (citing *VOSR Indus. v. Martin Props.*, 919 So. 2d 554, 556 (Fla. 4th DCA 2005)).

[35] *AG Group Investments, LLC v. All Realty Alliance Corp.*, 106 So. 3d 950, 951-52 (Fla. 3d DCA 2013); *Saidi v. Wasko*, 687 So. 2d 10, 11 (Fla. 5th DCA 1996); *Burns v. Bankamerica Nat. Trust Co.*, 719 So. 2d 999, 1001 (Fla. 5th DCA 1998) (citing *Riley v. Grissett*, 556 So. 2d 473, 475 (Fla. 1st DCA 1990)).

[36] *Abdoney v. York*, 903 So. 2d 981, 984 (Fla. 2d DCA 2005) (citing *Burns v. Bankamerica Nat'l Trust Co.*, 719 So. 2d 999, 1001 (Fla. 5th DCA 1998)).

[37] Fla. Stat. § 45.0315. However, the trial court may not extend the time to exercise the statutory right of redemption in response to a tenants' motion to set the terms of redemption. *YEMC Const. & Dev., Inc. v. Inter Ser, U.S.A., Inc.*, 884 So. 2d 446, 448 (Fla. 3d DCA 2004).

[38] *Green Emerald Homes, LLC v. 21st Mortgage Corporation*, 2019 WL 239801544 *2, Fla. L. Weekly D1449 (Fla. 2d DCA June 7, 2019); *De Sousa v. JP Morgan Chase, N.A.*, 170 So. 3d 928, 929 (Fla. 4th DCA 2015) (explaining that the third-party purchaser could protect its interest in the property by exercising its statutory right of redemption); *Eurovest, Ltd. v. Segall*, 528 So. 2d 482, 483 (Fla. 3d DCA 1988) ("[t]he inability of a subsequent purchaser

the amount of the indebtedness owed and raising a defense based on the five-year statute of limitations for breach of contract claims.[39] Courts have increasingly accepted challenges by third-party purchasers to the plaintiff's standing to bring a foreclosure action.[40] While there are older cases limiting a third-party purchaser's ability to defend against a foreclosure, more recent case law reflects a trend in favor of allowing defenses that go to the elements of the cause of action. This is a rapidly-developing area of the law so care should be taken to assess the particular circumstances of the case (with particular attention to whether the third party is a purchaser pendente lite) as well as the state of the law.

As a general proposition, a third-party purchaser takes its interest subject to the senior mortgage, and a third-party purchaser who obtained its interest after the lis pendens was recorded is also subject to the lis pendens, but the particular circumstances of a case may warrant an objection.[41] Third-party purchasers still are likely to

---

to contest the validity of a mortgage does not affect his equitable right of redemption."); *Beauchamp v. The Bank of N.Y, Tr. Co., N.A.*, 150 So. 3d 827 (Fla. 4th DCA 2014); *Clay Cty. Land Tr. No. 08-04-25-0078-014-27, Orange Park Tr. Servs., LLC v. JP Morgan Chase Bank, Nat'l Ass'n.*, 152 So. 3d 83, 85 (Fla. 1st DCA 2014).

[39] *Green Emerald Homes, LLC v. 21st Mortgage Corporation*, 2019 WL 239801544 *2, Fla. L. Weekly D1449 (Fla. 2d DCA June 7, 2019); *Wilmington Tr., N.A. v. Alvarez*, 239 So. 3d 1265, 1266 n.1 (Fla. 3d DCA 2018) (rejecting the argument that a subsequent purchaser lacked standing to assert the statute of limitations as a defense to a foreclosure case); *Clay Cty. Land Tr. No. 08-04-25-0078-014-27, Orange Park Tr. Servs., LLC v. JP Morgan Chase Bank, Nat'l Ass'n.*, 152 So. 3d 83, 85 (Fla. 1st DCA 2014) ("As the current owner of the property, appellant had standing to challenge [the bank's] affidavit as to the amount of the debt owed because it related to appellant's right of redemption, i.e., how much appellant would have to pay under the judgment in order to exercise its right to stop the foreclosure sale."); *but see Irwin v. Grogan-Cole*, 590 So. 2d 1102, 1104 (Fla. 5th DCA 1991) (holding that a subsequent purchaser who took subject to a superior mortgage could not challenge the running of the statute of limitations).

[40] The Second, Third, and Fourth District Courts of Appeal have rejected the idea that third-party purchasers lack the ability to raise certain defenses to a foreclosure. *3709 N. Flagler Drive Prodigy Land Trust v. Bank of America, N.A.*, 226 So. 3d 1040, 1041 (Fla. 4th DCA 2017) (holding that a third-party purchaser could challenge the plaintiff's standing to foreclose a note and mortgage); *Benzrent 1, LLC v. Wilmington Savings Fund Society, FSB*, 273 So. 3d 107, 109 (Fla. 3d DCA 2019) (finding that there was no inter-district conflict on this issue and determining that "because this Court had no binding precedent on this issue, the predecessor judge was duty bound to follow the Fourth District's decision in *3709 N. Flagler*"); *Green Emerald Homes, LLC v. 21st Mortgage Corporation*, 2019 WL 239801544 *2, Fla. L. Weekly D1449 (Fla. 2d DCA June 7, 2019) (rejecting the argument that a third-party purchaser lacked standing to raise defenses to a foreclosure and distinguishing prior cases based in part on procedural due process grounds).

[41] *Green Emerald Homes, LLC v. 21st Mortgage Corporation*, 2019 WL 239801544 at n.2, Fla. L. Weekly D1449 (Fla. 2d DCA June 7, 2019); *Wilmington Tr., N.A. v. Alvarez*, 239 So. 3d 1265, 1266 n.1 (Fla. 3d DCA 2018); *cf. YHT & Assocs., Inc. v. Nationstar Mortg. LLC*, 177 So. 3d 641, 643 (Fla. 2d DCA 2015) ("At the beginning of the foreclosure trial... YHT's attorney attempted to participate, but Nationstar objected because YHT was not a party. The court refused to allow YHT to participate."); *cf. Portfolio Investments Corp. v. Deutsche Bank Nat. Trust Co.*, 81 So. 3d 534, 536 (Fla. 3d DCA 2012) ("Portfolio was not a 'stranger to the record.' ... Deutsche Bank and Mendez understood that Portfolio, as the assignee of the Association's claim of lien, had stepped into the Association's shoes and had adopted the position raised by the Association in its answer to the complaint, and that Deutsche Bank

be limited in their ability to challenge the actual terms of a mortgage as though they were a party to the mortgage.[42] For example, a defense based on failure of the plaintiff to fulfill a contractual condition precedent is generally regarded as personal to the borrower, who was the party to the mortgage. Therefore, it is possible that a third-party purchaser of the subject property may not be able to raise it successfully.[43] Additionally, third-party purchasers have no right to attorney's fees established by contract

---

and Mendez did not object to Portfolio's participation in the litigation."); *Spinney v. Winter Park Bldg. & Loan Ass'n,* 120 Fla. 453, 162 So. 899 (Fla. 1935); *Zimmerman v. Hill,* 100 So. 2d 432 (Fla. 3d DCA 1958); *Irwin v. Grogan-Cole,* 590 So. 2d 1102, 1104 (Fla. 5th DCA 1991) (holding that a subsequent purchaser who took subject to a superior mortgage could not challenge the running of the statute of limitations); *Eurovest, Ltd. v. Segall,* 528 So. 2d 482, 483 (Fla. 3d DCA 1988) (a purchaser who takes title to property subject to a prior recorded mortgage is "estopped from contesting the validity of the mortgage."); *Nesbitt v. Citicorp Savings of Fla.,* 514 So. 2d 371 (Fla. 3d DCA 1987) (affirming trial court summary judgment of foreclosure over the purchaser's objection based on the mortgage being usurious); *CCM Pathfinder Palm Harbor Mgmt., LLC v. Unknown Heirs of Gendron,* 198 So. 3d 3, 7 (Fla. 2d DCA) ("[I]f a recorded mortgage is valid on its face, a subsequent purchaser 'is assumed to have recognized it as a valid lien against the property which he is buying.'") (quoting *Spinney v. Winter Park Bldg. & Loan Ass'n,* 120 Fla. 453, 162 So. 899, 904 (Fla. 1935); *Pealer v. Wilmington Tr. Nat'l Ass'n for MFRA Tr.,* 212 So. 3d 1137, 1138 (Fla. 2d DCA 2017) (Sleet, J., concurring) ("Therefore I question whether the Pealers' limited interest in the property provided them standing to challenge the bank's standing to foreclose or the admissibility of the bank's records at trial."). In light of recent precedent, care should be taken regarding treatment of a third party's purchaser's defenses.

[42] *Wells Fargo Bank, N.A. v. Rutledge,* 230 So. 3d 550 (Fla. 2d DCA 2017) (third-party purchaser lacked standing in bank's foreclosure action to raise forgery defense); *Wells Fargo Del. Tr. Co., N.A. for Vericrest Opportunity Loan Tr. 201-NPL1 v. Petrov,* 230 So. 3d 575 (Fla. 2d DCA 2017) (questioning whether third-party purchaser has standing to challenge arguments regarding loan servicer's alleged lack of authority); *Eurovest, Ltd. v. Segall,* 528 So. 2d 482, 483 (Fla. 3d DCA 1988) (a purchaser who takes title to property subject to a prior recorded mortgage is "estopped from contesting the validity of the mortgage."); *Nesbitt v. Citicorp Savings of Fla.,* 514 So. 2d 371 (Fla. 3d DCA 1987) (affirming trial court summary judgment of foreclosure over the purchaser's objection based on the mortgage being usurious); *CCM Pathfinder Palm Harbor Mgmt., LLC v. Unknown Heirs of Gendron,* 198 So. 3d 3, 7 (Fla. 2d DCA) ("[I]f a recorded mortgage is valid on its face, a subsequent purchaser 'is assumed to have recognized it as a valid lien against the property which he is buying.'").

[43] As noted before, the case law regarding the rights of third-party purchasers is developing. There are several decisions suggesting that a defense that is so personal to the borrower may not be available to a third-party purchaser. See *Green Emerald Homes, LLC v. 21st Mortgage Corporation,* 2019 WL 239801544 at n.2, Fla. L. Weekly D1449 (Fla. 2d DCA June 7, 2019) (finding that "there might be an argument that the failure to comply with [the contractual condition precedent in] paragraph twenty-two may be asserted by a named defendant to the suit that is not a party to the mortgage," but declining to express an opinion on that question); *Clay Cty. Land Tr. No. 08-04-25-0078-014-27, Orange Park Tr. Servs., LLC v. JP Morgan Chase Bank, Nat'l Ass'n,* 152 So. 3d 83, 84 (Fla. 1st DCA 2014) ("The borrower, Buckley, was the only party who could plead nonperformance of these conditions precedent as required by Florida Rule of Civil Procedure 1.120(c)."); *LaFaille v. Nationstar Mortg., LLC,* 197 So. 3d 1246, 1247 (Fla. 3d DCA 2016) ("[N]either of the appellants was a party to, or a 'borrower' under, the mortgage or note, and thus, have no standing to assert this defense.").

and statutory reciprocity provisions.⁴⁴ For the same reasons, third-party purchasers generally do not have standing to object to the foreclosure sale if they are purchasers' pendente lite.⁴⁵ This is a developing area of the law, however, so care should be taken when raising challenges to a third party's defenses.

10-3 Tenants

10-3:1 Tenancies Established Prior to Foreclosure

Parties in possession of the subject property, whether under a written or oral lease, are necessary parties to the foreclosure action.⁴⁶ While a tenant is a necessary party, no case explicitly holds that a tenant is an indispensable party. Instead, a tenant which has not been joined as a party to the foreclosure action simply continues to hold its possessory interest until its rights are adjudicated.⁴⁷

A foreclosure action where the tenant has been properly joined as a party terminates the tenant's possessory interest in the lease.⁴⁸ This result is based on the principle that the tenant's leasehold is extinguished simultaneously with his landlord's title, from whence it was derived.⁴⁹ The purchaser at sale thereafter does not step into a

---

⁴⁴ *Fla. Cmty. Bank, N.A. v. Red Rd. Residential, LLC*, 197 So. 3d 1112, 1116 (Fla. 3d DCA 2016); *PNC Bank, Nat'l Ass'n v. MDTR, LLC*, 243 So. 3d 456, 458-59 (Fla. 5th DCA 2018); *see also Novastar Mortg., Inc. v. Strassburger*, 855 So. 2d 130, 131 (Fla. 4th DCA 2003).

⁴⁵ *Whitburn, LLC v. Wells Fargo Bank, N.A.*, 190 So. 3d 1087, 1091-92 (Fla. 2d DCA 2015) ("Because Whitburn purchased the property in June 2013 after Wells Fargo filed its notice of lis pendens in December 2012, Whitburn took the property subject to the outcome of the litigation in Wells Fargo's case, including the foreclosure sale to which Wells Fargo was entitled as a result of the judgment entered in its favor. . . . Accordingly, Whitburn does not have standing to object to the sale or intervene in Wells Fargo's foreclosure proceeding."). Even bidders at a foreclosure sale have limited standing to object to the sale. *REO Properties Corp. v. Binder*, 946 So. 2d 572, 574 (Fla. 2d DCA 2006); *Jagodinski v. Washington Mut. Bank*, 63 So. 3d 791, 793 (Fla. 1st DCA 2011).

⁴⁶ *See Redding v. Stockton, Whatley, Davin & Co.*, 488 So. 2d 548, 549 (Fla. 5th DCA 1986) (holding that a foreclosure action is the proper proceeding to terminate a tenant's possessory interest in a property); *Commercial Laundries, Inc. v. Golf Course Towers Assocs.*, 568 So. 2d 501, 503 (Fla. 3d DCA 1990) (citing *Dundee Naval Stores v. McDowell*, 61 So. 108 (Fla. 1913)).

⁴⁷ *Dundee Naval Stores Co. v. McDowell*, 61 So. 108, 113 (Fla. 1913) ("failure to make the lessees or their assignee parties to the foreclosure proceedings may not affect the validity of the decree; and though the purchaser gets a title by virtue of the mortgages, the foreclosure, and the sale, which title includes a right of ultimate possession, yet, as the rights of the leaseholder have not been adjudicated, the title and right of possession acquired by the purchaser at the same are subject to the rights of the leaseholder under the duly executed and recorded lease until such rights are in some way duly terminated."); *Sedra Family Ltd. P'ship v. 4750, LLC*, 124 So. 3d 935, 936 (Fla. 4th DCA 2012) ("[b]ecause it was not a party to the original proceedings, the tenant still has a possessory interest which has not been foreclosed in the property").

⁴⁸ *Redding v. Stockton, Whatley, Davin & Co.*, 488 So. 2d 548, 549 (Fla. 5th DCA 1986), *cause dismissed*, 492 So. 2d 1334 (Fla. 1986).

⁴⁹ *Redding v. Stockton, Whatley, Davin & Co.*, 488 So. 2d 548, 549 (Fla. 5th DCA 1986), *cause dismissed*, 492 So. 2d 1334 (Fla. 1986); *see also Igbinadolor v. Deutsche Bank Nat'l Trust Co.*, 215 So. 3d 192 n.1 (Fla. 3d DCA 2017).

landlord-tenant relationship with the tenant.[50] Rather, the relationship at that point is owner and trespasser—the exact situation for which a writ of possession is required.

After the foreclosure sale, the Federal Protecting Tenants at Foreclosure Act (FPTFA)[51] and the Florida Residential Landlord and Tenant Act[52] entitle tenants to notice and time to vacate the foreclosed property, and potentially the honoring of their existing lease. The FPTFA does not preempt the Florida Act where the Florida Act is more protective of tenants, but the FPTFA does preempt the Florida Act where it is less protective.[53] The FPTFA and Florida's Act are consistent with regard to the class of tenants they protect.[54] However, unlike the Florida Act,[55] under the FPTFA a bona fide lease with a specific duration must be honored by the purchaser at the foreclosure sale for the lease's duration under its terms.[56] In addition, under the FPTFA, a bona fide tenant without a written lease or with a "lease terminable at will under State law" must be given 90 days to vacate after notice.[57] Under both acts, the tenant must pay rent to the purchaser.[58]

Neither of the acts and related rights apply to a holdover tenant who was the mortgagor of the property in the subject foreclosure, nor do the acts apply when the lease

---

[50] *Redding v. Stockton, Whatley, Davin & Co.*, 488 So. 2d 548, 549 (Fla. 5th DCA 1986), *cause dismissed*, 492 So. 2d 1334 (Fla. 1986).

[51] On June 23, 2018, the Economic Growth, Regulatory Relief, and Consumer Protection Act became effective, repealing the sunset provisions in the Federal Protecting Tenants at Foreclosure Act (FPTFA), which previously had expired on December 31, 2014. Pub. L. 115–74. The FPTFA contained protections intended to ensure that tenants facing eviction from a foreclosed property would have adequate time to find alternative housing. Following the FPTFA's expiration at the end of 2014, many states (including Florida) implemented their own versions of the law to continue protections.

[52] Fla. Stat. § 83.561, *et seq.*

[53] Fla. Stat. § 702(a) ("[N]othing under this section shall affect the requirements for termination of any Federal- or State-subsidized tenancy or of any State or local law that provides longer time periods or other additional protections for tenants.").

[54] Under the Fla. Stat. § 702(b), protections only apply if:

(1) the mortgagor or the child, spouse, or parent of the mortgagor under the contract is not the tenant;

(2) the lease or tenancy was the result of an arms-length transaction; and

(3) the lease or tenancy requires the receipt of rent that is not substantially less than fair market rent for the property or the unit's rent is reduced or subsidized due to a Federal, State, or local subsidy.

Similarly, under Fla. Stat. § 83.561(3)(a)-(c), protections do not apply if:

(a) The tenant is the mortgagor in the subject foreclosure or is the child, spouse, or parent of the mortgagor in the subject foreclosure.

(b) The tenant's rental agreement is not the result of an arm's length transaction.

(c) The tenant's rental agreement allows the tenant to pay rent that is substantially less than the fair market rent for the premises, unless the rent is reduced or subsidized due to a federal, state, or local subsidy.

[55] Fla. Stat. §§ 83.561(1)(a) and (2).

[56] Fla. Stat. § 702(a)(2)(A).

[57] Fla. Stat. § 702(a)(2)(B).

[58] Fla. Stat. § 702(b)(3); Fla. Stat. § 83.561(1)(c).

was not the result of an arms-length transaction.[59] The purchaser does not assume other various statutory obligations of a landlord for building maintenance and post-tenancy security deposit notices.[60] However, the purchaser is strictly prohibited from terminating utility services furnished to the tenant, preventing reasonable access to the property, and changing locks or removing personal property, and the purchaser may be liable for damages and attorney's fees in the event a violation occurs.[61]

10-3:2 Lessee Pendente Lite

A tenant taking possession mid-foreclosure is a lessee pendente lite.[62] As a consequence, a lessee pendente lite will be bound by the judgment in the action to which his landlord is a party.[63] Like a purchaser, a lessee pendente lite is not entitled to intervene or otherwise be made a party to the ongoing lawsuit.[64]

Lessee pendente lites' only rights in the pending foreclosure case derive from the Federal Protecting Tenants at Foreclosure Act (FPTFA) and the Florida Residential Landlord and Tenant Act, discussed in Section 10-3:1.

10-3:3 Writ of Possession

Following a final judgment of foreclosure where the tenant is joined as a party, the purchaser at foreclosure sale may obtain relief from the tenant's continued possession by obtaining a writ of possession.[65] The purchaser is not required to commence a separate eviction proceeding.[66]

---

[59] Fla. Stat. § 702(b); Fla. Stat. § 83.561(3).
[60] Fla. Stat. § 83.561(4).
[61] Fla. Stat. § 83.561(4); *see also* Fla. Stat. § 83.67.
[62] *Bymel v. Bank of Am., N.A.*, 159 So. 3d 345, 347 (Fla. 3d DCA 2015) (stating that a person who purchases property that is the subject of a foreclosure action where a lis pendens has been recorded is a purchaser pendente lite); *see also Igbinadolor v. Deutsche Bank Nat'l Trust Co.*, 215 So. 3d 192 n.1 (Fla. 3d DCA 2017) (describing a tenant who entered into a verbal lease agreement with the mortgagor well into the foreclosure proceedings as a lessee pendente lite).
[63] *Howard Cole & Co. v. Williams*, 27 So. 2d 352, 355 (Fla. 1946).
[64] *Bymel v. Bank of Am., N.A.*, 159 So. 3d 345, 347 (Fla. 3d DCA 2015) ("[W]hen property is purchased during a pending foreclosure action in which a lis pendens has been filed, the purchaser generally is not entitled to intervene in the pending foreclosure action."); *see also Trust No. 602W0 Dated 7/16/15, Dema Investments, LLC v. Wells Fargo Bank, N.A.*, 207 So. 3d 977, 978 (Fla. 5th DCA 2016) ("As a purchaser pendente lite, the Trust was not entitled to intervene in the foreclosure proceedings.").
[65] Fla. Stat. § 83.561 and Fla. R. Civ. P. 1.580 provide the procedure for such writs and an example can be found in Form 1.915. *See also Neuschatz v. Rabin*, 760 So. 2d 1018, 1018 (Fla. 4th DCA 2000) (citing *Martorano v. Spicola*, 148 So. 585, 586 (1933)); *Redding v. Stockton, Whatley, Davin & Co.*, 488 So. 2d 548, 549 (Fla. 5th DCA 1986), *cause dismissed*, 492 So. 2d 1334 (Fla. 1986).
[66] *Redding v. Stockton, Whatley, Davin & Co.*, 488 So. 2d 548, 549 (Fla. 5th DCA 1986), *cause dismissed*, 492 So. 2d 1334 (Fla. 1986) ("The relationship at that point was owner and trespasser—the exact situation for which a writ of possession is required. Redding's lease was extinguished simultaneously with his landlord's title, from whence it was derived.").

10-4 Governmental Entities

10-4:1 Local Government Liens

Certain liens have priority over a first mortgage regardless of the date of recordation, a phenomenon known as "superpriority." The plaintiff will be unable to foreclose such liens. An example of a superpriority lien is a tax lien imposed by the state of Florida.[67]

Local taxing districts also have the authority to impose liens on the subject property, which may be either recorded or unrecorded. These subordinate interests in the property should be alleged in the foreclosure complaint and identified with particularity.[68] The complaint also should include allegations to foreclose any local code enforcement liens on the property.[69] Plaintiffs should bear in mind that the limitation period for the enforcement of code enforcement liens is twenty years.[70]

10-4:2 Internal Revenue Service

The United States of America may be named as a junior lienholder by virtue of any tax lien on the subject property.[71] Prior recorded mortgages have priority over later recorded Internal Revenue Service liens.[72] If the mortgage is inferior to the federal lien, the sale will be subject to the government's lien if it consents that the property may be sold free of its lien and the proceeds divided as the parties may be entitled.[73]

---

[67] *See* Fla. Stat. § 197.122. Some special assessments also enjoy superpriority status. Fla. Stat. § 170.09. Tax deeds have priority status over other liens except for municipal liens. Fla. Stat. § 197.552. Further discussion of the subject of the priority of various kinds of liens may be found in *Argent Mortg. Co., LLC v. Wachovia Bank N.A.*, 52 So. 3d 796 (Fla. 5th DCA 2010); *Barton v. MetroJax Property Holdings, LLC*, 207 So. 3d 304, 306 (Fla. 3d DCA 2016) and *Miami-Dade Cty. Lansdowne Mortg., LLC*, 235 So. 3d 960, 961 (Fla. 3d DCA 2017).

[68] Fla. Stat. § 69.041 ("The complaint shall set forth with particularity the nature of the interest claimed by the state in such real property with respect to quiet title proceedings. In the case of mortgage or lien foreclosure, the complaint shall set forth with particularity the nature of the lien claimed by the state in such real property.").

[69] The authority and procedure by which municipalities may impose administrative fines and liens against property is set forth in the Local Government Code Enforcement Boards Act. Fla. Stat. § 162.09. A municipal ordinance cannot establish a superpriority status for code enforcement liens over prior recorded mortgages. *City of Palm Bay v. Wells Fargo Bank, N.A.*, 114 So. 3d 924 (Fla. 2013). However, courts have recognized that municipal code liens have priority according to its time of recordation. *Broward County v. Recupero*, 949 So. 2d 274, 276 (Fla. 4th DCA 2007).

[70] Fla. Stat. § 162.10; *City of Riviera Beach v. J & B Motel Corp.*, 213 So. 3d 1102, 1103 (Fla. 4th DCA 2017).

[71] 28 U.S.C. § 2410(a)(2).

[72] *In re Haas*, 31 F.3d 1081, 1086-87 (11th Cir. 1994).

[73] 28 U.S.C. § 2410(c).

CHAPTER 11

Discovery

Gaspar Forteza

11-1 Introduction

Discovery is an art. Parties are entitled to discovery of all non-privileged[1] information that is either relevant to any issue in the case, or that is likely to lead to the discovery of relevant, admissible evidence.[2] This is known as the "scope" of discovery. Trial courts have wide discretion in determining the scope of discovery, the timeframes for propounding and responding to discovery requests, the amount of discovery to be permitted and the sufficiency of responses.[3] Absent a clear abuse of that discretion or a departure from the essential requirements of law, the Florida appellate courts will defer to the discretion of the trial courts and will not disturb discovery-related rulings by certiorari review on appeal.[4] Even so, whether to grant certiorari[5] review and relief

---

[1] An exception to the general rule is that a party may obtain otherwise privileged materials prepared by another party, its counsel or other representative(s), in anticipation of litigation or for trial upon a showing that the party seeking the discovery has need of the materials in preparation of the case and is unable without undue hardship to obtain the substantial equivalent of the materials by other means. *See* Florida Rule of Civil Procedure 1.280(b)(4); *see also Butler v. Harter*, 152 So. 3d 705 (Fla. 1st DCA 2014) (generally, fact work product is discoverable upon showing of need; opinion work product is "nearly absolutely" privileged).

[2] *See* Fla. R. Civ. Pro. 1.280(b); *Allstate Ins. Co. v. Langston*, 655 So. 2d 91, 94 (Fla. 1995) ("Discovery in civil cases must be relevant to the subject matter of the case and must be admissible or reasonably calculated to lead to admissible evidence.") (citations omitted); *Amente v. Newman*, 653 So. 2d 1030 (Fla. 1995) (concept of relevancy is broader in discovery context than in trial context such that party may be permitted to discover relevant evidence that would be inadmissible at trial if it may lead to discovery of relevant evidence).

[3] *See Tumelaire v. Naples Estates Homeowners Ass'n, Inc.*, 137 So. 3d 596 598 (Fla. 2nd DCA 2014) (trial court's discretion is so broad with respect to discovery that a ruling from the trial court with respect to discovery will be "set aside on certiorari review [only] if it constitutes an abuse of discretion which would cause irreparable damage which cannot be remedied on appeal") (internal quotations marks and citation to authority omitted).

[4] *See Nucci v. Target Corp.*, 162 So. 3d 146 (Fla. 4th DCA 2015); *Racetrac Petroleum, Inc. v. Sewell*, 150 So. 2d 1247 (Fla. 3d DCA 2014).

[5] *See* Section 5-8. A Petition for Writ of Certiorari Review is a type of interlocutory appeal by which litigants can challenge a trial court's ruling(s) with respect to discovery matters before having to produce documents the trial court deemed subject to discovery under the Rules. Significantly, in addition to filing a Notice of Appeal with the trial court, the petition or other notice invoking the appellate court's jurisdiction must be filed with the appellate

is itself discretionary with the appellate court, and an appellate court may decline to grant relief even where a trial court departs from the essential requirements of law.[6]

11-2 Methods of Discovery

Residential mortgage foreclosure litigation typically lends itself to four methods of discovery: (1) Requests to Produce; (2) Requests for Admissions; (3) Interrogatories; and (4) Depositions. Each is discussed briefly below.

11-3 Requests to Produce (RTPs)

Although dubbed "requests," RTPs actually impose upon the party to whom they are directed a legal *requirement* to respond. Failure to respond may be met with motions to compel production, and orders granting motions to compel invite fee awards and/or further sanctions from the court against the non-producing party. Sanctions usually consist of, or include, reimbursement to the movant of reasonable costs and attorneys' fees associated with bringing the motion to compel.[7] More egregious violations of court-ordered production, such as serial non-compliance with court orders to produce, etc., invite more severe sanctions, including precluding the party from whom the materials were sought from introducing them into evidence at trial; the striking of pleadings; and the entry of either a dismissal of the plaintiff's claim, or a final judgment against the defendant, depending on which party failed to respond as required. Dismissal with prejudice is the ultimate sanction.

11-3:1 Propounding RTPs

Subject to the court's discretion, the rules do not limit the number of RTPs one party may propound upon another, provided they seek production or inspection of materials within the scope of discovery.[8] RTPs may be served upon a plaintiff any time after commencement of an action, and upon other parties either with service of the summons and complaint, or any time thereafter, subject to a discovery cut-off date, which can be determined by the court or sometimes agreed to by the parties.[9] Costs associated with the production of documents or other materials are generally recoverable by the prevailing party.[10]

11-3:2 Responding to RTPs

Responses to RTPs directed to parties are due within 30 days of service, or within 45 days if served with the summons and complaint.[11] The duty to respond extends to all materials within the "possession, custody, or control" of the party to whom the RTPs

---

court within 30 days of the lower court's order; otherwise the appellate court lacks jurisdiction. *See Hoyt v. Commonwealth Land Title Ins. Co.*, 532 So. 2d 72 (Fla. 2d DCA 1988); Florida Rules of Appellate Procedure 9.100(b) and (c).

[6] *See Nucci v. Target Corp.*, 162 So. 3d 146 (Fla. 4th DCA 2015).
[7] *See* Fla. R. Civ. P. 1.380(4).
[8] *See*, Fla. R. Civ. P. 1.350 (a).
[9] *See* Fla. R. Civ. P. 1.350(b).
[10] *See Collins v. Holland*, 409 So. 2d 1097 (Fla. 3d DCA 1982).
[11] *See* Fla. R. Civ. P. 1.350(b).

are directed.[12] In other words, such parties must produce or otherwise respond to the request for any document or material that is within the power of the party to obtain (e.g., documents maintained by third parties such as financial institutions, servicers, attorneys, other agents, etc.). It is not enough that the document is in the physical possession of another, provided the party required to produce the document has sufficient control over the one with physical possession to obtain the document for itself for discovery purposes.

11-3:2.1 Objections

Responses to RTPs need set forth only objections and reasons.[13] Parties served with RTPs may object to production of documents or other materials on numerous grounds including, but not limited to, the fact that the request seeks materials beyond the scope of discovery, is subject to privilege (e.g., attorney-client; work-product privilege; etc.); or where production of the documents would be unduly burdensome or oppressive. In addition, a party cannot be compelled to generate a document not already in existence at the time production is due.[14]

As a matter of good practice, a party asserting objections may want to schedule the objections for hearing. This renders unnecessary any motion to compel and facilitates the objecting party's opportunity to be heard first at the hearing instead of having to react and respond to the motion to compel from a defensive posture. In any case, prior to setting a hearing on the objections or on a motion to compel, parties must make a good faith effort to resolve their differences without judicial intervention. Except as they relate to privilege, courts deem waived any objection not raised by the date on which the response is due. Consequently, it is prudent to assert objections even when unaware of any documents responsive to a particular RTP, thereby preserving the objection in the event responsive documents extant at the time of the request are later discovered. However, discovery objections should also be carefully drafted and tailored to the particular request. Blanket objections and treating the requests in a boilerplate fashion could result in sanctions. Trial courts have even undertaken extreme measures, such as cancelling the entire mortgage itself.[15] In all cases where sanctions are sought against a litigant or its counsel, however, an evidentiary hearing is generally required. Although some courts have previously held that evidentiary hearings are required only in cases where the court was required to make a factual determination of whether the sanctionable conduct should be apportioned to the attorney or the litigant,[16] Florida courts generally favor an individual evidentiary hearing to determine the appropriateness of the sanction.[17]

---

[12] Fla. R. Civ. P. 1.350(a).
[13] *See Messer v. E.G. Pump Controls, Inc.*, 667 So. 2d 321 (Fla. 1st DCA 1995); *DeBartolo-Aventura, Inc. v. Hernandez*, 638 So. 2d 988 (Fla. 3rd DCA 1994).
[14] *See Allstate Ins. Co. v. Pinder*, 746 So. 2d 1255, 1256-57 (Fla. 5th DCA 1999) (party seeking production of documents cannot require the party to whom the request is directed to create a non-existing document).
[15] *Deutsche Bank Nat'l Tr. Co. v. Avila-Gonzalez*, 164 So. 3d 90, 93 (Fla. 3d DCA 2015) (reversing cancellation only for failure to consider the test for such a sanction under *Kozel v. Ostendorf*, 629 So. 2d 817, 818 (Fla.1993)).
[16] *See Deutsche Bank Nat'l Trust Co. v. Avila-Gonzalez*, 164 So. 3d 90, 93 (Fla. 3d DCA 2015); *Ledo v. Seavie Resources, LLC*, 149 So. 3d 707, 710 (Fla. 3d DCA 2014).
[17] *See Deutsche Bank Nat'l Tr. Co. v. Sombrero Beach Rd., LLC*, 260 So. 3d 424, 428 (Fla. 3d DCA 2018); *Bank of New York Mellon v. Johnson*, 270 So. 3d 1269, 1272 (Fla. 1st DCA 2019).

11-3:2.2 Production

Documents may be produced in one of two ways: (1) they may be made available for inspection and copying as they are kept in the usual course of business; or (2) they may be identified to correspond with categories of documents sought in the RTP.[18] For example, if Request #1 asks for "copies of all contracts entered into between Jon Doe and Sue Smith from January 1, 2013 to the present," the response might read, "Copies of all documents responsive to Request #1 are attached hereto as Exhibit "A." All documents produced should contain a numerical bate stamp beginning with page "1" and continuing sequentially through the last page of the last document produced, so as to avoid subsequent disputes over what was and was not produced. Unless directed otherwise by the court, documents produced in response to RTPs should not be filed with the court. Finally, with respect to documents withheld on the grounds of privilege, the party asserting the privilege must provide a "privilege log" describing the nature of the documents or other materials not produced in a manner that, without revealing information deemed privileged, enables the other parties to evaluate the privilege assertion.[19] The failure to file a timely privilege log can, in certain cases, constitute a waiver of the privilege.[20]

11-3:3 Inadvertent Production of Privileged Materials

Inadvertent disclosure of privileged materials does not automatically waive the privilege.[21] However, the party seeking to invoke it thereafter must, within 10 days of learning of the disclosure, serve written notice to the recipient that the privilege is being asserted. The notice must identify the documents, the nature of the privilege, and the date on which the inadvertent disclosure was discovered. Upon receipt of a timely notice, the party to whom the documents were inadvertently disclosed must "promptly" return them, sequester them or destroy them.[22] Significantly, a party does not waive a privilege objection simply by furnishing protected or privileged material to the party's own expert.[23]

11-3:4 No Duty to Supplement Responses

A party that responds to an RTP with a response that is complete when given has no duty to supplement the response to produce documents acquired thereafter.[24]

---

[18] Fla. R. Civ. P. 1.350(b).

[19] Fla. R. Civ. P. 1.280(b)(6).

[20] *See TIG Ins. Corp. of America v. Johnson*, 799 So. 2d 399 (Fla. 4th DCA 2001). *But see Fifth Third Bank v. ACA Plus, Inc.*, 73 So. 3d 850 (Fla. 5th DCA 2011) ("The trial court's subsequent finding of an implicit waiver, based on a failure to file a privilege log within thirty days of the date of service . . . constituted a departure from the essential requirements of law."). Moreover, the time in which to file a privilege log is tolled at least until court rules on non-privilege objections. *See DLJ Mortg. Capital, Inc. v. Fox*, 112 So. 3d 644 (Fla. 4th DCA 2013).

[21] Fla. R. Civ. P. 1.285(a).

[22] Fla. R. Civ. P. 1.285(b).

[23] *Mullins v. Tompkins*, 15 So. 3d 798 (Fla. 1st DCA 2009) (and citations therein).

[24] Fla. R. Civ. P. 1.280(f).

11-4 Requests for Admissions (RFAs)

Requests for Admission are often underutilized but carry at least three potential benefits. First, they enable cooperative litigants and their counsel to narrow the issues, saving time and money for both sides. Second, absent a timely response, RFAs are deemed admitted without further action by the parties or the court. Third, they can serve as a powerful tool in setting up at least one interrogatory; to wit, "If you denied any of the Requests for Admissions propounded contemporaneously herewith, state in detail and under oath all facts on which you base your denial." It is one thing for an attorney to stamp "denied" in response to every request to admit. It is quite another for the attorney's client to have to sit down and answer under oath how it is that he and/or his attorney denied, for example, that a signature on a promissory note appearing to be that of the client is not the client's signature.

11-4:1 Propounding RFAs

A party may serve up to 30 written requests upon any other party asking that the latter admit to the "truth of any matter within the scope of [proper discovery]," including "statements or opinions of fact, or of the application of law to fact, including the genuineness of any documents described in the request."[25] RFAs may be served upon a plaintiff any time after commencement of an action, and upon other parties either with service of the summons and complaint, or any time thereafter, subject to a discovery cut-off date, which can be determined by the court or, sometimes, agreed to by the parties. RFAs must be drafted carefully and with precision. Compound requests and general sloppiness in formulating the assertion to be admitted can render RFAs useless. As a general rule of thumb, drafters should consider following the allegations of carefully drafted pleadings. Copies of documents must be provided with RFAs unless they have already been provided or made available for inspection and copying.[26]

11-4:2 Responding to RFAs

Responses to RFAs directed to parties are due within 30 days of service, or within 45 days if served with the summons and complaint. Timely responses to RFAs are of paramount importance. Failure to respond timely constitutes an admission without further action on the part of the court or the party that propounded the RFAs.[27] Leave of court is required to withdraw such "technical" admissions, and it is not uncommon for courts to grant such motions in deference to a trial on the merits.[28] If such a motion is denied, however, those admissions can be difficult if not impossible to overcome. While there is case law standing for the proposition that entry of judgment based on technical admissions can be error where other evidence on the record refutes the admissions,[29] the

---

[25] Fla. R. Civ. P. 1.370(a).
[26] Fla. R. Civ. P. 1.370(a).
[27] Fla. R. Civ. P. 1.370(a).
[28] *See, e.g., Ramos v. Growing Together, Inc.*, 672 So. 2d 103, 104 (Fla. 4th DCA 1996); *Sher v. Liberty Mut. Ins. Co.*, 557 So. 2d 638 (Fla. 3d DCA 1990); *Habib v. Maison Du Vin Francais, Inc.*, 528 So. 2d 553 (Fla. 4th DCA 1988) *Melody Tours, Inc. v. Granville Market Letter, Inc.*, 413 So. 2d 450 (Fla. 5th DCA 1982).
[29] *See, e.g., Sterling v. City of West Palm Beach*, 595 So. 2d 284 (Fla. 4th DCA 1992) ("The use of admissions obtained through a technicality should not form a basis to preclude adjudication of a legitimate claim.").

Rule is very clear: "[a]ny matter admitted under this rule is conclusively established unless the court on motion permits withdrawal."[30]

11-4:2.1 Objections

Parties may object to RFAs on the same grounds as they may object to other types of discovery requests, but the objection must be specifically stated. Unless answered in the affirmative, the response must deny the matter asserted or explain why the matter asserted cannot be truthfully be answered by an admission or denial. Denials must "fairly meet" the substance of the matter asked to be admitted, and a qualified or partial admission must set forth the basis for why the assertion cannot be admitted in its entirety. Lack of information or knowledge is not a basis to admit or deny a request to admit unless the party providing the response avers that he or she "made a reasonable inquiry and that the information known or readily available . . . is insufficient" to allow the party to admit or deny.[31]

11-4:2.2 Admitting

Although courts may accept evidence that contradicts "technical admissions" (i.e., a failure to answer), the Rule provides that an admission conclusively establishes the truth of the matter admitted. The proponent need not introduce into evidence anything more than the admission to prove its veracity. At least one court has held that admissions obtained in a response to a request to admit need not even be introduced into evidence since the admission would not go to any contested issue of fact.[32] Significantly, an admission is binding only in the pending action and cannot be used against a party in any other proceeding.[33]

11-4:2.3 Denying

When in doubt, the default value is to deny a troublesome or otherwise unclear request for admission. While all parties and their counsel have a duty of candor, the response is not under oath. A "denial" merely represents that a party will not stipulate to the matter asserted but will require proof thereof. The penalty or "sanction" for requiring a party to prove the truth of a matter denied is an award of attorney's fees and costs incurred in proving that the assertion was in fact true.

11-5 Interrogatories

Interrogatories are simply written questions one party propounds upon another to which the other (person or entity) must respond under oath. Florida Supreme Court approved standard interrogatory forms may be found in "Appendix I" following the text of the Civil Procedure Rules and Forms, which are themselves found after the Rules of Civil Procedure in the Florida Rules of Court (Volume I—State) (2014). In any case, Florida Supreme Court form interrogatories should be used where applicable. They need not all be used, however, and they may be supplemented by additional

---

[30] Fla. R. Civ. P. 1.370(b).
[31] Fla. R. Civ. P. 1.370(a).
[32] *See Lutsch v. Smith*, 397 So. 2d 337 (Fla. 1st DCA 1981).
[33] Fla. R. Civ. P. 1.370(b).

interrogatories provided the total does not exceed the number of interrogatories permitted.

11-5:1 Propounding Interrogatories

Interrogatories may be served upon a plaintiff any time after suit is filed, and upon other parties either with service of the summons and complaint, or any time thereafter, subject to a discovery cut-off date, which can be determined by the court or, sometimes, agreed to by the parties. Interrogatories are limited to 30 per party in number, including subparts.[34]

Interrogatories can be quite helpful in determining the identity and contact information for prospective witnesses, as well as gaining at least some insight into the area(s) about which they might have relevant knowledge. Interrogatories may also prove helpful in identifying and locating documents and other materials subject to discovery, and in seeking quantification and calculations with respect to damages. At the same time, interrogatories may prove counterproductive to the extent they apprise the party to whom they are directed of questions that might be posed more strategically for the first time at a deposition. Responses to interrogatories usually represent a careful and dual effort of both counsel and client working in tandem. Although attorneys (are supposed to) prepare their clients for depositions, doing so can prove a much more difficult process than sitting down with a client and working together through responses to interrogatories. Those carefully crafted responses may conveniently find their way into the client's testimony at a subsequent deposition, thereby making it more rehearsed and less candid than it might otherwise have been.

11-5:2 Responding to Interrogatories

Responses to Interrogatories directed to parties are due within 30 days of service, or within 45 days if served with the summons and complaint. The answers must "stand on their own." In other words, except to the extent discussed in Section 11-5:2.3 below, they may not simply refer the reader to pleadings or other documents, even if it means retyping information contained therein.[35]

11-5:2.1 Objections

Parties may object to Interrogatories on the same grounds as they may object to other types of discovery requests. If only a partial objection is raised, the party should answer the balance of the Interrogatory to the best of his or her ability.

11-5:2.2 Answering in Individual or Corporate Capacity

Interrogatories propounded upon an individual person must be answered by that individual, albeit with or without aid of counsel. The answers must be under oath or affirmation. If the individual is a party, the answers to interrogatories constitute an admission of that party against interest and can be used by that party's opponent for any reason (e.g., as substantive evidence at summary judgment or trial). Moreover,

---

[34] Fla. R. Civ. P. 1.340(a).
[35] *See State Road Dept. v. Florida East Coast Ry. Co.*, 212 So. 2d 315 (Fla. 3rd DCA 1968).

an individual's false answers to interrogatories can result in prosecution for perjury. That said, the Rules provide that:

> An interrogatory otherwise proper is not objectionable merely because an answer to the interrogatory involves an opinion or contention that relates to fact or calls for a conclusion or asks for information not within the personal knowledge of the party. A party shall respond to such an interrogatory by giving the information the party has and the source on which the information is based. Such a qualified answer may not be used as direct evidence for or impeachment against the party giving the answer unless the court finds it otherwise admissible under the rules of evidence.[36]

With respect to interrogatories propounded upon corporations or other entities, the Authors' Comment [to the Rule]—1967 Rule provides that:

> ... an officer or agent of a corporation ... who answers interrogatories must 'furnish such information as is available to the party' on whose behalf he answers. This means that an officer or agent, who has not sufficient familiarity with the facts to answer the interrogatories either as of knowledge or on information, as may be the case in some large corporations, is required to make such inquiry as will enable him to supply the answers, when the information is accessible to the company on whose behalf he answers as, for example, where the information called for in the interrogatories is contained in the company's files.[37]

In other words, a corporate representative is entitled to rely on hearsay, general knowledge of company policy, reasonable inferences, and the like, provided he or she has made a good faith effort to determine what would, in fact, be the corporation's response were a corporate entity capable of answering for itself.

11-5:2.3 Option to Produce Records

If the information sought can be derived or ascertained from documents, records, or other materials as easily by the party propounding the interrogatories as by the party responding to them, the party responding may attach such documents, records and/or other materials to the answer in lieu of responding further.[38]

11-6 Depositions

A deposition is a court proceeding outside the presence of the judge or jury where an attorney asks questions of a witness, call the "deponent." A court reporter will be present to record (by one or more means) everything said on the record, so that a transcript of the deposition can be prepared, if ordered. Answers given at a deposition are under oath or affirmation and can be used in court for many purposes, often to impeach or undermine the deponent's testimony and credibility. As a general rule, leave of court is not required to take a deposition unless the plaintiff seeks to take a deposition within 30 days after service of a summons and complaint upon any defen-

---

[36] Fla. R. Civ. P. 1.340(b).
[37] Fla. R. Civ. P. 1.340. Author's Comment—1967.
[38] Fla. R. Civ. P. 1.340(c).

DISCOVERY 181

dant, unless the defendant has already initiated discovery demands of its own. A deponent may or may not be required to bring documents to the deposition, depending upon whether the Notice of Taking Deposition is "Duces Tecum," or not. If it is duces tecum, then the deponent is required to bring to the deposition documents identified in the Notice, usually by way of an attachment thereto. Thirty days advance notice must be provided to party-deponents noticed for deposition duces tecum.

11-6:1 Preparing the Deponent for Deposition

Thoroughly discussing the deposition with the deponent prior to the deposition is not only acceptable preparation, it is strongly encouraged and may constitute malpractice if not properly done, particularly when preparing a party-deponent. Attempting to "prepare" the deponent during the course of the deposition, however, is often referred to as "coaching." Coaching is not only improper, it borders and can cross over the line into the unethical. How one prepares a witness for deposition is largely a function of whether the deponent is a party to the action or not. In either case, the purpose of deposition preparation should not be to "tell the witness what to say," but to familiarize the witness with the process and to discern what the witness knows and assist him or her in how best to articulate it.

11-6:1.1 Party Deponent

A "party-deponent" is any person scheduled for a deposition who is named as a party in the lawsuit or is the representative of any entity named as a party in the lawsuit. Preparation of a party-deponent is usually easier than preparation of a non-party deponent because the attorney-client privilege shields a party-deponent from having to disclose information exchanged between counsel and the deponent in preparation for the deposition. While a deponent appearing in his or her individual capacity is not obligated to "prepare" for a deposition, the same cannot be said for a corporate representative. In addition to understanding the basic rules, purposes and intents of a deposition, a deponent testifying in a representative capacity must take special care to become familiar with documents likely to be discussed during the course of the deposition. As a general rule, the representative of a party seeking to foreclose a mortgage should become familiar with the following, and discuss them with counsel, before appearing for deposition:

- The promissory note;
- The mortgage;
- The "breach" or "demand" letter;
- The borrower's payment history;
- Any Power of Attorney or other document authorizing the deponent's company to act on behalf of a principal (e.g., a Trust);
- The "Hello-Goodbye Letter" sent to the borrower(s) upon a change in servicers;
- Servicing notes and correspondence with the borrower(s);
- Public/Agency Merger and Acquisition Records;
- Assignments of Mortgage;
- Any applicable Pooling and Servicing Agreement;

- Any Bailee letters;
- Contracts and/or other documents evidence purchase of the note;
- Any computer screen shots evidencing when the Plaintiff or its principal acquired ownership of the note;
- The pleadings (and, particularly, any affirmative defenses); and,
- Answers to interrogatories provided by the deponent's employer.

Significantly, parties must "designate with reasonable particularity the matters on which examination is requested." Parties seeking to depose the opposition will often request to be provided with the witness with the "most knowledge" regarding a specified topic. But Florida Rule of Civil Procedure 1.310(b)(6) does not require—or for that matter even contemplate—that a corporation produce the witness with the "most knowledge" on the specified topic(s). (In fact, a corporation may have good reason not to produce the "most knowledgeable" witness as its Rule 1.310(b)(6) designee.)[39]

The person designated to testify "represents the collective knowledge of the corporation, not of the individual deponent. "As the corporation's "voice" the witness does "not simply testify about matters within his or her personal knowledge, but rather is 'speaking for the corporation.'"[40] Rule 1.310(b)(6) streamlines the discovery process and gives the corporation the right to select and prepare a witness to testify on its behalf. Although in certain circumstances, litigants may seek to depose specific individuals in their corporate capacities, a borrower is generally not permitted to designate the lender's corporate representative to testify at deposition in a mortgage foreclosure action.[41]

11-6:1.2 Non-Party Deponent

Discussions between an attorney and a non-party deponent are discoverable, meaning the opposing party is entitled to inquire into those discussions during the course of the deposition or thereafter. Attorneys exchanging information with non-party deponents should proceed accordingly. Nonetheless, to facilitate preparation for deposing a non-party witness, it is advisable to confer with him or her prior to the deposition so as to gain as much knowledge as possible as to what might transpire at the deposition. It is important that the attorney knows in advance what to expect from the witness' testimony and how to solicit what the attorney wants from the witness' testimony.

11-6:2 Taking the Deposition

Examination and cross-examination of deponents may proceed as if they are witnesses at trial.[42]

---

[39] *See QBE Ins. Corp. v. Jorda Enters., Inc.*, 277 F.R.D. 676, 688–89 (S.D. Fla. 2012).
[40] *Carriage Hills Condominium, Inc. v. JBH Roofing & Constructors, Inc.*, 109 So. 3d 329 (Fla. 4th DCA 2013).
[41] *U.S. Bank Nat'l Ass'n as Tr. for Certificateholders of Structured Asset Mortgage Investments II, Inc., Bear Stearns Arm Tr., Mortgage Pass-Through Certificates, Series 2006-2 v. Williamson*, 273 So. 3d 190, 192 (Fla. 5th DCA 2019) ("... Bank, and not Williamson, has the authority to designate one or more of its officers, directors, managing agents, or other persons as its corporate representative to testify at deposition on its behalf.").
[42] Fla. R. Civ. P. 1.310(c).

11-6:3 Defending the Deposition of a Party-Deponent

Barring the extreme, and as a general rule, the only appropriate objections to be made while defending a deposition of a party-deponent are objections on the grounds of privilege (in which case the witness should be instructed not to answer), and objections as to the form of the question (in which case opposing counsel is entitled to know the basis for the objection).[43] Objections to form include, "lack of predicate" (without establishing the basis on which the question is purportedly asked), "calls for a legal conclusion" (without establishing first the deponent's qualifications to testify as to matters of law), "the question is compound," (it requires two or more answers), "assumes facts not in evidence" (similar to "lack of predicate"), etc.[44] However, one might also object to the extent a corporate representative was designated to testify as to certain issues only, but the attorney conducting the deposition asks questions beyond the scope of the designation. In any case, there is nothing inappropriate about such questions; the answers just may prove of no use at trial.

As a rule, the attorney defending the deposition will not ask any questions unless the deponent's testimony needs to be rehabilitated (e.g., he misspoke, contradicted himself, said "days" when he meant "months," etc.). Otherwise, the attorney can speak with the client in private cloaked with the attorney-client privilege.

11-7 Judicial Resolution of Discovery Disputes

As indicated in the Introduction and in Section 11-8 below, trial judges have broad discretion with respect to discovery matters. That discretion extends beyond just determining what falls within the scope of permissible discovery in a given case. It also extends into what sanctions to impose for the failure to respond sufficiently to discovery requests and, more egregiously, for the failure to comply with court orders regarding discovery.

11-7:1 Motions to Compel

A party dissatisfied with the opposing party's response to discovery requests may move the court to enter an order compelling a response or, at least a *better* response, as the case may be.[45] A motion to compel seeks an order from the court requiring the party served with the discovery requests to produce documents and/or answers to interrogatories the court finds to be non-privileged and within the broad scope of permissible discovery. The court may also compel a person or legal entity (through its representative) to appear for deposition. Where no response is received at all, most Florida trial court judges will grant Motions to Compel, ex parte (i.e., without a hear-

---

[43] *See* Fla. R Civ. P. 1.330(d)(3)(B); *David v. City of Jacksonville*, 534 So. 2d 784 (Fla. 1st DCA 1988) (failure to object to questions and answers during discovery deposition does not amount to waiver of right to make objections thereto at trial except as to errors and irregularities in manner of taking deposition, in form of questions or answers in oath or affirmation or in conduct of parties and errors of any kind that might be obviated, removed or cured if properly presented at taking of deposition).

[44] Leading questions invite objections to form as well, but only if they are asked of a neutral witness, or of a witness testifying for the party who is represented by the attorney asking the leading question.

[45] Fla. R. Civ. P. 1.380(a)(2).

ing or notice to the other party). Where only a partial, incomplete, evasive, or otherwise unsatisfactory response is filed, a party seeking to compel discovery should file a timely motion and schedule it for hearing before the party on whom discovery was served files and sets hearings on any objections and/or motions for protective order. Again, he or she, who is the first to set the matter for hearing on his or her own motion, is likely to get the floor first before the judge, thereby putting opposing counsel on the defensive. Prior to scheduling any such matter for hearing, however, it is incumbent that the movant has conferred, or attempted to confer, in good faith with the opposing party in effort to avoid the need for judicial intervention, and the fact of having made the "good faith" effort must be certified in the motion. The careful practitioner will ensure to review local Administrative Orders and the Circuit Court's Local Rules regarding resolving discovery disputes. The requirements for submitting Motions to Compel, in particular, often vary drastically from county to county with respect to both the availability of ex parte relief as well as unique certifications required prior to the submission of such motions.

11-7:2 Motions for Protective Orders

A motion for "protective order" seeks a court order relieving the recipient of discovery requests (including a subpoena or notice of deposition), from having to produce some or all of the discovery requested. Once again, the trial court has broad discretion.[46] Such motions should be filed and brought up for hearing as soon as reasonably practicable, so as not to cause unnecessary delay in the discovery process or otherwise give opposing counsel the upper hand in driving the discovery process.

Rule 1.280(c) of the Florida Rules of Civil Procedure sets out the process and enumerates the court's options succinctly. It reads in relevant part, as follows:

> Upon motion by a party or by the person from whom discovery is sought, and for good cause shown, the court . . . may make any order to protect a party or persons from annoyance, embarrassment, oppression, or undue burden or expense that just requires, including one or more of the following: (1) that the discovery not be had; (2) that the discovery may be had only on specified terms and conditions including the designation of the time or place; (that the discovery may be had only by a method of discovery other than that selected by the party seeking discovery; (4) that certain matters not be inquired into, or that the scope of the discovery be limited to certain matters; (5) that discovery be conducted with no one present except persons designated by the court; (6) that a deposition after being sealed be opened only by order of the court; (7) that a trade secret or other confidential research . . . not be disclosed or be disclosed only in a designated way; and (8) that the parties simultaneously file specified documents or information enclosed in sealed envelopes to be opened by direction of the court.

---

[46] *Friedman v. Heart Institute of Port St. Lucie, Inc.*, 863 So. 2d 189, 193-94 (Fla. 2003) ("In deciding whether a protective order is appropriate in a particular case, the court must balance the competing interest that would be served by granting discovery or by denying it. Thus, the discovery rules provide a framework for judicial analysis of challenges to discovery on the basis that the discovery will result in undue invasion of privacy. This framework allows for broad discovery in order to advance the state's important interest in the fair and efficient resolution of disputes while at the same time providing protective measures to minimize the impact of discovery on competing privacy interests.").

As with objections to discovery requests, it is advisable for the party seeking a protective order to file and schedule its motion for hearing before the opposing party files and sets a hearing on a Motion to Compel. As a general rule, he whose motion is scheduled for hearing first will usually get the floor first, thereby putting her opponent on the defensive. Moreover, the motion must be filed before the scheduled date of deposition.

11-7:3 Failure to Produce Discovery; Sanctions

Most commonly, an order granting a motion to compel or for a protective order will tax reasonable attorney's fees and costs in favor of the movant associated with having to bring the motion, provided there are no extenuating circumstances, and the motion includes the certification that the movant made, or attempted to make, a good faith effort to resolve the dispute without judicial intervention. This is not so much of a "sanction" as it is a disincentive to engage in dilatory discovery tactics.

Sanctions, per se, typically ensue for failure to comply with discovery-related court orders, and are limited by rule to five: (A) the information sought can be deemed established; (B) the disobedient party can be precluded from supporting or opposing certain claims or defenses, or may be prohibited from introducing evidence to refute those claims or defenses; (C) pleadings, or parts thereof, may be struck, or defaults entered; (D) the disobedient party may be held in contempt; and/or (E) the Court may invoke (A), (B) and/or (C) where a party has failed to comply with an order compelling examination of a person when that person's condition is at issue. Dismissal with prejudice is the "ultimate sanction."[47] Prior to imposing the "ultimate sanction," trial courts are required to conduct "*Kozel*" hearings, and make specific findings of fact with respect thereto.[48]

It is commonly held that the failure to respond timely to outstanding discovery requests constitutes a waiver of all objections, except those related to privilege. This, however, is not among the "sanctions" authorized by the rules. Trial courts have found that it is not a departure from the clear requirements of law or even an abuse of

---

[47] See *Deutsche Bank National Trust Co. v. LGC*, 107 So. 3d 486, 488 (Fla. 2d DCA 2013) (dismissal with prejudice for failure to comply with court discovery orders is the ultimate sanction and should be reserved for those aggravating circumstances in which a lesser sanction would fail to achieve a just result. The purpose of discovery sanctions is to ensure compliance with the trial court's order rather than to punish; dismissal with prejudice is frowned upon by the appellate courts, except in the most egregious circumstances of intentional defiance and contumacious disregard of the court's authority) (internal quotation marks and citations to authority omitted).

[48] In *Kozel v. Ostendorf*, 629 So. 2d 817, 818 (Fla. 1994), the Florida Supreme Court adopted a six-factor analysis a trial judge must undertake before dismissing a case with prejudice. Those factors are: (1) whether the attorney's disobedience was willful, deliberate or contumacious, rather than an act of neglect or inexperience; (2) whether the attorney has been previously sanctioned; (3) whether the client was personally involved in the act of disobedience; (4) whether the delay prejudiced the opposing party through undue expense, loss of evidence, or in some other fashion; (5) whether the attorney offered reasonable justification for non-compliance; and (6) whether the delay created significant problems of judicial administration. "Upon consideration of these factors," wrote the Court, "if a sanction less severe than dismissal with prejudice appears to be a viable alternative, the trial court should employ such an alternative."

discretion (in some circumstances) to deem objections (even as to privilege) waived as a sanction for not filing a timely response.[49] With respect to claims of privilege, Florida courts generally deem it a violation of the essential requirements of law to order production of documents claimed to be privileged, at least without first conducting a hearing and/or an in camera review of the materials claimed to be privileged.[50]

11-8 Certiorari Review

A petition for certiorari review by the appellate court is the appropriate means by which to challenge a trial court order compelling production of privileged or trade secret information.[51] It is interlocutory in nature, meaning that it can be filed prior to disposal of the case, provided it is properly filed within 30 days of the date on which the order to be challenged is issued.[52] The petition must contain a fully briefed analysis of the basis of jurisdiction, the facts, argument with citations of authority, and a request for relief.[53] Absent a clear abuse of discretion or a departure from the essential requirements of law,[54] Florida appellate courts will defer to the discretion of the trial courts and will not disturb their rulings on matters relating to discovery.[55] Even so, certiorari relief from Florida appellate courts is itself discretionary, and an appellate court may decline to grant relief even where a trial court departs from the essential requirements of law.[56]

---

[49] *See American Funding, Ltd. v. Hill*, 402 So. 2d 1369 (Fla. 1st DCA 1981); expressly disagreed with by *Austin v. Barnett Bank of South Florida, N.A.*, 472 So. 2d 830 (Fla. 4th DCA 1985) (untimely objections as to privilege not waived).

[50] *See Harley Shipbuilding Corp. v. Fast Cats Ferry Service, LLC*, 820 So. 2d 445 (Fla. 2nd DCA 2002); *see also Mariner Health Care of Metrowest, Inc. v. Best*, 879 So. 2d 65 (Fla. 5th DCA 2004) (in camera inspection of documents claimed to be privileged was required to determine if they were discoverable).

[51] *Westco, Inc. v. Scott Lewis' Gardening & Trimming, Inc.*, 26 So. 3d 620 (Fla. 4th DCA 2009); *Martin-Johnson, Inc. v. Savage*, 509 So. 2d 1097, 1099 (Fla. 1987) (review by certiorari is appropriate when a discovery order departs from the essential requirements of law, causing material injury to a petitioner throughout the remainder of the proceedings below and effectively leaving no adequate remedy on appeal); *but see Heekin v. Del Col*, 60 So. 3d 437 (Fla. 1st DCA 2011) ("Mere legal error is insufficient to constitute a departure from the essential requirements of law but the error must amount to a violation of a clearly established principle of law and resulting in a miscarriage of justice.") (internal quotation marks and citations to authority omitted).

[52] Fla. R. Civ. P. 9.100(c). In addition to filing a Notice of Appeal with the trial court, the petition or other notice invoking the appellate court's jurisdiction must be filed with the appellate court within 30 days of the lower court's order; otherwise the appellate court lacks jurisdiction. *See Hoyt v. Commonwealth Land Title Ins. Co.*, 532 So. 2d 72 (Fla. 2d DCA 1988); Fla. R. App. P. 9.100(b) and (c).

[53] Fla. R. App. P. 9.100(g).

[54] "A departure from the essential requirements of the law is more than simple legal error; rather it is 'a violation of a clearly established principle of law resulting in a miscarriage of justice.'" *Trucap Grantor Trust 2010-1 v. Pelt*, 84 So. 3d 369, 371 (Fla. 2nd DCA 2012) (citation to quoted authority omitted); *see also Haines City Community Development v. Heggs*, 658 So. 2d 523, 528 (Fla. 1995) (clarifying the certiorari standard and elaborating on the meaning and boundaries of "departure from the essential requirements of law").

[55] *See Nucci v. Target Corp.*, 162 So. 3d 146 (Fla. 4th DCA 2015); *see also Racetrac Petroleum, Inc. v. Sewell*, 150 So. 2d 1247 (Fla. 3d DCA 2014).

[56] *Nucci v. Target Corp.*, 162 So. 3d 146 (Fla. 4th DCA 2015).

11-9 Unique Considerations for Foreclosures

11-9:1 Local Rules

With the adoption of Rule 2.545(b) of the Florida Rules of Judicial Administration, the Supreme Court directed Florida Courts to "take charge of all cases at an early stage in the litigation and control the progress of the case thereafter until the case is determined."[57] In response, many circuit courts have adopted administrative orders calculated to streamline the often lengthy litigation process. For example, in the Twentieth Judicial Circuit for Lee County, the Court will generally issue a Residential Foreclosure Case Management Plan and Order requiring that all discovery requests be filed no later than 45 days from the date of the answer to the complaint and objections be filed no later than 20 days from receipt of that request. Responses with no objections may be filed within 30 days.[58] Accordingly, the careful practitioner will always review local rules and administrative orders to ensure that they do not afoul of the same.

11-9:2 Discovery and Final Judgment

A foreclosing Plaintiff's goal is generally to bring the matter to summary judgment and foreclosure sale as quickly as possible. Time is money! Mortgage balances increase, carrying costs increase (often lenders are paying insurance and taxes), the collateral property depreciates, etc. The foreclosure defendant's goal, on the other hand, is to buy time—time to negotiate a loan modification, short sale, or time to syphon more rental income from the subject property. And there exists no greater currency with which such time is purchased than the discovery process. Generally, the granting of summary judgment while there is outstanding discovery is reversible error.[59] This is because summary judgment will be granted when there is no dispute as to any genuine issues of material fact, and the defending mortgagor is certainly entitled to diligently engage in discovery to support his or her defense. Conversely, summary judgment is appropriate irrespective of whether discovery is outstanding when such discovery would not create a disputed issue of material fact, i.e., "would not yield any new information that the trial court either did not already know, or needed to make its ruling."[60] Furthermore, when the discovery motions are clearly delay tactics, the trial court is within its sound discretion to enter summary judgment, irrespective of whether discovery is pending or not. "If there is good faith discovery still in progress, the trial court should not grant the moving party's motion for summary judgment. . . . However, if the non-moving party does not act diligently in

---

[57] Fla. Stat. J. Admin. Rule 2.545.
[58] Fla. Stat. 20 J. Cir. 1.18.
[59] *See Osorto v. Deutsche Bank Nat. Trust Co.*, 88 So. 3d 261, 262–63 (Fla. 4th DCA 2012) ("The trial court 'should not . . . entertain a motion for summary judgment until . . . discovery [is] concluded.'" *Collazo v. Hupert*, 693 So. 2d 631, 631 (Fla. 3d DCA 1997). An order granting summary judgment while there is an outstanding request for production of documents is premature and the appellate court should reverse and remand for discovery to be completed. *Henderson v. Reyes*, 702 So. 2d 616, 616 (Fla. 3d DCA 1997)).
[60] *Estate of Herrera v. Berlo Indus., Inc.*, 840 So. 2d 272 (Fla. 3d DCA 2003); *See also A & B Discount Lumber & Supply, Inc. v. Mitchell*, 799 So. 2d 301 (Fla. 5th DCA 2001); *see also Crespo v. Florida Entm't Direct Support Org., Inc.*, 674 So. 2d 154 (Fla. 3d DCA 1996) ("A trial court has the discretion to deny a continuance of a summary judgment hearing where the outstanding discovery items are immaterial to the dispositive issues in the case.").

completing discovery or uses discovery methods to thwart and/or delay the hearing on the motion for summary judgment, the trial court is within its discretion to grant summary judgment even though there is discovery still pending."[61] Common sense is key for practical application of these principles. A mortgagor's request for a copy of the servicing agreement between the servicer Plaintiff and the owner of the note and mortgage may be relevant in some circumstances, but not in others where there are no servicers (naturally). However, in employing common sense, a foreclosing Plaintiff will take into account the three following important considerations: (1) the Court has broad discretion to tailor discovery; (2) "relevance" is always a rather subjective standard; and (3) sometimes judges get it wrong. Accordingly, the best practice is to be as forthcoming as possible with discovery to the summary judgment defendant. Producing documents generally costs very little in terms of actual costs, since most documentation relevant in foreclosure actions is electronic in nature. Boilerplate and broad objections to documents requested by foreclosure defendants often lead to an unnecessary and prolonged discovery process which only serves to achieve the defendants' goal of buying time. A policy of being forthcoming (even when not absolutely required) is usually rewarded with quicker final judgments and an appreciative judge.

11-9:3 A Foreclosure Plaintiff's Witness

Institutional mortgage foreclosure actions are often plagued by the problems of their Plaintiffs' unique business history. Residential mortgages have often undergone several assignments of interest and (most importantly) transfers of servicing from one corporate entity to another. This presents unique problems in post-*Glarum* litigation. *Glarum v. LaSalle Bank Nat. Ass'n*, 83 So. 3d 780 (Fla. 4th DCA 2011) a pivotal case in Florida foreclosure law which stands for the proposition that a mortgage servicer must be able to authenticate and support each and every element of the Business Exception Rule with respect to each document submitted in support of the Plaintiff's case. This includes statements, payment history, and of course, any Notice of Default that may be a condition precedent to the institution of the action. Notably, a witness should be familiar with the specific electronic management system within which such documents are kept, should know where the document originated, and be able to testify with personal knowledge as to the drafting and transmission of the document. Appellate courts routinely reverse final judgments on appeal when a sufficient foundation is not laid regarding the witness' personal knowledge of the elements required to establish the application of the Business Records Exception to hearsay.[62]

This is often a very high burden to a witness employed by an entity that did not generate these documents. Servicers change, and sometimes third-party vendors are employed by the servicers to generate documentation, such as notices and monthly statements. A foreclosing Plaintiff's attorney must therefore carefully prepare her

---

[61] *Weisser Realty Group, Inc. v. Porto Vita Prop. Owners Ass'n, Inc.*, 44 Fla. L. Weekly D1904 (Fla. 3d DCA July 24, 2019) (quoting *Martins v. PNC Bank, N.A.*, 170 So. 3d 932, 936-37 (Fla. 5th DCA 2015)); *see also Schwartz v. Bank of Am., N.A.*, 267 So. 3d 414 (Fla. 4th DCA 2019) ("The court determined that the appellants had not diligently conducted discovery, and it denied a motion for continuance. No abuse of discretion has been shown.").

[62] *See Maslak v. Wells Fargo Bank, N.A.*, 190 So. 3d 656 (Fla. 4th DCA 2016); *Channell v. Deutsche Bank Nat'l Trust Co.*, 173 So. 3d 1017, 1020 (Fla. 2d DCA 2015) (citing *Sas v. Fed. Nat'l Mortg. Ass'n*, 112 So.3d 778, 780 (Fla. 2d DCA 2013)).

witness to ensure that she has such requisite knowledge and is able to testify in a manner that will lay such a foundation. Likewise, a foreclosure defendant generally lacks valid objections to the entry of foreclosure, and a careful audit of the Plaintiff's witness' personal knowledge is often the only difference between final judgment and dismissal.[63]

---

[63] For a more detailed discussion of the Business Records Rule and admission of documentation of a prior servicer, *see* Chapter 13.

CHAPTER 12

Motions for Summary Judgment in Foreclosure Cases

Ileen J. Cantor

12-1 Introduction

This chapter provides an overview of summary judgment practice generally. It also examines the procedural and substantive factors particularly related to obtaining and opposing summary judgments in foreclosure lawsuits.[1]

12-1:1 Overview of Summary Judgment in Florida

Fla. R. Civ. P. 1.510 governs summary judgment, which is a procedural vehicle that permits a party to obtain a resolution of a case when a question of law is involved and no genuine (i.e., triable) issues of material fact[2] exist. Summary judgment can avoid the costs of protracted litigation when a defense or claim is meritless. It is fair to say that the jury is still out as to whether Rule 1.510, and the courts' interpretation of its standards, has led to an effective procedural mechanism to end baseless lawsuits, to save judicial resources, or to dispose of issues when it is clear that no genuine issue of material fact exists.[3] Nonetheless, when Florida's summary judgment procedure was enacted in 1950, it was intended to be an effective practical method to quickly resolve civil lawsuits.[4]

---

[1] Unless otherwise indicated, "foreclosure lawsuits" refer to those matters in which a plaintiff asserts claims to foreclose a mortgage lien encumbering residential properties due to a borrower's default under one or more of the provisions in the mortgage and the promissory note evidencing the underlying debt.

[2] A fact is material when it supports or negates an element in a legally sufficient claim or defense. Otherwise, it is irrelevant. A material fact is one which might affect the outcome of the case under governing law. *See Anderson v. Liberty Lobby, Inc.*, 477 U.S. 242, 248 (1986) (material facts are those which might affect the outcome of the case). To preclude summary judgment, the dispute about a material fact must also be "genuine," such that a reasonable jury could find in favor of the non-moving party. *Anderson v. Liberty Lobby, Inc.*, 477 U.S. 242, 248 (1986).

[3] *See* Leonard D. Pertnoy, *Summary Judgment in Florida: The Road Less Traveled*, 20 St. Thomas L. Rev. 69, 69 (2007) (the author's experience is that "winning a summary judgment in Florida is extremely difficult to achieve, and the tool of summary judgment is not being used in a manner that is consistent with the intent behind the enactment of" Rule 1.510).

[4] *See Jones v. Stoutenburgh*, 91 So. 2d 299, 302 (Fla. 1956) (The rule "is designed to provide trial judges with authority to terminate litigation without the necessity of a full trial if it

12-1:2 Legal Standard

Courts shall grant motions for summary judgment if the pleadings, depositions, answers to interrogatories, admissions, affidavits, and other materials as would be admissible in evidence[5] on file show that there is no genuine issue as to any material fact and that the moving party is entitled to a judgment as a matter of law.[6] In ruling on a motion for summary judgment, the trial court must construe all the evidence, and draw every possible inference therefrom, in a light most favorable to the nonmoving party.[7]

12-1:3 Burden of Proof[8]

The burden is initially on movants for summary judgment to conclusively demonstrate, through admissible evidence,[9] the nonexistence of any question of material

---

is apparent that there is no genuine issue of a material fact to be settled."); *Anderson v. Maddox*, 65 So. 2d 299, 300 (Fla. 1953) ("The plain purpose of this new rule is to obviate the expense and delay of summoning a jury in a case to try facts that are not in conflict."); *Keys Country Resort v. 1733 Overseas High., LLC*, 272 So. 3d 500, 503 (Fla. 3d DCA 2019) ("Summary judgment 'is designed to test the sufficiency of the evidence to determine if there is sufficient evidence at issue to justify a trial or formal hearing on the issues raised in the pleadings'" (citation omitted)).

[5] Rule 1.510(c) refers to such evidence as "summary judgment evidence."
[6] Fla. R. Civ. P. 1.510(c).
[7] *Moore v. Morris*, 475 So. 2d 666 (Fla. 1985); *Willis v. Gami Golden Glades, LLC*, 967 So. 2d 846, 848 (Fla. 2007); *Bowman v. Barker*, 172 So. 3d 1013, 1014 (Fla. 1st DCA 2015); *Cohen v. Arvin*, 878 So. 2d 403, 405 (Fla. 4th DCA 2004); *RV-7 Prop. v. Stefani De La O, Inc.*, 187 So. 3d 915, 917 (Fla. 3d DCA 2016).
[8] It is somewhat of a misnomer to characterize the burden at the summary judgment stage as a burden of "proof." There is no need to prove a fact at the summary judgment stage. Summary judgment evidence is not produced for the purpose of being weighed or to convince or persuade a fact-finder to resolve a disputed issue of fact. This is why a trial court errs if it takes live oral testimony at a summary judgment hearing or resolves a controverted issue of fact. *Campbell-Settle Pressure Grouting v. David M. Abel Constr. Co.*, 395 So. 2d 247, 248 (Fla. 3d DCA 1981). Summary judgment evidence is produced solely to demonstrate that, as a matter of law, there is or is not a dispute over a key fact that requires a trial. *See Florida Atl. Univ. Bd. of Trs. v. Lindsey*, 50 So. 3d 1205, 1206 (Fla. 4th DCA 2010) ("When a defendant moves for summary judgment, *the court is not called upon to determine whether the plaintiff can actually prove his cause of action*. Rather, the court's function is solely to determine whether the record conclusively shows that *the moving party proved a negative*, that is, 'the nonexistence of a genuine issue of a material fact." (citation omitted; emphasis added)). The only "proof," then, is proof that a dispute does or does not exist—not whether the movant can win at trial. It is legal error for a trial judge to weigh and discredit admissible evidence offered in opposition to a motion for summary judgment. *Hlad v. State*, 565 So. 2d 762, 776 (Fla. 5th DCA 1990). *See Charles E. Burkett & Associates, Inc. v. Vick*, 546 So. 2d 1190, 1191 (Fla. 5th DCA 1989) (holding that the trial court should not have attempted to resolve issue raised by conflicting affidavits as to amount due under the contractual agreement at issue through summary judgment).
[9] Although many cases interpreting Rule 1.510 refer to a movant's requirement to produce "*competent* evidence" to meet its initial burden, (*see Ciolli v. City of Palm Bay*, 59 So. 3d 295, 295 (Fla. 5th DCA 2011); *Jenkins v. W.L. Roberts, Inc.*, 851 So. 2d 781, 783 (Fla. 1st DCA 2003); *Castro v. Brazeau*, 873 So. 2d 516, 517 (Fla. 4th DCA 2004)), Rule 1.510(c) only and expressly requires "summary judgment evidence," defined as "admissible evidence." The word "competent" is nowhere to be found in Rule 1.510.

fact.[10] Courts have described the burden on the party moving for summary judgment as "heavy."[11] The movant has the burden to establish a negative, that the opposing party could never prevail at trial.[12] The opposing parties' evidentiary burden is not triggered until movants meet their initial burden.[13] Only where movants tender competent summary judgment evidence in support of their motion does the burden shift to the opposing party to come forward with opposing evidence.[14] Although nonmoving parties are not required to file anything in opposition, including an affidavit to counter a movant's affidavit, once their evidentiary burden is triggered, opposing parties must reveal a genuine issue of material fact through sufficient admissible counterevidence.[15]

Understanding the evidentiary burdens is key to winning or defeating a summary judgment motion. For if moving parties cannot meet their initial burden of establishing the absence of material disputed facts, they cannot prevail and there is nothing more opposing parties must do to defeat the motions (such as filing and serving written opposition and summary judgment evidence to show the existence of genuine issues of material fact).[16]

---

[10] *See Landers v. Milton*, 370 So. 2d 368, 370 (Fla. 1979); *Holl v. Talcott*, 191 So. 2d 40, 43-44 (Fla. 1966). *Holl v. Talcott*, 191 So. 2d 40, 43 (Fla. 1966). In essence, a movant must prove a negative—the nonexistence of a genuine issue of material fact. *See Grimsley v. Moody, Jones, Ingino & Morehead, P.A.*, 70 So. 3d 761, 762 (Fla. 4th DCA 2011) ("When a defendant moves for summary judgment, the court is not called upon to determine whether the plaintiff can actually prove his cause of action' . . . . Rather, the court's role is to determine whether the record conclusively shows that the moving party proved a negative, that is, 'the nonexistence of a genuine issue of a material fact.") (quoting *Winston Park, Ltd. v. City of Coconut Creek*, 872 So. 2d 415, 418 (Fla. 4th DCA 2004) (citations omitted)); *Holl v. Talcott*, 191 So. 2d 40, 43 (Fla. 1966) (A summary judgment movant is required to prove "a negative . . . the nonexistence of a genuine issue of material fact," before "it becomes necessary to determine the legal sufficiency of the affidavits or other evidence submitted by the party moved against.").

[11] *Hervey v. Alfonso*, 650 So. 2d 644, 646 (Fla. 2d DCA 1995); *Cox v. CSX Intermodal, Inc.*, 732 So. 2d 1092, 1095 (Fla. 1st DCA 1999).

[12] *Land Dev. Servs., Inc. v. Gulf View Townhomes, LLC*, 75 So. 3d 865, 868 (Fla. 2d DCA 2011).

[13] *See Landers v. Milton*, 370 So. 2d 368, 370 (Fla. 1979); *Land Dev. Servs., Inc. v. Gulf View Townhomes, LLC*, 75 So. 3d 865, 869 (Fla. 2d DCA 2011) (The nonmoving party "had no burden to come forward with the evidence necessary to prove [his] case."); *Raissi v. Valente*, 247 So. 3d 629 (Fla. 2d DCA 2018) (the nonmovant "was not required to defeat summary judgment when [the moving party] failed to meet her initial burden of showing the absence of any material fact").

[14] *See, e.g., Landers v. Milton*, 370 So. 2d 368, 370 (Fla. 1979); *Holl v. Talcott*, 191 So. 2d 40, 43-44 (Fla. 1966); *Wells Fargo Bank, N.A. v. Bilecki*, 192 So. 3d 559, 561 (Fla. 4th DCA 2016) (the trial court improperly placed the burden of proof on the lender bank to produce evidence it complied with conditions precedent in opposition to the homeowners' motion for summary judgment when it properly rested with the homeowners as movants, and because the homeowners did not produce timely, competent evidence in support of their motion, the burden should have never shifted to the bank).

[15] *See The Florida Bar v. Mogil*, 763 So. 2d 303, 307 (Fla. 2000).

[16] *Hamilton v. Bank of Palm Beach & Trust Co.*, 348 So. 2d 1190, 1191 (Fla. 4th DCA 1977) ("The cases are legion and need no citation that the burden of proof on [a] motion for summary judgment is upon the movant to affirmatively demonstrate that none of the issues of fact ostensibly raised by the pleadings is in actuality in dispute. Until the movant adduces some proof that no issue raised by the non-movant's pleading is genuine the non-movant

The movant's proof of the nonexistence of a genuine issue of fact must be conclusive, such that all reasonable inferences which may be drawn in favor of the opposing party are overcome.[17] Many courts continue to hold that if there is even the "slightest doubt" regarding the existence or nonexistence of a material fact, summary judgment cannot be granted.[18] However, the Florida Supreme Court explained many years ago that its use of the phrase "slightest doubt"[19] created some uncertainty, leading it to explain in a subsequent decision that what it really meant to say is that any doubt as to the existence or nonexistence of a genuine issue of material fact should be resolved against the movant.[20]

After the moving party has met its burden of proof, the opposing party must tender "competent evidence" or "counterevidence" showing a genuine issue of fact.[21] It is insufficient for the opponent to simply argue that an issue of fact exists.[22] Affidavits opposing summary judgment must identify admissible evidence revealing a genuine issue of material fact.[23] Nevertheless, the evidence offered in opposition to summary judgment need not be identical, or address the entire preliminaries, predicates, and details that would be required of a witness testifying live at trial.[24] To require all the details and formalities of live trial, witness testimony at the summary judgment stage would defeat the purpose of the summary judgment process by turning it into a trial instead of a search for issues.[25] Further, courts generally hold the summary judgment

---

need not file any proof to oppose the motion."); *Koresko v. Coe*, 683 So. 2d 602, 603 (Fla. 2d DCA 1996) (if the movant has not met its burden, the opponent has no obligation to refute).

[17] *Holl v. Talcott*, 191 So. 2d 40, 43 (Fla. 1966); *Moore v. Morris*, 475 So. 2d 666, 668 (Fla. 1985). But note that a moving party is not required to exclude every possible inference from other evidence that may have been available if it was not identified and properly filed by the parties before the summary judgment hearing. *See De Mesme v. Stephenson*, 498 So. 2d 673, 675 (Fla. 1st DCA 1986) ("[Appellee] was not required, as appellant seems to contend, to exclude every inference possible from other evidence that may have been available.").

[18] *See, e.g., Aloff v. Neff-Harmon, Inc.*, 463 So. 2d 291, 294 (Fla. 1st DCA 1984) ("A summary judgment is appropriate only when 'the facts are so crystalized that nothing remains but questions of law' and there is not the 'slightest doubt' as to any issue of material fact.") (quoting *Harris v. Lewis State Bank*, 436 So. 2d 338, 340 (Fla. 1st DCA 1983)).

[19] *Williams v. City of Lake City*, 62 So. 2d 732, 733 (Fla. 1953).

[20] *Manning v. Clark*, 71 So. 2d 508, 510 (Fla. 1954).

[21] *The Florida Bar v. Mogil*, 763 So. 2d 303, 307 (Fla. 2000) (quoting *Landers v. Milton*, 370 So. 2d 368, 370 (Fla. 1979)); *Valderrama v. Portfolio Recovery Assocs., LLC*, 972 So. 2d 239, 239 (Fla. 3d DCA 2007). *See also Dempsey v. Law Firm of Cauthen & Odham, P.A.*, 781 So. 2d 1141, 1143 (Fla 5th DCA 2001).

[22] *Landers v. Milton*, 370 So. 2d 368, 370 (Fla. 1979) (citing *Harvey Bldg., Inc. v. Haley*, 175 So. 2d 780 (Fla. 1965); *Farrey v. Bettendorf*, 96 So. 2d 889 (Fla. 1957)).

[23] *Panzera v. O'Neal*, 198 So. 3d 663, 665 (Fla. 2d DCA 2015) (citing *Byrd v. Leach*, 226 So. 2d 866, 868 (Fla. 4th DCA 1969)). The purpose of this requirement is "to ensure that there is an admissible evidentiary basis for the case rather than mere supposition or belief." *Alvarez v. Fla. Ins. Guar. Ass'n*, 661 So. 2d 1230, 1232 (Fla. 3d DCA 1995) (quoting *Pawlik v. Barnett Bank*, 528 So. 2d 965, 966 (Fla. 1st DCA 1988)).

[24] *Onewest Bank, FSB v. Jasinski*, 173 So. 3d 1009, 1013-14 (Fla. 2d DCA 2015) (citing *Holl v. Talcott*, 191 So. 2d 40, 45 (Fla. 1966)).

[25] *Onewest Bank, FSB v. Jasinski*, 173 So. 3d 1009, 1014 (Fla 2d DCA 2015) (citing *Holl v. Talcott*, 191 So. 2d 40, 45 (Fla. 1966)). In this regard, questions regarding the relative credibility or weight of the evidence cannot be resolved on summary judgment, but must be left

evidence offered by movants is to be more carefully and closely scrutinized than that offered by parties opposing summary judgment.[26]

12-1:3.1 Burden of Proof as to Motions for Summary Judgment Made Before an Answer Is Filed

A plaintiff who moves for summary judgment before a defendant has filed an answer[27] has a difficult burden.[28] The plaintiff, in addition to the already "heavy" burden to show the absence of a genuine issue of material fact, must also demonstrate conclusively and to a certainty from the record that no answer which the defendant might properly serve could present a genuine issue of material fact.[29] The Third District has characterized this burden as requiring a plaintiff to negate every possible defense to the action.[30]

12-1:3.2 Burden of Proof on a Plaintiff When a Defendant Raises Affirmative Defenses

Plaintiffs must not only establish that there exist no genuine issues of material fact regarding their own claims, but, when a defendant raises affirmative defenses, they must also either factually refute each affirmative defense or establish it is legally insuf-

---

for the trier of fact. *Hernandez v. United Auto. Ins. Co.*, 730 So. 2d 344, 345 (Fla. 3d DCA 1999) ("In ruling on a motion for summary judgment, it is well-established that the court may neither adjudge the credibility of the witnesses nor weigh the evidence.").

[26] *Onewest Bank, FSB v. Jasinski*, 173 So. 3d 1009, 1014 (Fla. 2d DCA 2015) (citing *Gonzalez v. Chase Home Fin. LLC*, 37 So. 3d 955, 958 (Fla. 3d DCA 2010). and *Humphrys v. Jarrell*, 104 So. 2d 404, 410 (Fla. 2d DCA 1958)).

[27] As discussed below, Rule 1.510(a) permits a plaintiff to move for summary judgment 20 days after suit has been filed, even if the defendant has not filed an answer. *Brakefield v. CIT Group/Consumer Fin., Inc.*, 787 So. 2d 115 (Fla. 2d DCA 2001).

[28] *Goncharuk v. HSBC Mortg. Servs.*, 62 So. 3d 680, 681 (Fla. 2d DCA 2011).

[29] *West Fla. Cmty. Builders v. Mitchell*, 528 So. 2d 979, 980 (Fla. 1988); *Hodkin v. Ledbetter*, 487 So. 2d 1214, 1217 (Fla. 4th DCA 1986); *Miles v. Robinson*, 803 So. 2d 864, 865 (Fla. 4th DCA 2002); *Beach Higher Power Corp. v. Granados*, 717 So. 2d 563, 565 (Fla. 3d DCA 1998); *Greene v. Lifestyle Builders*, 985 So. 2d 588 (Fla. 5th DCA 2008). *See also Getman v. Tracey Constr., Inc.*, 62 So. 3d 1289 (Fla. 2d DCA 2011).

[30] *Beach Higher Power Corp. v. Granados*, 717 So. 2d 563, 565 (Fla. 3d DCA 1998). For example, in *Raven v. Roosevelt Reo US LLC*, 44 Fla. L. Weekly D2096, 2019 WL 3807022, 2019 Fla. App. LEXIS 12464, *1 (Fla. 3d DCA Aug. 14, 2019), the foreclosure plaintiff filed a motion for summary judgment before the appellant had filed an answer. Nothing in the plaintiff's complaint, motion, or affidavit indicated it gave the appellant the requisite pre-suit notice. Further, the record did not clearly show the plaintiff's standing. *Id.* at *4. The Third District reversed the trial court's grant of final summary judgment. *Id.*

ficient.[31] Although it may seem obvious, plaintiffs are only required to refute those affirmative defenses raised in responsive "pleadings."[32]

An *affirmative defense* is a defense which admits the cause of action, but avoids liability, in whole or in part, by alleging an excuse, justification, or other matter negating or limiting liability.[33] The defendant has the burden of proving an affirmative defense.[34] Legally sufficient affirmative defenses must contain factual allegations that clearly set out the essential elements of the defense and cannot contain legal conclusions or formulaic recitations of a statute couched as factual allegations.[35] Vague, ambiguous, and conclusory statements unsupported by ultimate factual allegations are legally insuf-

---

[31] *Deutsche Bank Nat'l Tr. Co. v. Hagstrom*, 203 So. 3d 918, 923 (Fla. 2d DCA 2016) (Failure to comply with Fla. Stat. § 559.715 is not a legally sufficient affirmative defense to foreclosure that needs to be refuted upon bank's motion for summary judgment); *Haven Fed. Sav. & Loan Ass'n v. Kirian*, 579 So. 2d 730, 733 (Fla. 1991); *West Edge II v. Kunderas*, 910 So. 2d 953, 955 (Fla. 2d DCA 2005); *Congress Park Office Condos v. First-Citizens Bank & Trust Co.*, 105 So. 3d 602, 606 (Fla. 4th DCA 2013); *Jelic v. Citimortgage, Inc.*, 150 So. 3d 1223, 1225 (Fla. 4th DCA 2014) (quoting *Knight Energy Servs., Inc. v. Amoco Oil Co.*, 660 So. 2d 786, 788 (Fla. 4th DCA 1995)); *Sample v. Wells Fargo Bank, N.A.*, 150 So. 3d 1191, 1192 (Fla. 4th DCA 2014) (quoting *Alejandre v. Deutsche Bank Trust Co. Ams.*, 44 So. 3d 1288, 1289 (Fla. 4th DCA 2010)); *Olivera v. Bank of Am., N.A.*, 141 So. 3d 770, 773 (Fla. 2d DCA 2014); *Taylor v. Bayview Loan Servicing, LLC*, 74 So. 3d 1115, 1117 (Fla. 2d DCA 2011); *Goncharuk v. HSBC Mortg. Servs., Inc.*, 62 So. 3d 680, 682 (Fla. 2d DCA 2011) (reversing summary judgment for plaintiff's failure to address in its motion for summary judgment and affidavits the affirmative defense of lack of notice); *Lazuran v. Citimortgage, Inc.*, 35 So. 3d 189, 189-90 (Fla. 4th DCA 2010) (reversing summary judgment where the plaintiff failed to refute the affirmative defense of lack of notice); *Konsulian v. Busey Bank, N.A.*, 61 So. 3d 1283, 1285 (Fla. 2d DCA 2011).

[32] Fla. R. Civ. P. 1.110(d) provides that "a party shall set forth affirmatively . . . any . . . matter constituting an avoidance or affirmative defense." Application of this rule means "that affirmative defenses must be *pleaded* or they are considered waived." *Kersey v. City of Riviera Beach*, 337 So. 2d 995, 997 (Fla. 4th DCA 1976) (citations omitted; emphasis added); *see also* Fla. R. Civ. P. 1.140(b) ("Every defense in law or fact to a claim for relief in a pleading shall be asserted in the responsive pleading[.]"). Hence, defendants may not raise unpled affirmative defenses in opposition to, or in their own, summary judgment motion. *See* Section 12-1:4.

[33] *See Haven Fed. Sav. & Loan Ass'n v. Kirian*, 579 So. 2d 730, 733 (Fla. 1991); *St. Paul Mercury Ins. Co. v. Coucher*, 837 So. 2d 483 (Fla. 5th DCA 2002); *Wiggins v. Portmay Corp.*, 430 So. 2d 541, 542 (Fla. 1st DCA 1983) ("Affirmative defenses do not simply deny the facts of the opposing party's claim. They raise some new matter which defeats an otherwise apparently valid claim.").

[34] *See Hough v. Menses*, 95 So. 2d 410, 412 (Fla. 1957).

[35] *See Thompson v. Bank of N.Y.*, 862 So. 2d 768, 770 (Fla. 4th DCA 2003); *Zito v. Washington Federal Sav. & Loan Assoc.*, 318 So. 2d 175, 176 (Fla. 3rd DCA 1975) (affirmative defenses must be pled with certainty so that the adversary can compile the proper evidence). "Certainty is required when pleading defenses, and pleading conclusions of law unsupported by allegations of ultimate fact is legally insufficient. *Bliss v. Carmona*, 418 So. 2d 1017, 1019 (Fla. 3d DCA 1982); 40 Fla. Jur. 2d Pleadings §§ 28, 33 (1982)." *Cady v. Chevy Chase Sav. & Loan, Inc.*, 528 So. 2d 136, 138 (Fla. 4th DCA 1988).

ficient.[36] Certain defenses such as fraud or mistake require heightened pleading with specific (not general) allegations of each fraud element.[37]

Common affirmative defenses raised by borrower-defendants in foreclosure litigation include absence of *standing*,[38] lack of the requisite pre-suit/pre-acceleration notice delineated in section or paragraph 22 of most residential mortgage loans (routinely referred to as a "conditions precedent" defense[39]), and the statute of limitations.

---

[36] *See Southern Waste Sys., LLC v. J & A Transfer, Inc.*, 879 So. 2d 86, 87 (Fla. 4th DCA 2004); *Chris Craft Ind. v. Van Valkenberg*, 267 So. 2d 642, 645 (Fla. 1972); *Cady v. Chevy Chase Sav. & Loan, Inc.*, 528 So. 2d 136, 138 (Fla. 4th DCA 1988); *Bliss v. Carmona*, 418 So. 2d 1017, 1019 (Fla. 3d DCA 1982); *Congress Park Office Condos II, LLC v. First-Citizens Bank & Trust Co.*, 105 So. 3d 602 (Fla. 4th DCA 2013) (finding that an unclean hands affirmative defense in a mortgage foreclosure case was not pled with sufficient facts).

[37] *See* Fla. R. Civ. Pro. 1.120(b); *Cocoves v. Campbell*, 819 So. 2d 910, 913 (Fla. 4th DCA 2002) ("An affirmative defense of fraud that is not pleaded with particularity is deemed waived.").

[38] Although defendants routinely assert a lack of plaintiff's *standing* (to foreclose on the date the complaint is filed) as an affirmative defense in foreclosure lawsuits (*see Phadael v. Deutsche Bank Tr. Co. Ams.*, 83 So. 3d 893, 895 (Fla. 4th DCA 2012) ("[L]ack of standing is an affirmative defense that must be raised by the defendant and the failure to raise it generally results in waiver." (alteration in original)), the majority of Florida courts seemingly have, without expressly saying so, "transformed what should be a defendant's affirmative defense . . . into a jurisdictional prerequisite that must be established by the plaintiff to avoid a dismissal of the action." *Focht v. Wells Fargo Bank, N.A.*, 124 So. 3d 308, 312 (Fla. 2d DCA 2013) (Altenbernd, J., concurring); *Corrigan v. Bank of Am., N.A.*, 189 So. 3d 187, 195 (Fla. 2d DCA 2016) (Lucas, J., concurring). "As defenses go, standing has become something of a legal oddity. We treat it as an affirmative defense in that the defendant must put it in play by raising it in an appropriate pleading—ordinarily, the answer. Yet once injected into a case by a defendant's pleading, we say that it must be proved at trial by the plaintiff." *Winchel v. PennyMac Corp.*, 222 So. 3d 639 (Fla. 2d DCA 2017) (citations omitted). As a result, as a practice tip, foreclosure plaintiffs should establish there is no genuine issue of material fact as to "standing" even if it is not raised as an affirmative defense. Currently, "[a] plaintiff alleging standing as a holder must prove it is a holder of the note and mortgage both as of the time of trial and also that [it] had standing as of the time the foreclosure complaint was filed." *Peoples v. Sami II Trust 2006-AR6*, 178 So. 3d 67, 69 (Fla. 4th DCA 2015) (alteration in original) (quoting *Kiefert v. Nationstar Mortg., LLC*, 153 So. 3d 351, 352-54 (Fla. 1st DCA 2014)).

[39] The term *"condition precedent"* is used in the foreclosure context to refer to a contractual pre-suit requirement, here referring to the required notice and opportunity to cure normally set forth in paragraph 22 of most mortgages. This is not to be confused with the doctrines of condition precedent and condition subsequent referring to contract formation or performance *See Mitchell v. DiMare*, 936 So. 2d 1178, 1180 (Fla. 5th DCA 2006) ("A condition precedent is an act or event, other than a lapse of time, that must occur before a binding contract will arise. . . . A condition may be either a condition precedent to the formation of a contract or a condition precedent to performance under an existing contract."); *Gunderson v. Sch. Dist. of Hillsborough Cnty.*, 937 So. 2d 777, 779 (Fla. 1st DCA 2006) ("Provisions of a contract will only be considered conditions precedent or subsequent where the express wording of the disputed provision conditions formation of a contract and or performance of the contract on the completion of the conditions.").

12-1:4 Contents of the Motion for Summary Judgment

Rule 1.510(c) requires the motion to precisely identify the issues and the grounds upon which it is based and the substantial matters of law to be argued.[40] The requirement that a movant state with particularity the grounds upon which the movant will rely in seeking summary judgment was added in 1976 to eliminate surprise.[41] The rule relates to due process concerns[42] and is designed to prevent "ambush" by allowing the nonmoving party a full and fair opportunity to be prepared for the issues that will be argued at the summary judgment hearing.[43] Hence, it is a reversible error for a trial court to enter summary judgment based on arguments made at the hearing but not in the motion.[44]

A motion for summary judgment (or opposition thereto) must be restricted to the legal issues solely raised by the pleadings and its function is only to determine if the respective parties can produce adequate summary judgment evidence in support of (or in opposition to) the operative issues raised by the pleadings.[45] As a result, both moving

---

[40] *HSBC Mortg. Corp. v. Mullan*, 159 So. 3d 250, 252 (Fla. 2d DCA 2015) ("Trial courts are limited to the grounds raised in a motion for summary judgment.").

[41] *See* Rule 1.510(c) committee notes; *H.B. Adams Distribs., Inc. v. Admiral Air of Sarasota Cty., Inc.*, 805 So. 2d 852, 854 (Fla. 2d DCA 2001) (holding that the summary judgment motion violated Rule 1.510(c) because the motion failed to provide notice that count I was to be considered on summary judgment when the motion and its affidavit "did not identify count I as one of the matters to be argued" or address any facts relevant to count I); *Gee v. U.S. Bank Nat'l Ass'n*, 72 So. 3d 211, 215 (Fla. 5th DCA 2011) ("It is reversible error to enter summary judgment on a ground not raised with particularity in the motion." (quoting *Williams v. Bank of Am. Corp.*, 927 So. 2d 1091, 1093 (Fla. 4th DCA 2006)).

[42] The right to reasonable notice implicates constitutional due process concerns. "Procedural due process requires both fair notice and a real opportunity to be heard." *Borden v. Guardianship of Borden-Moore*, 818 So. 2d 604, 607 (Fla. 5th DCA 2002) (quoting *Keys Citizens for Responsible Gov't v. Fla. Keys Aqueduct Auth.*, 795 So. 2d 940, 948 (Fla. 2001)). *See Casa Inv. Co. v. Nestor*, 8 So. 3d 1219, 1221-22 (Fla. 3d DCA 2009) (Because the trial court granted an oral motion for summary judgment that was not properly noticed, the Third District ruled that the trial court deprived the nonmoving party of due process).

[43] *City of Cooper City v. Sunshine Wireless Co.*, 654 So. 2d 283 (Fla. 4th DCA 1995).

[44] *See HSBC Mortg. Corp. v. Mullan*, 159 So. 3d 250, 252-53 (Fla. 2d DCA 2015) ("[W]e conclude that the trial court committed reversible error in granting summary judgment on an issue not raised by East Bay."); *Gulf Insurance Co. v. Stofman*, 664 So. 2d 1083 (Fla. 4th DCA 1995); *Worley v. Sheffield*, 538 So. 2d 91, 92 (Fla. 1st DCA 1989); *Gee v. U.S. Bank Nat'l Ass'n*, 72 So. 3d 211, 215 (Fla. 5th DCA 2011) ("It is reversible error to enter summary judgment on a ground not raised with particularity in the motion [for summary judgment]." (quoting *Williams v. Bank of Am. Corp.*, 927 So. 2d 1091, 1093 (Fla. 4th DCA 2006))); *Deluxe Motel, Inc. v. Patel*, 727 So. 2d 299, 301 (Fla. 5th DCA 1999) ("[T]he trial court erred to the extent that, in entering judgment for the sellers, it relied on the arguments made at the hearing but not in the motion.").

[45] *Hart Properties, Inc. v. Slack*, 159 So. 2d 236, 239 (Fla. 1963). *Decosmo v. Fisher*, 683 So. 2d 659, 660 (Fla. 5th DCA 1996) ("Our courts have consistently ruled that a party who opposes summary judgment will not be permitted to alter the position of his or her previous pleadings, admissions, affidavits, depositions or testimony in order to defeat a summary judgment."). The Florida Supreme Court noted long ago that "[a] motion for summary judgment necessarily proceeds upon the theory that the legal issues are fully settled by the pleadings, and there exists no genuine dispute as to a material fact." *White v. Fletcher*, 90 So.

MOTIONS FOR SUMMARY JUDGMENT IN FORECLOSURE CASES 199

and nonmoving parties cannot raise unpled legal issues or unpled defenses.[46] Nevertheless, at least one court has held that the failure of an opposing party to object to a movant's attempt to raise unpled legal issues in a motion for summary judgment acts as a waiver akin to the failure of parties at trial to object to opposing parties' attempts to amend their pleadings by express or implied consent to conform to the evidence.[47]

12-1:4.1 Identification of Summary Judgment Evidence in the Motion

Under Rule 1.510(c), the motion must also specifically identify any affidavits, answers to interrogatories, admissions, depositions, and other materials as would be admissible in evidence (summary judgment evidence) on which the movant relies. As a result, the plain terms of Rule 1.510(c) do not permit a moving party to rely upon any summary judgment evidence that is not particularly pinpointed in the body of the motion. However, both plaintiffs and defendants in foreclosure litigation often fail to precisely point out their summary judgment evidence in the body of their respective motions for summary judgment. Nonetheless, a valid objection or opposing argument can be made to a trial court that it may not consider any summary judgment evidence that was not specifically identified in the motion because of the mandate in Rule 1.510(c). Failure to do so waives the procedural defect. In fact, several courts have held that parties may waive *any procedural* anomaly in a motion for summary judgment.[48] Thus, parties are well-advised to note their objections for the record.

12-1:5 Summary Judgment Evidence

Rule 1.510(c) defines "summary judgment evidence" as affidavits, answers to interrogatories, admissions,[49] depositions, and other items as would be admissible in

---

2d 129, 131-32 (Fla. 1956). *See Deluxe Motel, Inc. v. Patel*, 727 So. 2d 299, 301 (Fla. 5th DCA 1999).

[46] *See B.B.S. v. R.C.B.*, 252 So. 2d 837, 839 (Fla. 2d DCA 1971) ("An affirmative defense must be pleaded and not raised by a motion for summary judgment supported by an affidavit." (citations omitted)); *Accurate Metal Finishing Corp. v. Carmel*, 254 So. 2d 556, 557 (Fla. 3d DCA 1971) ("Affirmative defenses must be pleaded and it is not sufficient to sustain a defense to a summary judgment motion to allege such in affidavits." (citations omitted)); *Couchman v. Goodbody & Co.*, 231 So. 2d 842 (Fla. 4th DCA 1970); *Turf Express, Inc. v. Palmer*, 209 So. 2d 461 (Fla. 3d DCA 1968); *Danford v. Rockledge*, 387 So. 2d 968, 969 (Fla. 5th DCA 1980). The *Danford* court also ruled that the requirement that a motion for summary judgment be confined to the issues in the pleadings is a "procedural matter" that can be waived. Thus, parties would be well-advised to make a timely and written objection to opposing parties' attempts to raise new claims or defenses by way of a motion for summary judgment lest the issue be waived. *Danford v. Rockledge*, 387 So. 2d 968, 970 (Fla. 5th DCA 1980).

[47] *See Danford v. Rockledge*, 387 So. 2d 968, 970 (Fla. 5th DCA 1980); Fla. R. Civ. P. 1.190(b) ("[w]hen issues not raised by the pleadings are tried by express or implied consent of the parties, they shall be treated in all respects as if they had been raised in the pleadings.").

[48] *Fla. Holding 4800, LLC v. Lauderhill Lending, LLC*, 275 So. 3d 183 (Fla. 4th DCA 2019) ("A plaintiff may 'waive[] any procedural irregularity in [a] motion for summary judgment.'" (citations omitted)).

[49] *Technical admissions* are those theoretically made when a party fails to respond to requests for admission. Although a court normally has discretion to rely on a technically deemed

evidence. Deposition transcripts must be filed and served in compliance with Florida Rule of Civil Procedure 1.310(f)(3).

Rule 1.510(e) sets out the requisite form for affidavits used to support or oppose summary judgment. Affidavits must be based on personal knowledge, contain admissible testimony, show that the affiant is competent to testify, and attach sworn or certified copies of all or part of any documents referenced in the affidavit.[50] Affidavits made in bad faith subject the submitting party to sanctions or contempt.[51] Affidavits lacking statements of fact but containing mere conclusions or opinions are insufficient.[52] Supplemental affidavits may be allowed by the court.[53] The affidavits must

---

admission to support a summary judgment, it is error to do so if the record contains evidence contradicting the admission. *Walker v. City of Bartow Police Dep't (In re Forfeiture of 1982 Ford Mustang)*, 725 So. 2d 382, 385 (Fla. 2d DCA 1998); *see also Mahmoud v. King*, 824 So. 2d 248 (Fla. 4th DCA 2002) (holding, and citing like cases that hold, summary judgment is not proper based on a failure to respond to requests for admissions when the record otherwise reveals disputed issues of material fact); *Sher v. Liberty Mutual Insur. Co.*, 557 So. 2d 638, 639 (Fla. 3d DCA 1990) (disputed issues of fact precluded the entry of summary judgment since the record was replete with evidence that contradicted the admissions created by a failure to timely respond). Allegations in a verified mortgage complaint, and denials in a reply to an answer and affirmative defenses, have been considered record contradictions of technical admissions that should preclude summary judgment based on technical admissions. *See Wells Fargo Bank, N.A. v. Donaldson*, 165 So. 3d 40, 42 (Fla. 3d DCA 2015).

[50] Rule 1.510(e). The sworn or certified copy of documents referred to in an affidavit may also be served with the affidavit instead of attaching them to the affidavit itself. Rule 1.510(e). It is logical to conclude that any documents attached to an affidavit must also constitute admissible evidence. For example, demand or breach letters attached to an affidavit must be properly authenticated and overcome any hearsay objections. In other words, the affidavit must establish the proper predicate for the admission of documents attached thereto. Such documents do not become admissible merely because they are attached to an affidavit. *See BiFulco v. State Farm Mut. Auto. Ins. Co.*, 693 So. 2d 707, 709 (Fla. 4th DCA 1997) ("Merely attaching documents which are not sworn to or certified to a motion for summary judgment does not, without more, satisfy the procedural strictures inherent in Florida Rule of Civil Procedure 1.510(e)."); *Zoda v. Hedden*, 596 So. 2d 1225, 1226 (Fla. 2d DCA 1992) (unauthenticated documents referred to in the affidavit of appellee's counsel, which were not attached to his affidavit, constituted incompetent hearsay not sufficient to support summary judgment). Business records attached to an affidavit require the affiant to establish the business records exception to the hearsay rule. *See* Fla. Stat. § 90.803(6).

[51] Fla. R. Civ. P. 1.510(g).

[52] "[A] corporate officer's affidavit which merely states conclusions or opinion [is insufficient] even if it is based on personal knowledge." *Alvarez v. Florida Ins. Guar. Ass'n*, 661 So. 2d 1230, 1232 n.2 (Fla. 3d DCA 1995) (citing *Nour v. All State Pipe Supply Co.*, 487 So. 2d 1204, 1205 (Fla. 1st DCA 1986)); *see Land Dev. Servs. v. Gulf View Townhomes, LLC*, 75 So. 3d 865, 870 (Fla. 2d DCA 2011) (affidavit, containing assertion that movant was "not indebted" to the nonmoving party, was nothing more than a factual conclusion that could not support entry of summary judgment); *Lee-Booth, Inc. v. Fid. & Deposit Co. of Md.*, 399 So. 2d 531, 532 (Fla. 2d DCA 1981) (providing that statements of ultimate fact will not "justify entry of summary judgment"); *Buzzi v. Quality Serv. Station, Inc.*, 921 So. 2d 14, 15 (Fla. 3d DCA 2006) (noting that "'[a]n affidavit in support of summary judgment may not be based upon factual conclusions or conclusions of law'" (quoting *Florida Dep't of Fin. Servs. v. Associated Indus. Ins. Co.*, 868 So. 2d 600, 602 (Fla. 1st DCA 2004)).

[53] Rule 1.510(e).

indicate whether they are being made to support or oppose summary judgment as no less than one court has indicated that the same affidavit used to oppose summary judgment cannot be used to support the party's own motion for summary judgment.[54]

12-1:6 Partial Summary Judgment

Partial summary judgment is a very effective tool to narrow the issues before trial. Simply put, a partial summary judgment is any order that grants summary judgment but does not entirely dispose of the suit, leaving factual issues to be tried. Rule 1.510(a) authorizes a party to move for summary judgment upon all or any part of the movant's claim. For a plaintiff, it can be used to dispose of one or more affirmative defenses.[55] Moreover, at a summary judgment hearing (whether for final or partial summary judgment) in which a final judgment (disposing of the entire suit) is not rendered, or summary judgment is not granted as to all the relief sought by the moving party, a trial court judge shall, if practicable, enter an order specifying the facts that appear without substantial controversy.[56] Such an order can determine the extent to which the amount of damages or other relief is not in controversy, and may direct further proceedings in the suit as is "just."[57] The facts specified in the order are "deemed established" for the balance of the case, including at trial.[58] In effect, the court grants partial summary judgment as to those facts it finds are not substantially controverted, narrowing the factual issues for trial. Although uncommon, the First District wrote to expressly urge trial courts to detail in their summary judgment orders the material "facts that appear without substantial controversy" and those which stay "actually in good faith controverted."[59]

The same burden of proof applies to both complete and partial summary judgments. To illustrate, it is error for a trial court to grant partial summary judgment without considering affirmative defenses.[60]

---

[54] *Wells Fargo Bank, N.A. v. Bilecki*, 192 So. 3d 559, 561 (Fla. 4th DCA 2016).
[55] *See, e.g., Villareal v. Eres*, 128 So. 3d 93, 101 (Fla. 2d DCA 2013) (affirming order granting plaintiff's motion for partial summary judgment as to defendant's affirmative defense regarding settlement).
[56] Rule 1.510(d).
[57] Rule 1.510(d).
[58] Rule 1.510(d). Rule 1.510(d) seemingly contradicts this author's earlier assertion that a trial judge may not weigh evidence at the summary judgment stage, because the trial judge can enter a summary judgment order deeming certain facts established for use at trial when the fact-finder is obligated to weigh evidence. Further, Rule 1.510(d) appears to add a different or additional burden of proof for summary judgment. This is because if a party can convince the court, at a summary judgment hearing, that there is no "substantial controversy" (*not* the absence of a genuine issue of material fact) as to a given fact, that particular fact is deemed established (to the same effect as a binding admission of the subject fact).
[59] *Destin Pointe Owners' Ass'n v. Destin Parcel 160, Ltd.*, 44 Fla. L. Weekly D1869, 2019 WL 3282621, 2019 Fla. App. LEXIS 11460 *1 (Fla. 1st DCA July 22, 2019) (citing Fla. R. Civ. P. 1.510(d)).
[60] *Florida Dep't of Agric. v. Go Bungee*, 678 So. 2d 920, 921 (Fla. 5th DCA 1996).

12-1:7 Timing

A claimant (a party seeking affirmative relief upon a claim, counterclaim, cross-claim, or third-party claim)[61] may move for summary judgment at any time after the expiration of 20 days from the time a lawsuit or claim is initially filed or after service of a motion for summary judgment by the opposing party.[62] A defendant may move for summary judgment at any time.[63]

Despite the plain meaning of Rule 1.510, courts have held that a motion for summary judgment should not be made once trial begins.[64] The reasoning is as follows. Summary judgment proceedings are pre-trial in character.[65] Their purpose is to avoid the time and expense of a useless trial, not to delay trial.[66] Once the trial commences, the defendant then tests the sufficiency of the plaintiff's evidence, not by a motion for summary judgment, but by a motion for directed verdict or a motion for involuntary dismissal in nonjury matters.[67]

A motion for summary judgment, with the summary judgment evidence identified in the motion (unless it has already been filed with the court), must be served at least 20 days before the time fixed for the hearing.[68] Nonmoving parties must identify summary judgment evidence and serve it pursuant to Florida Rule of Judicial Administration 2.516—that is, by mail (if authorized) at least five days prior to the hearing or by e-mail no later than 5:00 p.m. two business days prior to the hearing.[69] An affidavit that is untimely served before the initial summary judgment hearing may be relied upon as timely in subsequent continued hearings on the same motion for summary judgment.[70]

---

[61] Rule. 1.510(a).

[62] Rule 1.510(a).

[63] Rule 1.510(b).

[64] *Gutierrez v. Bermudez*, 540 So. 2d 888, 890 (Fla. 5th DCA 1989) (citing *Fish Carburetor Corp. v. Great American Insurance Company*, 125 So. 2d 889, 891 (Fla. 1st DCA 1961)). The reasoning in *Gutierrez* was subsequently approved in *Ameriseal of North East Florida v. Leiffer*, 738 So. 2d 993, 995 (Fla. 5th DCA 1999). *See also Howarth Trust v. Howarth*, 310 So. 2d 57 (Fla. 1st DCA 1975); *Busbee-Bailey Tomato Co. v. Bailey*, 463 So. 2d 1255 (Fla. 1st DCA 1985).

[65] *Fish Carburetor Corp. v. Great American Insurance Company*, 125 So. 2d 889, 891 (Fla. 1st DCA 1961).

[66] *Fish Carburetor Corp. v. Great American Insurance Company*, 125 So. 2d 889, 891 (Fla. 1st DCA 1961).

[67] *Gutierrez v. Bermudez*, 540 So. 2d 888, 890 (Fla. 5th DCA 1989).

[68] Rule 1.510(c); *see In re Amends. to Fla. Rules of Civ. Pro.*, 257 So. 3d 66 (Fla. 2018) (As relevant here, the Court amended Rule 1.510 to directly reference Rule of Judicial Administration 2.516 (Service of Pleadings and Documents) and Rule 1.510(c) to treat evidence submitted served electronically or by e-mail the same as summary judgment evidence that is "delivered," among other things.); *see United States Bank v. Holbrook*, 226 So. 3d 363, 364 (Fla. 2d DCA 2017) (circuit court's consideration of evidence submitted for the first time at the summary judgment hearing was an error).

[69] Rule 1.510(c).

[70] *Wells Fargo Bank, N.A. v. Bilecki*, 192 So. 3d 559, 561 (Fla. 4th DCA 2016); *Rodriguez v. Tri-Square Constr., Inc.*, 635 So. 2d 125 (Fla. 3d DCA 1994). *But see Les Chateaux at Int'l Gardens Condo. Ass'n v. Cuevas & Assocs., P.A.*, 219 So. 3d 106 (Fla. 3d DCA 2017) (affirmed, in the absence of a transcript of the proceeding, the trial court's denial of the appellant's request to consider its untimely affidavit in opposition to the motion for summary judgment, and

The Third and Fourth District Courts of Appeal have held that the time set by Rule 1.510(c) is not jurisdictional and may be waived by the opposing party's failure to object or move for a continuance.[71]

The rules governing the computation of time and service are now found in the Florida Rules of Judicial Administration.[72] An understanding of these rules is crucial in determining the proper timing for service of motions for summary judgment as well as summary judgment evidence. Final summary judgments entered after a failure to timely serve these documents can constitute reversible error as untimely service may be considered prejudicial.[73] Yet several courts have held that the lack of timely notice can be waived by a failure to object to same or when there is evidence that the nonmovant had actual notice of the motion and hearing.[74]

Fla. R. Jud. Admin. 2.516 mandates service by electronic mail (e-mail) unless (1) an attorney obtains a court order excusing the attorney from e-mail service or (2) a pro se party has not designated an e-mail address for service.[75] For these latter categories, service may be made by other means such as mail, hand delivery, or by facsimile transmission.[76] Rule 2.516(d) also mandates that all documents must be filed with the court either before service or immediately thereafter except for those documents that may not be filed according to statutory law. As a practical matter, parties should file their respective summary judgment evidence so that it becomes part of the record for, among other things, motions for rehearing under Florida Rule of Civil Procedure 1.530 or appeal.

---

the trial court's denial of the appellant's motion for rehearing, which was accompanied by a new affidavit).

[71] *White v. Ocwen Loan Servicing*, 159 So. 3d 1009, 1011 (Fla. 3d DCA 2015) (Third District affirmed summary judgment entered on a counterclaim at trial even though the motion for summary judgment was filed only 16 days before trial. The court noted the opposing party's failure to object to the motion being heard at trial and otherwise ruled the procedural error was harmless. *Gutierrez v. Bermudez*, 540 So. 2d 888 (Fla. 5th DCA 1989)); *Blatch v. Wesley*, 238 So. 2d 308, 309 (Fla. 3d DCA 1970) (holding the time set by Rule 1.510 is not jurisdictional and may be waived by a failure to object or move for a continuance); *E & I, Inc. v. Excavators, Inc.*, 697 So. 2d 545, 546 (Fla. DCA 1997) ("We conclude that where, as in the present case, there was no objection to the insufficient notice prior to the hearing, at the hearing, nor in the motion for rehearing, the issue has been waived." *Blatch v. Wesley*, 238 So. 2d 308, 309 (Fla. 3d DCA 1970)).

[72] .*See* Florida Rules of Judicial Administration 2.514 and 2.516.

[73] *See Nelson v. Balkany*, 620 So. 2d 1138, 1139 (Fla. 3d DCA 1993). Needless to say, untimely service also expressly violates Rule 1.510(c).

[74] *See Vivona v. Colony Point 5 Condo. Ass'n*, 706 So. 2d 391 (Fla. 4th DCA 1998) (holding that any objection to the lack of notice to the hearing on a motion for summary judgment was waived where the opposing parties were given additional time to respond and, in their affidavits and memorandum, they did not raise any procedural objections, citing *Ultimate Corp. v. CG Data Corp.*, 575 So. 2d 1338, 1339 (Fla. 3d DCA 1991)); *E & I, Inc. v. Excavators, Inc.*, 697 So. 2d 545, 546 (Fla. 4th DCA 1997) (finding that the issue was waived where there was no objection to the insufficient notice, where the nonmovants filed affidavits in opposition to the motion, *and* the nonmovants had actual notice of the motion). Essentially, the analysis is centered on the issue of prejudice to the nonmovant.

[75] Fla. R. Jud. Admin. 2.516(b)(1).

[76] Fla. R. Jud. Admin. 2.516(b)(2).

Rule 2.516 states in no uncertain terms that service by e-mail is complete on the date it is sent.[77] Further, in 2019, Fla. R. Jud. Admin. 2.514 was amended so that services by e-mail and mail were no longer treated the same.[78] Because Rule 1.510(c) obligates movants to serve their motions and summary judgment evidence at least 20 days before the hearing, and Rule 2.516 states service by e-mail is complete on the day it is sent, motions and summary judgment evidence served by e-mail may be heard 20 days after they are served—and not 25 days before the hearing as many believe.[79]

12-1:8 Continuances and Pending Discovery Issues

Upon affidavit of a party seeking a continuance, Rule 1.510(f) gives a trial court discretion to continue a summary judgment hearing to allow a party to obtain affidavits, a deposition, or take discovery. One caveat is, once a summary judgment motion is set for hearing, parties who seek a continuance bear the burden of showing, by affidavit, the existence and availability of additional evidentiary matter, what it is and its relevance, what steps were taken to obtain it and that failure to have obtained such evidence sooner did not result from inexcusable delay by the parties seeking a continuance.[80] Parties seeking a continuance also bear the burden to demonstrate that further discovery would likely lead to material and relevant facts.[81] Likewise, it is reversible error for a trial court to grant summary judgment prior to the completion of relevant ongoing discovery.[82]

A party cannot later complain that it had insufficient time to oppose a summary judgment motion if that party did not seek a continuance by sworn affidavit, under Rule 1.510(f), before the hearing.[83] Parties cannot seek a continuance to obtain responses to outstanding discovery requests when those requests are related only to unpled defenses, and are therefore, irrelevant.[84] Courts interpreting Rule 1.510(f) primarily focus on the diligence of the nonmoving party in seeking discovery before

---

[77] Fla. R. Jud. Admin. 2.516(b)(1)(D).

[78] *See In re Amends. to Fla. Rules of Civ. Pro.*, 257 So. 3d 66, 68 (Fla. 2018) (removing the additional five days when service is made by e-mail).

[79] *See Ultimate Corp. v. CG Data Corp.*, 575 So. 2d 1338, 1339 (Fla. 3d DCA 1991); *Nelson v. Balkany*, 620 So. 2d 1138, 1139 (Fla. 3d DCA 1993) (finding a motion for summary judgment served by mail less than 25 days before the hearing violated rules 1.090(e) and 1.510(c)).

[80] *See McNutt v. Sherrill*, 141 So. 2d 309, 311 (Fla. 3d DCA 1962); *Carbonell v. BellSouth Telcoms.*, 675 So. 2d 705, 706 (Fla. 3d DCA 1996); *Giroux v. Ronald W. Williams Constr. Co.*, 705 So. 2d 663, 664-65 (Fla. 1st DCA 1998); *DeMesme v. Stephenson*, 498 So. 2d 673, 676 (Fla. 1st DCA 1986).

[81] *Trust Real Estate Ventures v. Desnick*, 44 Fla. L. Weekly D2016, 2019 WL 3675266, 2019 Fla. App. LEXIS 12199 *1 (Fla. 3d DCA Aug. 7, 2019) (citing *Barco Holdings, LLC v. Terminal Inv. Corp.*, 967 So. 2d 281, 289 (Fla. 3d DCA 2007)).

[82] *Skydive Space Ctr., Inc. v. Pohjolainen*, 275 So. 3d 825 (Fla. 5th DCA 2019) (reversible error to grant summary judgment with a pending motion to compel critical e-mails and a cloned hard drive for forensic examination).

[83] *See Titusville Assoc. v. Barnett Banks Trust Co.*, 591 So. 2d 609, 610 (Fla. 1991); *Leviton v. Philly Steak-Out, Inc.*, 533 So. 2d 905, 906 (Fla. 3d DCA 1988) (noting that when a party does not "request a continuance of the summary judgment hearing so that they could complete their discovery," the party "cannot now be heard to complain that they were not given a reasonable time to complete same").

[84] *Osorto v. Deutsche Bank Nat'l Trust Co.*, 88 So. 3d 261, 263 (Fla. 4th DCA 2012) ("if the incomplete discovery will not raise future disputed issues of material fact, summary judg-

the summary judgment hearing is set; in other words, whether the nonmoving party seeking a continuance took advantage of his or her opportunity to develop evidence before the hearing or whether, in fact, the motion for continuance is merely a dilatory tactic.[85]

Where there was more than a month's notice of the summary judgment hearing, the plaintiff's deposition was taken 28 days before the hearing, and the defendant had 16 days before the hearing to review the documents (defendant requested a continuance to study the subject documents), the trial court properly denied defendant's continuance to postpone the hearing.[86] Where the defendants conducted very little discovery over a seven-month period and did not request a continuance to complete discovery, the trial court properly granted summary judgment.[87] In one case, the plaintiff, about six months after the lawsuit was filed, first propounded discovery requests for interrogatories and production of documents.[88] One of the defendants then served a motion for summary judgment and timely objected to some of the requests for production.[89] Over two months later, the defendant served notice of a summary judgment hearing to be held on April 5th.[90] The plaintiff took no action until two weeks before the hearing, at which time the plaintiff noticed its motion for continuance and motion to compel for hearing on April 5th, the same day as defendant's summary judgment hearing.[91] The First District held that the trial court did not abuse its discretion in entering summary judgment, despite the pendency of discovery, because the plaintiff had not diligently sought discovery.[92]

Similarly, the trial court did not abuse its discretion in granting summary judgment, despite the pendency of discovery, where it had given the nonmoving party sufficient time to pursue discovery, but the party failed to do so.[93] The Second District affirmed an order granting summary judgment where the plaintiff failed to depose a witness even though the trial court had deferred ruling on the summary judgment for nearly two months to permit the plaintiff the opportunity to do so.[94] Where a party, who had conducted virtually no discovery, filed an unverified motion to continue that failed to address the necessary factors to warrant a continuance, and considering that the motion to continue was made more than one year after the suit had begun, the trial court properly denied the request for continuance and granted summary judgment.[95] Although the standard for considering requests for continuance is meant to permit

---

ment may be properly granted.") (citing *Estate of Herrera v. Berlo Indus., Inc.*, 840 So. 2d 272, 272 (Fla. 3d DCA 2003)).

[85] *See Schwartz v. Bank of Am., N.A.*, 267 So. 3d 414 (Fla. 4th DCA 2019) (The outstanding discovery the appellants complained of had been propounded only days before the summary judgment hearing which had been set several months earlier in a 2012 case. The Fourth District found no abuse of discretion of the trial court's finding that the appellants had not diligently conducted discovery.).

[86] *McNutt v. Sherrill*, 141 So. 2d 309, 311 (Fla. 3d DCA 1962).
[87] *Leviton v. Philly Steak-Out, Inc.*, 533 So. 2d 905, 906 (Fla. 3d DCA 1988).
[88] *Southern California Funding, Inc. v. Hutto*, 438 So. 2d 426, 431 (Fla. 1st DCA 1983).
[89] *Southern California Funding, Inc. v. Hutto*, 438 So. 2d 426, 431 (Fla. 1st DCA 1983).
[90] *Southern California Funding, Inc. v. Hutto*, 438 So. 2d 426, 431 (Fla. 1st DCA 1983).
[91] *Southern California Funding, Inc. v. Hutto*, 438 So. 2d 426, 431 (Fla. 1st DCA 1983).
[92] *Southern California Funding, Inc. v. Hutto*, 438 So. 2d 426, 431-32 (Fla. 1st DCA 1983).
[93] *Allen v. Shows*, 532 So. 2d 1304, 1305 (Fla. 2d DCA 1988).
[94] *Allen v. Shows*, 532 So. 2d 1304, 1305 (Fla. 2d DCA 1988).
[95] *DeMesme v. Stephenson*, 498 So. 2d 673, 676 (Fla. 1st DCA 1986).

a party sufficient time to conduct discovery and develop facts to oppose a summary judgment motion, it does not allow a party to delay pretrial discovery for years and then attempt to squeeze in discovery into the short period of time between a notice of hearing of the summary judgment motion and the actual summary judgment hearing.[96]

After a motion for summary judgment is filed and set for hearing, nonmoving parties cannot impede the hearing by initiating discovery.[97] A party does not have limitless time to engage in discovery before a summary judgment hearing.[98] As one court has said, there comes a time when discovery must end.[99] When additional discovery will not likely produce a genuine issue of material fact, discovery should end.[100]

On the other hand, where a party's affidavit establishes his inability to conclude discovery, his efforts to complete discovery, and that the failure to do so was not due to inaction on his part, it is an abuse of discretion to deny that party's motion for continuance.[101] It is premature to grant summary judgment when the nonmoving party, through no fault of its own, had not completed discovery.[102] In determining whether a trial court has abused its discretion in ruling on a motion for a continuance, appellate courts have considered the following factors: 1) whether the movant suffers injustice from the denial of the motion; 2) whether the underlying cause for the motion was unforeseen by the movant and whether the motion is based on dilatory tactics; and 3) whether prejudice and injustice (to the opposing party) will transpire if the motion is granted.[103] If both parties set a deposition by agreement to take place after the summary judgment hearing, it does not appear that the deposition had been scheduled to thwart the court's consideration of the summary judgment motion.[104] It is reversible error to enter summary judgment when the deposition of a party is pending.[105]

---

[96] *Building Educ. Corp. v. Ocean Bank*, 982 So. 2d 37, 40 (Fla. 3d DCA 2008).

[97] *Smith v. Smith*, 734 So. 2d 1144-45 (Fla. 5th DCA 1999).

[98] *Colby v. Ellis*, 562 So. 2d 356, 357 (Fla. 2d DCA 1990).

[99] *Colby v. Ellis*, 562 So. 2d 356, 357 (Fla. 2d DCA 1990).

[100] *Colby v. Ellis*, 562 So. 2d 356, 357 (Fla. 2d DCA 1990) (citing *Amey, Inc. v. Gulf Abstract & Title, Inc.*, 758 F.2d 1486, 1506 (11th Cir. 1985), *cert. denied*, 475 U.S. 1107 (1986)).

[101] *Giroux v. Ronald W. Williams Constr. Co.*, 705 So. 2d 663, 664-65 (Fla. 1st DCA 1998).

[102] *Commercial Bank of Kendall v. Heiman*, 322 So. 2d 564, 564 (Fla. 3d DCA 1975); *United States Bank v. Holbrook*, 226 So. 3d 363, 364 (Fla. 2d DCA 2017) (error to enter summary judgment before the movant had responded to any of the nonmoving party's discovery requests and who had, in fact, adamantly refused to sit for his deposition).

[103] *Baron v. Baron*, 941 So. 2d 1233, 1235-36 (Fla. 2d DCA 2006) (quoting *Myers v. Siegel*, 920 So. 2d 1241, 1242 (Fla. 5th DCA 2006)).

[104] *Smith v. Smith*, 734 So. 2d 1142, 1144 (Fla. 5th DCA 1999) (it is a reversible error to enter summary judgment when discovery is in progress and the deposition of a party is pending) (citations omitted).

[105] *Smith v. Smith*, 734 So. 2d 1142, 1144 (Fla. 5th DCA 1999); *Villages at Mango Key Home Owners Assoc., Inc. v. Hunter Development, Inc.*, 699 So. 2d 337 (Fla. 5th DCA 1997) (holding that summary judgment should not be granted when depositions are pending, i.e., had been scheduled before the summary judgment was set for hearing, unless a protective order is sought or entered); *Arguelles v. City of Orlando*, 855 So. 2d 1202, 1203 (Fla. 5th DCA 2003) (after appellant noticed the appellees' depositions, the appellee responded by filing a motion for summary judgment and setting same for hearing; court held that it was premature to consider summary judgment). It is a logical extension of this line of cases to reason that a summary judgment motion may not be considered if the nonmoving party fails to appear at a properly noticed deposition before the summary judgment is heard.

Attorneys would be well-advised to ensure that a sworn motion to continue a summary judgment hearing (that meets the requirements for an affidavit or is in the form of an affidavit), explaining the relevance of the necessary discovery as well as the diligent efforts of the party seeking a continuance to obtain the summary judgment evidence, is filed, or risk waiving their client's right to raise the issue at a later date.[106]

12-1:9 Pending Counterclaims

Can a trial court grant summary judgment as to all of one party's claims against another when there is a pending counterclaim against the party moving for summary judgment? Most courts hold that summary judgment can be granted for a plaintiff when a counterclaim remains pending, so long as the trial court stays execution of the summary judgment pending resolution of the counterclaim.[107] Alternatively, trial courts can enter an order granting summary judgment but delay the actual entry of a final summary judgment until the counterclaim is disposed. As a practical matter, delaying the entry of a final summary judgment (after a ruling by the court, in a written order, that a party is entitled to final summary judgment), or staying the execution of a final summary judgment, can help plaintiffs avoid forgotten counterclaims and the negative consequences resulting from execution of a final summary judgment when a later-decided counterclaim requires that final summary judgment be amended or vacated altogether.[108] Some courts have ruled it is reversible error to grant final summary judgment on an equitable foreclosure claim where the issues are sufficiently similar or related to a compulsory counterclaim to which the counterclaimant has a constitutional right to trial by jury (upon a timely demand) without being bound by the factual determinations in the final summary judgment of foreclosure decided by the court.[109]

---

[106] See *Fuller v. General Motors Corp.*, 353 So. 2d 1236, 1237 (Fla. 3d DCA 1978), *writ of certiorari denied*, 361 So. 2d 832 (Fla. 1978) (because the appellant did not, *inter alia*, move for a continuance to complete discovery, the trial court property proceeded with the summary judgment hearing without permitting the appellant the opportunity for any further discovery); *Howard v. Shirmer*, 334 So. 2d 103, 104 (Fla. 3d DCA 1976) (because plaintiffs did not move for a continuance to give them additional time to take a deposition, there was no merit in plaintiffs' argument that the court erred in entering summary judgment).

[107] See *Tooltrend, Inc. v. C.M.T. Utensili*, 707 So. 2d 1162, 1162 (Fla. 2d DCA 1998); *Millennium Group I, L.L.C. v. Attorneys Title Ins. Fund, Inc.*, 847 So. 2d 1115, 1117 (Fla. 1st DCA 2003) (stating that when summary judgment is granted for one party and a counterclaim on an original claim remains pending, the trial court should stay the execution of the judgment pending the resolution of the remaining claim); *Howell v. Miller*, 638 So. 2d 544 (Fla. 2d DCA 1994); *Carpenter v. Super Pools, Inc.*, 534 So. 2d 426 (Fla. 5th DCA 1988); *Zanathy v. Beach Harbor Club Ass'n, Inc.*, 343 So. 2d 625 (Fla. 2d DCA 1977).

[108] See *Tolin v. Doudov*, 626 So. 2d 1054, 1056 (Fla. 4th DCA 1993) (reversing and remanding for set-off of foreclosure "damages" against damages for breach of contract).

[109] *Del Rio v. Brandon*, 696 So. 2d 1197, 1198 (Fla. 3d DCA 1997) (quoting *Dykes v. Trustbank Sav., F.S.B.*, 567 So. 2d 958, 959 (Fla. 2d DCA 1990), *review denied*, 577 So. 2d 1330 (Fla. 1991)). This rule only applies if the counterclaim is both compulsory (involving similar or related issues of fact) and the counterclaimant is entitled to and timely demanded a jury trial.

12-1:10 Summary Judgment in Foreclosure Lawsuits

12-1:10.1 Summary Judgment of Foreclosure Claims

To obtain a final summary judgment of foreclosure, a plaintiff in a foreclosure lawsuit has the burden to conclusively establish the absence of any genuine issue of material fact as to the essential elements of its foreclosure claim. The essential elements of a foreclosure claim are (1) an agreement between the plaintiff and the borrowers, (2) a default by the borrowers, (3) an acceleration of the entire amount due to maturity,[110] and (4) the amount due by the borrowers under the note and mortgage.[111]

If a Defendant has filed an answer and affirmative defenses, the foreclosure plaintiff also has the burden to conclusively establish the absence of any genuine issue of material fact as to a Defendant's well-pled affirmative defenses or show they are legally insufficient,[112] presumably by memorandum of law.

As explained above,[113] a foreclosure plaintiff's burden must be met through the use of summary judgment evidence.

---

[110] *Acceleration* means that all future payments due under a promissory note become immediately due and payable. The majority of residential mortgages in Florida contain what are called *optional acceleration clauses* which simply means "the entire debt does not become due on the mere default of payment; rather, it become due when the creditor takes affirmative action to alert the debtor that he has exercised his option to accelerate." *Greene v. Bursey*, 733 So. 2d 1111, 1115 (Fla. 4th DCA 1999). Nearly all courts that have decided the issue hold that acceleration occurs when a foreclosure complaint is filed declaring all amounts due and payable. *See Locke v. State Farm Fire and Casualty Co.*, 509 So. 2d 1375 (Fla. 1st DCA 1987) (holding that the mortgagee had not enforced the optional acceleration clause in the mortgage until it filed its foreclosure complaint); *Fowler v. First Fed. Sav. & Loan Ass'n*, 643 So. 2d 30, 34 (Fla. 1st DCA 1994); *Seligman v. Bisz*, 123 Fla. 493, 167 So. 38 (Fla. 1936) (finding where acceleration is at the option of the mortgagee, the "institution of a suit for foreclosure is the exercise of the option to declare the whole of the principal sum and interest secured by the mortgage to be due and payable"); *Jaudon v. Equitable Life Assur. Soc. of United States*, 102 Fla. 782, 136 So. 517 (Fla. 1931) ("mere filing of suit to enforce the mortgage by foreclosure may sufficiently show [an] election to exercise [an] option to accelerate").

[111] *Black Point Assets, Inc. v. Fannie Mae*, 220 So. 3d 566, 568 (Fla. 5th DCA 2017); *Pealer v. Wilmington Tr. Nat'l Ass'n*, 212 So. 3d 1137, 1139 (Fla. 2d DCA 2017) (Sleet, J. concurring); *Ernest v. Carter*, 368 So. 2d 428, 429 (Fla. 2d DCA 1979); *Kelsey v. SunTrust Mortg., Inc.*, 131 So. 3d 825, 826 (Fla. 3d DCA 2014); *Bank of Am., N.A. v. Delgado*, 166 So. 3d 857, 859 (Fla. 3d DCA 2015). Although none of these cases mention *standing* as an element of a foreclosure complaint, as noted above, due to obscuring language used among Florida courts when discussing "standing," the best practice for foreclosure plaintiffs is to treat standing as an element of their claim. *Compare U.S. Bank Nat'l Ass'n v. Clarke*, 192 So. 3d 620, 622 (Fla. 4th DCA 2016) ("[S]tanding is a crucial element in any mortgage foreclosure proceeding and must be established at the inception of the lawsuit.") *with Jaffer v. Chase Home Fin., LLC*, 155 So. 3d 1199, 1202 (Fla. 4th DCA 2015) ("We have repeatedly held that standing is an affirmative defense and failure to raise it in a responsive pleading generally results in a waiver." (citations omitted)).

[112] *See* Section 12-1:3.2.

[113] *See* Section 12-1:5.

12-1:10.1a Business Records

Because mortgage loans, and the promissory notes they secure, are commercial documents that are commonly transferred, bought, and sold,[114] a central issue in any foreclosure suit is whether or not a foreclosing plaintiff can produce admissible evidence, for purposes of both summary judgment and trial, through its own records of regularly conducted business activity,[115] or through the business records of its mortgage loan servicer.[116] Other than the authenticity and admissibility of the mortgage and note,[117] business records are primarily used to prove a foreclosure plaintiff's case. These business records inevitably contain out of court statements offered to show the truth of the matter asserted. The hearsay exception for business records found in Fla. Stat. § 90.803(6) is therefore critical in any foreclosure lawsuit. It is especially important in summary judgment proceedings because summary judgment evidence must constitute *admissible* evidence. Ordinarily then, most, if not all, documents used to support plaintiffs' motions for summary judgment, must both be authenticated and overcome the business records exception to the evidentiary hearsay rule—typically by an affiant's testimony.

The underlying premise of the business records' exception to the hearsay rule is that business records are inherently trustworthy. Businesses depend on their records in their daily operations and routinely check them for accuracy in the course of running their respective business.[118]

To admit business record evidence under Fla. Stat. § 90.803(6), plaintiffs must establish the following foundation through the testimony of a records custodian or any qualified person[119]:

(1) that the record was made at or near the time of the event; (2) that it was made by or from information transmitted by a person with knowledge; (3) that it was kept in the ordinary course of a regularly conducted business activity; and (4) that it was a regular practice of that business to make such a record.[120]

---

[114] After all, the principal purpose of the Uniform Commercial Code is to support the transfer and market of negotiable instruments.

[115] Referred to herein as "business records."

[116] Business records in foreclosure suits (and those generally since the advent of personal computers, the internet, and networks used in most modern businesses), primarily consist of computerized or electronic records—that is printouts of data stored on computers or networks.

[117] These documents are generally self-authenticating. As contracts they are not hearsay and are admissible for their independent legal significance - to establish the existence of the contractual relationship and the rights and obligations of the parties to the note and mortgage, regardless of the truth of any assertions made in the documents. *Deutsche Bank Nat'l Tr. Co., Etc. v. Alaqua Prop.*, 190 So. 3d 662, 665 (Fla. 5th DCA 2016).

[118] *See, e.g., Bank of N.Y. v. Calloway*, 157 So. 3d 1064, 1071 (Fla. 4th DCA 2015) ("Businesses rely upon their records 'in the conduct of [their] daily affairs' and 'customarily check [them] for correctness during the course of the business activities.'" (quoting Charles W. Ehrhardt, Florida Evidence § 803.6 (2014 ed.)).

[119] *See CitiMortgage, Inc. v. Hoskinson*, 200 So. 3d 191, 192 (Fla. 5th DCA 2016) (A qualified witness with the requisite knowledge to lay the foundation for the business records exception is one who is "well enough acquainted with the activity to give the testimony." (citations omitted)).

[120] *See Yisrael v. State*, 993 So. 2d 952, 956 (Fla. 2008).

The person or affiant called upon to make this foundation for plaintiffs need not be the records custodian, the person who actually prepared the document,[121] or the one who entered the data.[122]

In recent years, there has been a proliferation of challenges (both at the trial and appellate levels) to the introduction of a predecessor's business records relied upon by the plaintiff or its mortgage loan servicer who maintains its business records.[123]

A plaintiff can meet the business records' exception to the hearsay rule when it needs to admit the records of a previous entity (or its own records that incorporate its predecessor's data) by (1) obtaining the proper foundational testimony directly from each of the plaintiff's predecessors[124] or (2) laying the proper predicate under Fla. Stat. § 90.803(6), testifying the successor business relies upon those records and showing that the circumstances otherwise indicate the records are trustworthy, typically through a process that checks the accuracy of a previous entity's records either before or after they are incorporated or boarded into the successor business' records.[125] It is not necessary that the witness have personal knowledge of the prior entity's business practice or participate in the actual boarding process.[126]

---

[121] *Onewest Bank, FSB v. Jasinski*, 173 So. 3d 1009, 1013 (Fla. 2d DCA 2015) (quoting *Bank of N.Y. v. Calloway*, 157 So. 3d 1064, 1073 (Fla. 4th DCA 2015) (quotation omitted)); *Hunter v. Aurora Loan Services, LLC*, 137 So. 3d 570, 573 (Fla. 1st DCA 2014) (quoting *Mazine v. M & I Bank*, 67 So. 3d 1129, 1132 (Fla. 1st DCA 2011)).

[122] *Glarum v. La Salle Bank*, 83 So. 3d 780, 782 n.2 (Fla. 4th DCA 2011).

[123] *See Glarum v. La Salle Bank*, 83 So. 3d 780, 782 (Fla. 4th DCA 2011); *Weisenberg v. Deutsche Bank Nat'l Trust Co.*, 89 So. 3d 1111, 1112 (Fla. 4th DCA 2012); *Cayea v. CitiMortgage, Inc.*, 138 So. 3d 1214, 1217 (Fla. 4th DCA 2014); *Hunter v. Aurora Loan Services, LLC*, 137 So. 3d 570, 573 (Fla. 1st DCA 2014); *Holt v. Calchas, LLC*, 155 So. 3d 499, 505 (Fla. 4th DCA 2015).

[124] By affidavit, or certification under Fla. Stat. § 90.902(11) and Fla. Stat. § 90.803(6)(a), from each previous loan servicer. *See Holt v. Calchas, LLC*, 155 So. 3d 499, 506 (Fla. 4th DCA 2015).

[125] *Ocwen Loan Servicing, LLC v. Gundersen*, 204 So. 3d 530, 533-34 (Fla. 4th DCA 2016); *Nationstar Mortgage, LLC v. Berdecia*, 169 So. 3d 209, 213-14 (Fla. 5th DCA 2015) (citing *Le v. U.S. Bank*, 165 So. 3d 776, 778 (Fla. 5th DCA 2015) and *Bank of N.Y. v. Calloway*, 157 So. 3d 1064, 1074 (Fla. 4th DCA 2015)); *WAMCO XXVIII, Ltd. v. Integrated Electronic Environments, Inc.*, 903 So. 2d 230, 233 (Fla. 2d DCA 2005); *Bank of N.Y. v. Calloway*, 157 So. 3d 1064, 1074 (Fla. 4th DCA 2015) (and the numerous cases cited therein); *Deutsche Bank Tr. Co. Ams. v. Frias*, 178 So. 3d 505, 508 (Fla. 4th DCA 2015) (reversing trial court's preclusion of records originating from prior servicers because although current servicer's testifying employee had not worked for any prior servicers, employee adequately established that the prior servicer's records met the business records exception and were checked for accuracy by current servicer); *Holt v. Calchas, LLC*, 155 So. 3d 499, 506 (Fla. 4th DCA 2015); *Cayea v. Citimortgage, Inc.*, 138 So. 3d 1214, 1217 (Fla. 4th DCA 2014) (the Fourth District, in *Cayea*, also provided another method for overcoming the business record exception: "Printouts of data prepared for trial may be admitted under the business records exception even if the printouts themselves are not kept in the ordinary course of business so long as a qualified witness testifies as to the manner of preparation, reliability, and trustworthiness."); *Hunter v. Aurora Loan Services, LLC*, 137 So. 3d 570, 573 (Fla. 1st DCA 2014); *In re Sagamore Partners, Ltd*, No. 11-3122, 2012 Bankr. LEXIS 3800 *12-13 (Bankr. S.D. Fla. Aug. 15, 2012) (interpreting Florida law).

[126] *See OneWest Bank, FSB v. Jasinski*, 173 So. 3d 1009, 1012-13 (Fla. 2d DCA 2015); *WAMCO XXVIII, Ltd. v. Integrated Elec. Env'ts, Inc.*, 903 So. 2d 230, 233 (Fla. 2d DCA 2005); *Le v. U.S. Bank*, 165 So. 3d 776, 777-78 (Fla. 5th DCA 2015); *Bank of N.Y. v. Calloway*, 157 So. 3d 1064,

12-1:10.1b Standing

Affidavits, verified complaints, deposition testimony, and note certifications can all be used by plaintiffs to show they have the right to enforce the note and the corresponding right to foreclose the mortgage lien, i.e., standing.[127]

Verified foreclosure complaints[128] can serve the same purpose as an affidavit in support of a motion for summary judgment.[129] Yet to be considered by a trial court, the allegations in the verified complaint must meet the same requirements governing affidavits.[130] Verifications, solely based on information and belief, are normally insufficient because they are conditional in nature.[131]

Fla. Stat. § 92.525(2) authorizes verification solely on information and belief only when "permitted by law." Fla. R. Civ. P. 1.115(e) (Rule 1.115) requires foreclosing plaintiffs to verify foreclosure complaints. That verification may be made on the best of the claimant's knowledge and belief. Because Fla. Stat. § 92.525(2) allows verifications based on information and belief when they are permitted by law and Rule 1.115(e) authorizes a verification to be based on the best of a claimant's knowledge and belief, an argument can be made that verified foreclosure complaints can constitute summary judgment evidence.[132]

Similarly, a certification attaching a copy of the original promissory note, made under penalty of perjury, that a foreclosing plaintiff is in possession of the original promissory note, can also serve as summary judgment evidence so long as the same requirements for affidavits are met.[133]

Given the recent statutory and rule changes[134] that require plaintiffs to effectively establish their right to enforce the note by verified and certified documents filed at

---

1072 (Fla. 4th DCA 2015); *Michel v. Bank of N.Y. Mellon*, 191 So. 3d 981, 983 (Fla. 2d DCA 2016).

[127] Case law focuses on standing to enforce the note, as opposed to the mortgage, because the mortgage generally passes as an incident to the debt. *Cutler v. U.S. Bank Nat'l Ass'n*, 109 So. 3d 224, 225 (Fla. 2d DCA 2012); *WM Specialty Mortg., LLC v. Salomon*, 874 So. 2d 680, 682 (Fla. 4th DCA 2004); *Johns v. Gillian*, 134 Fla. 575, 184 So. 140, 143 (Fla. 1938) ("[i]f the note or other debt secured by a mortgage [is] transferred without any formal assignment of the mortgage, or even a delivery of it, the mortgage in equity passes as an incident to the debt. . . .").

[128] Fla. R. Civ. P. 1.115(e) requires *verified* mortgage foreclosures claims.

[129] *See Rinzler v. Carson*, 262 So. 2d 661, 665 (Fla. 1972); *Booth v. Bd. of Pub. Instruction of Dade County*, 67 So. 2d 690, 691 (Fla. 1953); *Lindgren v. Deutsche Bank*, 115 So. 3d 1076, 1076 (Fla. 4th DCA 2013); *Ballinger v. Bay Gulf Credit Union*, 51 So. 3d 528, 529 (Fla. 2d DCA 2010).

[130] *Lindgren v. Deutsche Bank*, 115 So. 3d 1076 (Fla. 4th DCA 2013); *Boettcher v. IMC Mortg. Co.*, 871 So. 2d 1047, 1049 n.2 (Fla. 2d DCA 2004) (citing Rule 1.510(e)).

[131] *See Muss v. Lennar Fla. Partners*, 673 So. 2d 84, 85 (Fla. 4th DCA 1996). As mentioned, Fla. Stat. § 92.525(2) authorizes verification solely on information and belief only where "permitted by law."

[132] As noted above, the motion for summary judgment must state that the movant will rely upon a verified complaint if the movant intends to rely upon same in support of the summary judgment motion. Rule 1.510(c).

[133] This certification must now be filed by a foreclosing plaintiff at the initiation of a foreclosure lawsuit. Fla. R. Civ. P. 1.115(c).

[134] *See In re Amendments to the Fla. Rules of Civ. Procedure*, 153 So. 3d 258 (Fla. 2014). The amended rules were made in response to enactment of Fla. Stat. § 702.015.

the inception of the suit, the issue of who has the right to enforce the note should be easier to demonstrate when plaintiffs seek final judgment. Still, foreclosing plaintiffs cannot solely rely upon verified complaints and note certifications to establish standing[135] at summary judgment unless these documents otherwise meet the same requirements as affidavits under Rule 1.510(e).

Affidavits by foreclosing plaintiffs are almost always made by mortgage loan servicers, whether or not the servicer is actually the plaintiff. As a result, loan servicer affidavits used to show plaintiffs' right to enforce notes typically require loan servicer[136] witnesses to explain that they have personal knowledge based on their review of business records associated with the mortgage account,[137] that plaintiff possessed the original note with appropriate endorsements[138] at inception of the suit[139] and at the time of summary judgment.[140]

---

[135] As discussed above, the right to enforce the note and *standing* are considered equivalent legal concepts in foreclosure litigation.

[136] According to the Consumer Financial Protection Bureau, a mortgage lender is the financial institution that gives the mortgage loan. A mortgage servicer "handles the day-to-day tasks of managing your loan ... typically processes ... loan payments, responds to borrower inquiries, keeps track of principal and interest paid, manages ... escrow account[s], and may initiate foreclosure if ... too many loan payments are missed." What's the difference between a mortgage lender and a servicer?, http://www.consumerfinance.gov/askcfpb/198/whats-the-difference-between-a-mortgage-lender-and-a-servicer.html (last visited Aug. 21, 2017).

[137] Any business records referenced in affidavits must be attached to them. Rule 1.510(e) ("Sworn or certified copies of all papers or parts thereof referred to in an affidavit shall be attached thereto or served therewith.").

[138] Because possession of original promissory notes are the key to any foreclosure case, and the advent of electronic filing and service make it relatively onerous to physically file an original document in a court *file*, they are usually presented to the court at the time of the summary judgment hearing. This also helps guard against loss of the note by clerk or court staff. Consequently, *true and correct* copies of the original note (shown by sworn testimony) are almost always used to attach to summary judgment affidavits instead of the actual original note. However, a foreclosing plaintiff must produce and surrender the original note (a negotiable instrument) *before* the entry of a final summary judgment in order to take it out of the stream of commerce. See *Downing v. First Nat'l Bank of Lake City*, 81 So. 2d 486, 488 (Fla. 1955); *Deutsche Bank Nat'l Trust Co. v. Clarke*, 87 So. 3d 58, 60-61 (Fla. 4th DCA 2012); *Johnston v. Hudlett*, 32 So. 3d 700, 704 (Fla. 4th DCA 2010). It is this author's experience that upon surrender, some trial court judges stamp the promissory note as "cancelled." Plaintiffs' counsel will therefore be well advised to wait to surrender the original note until they are absolutely sure that the trial court is entering *final judgment* in plaintiffs' favor.

[139] When defendants raise *standing* as an affirmative defense. *See* Section 12-3:1.

[140] During the pendency of many foreclosure suits, foreclosing plaintiffs transfer their rights to enforce the note to another entity. Pursuant to Florida Rule of Civil Procedure 1.260, these plaintiffs almost always move to substitute the new entity in its place as the plaintiff. Although there are multiple cases holding these substituted plaintiffs acquire the *standing* of the original plaintiff, *see Brandenburg v. Residential Credit Solutions, Inc.*, 137 So. 3d 604, 605-06 (Fla. 4th DCA 2014); *U.S. Bank, Nat'l Ass'n v. Angeloni*, 199 So. 3d 492, 493 (Fla. 4th DCA 2016), the current consensus seems to be that a plaintiff (substituted or not) must prove its right to enforce the note both at the time of trial and also at the time the foreclosure complaint was filed. *See Russell v. Aurora Loan Servs., LLC*, 163 So. 3d 639, 642 (Fla. 2d DCA 2015); *Rigby v. Wells Fargo Bank, N.A.*, 84 So. 3d 1195, 1196 (Fla. 4th DCA 2012); *Kiefert v. Nationstar Mortg., LLC*, 153 So. 3d 351, 352 (Fla. 1st DCA 2014).

Foreclosure plaintiffs can also establish standing through what has now evolved as an evidentiary presumption called the *Ortiz* Presumption (or inference), named after the seminal case on the issue.[141] This presumption specifies that, if that a properly endorsed original note is introduced as evidence at a final hearing that matches the copy of the note attached to the initial complaint, this suffices to establish standing absent any testimony or other evidence to the contrary.[142]

Many foreclosure plaintiffs in Florida are trustees of various securitized trusts. Recently, the Fourth District, in reversing a final summary judgment in favor of the defendant based on standing, held that to prove standing a trustee-plaintiff is not required to identify or prove the trust upon which it acts.[143]

Florida courts also recognize the element of possession necessary to prove a plaintiff's right to enforce the note as a holder or a non-holder in possession can be met through *constructive* possession, that is by showing the foreclosure plaintiff's agent retained physical possession of the note while the plaintiff exercised control over it.[144]

12-1:10.1c The Loan Agreement

Proof that the borrower-defendants agreed to the terms of the mortgage loan is normally shown by the introduction of the note and mortgage, reflecting the borrower-defendants' signatures, into evidence. Officially recorded mortgages certified by the clerk are self-authenticating.[145] Commercial papers such as promissory notes, as well as the signatures thereon, are self-authenticating.[146] Yet defendants may specifically deny the validity of their signatures on promissory notes in their pleadings.[147] When this occurs, the burden is placed on plaintiffs to show the signatures are authentic.[148]

---

[141] *Ortiz v. PNC Bank*, 188 So. 3d 923 (Fla. 4th DCA 2016).

[142] *Clay Cty. Land Tr. #08-04-25-0078-014-27, Orange Park Tr. Servs., LLC v. JP Morgan Chase Bank, Nat'l Ass'n*, 152 So. 3d 83 (Fla. 1st DCA 2014); *Ortiz v. PNC Bank*, 188 So. 3d 923, 925 (Fla. 4th DCA 2016); *U.S. Bank N.A. v. Clarke*, 192 So. 3d 620, 622 (Fla. 4th DCA 2016); *Wells Fargo Bank v. Ousley*, 212 So. 3d 1056, 1058 (Fla. 1st DCA 2016); *Deutsche Bank Nat'l Trust Co., Etc. v. Alaqua Prop., Etc.*, 190 So. 3d 662, 663 (Fla. 5th DCA 2016); *US Bank Nat'l Ass'n v. Laird*, 200 So. 3d 176, 177 (Fla. 5th DCA 2016); *Meilleur v. HSBC Bank USA, N.A.*, 194 So. 3d 512 (Fla. 4th DCA 2016); *Bank of N.Y. Mellon v. Milford*, 206 So. 3d 137, 137-38 (Fla. 4th DCA 2016); *ALS-RVC, LLC v. Garvin*, 201 So. 3d 687, 691 (Fla. 4th DCA 2016).

[143] *Bank of N.Y. Mellon v. Ginsberg*, 221 So. 3d 1196, 1197 (Fla. 4th DCA 2017).

[144] *Caraccia v. U.S. Bank, N.A.*, 185 So. 3d 1277, 1279 (Fla. 4th DCA 2016); *Deakter v. Menendez*, 830 So. 2d 124, 128 (Fla. 3d DCA 2002); *Bush v. Belenke*, 381 So. 2d 315, 316 (Fla. 3d DCA 1980); *Phan v. Deutsche Bank Nat'l Tr. Co.*, 198 So. 3d 744, 748 (Fla. 2d DCA 2016).

[145] Fla. Stat. § 90.902(4).

[146] Fla. Stat. § 90.902(8); Fla. Stat. § 673.3081(1) ("each signature on [an] instrument is admitted unless specifically denied in the pleadings.").

[147] The official comment to Fla. Stat. § 673.3081, and common sense, indicate that a *specific* denial requires more than a general one. In other words, defendants cannot merely deny it is their signatures but must give reasons why they deny the authenticity of the signatures. This requirement appears to be related to due process and notice concerns. "The purpose of the requirement of a specific denial in the pleadings is to give the plaintiff notice of the defendant's claim of forgery or lack of authority as to the particular signature, and to afford the plaintiff an opportunity to investigate and obtain evidence." Fla. Stat. § 673.3081, official comment.

[148] Fla. Stat. § 673.3081(1).

At the same time, the signatures are presumed to be authentic.[149] Defendants must introduce some evidence that show the signature is forged or unauthorized, in order to overcome the presumption.[150]

As contracts, the foreclosure plaintiff does not need to establish the mortgage and note are business records because they are not hearsay. They are contracts that have independent legal significance that are introduced to show their legal effect (the existence of the contractual relationship and the rights and obligations of the parties), not to prove the truth of the matter asserted.[151]

12-1:10.1d Default

The borrower's default is ordinarily established by an affidavit attaching the business records of the loan payment history. Additional support can be provided by a copy of the pre-suit default notice[152] with the affiant's testimony confirming that to date, the borrower has not cured the default.

12-1:10.1e Conditions Precedent

There is a common misunderstanding among foreclosure litigants and the courts that a plaintiff must prove it has met conditions precedent as part of its prima facie case in chief or establish there is no genuine issue of fact that it has complied with any and all conditions precedent in order to obtain a final summary judgment of foreclosure.

However, a defendant's assertion that a plaintiff has failed to satisfy conditions precedent is commonly considered an affirmative defense, for which the defendant has the burden of proof.[153] Accordingly the only time plaintiffs need address conditions precedent at the summary judgment or trial stage of the litigation is when borrower-defendants have properly raised a condition precedent defense or properly denied, in

---

[149] Fla. Stat. § 673.3081(1).
[150] Fla. Stat. § 673.3081, official comment.
[151] *Deutsche Bank Nat'l Tr. Co., Etc. v. Alaqua Prop.*, 190 So. 3d 662, 665 (Fla. 5th DCA 2016).
[152] The pre-suit default notice must of course be authenticated and overcome any hearsay objections, in order to qualify as admissible summary judgment evidence. This is routinely done by affidavit.
[153] *Custer Med. Ctr. v. United Auto. Ins. Co.*, 62 So. 3d 1086, 1096 (Fla. 2010) (A "defending party's assertion that a plaintiff has failed to satisfy conditions precedent necessary to trigger contractual duties under an existing agreement is generally viewed as an affirmative defense, for which the defensive pleader has the burden of pleading and persuasion."); *Deutsche Bank Nat'l Trust Co. v. Quinion*, 198 So. 3d 701, 703 (Fla. 2d DCA 2016) (explaining that when the bank alleges compliance with conditions precedent, "the burden fell to the [borrowers] to first frame that issue [of noncompliance], specifically and with particularity, in their answer."); *Bank of Am., N.A. v. Asbury*, 165 So. 3d 808, 809 (Fla. 2d DCA 2015) (failure to raise non-compliance with condition precedent until trial barred it as a defense). *But see Palma v. JPMorgan Chase Bank, NA*, 208 So. 3d 771, 774 (Fla. 5th DCA 2016) (a sufficiently specific denial of the performance of a condition precedent shifts the burden to the plaintiff to prove compliance with the particular condition precedent, distinguishing *Custer Med. Ctr. v. United Auto. Ins. Co.*, 62 So. 3d 1086 (Fla. 2010) by interpreting *Custer* as applicable only to defendants who assert a condition precedent defense to avoid liability under an agreement).

their pleadings, a plaintiff's allegation that it has met conditions precedent.[154] Otherwise borrower-defendants waive the defense related to conditions precedent and thereby eliminate the issue from the foreclosure litigation.[155]

Fla. R. Civ. P. 1.120(c) permits the satisfaction of a condition precedent to be generally pled, and provides that a denial of such must be made "specifically and with particularity." A denial or defense to conditions precedent must therefore meet a heightened or special pleading requirement under Rule 1.120(c).[156] When a plaintiff alleges generally the occurrence of a condition precedent, and the defendant fails to deny the occurrence with particularity, then the defendant has no right to demand proof from the plaintiff of the occurrence of such condition and has waived the conditions precedent defense.[157] A defendant, therefore, has the burden of identifying the particular unfulfilled condition precedent before the burden reverts to the plaintiff to prove the satisfaction of the condition precedent, or at the summary judgment stage, to establish there is no genuine issue of fact that the plaintiff has complied with the specified condition precedent.[158]

The premise underlying Rule 1.120(c) is that pleadings should make absolutely clear what the issues are to be adjudicated in the litigation.[159] A general denial of compliance with conditions precedent fails to provide the requisite notice to a plaintiff of the type of proof a plaintiff will need to refute the defense at trial or at summary judgment.

Furthermore, in foreclosure suits, a plaintiff need only prove that it substantially complied with conditions precedent.[160] Moreover, a breach of a condition precedent does not preclude the enforcement of an otherwise valid contract, absent some prejudice.[161]

---

[154] *See Bank of Am. v. Asbury*, 165 So. 3d 808, 810 (Fla. 2d DCA 2015); *Cooke v. Ins. Co. of N. Am.*, 652 So. 2d 1154, 1156 (Fla. 2d DCA 1995); *Scarborough Assocs. v. Financial Federal Savings & Loan Ass'n of Dade Cnty.*, 647 So. 2d 1001, 1004 (Fla. 3d DCA 1994).

[155] *Bank of Am. v. Asbury*, 165 So. 3d 808, 809-10 (Fla. 2d DCA 2015). *Cooke v. Ins. Co. of N. Am.*, 652 So. 2d 1154, 1156 (Fla. 2d DCA 1995); *Scarborough Assocs. v. Financial Federal Savings & Loan Ass'n of Dade Cnty.*, 647 So. 2d 1001, 1004 (Fla. 3d DCA 1994).

[156] *Bank of Am. v. Asbury*, 165 So. 3d 808, 809-10 (Fla. 2d DCA 2015).

[157] *Bank of Am. v. Asbury*, 165 So. 3d 808, 811 (Fla. 2d DCA 2015); *Griffin v. Am. Gen. Life & Acc. Ins. Co.*, 752 So. 2d 621, 623 n.1 (Fla. 2d DCA 1999); *Cooke v. Ins. Co. of N. Am.*, 652 So. 2d 1154, 1156 (Fla. 2d DCA 1995); *Scarborough Assocs. v. Financial Federal Savings & Loan Ass'n of Dade Cnty.*, 647 So. 2d 1001, 1004 (Fla. 3d DCA 1994).

[158] *See In re Std. Jury Instructions-Contract & Bus. Cases*, 116 So. 3d 284, 319-21 (Fla. 2013); *Griffin v. Am. Gen. Life & Accident Ins. Co.*, 752 So. 2d 621, 623 n.1 (Fla. 2d DCA 1999); *Sheriff of Orange County v. Boultbee*, 595 So. 2d 985 (Fla. 5th DCA 1992); *Fidelity & Cas. Co. of New York v. Tiedtke*, 207 So. 2d 40 (Fla. 4th DCA 1968), *quashed on other grounds*, 222 So. 2d 206 (Fla. 1969).

[159] *Bank of Am. v. Asbury*, 165 So. 3d 808, 810-11 (Fla.2d DCA 2015).

[160] *Fannie Mae v. Hawthorne*, 197 So. 3d 1237, 1240 (Fla. 4th DCA 2016); *Lopez v. JP Morgan Chase*, 187 So. 3d 343, 345 (Fla. 4th DCA 2016); *Green Tree Servicing, LLC v. Milam*, 177 So. 3d 7, 13 (Fla. 2d DCA 2015); *Bank of N.Y. Mellon v. Nunez*, 180 So. 3d 160, 163 (Fla. 3d DCA 2015); *Bank of N.Y. v. Mieses*, 187 So. 3d 919 (Fla. 3d DCA 2016); *Bayview Loan Servicing, LLC v. Heefner*, 198 So. 3d 918, 920 (Fla. 5th DCA 2016); *Bank of N.Y. Mellon v. Johnson*, 185 So. 3d 594, 597 (Fla. 5th DCA 2016); *Bank of America v. Cadet*, 183 So. 3d 477, 478 (Fla. 3d DCA 2016); *Suntrust Mortg., Inc. v. Garcia*, 186 So. 3d 1036 (Fla. 3d DCA 2016).

[161] *Caraccia v. U.S. Bank, Nat'l Ass'n*, 185 So. 3d 1277, 1280 (Fla. 4th DCA 2016) (quoting *Gorel v. Bank of NY*, 165 So. 3d 44, 47 (Fla. 5th DCA 2015) ("Absent some prejudice, the breach

In short, if a defendant sufficiently pleads a condition precedent defense or a sufficiently specific denial, in order to prevail at summary judgment, a plaintiff must either establish there is no genuine issue of fact that the plaintiff substantially complied with the particular condition precedent[162] or that the defendant was not prejudiced by the lack of compliance.

12-1:10.1f Pre-Acceleration Default Notice[163]

The right of a plaintiff to accelerate all future payments due under the note upon a particular default is authorized by the loan agreement memorialized in the mortgage and note. Paragraph 22 of the vast majority of residential mortgage loans requires plaintiffs send a notice to borrower-defendants outlining various types of information listed in paragraph 22 before acceleration of all future payments due upon a default. Because acceleration is an element of a foreclosure claim, the sending of the paragraph 22 notice is commonly referred to as a condition precedent to foreclosure. However, as explained above, failure to meet a particular condition precedent must be sufficiently pled by defendants before it becomes an issue in the litigation.

An affirmative defense that alleged the Bank failed to comply with the notice requirements in paragraph 15 and 22 of the mortgage has been held to be sufficiently pled as a condition precedent defense.[164] Nonetheless, because the mortgage and note contain numerous provisions, it would seem to defeat the heightened pleading requirement of a condition precedent defense if a defendant was permitted to generally reference either the loan documents or even paragraph 22 itself, as paragraph 22 similarly contains at least six notice requirements.[165]

---

of a condition precedent does not constitute a defense to the enforcement of an otherwise valid contract.")); *Fannie Mae v. Hawthorne*, 197 So. 3d 1237 (Fla. 4th DCA 2016); *Bayview Loan Servicing, LLC v. Heefner*, 198 So. 3d 918, 919 (Fla. 5th DCA 2016); *Deutsche Bank Nat'l Trust Co. v. Hagstrom*, 203 So. 3d 918, 923 n.5 (Fla. 2d DCA 2016); *Vasilevskiy v. Wachovia Bank, N.A.*, 171 So. 3d 192, 192 (Fla. 5th DCA 2015).

[162] *See Lopez v. JP Morgan Chase Bank*, 187 So. 3d 343, 345 (Fla. 4th DCA 2016); *Bank of N.Y. Mellon v. Nunez*, 180 So. 3d 160, 162 (Fla. 3d DCA 2015); *Green Tree Servicing, LLC v. Milam*, 177 So. 3d 7, 13 (Fla. 2d DCA 2015).

[163] Commonly referred to in foreclosure litigation as, alternatively, the *breach letter, demand letter,* the *default notice,* or the *notice of intent to accelerate.*

[164] *Colon v. JP Morgan Chase Bank, N.A.*, 162 So. 3d 195, 197 (Fla. 5th DCA 2015); *DiSalvo v. SunTrust Mortg., Inc.*, 115 So. 3d 438, 439-41 (Fla. 2d DCA 2013) (stating that the defendant's denial "that they had received the required notice and alleg[ation] that SunTrust had not complied with any of the conditions precedent expressed in Section 22 of the mortgage . . . was legally sufficient to dispute SunTrust's allegations that all conditions precedent had been met.").

[165] Paragraph 22 of most residential mortgage loans contain the following, or nearly identical, language:

> Acceleration; Remedies. Lender shall give notice to Borrower prior to acceleration following Borrower's breach of any covenant or agreement in this Security Instrument (but not prior if acceleration under Section 18 unless Applicable Law provides otherwise). The notice shall specify: (a) the default; (b) the action required to cure the default: (c) a date, not less than 30 days from the date the notice is given to Borrower, by which the default must be cured; and (d) that failure to cure the default on or before the date specified in the notice may result in acceleration of the sums secured by this Security Instrument, foreclosure by judicial proceeding and sale of

In foreclosure summary judgment proceedings, if the properly pled condition precedent defense is based on paragraph 22, plaintiffs must authenticate and lay the proper predicate so that a copy of the actual pre-acceleration default notice sent to the borrower-defendant is contained in plaintiff's summary judgment evidence along with plaintiff's affidavit testimony that the notice was properly sent to the borrower-defendant.[166] The only other alternative available to plaintiffs is to rely upon court precedent to establish, via summary judgment evidence, that the defendants could not have been prejudiced by the lack of notice.[167] It seems obvious that it is easier for plaintiffs to obtain summary judgment by the former method—introducing the pre-acceleration notice with the relevant affidavit testimony in support of summary judgment.

Defendants who seek summary judgment premised on the lack of pre-acceleration default notice (breach letter) compliant with the terms of section or paragraph 22, must, as described above, first adequately raise the issue in their pleadings.[168] When defendants move for summary judgment, it is their burden to produce summary judgment evidence to show the plaintiff did not properly send the subject notice, or that the content of the subject notice was somehow deficient.[169] Defendants who move for summary judgment based on the insufficient content of a default notice must produce the default notice as summary judgment or admissible evidence because as movants, they have the burden of proof. In most instances this requires Defendants attest that the subject default notice is the notice they in fact received.

Further, it would be wise for Defendants moving for summary judgment on this premise to also show that there is no genuine issue of fact that they were in fact prejudiced by the lack of notice.

12-1:10.1g Amounts Due and Owing

The total amount presently owed by the borrower is proven through the mortgage and note,[170] business records containing loan payment history, and records establishing the variable interest rates for those mortgage loans that allow adjustable rates

---

    the Property. The notice shall further inform Borrower of the right to reinstate after acceleration and the right to assert in the foreclosure proceeding the non-existence of a default or any other defense of Borrower to acceleration and foreclosure.

[166] *See Colon v. JP Morgan Chase Bank, N.A.*, 162 So. 3d 195, 198 (Fla. 5th DCA 2015) (summary judgment reversed because the Bank never filed an authenticated copy of the breach letter in support of its motion for summary judgment).

[167] *See* Section 12-1:6.1e.

[168] Fla. R. Civ. P. 1.120(c) requires that a denial of conditions precedent "shall be made specifically and with particularity." The purpose of the rule is "to put the burden on the defendant to identify the specific condition that the plaintiff failed to perform—so that the plaintiff may be prepared to produce proof or cure the omission, if it can be cured." *Godshalk v. Countrywide Home Loans Servicing, L.P.*, 81 So. 3d 626, 626 (Fla. 5th DCA 2012).

[169] *See JP Morgan Chase Bank, N.A. v. Ostrander*, 201 So. 3d 1281, 1283 (Fla. 2d DCA 2016) (The owners' affidavits failed to satisfy their burden to prove a lack of notice because they did not address whether the bank fulfilled the notice requirement by sending the notice via first class mail, and, therefore, they were not entitled to summary judgment.).

[170] The mortgage and note contain the amount of the original principal, interest rates, authorized loan charges and fees (including for attorney fees and expenses of the suit), the date the loan was made, and variable or adjustable interest rates, if any.

but do not otherwise reflect whether the rate actually changed and if so, when and for how much.[171] Affidavits by plaintiffs' counsel (with accompanying and supporting documents) are used to establish the amount plaintiffs have incurred for attorney fees and costs of the foreclosure suit. An affidavit by a licensed attorney must also be used to show the reasonableness of the attorney fees sought.

12-1:10.1h Non-Borrower Defendants' Affirmative Defenses

A line of cases has developed as legal authority to nullify the affirmative defenses raised by those foreclosure defendants who are named because they acquired interests in the property after and subject to the plaintiff's validly recorded mortgage, e.g., subsequent owners and junior lienholders. Essentially, these cases hold that such defendants do not have standing to contest foreclosure.[172] Therefore, it would behoove foreclosure plaintiffs to ensure they raise these type of defendants' standing to contest foreclosure in the pleadings so that they can subsequently move for partial summary judgment as to these defendants' affirmative defenses.

---

[171] *Salauddin v. Bank of Am., N.A.*, 150 So. 3d 1189 (Fla. 4th DCA 2014).

[172] *Spinney v. Winter Park Bldg. & Loan Ass'n*, 120 Fla. 453, 162 So. 899, 904 (1935) ("[I]f a recorded mortgage is valid on its face, a subsequent purchaser 'is assumed to have recognized it as a valid lien against the property which he is buying."); *Clay Cty. Land Tr. #08-04-25-0078-014-27, Orange Park Tr. Servs., LLC v. JP Morgan Chase Bank, Nat'l Ass'n*, 152 So. 3d 83, 84 (Fla. 1st DCA 2014) ("Because appellant was not a party to the mortgage, appellee correctly asserts that appellant does not have standing to challenge any violation of these mortgage terms."); *LaFaille v. Nationstar Mortg., LLC*, 197 So. 3d 1246 (Fla. 3d DCA 2016) ("neither of the appellants was a party to, or a 'borrower' under, the mortgage or note, and thus, have no standing to assert this [conditions precedent] defense."); *Castillo v. Deutsche Bank Nat'l Trust*, 89 So. 3d 1069, 1069-70 (appellant who was not a party or third-party beneficiary of a common-law trust lacked the right to challenge the right of plaintiff, a trust, to bring the foreclosure action); *Irwin v. Grogan-Cole*, 590 So. 2d 1102, 1104 (Fla. 5th DCA 1991) (holding that a subsequent purchaser who took subject to a superior mortgage could not challenge the running of the statute of limitations); *Eurovest, Ltd. v. Segall*, 528 So. 2d 482, 483 (Fla. 3d DCA 1988) (a purchaser who takes title to property subject to a prior recorded mortgage is "estopped from contesting the validity of the mortgage."); *Nesbitt v. Citicorp Savings of Fla.*, 514 So. 2d 371 (Fla. 3d DCA 1987) (affirming trial court summary judgment of foreclosure over the purchaser's objection based on the mortgage being usurious); *Whitburn, LLC v. Wells Fargo Bank, N.A.*, 190 So. 3d 1087, 1091-92 (Fla. 2d DCA 2015) (a third-party purchaser's "interest in [a] foreclosure proceeding is not a legally cognizable interest because even though it now holds legal title to the property, it purchased the property subject to [the bank's] foreclosure proceeding and superior interest in the property."); *Pealer v. Wilmington Tr. Nat'l Ass'n*, 212 So. 3d 1137, 1138-39 (Fla. 2d DCA 2017) (Sleet, J., concurring) ("[U]ntil the Pealers assert their right of redemption and attempt to clear title to the property, their interest in the bank's foreclosure action on the note and mortgage is speculative and therefore insufficient to support their standing to challenge the bank's standing to foreclose or admission of evidence at trial.").

CHAPTER 13

Foreclosure Trials and Evidence

Jennifer Chapkin

13-1 Introduction

Foreclosure trials in Florida are conducted in any number of ways by differing jurisdictions. This chapter presents the general procedures for setting a trial, elements to be proven and typical exhibits required for presentation at trial, but is not intended to be exhaustive. Trials in foreclosure cases should be treated individually as the facts of each case dictate, and a trial lawyer's preparation should be guided by the local rules and the unique claims and defenses involved.

13-2 Setting Trials

Florida Rule of Civil Procedure 1.440 governs setting all cases for trial. A case must be at issue before it may be set for trial, and if the parties are forced to trial prematurely, the trial court commits reversible error.[1] Consequently, it is important to carefully consider whether a matter is at issue before proceeding to trial. Once a case is at issue, any party may serve a notice advising the court and all parties that trial may be scheduled.[2] The notice should include an estimate of the time needed for trial and whether the trial is to be by jury.[3] In Florida, mortgage foreclosure is an equitable proceeding which does not afford parties a right to a jury trial.[4] Where a compulsory counterclaim is asserted, a party is entitled to a jury trial on the issues raised which are shared by the equitable claim.[5] Upon receipt of a notice of readiness for trial, the

---

[1] *Lopez v. U.S. Bank*, 116 So. 3d 640 (Fla. 3d DCA 2013), *aff'd by Moise v. JP Morgan Chase Bank Nat'l Ass'n*, 137 So. 3d 1192 (Fla. 3d DCA 2014). A case is at issue "[a]fter any motions directed to the last pleading served has been disposed of or, if no such motions are served, 20 days after service of the last pleading." Fla. R. Civ. P. 1.440(a).

[2] Fla. R. Civ. P. 1.440(b).

[3] Fla. R. Civ. P. 1.440(b); Florida Statute § 702.01 (2012); *Kinney v. Countrywide Home Loans Servicing, L.P.*, 165 So. 3d 691 (Fla. 4th DCA 2015) (Foreclosures are to be tried without a jury).

[4] *Norris v. Paps*, 615 So. 2d 735, 737 (Fla. 2d DCA 1993).

[5] *Norris v.Paps*, 615 So. 2d 735, 737 (Fla. 2d DCA 1993); *Hightower v. Bigoney*, 156 So. 2d 501 (Fla. 1963) ("[W]e hold that the filing of a compulsory counterclaim for relief cognizable at law in an action for equitable relief does not constitute the counterclaimant's waiver to the right to a jury trial of the issues raised by said compulsory counterclaim, provided, jury trial is timely demanded.").

clerk is to submit the notice and case file to the court for setting of the trial.[6] In many foreclosure divisions, however, judges have specific procedures for advising of readiness for trial and a foreclosure clerk or case manager may be tasked with setting the trial without submission of the court file.

13-2:1 Readiness for Trial

An action is at issue after any motion directed to the last served pleading has been adjudicated.[7] For example, a motion to strike affirmative defenses is a motion directed to an answer and affirmative defenses, so while that motion remains pending, the pleadings cannot close.[8] If no such motion is filed, then 20 days after service of the last pleading is the trigger date for a case being at issue.[9] A party can also waive the opportunity to file a motion directed to the last pleading.[10] This is a common occurrence when a plaintiff elects to notice the matter for trial rather than file a reply or a motion directed at the answer and affirmative defenses. Note that while pleadings involving a counterclaim are intertwined with the original claim, pleadings involving a cross claim may be treated independently and do not preclude the case from being at issue and ready for trial.[11] Additionally, procedural readiness for trial should not be confused with practical readiness for trial. Pending discovery or a pending motion for leave to amend the pleadings will not prevent the pleadings from being closed.[12]

A case is said to be ready for trial when it is at issue but in this context the term "ready" is used in a legal sense to mean that the pleadings are closed. It does not necessarily mean the lawyers are prepared to try the case. Often the lawyers will not be ready for trial when the date is set because they will not have completed all discovery. However, the fact that discovery remains to be completed has no bearing on whether the case is at issue and it is not a valid reason to delay the entry of an order setting trial.[13]

13-2:2 Timing and Notice Requirements

Once a case is properly noticed as "at issue" the court may set the trial.[14] If the parties notice the case and it is in fact at issue, the trial court must act within a reasonable time period in scheduling the matter.[15] If a case is not specifically noticed, but the

---

[6] Fla. R. Civ. P. 1.440(b).

[7] Fla. R. Civ. P. 1.440(a).

[8] *Leeds v. C.C. Chemical Corp.*, 280 So. 2d 718 (Fla. 3d DCA 1973).

[9] Fla. R. Civ. P. 1.440(a).

[10] *Charter Review Comm'n of Orange County v. Scott*, 627 So. 2d 520, 522 (Fla. 5th DCA 1993), *quashed on other grounds*, 647 So. 2d 835 (Fla. 1994) (holding that when appellants "voluntarily proceeded with the hearing and fully participated without raising any objection under Rule 1.440, [they] waived any error pursuant to Rule 1.440.").

[11] Fla. R. Civ. P. 1.440(a).

[12] *Garcia v. Lincare, Inc.*, 906 So. 2d 1268 (Fla. 5th DCA 2005).

[13] Philip J. Padovano, *Florida Civil Practice*, § 15.2 [**3] (2004-2005 ed.).

[14] Fla. R. Civ. P. 1.440(c).

[15] *Rolle v. Birken*, 994 So. 2d 1129 (Fla. 3d DCA 2008); *City of Miami v. Dade County*, 321 So. 2d 140 (Fla. 3d DCA 1975) ("[I]t is the duty of, and the trial court is required, to enter an order setting the cause for trial after notice is given that the cause is ready for trial, and if, in fact, it is ready for trial.").

court identifies that the pleadings are closed, the court may *sua sponte* enter an order setting the trial.[16] The trial may not be set to take place less than 30 days from the service of the notice for trial (or the trial order if the court sets the trial).[17] The trial order should be served on all parties, even if they have been defaulted.[18]

13-3 Witnesses

Witnesses must be disclosed in accordance with the court's trial order. General statements such as reservation of a right to call "'any and all necessary' impeachment and rebuttal witnesses" is insufficient.[19] If a party attempts to call a witness who was not previously disclosed, it is within the purview of the court to exclude the witness.[20] The court's discretion should consider the ability to cure any possible prejudice to the surprised party, any possible intentional noncompliance (or bad faith noncompliance) with the trial order, or possible disruption of the efficient trial of the case.[21] Discretion takes into account local rules and customs, and the Florida Supreme Court has specifically endorsed this practice by local jurisdictions.[22] Where no prejudice occurs to the surprised party, or where the prejudice can be cured, the court should not strike the surprise witness.[23] Additionally, where the witness sought to be called is the sole or most important witness for the party, the trial court is to exercise caution to avoid depriving a party the opportunity to present evidence.[24]

---

[16] Fla. R. Civ. P. 1.440(c).

[17] *Precision Constructors, Inc. v. Valtec Construction Corp.*, 825 So. 2d 1062 (Fla. 3d DCA 2002).

[18] *Cellular Warehouse, Inc. v. GH Cellular, LLC*, 957 So. 2d 662 (Fla. 3d DCA 2007). Service of the trial order shall be in accordance with Fla. R. Civ. P. 1.080. *See* Fla. R. Civ. P. 1.440(c).

[19] *Binger v. King Pest Control*, 401 So. 2d 1310 (Fla. 1981).

[20] *Florida Marine Enterprises v. Bailey*, 632 So. 2d 649 (Fla. 4th DCA 1994) (finding no abuse of discretion when trial court struck a witness who was disclosed three days prior to trial and only by name).

[21] *Binger v. King Pest Control*, 401 So. 2d 1310 (Fla. 1981):

> ("The discretion to do so must not be exercised blindly, however, and should be guided largely by a determination as to whether use of the undisclosed witness will prejudice the objecting party. Prejudice in this sense refers to the surprise in fact of the objecting party, and it is not dependent on the adverse nature of the testimony. Other factors which may enter into the trial court's exercise of discretion are: (i) the objecting party's ability to cure the prejudice or, similarly, his independent knowledge of the existence of the witness; (ii) the calling party's possible intentional, or bad faith, noncompliance with the pretrial order; and (iii) the possible disruption of the orderly and efficient trial of the case (or other cases). If after considering these factors, and any others that are relevant, the trial court concludes that use of the undisclosed witness will not substantially endanger the fairness of the proceeding, the pretrial order mandating disclosure should be modified and the witness should be allowed to testify."). *See also Gutierrez v. Vargas*, 239 So. 3d 615 (Fla. Mar. 2018).

[22] *Florida Marine Enterprises v. Bailey*, 632 So. 2d 649 (Fla. 4th DCA 1994).

[23] *State v. Rolack*, 104 So. 3d 1286, 1288 (Fla. 5th DCA 2013) (trial court departed from the essential requirements of the law by striking a witness where any potential prejudice could be cured by affording an opportunity to depose the witness and a less extreme sanction was available to the trial court).

[24] *Deutsche Bank Nat'l Trust Co. v. Perez*, 180 So. 3d 1186, 1190 (Fla. 3d DCA 2015) (Defendant who was on notice that a corporate representative would testify for bank and made no effort to learn the identity of the witness or take a pretrial deposition was not prejudiced.). *Deut-*

13-3:1 Fact Witnesses

In a residential mortgage foreclosure trial, the plaintiff's primary witness is usually a records custodian or other representative of the mortgagee or loan servicer. The designated witness may testify regarding their individual knowledge, but primarily testifies about the collective knowledge of the company.[25] Generally, this testimony will be based upon the records maintained by the servicer, and possibly prior servicers of the loan. Proof of contractual authority to testify is not required for a witness to lay the foundation for the business records exception to hearsay.[26] The person who actually prepares the documents does not need to testify, as long as other circumstantial evidence and testimony can otherwise establish the trustworthiness of the information contained in the records.[27] It is not necessary that the witness be employed by the servicer or lender at the time the business records were created as long as the witness establishes the necessary foundation for admitting documents.[28] If prior servicer records are incorporated into the current servicer's records, it is important that the witness be able to testify that the accuracy of prior servicer records was verified.[29] This may be done by describing the process utilized to verify the data provided by a prior servicer, commonly referred to as the "boarding process."[30] Once the witness has testified regarding verification of the prior servicer's records, if nothing else in the record establishes that the loan information received from a prior servicer was untrustworthy, then the records may be accepted as those of the current servicer.[31]

13-3:2 Expert Witnesses

Florida Evidence Code, Sections 90.702 governs use of expert witnesses in all trials, including foreclosure actions.[32] Expert witnesses in foreclosure actions are rare, however, because these cases are fact-intensive and generally do not require special-

---

sche Bank Trust Co. Ams. v. Merced, 238 So. 3d 438, 441 (Fla. 5th DCA 2018) ("The effect of striking Deutsche Bank's sole witness was to deny it the right to introduce dispositive evidence.").

[25] *Carriage Hill v. JBH Roofing & Constructors, Inc.*, 109 So. 3d 329 (Fla. 4th DCA 2013).

[26] *U.S. Bank Nat'l Ass'n v. Clarke*, 192 So. 3d 620, 621 (Fla. 4th DCA 2016).

[27] *U.S. v. Parker*, 749 F.2d 628 (11th Cir. 1984); *U.S. v. Pfeiffer*, 539 F.2d 668 (8th Cir. 1976) ("The reason for excluding business records from the hearsay rule is their circumstantial guarantee of trustworthiness. It is not necessary that the declarant be present if the knowledge of the custodian of the record demonstrates that a document has been prepared and kept in the course of a regularly conducted business activity.").

[28] *Bank of America, N.A. v. Delgado*, 166 So. 3d 857, 860 (Fla. 3d DCA 2015).

[29] *WAMCO v. Integrated Elec. Environ., Inc.*, 903 So. 2d 230 (Fla. 2d DCA 2005); *Bank of New York v. Calloway*, 157 So. 3d 1064 (Fla. 4th DCA 2015); *AS Lily LLC v. Morgan*, 164 So. 3d 124 (Fla. 2d DCA 2015); *Bank of N.Y. Mellon v. Burgiel*, 248 So. 3d 237 (Fla. 5th DCA 2018).

[30] *Sas v. Federal Nat'l Mortg. Ass'n*, 165 So. 3d 849, 851 (Fla. 2d DCA 2015).

[31] *WAMCO v. Integrated Elec. Environ., Inc.*, 903 So. 2d 230 (Fla. 2d DCA 2005).

[32] "If scientific, technical, or other specialized knowledge will assist the trier of fact in understanding the evidence or in determining a fact in issue, a witness qualified as an expert by knowledge, skill, expertise, training, or education may testify about it in the form of an opinion; however, the opinion or otherwise, if: (1) the testimony is based upon sufficient facts or data; (2) the testimony is the product of reliable principles and methods; and (3) the witness has applied the principles and methods reliably to the facts of the case."

ized knowledge.[33] Use of an expert to testify as to whether a plaintiff has standing, or whether a mortgage is a binding contract, is improper as the interpretation of Florida law is not an appropriate subject for expert testimony.[34]

13-3:3 Subpoenas for Witness Testimony

For plaintiffs wishing to call a defendant homeowner to the stand, trial subpoenas may be necessary as defendants who are represented by counsel are not otherwise required to appear in person at trial.[35] A subpoena, however, may be issued by counsel of record in the case, and compels the attendance of the subject witness or party for testimony before the court.[36] If a witness is required to appear at trial pursuant to a subpoena and fails to appear, the court may initiate contempt proceedings by taking sworn testimony under oath regarding the service of a subpoena and then issuing a show cause order.[37] The striking of a defendant's pleadings at trial as a sanction for failure to appear pursuant to a subpoena is improper and will be reversed on appeal without a showing that the failure to appear was willful.[38]

13-4 Proof of Elements at Trial

Each element of a foreclosure action must be established at trial by competent testimony and evidence. The elements that must be proven in a Florida foreclosure trial are: 1) an agreement, 2) a default of that agreement, 3) acceleration of the amounts due and owing, and 4) the amount due.[39] The trial judge has broad discretion to admit or exclude evidence, but that discretion is limited by the rules of evidence.[40] Relevant evidence is that which tends to prove or disprove a material fact.[41] As a breach

---

[33] Fla. Stat. § 90.702; however, the facts or data upon which the expert relied to form his/her opinion do not need to be admitted into evidence if the facts or data are "of a type reasonably relied upon by experts in the subject to support the opinion expressed." Fla. Stat. § 90.704.

[34] *Hann v. Balogh*, 920 So. 2d 1250 (Fla. 2d DCA 2006), *Lee County v. Barnett Banks, Inc.*, 711 So. 2d 34 (Fla. 2d DCA 1999), *Siegel v. Husak*, 943 So. 2d 209 (Fla. 3d DCA 2006).

[35] Fla. R. Civ. P. 1.410(b)(1).

[36] Fla. R. Civ. P. 1.410(a) and (b).

[37] *See Paris v. Paris*, 427 So. 2d 1080 (trial judge is required to issue an Order to Show Cause prior to a hearing any charge of indirect criminal contempt, and the order must be premised upon a sworn affidavit or sworn testimony). *Also see Pugliese v. Pugliese*, 347 So. 2d 422 (Fla. 1977) (providing for civil contempt if the purpose of the proceeding is to coerce action or non-action, and including a purge provision so that "the contemnor 'carries the key to his cell in his own pocket.'" (*citing Demetree v. Stae*, 89 So. 2d 498 (Fla. 1956)) Furthermore, the Florida Supreme Court found that indirect criminal contempt may be found based on conduct outside the court's immediate presence, punishable "to vindicate the authority of the court." *Pugliese v. Pugliese*, 347 So. 2d 422 (Fla. 1977).

[38] *Trupei v. City of Lighthouse Point*, 506 So. 2d 19 (Fla. 4th DCA 1987) (striking of pleadings and entering a default is the most severe sanction, and requires the court to first make findings that the failure to appear was willful or done in bad faith, or was a deliberate and contumacious disregard of the court's authority).

[39] *Kelsey v. SunTrust Mortgage, Inc.*, 131 So.3d 825,826 (Fla. 3d DCA 2014). *Black Point Assets, Inc. v. Federal National Mortgage Association*, 220 So. 3d 566 (Fla. 5thDCA 2017).

[40] *Thigpen v. United Parcel Services, Inc.*, 990 So. 2d 639 (Fla. 4th DCA 2008).

[41] Fla. Stat. § 90.401.

of contract action, a mortgage foreclosure trial requires the introduction of certain exhibits which establish a valid contract, a material breach, and damages.[42] Florida Courts also recognize satisfaction of conditions precedent as an essential element to be proven at trial.[43] Below is a list of the most commonly utilized documents in a foreclosure trial. A summary of the evidentiary basis for the admission of the documents is included in Appendix A, 1-012.

   a. Original note

   b. Original/certified copy of the mortgage

   c. Original/certified copy of the assignment(s) of mortgage

   d. Loan payment history (including the date of default)

   e. Demand/Acceleration letter

   f. Proof of mailing demand/acceleration letter (return receipt card or letter log)

   g. Judgment figures (amounts due and owing which must correlate to the Loan payment history)

   h. Power of attorney (reflecting authority of the servicer to act on behalf of the named plaintiff or owner of the loan)[44]

   i. Pooling and servicing agreement and mortgage loan schedule

   j. Certified copy of association declarations (if an association has been named as a defendant and is contesting lien priority)

   k. Merger documents (if any prior lenders/holders have merged into or otherwise been acquired by another entity who subsequently sought to enforce or otherwise transfer/sell the loan)

13-4:1 The Contract: Mortgage and Note

The subject mortgage contract, along with the promissory note reflecting the debt secured by the mortgage, is the contract which must be introduced at a foreclosure trial. Florida courts have ruled that promissory notes are not hearsay.[45] If the original

---

[42] *See, e.g., J.J. Gumberg Co. v. Janis Services, Inc.*, 847 So. 2d 1048, 1049 (Fla. 4th DCA 2003).

[43] *Figueroa v. Federal Nat'l Mortg. Ass'n*, 180 So. 3d 1110 (Fla. 5th DCA 2015) (*quoting Gorel v. Bank of New York Mellon*, 165 So. 3d 44, 47 (Fla. 5th DCA 2015)) ("The subject mortgage provides that all notices to the borrower, which would include the default letter, must either be sent by first class mail or actually delivered to Appellant. '[A] mortgagee's right to the security for a mortgage is dependent upon its compliance with the terms of the mortgage contract, and it cannot foreclose until it has proven compliance.'").

[44] *Deutsche Bank Tr. Co. v. Merced*, 238 So. 3d 438 (Fla. 5th DCA 2018) ("Although the power of attorney was excluded, it was irrelevant to the witness's ability to testify on behalf of the loan servicer, PNC.") "Proof of contractual authority to testify is not required for a witness to lay the foundation for the business records exception to hearsay because the witness may testify to matters within his or her personal knowledge."

[45] *Deutsche Bank Nat'l Trust Co. Etc. v. Alaqua Prop., Etc.*, 190 So. 3d 662, 665 (Fla. 5th DCA 2016) ("An original promissory note is not hearsay and is admissible for its independent legal significance—to establish the existence of the contractual relationship and right and

note is available, it may be admitted as self-authenticating commercial paper.[46] If the original note has been filed with the clerk of court and is contained within the court file, the trial judge may not want to disturb the file by having the original removed. In this instance, the trial judge may take judicial notice of the original document being housed within the court file.[47] The original mortgage, if available, may accepted into evidence as self-authenticating as well.[48] If a copy of the mortgage is presented, its authenticity need not be separately proven as long as the copy is certified by the recorder's office responsible for maintaining the document.[49]

13-4:1.1 Lost Note

In order to obtain a final judgment at trial, the original note must be produced to the trial court or a satisfactory explanation must be given as to why the note cannot be produced.[50] If the note is missing at the time of trial, witness testimony and competent evidence may be used to re-establish the note, permitting the trial court to consider a copy of the note as the original. Enforcement of a lost note requires the plaintiff to prove that it was entitled to enforce the note at the time the instrument was lost, or that the plaintiff acquired ownership of the note from a person or entity who was entitled to enforce the instrument at the time of loss.[51]

A copy of the note, properly authenticated, may assist the plaintiff in providing proof of the terms of the instrument.[52] The plaintiff seeking to enforce a lost note at trial must also ensure adequate protection for the party the note is enforced against,

---

obligations of the parties to the note, regardless of the truth of any assertions made in the document.").

[46] Fla. Stat. § 90.902(8).

[47] Fla. Stat. § 90.202(6).

[48] Fla. Stat. § 90.202(4) (a document authorized by law to be recorded or filed and actually recorded or filed in a public office); note that while a document may be self-authenticating, this argument applies to the admissibility of a document and not to the weight assigned by the trial court.

[49] Fla. Stat. § 90.902(1); *Wells Fargo Bank v. Ousley*, 212 So. 3d 1056, 1058 (Fla. 1st DCA 2016).

[50] *Deutsche Bank Nat'l Trust Co. v. Huber*, 137 So. 3d 562, 564 ("This court has recognized that possession of the original note is a significant fact in deciding whether the possessor is entitled to enforce its terms." *Clarke*, 87 So. 3d at 61 (citing *Riggs v. Aurora Loan Servs., LLC*, 36 So. 3d 932, 933 (Fla. 4th DCA 2010)). Because a promissory note is a negotiable instrument, a plaintiff seeking to foreclose on a defendant *must produce the original note* (or provide satisfactory explanation of the failure to produce) *and surrender it to the court* or court clerk *before* the issuance of a final judgment in order to take it out of the stream of commerce. See, e.g., *Downing v. First Nat'l Bank of Lake City*, 81 So. 2d 486, 488 (Fla. 1955); *Clarke*, 87 So. 3d at 60-61; *Johnston v. Hudlett*, 32 So. 3d 700, 704 (Fla. 4th DCA 2010).

[51] *Beaumont v. Bank of New York Mellon*, 81 So. 3d 553, 554-55 (Fla. 5th DCA 2012).

[52] Fla. Stat. § 673.3091. Enforcement of lost, destroyed, or stolen instrument

(1) A person not in possession of an instrument is entitled to enforce the instrument if:

(a) The person seeking to enforce the instrument was entitled to enforce the instrument when loss of possession occurred, or has directly or indirectly acquired ownership of the instrument from a person who was entitled to enforce the instrument when loss of possession occurred;

(b) The loss of possession was not the result of a transfer by the person or a lawful seizure; and

in the event that a subsequent party later comes forward with the original and seeks to enforce it.[53]

13-4:1.2 Right to Enforce Contract ("Standing")

Standing to foreclose means that the plaintiff is entitled to enforce the note and mortgage obligation.[54] Every foreclosing plaintiff has the obligation to prove that it has

---

      (c) The person cannot reasonably obtain possession of the instrument because the instrument was destroyed, its whereabouts cannot be determined, or it is in the wrongful possession of an unknown person or a person that cannot be found or is not amenable to service of process.

  (2) A person seeking enforcement of an instrument under subsection (1) must prove the terms of the instrument and the person's right to enforce the instrument. If that proof is made, s. 673.3081 [proof of signatures and status as holder in due course] applies to the case as if the person seeking enforcement had produced the instrument. The court may not enter judgment in favor of the person seeking enforcement unless it finds that the person required to pay the instrument is adequately protected against loss that might occur by reason of a claim by another person to enforce the instrument. Adequate protection may be provided by any reasonable means.

[53] Fla. Stat. § 702.11. Adequate protections for lost, destroyed, or stolen notes in mortgage foreclosure:

  (1) In connection with a mortgage foreclosure, the following constitute reasonable means of providing adequate protection under s. 673.3091, if so found by the court:

      (a) A written indemnification agreement by a person reasonably believed sufficiently solvent to honor such an obligation;

      (b) A surety bond;

      (c) A letter of credit issued by a financial institution;

      (d) A deposit of cash collateral with the clerk of the court; or

      (e) Such other security as the court may deem appropriate under the circumstances.

[54] Every one of Florida's appellate courts have discussed standing at length, but the following excerpt from the Second District Court of Appeal aptly summarizes the law:

"Under section 673.3011, Florida Statutes (2014), a person entitled to enforce a negotiable instrument must be either: (1) the holder of the instrument, (2) a "nonholder in possession of the instrument who has the rights of a holder," or (3) a person not in possession but who has the right to enforce a lost, destroyed, or stolen instrument or an instrument paid by mistake. A holder is a person in possession of the negotiable instrument that is payable either to bearer or to the holder. § 671.201(21)(a), Fla. Stat. (2014). A person in possession of the instrument but who is not the original lender can still be a holder, but only if the instrument bears a special indorsement in his or her favor or a blank indorsement. *See McLean v. JP Morgan Chase Bank Nat'l Ass'n*, 79 So. 3d 170, 173 (Fla. 4th DCA 2012). Absent a special or blank indorsement, "the mere delivery of a note and mortgage, with intention to pass the title, upon a proper consideration, will vest the equitable interest in the person to whom it is so delivered." *Seffar v. Residential Credit Solutions, Inc.*, 160 So. 3d 122, 125 (Fla. 4th DCA 2015) (quoting *McLean*, 79 So. 3d at 173). However, possession of the instrument alone is an insufficient basis to prove standing to foreclose. *See Murray v. HSBC Bank USA*, 157 So. 3d 355, 358 (Fla. 4th DCA 2015). The person trying to

standing to foreclose at the time the complaint is filed.[55] If a plaintiff is substituted into the case after it is filed, but before trial, the substituted plaintiff must prove that its predecessor had standing as it will only acquire the standing of the prior plaintiff.[56] In addition, the newly substituted in plaintiff must also prove that it has standing at the time of trial.[57] The most straightforward way to demonstrate standing to foreclose (if the plaintiff is not the original mortgagee) is by attaching a true and correct copy of the note, bearing a blank indorsement, to the complaint.[58] In cases where plaintiff is asserting standing based upon its status as a "person entitled to enforce" because it is the holder of the instrument, proof who owns the note is not necessary or even relevant to the issue of standing.[59]

13-4:1.3 Additional Evidence of Standing

When a plaintiff does not have the benefit of possession of an endorsed note at the time the complaint is filed, standing to foreclose may be established through an assignment of the note.[60] Mortgage loans which are pooled as part of a securitized trust are subject to servicing agreements which may provide adequate foundation for a plaintiff to prove standing.[61] In these instances, copies of the pooling and servicing

---

enforce the instrument must demonstrate that he or she had standing as of the time the complaint is filed. *McLean*, 79 So. 3d at 173." *St. Clair v. U.S. Bank Nat'l Ass'n*, 173 So. 3d 1045, 1046 (Fla 2d DCA 2015).

[55] *Walsh v. Bank of New York Mellon Trust*, 219 So. 3d 929 (Fla. 5th DCA 2017) ("A crucial element in any mortgage foreclosure proceeding is that the party seeking foreclosure must demonstrate that it has standing to foreclose." *McLean v. JP Morgan Chase Bank Nat'l Ass'n*, 79 So. 3d 170, 173 (Fla. 4th DCA 2012) (citations omitted). Additionally, a "party must have standing to file suit at its inception and may not remedy this defect by subsequently obtaining standing." *Venture Holdings & Acquisitions Grp., LLC v. A.I.M Funding Grp., LLC*, 75 So. 3d 773, 776 (Fla. 4th DCA 2011). Thus, in order to prove standing, the bank was required to introduce admissible evidence that it (or its agent) possessed a properly-indorsed note at the inception of the case. *Focht v. Wells Fargo Bank, N.A*, 124 So. 3d 308, 310-11 (Fla. 2d DCA 2013).

[56] *Powers v. HSBC Bank USA, N.A.*, 202 So. 3d 121, 122, at *3 (Fla. 2d DCA 2016).

[57] *Creadon v. U.S. Bank, N.A.*, 166 So. 3d 952 (Fla. 2nd DCA 2015); *Focht v. Wells Fargo Bank, N.A.*, 124 So. 3d 308, 310 (Fla. 2d DCA 2013).

[58] *ALS-RVC, LLC v. Garvin*, 201 So. 3d 687, 691 (Fla. 4th DCA 2016) (citing *Ortiz v. PNC Bank, Nat'l Ass'n*, 188 So. 3d 923 (Fla. 4th DCA 2016)) ("[I]f a bank admits the original note, either endorsed to the bank or containing a blank endorsement, in the same condition as the copy it attached to the complaint, the evidence is sufficient to establish standing at the time the complaint is filed absent evidence to the contrary.").

[59] *HSBC Bank U.S.A, N.A. v. Buset*, 241 So. 3d 882 (Fla. 3d DCA 2018).

[60] *Verizzo v. Bank of N.Y. Mellon*, 220 So. 3d 1262 (Fla. 2d DCA 2017); *Caballero v. U.S. Bank Nat'l Ass'n*, 189 So. 3d 1044, 1046 (Fla. 2d DCA 2016); *Eaddy v. Bank of America, N.A.*, 197 So. 3d 1278, 1280 (Fla. 2d DCA 2016).

[61] *Deutsche Bank Nat'l Trust Co. v. Marciano*, 190 So. 3d 166 (Fla. 5th DCA 2016) (finding sufficient evidence of physical possession of the note prior to initiation of the foreclosure action where language in the pooling and servicing agreement reflected the transfer); *Bolous v. U.S. Bank Nat'l Ass'n*, 210 So. 3d 691, 694 (Fla. 4th 2016) ("We conclude that the pooling and servicing agreement's terms and corresponding mortgage loan schedule identifying the borrower's loan at issue, along with the other evidence presented through the analyst, was sufficient to demonstrate that the bank was the owner or holder of the borrower's note at the time the bank filed the original complaint.").

agreement (PSA), together with the mortgage loan schedule (MLS), that identifies that this particular loan was part of the trust, should be introduced to establish that the original plaintiff had standing at inception.[62] Standing may also be demonstrated by establishing that the foreclosing plaintiff's agent held physical possession of the note on the plaintiff's behalf, as long as the plaintiff retained the power to exercise control over the note.[63] For a complete discussion of standing, *see* Chapter 4: Standing to Foreclose.

13-4:2 Breach of Contract

Once the existence of a mortgage and note (and standing to enforce the same) are established, the plaintiff at a foreclosure trial must demonstrate that the contract was breached. This is perhaps the easiest element to demonstrate, because it can be accomplished by showing a default, or non-payment, of the mortgage obligation.[64] Most plaintiffs do so through the introduction of a loan payment history which reflects the last payment made (and consequently, the absence of required payments). Such records may be considered hearsay, but proper testimony may qualify them as a hearsay exception.[65] In order to demonstrate non-payment, however, the payment history must first be established as a record of regularly conducted business activity.[66] All of the business record testimony offered by a foreclosure plaintiff must be presented by a custodian or other qualified witness, unless it is otherwise certified.[67] Further, if the current plaintiff or servicer is not the original lender or if there was subsequent ser-

---

[62] *Bolous v. U.S. Bank, N.A.*, 210 So. 3d 691, 694 (Fla 4th DCA 2016); *HSBC Bank U.S.A. v. Alejandre*, 219 So. 3d 831 (Fla. 4th DCA 2017).

[63] *Caraccia v. U.S. Bank, Nat'l Ass'n*, 185 So. 3d 1277 (Fla. 4th DCA 2016) (*citing Deakter v. Menendez*, 830 So. 2d 124, 128 (Fla. 3d DCA 2002)) ("Even where a third party has physical possession of the note, so long as the plaintiff 'had the power to exercise control over it, then [the plaintiff] had constructive possession of the note.'").

[64] *Federal Home Loan Mortg. Corp. v. Taylor*, 318 So. 2d 203, 207 (Fla. 1st DCA 1975) ("It is fully established in the jurisprudence of this stat that an acceleration clause or promise in an installment note or mortgage confers a contract right upon the note or mortgage holder which he may elect to invoke upon default and to seek enforcement.").

[65] *Bank of America v. Delgado*, 166 So. 3d 857 (Fla. 3d DCA 2015); Florida Statute 90.803(6); *see also* Florida Statute § 90.803(7), which provides for a hearsay exception when a matter would regularly be included in a memorandum, report, record, or data compilation, but it is not included. The non-existence of the payment, for example, when a payment would normally be reflected in a payment history, may be established pursuant to this section.

[66] Fla. Stat. § 90.803(6): The following four elements must be met for a document to constitute a qualified business record:

(1) the record was made at or near the time of the event reflected;

(2) the record was made by, or from information transmitted by, a person with knowledge of the event reflected;

(3) the record was kept in the course of a regularly conducted business activity; and

(4) it was the regular practice of that business activity to make such memorandum, report, record, or data compilation.

[67] Fla. Stat. § 90.803(6).

FORECLOSURE TRIALS AND EVIDENCE

vice transfers of the loan, the qualified trial witness should be able to fully explain how the prior servicer's loan was 'boarded' into their system.[68]

13-4:3 Conditions Precedent

While there is no statutory requirement in Florida that notice be sent to a borrower advising of the lender's intent to foreclose, standard mortgages require notice, and the contract provision is enforceable as a condition precedent.[69] The standard Fannie Mae/Freddie Mac Uniform Instrument, which reflects the majority of Florida mortgages, includes as paragraph 22 the requirement that the lender provide notice to the borrower prior to acceleration.[70] Testimony supporting the notice provided must generally meet the requirements of the business record exception to the hearsay rule, similar to the payment history.[71] The notice of intended acceleration should be offered into evidence as a business record, but entry into evidence alone is not enough. The mortgage requires that the witness also confirm that the letter was sent via first class mail or actually delivered (if sent by other means).[72] For a comprehensive discussion

---

[68] *Sas v. Fannie Mae*, 165 So. 3d 849, 851 (Fla. 2d DCA 2015). Loan payment history was admissible under business records exception to hearsay rule, § 90.803(6), Fla. Stat., because successor servicer's records custodian's testimony established that successor servicer independently verified the accuracy of the records it received from the prior servicer using the successor servicer's verification procedures.

[69] *David v. Sun Federal Sav. & Loan Ass'n*, 461 So. 2d 93, 96 (Fla. 1984) ("The law does not require a mortgagee to notify a mortgagor of his intent to exercise his option to accelerate prior to instituting a foreclosure suit, but requires only that the option be exercised prior to tender of amounts due from the mortgagor.").

[70] Paragraph 22 of the standard mortgage reads as follows:

> Acceleration; Remedies. Lender shall give notice to Borrower prior to acceleration following Borrower's breach of any covenant or agreement in this Security Instrument (but not prior to acceleration under Section 18 unless Applicable Law provides otherwise). The notice shall specify: (a) the default; (b) the action required to cure the default; (c) a date, not less than 30 days from the date the notice is given to Borrower, by which the default must be cured; and (d) that failure to cure the default on or before the date, specified in the notice may result in acceleration of the sums secured by this Security Instrument, foreclosure by judicial proceeding and sale of the Property. The notice shall further inform Borrower of the right to reinstate after acceleration and the right to assert in the foreclosure proceeding the non-existence of a default or any other defense of Borrower to acceleration and foreclosure. If the default is not cured on or before the date specified in the notice, Lender at its option may require immediate payment in full of all sums secured by this Security Instrument without further demand and may foreclose this Security Instrument by judicial proceeding. Lender shall be entitled to collect all expenses incurred in pursuing the remedies provided in this Section 22, including, but not limited to, reasonable attorneys' fees and costs of title evidence.

[71] Fla. Stat. § 90.803(6); For a complete discussion of issues involving the notice of acceleration, *see* Chapter 2: Default and Acceleration.

[72] *Wells Fargo Bank, N.A. v. Cook*, 2D17-3913, 2019 Fla. App. LEXIS 11785 (Fla. 2d DCA July 26, 2019); *Allen v. Willmington Trust*, 216 So. 3d 685, 688 (Fla. 2d DCA 2017) ("mailing must be proven by producing additional evidence such as; proof of regular business practices, an affidavit swearing that the letter was mailed or return receipt card.").

Paragraph 15 of the standard mortgage reads as follows (in pertinent part):

of this condition precedent to mortgage foreclosure, *see* Chapter 2: Default and Acceleration. A copy of the standard Fannie Mae/Freddie Mac mortgage is also included in Appendix A, 1-018.

As an additional condition precedent, if the loan is an FHA-insured loan, plaintiff may be required to prove that it engages in the face-to-face meeting required by 24 C.F.R. § 203.604 (2012) prior to filing the foreclosure lawsuit.[73]

13-4:4 Damages

While the payment history may be utilized to demonstrate some damages in a foreclosure trial, practitioners must be diligent in establishing all additional damages incurred by the plaintiff.[74] These may include taxes and insurance paid on behalf of the mortgagor, as well as costs for property preservation.[75] The mortgage likely also permits recovery of attorneys' fees, but evidence of these must be presented as well in order to sustain a judgment which includes the fee totals.[76] If a defendant has been defaulted, notice and an opportunity to be heard at a hearing on unliquidated damages is still required.[77] Where the evidence at trial demonstrates damages, but does not fully support the claim for each amount claimed, a properly appealed final judgment may result in a remand to the trial court to ensure that the evidence will support the judgment amount.[78]

In some new filings, part of plaintiff's claim for damages is for a default on a loan modification. It is best practice to attach a copy of the modification agreement as an additional exhibit to the complaint. A copy of the modification agreement is admissible to the same extent as the original, as it not considered a negotiable instrument as

---

>Notices. All notices given by Borrower or Lender in connection with this Security Instrument must be in writing. Any notice to Borrower in connection with this Security Instrument shall be deemed to have been given to Borrower when mailed by first class mail or when actually delivered to Borrower's notice address if sent by other means. Notice to any one Borrower shall constitute notice to all Borrowers unless Applicable Law expressly requires otherwise.

[73] *Derouin v. Universal Am. Mortg. Co., LLC*, No. 2D17-1002, 2018 Fla. App. LEXIS 11800 (Fla. 2d DCA Aug. 22, 2018). For further discussion regarding HUD defenses/face-to-face meeting requirements, *see* Chapter 8, Section 8-4: FHA Home Loan Defenses.

[74] *Bank of America v. Delgado*, 166 So. 3d 857 (Fla. 3d DCA 2015) ("A foreclosure plaintiff proves the amount of indebtedness through the testimony of a competent witness who can authenticate the mortgagee's business records and confirm that they accurately reflect the amount owed on the mortgage."); *Peuguero v. Bank of Am., N.A.*, 169 So. 3d 1198 (Fla. 4th DCA 2015) (calculation of accrued interest must be supported by admissible evidence).

[75] *Wagner v. Bank of America, N.A.*, 143 So. 3d 447, 448 (Fla. 2d DCA 2014) (damages award at trial was not supported by competent, substantial evidence where payment history did not reflect damages for property inspections and costs of collection); *Doyle v. CitiMortgage, Inc.*, 162 So. 3d 340 (Fla. 2d DCA 2015) (evidence must support all figures included in the final judgment).

[76] *Boyette v. BAC Home Loans Servicing, LP*, 164 So. 3d 9 (Fla. 2d DCA 2015) (record did not reflect agreement for flat attorney fee, so fee was not supported by competent, substantial evidence).

[77] *Vercosa v. Fields*, 174 So. 3d 550, 552 (Fla. 4th DCA 2015).

[78] *Lasala v. Nationstar Mortg., LLC*, 197 So. 3d 1228, 1230 (Fla. 4th DCA 2016); *Deutsche Bank Nat'l Trust Co. v. Baker*, 199 So. 3d 967, 969 (Fla. 4th DCA 2016).

defined in Section 673.1041.[79] If a borrower is relying upon a purported loan modification to avoid the foreclosure claim, then it must be asserted as an affirmative defense and the burden of proving its existence is on the defendant.[80]

13-5 Burden of Proof

As in any breach of contract claim, to recover in a mortgage foreclosure each of the elements must be proven by a preponderance of the evidence.[81] Likewise, the burden to prove affirmative defenses and counterclaims is the defendant's to prove by a preponderance of the evidence.[82]

13-6 Motions for Involuntary Dismissal

At the close of plaintiff's case in chief at trial, a defendant may make a motion for involuntary dismissal.[83] The motion should be granted if the plaintiff has shown no right to relief by the basic presentation of its evidence.[84] The trial judge is not at liberty, however, to weigh evidence or credibility of witnesses at this stage, and must consider the motion in the light most favorable to the plaintiff (as the non-moving party).[85] The defendant does not waive their right to present their own case in chief by raising this motion, and the trial court may elect to withhold judgment until after the presentation of all evidence.[86] If the motion is granted, it is tantamount to an adjudication on the merits unless the trial court order indicates otherwise.[87]

---

[79] *Liukkonen v. Bayview Loan Servicing*, 243 So. 3d 981 (Fla. 4th DCA 2018).

[80] *Bank of N.Y. Mellon v. Bloedel*, 236 So. 3d 1164, 1167 (Fla. 2d DCA 2018). "The effect of a loan modification to a legal agreement, to the extent is would constitute an avoidance of all or part of the defendant's liability under the agreement, is an affirmative defense that must be pled and proven by the defendant."

[81] *Knowles v. C.I.T. Corp.*, 346 So. 2d 1042 (Fla. 1st DCA 1977).

[82] *Captains Table, Inc. v. Khouri*, 208 So. 2d 677 (Fla. 4th DCA 1968).

[83] Fla. R. Civ. P. 1.420(b); *Day v. Amini*, 550 So. 2d 169, 171 (Fla. 2d DCA 1989).

[84] Fla. R. Civ. P. 1.420(b).

[85] *Tillman v. Baskin*, 260 So. 2d 509 (Fla. 1972) ("We hold that a trial judge cannot weigh evidence when ruling on a defendant's Rule 1.420(b) F.R.C.P. motion for involuntary dismissal following the presentation of a prima facie case by a plaintiff."); *Bottalico v. Antonelli*, 695 So. 2d 363 (Fla. 4th DCA 1997) ("Upon the presentation of a *prima facie* case, as here, the trial court in a non-jury trial may not weigh and judge the credibility of the evidence when ruling upon a (motion for involuntary dismissal)."); *Perez v Perez*, 973 So. 2d 1227, 1231 (Fla. 4th DCA 2008) ("An involuntary dismissal is properly entered only where the evidence considered in the light most favorable to the non-moving party fails to establish a prima facie case.").

[86] Fla. R. Civ .P. 1.420(b).

[87] Fla. R. Civ. P. 1.420(b).

CHAPTER 14
Post-Judgment Motion Practice
Michael Starks

14-1 Introduction

There are times when the parties in a foreclosure need a do-over. In such circumstances, there are two Florida Rules of Civil Procedure that allow for such, namely Rules 1.530 and 1.540.[1] These two rules are important because, after more than 15 days after entry, except as provided by Rules 1.530 and 1.540, Florida Rules of Civil Procedure, the trial court has no authority to alter, modify, or vacate an order or judgment.[2]

These two rules are the subject of this chapter, as well as two other post-judgment topics, namely the mechanisms for objections to foreclosure sales and for seeking surplus funds from a foreclosure sale.

14-2 Rule 1.530 and Motions for Rehearing

Rule 1.530, titled "Motions for New Trial and Rehearing; Amendments of Judgments," states:

> (a) Jury and Non-Jury Actions. A new trial may be granted to all or any of the parties and on all or a part of the issues. On a motion for a rehearing of matters heard without a jury, including summary judgments, the court may open the judgment if one has been entered, take additional testimony, and enter a new judgment.
>
> (b) Time for Motion. A motion for new trial or for rehearing shall be served not later than 15 days after the return of the verdict in a jury action or the date of filing of the judgment in a non-jury action. A timely motion may be amended to state new grounds in the discretion of the court at any time before the motion is determined.
>
> (c) Time for Serving Affidavits. When a motion for a new trial is based on affidavits, the affidavits shall be served with the motion. The opposing party has 10

---

[1] "Except as provided by Rules 1.530 and 1.540, Florida Rules of Civil Procedure, the trial court has no authority to alter, modify or vacate an order or judgment." *Shelby Mut. Ins. Co. of Shelby, Ohio v. Pearson*, 236 So. 2d 1, 3 (Fla. 1970).
[2] *Deutsche Bank Nat'l Tr. Co. for Certificateholders of Morgan Stanley ABS Capital 1 Inc. Tr. 2003-NC10 v. Del Busto*, 254 So. 3d 1050, 1052 (Fla. 3d DCA 2018).

days after such service within which to serve opposing affidavits, which period may be extended for an additional period not exceeding 20 days either by the court for good cause shown or by the parties by written stipulation. The court may permit reply affidavits.

(d) On Initiative of Court. Not later than 15 days after entry of judgment or within the time of ruling on a timely motion for a rehearing or a new trial made by a party, the court of its own initiative may order a rehearing or a new trial for any reason for which it might have granted a rehearing or a new trial on motion of a party.

(e) When Motion Is Unnecessary; Non-Jury Case. When an action has been tried by the court without a jury, the sufficiency of the evidence to support the judgment may be raised on appeal whether or not the party raising the question has made any objection thereto in the trial court or made a motion for rehearing, for new trial, or to alter or amend the judgment.

(f) Order Granting to Specify Grounds. All orders granting a new trial shall specify the specific grounds therefor. If such an order is appealed and does not state the specific grounds, the appellate court shall relinquish its jurisdiction to the trial court for entry of an order specifying the grounds for granting the new trial.

(g) Motion to Alter or Amend a Judgment. A motion to alter or amend the judgment shall be served not later than 15 days after entry of the judgment, except that this rule does not affect the remedies in rule 1.540(b).

14-2:1 Appellate Considerations

Effective January 1, 2015, the filing of a notice of appeal after a timely motion for rehearing has been filed is no longer deemed an abandonment of that post-judgment motion. Specifically, Rule 9.020(i)[3] has been amended to eliminate the language providing that post-judgment motions are abandoned upon the filing of a notice of appeal. The amended rule allows an appeal to be held in abeyance until disposition of a post-judgment motion. Under Rule 9.110(l),[4] premature appeals were previously subject to dismissal, but the amendment thereto added language recognizing the exception provided in Rule 9.020(i) and recognizing that the lower tribunal retains jurisdiction to render a final order. The amendment further provides that the court may allow the parties time to obtain a final order. The definition of "rendition" was also amended to reflect these changes.[5]

Rule 1.530 decisions are generally reviewed on appeal for abuse of discretion but can be reviewed *de novo* if they involve pure questions of law.[6]

---

[3] *See* Fla. R. App. P. 9.020(i). *See In re Amendments to the Fla. Rules of Appellate Procedure*, 183 So. 3d 245 (Fla. 2014) (discussing amendment).

[4] *See* Fla. R. App. P. 9.110(*l*). *See In re Amendments to the Fla. Rules of Appellate Procedure*, 183 So. 3d 245 (Fla. 2014) (discussing amendment).

[5] *See In re Amendments to the Fla. Rules of Appellate Procedure*, 183 So. 3d 245 (Fla. 2014) (discussing amendment).

[6] *See Leach v. Salehpour*, 19 So. 3d 342, 344 (Fla. 2d DCA 2009) ("While there is no doubt that this court has jurisdiction to review the trial court's order, in order to apply the

The Florida Supreme Court resolved a split in the districts when it affirmed the 4th DCA's *en banc* opinion which held that a default judgment based on a complaint that fails to state a cause of action is not "void" but merely "voidable."[7] A merely voidable judgment must be challenged on that ground, if at all, immediately in a motion for rehearing under Rule 1.530, or on appeal, and cannot be challenged under Rule 1.540(b)(4) as void.[8] A judgment based on a complaint that fails to state a cause of action, where the party had notice of the proceedings and failed to address the issue, is merely "voidable" as opposed to "void".[9] Therefore, a voidable judgment must be attacked, on the ground of failure to state a cause of action, by Rule 1.530 and/or appeal.

The current version of Rule 1.530(b) provides 15 days for service of a motion for rehearing.[10] However, rehearing and appellate deadlines don't run from the date of entry or service of the order, but from "rendition of the order," that is, the date of the filing of the order by the court (and docketing by the clerk).[11] Most orders

---

proper standard of review we must examine whether the order was entered pursuant to Florida Rule of Civil Procedure 1.540 or 1.530. Leach brought this appeal pursuant to Florida Rule of Appellate Procedure 9.130(a)(5) as an appeal from an order that ruled on a motion filed pursuant to rule 1.540(b), which allows a trial court to 'relieve a party or party's legal representative from a final judgment, decree, order, or proceeding for' certain enumerated reasons. Such orders are appealable and reviewable under an abuse of discretion standard. Salehpour, however, contends that the trial court did not simply enter an order on a rule 1.540 motion, but instead granted a new trial on its own motion pursuant to rule 1.530(d). Appeals brought under rule 9.110(a)(4) are generally reviewed for an abuse of discretion but can be subject to de novo review if . . . they involve a pure question of law.").

[7] *The Bank of New York v. Condo. Ass'n of La Mer Estates, Inc.*, 175 So. 3d 282 (Fla. 2015), approving *Condominium Ass'n of La Mer Estates, Inc. v. Bank of New York Mellon Corp.*, 137 So. 3d 396, 400-01 (Fla. 4th DCA 2014) *(en banc)*.

[8] *The Bank of New York v. Condo. Ass'n of La Mer Estates, Inc.*, 175 So. 3d 282 (Fla. 2015), approving *Condominium Ass'n of La Mer Estates, Inc. v. Bank of New York Mellon Corp.*, 137 So. 3d 396, 400-01 (Fla. 4th DCA 2014) *(en banc)* ("The motion for relief in this case provided no other reason for vacating the judgment other than arguing that the complaint failed to state a cause of action. We hold that these allegations would render the judgment voidable, not void. The bank was properly notified of the proceedings, notified of the hearing on final judgment, and notified of the entry of the final judgment. It could have appeared in the proceedings and raised the pleading defects, or it could have raised the issue on direct appeal. 'A voidable judgment can be challenged by motion for rehearing or appeal and may be subject to collateral attack under specific circumstances, but it cannot be challenged at any time as void under rule 1.540(b)(4).'") (quoting *Sterling Factors Corp. v. U.S. Bank Nat. Ass'n*, 968 So. 2d 658, 667 (Fla. 2d DCA 2007)); *see also Dage v. Deutsche Bank Nat'l Trust Co.*, 95 So. 3d 1021, 1024 (Fla. 2d DCA 2012) ("Even if Deutsche Bank lacked standing when it filed suit, the final judgment is merely voidable, not void.") (citing *Jones-Bishop v. Estate of Sweeney*, 27 So. 3d 176, 177 (Fla. 5th DCA 2010)).

[9] *The Bank of New York v. Condo. Ass'n of La Mer Estates, Inc.*, 175 So. 3d 282 (Fla. 2015).

[10] *See In re Amend. Fla. Rules Civ. Pro.*, 131 So. 3d 643, 651 (Fla. 2013); *Redd v. Justice Admin. Comm'n*, 140 So. 3d 1085, 1088 n.1 (Fla. 2d DCA 2014).

[11] Florida no longer provides mailing time at all, but even when it did, the mailing time did not apply to orders of the court, but only to papers filed by a party. *See Dominguez v. Barakat*, 609 So. 2d 664 (Fla. 3d DCA 1992) ("Contrary to the appellants' position, the time for service was not extended by the five days provided by Fla.R.Civ.P. 1.090(e) because the final

on motions for rehearing are not appealable independent of the underlying final order.[12]

14-2:2 General Considerations

A motion for rehearing under Rule 1.530 can be addressed to any final order or decree.[13] The rule only applies to final orders.[14] Where a party does not get proper notice on a motion, and the court grants a rehearing on that basis under Rule 1.530, any prior due process violation is cured.[15]

A foreclosure sale must be set aside if a timely motion for rehearing was pending at the time of the sale because such a motion suspends rendition of the final order.[16]

A motion for "rehearing" targeting a non-final order is more aptly called a motion for "reconsideration."[17] Rule 1.530 motions for rehearing cannot be directed toward

---

judgment was mailed to counsel. As the rule specifically states, it applies only when there is 'a prescribed period after . . . *service* . . . and the notice or paper is served . . . by mail.' [e.s.] Fla.R.App.P. 1.090 (e). In contrast, the ten-day service requirement of Fla.R.Civ.P. 1.530(b) runs from 'the *filing* of the judgment.' [e.s.]"); *Nogales v. Countrywide Home Loans, Inc.*, 100 So. 3d 1161, 1162 n.1 (Fla. 2d DCA 2012) ("Moreover, the additional time allowed after service of a document by mail does not apply to the filing of a notice of appeal, which is measured from the date of rendition."). *See also* Florida Rules of Appellate Procedure P. 9.420(e), 9.110(b).

[12] *See* Fla. R. App. P. 9.130(a)(4) (stating, "Orders disposing of motions that suspend rendition are not reviewable separately from a review of the final order; provided that orders granting motions for new trial in jury and non-jury cases are reviewable by the method prescribed in rule 9.110"); *see also Wharton v. Dubose*, 458 So. 2d 411 (Fla. 4th DCA 1984) (holding that the granting of a motion for rehearing is "clearly not a final order" reviewable on appeal); *Cape Royal Realty, Inc. v. Kroll*, 804 So. 2d 605, 606-07 (Fla. 5th DCA 2002) (finding that an order granting a motion for rehearing was not reviewable).

[13] *Popescu v. Laguna Master Ass'n, Inc.*, 126 So. 3d 449, 449 (Fla. 4th DCA 2013).

[14] For instance, it is black letter law in Florida that an order determining entitlement to attorney's fees that does not also set the amount of fees is not final, not appealable, and is therefore interlocutory in nature (meaning there is no strict time limit to file a motion for rehearing). *See Miller v. Miller*, 801 So. 2d 1056, 1057 (Fla. 1st DCA 2001) ("We, however, decline to exercise our jurisdiction as to the former wife's entitlement to attorney's fees because the judgment does not set the amount of fees and thus, the issue is not ripe for our review."); *Alvis v. Alvis*, 95 So. 3d 910, 911 (Fla. 1st DCA 2012) ("The judgment does not set the amount of fees and thus is not a final order subject to review."); *Debolt v. Debolt*, 90 So. 3d 374, 374 (Fla. 1st DCA 2012) ("We, however, decline to exercise our jurisdiction as to the former wife's entitlement to attorney's fees because the order does not set the amount of fees, and thus, the issue is not ripe for review."); *Chaphe v. Chaphe*, 19 So. 3d 1019, 1024 (Fla. 1st DCA. 2009) ("A ruling which merely establishes entitlement to attorney's fees without setting the amount is not appealable.").

[15] *Porras v. Wachovia Bank NA*, 3D18-1382, 2019 WL 3309190, at *1 (Fla. 3d DCA July 24, 2019).

[16] *Wollman v. Levy*, 489 So. 2d 1239, 1239 (Fla. 3d DCA 1986); *Hoffman v. BankUnited, N.A.*, 137 So. 3d 1039 (Fla. 2d DCA 2014); *944 CWELT-2007 LLC v. Bank of America, N.A.*, 194 So. 3d 470, 471 (Fla. 3d DCA 2016).

[17] For a thorough and scholarly analysis of this issue, *see* James H. Wyman, *Reconsideration or Rehearing: Is There a Difference?*, Volume 83, No. 6, Florida Bar Journal (June 2009); the article can be found at the following link: http://www.floridabar.org/DIVCOM/JN

non-final orders such as an order granting a writ of possession.[18] Motions for reconsideration apply to non-final, interlocutory orders, and are based on a trial court's 'inherent authority to reconsider and, if deemed appropriate, alter or retract any of its non-final rulings prior to entry of the final judgment or order terminating an action.[19] Thus, a "motion for reconsideration" doesn't have an actual deadline and is more a creature of general practice and not of rule. A judge, including a successor judge, has the ability to reconsider any interlocutory order at any time.[20]

A movant is not entitled to a rehearing where there is no procedural error by the court and no new evidence is presented. Rehearing is not merely to convey displeasure to the court or to re-argue matters that were previously argued.[21] There is no basic and fundamental right to rehearing.[22]

A Rule 1.530 motion is required to preserve for appeal errors that first appear in the trial court's written order, such as a dismissal order for failure to appear at a case management conference, which must contain written findings covering the specific grounds.[23]

/JNJournal01.nsf/8c9f13012b96736985256aa900624829/0020ff826ad66c5f852575c50049d2b4?OpenDocument (last visited).

[18] *See Hollifield v. Renew & Co.*, 18 So. 3d 616, 617 (Fla. 1st DCA 2009).

[19] *Taufer v. Wells Fargo Bank, N.A.*, 278 So. 3d 335 (Fla. 3d DCA 2019).

[20] *Deemer v. Hallett Pontiac, Inc.*, 288 So. 2d 526, 527 (Fla. 3d DCA), *cert. denied*, 298 So. 2d 416 (Fla.1974). "[I]t is well settled that a trial court has the inherent authority to control its own interlocutory orders prior to final judgment." *North Shore Hospital, Inc. v. Barber*, 143 So. 2d 849, 851 (Fla. 1962); *see also Tieche v. Florida Physicians Ins. Reciprocal*, 431 So. 2d 287 (Fla. 5th DCA 1983) (dismissing appeal on non-final order of trial court setting aside a default under Rule 1.500(d), as it was well within the trial court's purview to review this type of order).

[21] *See Snell v. State*, 522 So. 2d 407 (Fla. 5th DCA 1988); *Banderas v. Advance Petroleum, Inc.*, 716 So. 2d 876 (Fla. 3d DCA 1998); *Goter v. Brown*, 682 So. 2d 155, 158 (Fla. 4th DCA 1996); *North Brevard County Hospital Dist., Inc. v. Florida Public Employees Relations Commission*, 392 So. 2d 556 (Fla. 1st DCA 1980); *Elliott v. Elliott*, 648 So. 2d 135 (Fla. 4th DCA 1994); *Whipple v. State*, 431 So. 2d 1011 (Fla. 2d DCA 1983).

[22] *See Stoner v. W. G., Inc.*, 300 So. 2d 268 (Fla. 2d DCA 1973).

[23] *Shelswell v. Bourdeau*, 239 So. 3d 707, 708-09 (Fla. 4th DCA 2018) ("Here, Shelswell, by way of her replacement trial attorney, did not raise the *Kozel* issue at any point in the proceedings below, such as through a motion for rehearing or clarification filed within fifteen days of the trial court's order. Fla. R. Civ. P. 1.530(b)."); *Vorbeck v. Betancourt*, 107 So. 3d 1142, 1147 (Fla. 3d DCA 2012); *Bank of Am., N.A. v. Ribaudo*, 199 So. 3d 407, 409 (Fla. 4th DCA 2016) (refusing to reverse a final order that failed to address the necessary *Kozel* factors because the appellant bank "did not raise [the issue] at the hearing on the motion to dismiss or by subsequently filing a motion for rehearing or reconsideration."); *Gozzo Dev., Inc. v. Prof'l Roofing Contractors, Inc.*, 211 So. 3d 145, 146 (Fla. 4th DCA 2017) (Lee, J., concurring) ("[A]ppellant cannot now be heard to complain about the trial court not making findings pursuant to *Kozel* when appellant failed to request the trial court to do so."); *Bank of N.Y. Mellon v. Sandhill*, 202 So. 3d 944, 945 (Fla. 5th DCA 2016) ("[I]n order to preserve as error the failure of the trial court to set forth its *Kozel* analysis in the order of dismissal, the Appellant was obligated to bring the matter to the trial court's attention by filing a timely motion for rehearing or clarification with a specific request for inclusion of the *Kozel* factor analysis in an amended order.").

Rule 1.530 does not provide rehearing relief from a denial of a Rule 1.540(b) motion for relief, because such an order of denial, though final, is not a "judgment."[24] Also, while there is a limited exception regarding non-party standing, the general rule remains, and best practice requires, that a non-party must seek and be granted leave to intervene before it will have standing to pursue relief under Rule 1.540(b).[25] For a non-party who does not fall under the limited exception in *Pearlman v. Pearlman*,[26] when leave to intervene is denied and that decision is not timely appealed, the non-party lacks standing to later file a 1.540(b) motion with the trial court.[27]

14-3 Rule 1.540 and Motions to Vacate Judgment

Florida Rule of Civil Procedure 1.540(b) sets forth several grounds upon which a court may relieve a party from a final judgment. Rule 1.540, titled "Relief from Judgment, Decrees, or Orders," states:

(a) Clerical Mistakes. Clerical mistakes in judgments, decrees, or other parts of the record and errors therein arising from oversight or omission may be corrected by the court at any time on its own initiative or on the motion of any party and after such notice, if any, as the court orders. During the pendency of an appeal such mistakes may be so corrected before the record on appeal is docketed in the appellate court, and thereafter while the appeal is pending may be so corrected with leave of the appellate court.

(b) Mistakes; Inadvertence; Excusable Neglect; Newly Discovered Evidence; Fraud; etc. On motion and upon such terms as are just, the court may relieve a party or a party's legal representative from a final judgment, decree, order, or proceeding for the following reasons: (1) mistake, inadvertence, surprise, or excusable neglect; (2) newly discovered evidence which by due diligence could not have been discovered in time to move for a new trial or rehearing; (3) fraud (whether heretofore denominated intrinsic or extrinsic), misrepresentation, or other misconduct of an adverse party; (4) that the judgment or decree is void; or (5) that the judgment or decree has been satisfied, released, or discharged, or a prior judgment or decree upon which it is based has been reversed or otherwise vacated, or it is no longer equitable that the judgment or decree should have prospective application. The motion shall be filed within a reasonable time, and for reasons (1), (2), and (3) not more than 1 year after the judgment, decree, order, or proceeding was entered or taken. A motion under this subdivision does not affect the finality of a judgment or decree or suspend its operation. This rule does not limit the power of a court to entertain an independent action to relieve a party from a judgment, decree, order, or proceeding or to set aside a judgment or decree for fraud upon the court.

---

[24] *Thornton v. Jabeen*, 683 So. 2d 150 (Fla. 3d DCA 1996).
[25] *Carlisle v. U.S. Bank, Nat'l Ass'n, as Tr. for the Benefit of Harborview 2005-10 Tr. Fund*, 225 So. 3d 893, 896 (Fla. 3d DCA 2017) ("Because Carlisle did not timely appeal the order denying his motion to intervene and does not fall within *Pearlman*'s limited exception, we find that Carlisle lacks standing to appeal the trial court's denial of his 1.540(b) motion, and dismiss the appeal.").
[26] *Pearlman v. Pearlman*, 405 So. 2d 764 (Fla. 3d DCA 1981).
[27] *Carlisle v. U.S. Bank, Nat'l Ass'n, as Tr. for the Benefit of Harborview 2005-10 Tr. Fund*, 225 So. 3d 893, 894-96 (Fla. 3d DCA 2017).

Writs of coram nobis, coram vobis, audita querela, and bills of review and bills in the nature of a bill of review are abolished, and the procedure for obtaining any relief from a judgment or decree shall be by motion as prescribed in these rules or by an independent action.

14-3:1 Appellate Considerations

Because a trial court is accorded broad discretion in determining Rule 1.540(b) motions,[28] the standard of review of an order denying a Rule 1.540(b) motion for relief from judgment is whether there has been an abuse of the trial court's discretion.[29] The Florida Rules of Appellate Procedure expressly permit appeals of orders on Rule 1.540 motions, unlike orders of Rule 1.530 motions.[30] A higher standard (than if the trial court had denied the motion) is applied to overturn the decision granting a motion to vacate.[31] Thus, a showing of gross abuse of discretion is necessary on appeal to justify reversal of the lower court's granting of a motion to vacate.[32]

While of course it is better to object to a Rule 1.540(b)(1)–(3) motion as untimely on the record, because the issue is jurisdictional, it can be raised for the first time on appeal.[33]

As with Rule 1.530, Rule 1.540 motions can only be directed to final orders.[34]

One use of Rule 1.540 can be to obtain a fresher judgment for appellate purposes, where the court failed to send the order to counsel within the appeal time.[35] However,

---

[28] *See Crowley v. Crowley*, 678 So. 2d 435, 438 (Fla. 4th DCA 1996).

[29] *See J.J.K. Int'l, Inc. v. Shivbaran*, 985 So. 2d 66, 68 (Fla. 4th DCA 2008). However, Rule 1.530 decisions, by contrast, are generally reviewed on appeal for abuse of discretion but can be reviewed de novo if they involve pure questions of law. *See Leach v. Salehpour*, 19 So. 3d 342, 344 (Fla. 2d DCA 2009) ("While there is no doubt that this court has jurisdiction to review the trial court's order, in order to apply the proper standard of review we must examine whether the order was entered pursuant to Florida Rule of Civil Procedure 1.540 or 1.530. Leach brought this appeal pursuant to Florida Rule of Appellate Procedure 9.130(a)(5) as an appeal from an order that ruled on a motion filed pursuant to rule 1.540(b), which allows a trial court to 'relieve a party or party's legal representative from a final judgment, decree, order, or proceeding for' certain enumerated reasons. Such orders are appealable and reviewable under an abuse of discretion standard.... Salehpour, however, contends that the trial court did not simply enter an order on a rule 1.540 motion, but instead granted a new trial on its own motion pursuant to rule 1.530(d).... Appeals brought under rule 9.110(a)(4) are generally reviewed for an abuse of discretion but can be subject to de novo review if... they involve a pure question of law.").

[30] *See* Fla. R. App. P. 9.130(a)(5).

[31] *Halpern v. Houser*, 949 So. 2d 1155, 1157 (Fla. 4th DCA 2007); *see also Bank of America, N.A. v. Lane*, 76 So. 3d 1007, 1008 (Fla. 1st DCA 2014).

[32] *Halpern v. Houser*, 949 So. 2d 1155, 1157 (Fla. 4th DCA 2007).

[33] *Linares v. Bank of Am., N.A.*, 278 So. 3d 330, 332 n.3 (Fla. 3d DCA 2019) (holding that the jurisdictional nature of Rule 1.540(b) allows the error to be raised for the first time on appeal); *Bank One, Nat'l Ass'n v. Batronie*, 884 So. 2d 346, 349 (Fla. 2d DCA 2004).

[34] *Taufer v. Wells Fargo Bank, N.A.*, 278 So. 3d 335 (Fla. 3d DCA 2019) ("Florida Rule of Civil Procedure 1.540 cannot be directed toward non-final orders such as the order granting the writ of possession.").

[35] *Diquollo v. TD Bank, N.A.*, 224 So. 3d 341, 342 (Fla. 5th DCA 2017) ("The trial court rendered a default final judgment in this matter on January 11, 2016, but Appellant, Ruenrudee Rowe Diquollo, did not receive a copy of the judgment until after the appeal time had run.

that non-receipt of the order must not be the result of a conscious decision by counsel to use a defective email system.[36] A default judgment based on a complaint that fails to state a cause of action is merely "voidable," which means the judgment must be challenged on that ground immediately in a motion for rehearing under Rule 1.530, or on appeal, and cannot be challenged under Rule 1.540(b)(4) as void.[37] Therefore, a judgment based on a complaint that fails to state a cause of action, where the party had notice of the proceedings and failed to address the issue, is merely voidable as opposed to void.[38] A voidable judgment must be attacked, on the ground of failure to state a cause of action, by Rule 1.530 and/or appeal.[39] A judgment that has an error in the legal description is merely voidable, not void.[40]

14-3:2 Evidentiary Hearing

An evidentiary hearing is unnecessary if a Rule 1.540(b) motion merely undertakes to rehash matters previously litigated at trial or raises inconsequential "de minimis" matters.[41] A motion seeking relief under Rule 1.540(b) warrants denial without an evidentiary hearing when the "allegations and accompanying affidavits fail to allege

---

This occurred because Appellee, TD Bank, N.A., furnished the trial court with an erroneous address for Appellant. After Appellant became aware of the entry of the judgment, on September 23, 2016, she filed a motion to vacate pursuant to Florida Rule of Civil Procedure 1.540(b). The trial court denied the motion without a hearing. Florida Rule of Civil Procedure 1.080(a) requires that all orders and documents filed in an action be served in conformity with Florida Rule of Judicial Administration 2.516. That rule provides that when a final judgment is entered against a party in default, the court must mail a conformed copy of it to the defaulting party at the address furnished by the party in whose favor the judgment is entered. *See* Fla. R. Jud. Admin. 2.516(h)(2).").

[36] *Emerald Coast Utils. Auth. v. Bear Marcus Pointe, LLC*, 227 So. 3d 752, 757-58 (Fla. 1st DCA 2017), *reh'g denied* (Oct. 6, 2017).

[37] *The Bank of New York v. Condo. Ass'n of La Mer Estates, Inc.*, 175 So. 3d 282 (Fla. 2015), *approving Condo. Ass'n of La Mer Estates, Inc. v. Bank of New York Mellon Corp.*, 137 So. 3d 396, 400-01 (Fla. 4th DCA 2014) (*en banc*) ("The motion for relief in this case provided no other reason for vacating the judgment other than arguing that the complaint failed to state a cause of action. We hold that these allegations would render the judgment voidable, not void. The bank was properly notified of the proceedings, notified of the hearing on final judgment, and notified of the entry of the final judgment. It could have appeared in the proceedings and raised the pleading defects, or it could have raised the issue on direct appeal. 'A voidable judgment can be challenged by motion for rehearing or appeal and may be subject to collateral attack under specific circumstances, but it cannot be challenged at any time as void under rule 1.540(b)(4).'") (quoting *Sterling Factors Corp. v. U.S. Bank Nat. Ass'n*, 968 So. 2d 658, 667 (Fla. 2d DCA 2007)). *See also Dage v. Deutsche Bank Nat'l Trust Co.*, 95 So. 3d 1021, 1024 (Fla. 2d DCA 2012) ("Even if Deutsche Bank lacked standing when it filed suit, the final judgment is merely voidable, not void.") (citing *Jones-Bishop v. Estate of Sweeney*, 27 So. 3d 176, 177 (Fla. 5th DCA 2010)).

[38] *The Bank of New York v. Condo. Ass'n of La Mer Estates, Inc.*, 175 So. 3d 282 (Fla. 2015).

[39] *The Bank of New York v. Condo. Ass'n of La Mer Estates, Inc.*, 175 So. 3d 282 (Fla. 2015), approving *Condo. Ass'n of La Mer Estates, Inc. v. Bank of New York Mellon Corp.*, 137 So. 3d 396, 400-01 (Fla. 4th DCA 2014) (en banc).

[40] *Cornelius v. Holzman*, 193 So. 3d 1029, 1032 (Fla. 4th DCA 2016).

[41] *Coleman (Parent) Holdings, Inc. v. Morgan Stanley & Co., Inc.*, 20 So. 3d 952, 955 (Fla. 4th DCA 2009).

a colorable entitlement to relief."[42] For instance, to entitle a movant to an evidentiary hearing on a motion for relief from judgment under Rule 1.540(b)(3), the motion must specify the fraud with particularity and explain why the fraud, if it exists, would entitle the movant to have the judgment set aside.[43] If a motion does not set forth a basis for relief on its face, then an evidentiary hearing is unnecessary, the time and expense of needless litigation is avoided, and the policy of preserving the finality of judgments is enhanced.[44] The matter alleged must affect the outcome of the case and not merely be "de minimis."[45] Thus, to obtain a hearing on a Rule 1.540(b)(3) motion, the law requires a movant "to demonstrate a prima facie case of fraud, not just nibble at the edges of the concept."[46] The evidence of fraud must be competent, sworn or verified.[47] Post-judgment discovery cannot commence on a motion for relief from judgment based upon unsworn allegations.[48]

14-3:3 One-Year Limitation Under Rule 1.540(b)(1) Through (3)

On the face of Rule 1.540(b)(1) through (3), a party must move for relief within a "reasonable time" that cannot exceed one year.[49] There is a necessity for "finality of litigation" which Florida courts have found prohibits them from giving parties a second chance at proof that they had available in the first instance, but overlooked or chose not to use.[50] Rule 1.540(b)(1) through (3) was not intended to allow parties to reopen lawsuits to assert new claims, or to offer new evidence omitted by oversight or inadvertence.[51] No party should be forced to bear the burden of relitigating a matter

---

[42] *Coleman (Parent) Holdings, Inc. v. Morgan Stanley & Co., Inc.*, 20 So. 3d 952, 954 (Fla. 4th DCA 2009).

[43] *Flemenbaum v. Flemenbaum*, 636 So. 2d 579, 580 (Fla. 4th DCA 1994).

[44] *Coleman (Parent) Holdings, Inc. v. Morgan Stanley & Co.*, 20 So. 3d 952, 955 (Fla. 4th DCA 2009).

[45] *Coleman (Parent) Holdings, Inc. v. Morgan Stanley & Co.*, 20 So. 3d 952, 955 (Fla. 4th DCA 2009).

[46] *Hembd v. Dauria*, 859 So. 2d 1238, 1240 (Fla. 4th DCA 2003).

[47] *Tikhomirov v. Bank of New .York Mellon*, 223 So. 3d 1112, 1113 (Fla. 3d DCA 2017) ("We find that the trial court did not abuse its discretion in denying the motion for relief from judgment. Appellant neither stated the alleged fraud with sufficient particularity nor explained why the purported fraud would entitle Appellant to have the judgment set aside. Indeed, Appellant presented no competent, sworn, or verified evidence of fraud in his motion to vacate. . . . Notwithstanding Appellant's concerns, incorrect or misleading assignments of mortgage are not by themselves indicative of fraud, as assignments of mortgages are not required to transfer mortgages.").

[48] *Rooney v. Wells Fargo Bank, N.A.*, 102 So. 3d 734, 736 (Fla. 4th DCA 2012) ("In order to present a colorable claim of entitlement to vacate a final judgment, a litigant must provide sworn proof to support the allegations of the motion. . . . We do not think that discovery can commence on a motion for relief from judgment based upon unsworn allegations. To do so would encourage fishing expeditions in post-judgment proceedings. Here, the Rooneys made multiple allegations, but none were sworn.") (emphasis in original).

[49] *See Florida Dep't of Revenue v. Pough*, 723 So. 2d 303 (Fla. 2d DCA 1998) (*per curiam*).

[50] *Viking Gen. Corp. v. Diversified Mortgage Investors*, 387 So. 2d 983, 985 (Fla. 2d DCA 1980); *see also Voce v. Wachovia Mortgage, FSB*, 174 So. 3d 545, 547 (Fla. 4th DCA 2015) (providing that once a case is beyond the 15-day window for a Rule 1.530 motion for rehearing, the trial court loses jurisdiction over the case except to enforce the judgment).

[51] *Viking Gen. Corp. v. Diversified Mortgage Investors*, 387 So. 2d 983, 985 (Fla. 2d DCA 1980).

due to the opponent's failure to take the necessary steps to protect his or her interests, particularly when this could have been easily done.[52]

Motions pursuant to Florida Rule of Civil Procedure 1.540(b) cannot be used as a substitute for a motion for rehearing or an appeal.[53] For instance, a borrower should not be permitted to allow herself to be defaulted, and then neither appeal nor move for rehearing,[54] and then be permitted to later challenge the bank's standing under a Rule 1.540 motion to vacate.[55]

Rule 1.540(b) applies to final orders as well as judgments.[56] There is only one year available to a judgment holder to vacate a final judgment due to an error in the legal description in the mortgage and judgment.[57]

It is important to note that an "amended" Rule 1.540(b)(1) through (3) motion that alleges new relief not argued in the original motion does not expand the one-year period.[58] Similarly, a party cannot escape its failure to appeal an adverse ruling by fil-

---

[52] *Allstate Ins. Co. v. Gulisano*, 722 So. 2d 216, 218 (Fla. 2d DCA 1998).
[53] *See Curbelo v. Ullman*, 571 So.2d 443, 445 (Fla. 1990) (finding that Rule 1.540 is not a substitute for a timely 1.530 motion or an appeal); *see Commonwealth Land Title Ins. Co. v. Freeman*, 884 So. 2d 164, 167 (Fla. 2d DCA 2004).
[54] *See, e.g., Lovett v. Nat'l Collegiate Student Loan Trust 2004-1*, 149 So. 3d 735 (Fla. 5th DCA 2014).
[55] *Beaulieu v. JP Morgan Chase Bank, N.A.*, 80 So. 3d 365, 365-66 (Fla. 4th DCA 2012).
[56] *De La Osa v. Wells Fargo Bank, N.A.*, 208 So. 3d 259, 261 (Fla. 3d DCA 2016) (rehearing *en banc*). *See also Courtney v. Catalina, Ltd.*, 130 So. 3d 739, 740 (Fla. 3d DCA 2014) ("Courtney's attorney filed a verified motion to vacate the order of dismissal [for failure to prosecute] pursuant to Florida Rule of Civil Procedure 1.540(b)(4), which authorizes a trial court to afford relief to a party when '[a] judgment or decree is void.'"); *Deutsche Bank Nat. Trust Co. v. Basanta*, 88 So. 3d 216, 218 (Fla. 3d DCA 2011); *Boosinger v. Davis*, 46 So. 3d 152, 154 (Fla. 2d DCA 2010). *Cf. State Department of Revenue v. Haughton*, 188 So. 3d 32 (Fla. 3d DCA 2016) (reversing trial court order denying Rule 1.540(b)(4) motion; holding that pursuant to Rule 1.540(b)(b)(4), trial court should have set aside "order" entered without notice as void).
[57] *Epstein v. Bank of Am.*, 162 So. 3d 159, 161 (Fla. 4th DCA 2015) (motion to vacate judgment with erroneous legal description held time-barred under Rule 1.540(b)); *Cornelius v. Holzman*, 193 So. 3d 1029, 1032 (Fla. 4th DCA 2016) (same); *Lucas v. Barnett Bank of Lee Cty.*, 705 So. 2d 115, 116 (Fla. 2d DCA 1998) ("When a mortgage contains an incorrect legal description, a court may correct the mistake before foreclosure. If, however, the mistaken legal description is not corrected before final judgment of foreclosure, and the mistake is carried into the advertisement for sale and the foreclosure deed, a court cannot reform the mistake in the deed and judgment; rather, the foreclosure process must begin anew.... The reason behind this policy is that, if the mortgage is not reforeclosed, the purchaser would have obtained title to a property that was not properly ordered for sale, advertised, or sold. While the mortgagee who bid its mortgage at the sale might have understood exactly what property was being offered, other potential bidders at the sale might not have had the same understanding.... As the *Fisher* court noted, the mortgage may be reformed if a sufficient showing is made, and the reformed mortgage may be foreclosed. But first, the deed to the property must be canceled, and the original foreclosure judgment set aside, such that the parties are returned to their original status.").
[58] *Cornelius v. Holzman*, 193 So. 3d 1029, 1032 (Fla. 4th DCA 2016) ("Although the lender also filed a motion to vacate on February 14, 2014, the lender moved under rule 1.190, an incorrect rule, and the trial court summarily denied it. The amended motion to amend final judgment asserted some arguments similar to the motion to vacate, but it also requested

ing a Rule 1.540(b) motion and then appealing its denial, because Rule 1.540(b) is not designed to correct judicial error, but party error.[59]

While of course it is better to object to a Rule 1.540(b)(1)–(3) motion as untimely on the record, because the issue is jurisdictional, it can be raised for the first time on appeal.[60]

14-3:4 Procedure Under Rule 1.540(b)(1); Mistake, Inadvertence, Surprise, or Excusable Neglect

Under Rule 1.530(b)(1), to obtain relief from a default judgment for excusable neglect under Florida Rule of Civil Procedure 1.540(b)(1), a party must show excusable neglect, a meritorious defense,[61] and due diligence after learning of the default.[62] The court must deny the motion if any one of the three elements is not established.[63] However, it must grant the motion to set aside default if there is reasonable doubt as to whether the moving party is entitled to relief.[64]

The excusable neglect prong[65] and due diligence prong[66] must be established with sworn testimony such as an affidavit. The meritorious defense prong, where the

---

new relief. This rendered the amended motion to amend final judgment a new motion that was untimely under rule 1.540(b). In short, the trial court lacked jurisdiction to rule on the motion. Absent an exception from subsections (4) or (5), the trial court lost jurisdiction over the case to address the lender's claim.").

[59] See *Curbelo v. Ullman*, 571 So.2d 443, 445 (Fla. 1990) (finding that Rule 1.540 is not a substitute for a timely 1.530 motion or an appeal); see also *Baez v. Perez*, 201 So.3d 692, 694 (Fla. 4th DCA 2016) ("Even Perez acknowledges that her allegations amount to judicial error. These are issues which could have been raised in an appeal from the final judgment or from the order confirming the sale over objections on these very grounds. These issues do not constitute mistake or excusable neglect remediable through 1.540 relief.").

[60] *Linares v. Bank of Am., N.A.*, 278 So. 3d 330, 332 n.3 (Fla. 3d DCA 2019) (holding that the jurisdictional nature of Rule 1.540(b) allows the error to be raised for the first time on appeal); *Bank One, Nat'l Ass'n v. Batronie*, 884 So. 2d 346, 349 (Fla. 2d DCA 2004).

[61] In the context of a motion to set aside a default, "meritorious" means simply that the defendant plans to raise a defense that may have some merit. The movant need only show that the defense it has raised is meritorious, not that it is likely to succeed. See *Rice v. James*, 740 So. 2d 7 (Fla. 1st DCA 1999). A general denial does not rise to the level of a meritorious defense, but affirmative defenses, even when pled with minimal specificity, can qualify as meritorious. *Household Fin. Corp., III v. Mitchell*, 51 So. 3d 1238, 1241 (Fla. 1st DCA 2011).

[62] See *Szucs v. Qualico Dev., Inc.*, 893 So. 2d 708, 711 (Fla. 2d DCA 2005) ("But the court is called upon to consider due diligence upon learning of the entry of the default, not four months later when the plaintiffs filed a motion for summary judgment."); *L.B.T. Corp. v. Camacho*, 429 So. 2d 88, 90 (Fla. 5th DCA 1983); *Bags by Ande, Inc. v. Schilling*, 406 So. 2d 536, 537 (Fla. 4th DCA 1981).

[63] See *Schwartz v. Business Cards Tomorrow, Inc.*, 644 So. 2d 611 (Fla. 4th DCA 1994).

[64] *Household Fin. Corp., III v. Mitchell*, 51 So. 3d 1238, 1241 (Fla. 1st DCA 2011).

[65] *Geer v. Jacobsen*, 880 So. 2d 717, 720 (Fla. 2d DCA 2004); *Steinhardt v. Intercondominium Group, Inc.*, 771 So. 2d 614, 614 (Fla. 4th DCA 2000); *Halpern v. Houser*, 949 So. 2d 1155, 1157 (Fla. 4th DCA 2007).

[66] *Lazcar Int'l, Inc. v. Caraballo*, 957 So. 2d 1191, 1192 (Fla. 3d DCA 2007) ("Unsworn argument of counsel is insufficient to satisfy the due diligence element of a motion to vacate a default final judgment.").

movant is alleging a legal defense, may be shown by attaching either an unverified pleading or motion, or an affidavit,[67] to the motion to vacate. But if the affirmative defense requires facts to be proven in order to establish it, the safer approach is to include the facts in an affidavit with the motion to vacate.[68]

On the face of Rule 1.540(b)(1), a party must move for relief within one year.[69] Since the rule provides for an entire year, the existence of "due diligence" in seeking relief upon discovery of the ground for vacatur under (b)(1), which is not even mentioned in the rule's express language, is a judgment call for the judge up to one year.[70]

One use of Rule 1.540 can be to obtain a fresher judgment for appellate purposes, where the court failed to send the order to counsel within the appeal time.[71] However, that non-receipt of the order must not be the result of a conscious decision by counsel to use a defective email system, which is not "excusable neglect."[72]

14-3:5 Procedure Under Rule 1.540(b)(2): Newly Discovered Evidence

That judgments of trial courts are presumed final is axiomatic in our system of justice.[73] This finality is eroded by vacating judgments based on a claim of "newly discovered evidence," and consequently, this remedy should be seldom granted and only when the party seeking relief has exercised due diligence.[74] It is the movant's burden to establish the exercise of due diligence, and it is not sufficient to merely show that the evidence was not discovered or known to counsel until after trial.[75] The movant must make his or her pre-trial vigilance apparent.[76] However, the necessary finality of litigation prohibits courts from giving parties a second chance at proof they had

---

[67] *American Network Transp. Mgmt. v. A Super-Limo Co.*, 857 So. 2d 313, 315 (Fla. 2d DCA 2003).

[68] *See Westinghouse Elevator Co. v. DFS Constr. Co.*, 438 So. 2d 125, 126 (Fla. 2d DCA 1983) ("An unverified answer may be sufficient if the issue involved is a matter of law, not a matter of proof, i.e., an answer alleging that the statute of limitations precludes the action.").

[69] *Florida Dep't of Revenue v. Pough*, 723 So. 2d 303 (Fla. 2d DCA 1998) (per curiam).

[70] *Fields v. Beneficial Florida, Inc.*, 208 So. 3d 278, 280 (Fla. 5th DCA 2016).

[71] *Diquollo v. TD Bank, N.A.*, 224 So. 3d 341, 342 (Fla. 5th DCA 2017) ("The trial court rendered a default final judgment in this matter on January 11, 2016, but Appellant, Ruenrudee Rowe Diquollo, did not receive a copy of the judgment until after the appeal time had run. This occurred because Appellee, TD Bank, N.A., furnished the trial court with an erroneous address for Appellant. After Appellant became aware of the entry of the judgment, on September 23, 2016, she filed a motion to vacate pursuant to Florida Rule of Civil Procedure 1.540(b). The trial court denied the motion without a hearing. Florida Rule of Civil Procedure 1.080(a) requires that all orders and documents filed in an action be served in conformity with Florida Rule of Judicial Administration 2.516. That rule provides that when a final judgment is entered against a party in default, the court must mail a conformed copy of it to the defaulting party at the address furnished by the party in whose favor the judgment is entered. See Fla. R. Jud. Admin. 2.516(h)(2).").

[72] *Emerald Coast Utils. Auth. v. Bear Marcus Pointe, LLC*, 227 So. 3d 752, 757-58 (Fla. 1st DCA 2017), *reh'g denied* (Oct. 6, 2017).

[73] *Bane v. Bane*, 775 So. 2d 938, 941 (Fla. 2000).

[74] *Brown v. McMillian*, 737 So. 2d 570, 571 (Fla. 1st DCA 1999).

[75] *King v. Harrington*, 411 So. 2d 912, 915 (Fla. 2d DCA 1982).

[76] *Cleveland v. Crown Fin., LLC*, 212 So. 3d 1065, 1069 (Fla. 1st DCA 2017).

available in the first instance but chose not to use.[77] On the face of Rule 1.540(b)(2), a party must move for relief within one year.[78]

14-3:6 Procedure Under Rule 1.540(b)(3): Fraud, Misrepresentation, or Other Misconduct by a Party

Under Rule 1.540(b)(3), to obtain relief from a final judgment based on fraud, misrepresentation or other misconduct of a party, the movant must, at a minimum, specify the alleged fraud with particularity and not just conclusions, and explain why the fraud, if it exists, would entitle the movant to have the judgment set aside.[79]

A mere allegation of fraud in a motion to vacate under Rule 1.540(b)(3) is not enough to merit vacatur, or even an evidentiary hearing: "In many cases, the term 'fraud' is loosely used to label all conduct which has displeased an opposing party."[80] It must be emphasized that *evidence*, not argument, is required.[81]

Importantly, Rule 1.540(b)(3) now does away with the old "intrinsic" versus "extrinsic" fraud distinction, meaning that all Rule 1.540(b)(3) motions based on fraud must now be brought within one year.[82] However, the "rule does not limit the power of a court to entertain an independent action to relieve a party from a judgment, decree, order, or proceeding or to set aside a judgment or decree for fraud upon the court."[83] "While a claim of intrinsic fraud must be brought under rule 1.540(b)(3), a claim of extrinsic fraud—also known as fraud upon the court—may be brought under the rule or may be brought at any time as an independent action challenging the final judgment."[84] On the other hand, false affidavits have always been considered "intrinsic

---

[77] *Cleveland v. Crown Fin., LLC*, 212 So. 3d 1065, 1068-69 (Fla. 1st DCA 2017).

[78] *Florida Dep't of Revenue v. Pough*, 723 So. 2d 303 (Fla. 2d DCA 1998) (per curiam).

[79] *See, e.g., Flemenbaum v. Flemenbaum*, 636 So. 2d 579, 580 (Fla. 4th DCA 1994); *Townsend v. Lane*, 659 So. 2d 720 (Fla. 5th DCA 1995); *Hembd v. Dauria*, 859 So. 2d 1238, 1239-40 (Fla. 4th DCA 2003).

[80] *Flemenbaum v. Flemenbaum*, 636 So. 2d 579, 580 (Fla. 4th DCA 1994).

[81] *See Bank of N.Y. Mellon v. Estate of Peterson*, 208 So. 3d 1218, 1222 (Fla. 2d DCA 2017) ("First, the Estate contends that the substance of its argument in the trial court would have allowed the court, on its own, to set aside the final judgment under rule 1.540(b)(3), which permits the court to vacate a final judgment based on the misconduct of an adverse party. However, it is incumbent on the party seeking to vacate a judgment under that rule to come forward with evidence to support its position, . . . and arguments of counsel do not constitute evidence, . . . Here, counsel for the Estate argued at the hearing that the Bank engaged in improper ex parte dealings with the court; however, this argument, which is frankly contradicted by the record on appeal, does not constitute evidence of any actual misconduct. In the absence of any such evidence, the record cannot support this argument as a basis for affirmance.").

[82] "Extrinsic fraud" used to be accorded more time to attack, but no more under Rule 1.540(b)(3) (. . . fraud (whether heretofore denominated intrinsic or extrinsic)). Now all alleged fraud is treated the same under Rule 1.540(b)(3).

[83] Fla. R. Civ. P. 1.540(b); *Linares v. Bank of Am., N.A.*, 278 So. 3d 330, 332 n.3 (Fla. 3d DCA 2019).

[84] *Bank One, N.A. v. Batronie*, 884 So. 2d 346, 348 n.1 (Fla. 2d DCA 2004); *Linares v. Bank of Am., N.A.*, 278 So. 3d 330, 332 n.2 (Fla. 3d DCA 2019).

fraud" which must be attacked within one year under Rule 1.540.[85] The court decides if the assertions raised amount to extrinsic fraud or intrinsic fraud.[86]

A Rule 1.540(b) motion based on fraud, if denied, operates as res judicata not only against successive Rule 1.540(b) motions,[87] but also against an independent action asserting the same grounds.[88]

An evidentiary hearing is unnecessary if a Rule 1.540(b)(3) motion merely undertakes to rehash matters previously litigated at trial or raises inconsequential "de minimis" matters.[89] For instance, to entitle a movant to an evidentiary hearing on a motion for relief from judgment under Rule 1.540(b)(3), the motion must specify the fraud with particularity and explain why the fraud, if it exists, would entitle the movant to have the judgment set aside.[90] This rule covers not only affirmative misrepresentations, but also material omissions as well.[91] If a motion does not set forth a basis for relief on its face, then an evidentiary hearing is unnecessary, the time and expense of needless litigation is avoided, and the policy of preserving the finality of judgments is enhanced.[92] The matter alleged must affect the outcome of the case and not merely be "de minimis."[93] Thus, to obtain a hearing on a Rule 1.540(b)(3) motion, the law requires a movant "to demonstrate a prima facie case of fraud, not just nibble at the edges of the concept."[94] The evidence of fraud must be competent, sworn or verified.[95]

---

[85] *Parker v. Parker*, 950 So. 2d 388, 391 (Fla.2007) (citing *DeClaire v. Yohanan*, 453 So. 2d 375, 377 (Fla.1984), *superseded by rule on other grounds* as stated in *Lefler v. Lefler*, 776 So. 2d 319 (Fla. 4th DCA 2001)); *State v. Speights*, 864 So. 2d 73 (Fla. 1st DCA 2003) (*per curiam*).

[86] *Linares v. Bank of Am., N.A.*, 278 So. 3d 330, 332 n.2 (Fla. 3d DCA 2019).

[87] *State, DOT v. Bailey*, 603 So. 2d 1384, 1386 (Fla. 1st DCA 1992) ("Under Rule 1.540(b), a party is generally precluded from bringing a successive motion which merely alleges matters which were or could have been alleged in the initial motion for post-judgment relief.").

[88] *Manzaro v. D'Alessandro*, 229 So. 3d 843, 845-46 (Fla. 4th DCA 2017) ("Regardless, whether or not a court has theoretical jurisdiction over an independent action for relief from a judgment entered by a different court is not dispositive on the issue of the frivolity of the Appellant's complaint in this case. Even if the Palm Beach Circuit Court had jurisdiction to entertain the independent action, it would have been precluded by . . . res judicata, due to the multiple earlier final orders denying the same relief requested in this proceeding [under Rule 1.540].") (citing *Pearce v. Sandler*, 219 So. 3d 961, 966 (Fla. 3d DCA 2017).

[89] *Coleman (Parent) Holdings, Inc. v. Morgan Stanley & Co., Inc.*, 20 So. 3d 952, 955 (Fla. 4th DCA 2009).

[90] *Flemenbaum v. Flemenbaum*, 636 So. 2d 579, 580 (Fla. 4th DCA 1994).

[91] See *Crowley v. Crowley*, 678 So. 2d 435, 438 (Fla. 4th DCA 1996).

[92] *Coleman (Parent) Holdings, Inc. v. Morgan Stanley & Co.*, 20 So. 3d 952, 955 (Fla. 4th DCA 2009).

[93] *Coleman (Parent) Holdings, Inc. v. Morgan Stanley & Co.*, 20 So. 3d 952, 955 (Fla. 4th DCA 2009).

[94] *Hembd v. Dauria*, 859 So. 2d 1238, 1240 (Fla. 4th DCA 2003).

[95] *Tikhomirov v. Bank of New York Mellon*, 223 So. 3d 1112, 1113 (Fla. 3d DCA 2017) ("We find that the trial court did not abuse its discretion in denying the motion for relief from judgment. Appellant neither stated the alleged fraud with sufficient particularity nor explained why the purported fraud would entitle Appellant to have the judgment set aside. Indeed, Appellant presented no competent, sworn, or verified evidence of fraud in his motion to vacate. . . . Notwithstanding Appellant's concerns, incorrect or misleading assignments of

14-3:7 Procedure Under Rule 1.540(b)(4): Voidness

A motion can be brought even after one year has passed to attack a void final order or judgment under Rule 1.540(b)(4), as long as it is brought within a "reasonable time."[96] But whether an order is void as opposed to voidable is not always easy to discern because there are three types of jurisdiction: personal, subject-matter, and procedural jurisdiction.[97] In general, a void judgment is so defective that it is deemed never to have had legal force and effect.[98] Generally speaking, a judgment is void if: (1) the trial court lacks subject matter jurisdiction; (2) the trial court lacks personal jurisdiction over the party; or (3) if, in the proceedings leading up to the judgment, there is a violation of the due process guarantee of notice and an opportunity to be heard.[99]

A default judgment based on a complaint that fails to state a cause of action is merely "voidable," which means the judgment must be challenged on that ground immediately in a motion for rehearing under Rule 1.530, or on appeal, and cannot be challenged under Rule 1.540(b)(4) as void.[100] A judgment based on a complaint that fails to state a cause of action, where the party had notice of the proceedings and failed to address the issue, is merely voidable as opposed to void.[101] A voidable judgment must be attacked, on the ground of failure to state a cause of action, by Rule 1.530

---

mortgage are not by themselves indicative of fraud, as assignments of mortgages are not required to transfer mortgages.").

[96] *Lamoise Grp., LLC v. Edgewater S. Beach Condo. Ass'n,* 278 So. 3d 796 (Fla. 3d DCA 2019).

[97] *U.S. Bank Nat. Ass'n v. Anthony-Irish,* 204 So. 3d 57, 62 (Fla. 5th DCA 2016) ("Rule 1.540(b) provides a limited avenue for collaterally attacking final judgments when certain errors are alleged. Even the limited grounds established by rule 1.540(b) must be brought within a reasonable time. . . . The only exception to this time limitation is for defects in the court's subject-matter jurisdiction. U.S. Bank brought its motion under rule 1.540(b) more than four years after the order it challenged was entered, which was not a reasonable time in this case. Further, U.S. Bank cannot show that the court lacked subject-matter jurisdiction. Accordingly, we affirm the trial court's denial of U.S. Bank's 1.540(b) motion.").

[98] *Dabas v. Boston Inv'r Grp., Inc.,* 231 So. 3d 542, 545 (Fla. 3d DCA 2017).

[99] *Lamoise Grp., LLC v. Edgewater S. Beach Condo. Ass'n,* 278 So. 3d 796 (Fla. 3d DCA 2019).

[100] *The Bank of New York v. Condo. Ass'n of La Mer Estates, Inc.,* 175 So. 3d 282 (Fla. 2015), *approving Condo. Ass'n of La Mer Estates, Inc. v. Bank of New York Mellon Corp.,* 137 So. 3d 396, 400-01 (Fla. 4th DCA 2014) (*en banc*) ("The motion for relief in this case provided no other reason for vacating the judgment other than arguing that the complaint failed to state a cause of action. We hold that these allegations would render the judgment voidable, not void. The bank was properly notified of the proceedings, notified of the hearing on final judgment, and notified of the entry of the final judgment. It could have appeared in the proceedings and raised the pleading defects, or it could have raised the issue on direct appeal. 'A voidable judgment can be challenged by motion for rehearing or appeal and may be subject to collateral attack under specific circumstances, but it cannot be challenged at any time as void under rule 1.540(b)(4).'") (quoting *Sterling Factors Corp. v. U.S. Bank Nat. Ass'n,* 968 So. 2d 658, 667 (Fla. 2d DCA 2007)); *see also Dage v. Deutsche Bank Nat'l Trust Co.,* 95 So. 3d 1021, 1024 (Fla. 2d DCA 2012) ("Even if Deutsche Bank lacked standing when it filed suit, the final judgment is merely voidable, not void.") (citing *Jones-Bishop v. Estate of Sweeney,* 27 So. 3d 176, 177 (Fla. 5th DCA 2010)).

[101] *The Bank of New York v. Condo. Ass'n of La Mer Estates, Inc.,* 175 So. 3d 282 (Fla. 2015).

and/or appeal.[102] A final judgment is not rendered void, but merely voidable, by the judgment holder (as opposed to some other affected property owner), by an error in the legal description in the mortgage and judgment.[103] A judgment that is voidable due to an error in the legal description can be attacked within one year under Rule 1.540(b)(1).[104]

Judgments based on illegally enacted statutes are void and thus can be attacked under Rule 1.540(b)(4), but judgments based on legally enacted statutes whose provisions violate the Constitution are merely voidable and cannot be attacked under that sub-paragraph.[105]

The failure to include the sole title owner in a mortgage foreclosure action results in a void final judgment.[106] This is so because the fee simple title holder is an indispensable party in an action to foreclose a mortgage on property.[107] However, if there are multiple title owners and at least one is named, the resulting judgment is merely voidable by the unnamed owners.[108] Thus, in cases where there are multiple owners of

---

[102] *The Bank of New York v. Condo. Ass'n of La Mer Estates, Inc.*, 175 So. 3d 282 (Fla. 2015), *approving Condo. Ass'n of La Mer Estates, Inc. v. Bank of New York Mellon Corp.*, 137 So. 3d 396, 400-01 (Fla. 4th DCA 2014) (*en banc*).

[103] *Epstein v. Bank of Am.*, 162 So. 3d 159, 161 (Fla. 4th DCA 2015) (motion to vacate judgment with erroneous legal description held time-barred under Rule 1.540(b)); *Cornelius v. Holzman*, 193 So. 3d 1029, 1032 (Fla. 4th DCA 2016) (same); *Lucas v. Barnett Bank of Lee Cty.*, 705 So. 2d 115, 116 (Fla. 2d DCA 1998) ("When a mortgage contains an incorrect legal description, a court may correct the mistake before foreclosure. If, however, the mistaken legal description is not corrected before final judgment of foreclosure, and the mistake is carried into the advertisement for sale and the foreclosure deed, a court cannot reform the mistake in the deed and judgment; rather, the foreclosure process must begin anew. . . . The reason behind this policy is that, if the mortgage is not reforeclosed, the purchaser would have obtained title to a property that was not properly ordered for sale, advertised, or sold. While the mortgagee who bid its mortgage at the sale might have understood exactly what property was being offered, other potential bidders at the sale might not have had the same understanding. . . . As the *Fisher* court noted, the mortgage may be reformed if a sufficient showing is made, and the reformed mortgage may be foreclosed. But first, the deed to the property must be canceled, and the original foreclosure judgment set aside, such that the parties are returned to their original status.").

[104] *Cornelius v. Holzman*, 193 So. 3d 1029, 1032 (Fla. 4th DCA 2016) ("Here, the allegation must have been under subsection (1), because the lender argued the legal description was incorrect.").

[105] *Attorney Gen. v. Nationwide Pools, Inc.*, 270 So. 3d 406 (Fla. 4th DCA 2019) (Rule 1.540(b)(4) not properly used because, "[a]ssuming for purposes of this opinion that the statute violated the First Amendment, the statute was not improperly enacted. Instead, it was a legally enacted statute whose provisions violate the Constitution. As a result, the judgment would have been voidable.").

[106] *FL Homes 1 LLC v. Kokolis Tr. of Toula Kokolis Revocable Tr.*, 271 So. 3d 6, 9 (Fla. 4th DCA 2019).

[107] *Citibank, N.A. v. Villanueva*, 174 So. 3d 612, 613 (Fla. 4th DCA 2015) (citing *Oakland Props. Corp. v. Hogan*, 96 Fla. 40, 117 So. 846, 848 (1928)).

[108] *FL Homes 1 LLC v. Kokolis Tr. of Toula Kokolis Revocable Tr.*, 271 So. 3d 6, 10 (Fla. 4th DCA 2019); *R.W. Holding Corp. v. R.I.W. Waterproofing & Decorating Co., Inc.*, 131 Fla. 424, 179 So. 753 (1938) (title owners for two of three parcels of land named in foreclosure action, but title owner of third parcel omitted); *Key West Wharf & Coal Co. v. Porter*, 63 Fla. 448, 58 So. 599 (1912) (mortgagor named in foreclosure action, but not others whom the mortgagor

property, but one or more of the property owners is omitted, "a foreclosure suit may be maintained even though the holder of the legal title to the property is not a party to the foreclosure, but . . . the decree only establishes the rights of persons who are parties."[109]

A voluntary dismissal of the complaint and counterclaims does not allow dismissal of a pending cross claim by a non-party to the voluntary dismissal, and a dismissal of that cross claim without notice to the cross claimant is void.[110]

Rule 1.540(b)(4) has application in a number of different foreclosure-related scenarios. For instance, sometimes a junior lienor such as a second mortgagee or an association may attempt to foreclose out a senior lienor. This is inappropriate, and any such judgment is a "nullity," "void," and not useful for purposes of res judicata against the senior lienholder.[111] The Florida Supreme Court has held that "the law is pretty well settled that a first or senior mortgagee is not a necessary or even proper party to foreclosure proceedings brought by a second or junior mortgagee."[112] That is, "persons holding mortgages or liens prior to the mortgage under foreclosure are neither necessary or proper parties to the action."[113] It is "not proper in foreclosure proceedings to try a claim of title superior or paramount to that of the mortgagor, and even if a party having title is made a party and judgment entered after a hearing, it will not bind his interest."[114] A judgment in a foreclosure action that favors a junior lienor over a primary lienor is a "nullity" and does not bind the primary lienor.[115] The resulting foreclosure judgment could be ignored, but this is most certainly not recommended; the risk-averse lender should defend any such foreclosure, and most certainly any declaratory relief or quiet title action, targeting its senior lien interest.[116] This is particularly true because a recent Florida Supreme Court case seems to suggest that, despite (but

---

had conveyed portions of the premises to); *Sudhoff v. Fed. Nat'l Mortg. Ass'n*, 942 So. 2d 425 (Fla. 5th DCA 2006) (husband named in foreclosure lawsuit, but not wife).

[109] *Pan Am. Bank of Miami v. City of Miami Beach*, 198 So. 2d 45, 47 (Fla. 3d DCA 1967).

[110] *Lamoise Grp., LLC v. Edgewater S. Beach Condo. Ass'n*, 278 So. 3d 796 (Fla. 3d DCA 2019).

[111] See *Wells Fargo Bank, N.A. v. Rutledge*, 148 So. 3d 533 (Fla. 2d DCA 2014) ("Wells Fargo, as the superior lien holder, was not a proper party to Harbor Towers' foreclosure action. . . . Because it was not required to participate in the county court foreclosure action, Wells Fargo's failure to participate cannot form the basis of a laches argument."); *U.S. Bank Nat'l Ass'n v. Bevans*, 138 So. 3d 1185, 1187 (Fla. 3d DCA 2014) (explaining that "the final judgment of foreclosure entered in favor of the Association in the Association's foreclosure action did not eliminate the Bank's senior mortgage interest because '[f]oreclosure does not terminate interests in the foreclosed real estate that are senior to the mortgage being foreclosed'" (quoting *Garcia v. Stewart*, 906 So. 2d 1117, 1120 (Fla. 4th DCA 2005))).

[112] *Cone Bros. Constr. Co. v. Moore*, 141 Fla. 420, 426 (1940).

[113] *Cone Bros. Constr. Co. v. Moore*, 141 Fla. 420, 426 (1940).

[114] *Cone Bros. Constr. Co. v. Moore*, 141 Fla. 420, 426 (1940).

[115] *CitiMortgage, Inc. v. Wachovia Bank*, 24 So. 3d 641, 642-43 (Fla. 2d DCA 2009).

[116] It should be pointed out, however, that the Second District Court of Appeal has held that even a quiet title action in which a judgment has been obtained, stating that a senior lien was foreclosed by an earlier foreclosure, may not be dispositive of the issue. *Bank of Am., N.A. v. Kipps Colony II Condo. Ass'n, Inc.*, 201 So. 3d 670, 676 (Fla. 2d DCA 2016) ("Moreover, the quiet title judgment did not resolve this issue. Rule 1.540(b)(5) provides that the court may relieve a party from a final judgment where 'a prior judgment or decree upon which [the challenged judgment] is based has been reversed or otherwise vacated.' The rule also 'does not limit the power of a court to entertain an independent action to relieve

not citing in any way) earlier precedent,[117] a bank is not free to ignore an attack on its mortgage, and has only one year to move to vacate because the judgment for failure to state a cause of action on these facts merely renders the judgment voidable, not void.[118]

Another scenario where Rule 1.540(b)(4) can be used is when an association files its own lien and foreclosure after an investor has already filed its own lis pendens.[119] In such a situation, any judgment or title obtained in the association's action is arguably void under *Quadomain* and Rule 1.540(b)(4) for lack of subject matter jurisdiction.[120] In other words, the association must litigate in the prior action with the prior lis pendens, if at all.[121] An order entered without subject matter jurisdiction is void.[122] It must be stated that the potency of *Quadomain* has been largely diluted by later decisions of the

---

a party from a judgment, decree, order, or proceeding or to set aside a judgment or decree for fraud upon the court.'").

[117] *Cone Bros. Constr. Co. v. Moore*, 141 Fla. 420, 426 (1940). However, *Cone Bros.* is still good law and seems to suggest that the reason the judgment naming a senior lienor is void is a question of judicial power, not of pleading. *See also Puryear v. State*, 810 So. 2d 901, 905 (Fla. 2002) ("We take this opportunity to expressly state that this Court does not intentionally overrule itself sub silentio. Where a court encounters an express holding from this Court on a specific issue and a subsequent contrary dicta statement on the same specific issue, the court is to apply our express holding in the former decision until such time as this Court recedes from the express holding.").

[118] *The Bank of New York v. Condo. Ass'n of La Mer Estates, Inc.*, 175 So. 3d 282 (Fla. 2015), approving *Condo. Ass'n of La Mer Estates, Inc. v. Bank of New York Mellon Corp.*, 137 So. 3d 396, 400-01 (Fla. 4th DCA 2014) (en banc).

[119] *The Bank of New York v. Condo. Ass'n of La Mer Estates, Inc.*, 175 So. 3d 282 (Fla. 2015), approving *Condo. Ass'n of La Mer Estates, Inc. v. Bank of New York Mellon Corp.*, 137 So. 3d 396, 400-01 (Fla. 4th DCA 2014) (*en banc*) ("The motion for relief in this case provided no other reason for vacating the judgment other than arguing that the complaint failed to state a cause of action. We hold that these allegations would render the judgment voidable, not void. The bank was properly notified of the proceedings, notified of the hearing on final judgment, and notified of the entry of the final judgment. It could have appeared in the proceedings and raised the pleading defects, or it could have raised the issue on direct appeal. 'A voidable judgment can be challenged by motion for rehearing or appeal and may be subject to collateral attack under specific circumstances, but it cannot be challenged at any time as void under rule 1.540(b)(4).'") (quoting *Sterling Factors Corp. v. U.S. Bank Nat. Ass'n*, 968 So. 2d 658, 667 (Fla. 2d DCA 2007)). The Florida Statutes specifically provide that "the recording of [a] notice of lis pendens . . . constitutes a bar to the enforcement against the property described in the notice of all interests and liens . . . unrecorded at the time of recording the notice *unless* the holder of any such unrecorded interest or lien intervenes in such proceedings within 30 days after the recording of the notice." Fla. Stat. § 48.23(1)(d) (emphasis added).

[120] *U.S. Bank Nat'l Ass'n v. Quadomain Condo. Ass'n, Inc.*, 103 So. 3d 977, 978-80 (Fla. 4th DCA 2012). However, the flip side is not true; banks with mortgages recorded prior to the association's lis pendens need not litigate in the association's foreclosure in order to have a valid judgment. *See CitiMortgage, Inc. v. Flowers*, 189 So. 3d 1032 (Fla. 4th DCA 2016). *Quadomain* only applies to interests which were unrecorded at the time of the initial lis pendens. *Id.*

[121] *See Baron v. Aiello*, 319 So. 2d 198, 200 (Fla. 3d DCA 1975) (holding that a judgment lienholder's attempt to foreclose said lien came too late when the action was commenced after the first mortgagee recorded a lis pendens). *Cf. CitiMortgage, Inc. v. Flowers*, 189 So. 3d 1032 (Fla. 4th DCA 2016).

[122] *Cesaire v. State*, 811 So. 2d 816, 817 (Fla. 4th DCA 2002). *Cf. CitiMortgage, Inc. v. Flowers*, 189 So. 3d 1032 (Fla. 4th DCA 2016).

Fourth District Court of Appeal, at least in cases (and here it attempted to distinguish *Quadomain*) where the association is not attempting to take title from the bank and is only suing a delinquent homeowner.[123] This gutting of *Quadomain* occurred by the construction of an association's declaration as a "recorded interest" under § 48.23, Fla. Stat.[124] An association's declaration will almost always predate the subject mortgage and a lis pendens in a related foreclosure action; but where it does not, *Quadomain* applies. However, if the bank does not record a lis pendens before the association files its foreclosure, the association is free to file its own action regardless of *Quadomain*.[125]

Or, sometimes an association will not serve the bank properly with process, but the clerk will default the bank anyway.[126] Any judgment or title obtained without proper service of process can be vacated under Rule 1.540(b)(4) because if process was not perfected, then the trial court lacked jurisdiction.[127] An order entered without personal jurisdiction is void.[128] If the default and judgment are vacated as void, it has been ruled that the resulting sale must be vacated as well.[129]

Also, if a party obtains a judgment for relief that was not pled, that renders the judgment void and subject to vacatur under rule 1.540(b)(4).[130]

---

[123] *Jallali v. Knightsbridge Vill. Homeowners Ass'n, Inc.*, 211 So. 3d 216, 221 (Fla. 4th DCA 2017), *rev. denied*, No. SC17-409, 2017 WL 2559143 (Fla. June 13, 2017).

[124] *See also Jallali v. Knightsbridge Vill. Homeowners Ass'n, Inc.*, 211 So. 3d 216 (Fla. 4th DCA 2017), *rev. denied*, No. SC17-409, 2017 WL 2559143 (Fla. June 13, 2017); *Fountainspring II Homeowners Ass'n, Inc. v. Veliz*, 212 So. 3d 1049, 1050 (Fla. 4th DCA 2017) ("We agree with the association. Since its claim of lien dated back to its 1989 Declaration, its recorded interest predated the bank's notice of lis pendens. Thus, the foreclosure action instituted to pursue the association's claim is not precluded by the bank's pending foreclosure action. Our holding is consistent with this court's recent opinion in *Jallali v. Knightsbridge Vill. Homeowners Ass'n*, . . .").

[125] *U.S. Bank Nat. Ass'n v. Bevans*, 138 So. 3d 1185, 1189 (Fla. 3d DCA 2014).

[126] *HSBC Bank USA, National Association v. Centre Court Ridge Condo. Ass'n, Inc.*, 147 So. 3d 593, 594 (Fla. 5th DCA 2014).

[127] *Pelycado Onroerend Goed B.V. v. Ruthenberg*, 635 So. 2d 1001, 1005 (Fla. 5th DCA 1994) (holding a trial court lacks jurisdiction when a party fails to strictly comply with the statutes regarding service).

[128] *Carter v. Kingsley Bank*, 587 So. 2d 567, 569 (Fla. 1st DCA 1991) ("The Carters next argue that the court did not have personal jurisdiction over them. Kingsley Bank did not even attempt to answer this argument with regard to Paul Carter. The undisputed facts show that he was never served with process and a copy of the complaint and did not appear at any hearing or file any paper with the court. The deficiency judgment is manifestly void as to him.").

[129] *Fremont Reorganizing Corp. v. The Grand Condo. Ass'n, Inc.*, No. 11-15916 CC 05, 2017 WL 3317502, at *2 (Fla. Cir. Ct. 2017) ("Secondly, it is undeniable that the sheriff's deed, and resulting sheriff's sale, were based *solely* upon the void (and now vacated) final judgment of foreclosure, which was itself based *solely* upon the void (and now vacated) default. It thus inexorably follows that the subsequent transactions predicated upon these void decrees are likewise void.") (emphasis in original).

[130] *Deutsche Bank Nat. Trust Co. v. Patino*, 192 So. 3d 637, 638 (Fla. 1st DCA 2016) ("Our review of the pleadings and the trial transcript show that Appellee did not affirmatively plead for or seek a determination at trial that the mortgage lien be cancelled or declared to be 'no longer of legal effect.' Accordingly, the trial court lacked jurisdiction to grant Appellee this relief, rendering this portion of the judgment void."); *BAC Home Loans Servicing, Inc. v. Headley*, 130 So. 3d 703, 704-07 (Fla. 3d DCA 2013).

Finally, arguably, a dismissal of a foreclosure action that occurs without an evidentiary hearing[131] on the six factors identified in *Kozel v. Ostendorf*,[132] can be challenged as "void" because Florida law requires an evidentiary hearing.[133] Florida law also requires an evidentiary hearing before an action can be dismissed as a sanction for discovery violations.[134] And where the law requires an evidentiary hearing, failure to hear the matter is a violation of due process.[135] Banks are also entitled to due process.[136] When a court fails to give one party the opportunity to present witnesses or testify on his or her own behalf, the court has violated that party's fundamental right to procedural due process.[137] Further, proper notice of an evidentiary hearing must be

---

[131] *Paxton v. Williams Scotsman, Inc.*, 924 So. 2d 37 (Fla. 5th DCA 2006); *TICO Ins. Co. v. Schonning*, 960 So. 2d 6 (Fla. 3d DCA 2005) ("Because the pleadings were struck in the absence of an evidentiary hearing, we reverse."); *Heritage Circle Condo. Ass'n, Inc. v. State of Florida*, 121 So. 3d 1141 (Fla. 4th DCA 2013); *Ross v. City of Tarpon Springs*, 802 So. 2d 473 (Fla. 2d DCA 2001) (reversed and remanded for evidentiary hearing).

[132] *Kozel v. Ostendorf*, 629 So. 2d 817 (Fla. 1994).

[133] The Second District Court of Appeal has held that the *Kozel* factors need only be considered on a dismissal with prejudice or its functional equivalent (such as when the statute of limitations has run), but certified conflict with the First and Third District Courts of Appeal on the issue. *See Fed. Nat. Mort. Ass'n v. Linner*, 193 So. 3d 1010, 1013 (Fla. 2d DCA 2016) ("However, it appears that the First District applies the *Kozel* factors when dismissal is entered as a sanction, even if the dismissal is without prejudice.... The Third District has also applied the *Kozel* factors to a dismissal without prejudice entered as a sanction where the sanctioned party was required to file a new case in order to pursue its claims.... It is not reversible error for a trial court to fail to consider the *Kozel* factors before dismissing a case without prejudice. The factors set forth in *Kozel* apply to dismissals with prejudice because such dismissals dispose of a case and may run the risk of punishing the litigant too harshly for counsel's conduct.... When a case is dismissed without prejudice, a litigant may still have his or her day in court, even if the case needs to be refiled. The concern underlying the *Kozel* factors is simply not presented by a dismissal without prejudice. Accordingly, we hold that for sanctions falling short of dismissal with prejudice or its functional equivalent, a trial court does not err by failing to consider the *Kozel* factors. Here, because the trial court dismissed the case without prejudice, any failure to apply Kozel does not require reversal. We certify conflict with *Cook*, 178 So. 3d 548; *Parrish*, 146 So. 3d 526; *Ellison*, 141 So. 3d 1290; and *Wild*, 164 So. 3d 94.").

[134] *See, e.g., Belflower v. Cushman & Wakefield of Fla., Inc.*, 510 So. 2d 1130 (Fla. 2d DCA 1987); *Austin v. Papol*, 464 So. 2d 1338 (Fla. 2d DCA 1985).

[135] *See Yoxsimer v. Yoxsimer*, 918 So. 2d 997 (Fla. 2d DCA 2006) (trial court was required to conduct a hearing in marriage dissolution action following wife's exceptions to magistrate's recommendation of order compelling wife to return to the state with the parties' children; due process and state rules of procedure mandated hearing); *Thurner v. Thurner*, 584 So. 2d 150 (Fla. 2d DCA 1991) (procedural due process of law requires that indirect criminal contempt proceedings be conducted in conformity with rule governing such proceedings); *Greene v. Seigle*, 745 So. 2d 411 (Fla. 4th DCA 1999) ("An elementary and fundamental requirement of due process in any proceeding which is to be accorded finality is notice reasonably calculated, under all the circumstances, to apprise interested parties of the pendency of the action and afford them an opportunity to present their objections."); *Mullane v. Central Hanover Bank & Trust Co.*, 339 U.S. 306, 314 (1950); *Quay Dev., Inc. v. Elegante Bldg. Corp.*, 392 So. 2d 901, 903 (Fla.1981).

[136] *See BAC Home Loans Servicing, Inc. v. Headley*, 130 So. 3d 703, 704-07 (Fla. 3d DCA 2013).

[137] *Douglas v. Johnson*, 65 So. 3d 605 (Fla. 2d DCA 2011). *See also Lezcano v. Estate of Hidalgo*, 88 So. 3d 306 (Fla. 3d DCA 2012).

given so as to avoid surprise.[138] As testimony must be taken, notice of the required evidentiary hearing must be provided to the parties in order to avoid surprise and ensure due process.[139] The constitutional guarantee of due process requires that each litigant be given a full and fair opportunity to be heard.[140] The right to be heard at an evidentiary hearing includes more than simply being allowed to be present and to speak.[141] Instead, the right to be heard includes the right to introduce evidence at a meaningful time and in a meaningful manner.[142] It also includes the opportunity to cross-examine witnesses and to be heard on questions of law.[143] Arguably, a dismissal-as-sanction order that did not provide an evidentiary hearing could be challenged as void under Rule 1.540(b)(4) for failure to accord procedural due process.

However, if a trial court awards post-sale surplus to the wrong party, it does not make the order void, but only erroneous, such that Rule 1.540(b)(4) cannot be used in such a case.[144]

14-3:8 Procedure Under Rule 1.540(b)(5): When a Judgment Has Been Satisfied, Released, Discharged, or It Is No Longer Equitable to Enforce It

Subparagraph (b)(5) of Rule 1.540 is not used as often as the other subparagraphs, but is still important. Florida Rule of Civil Procedure 1.540(b)(5) provides that a court may relieve a party from a final judgment where "the judgment or decree has been satisfied, released, or discharged . . . or it is no longer equitable that the judgment should have prospective application."[145] There is no one-year limit to the time within which a motion for relief from judgment may be made under Rule 1.540(b)(5), but the motion must be filed within a "reasonable time."[146] Additionally, the rule limits

---

[138] *Herranz v. Siam*, 2 So. 3d 1105 (Fla. 3d DCA 2009).

[139] *Juliano v. Juliano*, 687 So. 2d 910, 911 (Fla. 3d DCA 1997) ("It is expected that motion calendar hearings are for the purpose of resolving matters which require little time and are limited to arguments of counsel. While there is nothing to prevent the trial court from hearing testimony in uncontested matters, or by agreement of all involved, testimony in disputed matters comes as a surprise at motion calendar. Accordingly, to avoid sandbagging of parties, if the court is to allow testimony in disputed motion calendar hearings, specific notice of such intention must be given, with a sufficient interval to prepare and adequate opportunity to present contrary testimony prior to ruling.").

[140] *County of Pasco v. Riehl*, 635 So. 2d 17, 18 (Fla.1994); *E.I. DuPont De Nemours & Co. v. Lambert*, 654 So. 2d 226, 228 (Fla. 2d DCA 1995); *Edelman v. Breed*, 836 So. 2d 1092, 1094 (Fla. 5th DCA 2003).

[141] *Baron v. Baron*, 941 So. 2d 1233, 1236 (Fla. 2d DCA 2006).

[142] *Baron v. Baron*, 941 So. 2d 1233, 1236 (Fla. 2d DCA 2006); *Brinkley v. County of Flagler*, 769 So. 2d 468, 472 (Fla. 5th DCA 2000).

[143] *Baron v. Baron*, 941 So. 2d 1233, 1236 (Fla. 2d DCA 2006).

[144] *Eduartez v. Fed. Nat'l Mortg. Ass'n*, 251 So. 3d 227 (Fla. 3d DCA 2018) ("That the trial court might have disbursed the proceeds to the wrong person would not mean the trial court lacked jurisdiction, but simply that the trial court committed reversible error. Rule 1.540 is unavailable to remedy legal error."), *rev'd on other grounds, Eduartez v. Fed. Nat'l Mortgage Ass'n*, SC18-1436, 2018 WL 6434740, at *1 (Fla. Dec. 7, 2018).

[145] *JP Morgan Chase Bank, N.A. v. Hernandez*, 99 So. 3d 508 (Fla. 3d DCA 2011).

[146] *See* Fla. R. Civ. P. 1.540(b)(5).

the equities to "ones that come to fruition after the final judgment."[147] Rule 1.540(b)(5) merely requires a showing of significant new evidence or substantial changes in circumstances arising after the entry of judgment making it "no longer equitable" for the trial court to enforce the order.[148]

A successful Rule 1.540(b)(5) motion returns the case and the parties to the same position that they were in before the court entered the judgment.[149]

The primary use of this provision in the foreclosure context is when post-judgment (or even post-certificate of title), the bank and borrower wish to vacate the prior judgment and enter into a loan modification, because "it is no longer equitable that the judgment or decree should have prospective application."[150] Vacatur in such cases is needed because, technically, a note and mortgage cannot otherwise be modified once there is a judgment of foreclosure because of the loan's merger into the final judgment—unless there is vacatur.[151] Nor can the lender retrieve the original loan documents after a judgment of foreclosure,[152] which in modification cases the lender needs in case of future default, because the note and mortgage are collateral and must not be shredded, which they will be, if they are left in the court file long enough.

Settlement is heavily favored under Florida jurisprudence. The public policy of the State of Florida, as articulated in numerous court decisions, highly favors settlement agreements among parties and will seek to enforce them whenever possible.[153] To force the borrower and lender into a final judgment and sale, by denying vacatur of a sale or final judgment (or both), that unless vacated will deter any attempts at a loan modification, would have a chilling effect on settlement negotiations, a result that helps no one.[154] An order refusing to vacate the final judgment and resulting title could

---

[147] *Baker v. Baker*, 920 So. 2d 689, 692 (Fla. 2d DCA 2006); *See Bank of N.Y. Mellon v. Estate of Peterson*, 208 So. 3d 1218, 1222 (Fla. 2d DCA 2017) ("At its core, there must be some new postjudgment fact or occurrence that requires the trial court, in equity, to recede from its prior order or judgment.").

[148] *Pure H20 Biotech., Inc. v. Mazziotti*, 937 So. 2d 242, 244 (Fla. 4th DCA 2006).

[149] *Bane v. Bane*, 775 So. 2d 938, 941 (Fla. 2000).

[150] Fla. R. Civ. P. 1.540(b)(5).

[151] *One 79th Street Estates, Inc. v. American Investment Services*, 47 So. 3d 886, 889 & n.4 (Fla. 3d DCA 2010) (addressing the impact of a post-judgment settlement agreement, while acknowledging the merger of the loan documents into the final judgment: "The 'reinstatement' of a mortgage after the entry of a foreclosure judgment is considerably more difficult than merely rescheduling a judicial sale date. Reinstatement signifies that the mortgage is returned to its pre-default status as an effective instrument, by definition anticipating that any foreclosure judgment is vacated and the lawsuit dismissed.... A reinstatement of a mortgage after acceleration and foreclosure can accomplish the intended result only if the foreclosure judgment is vacated.").

[152] *Johnston v. Hudlett*, 32 So. 3d 700 (Fla. 4th DCA 2010).

[153] *See Sun Mircosystems of California, Inc. v. Engineering and Manufacturing. Systems, C.A.*, 682 So. 2d 219, 220 (Fla. 3d DCA 1996) (citing *Robbie v. City of Miami*, 469 So. 2d 1384 (Fla. 1985)); *American Express Travel Related Services, Co. v. Marrod, Inc.*, 637 So. 2d 4 (Fla. 3d DCA 1994).

[154] *See Wells Fargo Bank, N.A. v. Lupica*, 36 So. 3d 875, 876 (Fla. 5th DCA 2010) ("The trial court then entered a final order denying the motions [to cancel sale and to vacate sale]. The purported basis for the denial of Wells Fargo's two unopposed motions was the failure to attach a stipulation and/or a copy of the loan modification or forbearance agreement signed by all parties. The trial judge further suggested that the parties should have dis-

force foreclosure and eviction: an illogical result that neither party desires when a loan is modified. Rule 1.540(b)(5) can be used, at any time, to resolve this issue.

However, if the judgment is vacated, the original loan documents can and should be retrieved. When moving for the return of the original loan documents after vacating a foreclosure judgment, it is wise to include a provision in the return order that in the event the court or clerk has stamped "cancelled" or anything of similar import on the note and/or mortgage, that said stamp is vacated and the original loan documents reinstated.[155]

---

cussed the modification of the loan prior to entry of the final judgment 'which could have avoided unnecessary consumption of the time of two courts.' Foreclosures are equitable proceedings under Florida law and settlements between litigants are favored. The trial court's denial of Wells Fargo's unopposed motions flies in the face of these principles. Furthermore, it was not necessary for Wells Fargo to have attached a stipulation and/or copy of a signed loan modification or forbearance agreement. There was no basis for the trial court to reject Wells Fargo's counsel's representation, as an officer of the court, that an agreement had been reached between the parties—particularly where the Lupicas never disputed such representation. The trial court's actions constituted a gross abuse of discretion."); *Wells Fargo Bank, NA v. Giglio,* 123 So. 3d 60, 60-61 (Fla. 4th DCA 2013) ("Wells Fargo's motion relied upon section 702.07, Florida Statutes (2011), as well as Florida Rule of Civil Procedure 1.540(b)(5). We have held that section 702.07 'standing alone does not create an independent, substantive right to vacate a judgment of foreclosure for any reason,' and that the statute must be read together with Rule 1.540 which 'provides the avenue' for such relief.... The pertinent part of Rule 1.540(b)(5) relied upon by Wells Fargo requires the movant to demonstrate that 'it is no longer equitable that the judgment or decree should have prospective application.' Florida Rule of Civil Procedure 1.540(b)(5). Subsection (b)(5) was designed to provide 'extraordinary relief' in exceptional circumstances and is to be narrowly construed.... As one would expect, relief under Rule 1.540(b)(5) is typically sought by a party against whom the subject judgment is entered—not, as in this case, the beneficiary of the judgment. But nothing in the rule suggests that Wells Fargo lacked an ability to seek vacatur of a judgment it received, relief Giglio did not oppose. The trial court nevertheless concluded that: (a) Wells Fargo's motion failed to allege sufficient grounds under Rule 1.540; (b) the clerk could not return the original note because it was cancelled and incorporated into the final judgment; and (c) that as a result of the final judgment, Wells Fargo's request for dismissal was moot. As the trial court had vacated the foreclosure sale, its order denying the related relief requested left the parties in legal limbo. A final judgment and lis pendens remained of record even though the mortgage had been reinstated, and Wells Fargo was denied possession of its original loan documents, thereby impeding its ability to seek relief in the event of a further default. We hold that the trial court, having vacated the foreclosure sale, abused its discretion in refusing to grant the related collateral relief requested by Wells Fargo, which refusal prevented the parties from concluding their settlement.... The trial court clearly had jurisdiction to consider Wells Fargo's Rule 1.540(b)(5) motion; and in light of the parties' settlement—a result the law seeks to encourage—the relief requested should have been granted."). *See* Fla. Stat. § 702.07 ("Power of courts and judges to set aside foreclosure decrees at any time before sale.—The circuit courts of this state, and the judges thereof at chambers, shall have jurisdiction, power, and authority to rescind, vacate, and set aside a decree of foreclosure of a mortgage of property at any time before the sale thereof has been actually made pursuant to the terms of such decree, and to dismiss the foreclosure proceeding upon the payment of all court costs.").

[155] *HSBC Bank USA, N.A. v. Angelini,* 2016 WL 3547023, at *1 (Fla. Cir. Ct. June 29, 2016) ("In the event the Court or Clerk may have stamped 'cancelled' or the like on the original Note and Mortgage, due to the prior, now-reversed foreclosure judgment, the Note and Mortgage are *nunc pro tunc* declared reinstated, un-cancelled, and re-validated as effective Loan

Sometimes a court will penalize a lender, after a sale has been cancelled or set aside due to attempts at settlement, by refusing to re-set a sale after a judgment when settlement attempts fail. A Rule 1.540(b)(5) motion can target such an order if vacatur or cancellation of the sale was an attempted resolution via some method that doesn't entail a judicial sale, such as a short sale. Refusing to reset the sale if the attempted settlement fails is not equitably prospective in application, in essence, because it strips a lender of its security interest and ability to obtain a deficiency judgment (which cannot exist absent a sale).[156] Absent extraordinary circumstances, courts cannot refuse to re-set a sale, and trial courts have been overturned for failing to reset a sale.[157]

14-3:9 Uses of Rule 1.540(a) to Correct Clerical Errors

Rule 1.540(a) is not used as much as 1.540(b), but it allows a court to correct a clerical error "at any time on its own initiative."[158] Sub-section (a) of Rule 1.540 allows the trial court to correct errors "arising from oversight or omission ... at any time on its own initiative or on the motion of any party and after such notice, if any, as the court orders." The clerical mistakes referred to by subsection (a) are only "errors or mistakes arising from accidental slip or omission, and not errors or mistakes in the substance of what is decided by the judgment or order."[159] Hence, the rule is essentially designed to correct typographical errors and the like rather than to address due process violations or substantive errors in a judgment.[160] However, the clerical errors are supposed to be small, not substantive. Reliance on this rule to get around Rule 1.540(b)'s time limitations is risky since there are many cases holding that an error is not "clerical" and not redressable by the rule.[161] Yet, one court allowed Deutsche Bank to amend its erroneously abbreviated name in a judgment and certificate of

---

Documents, and are declared as enforceable as if they bore no such stamp.") (citing Fla. Sat. § 702.07 and § 702.08).

[156] Fla. Stat. § 45.031(1) (following entry of a final judgment, the court "shall direct the clerk to sell the property at public sale" no more than 35 days from entry of the final judgment, unless plaintiff consents to an extension); *see also LR5A-JV v. Little House, LLC*, 50 So. 3d 691, 695-96 (Fla. 5th DCA 2010); *Bankers Trust Co. v. Edwards*, 849 So. 2d 1160, 1161 (Fla. 1st DCA 2003); *Chrestensen v. Eurogest, Inc.*, 906 So. 2d 343, 345 (Fla. 4th DCA 2005); *David v. Sun Federal Sav. & Loan Ass'n*, 461 So. 2d 93, 95 (Fla. 1984); *Campbell v. Werner*, 232 So. 2d 252, 256 (Fla. 3d DCA 1970). *See also* Fla. Stat. § 95.11(5)(h).

[157] *Bankers Trust Co. of California, N.A. v. Weidner*, 688 So. 2d 453, 454 (Fla. 5th DCA 1997); *Republic Fed. Bank, N.A. v. Doyle*, 19 So. 3d 1053, 1054 (Fla. 3d DCA 2009).

[158] *Moforis v. Moforis*, 977 So. 2d 786, 788 (Fla. 4th DCA 2008).

[159] *Byers v. Callahan*, 848 So. 2d 1180, 1184 (Fla. 2d DCA 2003) (quoting *Keller v. Belcher*, 256 So. 2d 561, 563 (Fla. 3d DCA 1971)).

[160] *Purdue v. R.J. Reynolds Tobacco Co.*, 259 So. 3d 918, 921 (Fla. 2d DCA 2018).

[161] *See, e.g., Purdue v. R.J. Reynolds Tobacco Co.*, 259 So. 3d 918, 921 (Fla. 2d DCA 2018) ("Here, Purdue does not allege that there is an error in the order of dismissal itself. Thus, she has not alleged an error that is cognizable under rule 1.540(a). Her reliance on *DiPiazza v. Palm Beach Mall, Inc.*, 722 So.2d 831 (Fla. 2d DCA 1998), where the order at issue accidentally dismissed all defendants rather than only one, and *Underwriters at Lloyd's London v. Rolly Marine Service, Inc.*, 475 So.2d 265 (Fla. 4th DCA 1985), where a mistake in an order entered by the clerk caused the case to be dismissed rather than transferred, is unavailing because those cases did involve actual errors in the orders themselves rather than in the process of transmitting them. Accordingly, Purdue is not entitled to relief under rule 1.540(a).").

title which had caused a title defect affecting its sale to a third party, which arguably had substantive effect.[162] Since the court held that a name change had no substantive effect, the court refused to allow the borrower to use the amendment to kick-start a new rehearing or appellate period, stating that she should have appealed the original judgment.[163]

14-4 Post-Judgment Objections to Sale

Section 45.031, Florida Statutes, titled "Judicial sales procedure," addresses judicial foreclosure sales and sets forth the procedures that "may be followed as an alternative to any other sale procedure if so ordered by the court."[164] Under section 45.031, the trial court, "[i]n the order or final judgment," "shall direct the clerk to sell the property at public sale on a specified day."[165] A notice of sale shall then be published at certain times and shall contain certain information, including "[t]he time and place of sale."[166] The winning bidder is required to post a deposit "[a]t the time of the sale" and must pay the remaining balance within a prescribed period.[167] "After a sale of the property," the clerk is required to "promptly file a certificate of sale."[168] "If no objections to the sale are filed within 10 days after filing the certificate of sale," the clerk is then required to file a "certificate of title."[169] Upon the filing of the certificate of title, "the sale shall stand confirmed."[170]

Section 45.031, Florida Statutes,[171] authorizes objections to judicial foreclosure sales[172] if timely made, and states in pertinent part:

---

[162] *Bazzichelli v. Deutsche Bank Tr. Co. Americas*, 274 So. 3d 414 (Fla. 3d DCA 2019), *reh'g denied* (May 29, 2019).

[163] *Bazzichelli v. Deutsche Bank Tr. Co. Americas*, 274 So. 3d 414 (Fla. 3d DCA 2019), *reh'g denied* (May 29, 2019).

[164] *Bank of New York Mellon v. Glenville*, 252 So. 3d 1120, 1122 (Fla. 2018) (quoting § 45.031, Fla. Stat.).

[165] *Bank of New York Mellon v. Glenville*, 252 So. 3d 1120, 1122 (Fla. 2018) (quoting § 45.031(1)(a), Fla. Stat.).

[166] *Bank of New York Mellon v. Glenville*, 252 So. 3d 1120, 1122 (Fla. 2018) (quoting § 45.031(2), Fla. Stat.).

[167] *Bank of New York Mellon v. Glenville*, 252 So. 3d 1120, 1122 (Fla. 2018) (quoting § 45.031(3), Fla. Stat.).

[168] *Bank of New York Mellon v. Glenville*, 252 So. 3d 1120, 1122 (Fla. 2018) (quoting § 45.031(4), Fla. Stat.).

[169] *Bank of New York Mellon v. Glenville*, 252 So. 3d 1120, 1122 (Fla. 2018) (quoting § 45.031(5), Fla. Stat.).

[170] *Bank of New York Mellon v. Glenville*, 252 So. 3d 1120, 1122 (Fla. 2018) (quoting § 45.031(6), Fla. Stat.).

[171] Florida courts apply these sections to foreclosures by associations as well. *See Chase Financial Services, LLC. v. Edelsberg*, 129 So. 3d 1139, 1141-42 (Fla. 3d DCA 2013); *Aegis Props. of S. Fla., LLC v. Avalon Master Homeowner Ass'n, Inc.*, 37 So. 3d 960 (Fla. 4th DCA 2010) (applying Chapter 45 procedure to a homeowner association's lien foreclosure action). *See* Fla. Stat. § 720.3085(1)(c) (providing that an "association may bring an action in its name to foreclose a lien for assessments in the same manner in which a mortgage of real property is foreclosed").

[172] One ground for objection is failure to properly notice the sale. *Cf. Karapetyan v. Deutsche Bank Nat'l Trust Co.*, 220 So. 3d 542, 543 (Fla. 3d DCA 2017) ("The borrowers argue that the notice of the foreclosure sale did not comply with section 45.031(2), Florida Statutes

(4) CERTIFICATION OF SALE.—After a sale of the property the clerk shall promptly file a certificate of sale and serve a copy of it on each party. . . .

(5) CERTIFICATE OF TITLE.—If no objections to the sale are filed within 10 days after filing the certificate of sale, the clerk shall file a certificate of title. . . .

(8) VALUE OF PROPERTY.—The amount of the bid for the property at the sale shall be conclusively presumed to be sufficient consideration for the sale. Any party may serve an objection to the amount of the bid within 10 days after the clerk files the certificate of sale. If timely objections to the bid are served, the objections shall be heard by the court. Service of objections to the amount of the bid does not affect or cloud the title of the purchaser in any manner. If the case is one in which a deficiency judgment may be sought and application is made for a deficiency, the amount bid at the sale may be considered by the court as one of the factors in determining a deficiency under the usual equitable principles.

Fla Stat. §§ 45.031(4), (5), (8).

The right of redemption, per Fla. Stat. § 45.0315, extends until the later of the filing of a certificate of sale by the clerk or the time specified in the final judgment.[173] Once the right of redemption expires, the only way for the borrower to have her redemption rights revested is to get the judicial sale set aside.[174] If the United States of America is a defendant, it has a special right of redemption following the judicial sale and unique procedures governing its redemption under 28 U.S.C. § 2410(c) and (d).

The statute on its face requires that the objection be filed,[175] not merely served, within 10 days after the filing of the certificate of sale, but is somewhat ambiguous.

(2015), . . . Here, there is no dispute that the notice of foreclosure sale was printed in the Daily Business Review on Friday, April 15, 2016, and again on Friday, April 22, 2016. The sale took place on May 4, 2016, more than the required five days after the April 22, 2016 date of the second publication. Appellants suggest that because the first publication occurred on April 15, 2016, we must consider that to be the beginning of an initial one-week period ending on April 21, 2016. The appellants further contend that the statute requires a second one-week period which, in this case, is the period from April 22 through April 29, 2016. They argue that this interpretation requires that the second publication occur on April 29, 2016 because it is the final day of the second full week. Under that methodology, the May 4, 2016 sale date falls short of the five-day statutory requirement, once the intervening weekends are considered. We reject this interpretation of the statute. Publication occurred once during the week of April 15, 2016, and once again during the week of April 22, 2016, satisfying the 'once a week for 2 consecutive weeks' requirement in the statute. Accordingly, we affirm the order on appeal.").

[173] Fla. Stat. § 45.0315.
[174] *JRBL Dev., Inc. v. Maiello*, 872 So. 2d 362, 363 (Fla. 2d DCA 2004).
[175] *Cf.* Fla. Stat. § 45.031(5) ("If no objections to the sale are *filed* within 10 days after filing the certificate of sale, the clerk shall file a certificate of title . . .") (emphasis added), with Fla. Sat. § 45.031(8) ("If timely objections to the bid are *served*, the objections shall be heard by the court.") (emphasis added). Thus, a wise practitioner will ensure that both are done, and that the service method complies with Rule 2.516 of the Florida Rules of Judicial Administration. *Cf. Wheaton v. Wheaton*, 261 So. 3d 1236, 1237 (Fla. 2019).

The 10 days to object has been held to be jurisdictional.[176] But there is contrary authority.[177]

The timely objector is entitled to an evidentiary hearing.[178] For the court to "hear" objections as required by § 45.031(8), Florida Statutes, the court must provide both notice and an opportunity for any interested party to address those objections.[179] Further, it is reversible error for a trial court to deny a party an evidentiary hearing to which the objector is entitled.[180] The Clerk of the Court lacks authority to issue a certificate of title when an objection to a foreclosure sale is timely filed.[181] Also, a foreclosure sale must be set aside if a timely motion for rehearing was pending at the time of the sale.[182]

Under Florida law, actions involving foreclosure of property are brought in courts of equity. The Florida Legislature recognized the need for equitable remedies in foreclosure actions and, thus, codified that foreclosure cases involving mortgages will be tried in equity courts.[183] The Florida Supreme Court has said that only one of several equitable factors is needed to vacate a sale, including gross inadequacy of consideration, surprise, accident, or mistake imposed on complainant, and irregularity in the conduct of the sale.[184] A judicial sale may on a proper showing made, be vacated and set aside on any or all of these grounds, and proof of an inadequate bid price is not a necessary requirement in an action to set aside a judicial foreclosure sale.[185]

---

[176] *Ryan v. Countrywide Home Loans, Inc.*, 743 So. 2d 36, 38 (Fla. 2d DCA 1999) ("Accordingly, because Countrywide did not file a timely motion challenging the judicial sale and because the motion it did file could not relate back to a timely date, the trial court was without authority to set aside the sale.").

[177] See *Surratt v. Fleming*, 309 So. 2d 614, 615 (Fla. 1st DCA 1975) ("The trial court had jurisdiction to consider the motion to vacate and set aside sale though the time had expired to appeal the judgment. Courts of equity have general jurisdiction over judicial sales made under their orders and may set aside or vacate sales even after confirmation.") (citing *Marsh v. Marsh*, 72 Fla. 142, 72 So. 638 (1916)).

[178] *Regner v. Amtrust Bank*, 71 So. 3d 907, 907 (Fla. 4th DCA 2011).

[179] *U.S. Bank Nat'l Ass'n v. Bjeljac*, 43 So. 3d 851, 853 (Fla. 5th DCA 2010).

[180] *Avi-Isaac v. Wells Fargo Bank, N.A.*, 59 So. 3d 174, 177 (Fla. 2d DCA 2011).

[181] *Opportunity Funding I, LLC v. Otetchestvennyi*, 909 So. 2d 361, 362 (Fla. 4th DCA 2005).

[182] *Wollman v. Levy*, 489 So. 2d 1239, 1239 (Fla. 3d DCA 1986); *Hoffman v. BankUnited, N.A.*, 137 So. 3d 1039 (Fla. 2d DCA 2014).

[183] *Arsali v. Chase Home Finance LLC*, 121 So. 3d 511, 517 (Fla. 2013). *See* Fla. Stat. § 702.01 ("All mortgages shall be foreclosed in equity. In a mortgage foreclosure action, the court shall sever for separate trial all counterclaims against the foreclosing mortgagee. The foreclosure claim shall, if tried, be tried to the court without a jury.").

[184] See generally, *Arsali v. Chase Home Finance LLC*, 121 So. 3d 511 (Fla. 2013).

[185] See generally, *Arsali v. Chase Home Finance LLC*, 121 So. 3d 511 (Fla. 2013). In *Arsali*, the Florida Supreme Court hinted that Rule 1.540(b) could be used in a foreclosure sale context. *Arsali v. Chase Home Finance LLC*, 121 So. 3d 511, 517 (Fla. 2013) ("We note that none of the parties argued that Florida Rule of Civil Procedure 1.540(b) (Relief From Judgment, Degrees, or Orders—Mistakes; Inadvertence; Excusable Neglect; Newly Discovered Evidence; Fraud; etc.) should apply in this case. And because the borrowers' timely objection (i.e., motion to vacate) was not brought before the trial court under rule 1.540, we decline to address any application of the rule in this case.").

The fact that the mortgagor purports that he is attempting to negotiate a loan mod is not a basis to stop or vacate a sale.[186] While the Real Estate Settlement Procedures Act ("RESPA") and its implementing regulations, Regulation X, 12 C.F.R. 1024.41(g), do provide that a sale should be stopped in some circumstances if a loss mitigation application is complete,[187] Regulation X, by incorporating RESPA's damages provision, directs that its sole enforcement mechanism is monetary damages.[188] Because 12 U.S.C. § 2605(f) authorizes *only* monetary damages, specifically, actual damages resulting from the RESPA violation and, in the case of "a pattern or practice of noncompliance," statutory damages not to exceed $2,000, a Regulation X or RESPA violation is not a basis to stop or vacate a sale. While no Florida case seems to have directly addressed the issue, a legion of other jurisdictions have uniformly rejected making RESPA and Regulation X into a foreclosure defense.[189]

---

[186] *Salazar v. HSBC Bank, USA, NA*, 158 So. 3d 699, 700 (Fla. 3d DCA 2015) ("Seven months later, in July of 2009, Salazar's condominium was sold and a certificate of sale was filed by the clerk of the court. Salazar, in a single motion, objected to the sale and moved to set aside the final judgment claiming only that he had been working with his lender, HSBC, to modify the now foreclosed loan and that HSBC had advised him not to worry about the default or the judgment because they would work it out. Although these grounds were legally insufficient to nullify the foreclosure sale, the sale was vacated.").

[187] When the application is rendered complete—either in actuality or facially—more than thirty-seven (37) days before the foreclosure sale, the evaluation procedures under Subsection (c) are triggered. *See* 12 C.F.R. § 1024.41(c).

[188] 12 C.F.R. 1024.41(a) ("Enforcement and limitations. A borrower may enforce the provisions of this section pursuant to section 6(f) of RESPA (12 U.S.C. 2605(f)). Nothing in § 1024.41 imposes a duty on a servicer to provide any borrower with any specific loss mitigation option. Nothing in § 1024.41 should be construed to create a right for a borrower to enforce the terms of any agreement between a servicer and the owner or assignee of a mortgage loan, including with respect to the evaluation for, or offer of, any loss mitigation option or to eliminate any such right that may exist pursuant to applicable law.").

[189] *See, e.g., Phillips v. Green Tree Servicing LLC*, No. 15-13582, 2016 WL 627903, at *3 (E.D. Mich. Feb. 17, 2016) ("Plaintiff alleges that defendant violated various provisions of the Real Estate Settlement Procedures Act and corresponding regulations. However, the principal relief sought by plaintiff—to set aside the sheriff's sale—is unavailable to her under RESPA."); *Ray v. TCF Nat'l Bank*, No. 1-15-0001, 2015 WL 9590282, at *7 (Ill. App. Ct. Dec. 31, 2015) ("Section 2605(f) of RESPA only provides for monetary damages in the amount of actual damages, additional damages and costs and fees associated with obtaining those damages.... Accordingly, not only is the Code of Federal Regulations not applicable here, but the provisions relied upon by Ray do not provide her with the relief she now seeks, which is to reverse the trial court's judgment of foreclosure for failing to make her aware of and provide her with unidentified alternative loss mitigation programs."); *Fed. Nat'l Mortg. Ass'n v. Karastamatis*, 52 Misc. 3d 1007, 1009–10, 36 N.Y.S.3d 360, 362–63 (N.Y. Sup. Ct. 2016) ("While regulatory provisions, particularly those referred to as Regulation X, obligate some mortgage foreclosure plaintiffs to conform to review standards and to seek stays or adjournments of the prosecution of their foreclosure claims in impending or pending action in state courts or elsewhere, they do not provide defendant mortgagors with any viable defense to a New York mortgage foreclosure action or any right to obtain a stay of proceedings in such actions or to obtain a vacatur of or orders or judgments issued in such actions. Instead, the regulations merely provide a federal monetary remedy ... upon proof of their violation of one or more of the regulations."); *Roosevelt Cayman Asset Co. II v. Mercado*, No. 15-2314 (BJM), 2016 WL 3976627, at *4 (D.P.R. July 22, 2016) ("Further, even if it were found that Cayman violated any of the CFPB regulations, the statute does not provide for injunctive relief or a stay or adjourning of the prosecution of the impending fore-

A borrower cannot challenge the underlying foreclosure judgment by attacking the sale.[190]

14-5 Post-Judgment Claims for Surplus Funds

Section 45.031 was amended in 2006 to require that the final judgment of foreclosure, the notice of sale, and the certificate of disbursements include certain language informing subordinate lienholders and other persons claiming a right to any surplus funds that they must file a claim with the clerk of court within "60 days after the sale."[191] Various districts had interpreted "after the sale" as beginning at different times, so the Florida Supreme Court accepted conflict jurisdiction between the Fourth and Second Districts and rejected both of their approaches, instead holding, as a matter of pure statutory construction, that the 60 days to seek a surplus ran from the clerk's issuance of the certificate of disbursements.[192] However, this debate has been rendered moot because, effective July 1, 2019, the Legislature passed Committee Substitute for Committee Substitute for House Bill 1361 which, among other things, amends sec-

---

closure action. . . . This indicates that a servicer is not required to allege compliance with these regulations in a foreclosure complaint, as noncompliance with these rules will not bar a pending foreclosure action."); *Ayala v. Pacific Coast Nat'l Bank*, No. 5:16-cv-00723, 2016 WL 1700376, at *2 (C.D. Cal. April 27, 2016) ("As to the [RESPA] claim, it does not appear that the Act provides for injunctive relief, and therefore cannot be used to enjoin (even temporarily) the impending foreclosure."); *Clark v. Ocwen Loan Servicing, LLC*, No. 1:15-cv-659, 2015 WL 6159447, at *6 (W.D. Mich. Oct. 20, 2015) ("Ocwen contends that RESPA does not permit the Court to issue an order to set aside the foreclosure sale or to require Ocwen to review his eligibility for a modification to his loan. The Court agrees with other courts which have held that RESPA does not provide for injunctive relief."); *Caggins v. Bank of N.Y. Mellon*, No. 1511124, 2015 WL 4041350, at *2 (E.D. Mich. July 1, 2015) ("There is no provision found in RESPA under which Plaintiff can seek to have foreclosure proceedings nullified, or force Defendants to negotiate a loan modification."); *Houle v. Green Tree Servicing, LLC*, No. 14-CV-14654, 2015 WL 1867526, at *4 (E.D. Mich. Apr. 23, 2015) ("Due to the alleged violations, plaintiff seeks to have the foreclosure sale set aside, to have his loan modification properly evaluated, and to recover damages under RESPA. The principal relief sought by plaintiff-to set aside the sheriff's sale-is unavailable to him under RESPA.").

[190] *Aparicio v. Deutsche Bank Nat'l Tr. Co.*, 278 So. 3d 814 (Fla. 3d DCA 2019) ("Here, in pursuing relief from the sale, the borrowers failed to allege 'one or more adequate equitable factors and make a proper showing to the trial court that they exist[ed],' in the proceedings below. . . . Instead, they embarked on an impermissible mission designed to once again elucidate the infirmities in the underlying judgment."); *Flagstar Bank, F.S.B. v. Cleveland*, 87 So. 3d 63, 65 (Fla. 4th DCA 2012) ("This court has long held, however, that '[a] trial court is without jurisdiction to entertain a second motion for relief from judgment which attempts to relitigate matters settled by a prior order denying relief.'") (quoting *Steeprow Enters., Inc. v. Lennar Homes, Inc.*, 590 So. 2d 21, 23 (Fla. 4th DCA 1991)); *De Ardila v. Chase Manhattan Mortg. Corp.*, 826 So. 2d 419, 421 (Fla. 3d DCA 2002) ("[W]e cannot escape the conclusion that what occurred was a rehearing of a rehearing, and ultimately an untimely appeal.").

[191] *Bank of New York Mellon v. Glenville*, 252 So. 3d 1120, 1123 (Fla. 2018) (citing ch. 2006-175, § 1, at 2, 3, 5, Laws of Fla. (amending § 45.031(1)(a), (2)(f), (7)(b), Fla. Stat., respectively)).

[192] *Bank of New York Mellon v. Glenville*, 252 So. 3d 1120, 1123 (Fla. 2018) (citing § 45.032(3), Fla. Stat.). The Third District had followed the Second District, and its decision doing so was also quashed in *Eduartez v. Fed. Nat'l Mortgage Ass'n*, SC18-1436, 2018 WL 6434740, at *1 (Fla. Dec. 7, 2018).

tions 45.031 and 45.032, as well as certain related sections of the Florida Statutes, to change the time period within which title owners, subordinate lienholders, and other persons must file a claim to the surplus amount.[193]

Section 45.032(2) provides that "there is established a rebuttable legal presumption that the owner of record on the date of the filing of a lis pendens is the person entitled to surplus funds after payment of subordinate lienholders who have timely filed a claim."[194] If the owner of record claims the surplus before the date the clerk reports it as unclaimed and there is no subordinate lienholder, the court shall order the clerk to deduct any applicable service charges from the surplus and pay the remainder to the owner of record.[195] The clerk may establish a reasonable requirement that the owner of record prove his or her identity before receiving the disbursement.[196] If any other person claims the surplus or if the owner of record files a claim for the surplus but acknowledges that one or more other persons may be entitled to part or all of the surplus, the court shall set an evidentiary hearing to determine entitlement to the surplus.[197] At the evidentiary hearing, an equity assignee has the burden of proving that he or she is entitled to some or all of the surplus funds.[198] The court may grant summary judgment to a subordinate lienholder prior to or at the evidentiary hearing.[199] The court shall consider the factors in § 45.033 when hearing a claim that any person other than a subordinate lienholder or the owner of record is entitled to the surplus funds.[200]

Section 45.032(3)(b) now provides that, "[o]ne year after the sale, any surplus remaining with the clerk of the court that has not been disbursed as provided herein is presumed unclaimed as set forth in s. 717.113 and must be reported and remitted to the department in accordance with ss. 717.117 and 717.119, unless there is a pending court proceeding regarding entitlement to the surplus."[201] "At the conclusion of any court proceeding and any appeal regarding entitlement to the surplus, the clerk of the court shall report and remit the unclaimed property to the department if directed by a court order, to another entity if directed by the court order, or, if not directed by the court order, to the owner of record."[202] "For purposes of establishing entitlement to the surplus after the property has been remitted to the department, only the owner of record reported by the clerk of the court, or the beneficiary, as defined in s. 731.201, of a deceased owner of record reported by the clerk, is entitled to the surplus."[203] A surplus of less than $10 escheats to the clerk.[204]

An association does not need to have recorded a lien in order to have a right to the surplus because the lien in favor of the association is created by the statute

---

[193] *See* Fla. Stat. § 45.032(3)(a)-(c). The bill, which provided for an effective date of July 1, 2019, was signed by Governor Scott on March 21, 2018. *See* ch. 2018-71, Laws of Fla.
[194] Fla. Stat. § 45.032(2).
[195] Fla. Stat. § 45.032(3)(b). This replaces the previously applicable 60-day period.
[196] Fla. Stat. § 45.032(3)(b).
[197] Fla. Stat. § 45.032(3)(b).
[198] Fla. Stat. § 45.032(3)(b).
[199] Fla. Stat. § 45.032(3)(b).
[200] Fla. Stat. § 45.032(3)(b).
[201] Fla. Stat. § 45.032(3)(c).
[202] Fla. Stat. § 45.032(3)(c).
[203] Fla. Stat. § 45.032(3)(c).
[204] Fla. Stat. § 45.032(3)(c).

itself."[205] The Second District has relied on § 45.032(2)'s rebuttable presumption to reject a mortgagor's attempts to claim entitlement to a surplus when a third party who held title at the time of the lis pendens' filing claimed entitlement.[206]

"Proceedings regarding surplus funds in a foreclosure case do not in any manner affect or cloud the title of the purchaser at the foreclosure sale of the property."[207]

---

[205] *Calendar v. Stonebridge Gardens Section III Condo. Ass'n, Inc.*, 234 So. 3d 18, 19-20 (Fla. 4th DCA 2017) ("We agree with this reasoning and we hold that the lien in favor of the association was created by the statute itself. Since there is no indication that a first mortgage was at issue in this case, the association was not required to file a claim to validate its lien." [in order to obtain surplus funds]) (citing Fla. Stat. § 718.116(5)(a)).

[206] *2017 Bell Ranch Residential Land Tr. v. Burrill*, 264 So. 3d 295, 297 (Fla. 2d DCA 2019) ("Section 45.033(1) iterates that there is 'a rebuttable presumption that the owner of record of real property on the date of the filing of a lis pendens is the person entitled to surplus funds.' Significantly, under section 45.033(2) the presumption may be rebutted 'only by' proof of either a voluntary or involuntary transfer or assignment from the record owner to the claimant of the right to collect the surplus. (Emphasis added.).").

[207] Fla. Stat. § 45.032(4).

CHAPTER 15

Sanctions

Morgan Weinstein

15-1 Introduction

Foreclosure cases follow the typical litigation process in Florida. The filing of a complaint precipitates a motion to dismiss or an answer, often along with discovery by at least one of the parties. Eventually, the plaintiff may file a reply to any affirmative defenses raised by the defendant and there may be a trial. At each step of this process, a motion or pleading, or any other paper, may be thought to be either frivolous or taken for the purpose of delay. Additionally, one or more of the parties may violate or allegedly violate one of the rules of procedure governing discovery or appeals, or a court order. A court can also sanction a party for spoliation of evidence.[1] The recourse for an aggrieved party under these circumstances is to seek sanctions.

Sanctions may only be made pursuant to rule, pursuant to statute, or pursuant to the courts' inherent authority.[2] Sanctions may include monetary fines and may become severe, up to the point of dismissal of a plaintiff's claim or the striking of a defendant's pleadings.[3] Where a rule or statute provides for sanctions, the courts should look to the rule or statute, and should refrain from utilizing their limited inherent authority to enter sanctions.[4] While technically not a sanction against the party, a court can also refer a party's attorney to The Florida Bar for violating the duty of candor, such as by failing to cite controlling authority, or for impugning the integrity of the judiciary in a court filing.[5]

---

[1] For a thorough discussion of spoliation sanctions, *see* Patrick John McGinley, 10 Fla. Prac., Workers' Comp. § 40:5–40:11 (2019 ed.) (spoliation chapter by Michael Starks), which discusses the full picture of this legal hydra, which is a complex and intertwined concept that has developed over time, it is necessary to break spoliation down into its various components and analyze it under a number of interrelated rubrics, including "Remedy" (sanctions or tort damages?), "Identity" (plaintiff, defendant, or third-party spoliator?), "Culpability" (negligent, intentional, or bad faith?), "Prejudice" (How much has non-spoliator been prejudiced, and can the prejudice be remedied?), "Quality" (primary or secondary evidence?), "Duty" (is a duty required before a court applies a remedy, and if so what is the source of the duty?).

[2] *Moakley v. Smallwood*, 826 So. 2d 221, 223 (Fla. 2002) (quoting *Bane v. Bane*, 775 So. 2d 938, 940 (Fla. 2000) (citing *United States Sav. Bank v. Pittman*, 86 So. 567, 572 (Fla. 1920)).

[3] *Kozel v. Ostendorf*, 629 So. 2d 817, *passim* (Fla. 1993).

[4] *Moakley v. Smallwood*, 826 So. 2d 221, 227 (Fla. 2002).

[5] *See Bank of New York Mellon v. Atkin*, 2019 WL 3820572, n. 1 (Fla. Cir. Ct. July 31, 2019) (referring attorney to The Florida Bar for failure to cite controlling authorities and impugn-

15-2 Courts' Inherent Authority to Sanction

15-2:1 Courts' Authority to Sanction

The courts of the State of Florida are possessed of a broad, discretionary power to impose silence, respect, and decorum, as well as to ensure that parties' actions are consistent with court mandates.[6] This inherent power of the courts to hold parties or counsel in contempt of court may be exercised in attempts to enforce and ensure compliance with orders.[7]

Contempt sanctions fall into two basic categories: criminal contempt and civil contempt.[8] The threshold of whether a sanction is criminal or civil in nature turns, on a case-by-case basis, upon the character and purpose of the sanctions involved.[9]

Additionally, the courts have the inherent authority to sanction abusive litigants, in order to safeguard the right to access the courts.[10] Generally, a court may only enter sanctions in the form of attorney's fees when such fees are expressly provided by statute, rule or contract; however, the courts possess the inherent authority to assess fees for misconduct during the course of litigation.[11]

15-2:2 Differences Between Contempt and Sanctions

Criminal contempt sanctions have punishment as their traditional purpose, usually for violation of a court order.[12] In the case of criminal contempt, the contemnor is afforded the constitutional due process protections normally afforded to criminal defendants, including the right to be represented by counsel, the right to the reasonable doubt standard of proof, the right to not incriminate oneself, jury trial rights in cases involving imprisonment lasting more than six months, and protections afforded under the

---

ing integrity of the court); *Bank of Am., N.A. v. Atkin*, 271 So. 3d 145, 147 (Fla. 3d DCA 2019) (referring attorney to The Florida Bar for impugning integrity of the courts); *Bank of Am., N.A. v. Atkin*, 43 Fla. L. Weekly D2799 (Fla. 3d DCA Dec. 14, 2018) (order to show cause to attorney as to why he should not be sanctioned for impugning the judiciary); *Aquasol Condo. Ass'n v. HSBC Bank USA, Nat'l Ass'n*, 2018 Fla. App. LEXIS 17361 (Fla. 3d DCA Dec. 5, 2018) (referring attorney to The Florida Bar for impugning integrity of the courts and awarding fees up to $5,000 against attorney as sanction); *Aquasol Condo. Ass'n v. HSBC Bank USA, Nat'l Ass'n*, 2018 Fla. App. LEXIS 14313 (Fla. 3d DCA Sept. 26, 2018) (order to show cause to attorney for failure to cite controlling authorities and impugning integrity of the courts).

[6] *Parisi v. Broward County*, 769 So. 2d 359, 363 (Fla. 2000).
[7] *Fla. Bar v. Palmer* 149 So. 3d 1118, 1120 (Fla. 2013).
[8] *Parisi v. Broward County*, 769 So. 2d 359, 363-64 (Fla. 2000).
[9] *Parisi v. Broward County*, 769 So. 2d 359, 363-64 (Fla. 2000) (quoting *International Union, United Mine Workers v. Bagwell*, 512 U.S. 821, 831-32 (1994)).
[10] *Hastings v. State*, 79 So. 3d 739, 742 (Fla. 2011). *See also Petsoules v. State*, 140 So. 3d 1284 (Fla. 5th DCA 2013) (discussing this authority in the context of pro se litigants); *Robinson v. State*, 84 So. 3d 1130 (Fla. 5th DCA 2012) (prohibiting a party from further pro se filings); *Durie v. State*, 69 So. 3d 274, 276 (reasoning that sanctions may be the only mechanism to prevent further spurious or nonmeritorious filings).
[11] *Moakley v. Smallwood*, 826 So. 2d 221, 223 (Fla. 2002) (quoting *Bane v. Bane*, 775 So. 2d 938, 940 (Fla. 2000) (citing *United States Sav. Bank v. Pittman*, 86 So. 567, 572 (Fla. 1920)).
[12] *Parisi v. Broward County*, 769 So. 2d 359, 363-64 (Fla. 2000) (quoting *Bowen v. Bowen*, 471 So. 2d 1274, 1277 (Fla. 1985)).

Florida Rules of Criminal Procedure.[13] In the event that the contemnor's alleged conduct includes disrespect to or criticism of the judge, the judge must disqualify himself or herself from presiding at the hearing, due to the subject due process constraints imposed on the process.[14]

Alternatively, civil contempt sanctions are remedial or for the benefit of the aggrieved party.[15] Civil contempt sanctions come with fewer procedural protections.[16] Civil contempt sanctions require only notice and an opportunity to be heard.[17] In a civil contempt proceeding, the contemnor must be afforded the ability to purge the contempt and cure the problem.[18]

Civil contempt sanctions may be either compensatory or coercive.[19] Coercive sanctions may include, without limitation, incarceration, garnishment of wages and the revocation of a driver's license.[20] Notwithstanding the fact that the sanction may include incarceration, a contempt order may still technically be civil, if and only if it provides a provision allowing the contemnor to purge.[21] The ability to purge means that the contemnor must possess the ability to avoid further incarceration.[22] Trial courts may also dismiss actions determined to be frivolous.[23] Civil contempt sanctions may not be entered where a party acts recklessly, rather than intentionally.[24]

The courts' inherent authority to sanction bad faith conduct during the course of litigation is altogether separate from the courts' contempt powers, but presents an additional form of sanctions that the courts may enter.[25]

---

[13] *Parisi v. Broward County*, 769 So. 2d 359, 364 (Fla. 2000) (quoting *International Union, United Mine Workers v. Bagwell*, 512 U.S. 821, 826 (1994)). See also Fla. R. Crim. Pro. 3.830; 3.840.

[14] Fla. R. Crim. P. 3.840(e). See also *Rosenwater v. Deutsche Bank Nat'l Trust Co.*, 220 So. 3d 1204 (Fla. 4th DCA 2017).

[15] *Parisi v. Broward County*, 769 So. 2d 359, 363-64 (Fla. 2000) (quoting *International Union, United Mine Workers v. Bagwell*, 512 U.S. 821, 827-28 (1994)). See also *Fa. Bar. v. Forrester*, 916 So. 2d 647, 651 (Fla. 2005).

[16] *Parisi v. Broward County*, 769 So. 2d 359, 365 (Fla. 2000) (quoting *International Union, United Mine Workers v. Bagwell*, 512 U.S. 821, 831 (1994)).

[17] *Parisi v. Broward County*, 769 So. 2d 359, 365 (Fla. 2000) (quoting *International Union, United Mine Workers v. Bagwell*, 512 U.S. 821, 827 (1994)).

[18] *Parisi v. Broward County*, 769 So. 2d 359, 365 (Fla. 2000) (citing *International Union, United Mine Workers v. Bagwell*, 512 U.S. 821, 829 (1994)). See also *Fa. Bar. v. Forrester*, 916 So. 2d 647, 651 (Fla. 2005) (reasoning that the purge provision is the "hallmark" of civil contempt).

[19] *Parisi v. Broward County*, 769 So. 2d 359, 363-64 (Fla. 2000).

[20] *Parisi v. Broward County*, 769 So. 2d 359, 365 (Fla. 2000) (quoting *Gregory v. Rice*, 727 So. 2d 251 (Fla. 1999)).

[21] *Parisi v. Broward County*, 769 So. 2d 359, 365 (Fla. 2000) (quoting *Gregory v. Rice*, 727 So. 2d 251 (Fla. 1999)).

[22] *Ross Dress for Less Va., Inc. v. Castro*, 134 So. 3d 511, 523 (Fla. 3d DCA 2014) (discussing the ability of a contemnor to carry "the key to his cell in his own pocket").

[23] *Wilson v. Salamon*, 923 So. 2d 363, 367 n.3 (Fla. 2006).

[24] *Fore v. State*, 201 So. 3d 839 (Fla. 4th DCA 2016).

[25] *Moakley v. Smallwood*, 826 So. 2d 221, *passim* (Fla. 2002).

15-2:3 Limitations on the Inherent Authority to Sanction

The purpose of the inherent authority to enter sanctions for contempt is twofold: first, it enforces compliance with prior orders.[26] Secondly, the sanction seeks to modify the behavior of the sanctioned party.[27] However, the inherent contempt power of judges is a power that is noted as being consistently ripe for abuse, because the judge is responsible not only for identifying, pursuing and adjudicating any potentially contumacious activity, but is also responsible for entering any sanctions stemming from that judge's adjudication.[28] A judge is barred from basing contempt upon noncompliance with an order on anything other than what is expressly and clearly contained within the order.[29] Moreover, consideration must be paid to the potential contemnor's financial situation, particularly where a contempt order may provide for incarceration.[30]

Additionally, there are certain limits on when courts may impose sanctions and which sanctions courts may impose. Courts should not deny access to courts, but may limit access due to abusive or frivolous filings.[31] In terms of awarding attorney's fees as a sanction, the courts' ability is narrow, and should only be exercised where a party has exhibited egregious conduct or acted in bad faith.[32] Where a statute or rule provides for sanctions, then that sanction or rule should be utilized, instead of the courts' inherent authority.[33]

With regard to which sanctions courts may impose, courts may not impose sanctions where they do not possess jurisdiction to do so. In a foreclosure action, it was determined that the courts do not have the inherent authority to strike a notice of voluntary dismissal, for the purpose of effectuating a dismissal with prejudice.[34] Moreover, where a court issues an order to show cause, and the factual basis underlying that order, taken as true, would not constitute contempt, an appellate court may issue a writ of prohibition.[35]

Pro se borrowers may also be sanctioned under the court's inherent authority by committing fraud on the court, such as by trying to pass off a satisfaction of an old mortgage as being a satisfaction of the mortgage in the subject foreclosure or engaging in a systematic conduct designed to harass litigants and their attorneys and to

---

[26] *Parisi v. Broward County*, 769 So. 2d 359, 364 (Fla. 2000) (quoting *International Union, United Mine Workers v. Bagwell*, 512 U.S. 821, 828 (1994)).

[27] *Parisi v. Broward County*, 769 So. 2d 359, 364 (Fla. 2000) (quoting *International Union, United Mine Workers v. Bagwell*, 512 U.S. 821, 828 (1994)).

[28] *Parisi v. Broward County*, 769 So. 2d 359, 363 (Fla. 2000).

[29] *Oasis Builders, LLC v. McHugh*, 138 So. 3d 1218, 1220-21 (Fla. 4th DCA 2014); *Rojo v. Rojo*, 84 So. 3d 1259, 1262 (Fla. 3d DCA 2012).

[30] *Creative Choice Homes, II, Ltd. v. Keystone Guard Servs.*, 137 So. 3d 1144, 1147 (Fla. 3d DCA 2014).

[31] *Durie v. State*, 69 So. 3d 274, 276 (Fla. 2011); *Fla. Bar v. Kivisto*, 62 So. 3d 1137, 1139-40 (Fla. 2011).

[32] *Moakley v. Smallwood*, 826 So. 2d 221, 224 (Fla. 2002) (discussing the inequitable conduct doctrine as authorizing fees without requiring statutory authority). *See also Diaz v. Diaz*, 826 So. 2d 229, 232 (Fla. 2002) (holding that a court does not have inherent authority to sanction a party for pursuing a claim that the court deems to be a "long shot").

[33] *Moakley v. Smallwood*, 826 So. 2d 221, 227 (Fla. 2002).

[34] *Pino v. Bank of N.Y.*, 121 So. 3d 23, 44 (Fla. 2013).

[35] *Yacenda Hudson & Amina McNeil & DItech Fin., LLC v. Marin*, So. 3d 148 (Fla. 3d DCA 2018).

delay foreclosure.[36] A lesser sanction available to the court is to require that a pro se borrower obtain counsel.[37]

15-3 Sanctions Pursuant to Rule

15-3:1 Introduction

The Florida Rules of Civil Procedure provide for sanctions, pursuant to rule, at the trial court level in foreclosure cases. There are a number of rules which include a sanction component.[38] However, the main rule utilized in attempts to procure or defend against sanctions in a foreclosure action is Rule 1.380, Florida Rules of Civil Procedure, titled "Failure to Make Discovery; Sanctions."

15-3:2 Sanctions for Discovery Violations

Rule 1.380 provides that any party may apply for an order compelling discovery.[39] If a party fails to respond to discovery, the discovering party may move for an order to compel that discovery.[40] A discovery response that is challenged on the basis that it is incomplete or evasive is treated as though there was a failure to answer the discovery in its entirety.[41] The motion must include a certification that the party seeking the order has, in good faith, conferred with the allegedly non-producing party.[42]

If a court enters an order compelling discovery, and there is subsequent noncompliance with the order, then Rule 1.380 empowers the court to enter sanctions. The trial court has discretion as to whether to sanction a party for failure to comply with a discovery order.[43] In the case of a deponent at a deposition, if the deponent fails to answer or to be sworn in, following an order requiring the deponent to do so, the court may hold the deponent in contempt.[44] Further, if a party or a party's representative fails to obey an order regarding discovery, the court is empowered to order

---

[36] *See U.S. Bank v. King-Fenn*, 2012 WL 4983784 (Fla. Cir. Ct. Oct. 17, 2012) (due to abuse of system and failure to obtain counsel as ordered and fraud on the court, striking answer and all other papers they filed in the case, and judicially default borrower); Default and the Striking of Uribe's Pleadings, which is published at *Wells Fargo Bank, N.A. v. Uribe*, No. 2012-CA-5930, 2018 WL 1936303, (Fla. Cir. Ct. Orange 2018) (striking pro se borrower's pleadings and judicially defaulting him due to fraud on the court by creating a Florida entity for the purpose of impersonating a California entity so as to defeat standing to foreclose).

[37] *Wells Fargo Bank, N.A v. Uribe*, 2018 WL 3635764 (Fla. Cir. Ct. July 24, 2018) (forbidding borrower from pro se representation due to abuse of court system); *Bank of America, N.A. v. King-Fenn*, 2011 WL 3515682 (Fla. Cir. Ct. Aug. 10, 2011) (forbidding pro se representation due to abuse of court system and directing borrowers to obtain counsel).

[38] *See* Fla. R. Civ. P. 1.201(c)(4); Fla. R. Civ. P. 1.280(g); Fla. R. Civ. P. 1.442(g); Fla. R. Civ. P. 1.720(f); Fla. R. Civ. P. 1.730(c); and Fla. R. Civ. P. 1.820(a). Rules 1.720 and 1.730 deal with mediation, in which a party may be sanctioned for various conduct leading up to and during a mediation in a case.

[39] Fla. R. Civ. P. 1.380(a).

[40] Fla. R. Civ. P. 1.380(a)(2).

[41] Fla. R. Civ. P. 1.380(a)(3).

[42] Fla. R. Civ. P. 1.380(a)(2).

[43] *EMM Enters. Two, LLC v. Fromberg, Perlow & Kornik, P.A.*, 202 So. 3d 932 (Fla. 4th DCA 2016).

[44] Fla. R. Civ. P. 1.380(b)(1).

that the subject matter of the testimony be taken to be established, refusing to allow the party to support or oppose certain claims or defenses or introduce matters into evidence, striking pleadings or parts thereof, staying the matter, dismissing the action or any part thereof, or entering a default judgment, treating the matter as a contempt of court.[45] However, if the would-be sanctioned party can show an inability to produce the person for examination, the court's powers become limited.[46]

Additionally, with regard to requests for admissions, should there be a failure to admit the genuineness of any genuine document or the truth of any truthful matter, then the party seeking discovery may move for an order requiring the party avoiding admissions to pay the reasonable expenses involved in pursuing the discovery, including attorney's fees.[47] Rule 1.380(c) contains exceptions, whereby a non-admitting party may not be sanctioned if the request was objectionable, the admission sought was of no substantial importance, or there was other good reason for failing to admit to the request.[48]

15-3:3 Limitations on Sanctions for Discovery Violations

The purpose of Rule 1.380 is to promote the orderly movement of litigation.[49] Sanctions under Rule 1.380 are to be applied on a sliding scale of severity, with the ultimate sanction of dismissal or the striking of pleadings being reserved only for cases in which there has been a protracted history of discovery abuses, numerous motions to compel, the entry of prior sanctions, and obvious prejudice.[50]

To determine whether dismissal is warranted, rather than a less severe sanction, courts are guided by the following six factors: willfulness; prior sanctions of the attorney; whether the client was involved in the act of disobedience, rather than counsel being solely responsible for the act or neglect; prejudice; whether there was a reasonable justification for noncompliance; and the extent to which the delay effected judicial administration.[51]

Absent an explicit finding of willfulness or deliberate disregard for an order, the trial court should not dismiss a case or strike a party's pleadings due to discovery violations.[52] Further, without a determination that prejudice will occur, a trial court abuses its discretion in dismissing a case or striking a witness.[53] Where a trial court makes a finding as to a number of the six factors, but does not make a finding on each factor, it is reversible error for the court to enter a dismissal.[54] Likewise, where a trial court does not articulate a reason for dismissal, an appellate court may speculate as to the reason for dismissal and determine that the trial court did not consider

---

[45] Fla. R. Civ. P. 1.380(b)(2)(A)-(D).
[46] Fla. R. Civ. P. 1.380(b)(2)(E).
[47] Fla. R. Civ. P. 1.380(c).
[48] Fla. R. Civ. P. 1.380(c).
[49] *PNC Bank, NA v. Duque*, 137 So. 3d 476, 478 (Fla. 4th DCA 2014).
[50] *Ham v. Dunmire*, 891 So. 2d 492, 499 (Fla. 2004).
[51] *Kozel v. Ostendorf*, 629 So. 2d 817, 818 (Fla. 1993); *PNC Bank, NA v. Duque*, 137 So. 3d 476, 478 (Fla. 4th DCA 2014).
[52] *Chmura v. Sam Rodgers Props.*, 2 So. 3d 984, 986 (Fla. 2d DCA 2008).
[53] *Bank of New York Mellon v. Pearson*, 212 So. 3d 1071, 1072 (Fla. 3d DCA 2017).
[54] *EMM Enters. Two, LLC v. Fromberg, Perlow & Kornik, P.A.*, 202 So. 3d 932 (Fla. 4th DCA 2016).

the relevant factors.[55] Even where the reason for dismissal seems to be apparent and outside the realm of dispute, an evidentiary hearing and a factual determination are nevertheless required.[56]

However, there is a question as to whether such orders are reviewable in particular circumstances. A failure to consider any of the subject factors is an independent basis for remand, so that the correct standard can be applied.[57] And a court may decline to reach the issue of the sufficiency of the order if the court finds compliance with prior orders.[58] Nevertheless, courts have held that an error in failing to make these findings is not automatically preserved.[59] Preservation, now, may require a transcript of the hearing demonstrating an objection was raised, the filing of a motion for rehearing, or both.[60]

15-4 Sanctions Pursuant to Statute

15-4:1 Sanctions for Frivolous Claims and Defenses, and Unreasonable Delay

Section 57.105, Florida Statutes governs generally sanctions in civil cases, including sanctions in cases for the foreclosure of mortgages. Under Section 57.105, sanctions may be awarded on the court's own initiative or by motion of a party to the case.[61] Sanctions pursuant to this statute are awarded where a party or their attorney knew or should have known that a claim or defense by a party was either not supported by the necessary material facts or would not be supported by the application of then-existing law.[62] Also, where an action is taken for the purposes of delay, the court may award sanctions to the aggrieved party.[63] These sanctions may not include costs.[64] In certain circumstances, though, travel costs and travel time may be awarded as a sanction, particularly where a party was aware that their actions could result in unnecessary litigation.[65]

However, good faith is a defense to the imposition of sanctions and, in the case of sanctions own the court's own initiative, such sanctions must be entered prior to a voluntary dismissal or settlement.[66] The reason for the good faith exception is that Section 57.105 is meant to provide sanctions in order to deter the filing of frivolous

---

[55] *Bank of N.Y. Mellon v. Diaz*, 232 So. 3d 435, 439 (Fla. 4th DCA 2017).
[56] *Deutsche Bank Nat'l Trust Co. v. Sombrero Beach Rd., LLC*, 260 So. 3d 424, 428-29 (Fla. 3d DCA 2018).
[57] *Ham v. Dunmire*, 891 So. 2d 492, 499-500 (Fla. 2004).
[58] *See Bank of N.Y. Mellon v. Johnson*, 270 So. 3d 1269, 1271-72 (Fla. 1st DCA 2019).
[59] *See Bank of Am., N.A. v. Ribaudo*, 199 So. 3d 407, 408 (Fla. 4th DCA 2016) (reasoning that the issue is reviewable "provided that the error has been preserved").
[60] *See Bank of Am., N.A. v. Ribaudo*, 199 So. 3d 407, 408 (Fla. 4th DCA 2016); *Bank of New York Mellon v. Sandhill*, 202 So. 3d 944, 945-46 (Fla. 5th DCA 2016) (holding that a party is "obligated to bring the matter to the trial court's attention by filing a timely motion for rehearing or clarification").
[61] Fla. Stat. § 57.105(1).
[62] Fla. Stat. § 57.105(1)(a)-(b).
[63] Fla. Stat. § 57.105(2).
[64] *Heldt-Pope v. Thibault*, 198 So. 3d 650, 652 (Fla. 2d DCA 2015).
[65] *Bank of N.Y. v. Obermeyer*, 260 So. 3d 1155, 1156 (Fla. 3d DCA 2018).
[66] Florida Statute § 57.105(3)(a)-(d); *Pino v. Bank of N.Y.*, 121 So. 3d 23, *passim* (Fla. 2013).

claim and defenses, as well as the pursuit of litigation for the purpose of unreasonable delay.[67]

15-4:2 Safe Harbor from Sanctions

Section 57.105 provides a safe harbor period of 21 days, in which the offending motion or pleading may be withdrawn.[68] Any party that wishes to file a motion for sanctions under the statute must serve the motion on the party against whom they are seeking sanctions, but may not file the motion with the court until 21 days has elapsed from the date that the motion was served on the offending party.[69] Where a party contemplates filing a subsequent or amended motion for sanctions, that motion carries its own separate and independent 21-day safe harbor period.[70] The motion, when served but not filed, may not be a document filed in a court proceeding, meaning that certain service requirements would not apply to such a motion.[71] This issue is not settled law, and conflict has been certified to the Florida Supreme Court.

The safe harbor provision is not simply a notice provision; it creates an opportunity to avoid a sanction.[72] Prior to the time for filing the motion, the non-moving party may freely withdraw or correct the alleged offense.[73] In the event that a party fails to comply with the safe harbor period afforded by Section 57.105(4), a trial court may not grant the motion for sanctions and an appellate court must reverse an order granting the motion.[74] However, under special circumstances in which a party informs the opposing party of its intent to seek sanctions and more than 21 days elapses, if there is an absence of strict compliance with Section 57.105(4), a trial court may be able to award attorney's fees on its own initiative, pursuant to Section 57.105(1).[75] This ability is an unsettled question of law, as certain courts require strict compliance with the service requirements in the Florida Rules of Judicial Administration.[76]

---

[67] *Bionetics Corp. v. Kenniasty*, 69 So. 3d 943, 944 (Fla. 2011).
[68] *Pino v. Bank of N.Y.*, 121 So. 3d 23, 28 (Fla. 2013).
[69] Fla. Stat. § 57.105(4).
[70] *Lago v. Kame*, 120 So. 3d 73, 75 (Fla. 4th DCA 2013).
[71] *See, e.g., Isla Blue Devel., LLC v. Moore*, 223 So. 3d 1097 (Fla. 2d DCA 2017) (certifying conflict with *Matte v. Caplan*, 140 So. 3d 686 (Fla. 4th DCA 2014)); *Denino v. Abbate*, 247 So. 3d 48, 50 (Fla. 2d DCA 2018) (holding e-mail service requirements did not apply to sanctions and certifying conflict); *see also Wheaton v. Wheaton*, 261 So. 3d 1236, 1243-44 (Fla. 2019) (discussing *Matte* in *dicta, but holding that* "[t]he plain language of section 768.79 and rule 1.442 do not require service by email. Moreover, because a proposal for settlement is a document that is required to be served on the party to whom it is made, rule 2.516 does not apply").
[72] *Walker v. Cash Register Auto Ins. of Leon County, Inc.*, 946 So. 2d 66, 71 (Fla. 1st DCA 2006).
[73] Fla. Stat. § 57.105(4).
[74] *Lago v. Kame*, 120 So. 3d 73, 74-75 (Fla. 4th DCA 2013).
[75] *HFC Collection Ctr., Inc. v. Alexander*, 190 So. 3d 1114, 1119 (Fla. 5th DCA 2016).
[76] *Goersch v. City of Satellite Beach*, 252 So. 3d 309 (Fla. 5th DCA 2018).

CHAPTER 16

Attorney's Fees in Foreclosure Actions

Richard Slaughter McIver

16-1 Introduction

16-1:1 The "American Rule" on Attorney's Fees

In Florida, the general rule is that attorney's fees may be awarded to a party in a lawsuit by a court only when authorized by statute or by agreement of the parties.[1] This is referred to as the "American Rule." It applies throughout most jurisdictions in the United States, which have rejected the English rule permitting the award of costs and fees to the prevailing party under common law.[2] An award of attorney's fees is considered to be in derogation of the common law.[3] Furthermore, it is well established that contracts and statutes awarding attorney's fees must be strictly construed.[4]

16-2 The Note and Mortgage Contracts

16-2:1 The Terms of the Note and Mortgage Control

There is no Florida statute which specifically provides that a prevailing party is entitled to recover attorney's fees in a mortgage foreclosure action. With some exceptions, discussed below, the parties can only recover attorney's fees if the note, mortgage or other loan documents provide for payment of such fees. The vast majority of residential and commercial mortgages held by institutions provide that the lender is entitled to recover its attorney's fees incurred in enforcing the mortgage.

The typical residential mortgage utilizing the Fannie Mae/Freddie Mac Uniform Instrument has several provisions regarding the borrower's obligation to pay attorney's fees in the event of default. The Uniform Instrument provides that a lender may be entitled to attorneys' fees for protection of its security interest in legal proceed-

---

[1] *Florida Patient's Comp. Fund v. Rowe*, 472 So. 2d 1145, 1148 (Fla. 1985); *State Farm Fire & Cas. Co. v. Palma*, 629 So. 2d 830 (Fla. 1993).
[2] *Alyeska Pipeline Serv. Co. v. Wilderness Society*, 421 U.S. 240, 249 (1975).
[3] *Rivera v. Deauville Hotel, Employers Service Corp.*, 277 So. 2d 265 (Fla. 1973).
[4] *Dade County v. Pena*, 664 So. 2d 959 (Fla. 1995); *Trytek v. Gale Industries, Inc.*, 3 So. 3d 1194 (Fla. 2009); *Campbell v. Goldman*, 959 So. 2d 223, 227 (Fla. 2007).

ings, including bankruptcy, probate, condemnation or forfeiture, code enforcement or other laws or regulations (Paragraph 9), upon reinstatement by a borrower for a payment default (Paragraph 19), in foreclosure (Paragraph 22), and attorney's fees awarded on appeal (Paragraph 24).

In addition, a mortgagee may be entitled to attorney's fees when "any default has occurred that allows the mortgagee to institute a foreclosure action or collect the monies payable under the note," even if the foreclosure remedy sought is denied.[5] Likewise, where a mortgage provides that the lender may recover fees upon default, the lender may recover fees even if foreclosure is denied.[6] However, if a mortgage does not have a contractual provision regarding the award of attorney's fees, or if it is found that there is no valid mortgage contract between the parties to the suit, no fees may generally be awarded.[7]

In rare cases, the loan documents do not contain provisions for payment of attorney's fees in favor of the mortgagee, and in such cases, the mortgagee is generally not entitled to recover fees in foreclosing the mortgage.[8] If the loan documents do not contain enforceable attorney's fee provisions, a practitioner may consider using the Offer of Judgment and Demand for Judgment statute[9] and Proposal for Settlement rule[10] to shift responsibility for attorney's fees, discussed below in Section 16-5.

16-2:2 Reciprocal Provisions of Fla. Stat. § 57.105(7) Apply to Foreclosure Actions

If a mortgage contains a provision allowing attorney's fees when the holder of the note and mortgage is required to take any action to enforce it, Fla. Stat. § 57.105(7) provides that the court may also allow reasonable attorney's fees to the other party when that party prevails in any action with respect to the mortgage.[11] In other words, the statute makes a unilateral provision on attorney's fees in favor of one party reciprocal, or available to either party to the mortgage.[12] Application of this statute is discretionary, however, and is not mandatory.[13]

16-2:3 No Contract, No Fees

It has been found in non-foreclosure cases that if there is no contract between the parties, then no attorney's fees may be awarded to the prevailing party.[14] The same rule

---

[5] *Maw v. Abinales*, 463 So. 2d 1245 (Fla. 2d DCA 1985).

[6] *Savarese v. Schoner*, 464 So. 2d 695, 696 (Fla. 2d DCA 1985); *Siemer v. Geringer*, 617 So. 2d 1155 (Fla. 4th DCA 1993); *Rockwood v. DeRosa*, 279 So. 2d 54 (Fla. 4th DCA 1973).

[7] *The Bank of New York Mellon v. Mestre*, 159 So. 3d 953 (Fla. 5th DCA 2015); *Edrisi v. Sarnoff*, 715 So. 2d 1124 (Fla. 3d DCA 1998).

[8] *Edrisi v. Sarnoff*, 715 So. 2d 1124 (Fla. 3d DCA 1998).

[9] Fla. Stat. § 768.79.

[10] Fla. R. Civ. P. 1.442.

[11] Fla. Stat. § 57.105(7).

[12] *Mihalyi v. LaSalle Bank, N.A*, 162 So. 3d 113 (Fla. 4th DCA 2014).

[13] *Spartan Holdco, LLC v. Cheeburger Cheeburger Restaurants*, 2011 WL 6024487, at *3 (M.D. Fla. Nov. 18, 2011).

[14] *HFC Collection Center, Inc. v. Alexander*, 190 So. 3d 1114 (Fla. 5th DCA 2016); *Fielder v. Weinstein Design Group, Inc.*, 842 So. 2d 879 (Fla. 4th DCA 2003); *Hanna v. Beverly*

applies in foreclosure cases.[15] If the Court finds that there was no mortgage contract between the parties to the foreclosure action, it is error to award attorney's fees to the prevailing party. For example, an award of attorney's fees against a bank that brought a foreclosure action against a trust that did not sign the mortgage was error.[16] Where a court found that the mortgagors' signatures were forged, there was no valid contract between the parties, and thus no attorney's fees may be awarded.[17] Likewise, where a defendant in a foreclosure action successfully employs a defense strategy that she is not a party to the contract, it is very difficult for the prevailing defendant to meet her threshold burden that she is in fact a party to the contract, and thus entitled to fees under that previously disavowed contract.[18] It has also been held that where a party is not personally responsible for payment of a non-recourse note and mortgage, that party is not entitled to recover attorney's fees if it is the prevailing party on a suit on that note and mortgage.[19] In addition, a mortgagor that obtains dismissal of a foreclosure complaint on the grounds that the plaintiff lacks standing to sue on the note and mortgage may not be entitled to recover attorney's fees based upon those same contracts (i.e., no contract existed between the parties and thus no fees should be awarded to the prevailing party).[20] The Fourth District, in an *en banc* decision, made it clear that if the defendant prevails on a theory of the plaintiff's lack of standing, the defendant is not entitled to recover attorney's fees (saying "NO STANDING = NO FEES").[21] However, it appears that there is a split of opinion among the appellate courts, as the Fifth District has held that a mortgagor that prevails on the issue of a lender's standing may be entitled to recover attorney's fees.[22] The Florida Supreme Court recently concluded that it had "improvidently" granted jurisdiction in overruling the Fourth DCA's "no standing, no attorney's fees" decision in the *Glass* case, and withdrew its earlier decision.[23]

Enterprises-Florida, 738 So. 2d 424 (Fla. 4th DCA 1999); *Warfield v. Stewart*, 434 Fed. Appx. 777, 784 (11th Cir. 2011); *Stewart v. Tasnet, Inc.*, 718 So. 2d 820, 821 (Fla. 2d DCA 1998).

[15] *Novastar Mortgage, Inc. v. Strassburger*, 855 So. 2d 130 (Fla. 4th DCA 2003).

[16] *HSBC Bank USA, N.A. v. Frenkel*, 208 So. 3d 156 (Fla. 3d DCA 2016).

[17] *Bank of New York Mellon v. Mestre*, 159 So. 3d 953 (Fla. 5th DCA 2015).

[18] *Florida Community Bank, N.A. v. Red Road Residential, LLC*, 197 So. 3d 1112 (Fla. 3d DCA 2016).

[19] *Suchman Corp. Park, Inc. v. Greenstein*, 600 So. 2d 532 (Fla. 3d DCA 1992).

[20] *Bank of New York Mellon Trust Company, N.A. v. Fitzgerald*, 215 So. 3d 116 (Fla. 3d DCA 2017); *Nationstar Mortgage LLC v. Glass*, 219 So. 3d 896 (Fla. 4th DCA 2017), *cert. dismissed*, 268 So.3d 676 (Fla. 2019).

[21] *Deutsche Bank Trust Company Americas v. Page*, 274 So. 3d 1116 (Fla. 4th DCA 2019), *rev. granted*, Case No. SC19-1137. See also *Fassy v. Bank of New York Mellon*, 273 So. 3d 52 (Fla. 4th DCA 2019); *Rennick v. Wilmington Savings Fund Society, FSB*, 276 So. 3d 29 (Fla. 4th DCA 2019); *Nationstar Mortgage, LLC v. Faramarz*, 275 So. 3d 668 (4th DCA 2019).

[22] *Madl v. Wells Fargo Bank, N.A.*, 244 So. 3d 1134 (Fla. 5th DCA 2017); *Harris v. Bank of New York Mellon*, 2018 WL 6816177 (Fla. 2nd DCA 2018); *but see*, *Hopson v. Deutsche Bank*, 278 So. 3d 306 (Fla. 2nd DCA 2019).

[23] *Nationstar Mortgage LLC v. Glass*, 219 So. 3d 896 (Fla. 4th DCA 2017), *cert. dismissed*, 268 So. 3d 676 (Fla. 2019).

16-3 Procedures to Recover Attorney's Fees

16-3:1 Pleading Requirement

The Florida Supreme Court has made it clear that it is necessary for a party to plead any claim for attorney's fees for that party to recover its fees, and that failure to do so constitutes a waiver of the claim.[24] Thus, it is critical that any claim for attorney's fees must be pled in the complaint or answer. However, the Supreme Court also held that if a party is on notice that an opponent claims entitlement to attorney's fees, and by its conduct recognizes or acquiesces to that claim or otherwise fails to object to the failure to plead entitlement, that party waives any objection to the failure to plead a claim for attorney's fees.[25] Failing to allege entitlement to attorney's fees in an answer or complaint may constitute a waiver of any claim for fees.[26] There are some exceptions to the general pleading requirement. For example, a defendant who files a motion to dismiss, prior to filing any responsive pleading to the complaint, may be entitled to recover attorney's fees upon the dismissal of the action, if the defendant's motion for attorney's fees is otherwise timely filed.[27] However, a party filing a "notice of intent to seek attorney's fees" in a deficiency action filed after completion of a foreclosure was not entitled to recover attorney's fees, as the notice was not a pleading and did not provide sufficient notice of the defendants' claim that they would seek to recover their fees.[28] The effect of waiver can work against a plaintiff, too. A plaintiff's failure to raise the issue of the defendant's failure to plead entitlement to fees may constitute the waiver of the plaintiff's objection to such lack of pleading.[29] Note that the specific statutory or contractual basis for a claim for attorney's fees need not be specially pled, and that failure to plead the basis of such a claim will not result in waiver of the claim.[30] The better practice, however, is to plead the legal and factual basis for any claim for fees.

16-3:2 Prevailing Party

To recover attorney's fees in an action on a contract, the party must be construed as the party that prevailed or succeeded on "any significant issue in litigation which achieves some of the benefit the parties sought in bringing suit."[31] A mortgagee that obtains a judgment of foreclosure is entitled to recover its attorney's fees, provided that it pleads and proves that the mortgagee has obligated itself to pay a reasonable attorney's fee for bringing the action.[32] Conversely, a mortgagor who succeeds in having a foreclosure action dismissed (either voluntarily or involuntarily) is the prevailing

---

[24] *Stockman v. Downs*, 573 So. 2d 835 (Fla. 1991).
[25] *Stockman v. Downs*, 573 So. 2d 835, 838 (Fla. 1991).
[26] *Concrete & Lumber Enterprises Corp. v. Guaranty Business Credit Corp.*, 829 So. 2d 247 (Fla. 3d DCA 2002).
[27] *Green v. Sun Harbor Homeowners' Ass'n, Inc.*, 730 So. 2d 1261 (Fla. 1998); *Nudel v. Flagstar Bank, FSB*, 60 So. 3d 1163 (Fla. 4th DCA 2011).
[28] *BMR Funding, LLC v. DDR. Corp.*, 67 So. 3d 1137 (Fla. 2d DCA 2011).
[29] *BankUnited, N.A. v. Ajabshir*, 207 So. 3d 354 (Fla. 3d DCA 2016).
[30] *Caulfield v. Cantele*, 837 So. 2d 371 (Fla. 2002).
[31] *Hensley v. Eckerhart*, 461 U.S. 424, 103 S. Ct. 1933, 76 L. Ed.2d 40 (1983); *Moritz v. Hoyt Enterprises, Inc.*, 604 So. 2d 807 (Fla. 1992); *Prosperi v. Code, Inc.*, 626 So. 2d 1360 (Fla. 1993); *Trytek v. Gale Industries, Inc.*, 3 So. 3d 1194 (Fla. 2009).
[32] *Buchanan & Crowder, Inc. v. Kreamer*, 162 So. 500 (Fla. 1935).

party and may be entitled to recover attorney's fees incurred in defending the action.[33] Or, if the plaintiff voluntarily dismisses the foreclosure action, prior to a determination on the merits, the defendant may be the prevailing party and entitled to attorney's fees.[34] However, the determination of which party is the prevailing party must take into account the litigation as a whole, and the "substance of litigation outcomes—not just procedural maneuvers," to determine which party prevailed on the significant issues.[35] In a case where both parties prevailed on significant claims in complex and protracted litigation, neither party may be awarded fees.[36] In another case with multiple claims, where each claim is separate and distinct and would support an independent action, the prevailing party was entitled to an award of attorney's fees for those fees generated in connection with that claim.[37] When a plaintiff is not a prevailing party on a reformation count, which is "outside the terms of the contract," and prevails on the foreclosure of that mortgage contract, the defendant was not entitled to attorney's fees.[38] However, there is no prevailing party upon the settlement of a case, such as when the parties have agreed to a short sale of the property, or the defendant mortgagor pays the amounts due the mortgagee.[39] Note that an attorney representing himself in a mortgage foreclosure action is entitled to recover attorney's fees when successfully defending a foreclosure action,[40] and that an attorney who has withdrawn as attorney of record for the mortgagor in a foreclosure has no claim for attorney's fees upon dismissal of that case.[41] Also, a lawyer does not have standing to bring a claim for fees on his own behalf, as the claim for fees belongs to the client, and not the lawyer.[42]

16-3:3 Time for Filing of Motion

The Florida Rules of Civil Procedure provide that the time for filing a motion for attorney's fees is no later than 30 days after filing of the judgment, including a judgment of dismissal, or the service of a notice of voluntary dismissal.[43] The 30-day time period may be extended by filing a motion under Rule 1.090(b), for cause shown prior to the

---

[33] *Bank of New York v. Williams*, 979 So. 2d 347 (Fla. 1st DCA 2008); *Valcarcel v. Chase Bank USA, N.A.*, 54 So. 3d 989 (Fla. 4th DCA 2010); *Nudel v. Flagstar Bank, FSB*, 60 So. 3d 1163 (Fla. 4th DCA 2011).

[34] *Grosso v. HSBC Bank USA, N.A., as Trustee on Behalf of Ace Securities Corp.*, 275 So. 3d 642 (Fla. 4th DCA 2019); *see also Venezia v. JP Morgan Mortgage Acquisition Corp.*, 279 So. 3d 145 (Fla. 4th DCA 2019).

[35] *Tubbs v. Mechanik Nuccio Hearne & Webster, P.A.*, 125 So. 3d 1034 (Fla. 2d DCA 2013).

[36] *HHA Borrower, LLC. v. W.G. Yates & Sons Constr. Co.*, 266 So. 3d 1267, 1268 (Fla. 5th DCA 2019).

[37] *Padgett v. Kessinger*, 190 So. 3d 105 (Fla. 4th DCA 2015).

[38] *Deutsche Bank, Nat'l Tr. Co. as Tr. for Holders of the BCAP LLC Tr. 2007-AA1 v. Quintela*, 268 So. 3d 156, 158 (Fla. 4th DCA 2019).

[39] *Kelly v. BankUnited, FSB*, 159 So. 3d 403 (Fla. 4th DCA 2015); *Padow v. Knollwood Club Association, Inc.*, 839 So. 2d 744 (Fla. 4th DCA 2003); *Boxer Max Corporation v. Cane A. Sucre, Inc.*, 905 So. 2d 916 (Fla. 3d DCA 2005); *Bonfiglio v. EMC Mortgage Corporation*, 935 So. 2d 561 (Fla. 4th DCA 2006); *Washington Mutual Bank, F.A. v. Shelton*, 892 So. 2d 547 (Fla. 2d DCA 2005).

[40] *McClung v. Posey*, 514 So. 2d 1139 (Fla. 5th DCA 1987), *Nunez v. Allen*, 2019 WL 5089715 (Fla. 5th DCA 2019).

[41] *Cacho v. Bank of New York Mellon*, 124 So. 3d 943 (Fla. 3d DCA 2013).

[42] *Bonfiglio v. EMC Mortgage Corporation*, 935 So. 2d 561 (Fla. 4th DCA 2006).

[43] Fla. R. Civ. P. 1.525.

expiration of the deadline, or upon a showing of excusable neglect, after the expiration of the deadline.[44] The failure to timely file a motion for fees or show excusable neglect will result in the denial of a request for attorney's fees, as Fla. R. Civ. P 1.525 establishes a "bright line" time requirement for filing such motions.[45] The Florida Supreme Court has clarified that a motion filed prior to the entry of a final judgment is also considered timely.[46]

16-3:4 Burden of Proof and Evidence Required

It is well established that the burden to establish the right to attorney's fees is always on the claimant, and he must show the circumstances that justify the award as well as prove the reasonableness of the fee awarded.[47] The party asserting a right to attorney's fees under a written contract has the burden not only of demonstrating its general right of recovery, but also the reasonable amount due for asserting or defending the contract right.[48] Furthermore, the mere fact that the contract contains an attorney's fee provision is not, by itself, enough to show that the prevailing party is entitled to recover fees. The contract must contain specific language permitting the recovery of fees under the facts and circumstances of the case before the court.[49] Attorney's fees are not necessarily recoverable as to any and all litigation relating to a contract with an attorney's fee clause.[50] Furthermore, if the attorney's fees are recoverable only upon the "breach of the agreement by either party," and the court did not find any such breach, no fees may be awarded.[51]

16-3:5 Must Prove Fees Are Reasonable

The party seeking fees must prove that the attorney's fees sought are reasonable.[52] The prevailing party's attorney should keep accurate time records,[53] but the failure to put the time records in evidence is not necessarily fatal to the claim for fees.[54] In addition, the party must prove the amount of time actually spent in the case, and the court must make specific findings regarding the number of hours and the amount of a reasonable hourly rate.[55] An expert witness must testify as to the reasonableness of the hours spent and the hourly rate, and the failure to do so may result in reversal of the attorney's fee award.[56] The testimony of the expert witness is not binding upon the trial

---

[44] *State of Florida, Department of Transportation v. SouthTrust Bank*, 886 So. 2d 393 (Fla. 1st DCA 2004).
[45] *Hovercraft of South Florida, LLC v. Reynolds*, 211 So. 3d 1073 (Fla. 5th DCA 2017).
[46] *Barco v. School Board of Pinellas County*, 975 So. 2d 1116 (Fla. 2008).
[47] *Leonard v. Cook & Pruitt Masonry, Inc.*, 126 So. 2d 136, 139 (Fla. 1960).
[48] *Plapinger v. E. States Properties Realty Corp.*, 716 So. 2d 315, 318 (Fla. 5th DCA 1998).
[49] *Village 45 Partners, LLC v. Racetrac Petroleum Inc.*, 831 So. 2d 758 (Fla. 4th DCA 2002).
[50] *Bowman v. Kingsland Dev., Inc.*, 432 So. 2d 660 (Fla. 5th DCA 1983).
[51] *Dan Galasso Waste Serv., Inc. v. Hemery*, 528 So. 2d 1356, 1358 (Fla. 3d DCA 1988).
[52] *Fraser v. Security and Inv. Corp.*, 615 So. 2d 841 (Fla. 4th DCA 1993).
[53] *Florida Patient's Compensation Fund v. Rowe*, 472 So. 2d 1145 (Fla. 1985).
[54] *Brevard Community College v. Barber*, 488 So. 2d 93 (Fla. 1st DCA 1986); *Executive Square, Ltd. v. Delray Executive Square, Ltd.*, 553 So. 2d 803 (Fla. 4th DCA 1989).
[55] *Young v. Taubman*, 855 So. 2d 184 (Fla. 4th DCA 2003).
[56] *Palmetto Federal Savings and Loan Ass'n v. Day*, 512 So. 2d 332 (Fla. 3d DCA 1987); *Aldama v. JPMorgan Chase Bank, N.A.*, 194 So. 3d 543 (Fla. 3d DCA 2016); *Miller v. Bank of New York Mellon*, 149 So. 3d 1198 (Fla. 4th DCA 2014).

court, but it is persuasive.[57] The billing records of the opposing party are relevant to the issue of reasonableness of time expended in litigating a claim for attorney's fees.[58]

Florida has adopted the "Lodestar" approach utilized by the federal courts as an objective structure to determine whether attorney's fees are reasonable.[59] The Florida Supreme Court identified the following factors in *Rowe* for the court to examine in making its determination regarding the reasonableness of attorney's fees sought by a party:

> (1) The time and labor required, the novelty and difficulty of the question involved, and the skill requisite to perform the legal service properly; (2) The likelihood, if apparent to the client, that the acceptance of the particular employment will preclude other employment by the lawyer; (3) The fee customarily charged in the locality for similar legal services; (4) The amount involved and the results obtained; (5) The time limitations imposed by the client or by the circumstances; (6) The nature and length of the professional relationship with the client; (7) The experience, reputation, and ability of the lawyer or lawyers performing the services; (8) Whether the fee is fixed or contingent.[60]

The federal lodestar approach establishes a "strong presumption" that the lodestar represents the "reasonable fee."[61]

16-3:6 Fees to Determine Party's Entitlement to Attorney's Fees, But Generally Not the Amount of Fees

The Florida Supreme Court has held that a party may be entitled to recover attorney's fees to litigate whether that party is entitled to recover attorney's fees in an insurance matter.[62] This rule has been extended to other civil litigation matters based upon a breach of contract.[63] Thus, a prevailing party in a mortgage foreclosure action may recover its attorney's fees in obtaining an award of entitlement. However, the general rule is that a party may not recover fees in litigating the *amount* of the fees.[64] An exception to this rule may be found where the language of the contract is broad enough to provide for an award of fees for "any litigation" between the parties.[65] Fur-

---

[57] *Manatee County v. Harbor Ventures, Inc.*, 305 So. 2d 299 (Fla. 2d DCA1974); *Ruwitch v. First National Bank of Miami*, 327 So. 2d 833 (Fla. 3d DCA 1976).
[58] *Paton v. GEICO General Ins. Co.*, 190 So. 3d 1047 (Fla. 2016).
[59] *Florida Patient's Comp. Fund v. Rowe*, 472 So. 2d 1145 (Fla. 1985).
[60] *Florida Patient's Comp. Fund v. Rowe*, 472 So. 2d 1145, 1150 (Fla. 1985), *holding modified by Standard Guar. Ins. Co. v. Quanstrom*, 555 So. 2d 828 (Fla. 1990).
[61] *Progressive Exp. Ins. Co. v. Schultz*, 948 So. 2d 1027, 1030 (Fla. 5th DCA 2007).
[62] *State Farm Fire & Casualty Co. v. Palma*, 629 So. 2d 830 (Fla. 1993).
[63] *Mediplex Construction of Fla., Inc. v. Schaub*, 856 So. 2d 13 (Fla. 4th DCA 2003).
[64] *State Farm Fire & Casualty Co. v. Palma*, 629 So. 2d 830 (Fla. 1993); *National Portland Cement Co. v. Goudie*, 718 So. 2d 274 (Fla. 2d DCA 1998); *Mediplex Const. of Florida, Inc. v. Schaub*, 856 So. 2d 13 (Fla. 4th DCA 2003); *Allstate Indemnity Co. v. Hicks*, 880 So. 2d 772 (Fla. 5th DCA 2004); *Windsor Falls Condominium Association, Inc. v. Davis*, 265 So. 3d 709 (Fla. 1st DCA 2019); *Obermeyer v. Bank of New York*, 272 So. 3d 430 (Mem.) (Fla. 3d DCA 2019).
[65] *Waverly at Las Olas Condo. Ass'n, Inc. v. Waverly Las Olas, LLC*, 88 So. 2d 386 (2012); *Trial Practices, Inc. v. Hahn Loeser & Parks, LLP for Antaramian*, 228 So. 3d 1184 (Fla. 2d DCA

thermore, an order on attorney's fees is not final and may not be appealed until the amount of fees is determined by the trial court, as an order on the issue of entitlement only is not ripe for review.[66]

16-3:7 Contingency Fee Multipliers

In limited cases, the prevailing party may seek a "multiplier" of the attorney's fees awarded in cases based upon the contingent nature of the fee agreement the party had with its attorney. Those cases may include contract cases, and the Supreme Court has held that "in no case should the court-awarded fee exceed the fee agreement reached by the attorney and his client."[67] A threshold determination is that any contingency fee agreement must be in writing between the lawyer and client; otherwise they are unconscionable and of no effect.[68] Contingency contracts that do not comply with the Florida Rule of Professional Conduct 4-1.5(f)(1) offend public policy and are antagonistic to the public interest.[69] Without a valid contingency fee agreement, no contingency risk multiplier can be used.[70]

The Supreme Court has established principles regarding when a multiplier should be applied to a fee award: (1) whether the relevant market requires a contingency fee multiplier to obtain competent counsel; (2) whether the attorney was able to mitigate the risk of non-payment in any way; and (3) whether any of the factors set forth in *Rowe* are applicable, especially, the amount involved, the results obtained, and the type of fee arrangement between the attorney and the client.[71] The Supreme Court rejected a holding of the Fifth District that multipliers may only be awarded in "rare" and "exceptional" circumstances, finding that there is no such requirement.[72] Accordingly, whether or not a contingent fee multiplier should be awarded will be based upon the facts of each case. If a party does not testify that he had difficulty obtaining competent counsel to represent him, he is not entitled to a multiplier.[73] Further, if a party cannot demonstrate that he unable to obtain competent counsel without a multiplier, then one should not be awarded.[74] A court award of a multiplier of 2.5 was upheld in a mortgage foreclosure case where the mortgagor prevailed, and success seemed

---

2017) (holding that attorneys' fees incurred in litigating the amount of fees were encompassed by a broadly drafted contract provision and were therefore appropriate), *quashed on other grounds*, 260 So. 3d 167 (Fla. 2018); *but see Paladyne Corp. v. Weindruch,* 867 So. 2d 630 (Fla. 5th DCA 2004); *Burton Family Partnership v. Luani Plaza, Inc.,* 2019 WL 2844271 (Fla. 3d DCA 2019).

[66] *Miller v. Miller,* 801 So. 2d 1056 (Fla. 1st DCA 2001); *Alvis v. Alvis,* 95 So. 3d 910 (Fla. 1st DCA 2012); *Debolt v. Debolt,* 90 So. 3d 374 (Fla. 1st DCA 2012).

[67] *Florida Patient's Comp. Fund v. Rowe,* 472 So. 2d 1145, 1148 (Fla. 1985).

[68] *Foodtown Inc. of Jacksonville v. Argonaut Ins. Co.,* 102 F. 3d 483, 485 (11th Cir.1996); *FIGA v. R. V.M.P. Corp.,* 681 F.Supp. 806, 810 (S.D. Fla. 1988).

[69] *Chandris, S.A. v. Yanakakis,* 668 So. 2d 180, 185 (Fla. 1995); *Brickell Place Condo Association, Inc. v. Ganguzza & Associates, P.A.,* 31 So. 3d 287, 290 (Fla. 3d DCA 2010).

[70] *Pompano Ledger v. Greater Pompano Beach Chamber of Commerce,* 802 So. 2d 438, 438-39 (Fla. 4th DCA 2001); *Wolfe v. Nazaire,* 758 So. 2d 730, 734 (Fla. 4th DCA 2000).

[71] *Standard Guaranty Insurance Co. v. Quanstrom,* 555 So. 2d 828 (Fla. 1990).

[72] *Joyce v Federated National Insurance Co.,* 228 So. 3d 1122 (Fla. 2017).

[73] *Progressive Exp. Ins. Co. v. Schultz,* 948 So. 2d 1027, 1030-33 (Fla. 5th DCA 2007); *see also Indymac Federal Bank FSB v. Machado,* 2010 WL 8250945 (Fla. Cir. Ct. Palm Beach July 1, 2010).

[74] *Florida Peninsula Ins. Co. v. Wagner,* 196 So. 3d 419 (Fla. 2d DCA 2016).

unlikely at the outset of the case, because the mortgagor had no ability to pay attorney, a default had been entered, six months had passed, and mortgagor's attorney was the only attorney in the area who would undertake mortgage foreclosure defense on a contingency contract.[75] The same appellate court, however, reversed a multiplier award of $176,992.64 of attorney's fees, in a case involving $6,000 in actual and statutory damages under the Florida Consumer Collection Practices Act.[76] Similarly, a multiplier awarded in a construction lien case was reversed by the appellate court where the evidence indicated that both parties were able to obtain competent counsel when the dispute arose, even though the issues raised by the defendant were novel and complex.[77] When the attorney is able to mitigate his/her risk of non-payment, a multiplier is usually not warranted.[78] A trial judge's denial of a fee multiplier was found not to be an abuse of discretion by the appellate court in a landlord tenant dispute, where the evidence showed that any number of attorneys would have agreed to take the case on an hourly or contingent fee basis.[79] A number of circuit judges at the trial court level have rejected fee multipliers in mortgage foreclosure cases as well.[80]

16-3:8 Recovery of Attorney's Fees Incurred in Bankruptcy

A foreclosure trial court does not have jurisdiction to award attorney's fees incurred in a bankruptcy proceeding, as the bankruptcy court is the appropriate forum to determine a creditor's right to recover attorney's fees.[81] Federal law grants the bankruptcy court exclusive jurisdiction to award attorney's fees incurred in that forum.[82] Accordingly, an award of attorney's fees must be obtained in the bankruptcy court.

16-3:9 Recovery of Attorney's Fees on Appeal

To recover attorney's fees on appeal, the prevailing party on appeal must be entitled to attorney's fees pursuant to a contract or statute, and a motion for appellate fees must be filed with the appellate court.[83] Where appellate litigation ends in a "tie," with each party prevailing in part and losing in part on significant issues, it is appropriate

---

[75] *J.P. Morgan Acquisition Corporation v. Golden*, 98 So. 3d 220 (Fla. 2d DCA 2015).

[76] *Dish Network Service LLC v. Myers*, 87 So. 3d 72 (Fla. 2d DCA 2012).

[77] *Michnal v. Palm Coast Development, Inc.*, 842 So. 2d 927 (Fla. 4th DCA 2003).

[78] *Pompano Ledger v. Greater Pompano Beach Chamber of Commerce*, 802 So. 2d 438 (Fla. 4th DCA 2001); *Citizens Property Insurance Corp. v. River Oaks Condo. II Ass'n, Inc.*, 190 So. 3d 1110 (Fla. 2d DCA 2016).

[79] *Katz Deli of Aventura, Inc. v. Waterways Plaza, LLC*, 183 So. 3d 374 (Fla. 3d DCA 2013).

[80] *The Bank of New York Mellon v. Horton*, 2017 WL 538317 (Fla. Cir. Ct. Broward Feb. 9, 2017); *Bank of America v. Ruiz*, 2016 WL 6726326 (Fla. Cir. Ct. 6th Jud. Cir. Oct. 27, 2016); *Chase Home Finance LLC v. Guerrero*, 2015 WL 10945252 (Fla. Cir. Ct. Miami-Dade June 15, 2015); *Wilmington Trust Co. v. Hines*, 2016 WL 3356996 (Fla. Cir. Ct. Bay Mar. 9, 2016); *Wilmington Bank v. Garcia*, 2015 WL 11022890 (Fla. Cir. Ct. Broward Nov. 20, 2015); *HSBC Bank USA, N.A. v. Angelini*, 2016 WL 4702598 (Fla. Cir. Ct. Broward Aug. 31, 2016).

[81] *Pastore-Borroto Dev., Inc. v. Marevista Apartments, M.B., Inc.*, 596 So. 2d 526 (Fla. 3d DCA 1992); *Florida Fed. Sav. & Loan Ass'n v. Sanchez*, 553 So. 2d 1254 (Fla. 3d DCA 1989); *Hoffman v. Wells Fargo Bank Minnesota*, 987 So. 2d 206 (Fla. 5th DCA 2008).

[82] 11 U.S.C. § 506(b); *In re Aldrovandi*, 568 B.R. 154 (Bankr. M.D. Fla. 2017); *Dvorak v. First Family Bank*, 639 So. 2d 1076 (Fla. 5th DCA 1994).

[83] Fla. R. App. P. 9.400(b).

to deny a motion for appellate attorney's fees.[84] The lower court has no jurisdiction to award attorney's fees incurred on appeal of a foreclosure matter, without a mandate from the appellate court.[85] The attorney's fee motion must be filed no later than the time for service of the reply brief.[86] Unlike the rule in the lower courts as discussed above, a motion for fees must specify the particular contractual, statutory or other substantive basis for an award of fees on appeal.[87] A party's response to a motion for attorney's fees must be filed within 15 days.[88] The failure to file a timely response to a motion for fees may constitute a waiver of the right to oppose an award of fees.[89]

If the appellate court grants the motion for attorney's fees, the court typically remands the case to the lower court to determine the amount of fees to be awarded.[90] If the case is reversed and remanded for further action, such as trial, the attorney's fees awarded by the appellate court should be conditioned upon the successful party on appeal prevailing at trial.[91] The prevailing party must file its motion for costs in the lower court within 45 days after rendition of the appellate court's order.[92] Note that the time period to file a motion for costs was revised from 30 days to 45 days by an amendment to Rule 9.400(a) in 2014.[93] Failure to timely file a motion for costs precludes an order awarding such costs.[94] Review of orders rendered by the lower court on the amount of fees "shall be by motion filed" in the appellate court within 30 days of rendition.[95] The standard of review of an order granting a motion for appellate attorney's fees is abuse of discretion.[96]

16-4 Attorney's Fees as a Sanction

16-4:1 Court's Inherent Authority to Assess Attorney's Fees as a Sanction

Florida has long recognized a limited exception to the general American Rule in situations involving inequitable conduct, and the Florida Supreme Court has held that a court has inherent authority to impose sanctions, including attorney's fees, under the "inequitable conduct doctrine."[97] It is reserved for those extreme cases where a

---

[84] *Ashear v. Sklarey*, 239 So. 3d 786 (Fla. 3d DCA 2018).
[85] *Schere v. Z.F., Inc.*, 578 So. 2d 739, 740 (Fla. 3d DCA 1991).
[86] Fla. R. App. P. 9.400(b); *Advanced Chiropractic & Rehab. Ctr., Corp. v. United Auto. Ins. Co.*, 140 So. 3d 529, 533 (Fla. 2014).
[87] *United Services Auto. Ass'n v. Phillips*, 775 So. 2d 921 (Fla. 2000).
[88] Fla. R. App. P. 9.300(a).
[89] *Homestead Ins. Co. v. Poole, Masters & Goldstein, C.P.A., P.A.*, 604 So. 2d 825, 827 (Fla. 4th DCA 1991).
[90] *Jones v. Florida Ins. Guar. Ass'n, Inc.*, 908 So. 2d 435, 438 (Fla. 2005).
[91] *Sabina v. Dahlia Corporation*, 678 So. 2d 822 (Fla. 2nd DCA 1996); *Balmaseda v. Okay Ins. Exch. of Am., LLC*, 240 So. 3d 146 (Fla. 3rd DCA 2018); *Johnson v. Maroone Ford, LLC*, 944 So. 2d 1059 (Fla. 4th DCA 2006).
[92] Fla. R. App. P. 9.400(a).
[93] *In re Amendments to Florida Rules of Appellate Procedure*, 183 So. 3d 245 (Fla. 2014).
[94] *Abraham v. S.N.W. Corp.*, 549 So. 2d 776 (Fla. 4th DCA 1989).
[95] Fla. R. App. P. 9.400(c).
[96] *Pellar v. Granger Asphalt Paving, Inc.*, 687 So. 2d 282, 285 (Fla. 1st DCA 1997).
[97] *Florida Patient's Comp. Fund v. Rowe*, 472 So. 2d 1145 (Fla. 1985); *Bitterman v. Bitterman*, 714 So. 2d 356 (Fla. 1998).

party acts "in bad faith, vexatiously, wantonly, or for oppressive reasons."[98] A trial court possesses the inherent authority to impose attorney's fees against an attorney for bad faith conduct during the course of litigation.[99] A trial court's exercise of its inherent authority must be based upon an express finding of bad faith conduct and must be supported by detailed factual findings describing the specific acts of bad faith that resulted in unnecessary incurrence of attorney's fees.[100] In addition, the amount of fees awarded must be directly related to the attorney's fees and costs that the opposing party has incurred as a result of the specific bad faith of the attorney, and the sanctioned attorney must be provided with notice and an opportunity to be heard before the sanction is imposed.[101] The Florida Supreme Court has recognized a court's authority to impose sanctions for bad faith of an attorney in foreclosure actions as early as 1920.[102] An attorney may also be sanctioned in a foreclosure matter for acting in his own interest and not on behalf of his client.[103] The attorney and his client may be held jointly responsible for the attorney's bad faith conduct, or the court in its discretion may apportion the order of attorney's fees against the attorney or the client based upon its determination of each party's participation in the bad faith conduct.[104] Despite the inherent authority of a court to award sanctions, if a "specific statute or rule applies, the court should rely upon the applicable rule or statute rather than on inherent authority."[105]

16-4:2 Attorney's Fees for Raising Unsupported Claim or Defense or for Unreasonable Delay Under Fla. Stat. § 57.105(1) & (2)

Fla. Stat. § 57.105(1) provides a mechanism for a prevailing party to recover attorney's fees against a losing party and its attorney, if the court finds that the losing party or its attorney knew or should have known that a claim or defense when initially presented to the court (or at any time before trial) was a) not supported by the material facts necessary to establish the claim or defense, or b) would not be supported by the application of then-existing law to those material facts.[106] In addition, the statute provides that a party may obtain an award of its reasonable expenses, which may include attorney's fees, incurred in obtaining an order determining that an opposing party's actions were frivolous or taken primarily for the purpose of unreasonable delay.[107] This statute has been found to be applicable in mortgage foreclosure actions, where the defendants and their counsel asserted defenses which they know or should have known are not supported by the material facts of the case, results in an award of costs and attorney's fees, plus "delay damages" in the form of interest on the note and mortgage while

---

[98] *Foster v. Tourtellotte*, 704 F.2d 1109 (9th Cir. 1983) (quoting *F.D. Rich Co. v. United States ex rel. Industrial Lumber Co.*, 417 U.S. 116 (1974).
[99] *Moakley v. Smallwood*, 826 So. 2d 221 (Fla. 2002).
[100] *Moakley v. Smallwood*, 826 So. 2d 221 (Fla. 2002).
[101] *Moakley v. Smallwood*, 826 So. 2d 221 (Fla. 2002).
[102] *United States Sav. Bank v. Pittman*, 86 So. 567 (Fla. 1920).
[103] *Goldfarb v. Daitch*, 696 So. 2d 1199 (Fla. 3d DCA 1997).
[104] *Schiderman v. Fitness Innovations & Technology, Inc.*, 994 So. 2d 508 (Fla. 4th DCA 2008); *Bennett v. Berges*, 50 So. 3d 1154 (Fla. 4th DCA 2010).
[105] *Moakley v. Smallwood*, 826 So. 2d 221 (Fla. 2002); *Koch v. Koch*, 47 So. 3d 320 (Fla. 2d DCA 2010).
[106] Fla. Stat. § 57.105(1).
[107] Fla. Stat. § 57.105(2); *Bionetics Corp. v. Kenniasty*, 69 So. 3d 943, 944 (Fla. 2011).

the case was delayed.[108] The filing of frivolous pleadings by an attorney related to the tender of a "unilateral note" by the borrowers in an attempt to "satisfy" a foreclosure judgment resulted in an award of sanctions against the borrowers and their attorney, and a suspension of the attorney by the Florida Bar for ethical violations.[109] An appellate court may award attorney's fees against an appellant (and its lawyers) for filing a frivolous appeal.[110]

Fla. Stat. § 57.105(2) provides that if a moving party proves by a preponderance of the evidence that any action taken by the opposing party, including but not limited to, the filing of any pleading, the assertion of or response to any discovery, the assertion of any claim or defense, or the response to any request by any other party, was taken primarily for the purpose of unreasonable delay, the court "shall" award damages to the moving party, which may include attorney's fees or other loss resulting from the delay.[111]

The statute further provides that no sanctions may be awarded if the court finds that the claims or defenses were initially presented to the court as a good faith argument for the extension, modification or reversal of existing law with a reasonable expectation of success, or if the attorney acted in good faith, based upon the representations of his or her client as to the existence of material facts.[112] For example, a defendant raised a defense that her homestead was not subject to the forced sale to satisfy a judgment, the issue was not so clear as to make defense frivolous or completely untenable, and thus an award of attorney's fees was not warranted.[113]

16-4:3 Procedure to Obtain Attorney's Fees or Other Sanctions Under Fla. Stat. § 57.105(1) & (2)

A motion by a party seeking sanctions under Fla. Stat. § 57.105(1) & (2) must be served, but may not be filed with or presented to the court, unless within 21 days after the service of the motion, the challenged paper, claim, defense, contention, allegation or denial is not withdrawn or appropriately corrected.[114] The failure to serve the 21-day notice, sometimes referred to as a "safe harbor" notice, is fatal to the claim for sanctions under § 57.105.[115] A letter sent by an attorney did not meet the statutory requirements, and attorney's fees are properly denied if the proposed motion is not served at least 21 days before it is filed.[116] An appellant's motion for fees that was prematurely filed before an appellee had filed any briefs in an appeal, resulted in the motion being stricken, as there is nothing for the appellee to withdraw.[117] Waiting to

---

[108] *Korte v. U.S. Bank Nat. Ass'n.*, 64 So. 3d 134 (Fla. 4th DCA 2011).

[109] *JPMorgan Chase Bank, N.A. v. Hernandez*, 99 So. 3d 508, 513 (Fla. 3d DCA 2011); *The Florida Bar v. Woods*, 131 So. 3d 791 (Fla. 2013).

[110] *The Law Offices of Lynn W. Martin, P.A. v. Madson*, 144 So. 3d 707 (Fla. 1st DCA 2014); *Visoly v. Security Pac. Credit Corp.*, 768 So. 2d 482 (Fla. 3d DCA 2000).

[111] Fla. Stat. § 57.105(2).

[112] Fla. Stat. § 57.105(3).

[113] *Brinson v. Creative Aluminum Products, Inc.*, 519 So. 2d 59 (Fla. 2d DCA 1988).

[114] Fla. Stat. § 57.105(4).

[115] *City of North Miami Beach v. Berrio*, 64 So. 3d 713 (Fla. 3d DCA 2011).

[116] *Nathan v. Bates*, 998 So. 2d 1178 (Fla. 3d DCA 2008); *Nedd v. Gary*, 35 So. 3d 1028 (Fla. 3d DCA 2010).

[117] *Reznek v. Chase Home Finance, LLC*, 152 So. 3d 793 (Fla. 3d DCA 2014).

serve the motion until after the litigation is concluded does not give the opposing party sufficient time to withdraw the objectionable pleading.[118] Note that the Florida Supreme Court has held that proposals for settlement do not need to be served pursuant to Rule 2.516.[119] The Fourth District Court of Appeal receded from its prior position in an *en banc* decision that a § 57.105 safe harbor notice must be served in accordance with Rule 2.516.[120]

16-5 Offers of Judgment and Proposals for Settlement

16-5.1 Offer of Judgment and Demand for Judgment—Fla. Stat. § 768.79

Fla. Stat. § 768.79 is Florida's Offer of Judgment and Demand for Judgment statute, which provides that a party may be entitled to recover attorney's fees in "any civil action for damages" if an offer or demand for judgment is not accepted, and certain other conditions are met.[121] For example, a defendant may file an offer of judgment, and if the offer is not accepted by the plaintiff within 30 days, and the judgment is one of no liability or the judgment obtained by the plaintiff is at least 25 percent less than the offer, the defendant is entitled to recover attorney's fees.[122] Likewise, a plaintiff may make a demand for judgment, which if not accepted within 30 days, and the plaintiff recovers at least 25 percent more than the offer, he or she is entitled to recover reasonable attorney's fees incurred from the date of the filing of the demand.[123] The statute appears to have limited applicability in foreclosure actions, which are equitable in nature, but at least one court has held that the statute applies in a foreclosure action, where defendants who did not sign the mortgage were seeking monetary damages from the foreclosing lender, and otherwise complied with the statute.[124]

16-5.2 Procedural Rule Governing Offers of Judgment—Rule 1.442

A party seeking fees under the offer of judgment statute must comply with Rule 1.442. A proposal shall be in writing and shall identify the applicable Florida law under which it is being made. A proposal shall: (A) name the party or parties making the proposal and the party or parties to whom the proposal is being made; (B) state that the proposal resolves all damages that would otherwise be awarded in a final judgment in the action in which the proposal is served, subject to subdivision (F); (C) state with particularity any relevant conditions; (D) state the total amount of the proposal and state with particularity all nonmonetary terms of the proposal; (E) state with particularity the amount proposed to settle a claim for punitive damages, if any; (F) state whether the proposal includes attorneys' fees and whether attorneys' fees are part of the legal

---

[118] *Anchor Towing, Inc. v. Florida Dep't. of Transp.*, 10 So. 3d 670 (Fla. 3d DCA 2009); *Burgos v. Burgos*, 948 So. 2d 918, 919 (Fla. 4th DCA 2007).

[119] *Wheaton v. Wheaton*, 261 F.3d 1236 (Fla. 2019).

[120] *Law Offices of Fred Cohen, P.A. v. H.E.C. Cleaning, LLC*, 2020 WL 559240 (Fla. 4th DCA 2020).

[121] Fla. Stat. § 768.79(1).

[122] Fla.Stat. § 768.79(1).

[123] Fla.Stat. § 768.79(1).

[124] *Novastar Mortg., Inc. v. Strassburger*, 855 So. 2d 130, 131 (Fla. 4th DCA 2003).

claim; and (G) include a certificate of service in the form required by rule 1.080.[125] In addition, the offer must be served on the party or parties to whom it is made, but not filed unless necessary to enforce the provisions of the rule.[126] The offer of judgment statute and this rule of procedure are both in derogation of the common law, and thus must be strictly construed.[127]

16-6 Wrongful Act Doctrine

16-6:1 The Doctrine

Another narrow exception to the American Rule on recovery of attorney's fees is referred to as the "wrongful act doctrine," where the wrongful act of a party has caused the claimant to be in litigation with third parties, causing the claimant to incur attorney's fees to defend itself.[128] This doctrine would likely have limited applicability to mortgage foreclosure actions, and some courts have questioned its viability in Florida, as the Florida Supreme Court has apparently never recognized it.[129] However, there are a number of lower Florida courts that have held that the doctrine is "well established," and have awarded fees to the claimant under the doctrine.[130] Attorney's fees sought under the wrongful act doctrine are special damages, and must be specifically pled.[131]

---

[125] Fla. R. Civ. P. 1.442(c).
[126] Fla. R. Civ. P. 1.442(d).
[127] *Campbell v. Goldman*, 959 So. 2d 223 (Fla. 2007).
[128] *Reiterer v. Monteil*, 98 So. 3d 586 (Fla. 2d DCA 2012); *City of Tallahassee v. Blankenship & Lee*, 736 So. 2d 29 (Fla. 1st DCA 1999); *State Farm Fire & Cas. Co. v. Pritcher*, 546 So. 2d 1060, 1061 (Fla. 3d DCA 1989).
[129] *Osorio v. State Farm Bank, F.S.B.*, 746 F.3d 1242 (11th Cir. 2014).
[130] *Glace & Radcliffe, Inc. v. City of Live Oak*, 471 So. 2d 144 (Fla. 1st DCA 1985); *Auto-Owners Ins. Co. v. Hooks*, 463 So. 2d 468 (Fla. 1st DCA 1985); *Northamerican Van Lines, Inc. v. Roper*, 429 So. 2d 750 (Fla. 1st DCA 1983); *but see State Farm Fire & Casualty Company v. Pritcher*, 546 So. 2d 100 (Fla. 3d DCA 1989).
[131] *Robbins v. McGrath*, 955 So. 2d 633 (Fla. 1st DCA 2007).

CHAPTER 17

Bankruptcy

Nicole Mariani Noel

17-1 Introduction

The filing of a bankruptcy petition is a common occurrence during a mortgage foreclosure action. In general, the mortgagor may file under Chapter 7 of Title 11 of the Unites States Code,[1] which is the liquidation provision, or under Chapters 11 or 13, which are reorganization or repayment provisions, respectively.[2] Under Chapter 7, all of the mortgagor's non-exempt assets are liquidated to pay debts by an independent third-party trustee. Under Chapters 11 and 13, the mortgagor keeps his assets and uses his income to pay some of his debts over a specified period of time through a plan of reorganization (Chapter 11) or a repayment plan (Chapter 13). A Chapter 13 repayment plan typically lasts five years,[3] but a reorganization plan under Chapter 11 can be much longer.

Bankruptcy law is controlled mainly by the Bankruptcy Code and cases interpreting it. However, the Bankruptcy Code and bankruptcy judges defer to state law on many issues, such as the nature of the mortgagor's interest in property. Bankruptcy courts are divisions of the federal district courts, and each has its own local rules and administrative orders.[4] This section is intended to provide a basic overview of the effect of bankruptcy on a foreclosure action and is not a comprehensive discussion of bankruptcy law. Where a foreclosure is affected by the mortgagor's filing of a bankruptcy petition, a bankruptcy lawyer should be consulted to navigate the unique and voluminous laws pertaining to bankruptcy.

17-2 Mortgagee's Interest in Bankruptcy Proceedings

The interests of creditors in bankruptcy proceedings are either "secured claims" or "unsecured claims." Mortgagees have a secured claim on account of the mortgage lien. However, if the total mortgage debt exceeds the fair market value of the mortgaged property, the mortgagee may be entitled to an unsecured deficiency claim in

---

[1] Herein abbreviated the "Bankruptcy Code."
[2] Whether a mortgagor files under Chapter 11 or 13 generally depends upon the amount of debt he or she has. Chapter 13 has less onerous reporting requirements, but the amount of debt allowed is currently limited to $394,725 in total unsecured debt and $1,184,200 in total secured debt (effective until April 1, 2019).
[3] 11 U.S.C. § 1322(d).
[4] 28 U.S.C.A. § 1334; Fed. Rules Bankr. Proc. 9029.

the bankruptcy case.[5] As a general principal, the mortgage itself, as an *in rem* claim, survives the bankruptcy case, unless otherwise affected.[6]

17-3 Automatic Stay

17-3:1 Effect of the Automatic Stay

When a bankruptcy petition is filed, the Bankruptcy Code acts to enjoin all legal action against the bankruptcy mortgagor—called "the debtor" in bankruptcy proceedings. The automatic stay prohibits the commencement or continuation of any "judicial, administrative, or other action or proceeding against the debtor" that arose before the petition was filed.[7] Penalties for violating the automatic stay include contempt, punitive damages and attorney's fees.[8]

The filing of a bankruptcy petition creates a "bankruptcy estate," consisting of all of the mortgagor's assets, including causes of action possessed by the mortgagor. The automatic stay prohibits taking action to recover property of the bankruptcy estate.[9] Consequently, a pending foreclosure action is immediately stayed by the initiation of a bankruptcy proceeding if the mortgagor or title owner is the bankruptcy debtor or codebtor, or if the property which is the subject of the foreclosure is property of the estate.[10] Upon the filing of bankruptcy, foreclosure practitioners should cancel any scheduled hearings, suspend discovery efforts, and advise the court to the extent necessary to cancel trials or pending foreclosure sales. Actions taken in violation of

---

[5] However, as explained more fully in Section 17-5, it is important that the mortgagee must take some action notifying the mortgagor or the trustee of the mortgagee's intention to assert an unsecured claim. *See, e.g., In re Brooks*, 407 B.R. 429, 433 (Bankr. M.D. Fla. 2009) (allowing amendment to wholly secured proof of claim to assert unsecured deficiency component where debtor was on notice that mortgagee might assert an unsecured component to proof of claim); *c.f. In re Jackson*, 482 B.R. 659, 664 (Bankr. S.D. Fla. 2012) (disallowing amendment to wholly secured proof of claim to assert unsecured deficiency component where mortgagee provided no indication that it might assert an unsecured component to proof of claim).

[6] *Johnson v. Home State Bank*, 501 U.S. 78, 84 (1991) ("[A] bankruptcy discharge extinguishes only one mode of enforcing a claim, namely, an action against the debtor *in personam*, while leaving intact another, namely, an action against the debtor *in rem*."). This general rule applies so long as the mortgagor does not invalidate the lien during the course of the bankruptcy case (*see* strip offs and strip downs discussed, *infra*). 11 U.S.C. § 1141(c) also includes an exception to this general rule in certain Chapter 11 cases. *See In re S. White Transp., Inc.*, 725 F.3d 494, 498 (5th Cir. 2013) (declining to apply 11 U.S.C. § 1141(c) in a Chapter 11 case in which the secured creditor did not materially participate). *See also Butner v. U.S.*, 440 U.S. 48, 99 S. Ct. 914 (1979) ("Property interests are created and defined by state law. Unless some federal interest requires a different result, there is no reason why such interests should be analyzed differently simply because an interested party is involved in a bankruptcy proceeding.").

[7] 11 U.S.C.§ 362(a)(1)-(2).

[8] 11 U.S.C. § 362(h); *also see Jove Engineering, Inc v. IRS*, 92 F.3d 1539, 1555-57 (11th Cir. 1996).

[9] 11 U.S.C. § 362(a)(2)-(3); 11 U.S.C. § 541(a)(1).

[10] *See* 11 U.S.C. § 362(a); 11 U.S.C.§ 1301.

the stay are void as a matter of law.[11] Further, developing case law suggests that failing to undo actions which were inadvertently taken in violation of the stay could also give rise to sanctions for violation of the automatic stay.[12]

Notably, however, in most instances the automatic stay does not preclude continuation of an action on a promissory note or guaranty against a non-debtor co-obligor or guarantor, unless the mortgagor files under Chapter 13 and the debt at issue is a consumer debt.[13] This is because the automatic stay under Section 362 of the Bankruptcy Code only extends to the debtor and property of the debtor.[14]

17-3:2 Termination of the Automatic Stay

The automatic bankruptcy stay can terminate automatically when the bankruptcy case is closed or dismissed.[15] However, a mortgagee who does not want to wait for the bankruptcy stay to expire as a matter of law can move the bankruptcy court for relief from the automatic stay by filing a motion for relief from stay.[16] If no request for relief from the automatic stay is filed, the foreclosure action remains stayed until the bankruptcy concludes by operation of law.[17] Once the automatic stay is lifted, the foreclosure trial court must be notified by one of the parties through filing a copy of the bankruptcy court order that authorized the termination of the stay, or similar documents which terminated the stay. In some jurisdictions, the local Chapter 13 model plan provides that the stay is automatically lifted if the plan provides for surrender of the property, direct payment to the lender, or where the plan does not provide for

---

[11] *Borg-Warner Acceptance Corp. v. Hall*, 685 F.2d 1306, 1308 (11th Cir. 1982); *see also Barton-Malow Co. v. Gorman Co. of Ocala, Inc.*, 558 So. 2d 519, 521 (Fla. 5th DCA 1990); *Personalized Air Conditioning, Inc. v. C.M. Sys. of Pinellas Cty., Inc.*, 522 So. 2d 465, 466 (Fla. 4th DCA 1988).

[12] *In re Keen*, 301 B.R. 749 (2003).

[13] *See* 11 U.S.C. § 1301 which provides as follows:

> after the order for relief under this chapter, a creditor may not act, or commence or continue any civil action, to collect all or any part of a consumer debt of the debtor from any individual that is liable on such debt with the debtor, or that secured debt, unless—(1) such individual became liable on or secured such debt in the ordinary course of such individual's business; or (2) the case is closed, dismissed, or converted to a case under chapter 7 or 11 of this title.

11 U.S.C. § 1301. *See also In re Bertolami*, 235 B.R. 493, 495 (Bankr. S.D. Fla. 1999)

[14] *In re Sunbeam Sec. Litig.*, 261 B.R. 534, 536 (S.D. Fla. 2001) ("The law makes clear (and no party disagrees) that the automatic stay provisions of section 362(a) generally are not available to third-party non-debtors."). However, it has become common for a court to extend the stay or issue an injunction against actions targeting third-party non-debtors, where the stay is in the interest of preserving the estate or of benefit to the debtor and the success of its reorganization.

[15] *In re Laurent*, 193 Fed. Appx. 831 (11th Cir. 2006); 11 U.S.C. 362(c)(2). The automatic stay does not terminate automatically upon the administrative closing of a Chapter 11 case involving an individual debtor.

[16] The basis for stay relief is found in 11 U.S.C. § 362(d). In general, a mortgagee will receive stay relief for cause, specifically, if it is undersecured, the mortgagor is not making payments or maintaining taxes and insurance on the property, or where the property is not necessary for a reorganization. 11 U.S.C. § 362(d).

[17] Automatic expiration of the automatic stay is governed by 11 U.S.C. § 362(c).

any payment/treatment to the mortgagee.[18] However, given the severe penalties for violating the automatic stay, the safer course of action is to obtain an order granting stay relief.[19] An order granting stay relief allows the mortgagee to proceed against the property *in rem* but not against the mortgagor personally.[20] The bankruptcy court will usually enter an order terminating the automatic stay if there is insufficient equity in the property, there has been a default in taxes or insurance, the mortgagor does not provide the creditor with payments or a replacement lien on other property sufficient to protect the mortgagee during the pendency of the bankruptcy case and if the property is not necessary to an effective reorganization or repayment plan in a Chapter 11 or 13 case.[21] Bankruptcy courts will also grant stay relief if the Bankruptcy Petition was filed in bad faith.[22] At least one bankruptcy court has allowed stay relief where the prepetition agreement between the mortgagor and mortgagee provided for stay relief in the event of a bankruptcy and there was evidence that the bankruptcy was filed solely to delay or frustrate the efforts of the mortgagee to recover its property.[23] The bankruptcy court can also grant stay relief retroactively.[24] By contrast, courts usually do not allow stay relief if the fair market value of the property is greatly in excess of the amount of the outstanding mortgage debt.[25]

17-3:3 Repeat Filers

With the increase of foreclosure volume in 2009, practitioners also experienced an increase in bankruptcy filings, and subsequently, repeat filings. Often, one debtor will file multiple cases and obtain multiple stays to delay the foreclosure action, or otherwise halt the process through sales cancellations. Other times, spouses or co-owners will time their individual filings to overlap to prevent any foreclosure action from proceeding. In recent years, we have also seen a new scheme develop where the mortgagor transfers a portion of the property to a third party to obtain the benefit of the automatic stay. Sections 362(c)(3) and (c)(4) reflect Congress' efforts to curb such

---

[18] *See* M.D. Fla. Bankr. L. R. Ch. 13 Model Plan.

[19] The Bankruptcy Code does not provide for stay relief during a pending bankruptcy case on the basis of a confirmed repayment plan or through local rules. As such, the use of a plan or local rules to authorize stay relief is considered by some to be tenuous. Moreover, the penalties for violating the automatic stay are severe and include contempt, punitive damages and attorney's fees. 11 U.S.C. § 362(h); *also see Jove Engineering, Inc v. IRS*, 92 F.3d 1539, 1555-57 (11th Cir. 1996).

[20] Actions against the mortgagor personally are prohibited by 11 U.S.C. § 362(a) during the pendency of the bankruptcy case and then by 11 U.S.C. § 524(a) after the mortgagor receives a discharge.

[21] 11 U.S.C. § 362(d); *In re Albany Partners, Ltd.*, 749 F.2d 670, 673 (11th Cir. 1984).

[22] *In re Phoenix Piccadilly, Ltd.*, 849 F.2d 1393, 1395 (11th Cir. 1988).

[23] *In re Citadel Properties, Inc.*, 86 B.R. 275, 277 (Bankr. M.D. Fla. 1988).

[24] See 11 U.S.C. § 362(d). *In re Barr*, 318 B.R. 592, 598 (Bankr. M.D. Fla. 2004); *In re Williford*, 294 Fed. Appx. 518, 522 (11th Cir. 2008); *In re Albany Partners, Ltd.*, 749 F.2d 670, 673 (11th Cir. 1984).

[25] The precise value of the property in excess of amount of the mortgage necessary for the court to award or deny stay relief varies and can depend on factors such as whether the property is deteriorating in value. *In re Senior Care Properties, Inc.*, 137 B.R. 527, 529 (Bankr. N.D. Fla. 1992) (finding 18% excess in value of property over amount of mortgage warranted denial of stay relief); *see also In re O'Quinn*, 98 B.R. 86, 89 (Bankr. M.D. Fla. 1989).

abuse of the bankruptcy process.[26] Section 362(c)(3) provides that where a debtor had a prior case dismissed within the last year (other than for reasons under Section 707(b)), then the automatic stay will go into effect upon the new filing, but only last for thirty (30) days unless the debtor seeks to extend the stay within that thirty (30) day period and demonstrates that the new case was filed in good faith. However, the majority of courts have held that upon the thirty-one (31) day only the stay as to the debtor expires and the stay as to the estate will continue.[27] Best practice is to file a motion to determine that the stay has terminated by operation of law and request the court enter a comfort order allowing the *in rem* foreclosure action to proceed.[28] However, if the debtor has had two cases which were dismissed within the last year, then pursuant to Section 362(c)(4), the automatic stay does not go into effect upon the filing of the third case within a one-year period.[29]

Section 362(d)(4) provides another path for a mortgagee to seek extraordinary relief where a debtor is filing multiple bankruptcy cases with the intent to delay or hinder the mortgagee's efforts to foreclose on real property. The Court, upon finding that the debtor was involved in a "scheme to delay, hinder and defraud creditors" by either transferring ownership without court or lender approval or by filing multiple bankruptcy cases affecting the property, may order a two-year injunction or "prospective relief" preventing the debtor, or any subsequent party in interest, from obtaining a stay in a subsequent case.[30] Upon recording a certified copy of the order in the public records where the foreclosure is pending, no bankruptcy petition filed by anyone or any entity, whether voluntarily or involuntarily, in any United States Bankruptcy Court, may impose the stay as to the subject real property for the prescribed period.

17-4 Violations of Automatic Stay

Foreclosure practitioners must be aware of the consequences of proceeding with foreclosure while an automatic bankruptcy stay is in effect. As previously indicated, orders entered by the trial court in the foreclosure proceeding are void if they are entered while the automatic stay is in effect, unless the mortgagee receives retroactive stay relief.[31] Furthermore, a bankruptcy court may initiate contempt proceedings

---

[26] 11 U.S.C. §§ 362(c)(3) and (c)(4).

[27] Courts that subscribe to the majority opinion refer to this as the "Sliver of the Stay." Courts following the majority view: *Witkowski v. Knight (In re Witkowski)*, 523 B.R. 291, 296-97 (1st Cir. B.A.P. 2014); *Holcomb v. Hardeman (In re Holcomb)*, 380 B.R. 813, 815-16 (10th Cir. B.A.P. 2008); *Jumpp v. Chase Home Fin., LLC (In re Jumpp)*, 356 B.R. 789, 793-97 (1st Cir. B.A.P. 2006).
   Minority view: *Reswick v. Reswick (In re Reswick)*, 446 B.R. 362, 365-73 (9th Cir. B.A.P. 2011).

[28] 11 U.S.C. § 362(j).

[29] For example, where the debtor has two prior cases and the dates of dismissal were January 2, 2018 and June 2, 2018, if the debtor files a third case on or before January 1, 2019, then the automatic stay will not go into effect upon filing. If the debtor files on January 3, 2019, then the stay would go into effect as being outside the one (1) year period.

[30] 11 U.S.C. § 362(d)(4).

[31] *In re Clarke*, 373 B.R. 769 (Bankr. S.D. Fla. 2006); *In re Barr*, 318 B.R. 592, 598 (Bankr. M.D. Fla. 2004).

and issue sanctions upon finding a violation of the automatic stay.[32] Even an inadvertent violation of the automatic stay may form the basis of a stay violation action against the mortgagee.[33] Once the automatic stay has terminated, a mortgagee can proceed with its *in rem* foreclosure action, except to the extent that it may not seek a personal judgment against the mortgagor, unless the mortgagor's case has been dismissed without a discharge, the debtor has reaffirmed the debt in a Chapter 7 scenario or the mortgagee's debt has been excepted from discharge under Section 523 of the Bankruptcy Code.

17-5 Proofs of Claim

The Federal Rules of Bankruptcy Procedure were amended in December 2017 to provide that all creditors, including a secured creditor, must file a proof of claim in Chapters 7, 11, and 13 in order to have an allowed claim.[34] In a Chapter 7 case, the Chapter 7 trustee sets a "claims bar date" if the trustee believes that the mortgagor has assets. Under Chapters 11 and 13, the deadline to file claims is set by statute.[35] The deadline to file a proof of claim is usually found on the bankruptcy case docket. The proof of claim form can be found on the United States Courts' website under Bankruptcy forms. A mortgagee who is over secured (i.e. the value of the property is more than the mortgage debt) may preserve the right to accrued interest and fees, including attorney's fees, in a proof of claim if the underlying agreement provides for these items.[36] A mortgagee who is under-secured (i.e. its equity in the property is worth less than the debt) may preserve the right to an unsecured deficiency claim.[37] In general, a mortgagee may amend a timely filed proof claim to account for a change in circumstances, provided the original proof of claim contemplates the change.[38] It is

---

[32] *Matter of Crum*, 55 B.R. 455 (Bankr. M.D. Fla. 1985) ("It is quite evident and obvious that the only way the bankruptcy court can put teeth into its power to enforce the automatic stay is through the threat of contempt proceeding."); U.S.C. 362(h) (providing that an individual who is injured as a result of violations of an automatic stay may recover actual and punitive damages).

[33] *In re Price*, 42 F.3d 1068 (7th Cir. 1994) (errors, even if computer-generated, are willful violations of the stay when a creditor had actual notice of the bankruptcy); *but see In re Hamrick*, 175 B.R. 890, 893-94 (W.D.N.C. 1994) (a letter to debtor demanding payment was not a "willful" violation of the automatic stay where it resulted from an innocent clerical error); *In re Atkins*, 176 B.R. 998, 1008 (Bankr. D. Minn. 1994) (a "willful" violation requires the creditor to act deliberately with knowledge of the bankruptcy petition; a creditor's negligent omission or forgetfulness is not a willful violation of stay); *In re Crispell*, 73 B.R. 375, 379 (Bankr. E.D. Mo. 1987) (debits made to debtor's account were made by reason of bank's error in not terminating automatic debit feature and, therefore, not a "willful" violation).

[34] *See* Fed. R. Bankr. P. 3002(a) as well as Committee Notes on Rules pertaining to the 2017 Amendment.

[35] *See* Fed. R. Bankr. P. 3002(c).

[36] 11 U.S.C. § 506(b).

[37] *In re Jackson*, 482 B.R. 659, 664 (Bankr. S.D. Fla. 2012) (amended proof of claim for estimated unsecured deficiency disallowed where creditor filed a fully secured proof of claim and did not indicate any portion was unsecured); *also see In re Wright*, 486 B.R. 491, 506 (Bankr. D. Ariz. 2012) (creditor prohibited from receiving unsecured deficiency claim where it did not follow state law procedures required to secure deficiency claim).

[38] *In re Jackson*, 482 B.R. 659, 664 (Bankr. S.D. Fla. 2012) ("In general, 'amendment is permitted only where the original claim provided notice to the court of the existence, nature, and amount of the claim and that it was the creditors' intent to hold the estate liable.'")

important to note that the manner in which a claim is filed may be considered an election of remedy and preclude the mortgagee from later taking an inconsistent position in enforcing its lien.[39] During 2017, the U.S. Supreme Court ruled that filing a proof of claim for a time-barred debt did not constitute a violation of the Fair Debt Collection Practices Act.[40] However, the filing of a time-barred debt can give rise to an objection to claim.

17-6 Strip Offs and Strip Downs

17-6:1 A Matter of Equity

"Strip offs" and "strip downs" both arise when the mortgagee is under-secured, meaning the value of the property is less than the amount owed on the mortgage debt. Depending on the jurisdiction, a strip off or strip down can be accomplished through motion, adversary proceeding, or plan treatment where the court makes a finding as to the fair market value of the property.

A "strip off" refers to the removal (or voiding) of a mortgage lien with no equity. Stated differently, a strip off occurs where the court finds the fair market value of the property is less than the amount owed on the first mortgage lien, leaving no equity to support the second mortgage lien, and the bankruptcy court orders a judicial removal of the second lien from the property.[41] The junior mortgagee in such a case receives a wholly unsecured claim in the bankruptcy for the amount of the mortgage debt outstanding. A strip off cannot occur in connection with a first priority mortgage because the holder of a first priority mortgage always has equity in the property sufficient to prevent complete removal of the lien.[42]

A "strip down" (also called "cramdown"), on the other hand, refers to a reduction in the amount of the mortgage debt to match the fair market value of the property. In the case of a strip down, any excess in the amount owed on the mortgage over the fair market value of the property would be treated as an unsecured claim in the bankruptcy.[43] After a successful strip down, the mortgagee has two claims often referred to as a bifurcated claim, in the bankruptcy: one claim which is secured up

---

(quoting *United States v. Int'l Horizons, Inc. (In re Int'l Horizons, Inc.)*, 751 F.2d 1213, 1216 (11th Cir.1985)).

[39] *In re Barrera*, 2016 WL 6990876 (Bankr. M.D. Fla. Nov. 29, 2016) (secured creditor had waived its judgment lien where creditor filed a wholly unsecured claim and received distribution on account of the wholly unsecured claim in the Chapter 7 case).

[40] *Midland Funding, LLC v. Johnson*, 137 S. Ct. 1407, 1409 (2017).

[41] The same analysis would apply where there are additional liens on the property, such as an HOA/COA lien. The issue is whether the fair market value of the property is in excess of the lien just ahead in priority of the one the mortgagor is seeking to remove.

[42] For example, if the first priority mortgagee is owed $100,000; the second priority mortgagee is owed $50,000; and the court finds the fair market value of the property is $90,000, the second priority mortgage may be stripped off, leaving the second priority mortgagee with only an unsecured claim in the bankruptcy for $50,000. In that case, upon entry of a discharge, the second mortgagee no longer has a lien on the property.

[43] For example, if the first priority mortgagee is owed $100,000 and the court finds the fair market value of the property is $90,000, the mortgage debt may be stripped down to $90,000. In that case, the mortgagor only has to pay $90,000 through the plan and mortgagee has an unsecured claim for $10,000. The $10,000 is no longer secured by the property. Barring

to the fair market value of the property as determined by the bankruptcy court and a second claim for the difference between the fair market value of the property and the remaining amount of the mortgage debt outstanding. In a case under Chapter 7 of the Bankruptcy Code, the debtor cannot strip off or strip down a lien.[44] Further, in most cases, where the mortgagor's spouse is a co-owner the property and the spouse is not a debtor in the current bankruptcy case, a mortgagor may not strip off or strip down a mortgage in a case pending under any chapter of the Bankruptcy Code.[45]

17-6:2 Principal Residences

Under Chapter 13 of the Bankruptcy Code, if the property at issue is the mortgagor's principal residence the mortgage cannot be stripped down.[46] The case law on what constitutes the mortgagor's principal residence is not uniform. For example, some bankruptcy courts find that the property is the mortgagor's principal residence if any part of the property is used as the mortgagor's residence, notwithstanding other uses of the property.[47] Other courts have taken the exact opposite view, holding that a claim secured even in part by real property that is not a mortgagor's principal residence is subject to strip down.[48] Still other bankruptcy courts have analyzed the transaction between the mortgagor and the mortgagee to determine the predominant character of the transaction, and what the mortgagee bargained to be within the scope of its lien.[49] If the property is not the mortgagor's principal residence and the bankruptcy court orders the strip down, it will not be effective unless the mortgagor receives a bankruptcy discharge.[50] Chapter 11 of the Bankruptcy Code contains a similar prohibition on stripping down a lien on a principal residence and as a result, strip downs in a Chapter 11 bankruptcy case are treated the same as in a Chapter 13 bankruptcy case; however, in the case of a business debtor, the strip down is typically effective upon confirmation.[51]

On the other hand, a mortgagor in a Chapter 13 bankruptcy may strip off a wholly unsecured second lien where the bankruptcy court rules that the value of the property is less than the amount of the first mortgage.[52] In a Chapter 20 scenario, the mortgagor who successfully strips off a second lien need not receive a bankruptcy

---

a court order to the contrary, the mortgagor must receive a bankruptcy discharge for the strip down/strip off to be effective.

[44] *Bank of Am., N.A. v. Caulkett*, 135 S. Ct. 1995, 1997 (2015) (Chapter 7 debtor cannot strip off a lien); *Dewsnup v. Timm*, 502 U.S. 410, 413 (1992) (Chapter 7 debtor cannot strip down a lien).

[45] *See In re Pierre*, 468 B.R. 419, 426 (Bankr. M.D. Fla. 2012); *In re Alvarez*, 67 Collier Bankr. Cas. 2d 739 (Bankr. S.D. Fla. 2012); *but see In re Janitor*, BR 10-22594-JAD, 2011 WL 7109363, at *3 (Bankr. W.D. Pa. 2011).

[46] *Nobelman v. Am. Sav. Bank*, 508 U.S. 324, 324 (1993).

[47] *In re Macaluso*, 254 B.R. 799 (Bankr. W.D.N.Y. 2000).

[48] *Scarborough v. Chase Manhattan Mortg. Corp.*, 461 F.3d 406, 414 (3d Cir. 2006); *see also Lomas Mtg., Inc. v. Louis*, 82 F.3d 1 (1st Cir. 1996).

[49] *In re Zaldivar*, 441 B.R. 389, 390 (Bankr. S.D. Fla. 2011).

[50] *In re Colbourne*, 550 Fed. Appx. 687, 688 (11th Cir. 2013).

[51] *In re Silva*, 63 Collier Bankr. Cas. 2d 400 (Bankr. S.D. Fla. 2010).

[52] *In re Scantling*, 754 F.3d 1323, 1329 (11th Cir. 2014).

discharge in order to effectuate the lien strip.[53] Again, Chapter 11 strip offs are treated similarly.[54]

17-7 Discharge and Dischargeability

With few exceptions, a bankruptcy discharge operates to relieve the mortgagor from any personal liability for his mortgage debt.[55] Discharge under Sections 727, 1141 and 1328 of the Bankruptcy Code, and the dischargeability of a particular debt under Section 523 of the Bankruptcy Code operate very differently. A mortgagee may file an action to prevent the mortgagor from receiving a general discharge of all the mortgagor's debts under Sections 727, 1141 or 1328 of the Bankruptcy Code, as applicable. Alternatively, in a bankruptcy case pending under any chapter, the mortgagee may file an action to prevent discharge of the mortgagee's particular debt under Section 523 of the Bankruptcy Code.[56] The standards for discharge and dischargeability are set forth in the respective sections of the Bankruptcy Code.[57]

In general, in a Chapter 7 case where the debtor is an individual, the mortgagor receives a discharge of all debts under Sections 727, 60 days from the date of the first scheduled meeting of creditors under Section 341 of the Bankruptcy Code (the "341 Meeting") unless a creditor files an objection to the mortgagor's discharge, or the deadline to object is extended.[58] In contrast to a mortgagor in a Chapter 7 bankruptcy case, a mortgagor in a Chapter 13 case receives a discharge of all debts upon completion of a repayment plan[59] and in a Chapter 11 case, upon completion of a reorganization plan in a case where the debtor is an individual, so long as there is no pending objection to the mortgagor's discharge.[60]

The deadline to object to the mortgagor's discharge in cases under Chapters 7 and 13 is 60 days from the date of the first scheduled 341 Meeting. The deadline to object to the mortgagor's discharge in cases under Chapter 11 is no later than the first date set for the confirmation of the plan of reorganization hearing.[61] The deadline to file

---

[53] A "Chapter 20" is a Chapter 13 case filed shortly after a Chapter 7 case in which the debtor obtained a discharge of all of the debtor's debts. *In re Scantling*, 754 F.3d 1323, 1329 (11th Cir. 2014).

[54] *In re Doyle*, 63 Bankr. Ct. Dec. 114 (Bankr. M.D. Fla. 2016).

[55] *See* 11 U.S.C. §§ 727, 1141 and 1328.

[56] A creditor may file both discharge and dischargeability actions but generally, the discharge action will be tried first since it has the effect of excepting all debts from discharge resolving the need for a separate dischargeability action.

[57] *See* 11 U.S.C. §§ 523 (applies to a case under any chapter), 727 (applies only to Chapter 7 cases), 1141 (applies only to Chapter 11 cases) and 1328 (applies only to Chapter 13 cases). Although an action to prevent the overall discharge of all debts is generally easier to prove, an action under 11 U.S.C. § 523 is preferable because 11 U.S.C. § 523 excepts discharge of only the mortgagee's debt; all other debts are discharged, obviating the need to fight with other creditors over the mortgagor's remaining assets.

[58] Fed. R. Bankr. P. 4004(c). A corporate or business debtor is not eligible for a discharge.

[59] 11 U.S.C. § 1141(d)(1).

[60] *See* 11 U.S.C. § 1328(a); *but see* 11 U.S.C. § 1328(b). A corporate or business debtor is not eligible for a discharge.

[61] Fed. R. Bankr. P. 4004(a).

a complaint to determine dischargeability is also 60 days from the date of the first scheduled 341 Meeting in a case under any chapter of the Code.[62]

Any deadline to object to discharge or file a complaint to determine dischargeability may be extended by filing a motion and showing "cause."[63] Any such motion must be filed prior to the expiration of the initial deadline or any court-approved extended deadline.[64] Any motion to extend the deadline to file an objection to discharge under Sections 727, 1141 and 1328 or dischargeability under Section 523 should be separately stated since these deadlines are governed by different provisions of the Bankruptcy Code.[65]

When a mortgagor receives a discharge in bankruptcy, he or she is no longer subject to a personal deficiency judgment if the value of the property is not sufficient to satisfy the judgment.[66] Where the mortgage lien itself is not eliminated or avoided in the course of the bankruptcy, the foreclosure of the property itself is still proper.[67]

One exception to discharge can be found in Chapter 13 cases under Sections 1322(b)(5) and 1328(a)(1). Chapter 13 permits a mortgagor to cure any existing pre-petition default over a sixty (60) month period and maintains the ongoing regular monthly payments, commonly referred to as "cure and maintain."[68] This allows a mortgagor who is significantly in arrears to catch up on payments and come out of bankruptcy current on his or her mortgage obligation. However, where the last payment under the loan documents comes due after the last payment under the sixty (60) month plan, the secured claim shall be deemed long-term debt within the meaning of Section 1322(b)(5) and shall be deemed non-dischargeable under Section 1328(a). Further, certain courts have held that where the mortgage debt is paid direct and outside of the Chapter 13 plan, the debt is similarly not subject to the discharge.[69]

17-8 Statement of Intentions and Surrender

Individual debtors in bankruptcy are required to file a statement of intention, under penalty of perjury, reflecting the debtor's desire to redeem the property, reaffirm the mortgage debt, or surrender the property.[70] If the mortgagor chooses to redeem the property, he or she can remove the lien (and keep the property) by paying the mort-

---

[62] Fed. R. Bankr. P. 4007(c).
[63] Fed. R. Bankr. P. 4004 (b); Fed. R. Bankr. P. 4007 (c); *also see Kontrick v. Ryan*, 540 U.S. 443, 443 (2004). The deadline to object to discharge under 1328(f) is 60 days from the date of the first scheduled 341 Meeting—just like in a Chapter 7 case. Fed. R. Bankr. P. 4004(a).
[64] Fed. R. B. P. 4004 (b).
[65] However, some courts have found that where the motion for extension of time refers to Section 727, but articulates facts which indicate a violation of 523, the creditor received an extension of both deadlines. *In re Weinstein*, 234 B.R. 862, 865 (Bankr. E.D.N.Y. 1999).
[66] *Deutsche Bank Trust Co. Americas v. Nash*, 136 So. 3d 1267 (Fla. 2d DCA 2014); 11 U.S.C. § 524(a)(1) (discharge voids a judgment only to the extent that the judgment is one of personal liability).
[67] *Deutsche Bank Trust Co. Americas v. Nash*, 136 So. 3d 1267 (Fla. 2d DCA 2014).
[68] 11 U.S.C. 1322(b)(5) and 11 U.S.C. 1328(a)(1).
[69] . *Dukes v. Suncoast Credit Union (In re Dukes)*, 909 F.3d 1306 (11th Cir. 2018).
[70] 11 U.S.C. 521(a)(2)(A); *In re Record*, 347 B.R. 450 (M.D. Fla. 2006) (automatic stay is terminated where debtor fails to timely file, or timely act upon statement of intention) (citing 11 U.S.C. 362(h)).

gagee a lump sum amount equal to the lesser of the fair market value of the property or the amount of the outstanding mortgage on the date the bankruptcy petition is filed.[71] Similarly, the mortgagor may also keep the property by entering into an agreement with the mortgagee for repayment of the mortgage debt over time.[72] This is called "reaffirming" the debt. If the mortgagor chooses this option, the mortgagor becomes personally liable on the debt again, notwithstanding the bankruptcy discharge.[73] Finally, the mortgagor may give up the property by choosing to surrender the collateral to the mortgagee who disposes of it pursuant to state law.[74]

Initially, if the bankruptcy case is filed under Chapter 7 of the Bankruptcy Code, the property is surrendered to the Chapter 7 trustee.[75] If the property has little or no value in excess of the mortgage debt outstanding, the Chapter 7 trustee should abandon the property to the mortgagee.[76] However, even where property is abandoned by the mortgagor and the Chapter 7 trustee, in order to foreclose, the mortgagee must still obtain stay relief, or wait until closing of the case, dismissal of the case, or discharge of the mortgagor.

If a mortgagor surrenders the property and the mortgagee obtains stay relief, the mortgagor must not impede the secured creditor's efforts to recover the property through the appropriate legal process.[77] Although the mortgagor cannot impede the creditor's efforts, the mortgagor does not have to actively assist the mortgagee in its efforts to obtain title and possession of the property.[78] If the mortgagor contests the foreclosure action after surrendering the property, the mortgagee can try to obtain relief in the state court foreclosure action by way of judicial estoppel, but the mortgagee may need to file a motion to reopen the bankruptcy case and to compel the mortgagor to surrender the property. Notably, some bankruptcy courts allow the mortgagor to assert certain defenses, such as standing despite having surrendered

---

[71] *Taylor v. AGE Fed. Credit Union (In re Taylor)*, 3 F.3d 1512, 1514 (11th Cir. 1993) (discussing redemption under Chapter 7 of the Bankruptcy Code); *In re Menasche*, 301 B.R. 757, 760 (Bankr. S.D. Fla. 2003) (declining to allow debtor to redeem collateral under Chapter 13 of the Bankruptcy Code because Chapter 13 Plan provided for payments over time after debt had been accelerated).

[72] *In re Taylor*, 3 F.3d 1512, 1514 (11th Cir. 1993).

[73] 11 U.S.C. § 524(c).

[74] *In re Taylor*, 3 F.3d 1512, 1514 (11th Cir. 1993).

[75] *In re Failla*, 838 F.3d 1170, 1175 (11th Cir. 2016).

[76] 11 U.S.C. § 554; *In re Failla*, 838 F.3d 1170, 1176 (11th Cir. 2016).

[77] *In re Failla*, 838 F.3d 1170, 1175 (11th Cir. 2016); *In re Scott*, 567 B.R. 847, 851 (Bankr. S.D. Fla. 2017) (debtor was bound by Chapter 13 Plan which required surrender to creditor); *see also Rivera v. Bank of Am., N.A. ex rel. BAC Home Loans Servicing, L.P.*, 190 So. 3d 267 (Fla. 5th DCA 2016) (dismissing mortgagor's appeal where mortgagor filed bankruptcy and surrendered the property); *but see In re Ayala*, No. 6:11-BK-15964-RAC, 2017 WL 2874499, at *3 (Bankr. M.D. Fla. Apr. 17, 2017) (bankruptcy case could not be reopened to enforce mortgagors' stated intention to surrender property where case had been closed for more than 2 1/2 years and mortgagee had accepted payments); *Wilmington Savings Society v. Steele*, 2017 WL 2870985 (Fla. Cir. Ct.) (affirmative defense that mortgagor was estopped from contesting foreclosure because he surrendered property was waived where mortgagor failed to raise the issue until after filing a motion for summary judgment).

[78] *In re Plummer*, 513 B.R. 135, 143 (Bankr. M.D. Fla. 2014) ("'Surrender' does not require the debtor to turn over physical possession of the collateral; the Bankruptcy Code uses the word 'deliver' when it intends physical turnover of property.").

the property.[79] Other bankruptcy courts have declined to compel the mortgagor to surrender the property where a loan modification was entered into post-bankruptcy discharge and where a long period of time has lapsed between the bankruptcy discharge and the motion to compel surrender.[80] Yet other bankruptcy courts will compel surrender where a long period of time has lapsed between the discharge date and the date the mortgagee moves to compel surrender.[81]

17-9 Dismissal

An automatic stay imposed as a result of bankruptcy is lifted by operation of law if the bankruptcy case is dismissed.[82] Among other reasons, bankruptcies may be dismissed by the bankruptcy court if they were filed in bad faith,[83] if the mortgagor fails to appear at the 341 Meeting or if they have failed to filed required pleadings,[84] or if the mortgagor is found to have unreasonably delayed the proceedings.[85] The bankruptcy court may dismiss a case filed under Chapter 11 or 13 as having been filed in bad faith if the filing evidences an intent to abuse the judicial process, particularly when there is no realistic possibility of an effective reorganization and it is evident that the mortgagor seeks merely to delay or frustrate the legitimate efforts of secured creditors to enforce their rights.[86] Courts can also dismiss a case where assets are transferred to a new entity on the eve of a bankruptcy filing so that the new entity can obtain the benefit of the automatic stay and other aspects of bankruptcy, commonly referred to as the new debtor syndrome.[87] Similarly, a case filed under Chapter 7 may be dismissed for pre-petition bad faith, too.[88]

---

[79] *In re Karim Craig Thomas, and Kelly Mitchell Thomas*, Case No. 12-38513-EPK, Bankr. Southern District of Florida ECF No.66.

[80] *In re Richard Kurzban and Dalain Kurzban*, Case No. 09-30656-LMI, Bankr. Southern District of Florida, ECF No. 39.

[81] *In re Janet Deloris Keddo*, Case No. 14-28640-JKO, Bankr. Southern District of Florida, ECF No. 36.

[82] 11 U.S.C. 362(c)(2); *In re Hill*, 305 B.R. 100, 104 (Bankr. M.D. Fla. 2003) ("Although a case may remain open after dismissal, the automatic stay of § 362 of the Bankruptcy Code terminates when the case is dismissed.").

[83] *In re Piazza*, 719 F.3d 1253 (11th Cir. 2013); *In re Kollar*, 357 B.R. 657 (M.D. Fla. 2006) (dismissal for filing bankruptcy solely to thwart creditor's enforcement of lien rights).

[84] *In re Steinmetz Group, Ltd.*, 85 B.R. 633 (S.D. Fla. 1988). However, in practice, the bankruptcy case is rarely, if ever dismissed for failure to attend the first scheduled 341 Meeting.

[85] *In re Clark*, 107 B.R. 376 (S.D. Fla. 1988); 11 U.S.C. § 1112(b).

[86] *In re Albany Partners, Ltd.*, 749 F.2d 670, 674 (11th Cir. 1984).

[87] *In re Yukon Enters., Inc.*, 39 B.R. 919, 921 (Bankr. C.D. Cal. 1984) ("Indicia of the new debtor syndrome include: (1) transfer of distressed property into a newly created corporation; (2) transfer occurring within a close proximity to the bankruptcy filing; (3) transfer for no consideration; (4) the debtor has no assets other than the recently transferred property; (5) the debtor has no or minimal unsecured debt; (6) the debtor has no employees and no ongoing business; and (7) the debtor has no means, other than the transferred property, to service the debt on the property."). *See also In re Duvar Apt. Inc.*, 205 B.R. 196, 200 (9th Cir. BAP 1996). *In re SR Real Estate Holdings, LLC*, 506 B.R. 121 (Bankr. S.D. Cal. 2014) (broadened the criteria to include whether the corporation was created for the sole purpose of filing bankruptcy and bringing the action under the Bankruptcy Court's jurisdiction and control to "delay and hinder the First Lienholders in their bona fide efforts to realize upon their collateral.").

[88] *In re Piazza*, 719 F.3d 1253, 1271 (11th Cir. 2013).

CHAPTER 18

Appeals

Heidi Bassett

18-1 Introduction

Florida's district courts of appeal provide review of judgments and other orders entered by circuit courts in mortgage foreclosure actions.[1] The state is divided into five districts for purposes of appellate review.[2] The Florida Supreme Court has jurisdiction to consider rulings by all the various appellate districts, although cases are rarely accepted for review by the Supreme Court.[3] Consequently, foreclosure appeals are decided primarily in the five district courts. A decision made by one district binds all trial courts within that district, but also binds trial courts in other districts if those districts have not yet ruled on the issue and there is no inter-district conflict.[4]

In addition to the information contained in this chapter, you'll find discussions about appellate treatment of various cases, examples of reversible error and application of standards of review throughout the other chapters in this book. This chapter will primarily discuss the mechanics of an appeal in a foreclosure action.

18-2 Initiating an Appeal

Initiating an appeal requires that the appealing party file a petition or a notice of appeal (depending on the nature of the appeal) with the trial court, attaching the order

---

[1] Fla. R. App. P. 9.030(b) governs the jurisdiction of the district courts of appeal for final orders of trial courts and non-final orders of circuit courts. It also provides for certiorari jurisdiction and extraordinary writs.

[2] The District Courts of Appeal and their respective circuit court jurisdictions are as follows:
- First District Court of Appeal (located in Tallahassee)—1st, 2nd, 3rd, 4th, 8th and 14th Circuits
- Second District Court of Appeal (located in Lakeland and Tampa)—6th, 10th, 12th, 13th and 20th Circuits
- Third District Court of Appeal (located in Miami)—11th and 16th Circuits
- Fourth District Court of Appeal (located in West Palm Beach)—15th, 17th and 19th Circuits
- Fifth District Court of Appeal (located in Daytona Beach)—5th, 7th, 9th and 18th Circuits

[3] Fla. R. App. P. 9.030(a).

[4] See Sys. Components Corp. v. Florida Dep't of Trans., 14 So. 3d 967, 973 n. 4 (Fla 2009).

being appealed and advising that the subject order is being appealed to the appellate court with appropriate jurisdiction.[5] Even if the appellant files a notice of appeal in the wrong lower court, it will be transferred by the clerk to the correct court.[6] At the same time of the filing of a notice of appeal, the appellant must also pay a filing fee to the circuit court clerk, part of which is then paid by the circuit court to the applicable appellate court.[7] If the filing fee is not timely paid, the appellate court will issue an order warning that non-payment may result in the eventual dismissal of the appeal, but the non-payment of a filing fee at the same time as a notice of appeal will not automatically result in the immediate dismissal of an appeal because the filing fee is not jurisdictional.[8]

18-3 Preservation of Error

Not all orders entered by a trial court are appropriate for review. Any foreclosure litigant who takes an appeal must have properly preserved the record for appellate review.[9] Preserving the record includes making timely, contemporaneous objections, stating the legal basis for the objections, and obtaining an adverse ruling in the trial court.[10] It is imperative that an appellant preserves its position as to the alleged error made by the trial court and that the record does not indicate that the appellant invited an error by the trial court judge solely for the purpose of taking advantage of the ruling on appeal.[11] It is also the appellant's responsibility to ensure that the record is complete, and that it reflects the specific error made by the trial judge.[12] Appellants

---

[5] For exmple, a Notice of Appeal filed with the intent to appeal an order entered by a judge in the 15th Judicial Circuit of Palm Beach County should reference that the appeal is being taken to the Fourth District Court of Appeal.

[6] *See Alfonso v. Dep't of Envtl. Regulation*, 616 So. 2d 44, 47 (Fla. 1993) (the date of filing for jurisdictional purposes is the date of filing in the incorrect court).

[7] Fla. R. App. P. 9.110(b).

[8] *Jones v. Peninsula Motor Club, Inc.*, 558 So. 2d 517, 518 (Fla. 1st DCA 1990); *Mills v. Avon Park Motor Co.*, 223 So. 2d 802 (Fla. 2d DCA 1969) (filing fee to clerk of circuit court is not jurisdictional).

[9] *Sanchez v. State*, 909 So. 2d 981, 984 (Fla. 5th DCA 2005):

> Commonly referred to as the contemporaneous objection rule, a litigant must preserve a specific issue by: 1) making a timely contemporaneous objection in the trial court; 2) stating the legal grounds for that objection; and 3) raising the specific argument in the appellate court that was asserted as the legal ground for the objection or motion made in the trial court.

Citing Harrell v. State, 894 So. 2d 935 (Fla. 2005).

[10] *Applegate v. Barnett Bank of Tallahassee*, 377 So. 2d 1150 (Fla. 1979); *see also Aills v. Boemi*, 29 So. 3d 1105-108 (Fla. 2010) ("Proper preservation of error for appellate review generally requires three components. First, the party must make a timely, contemporaneous objection at the time of the alleged error. Second, the party must state a legal ground for that objection. Third, [i]n order for an argument to be cognizable on appeal, it must be the specific contention asserted as legal ground for the objection, exception, or motion below.") (internal citations omitted).

[11] *Goodwin v. State*, 751 So. 2d 537, 544 (Fla. 1999) ("Under the invited-error doctrine, a party may not make or invite error at trial and then take advantage of the error on appeal.").

[12] *Cohen v. Cohen*, 158 Fla. 802, 805 (1947) ("When one appeals from the judgment or decree of a trial judge, he impliedly represents that the record on appeal does reflect harmful error of the trial judge.").

may not rely on any inferences or evidence which are not made part of the appellate record.[13] This presents a challenge to foreclosure litigants who did not anticipate an appeal prior to the entry of the order they now wish to appeal, because they may not have taken necessary steps to retain a court reporter or otherwise preserve what was said at a hearing or trial. There are only limited exceptions to the necessity of a transcript, so litigants should err on the side of preservation of their arguments through use of a court reporter.[14]

In extremely limited circumstances, the appellate court has the inherent authority to review "fundamental errors" of the trial court even in the absence of a timely objection by the appealing party. Fundamental errors may occur in a foreclosure action when the trial court lacks subject matter jurisdiction or denies due process to a litigant.[15]

18-4 Types of Appeals Used in Foreclosure

18-4:1 Final Appeal

For an order to be considered "final" for purposes of appellate review, it must conclude the judicial labor in a case.[16] A final judgment of foreclosure, a judgment in favor of a defendant, or an order dismissing a foreclosure action without leave to amend are all examples of final, appealable orders as long as they contain language of finality sufficient to conclude the case.[17] Examples of final, appealable orders which occur

---

[13] *Cohen v. Cohen*, 158 Fla. 802, 806 (1947) (*see concurrence*) ("When counsel, in oral argument or in brief, attempt to fortify the record on appeal by matters dehors the record, it has a great tendency to impress the appellate court that the appeal was improvidently taken, and that counsel is unwilling to rely upon the record to establish error. Without further reference to the impropriety of such action, it is evidence of weakness of position, and has a tendency to obscure the presentation of matters which might have merit.").

[14] Where the order being appealed is the product of a non-evidentiary hearing consisting only of legal argument, the absence of a transcript will not necessarily be fatal to an appeal. *See Rollet v. de Bizemont*, 159 So. 3d 351 (Fla. 3d DCA 2015); *Shahar v. Green Tree Serv. LLC*, 125 So. 3d 251 (Fla. 4th DCA 2013); *Fish Tale Sales & Serv., Inc. v. Nice*, 106 So. 3d 57 (Fla. 2d DCA 2013). However, where a transcript is necessary but is not available because no court reporter was present or the transcript is otherwise unavailable, parties may seek to recreate the record by way of Florida Rule of Appellate Procedure 9.200(b)(4). Only when the litigants have unsuccessfully attempted to recreate the record pursuant to the rule with the appellate court, consider remanding the case for a new trial in order to produce a transcript. *Miranda v. RBS Citizens, N.A.*, 2018 WL 3862706 (Fla. 3d DCA Aug. 15, 2018).

[15] *See Dep't of Rev. ex rel. Smith v. Selles*, 47 So. 3d 916, 918 (Fla. 1st DCA 2010); *Withers v. Blomberg*, 41 So. 3d 398, 401 (Fla. 3d DCA 2010).

[16] *City of Tallahassee v Big Bend PBA*, 703 So. 2d 1066, 1069 (Fla. 1st DCA 1997) ("For an order to be deemed 'final,' the traditional test for determining finality- that the order reflects an end to judicial labor- must be met.") (*citing Carlton v. Wal-Mart Stores*, 621 So. 2d 451, 452 (Fla. 1st DCA 1993)); *see also Hoffman v. Hall*, 817 So. 2d 1057 (Fla. 1st DCA 2002).

[17] *Hoffman v. Hall*, 817 So. 2d 1057, 1058 (Fla. 1st DCA 2002) ("Particular words and phrases are not essential to finality of an order."). Some particular phrases are frequently utilized, however, to signal finality. *Raymond James & Assocs., Inc. v. Godshall*, 851 So. 2d 879, 880 (Fla. 1st DCA 2003) (identifying the phrase "for which such sum let execution issue" as traditional language of finality); *Orsonio v. Fuller, Maliah & Assocs.*, 857 So. 2d 973, 975 fn.1 (Fla. 3d DCA 2003) (identifying "that plaintiff shall take nothing by the action and go hence without day" as language of finality).

infrequently but are possible in foreclosures are orders which adjudicate only one of several causes of action and orders which end the case for one (or more, but less than all) of the parties.[18] An appellate court which is reviewing a final order may also review any underlying non-final orders (called interlocutory orders) which were necessary in reaching the final order.[19]

An order which simply grants summary judgment or dismisses an action but does so without prejudice to amend (and the claim is amendable) does not constitute a final, appealable order.[20] In these instances, the appellate court may elect to relinquish jurisdiction to the trial court, so that the appellant may secure entry of a final, appealable order.[21]

Appeal of a final order must be taken no more than thirty days after rendition of the final order.[22] Rendition does not occur until the clerk of the trial court stamps and files the order, so when calendaring a deadline for appeal, it is critical to note the date of rendition as reflected on the trial court's docket.[23] For example, rendition of a final judgment frequently does not occur on the same date that the judgment is executed because of the sheer volume the circuit court clerks must process, so while a trial court judge has signed the order, it may still be awaiting rendition. Failure to timely invoke the appellate court's jurisdiction will forfeit the right to appeal.[24]

A timely and authorized motion for rehearing filed within 15 days of rendition of the order a party intends to appeal will suspend rendition of the order until the motion for rehearing is adjudicated.[25] It is critical to note, however, that motions for rehearing must only be sought when actually authorized, because a motion for rehearing that is not authorized will not suspend rendition of the order, and the thirty day clock may start running.[26] For further discussion about motions for rehearing, see Section 18-9.

18-4:1.1 The Record on Final Appeal

In considering the appeal, the appellate court's review is limited to the "record," which is comprised of any evidence which was presented to the trial court, transcripts of proceedings, depositions, and any documents which were made part of the lower court's

---

[18] *See Mendez v. W. Flagler Family As'n. Inc.*, 303 So. 2d 1, 5 (Fla. 1974) *and Miami-Dade Water & Sewer Auth. v. Metro. Dade Cty.*, 469 So. 2d 813, 814 (Fla. 3d DCA 1985).

[19] Fla. R. App. P. 9.110(h); *see also Blackburn v. Boulis*, 184 So. 3d 565, 567 (Fla. 4th DCA 2016).

[20] *See Augustin v. Blount*, 573 So. 2d 104 (Fla. 1st DCA 1991).

[21] *Shamrock Jewelers, Inc. v. Schillaci*, 126 So. 3d 1073, 1075 (Fla. 4th DCA 2011) ("Where an appellant has prematurely filed an appeal, our procedure is to relinquish jurisdiction to the circuit court to give the appellant an opportunity to obtain a final appealable order.") (*citing Dobrick v. Discovery Cruises, Inc.*, 581 So. 2d 645 (Fla. 4th DCA 1991)).

[22] Fla. R. App. P. 9.110(b).

[23] Fla. R. App. P. 9.020(i).

[24] Fla. Stat. §59.081(2).

[25] *Smith v. Weede*, 433 So. 2d 992 (Fla. 5th DCA 1983); Fla. R. App. P. 9.020(g).

[26] For example, a Motion for Rehearing is not authorized following an order denying a Motion to Vacate Final Judgment. Consequently, such a motion does not suspend rendition of the order which denied the Motion to Vacate Final Judgment. *Smith v. Weede*, 433 So. 2d 992 (Fla. 5th DCA 1983).

file (discovery, pleadings, affidavits, etc.).[27] It follows that documents which are simply filed with the trial court but are never called to the attention of the trial court judge are not properly made part of the record, because the trial court never had an opportunity to rule on any requested relief.[28] The clerk of the court which entered the appealed order is to prepare the record on appeal within fifty days and serve an index to the record upon the parties.[29]

Within ten days of filing the notice of appeal, the appellant may direct the clerk to include or exclude certain documents in the record.[30] This assists the clerk in ensuring that relevant documents are included without unnecessarily including everything in the trial court's file. Following the appellant's directions to the clerk, the appellee may direct the clerk to include additional documents or evidence within twenty days of the filing of the notice of appeal.[31]

In rare circumstances where the parties may not record a transcript of the proceedings, a record may be created through preparation of a statement of the evidence.[32] The appellant first prepares a written statement that reflects the proceedings as accurately as possible, then serves the drafted statement on all parties (but does not file it with the court). Opposing parties then have fifteen days during which to object or propose amendments. The lower court judge will review the statement and will approve it only where the proceedings are fresh enough that the judge can confirm its accuracy. The district court will not consider statements of evidence that are not approved by the lower court.[33]

18-4:1.2 Supplementation of Record

After the record is prepared, the parties may identify documents or transcripts which were not included in the clerk's initial transmission, but will be necessary for the appellate court to review the matter. In this instance, the record may be supplemented by agreement of the parties or by the court.[34] If the parties do not take this initiative, but the court determines that the record is incomplete, it will direct a party to submit the omitted parts of the record.[35]

18-4:1.3 Timing of Briefs

In a final appeal, the appellant's initial brief must be filed within 70 days of the filing of the notice of appeal.[36] The appellee may then file an answer brief within thirty days

---

[27] Fla. R. App. P. 9.200(a).
[28] *See Braddy v. State*, 111 So. 3d 810 (Fla. 2012) (Contemporaneous objection rule requires that trial court knows that an objection was made, clearly understands the nature of the objection, and denies that request.).
[29] Fla. R. App. P. 9.110(e).
[30] Fla. R. App. P. 9.200(a).
[31] Fla. R. App. P. 9.200(a)(2).
[32] Fla. R. App. P. 9.200(b)(5).
[33] *See Schmidt v. Schmidt*, 997 So. 2d 2d 451, 451-53 (Fla. 2d DCA 2008).
[34] Fla. R. App. P. 9.200(f).
[35] Fla. R. App. P. 9.200(f) ("No proceeding shall be determined, because of an incomplete record, until an opportunity to supplement the record has been given.").
[36] Fla. R. App. P. 9.110(f).

of the initial brief, and finally, the appellant has the last word and may file a reply brief within thirty days following the answer brief.[37]

18-4:2 Non-Final Appeals

The Florida Rules of Appellate Procedure also provide for the filing of non-final appeals, which are appeals that do not, by their own effect, end the judicial labor in a case. Non-final appeals must be specifically authorized by Florida Rule of Appellate Procedure 9.130. The most common non-final appeal in a foreclosure context is a trial court's order on a motion for relief from judgment.[38] Other examples of non-final, appealable orders are orders on motions to vacate a default, orders on motions to quash service of process and orders on objections to sale.[39]

18-4:2.1 The Record on Non-Final Appeal

One of the notable differences between final and non-final appeals is the record. In a non-final appeal, the clerk does not prepare a record on appeal unless ordered to do so by the appellate court.[40] Instead, it is the appellant's duty to create an appendix to the initial brief, attaching all relevant documents which appear in the trial court's file and which the appellate court must review in deciding the case.

18-4:2.2 Timing of Briefs

While both final and non-final appeals provide litigants 30 days from rendition to file the appeal, the time for briefing following the notice of appeal is abridged when the appeal is of a non-final nature. In this instance, the appellant has just 15 days to prepare the initial brief.[41] The timing for the answer brief and reply brief is again thirty days for each.[42]

18-4:3 Interlocutory Appeals and Writs

Florida appellate courts may utilize various extraordinary writs in order to exercise jurisdiction where a plenary (or final) appeal is not appropriate. It must be noted initially that exercise of writ jurisdiction in foreclosure litigation (and in Florida generally) is extremely rare, so litigants should be particularly judicious in determining whether to petition for the issuance of a writ.[43] When seeking issuance of a writ, the

---

[37] Fla. R. App. P. 9.210.
[38] Fla. R. App. P. 9.130(a)(3); Fla. R. Civ. P. 1.540(b).
[39] *Local No. 666, Concrete Products and Material Yard Workers, Laborers Int'l Union of North America, AFL-CIO v. Dennis*, 453 So. 2d 1138 (Fla. 4th DCA 1984) (appeal from a non-final order denying motion to quash service is appropriate under Fla. R. App.P. 9.130(a)(3)(C)(1)); *Hoyt v. State*, 810 So. 2d 1007 (Fla. 4th DCA 2002) (order denying objection to foreclosure sale is a non-final, appealable order).
[40] Fla. R. App. P. 9.130(d).
[41] Fla. R. App. P. 9.130(e).
[42] Fla. R. App. P. 9.130(e); Fla R. App. P. 9.210.
[43] *Baptist Medical Center of Beaches, Inc. v. Rhodin*, 40 So. 3d 112 (Fla. 1st DCA 2010) (certiorari jurisdiction is subject to strict prerequisites, is not available as a matter of right, and should be used in very limited circumstances); *Joseph v. State*, 103 So. 3d 227 (Fla. 4th DCA

parties are not appellant and appellee, but instead are petitioner and respondent.[44] The petitioner does not file a notice of appeal or an initial brief, but invokes the appellate court's jurisdiction by filing the petition itself, which also acts as the initial brief.[45] If the petition reflects a cognizable basis for relief on its face, the appellate court will order the respondent to file a response to the petition, and the petitioner will have the last opportunity to be heard by way of a reply to the response.[46] If the petition does not meet the initial threshold, the appellate court may deny the petition without the need for input from the respondent.[47] Not all writs are appropriate for foreclosure litigation, but the following are sometimes used within the foreclosure context:

18-4:3.1 Certiorari

Appellate courts have jurisdiction to issue writs of certiorari when enforcement of a lower court's interlocutory order would result in irreparable harm to the petitioner which cannot be cured on a direct appeal.[48] For example, discovery orders may be appealed through certiorari jurisdiction if the discovery order departs from the essential requirements of the law, causing material injury through the remainder of the proceedings and leaving no adequate remedy on appeal.[49]

18-4:3.2 Mandamus

Florida's district courts also have jurisdiction to issue a writ of mandamus to compel an official to perform a duty or act which is required by law.[50] For example, if a foreclosure judgment has been entered, sale has concluded, and the clerk of court refuses to issue certificate of title, mandamus may be appropriate.[51]

18-4:3.3 Prohibition

A writ of prohibition restrains the trial court from taking action where the court does not have the judicial power to do so.[52] Prohibition is an appropriate vehicle in which to

---

2012) (writ of prohibition is an extraordinary writ and not available if other adequate remedies exist).

[44] Fla. R. App. P. 9.100(b)(1) and (e)(1).
[45] Fla. R. App. P. 9.100(c)(1) and (e)(2).
[46] Fla. R. App. P. 9.100(h), (j), and (k).
[47] Fla. R. App. P. 9.100(h).
[48] Fla. R. App. P. 9.030(b); *Jaye v. Royal Saxon, Inc.*, 720 So. 2d 214 (Fla. 1998).
[49] *Allstate Ins. Co. v. Langston*, 655 So. 2d 91 (Fla. 1995); *Martin-Johnson, Inc. v. Savage*, 509 So. 2d 1097 (Fla. 1987) (Information which may cause material injury includes "cat out of the bag" material that could be used to injure a person outside the context of the litigation.).
[50] *State ex rel. Buchwalter v. City of Lakeland*, 150 S. 508, 511 (Fla. 1933).
[51] *SR Acquisitions-Fla. City, LLC v. San Remo Homes at Fla. City, LLC*, 78 So. 3d 636, 638 (Fla. 3d DCA 2011) ("It is well settled that mandamus will lie where the petitioner has a clear legal right to the performance of the particular duty sought and that he has no other legal method for obtaining relief."). Mandamus may also be used to compel a trial court judge to rule on a pending motion where there is no valid reason to reserve ruling on the matter. Note that writ relief is rare, so all efforts to accomplish the desired result must be made before seeking the assistance of the court in compelling a ministerial duty.
[52] Fla. R. App. P. 9.030(b)(3).

challenge subject matter jurisdiction[53] or to appeal the denial of a motion to disqualify the trial judge.[54]

18-5 Stay of Action Pending Appeal

Mortgagors who have final judgments of foreclosure entered against them frequently seek a stay of the foreclosure sale while the appeal is pending. It is important to mortgagors in particular to understand that filing a notice of appeal does not automatically stay the sale.[55] A motion must be made in the lower court which entered the judgment and ordered the sale.[56]

The appellate rules grant jurisdiction to the trial court for the purpose of considering whether a stay is appropriate.[57] The lower court may also reserve jurisdiction (and usually does in the case of a final judgment of foreclosure) to adjudicate collateral issues relating to attorney fees and costs.[58] In considering whether to grant a stay, the trial court should consider what is necessary to protect the judgment holder (the plaintiff in a foreclosure).[59] The trial court may also order a stay conditioned upon the posting of a bond.[60]

18-6 Standards of Review

An appellate court's review of any case is framed by an appropriate standard of review, based on the nature of the order being appealed. In some cases, a "mixed" standard of review may be utilized where the appellate court is called upon to conduct two or more distinct reviews in the same underlying case.[61]

---

[53] *Phillips v. State*, 69 So. 3d 951 (Fla. 2d DCA 2010).
[54] *Hayslip v. Douglaw*, 400 So. 2d 553 (Fla. 4th DCA 1981).
[55] Only limited circumstances warrant an automatic stay, such as the appeal of a purely monetary judgment or when the state or a public officer seeks appellate review of an administrative action. Fla R. App. P. 9.310(b)(1) and (2). Neither of these exceptions are relevant to foreclosure actions.
[56] Fla. R. App. P. 9.310(a).
[57] Fla. R. App. P. 9.310(a). As foreclosure is not purely a money judgment, there is no automatic stay of the sale. Fla. R. App. P. 9.310(b).
[58] *Travelers Indem. Co. v. Hutchins*, 489 So. 2d 208, 209-10 (Fla. 2d DCA 1986).
[59] *Pabian v. Pabian*, 469 So. 2d 189 (Fla. 4th DCA 1985) (trial court should consider factors relevant to the individual case to determine what should be done to protect the judgment holder). In foreclosure, consideration of a stay may include whether the mortgagor has preserved the property, paid taxes and insurance, and performed maintenance, which may demonstrate a lower likelihood of waste during the stay, if one is ordered.
[60] Fla. R. App. P. 9.310(c); *Pabian v. Pabian*, 469 So. 2d 189 (Fla. 4th DCA 1985).
[61] Florida's Second District Court of Appeal provided a noteworthy example of a "mixed" standard of review in *Jarrard v. Jarrard*:

> Most commonly, the appellate court reviews the findings of fact to assure they are supported by competent, substantial evidence. Occasionally, the appellate court reviews the findings of fact to assure they are supported by competent, substantial evidence. Occasionally, the appellate court is called upon to review de novo the trial court's decision as to applicable law. In so doing, the appellate court provides only a modest presumption of correctness to the trial court because the issue is almost always one that is exclusively a pure issue of law upon which the trial court has no greater insight than the appellate court. Finally, the appellate court reviews the trial

18-6:1 De Novo

The standard of review for pure questions of law, where factual determinations are not relevant to the issue on appeal, is de novo.[62] Consequently, the standard of review on summary judgment is de novo,[63] as is the standard of review on an order granting a motion to dismiss.[64] The de novo standard is also applied when an appellate court is called upon to consider whether a foreclosing plaintiff proved its standing in the trial court.[65] De novo review means that the appellate court reviews the issue on appeal without deference to the legal conclusions of the trial court.[66]

18-6:2 Abuse of Discretion

A trial court's rulings on the admissibility of evidence are reviewed for abuse of discretion.[67] Other examples of orders reviewed for an abuse of discretion in foreclosure actions include orders on motions to vacate, or objections to, the foreclosure sale,[68] orders granting a deficiency decree,[69] orders on motions to vacate defaults,[70] and orders on motions to vacate final judgments.[71] To find abuse of discretion, the appellate court must necessarily find that no reasonable person in similar circumstances would have made the same ruling as made by the trial court.[72]

18-6:3 Competent, Substantial Evidence

Factual findings made by the trial judge regarding the sufficiency of evidence at a trial are evaluated by appellate courts for competent, substantial evidence.[73]

---

court's legal conclusion, which was reached by the application of the law to the facts. As stated earlier, the review of this legal conclusion is reviewed with a recognition that the factual component was determined by the trial judge and that all factual determinations may not have been expressly stated in the order. The interrelationships between the findings of fact and the conclusions of law is what makes the standard of review "mixed." 157 So. 3d 332, 337-38 (Fla. 2d DCA 2015).

[62] *Armstrong v. Harris*, 773 So. 2d 7, 11 (Fla. 2000).
[63] *Gonzalez v. Deutsche Bank Nat'l Trust Co.*, 95 So. 3d 251 (Fla. 2d DCA 2012).
[64] *Belcher Center, LLC v. Belcher Center, Inc.*, 883 So. 2d 338 (Fla. 2d DCA 2004).
[65] *Boyd v. Wells Fargo Bank, N.A.*, 143 So. 3d 1128, 1129 (Fla. 4th DCA 2014).
[66] *Bush v. Holmes*, 919 So. 2d 392, 400 (Fla. 2006) ("in a de novo review, 'no deference is given to the judgment of the lower courts.'") (citing *D'Angelo v. Fitzmaurice*, 863 So. 2d 311, 314 (Fla. 2003)).
[67] *Sottilaro v. Figueroa, 86 So. 3d 505, 507 (Fla. 2d DCA), review denied*, 103 So. 3d 139 (Fla. 2012).
[68] *U.S. Bank, N.A. v. Vogel*, 137 So. 3d 491, 493 (Fla. 4th DCA 2014).
[69] *Builders Finance Co., Inc., of St. Petersburg v. Ridgewood Homesites, Inc.*, 157 So. 2d 551, 552-53 (Fla. 2d DCA 1963).
[70] *Elliott v. Aurora Loan Services, LLC*, 31 So. 3d 304, 306 (Fla. 4th DCA 2010).
[71] *Foche Mortg., LLC v. CitiMortgage, Inc.*, 163 So. 3d 525, 526 (Fla. 3d DCA 2015).
[72] *Canakaris v. Canakaris*, 382 So. 2d 1197, 1203 (Fla. 1980) ("*If reasonable men* could differ as to the propriety of the action taken by the trial court, then the action is not reasonable and there can be no finding of an abuse of discretion."); *Delno v. Market Ry. Co.*, 124 F.2d 965, 967 (9th Cir. 1942) ("Discretion has been abused where the decision is arbitrary, fanciful or unreasonable.") (internal quotation marks and citations omitted).
[73] *Procacci v. Solomon, 317 So. 2d 467, 468 (Fla. 4th DCA 1975); State, Florida Highway Patrol v. Forfeiture of Twenty Nine, etc.*, 802 So. 2d 1171, 1172 (Fla. 3d DCA 2001).

18-7 Oral Argument

The appellate court may decide oral argument is warranted in any case, and either party may request oral argument.[74] A party's request is made by filing and serving a one-page document titled Request for Oral Argument. If a party requests argument, the request must be made no later than fifteen days after the last brief is due to be served.[75] Should the court decide argument is appropriate, it will schedule argument and send a notice to the parties identifying the date and time at which the matter will be considered by a panel of three judges. At oral argument, each side is typically afforded twenty minutes for argument, but the court has the right to limit or extend argument. The court may also decide to forego argument and decide the case on the briefs, in which case it will issue an order dispensing with argument. Even if the court dispenses with argument, the case will be decided by a panel of three judges.

If a matter is set for oral argument, attorneys should take note that the twenty minutes allotted for each side is not a twenty-minute presentation or speech. Frequently, attorneys will have time for little more than an introductory statement before the panel begins questioning. The court will already be familiar with the case, as court staff prepares a bench brief for the panel to review. Attorneys for the parties must be prepared to discuss the legal issues, the record on appeal, key facts, and procedural history. It is also imperative to be able to quickly reference page numbers in the record and to discuss the application of seminal cases that apply to the arguments.

The panel of judges will not issue a ruling at oral argument, but will take the case under advisement and issue a ruling after deliberation.

18-8 Attorneys' Fees on Appeal

In all Florida appeals, the prevailing party is entitled to attorneys' fees only if there are contractual or statutory grounds for attorneys' fees at the trial level.[76] Attorneys' fees in foreclosure appeals are controlled by the terms of the mortgage contract.[77] Where the mortgage calls for the mortgagee's attorney's fees to be paid in the event of a foreclosure, the mortgagor is also entitled to the payment of fees in the event the case is dismissed or judgment is entered for the mortgagor.[78] The prevailing party in an appeal may also be entitled to payment of costs, including filing fees, service of process, and charges for preparation of the record and transcripts.[79]

A party in a foreclosure appeal must file a motion seeking attorneys' fees before the party knows whether it is entitled to such an award (because the appeal has not yet been decided). The motion must be filed within the time for filing the reply brief in an appeal, or within the time for service of a petitioner's reply in a case seeking an extraordinary writ.[80]

---

[74] Fla. R. App. P. 9.320.
[75] Fla. R. App. P. 9.320(a).
[76] Fla. Stat. 59.46.
[77] *Nudel v. Flagstar Bank, FSB*, 60 So. 3d 1163, 1164-65 (Fla. 4th DCA 2011); see also Fla. R. App. P. 9.400(b).
[78] Fla. Stat. §57.105(7).
[79] Fla. R. App. P. 9.400(a).
[80] 1 Fla. R. App. P. 9.400(b)(1)-(2).

18-9 Rehearing and Clarification

When an appellate court renders its decision, such a ruling it is not final until a mandate is issued fifteen days following the issuance of the ruling.[81] During that fifteen day period, either party may seek rehearing or clarification.[82] However, litigants should be cautioned that rehearing and clarification are very rarely granted, and are not to be utilized as a vehicle to reargue the case or disagree with the ruling on appeal.[83] A motion for rehearing on appeal must state with particularity the points of law or fact that the court has overlooked or misapprehended it its decision.[84] A motion for clarification must state with particularity the points of law or facts that the movant believes are in need of clarification.[85]

If a motion seeking rehearing or clarification is filed, the party opposing the motion may file a response within ten days.[86] No party may file more than one motion seeking rehearing or clarification in an appeal, so if one is warranted, all grounds for seeking relief must be articulated in the motion.[87]

18-10 Supreme Court Jurisdiction

While it is extremely rare, the Florida Supreme Court occasionally exercises discretionary jurisdiction over a foreclosure case. Even the jurisdiction of the Supreme Court is fettered, however, and foreclosure cases which reach such a level do so primarily as a result of two circumstances:

1. A decision of one of the district courts of appeal passes upon a "question certified to be of great public importance";[88] or

2. A decision of one of the district courts of appeal is "certified to be in direct conflict" with a decision from another district court of appeal.[89]

Absent either of these circumstances (and usually only at the request of a district court of appeal), the Florida Supreme Court is not likely to exercise discretionary jurisdiction, and litigants should not view the Supreme Court as an opportunity to relitigate the issues on appeal.

---

[81] Fla. R. App. P. 9.340(a).

[82] Fla. R. App. P. 9.330(a).

[83] *Elliott v. Elliott*, 648 So. 2d 135, 135-36 (Fla. 4th DCA 1994) ("[D]isagreeing with the court's conclusion; rearguing matters already discussed in briefs and oral arguments and necessarily considered by the court; requesting the court to change its mind on matters already presented and argued; ventilating displeasure with the court's conclusion. These are the most common examples of abuse.").

[84] Fla. R. App. P. 9.330(a).

[85] Fla. R. App. P. 9.330(a).

[86] Fla. R. App. P. 9.330(a).

[87] Fla. R. App. P. 9.330(b).

[88] Fla. R. App. P. 9.030(a)(2)(A)(v); *Arsali v. Chase Home Finance LLC*, 121 So. 3d 511 (Fla. 2013).

[89] Fla. R. App. P. 9.030(a)(2)(A)(vi); *Bank of New York Mellon v. Condo. Ass'n of La Mer Estates, Inc.*, 175 So. 3d 282 (Fla. 2015).

CHAPTER 19

Deficiency Judgments

Steven C. Weitz

19-1 Introduction

When a borrower executes a note, they are signing a promise to repay the lender a specified amount of money. Through the foreclosure process, the property is sold at a public auction in an attempt to recoup the lender's losses. Frequently, however, the amount recovered through the sale of the property does not fully recoup the lender's losses. When this happens, the lender is entitled to recover a deficiency amount from the note signor.[1]

A deficiency judgment is a money judgment against the note signor for the difference between the indebtedness owed and the fair market value of the subject property. Florida Statute § 702.06 authorizes deficiency judgments, but limits the amount of the deficiency judgment based on specific calculations:

> In all suits for the foreclosure of mortgages heretofore or hereafter executed the entry of a deficiency decree for any portion of a deficiency, should one exist, shall be within the sound discretion of the court; however in the case of an owner-occupied residential property, the amount of the deficiency may not exceed the difference between the judgment amount, on in the case of a short sale, the outstanding debt, and the fair market value on the date of sale.[2]

19-2 Jurisdiction

19-2:1 In Personam Jurisdiction

In order for a court to have jurisdiction to enter a deficiency judgment against a note signor, the note signor must have been served pursuant to Florida Statute § 48.031 in the foreclosure action, or must have later availed themselves to the court's jurisdiction. In Florida, service on a defendant is authorized via publication in foreclosure

---

[1] The term borrower is sometimes used to include all mortgagors, but not every mortgagor is a note signor. Frequently, two people may execute the mortgage to perfect a security interest, but only one of them may execute the note. A deficiency judgment can only be sought against a party who signed the note, that is personally obligated to repay the debt.

[2] Fla. Stat. § 702.06.

actions.[3] Publication, however, only confers in rem jurisdiction upon the court.[4] Therefore, when service upon the note signor in the foreclosure action is conducted via publication, the foreclosure judgment obtained is an in rem judgment (against the property) simply authorizing a foreclosure sale and not a deficiency judgment.

A deficiency judgment, meanwhile, is an in personam judgment (against the person), in that it is a money judgment with recovery sought against the actual note signor. In an action for a money judgment, the court necessitates in personam judgment and therefore, personal service pursuant to Florida Statute § 48.031 upon the note signor is required.[5]

If in personam jurisdiction was obtained in the foreclosure and the final judgment retains jurisdiction for the court to enter a deficiency judgment, then the motion for deficiency is a continuance of the foreclosure proceedings.[6] In such event, it is unnecessary to re-establish personal jurisdiction.[7]

19-2:2 Rights of Assignees

An assignee of the right to recover a mortgage foreclosure deficiency can file an action to recover a deficiency under Florida Statute § 702.06.[8] Additionally, courts have the discretion to allow assignees to join the underlying foreclosure action to pursue the deficiency decree.[9] The assignee stands in the shoes of the assignor and the amount paid by an assignee is legally irrelevant to the issue of whether the assignee is entitled to a deficiency judgment.[10]

19-2:3 Where a Claim Can Be Brought

Florida Statute § 702.06 provides the right to sue at common law to recover a deficiency, unless the court in the foreclosure action has granted or denied a claim for a deficiency judgment. In many instances, the foreclosure judgment includes a reservation of the court's jurisdiction to enter a deficiency judgment. In such an instance, the judgment holder may either seek a deficiency judgment in the existing foreclosure action or through an independent action at law for a deficiency judgment.[11]

---

[3] Fla. Stat. § 49.011(1).
[4] See Zieman v. Cosio, 578 So. 2d 332 (Fla. 3d DCA 1991).
[5] See Zieman v. Cosio, 578 So. 2d 332 (Fla. 3d DCA 1991).
[6] Timmers v. Harbor Fed. Sav. & Loan Ass'n, 548 So. 2d 282, 283 (Fla. 1st DCA 1989) (the law contemplates a continuance of the proceedings for entry of a deficiency judgment as a means of avoiding the expense and inconvenience of an additional suit at law to obtain the balance of the obligation owed by a debtor); L.A.D. Prop. Ventures v. First Bank, 19 So. 3d 1126 (Fla. 2d DCA 2009); TD Bank, N.A. v. Graubard, 172 So. 3d 550 (Fla. 5th DCA 2015).
[7] Timmers v. Harbor Fed. Sav. & Loan Ass'n, 548 So. 2d 282, 283 (Fla. 1st DCA 1989); L.A.D. Prop. Ventures v. First Bank, 19 So. 3d 1126 (Fla. 2d DCA 2009).
[8] Dyck-O'Neal, Inc. v. Lanham, 257 So. 3d 1 (Fla. 2018); Franklin v. Regions Bank, 25 So. 3d 621 (Fla. 4th DCA 2009).
[9] Franklin v. Regions Bank, 25 So. 3d 621, 622 (Fla. 4th DCA 2009); Collins Asset Grp., LLC v. Prop. Asset Mgmt., Inc., 197 So. 3d 87 (Fla. 1st DCA 2016).
[10] Thomas v. Premier Capital, Inc., 906 So. 2d 1139, 1141 (Fla. 3d DCA 2005); Ahmad v. Cobb Corner, Inc., 762 So. 2d 944, 948 (Fla. 4th DCA 2000).
[11] Dyck-O'Neal v. Lanham, 257 So. 3d 1 (Fla. 2018).

19-3 Calculation of Deficiency Amounts

A mortgagee in a foreclosure action–or its assignee–is entitled to recover its full judgment debt, including post-judgment interest and costs, less the fair market value of the property.[12]

19-3:1 Burden of Proof

The granting of a deficiency judgment is the rule rather than the exception.[13] The reintroduction of a final judgment of foreclosure is not necessary to establish a lender's right to a deficiency judgment in the same case; therefore, the determination of the fair market value is typically the main issue of contest in a deficiency judgment proceeding.[14]

The initial burden of proving fair market value is placed on the lender; however, it is a burden easily met. Initially, the lender simply has to introduce the sale price at the foreclosure auction (or short sale, if deficiency is not waived in the agreement) in evidence. As Florida courts issue a certificate of sale, providing evidence of the sale price is simple.[15] Upon the introduction of the sale price, the burden then shifts to the note signor to prove the fair market value of the property is something different than the presented sale price. The "proper rule is that upon the introduction of the evidence of the sale price, the defendant has the burden of going forward and presenting such evidence as he shall find proper concerning the fair market value of the property."[16] In the absence of evidence presented by the defendant, the trial court has the power to act upon the assumption that the sale price reflects the fair market value.[17] In fact, a "legal presumption exists that the foreclosure sale price equals the fair market value of the property."[18]

The same burden-shifting framework also applies to deficiency judgments after short sales.[19] In fact, the presumption that the short sale price was the fair market

---

[12] *MR&F Enterprises v. Citicorp Savings of Florida*, 764 So. 2d 783 (Fla. 3d DCA 2000); *Morgan v. Kelly*, 642 So. 2d 1117 (Fla. 3d DCA 1994); *Norwest Bank Owatonna, N.A. v. Millard*, 522 So. 2d 546 (Fla. 4th DCA 1988) (citing *CSI Servs., Ltd. v. Hawkins Concrete Constr. Co.*, 516 So. 2d 337, 338 (Fla. 1st DCA 1987)). See *R.K. Cooper Constr. Co. v. Fulton*, 216 So. 2d 11 (Fla. 1968); *Liberty Bus. Credit Corp. v. Schaffer/Dunadry*, 589 So. 2d 451 (Fla. 2d DCA 1991); *Flagship State Bank of Jacksonville v. Drew Equip. Co.*, 392 So. 2d 609 (Fla. 5th DCA 1981). *Martinec v. Early Bird Int'l, Inc.*, 262 So. 3d 205, 206 (Fla. 4th DCA 2018) ("If the amount of the final judgment is increased due to encumbrances, those same encumbrances cannot be used to decrease the market value of the property.").

[13] *S/D Enterprises v. Chase Manhattan Bank*, 374 So. 2d 1121 (Fla. 3d DCA 1979); *Thomas v. Premier Capital, Inc.*, 906 So. 2d 1139 (Fla. 3d DCA 2005).

[14] *TD Bank, N.A. v. Graubard*, 172 So. 3d 550, 553 (Fla. 5th DCA 2015).

[15] *See* Fla. Stat. § 45.031.

[16] *Fara Manufacturing Co., Inc. v. First Federal Savings and Loan Association of Miami*, 366 So. 2d 164, 165 (Fla. 3d DCA 1979).

[17] *Fara Manufacturing Co., Inc. v. First Federal Savings and Loan Association of Miami*, 366 So. 2d 164, 165 (Fla. 3d DCA 1979).

[18] *Vantium Capital, Inc. v. Hobson*, 137 So. 3d 497 (Fla. 4th DCA 2014).

[19] *Branch Banking & Tr. Co. v. Park Circle, LLC*, No. 2:13-cv-25-FtM-38CM, 2014 WL 1870606 (M.D. Fla. May 8, 2014); *PNC Bank, N.A. v. Monument Ctr., LLC*, No: 6:15-cv-859-Orl-40DAB, 2016 WL 4435698 (M.D. Fla. July 27, 2016).

value may carry more weight as short sales are generally done at the request of the obligor.[20]

When there is a dispute over the fair market value of the property at the time of the sale, an evidentiary hearing is required. Often both sides will have appraisals done to establish the fair market value, but appraisals cannot be considered by the court unless the appraisal is: (1) properly admitted into evidence; and (2) an evaluation of the value of the property is conducted at the time of the sale.[21]

19-3:2 Judge's Discretion

The court is given discretion to determine if there are any "equitable considerations" that warrant a reduction in the actual deficiency.[22] However, this discretion is not unfettered. The court cannot exercise its discretion without first determining how much the property is worth at the time of the sale, either through the sale price or other evidence of fair market value.[23] If the court then decides to reduce the deficiency amount, the court must state any legal or equitable principles relied upon.[24] When a court does not state any legal or equitable principles justifying an award for less than the full amount of the deficiency, it is an abuse of discretion.[25]

In most cases, foreclosure sale bidding begins at $100.00 and frequently, the lender is the high bidder for that amount, or some other nominal amount. Upon introduction of the certificate of sale indicating a high bid at auction of $100, presumption would be placed that this is the fair market value and shift the burden to the note signor to present evidence to the contrary.[26] In such cases, the note signor should try to prove the fair market value of the property is higher than the sale price, thereby decreasing the amount of the deficiency judgment. However, even absent evidence from the defendant, in cases where the successful bid is clearly a nominal amount, the court may require an appraisal as close to the date of the foreclosure sale as possible and an affidavit attesting to the value within the appraisal in order to determine the fair market value. If the appraisal is far in excess of the successful bid, then the court would most likely intervene and exercise its discretion to value the property at a more appropriate level.

19-3:3 Timing of Appraisals

The lender must establish the value of the property on the date of the sale. It is not, however, necessarily a requirement for the appraisal of the property to be conducted

---

[20] *Branch Banking & Tr. Co. v. Park Circle, LLC*, No. 2:13-cv-25-FtM-38CM, 2014 WL 1870606 (M.D. Fla. May 8, 2014); *PNC Bank, N.A. v. Monument Ctr., LLC*, No: 6:15-cv-859-Orl-40DAB, 2016 WL 4435698 (M.D. Fla. July 27, 2016).

[21] *Flagship State Bank of Jacksonville v. Drew Equip. Co.*, 392 So. 2d 609, 610 (Fla. 5th DCA 1981).

[22] *Chidnese v. McCollem*, 695 So. 2d 936 (Fla. 4th DCA 1997) (*citing Federal Deposit Ins. Corp. v. Morley*, 915 F.2d 1517 (11th Cir. 1990)).

[23] *Chidnese v. McCollem*, 695 So. 2d 936, 938 (Fla. 4th DCA 1997).

[24] *Vantium Capital, Inc. v. Hobson*, 137 So. 3d 497 (Fla. 4th DCA 2014) (*citing Morgan v. Kelly*, 642 So. 2d 1117 (Fla. 3d DCA 1994)).

[25] *Chidnese v. McCollem*, 695 So. 2d 936 (Fla. 4th DCA 1997); *Morgan v. Kelly*, 642 So. 2d 1117 (Fla. 3d DCA 1994).

[26] *Fara Manufacturing Co., Inc. v. First Federal Savings and Loan Association of Miami*, 366 So. 2d 164 (Fla. 3d DCA 1979).

on the day of the sale. A party seeking a deficiency judgment may provide testimony to link the value of property on the date of an appraisal to the value of property on the date of the foreclosure sale.[27] For instance, where the appraisal is conducted long after the foreclosure sale, but the appraiser determined the value was the same on the date of the foreclosure sale, the appraisal may still be accepted.[28] The key factor is whether there is evidence of the value of the property at the time of the sale. Similar to the other aspects of a deficiency judgment, the trial court's decision of whether or not to admit an appraisal into evidence is reviewed for abuse of discretion if appealed.[29]

19-3:4 Defenses

Equitable defenses available in a foreclosure action in which a deficiency is sought are also available in a subsequent legal action to collect the deficiency.[30]

Personal defenses to the amounts owed–such as inspection fees and late charges–may be asserted as a setoff against a deficiency judgment claim.[31]

Florida Statute § 559.715 does not create a condition precedent to seeking a deficiency judgment.[32]

19-4 Statute of Limitations

In 2013, Florida's House Bill 87 amended Florida Statute § 95.11, which governs the statute of limitations to pursue a deficiency judgment. The alteration decreased the statute of limitations for claims of a deficiency related to notes secured by a mortgage against a one-family to four-family residential property unit from five years to one year. The 2013 amendment applies to actions commenced after July 1, 2013. For those actions that began prior to July 1, 2013, the statute of limitations remains no later than five years after the action accrued, but in any event, no later than July 1, 2014. As such, § 95.11(5)(h) requires that, moving forward, all deficiency judgment actions related to notes secured by residential properties are governed by the one-year statute of

---

[27] *743 Mahoney, LLC v. MDC 5, LLC*, 204 So. 3d 116 (Fla. 2d DCA 2016).
[28] *PB Surf, LTD v. Beach Community Bank, RFP, LLC*, 139 So. 3d 463 (Fla. 1st DCA 2014) (*citing Beach Cmty. Bank v. First Brownsville Co.*, 85 So. 3d 1119 (Fla. 1st DCA 2012)).
[29] *Eagle's Crest LLC v. Republic Bank*, 42 So. 3d 848, 850 (Fla. 2d DCA 2010).
[30] *Romagnoli v. SR Acquisitions - Homestead, LLC*, 218 So. 3d 955 (Fla. 3d DCA 2017) (citing *PMI Mortg. Ins. Co. v. Cavendar*, 615 So. 2d 710, 712 (Fla. 3d DCA 1993)) (quoting with approval cases holding that an action at law for a deficiency judgment is subject to equitable defenses); *Frumkes v. The Mortg. Guarantee Corp.*, 173 So. 2d 738, 741 (Fla. 3d DCA 1965) ("equitable considerations which could have been urged in opposition to a proper and timely application for deficiency decree in a foreclosure suit, may be asserted with similar purpose and effect in a law action for deficiency"); *Frank v. Levine*, 159 So. 2d 665, 666 (Fla. 3d DCA 1964) ("there would appear to be no reason why equitable considerations sufficient to limit a deficiency award in equity should not serve equally when pleaded and proved in an action at law to recover a mortgage foreclosure sale deficiency"); *Dyck-O'Neal, Inc. v. Norton*, 267 So. 3d 478, 482 (Fla. 2d DCA 2019) ("an equitable estoppel defense requires pleading and proof of (1) a representation about a material fact that is contrary to a later asserted position; (2) reliance on that representation; and (3) a detrimental change in position as a result of that reliance.").
[31] *Hudson v. U.S. Bank Nat'l Ass'n*, 240 So. 3d 34 (Fla. 4th DCA 2018).
[32] *Dyck-O'neal, Inc. v. Lanham*, 264 So. 3d 1115 (Fla. 1st DCA, 2019).

limitations. The limitations period commences on the day after "the certificate"[33] is issued by the clerk of court or the day after the mortgagee accepts a deed in lieu of foreclosure.[34] The one-year statute of limitations for a deficiency judgment does not apply to a judgment sought following a short sale.[35] The statute of limitations for seeking a deficiency judgment after a short sale is five years.[36]

19-5 Deficiency Judgments Unavailable

19-5:1 Waiver of Deficiency–Settlement

In some circumstances, a lender may be prohibited from pursuing a deficiency judgment. If the lender has waived the right to pursue a deficiency as part of a settlement, then the lender has voluntarily relinquished its right to seek a deficiency. The offer of a waiver of deficiency has become a common bargaining chip used in order to entice note signors to consent to judgment. Similarly, a waiver of deficiency is commonly included in short sale agreements between note signors and lenders. When multiple borrowers have executed the note, the lender can offer a waiver of deficiency for both note signors or for just one of them and still retain the right to pursue a deficiency against the other.

19-5:2 Discharged in Bankruptcy

The last situation in which a lender is prohibited from pursuing a deficiency judgment occurs where the note signor files for liquidation under Chapter 7 of the Bankruptcy Code and is granted a discharge. A Chapter 7 discharge releases individual debtors from personal liability for most debts. The discharge of personal liability prevents a money judgment (deficiency) from being entered against the debtor on those specific debts, leaving only in rem claims.[37] Therefore, a Chapter 7 discharge extinguishes the ability to obtain a deficiency against the discharged note signor. For a complete discussion about the effects of a bankruptcy discharge in the foreclosure context, see Chapter 17: Bankruptcy.

---

[33] Florida Statute § 95.11(5)(h) does not specify whether it is here referencing "the certificate" of sale, or the certificate of title. In an abundance of caution, wise lawyers will use the earlier date as the start date for the deficiency statute of limitations.

[34] *See* Fla. Stat. § 95.11(5)(h) (2018). *Dyck-O'Neal, Inc. v. Norton*, 267 So. 3d 478, 481 (Fla. 2d DCA 2019).

[35] *Bush v. Whitney Bank*, 219 So. 3d 257 (Fla. 5th DCA 2017) (one-year statute of limitations in Florida Statute § 95.11(5)(h) of the Florida Statutes (2015) did not apply to bank's action [to collect amounts outstanding after successful short sale].). *Whitney Bank v. Grant*, 223 So. 3d 476 (Fla. 1st DCA 2017).

[36] *Whitney Bank v. Grant*, 223 So. 3d 476 (Fla. 1st DCA 2017); Fla. Stat. § 95.11(2)(b) (2018).

[37] *See Johnson v. Home State Bank*, 501 U.S. 78 (1991).

APPENDIX A
Forms and Samples

1-001 SAMPLE COMPLAINT (HOLDERS AND NON-HOLDERS IN POSSESSION) – PREPARED BY SARAH WEITZ

The following sample is for purposes of guidance only and care should be taken to check the case law for any decisions that may impact the claims, and to tailor the counts to the facts of the specific case.

                                                IN THE CIRCUIT COURT OF THE [__]TH
                                                JUDICIAL CIRCUIT IN AND FOR
                                                [_____] COUNTY, FLORIDA

                                                CASE NO.

ANY BANK, N.A.

        Plaintiff,

v.

JOE BORROWER, BARBARA BORROWER,
SECOND MORTGAGEE, BANK N.A., DEL
BOCA VISTA HOMEOWNER'S ASSOCIATION,
UKNOWN TENANT IN POSSESSION #1, and
ANY AND ALL UNKNOWN PARTIES
CLAIMING BY, THROUGH, UNDER, AND
AGAINST THE HEREIN NAMED INDIVIDUAL
DEFENDANT(S) WHO ARE NOT KNOWN TO
BE DEAD OR ALIVE, WHETHER SAID
UNKNOWN PARTIES MAY CLAIM AN
INTEREST AS SPOUSES, HEIRS, DEVISEES,
GRANTEES, OR OTHER CLAIMANTS,
        Defendants.
_____/

VERIFIED COMPLAINT FOR MORTGAGE FORECLOSURE

Plaintiff, ANY BANK, N.A., sues Defendants, JOE BORROWER; BARBARA BORROWER; SECOND MORTGAGEE BANK, N.A.; DEL BOCA VISTA HOMEOWNER'S ASSOCIATION; UNKNOWN TENANT IN POSSESSION #1; and ANY AND ALL UNKNOWN PARTIES CLAIMING BY, THROUGH, UNDER, AND AGAINST THE HEREIN

NAMED INDIVIDUAL DEFENDANT(S) WHO ARE NOT KNOWN TO BE DEAD OR ALIVE, WHETHER SAID UNKNOWN PARTIES MAY CLAIM AN INTEREST AS SPOUSES, HEIRS, DEVISEES, GRANTEES, OR OTHER CLAIMANTS and alleges:

Count for Mortgage Foreclosure

1. This is an action to foreclose a mortgage on real property located in [_____] County, Florida and venue is proper in this county.

2. The Court has jurisdiction over this action.

3. On [_____], 20[__], JOE BORROWER executed and delivered a promissory note and he and BARBARA BORROWER executed and delivered a mortgage securing payment of the same to [original lender] which was recorded on [_____], 20[__] in official records book [____], page [____] of the Public Records of [_____] County, Florida, which mortgaged the property described therein, then owned by and in the possession of said Defendants. A copy of said Note with affixed allonge ("Note") as well as the Mortgage ("Mortgage," and collectively, "the Loan Documents") is attached to this Complaint as Composite Exhibit "A."

4. Plaintiff is the owner and holder of the Note secured by the Mortgage, and is entitled to enforce its terms, having acquired physical possession of the Note before filing this action.

[Alternatively: Plaintiff is a person entitled to enforce the note under applicable law because . . . (*allege specific facts*) . . .]

[Alternatively: Plaintiff has been delegated the authority to institute a mortgage foreclosure action on behalf of . . . (*name of holder*) . . . , the holder of the original note. The document(s) that grant(s) plaintiff the authority to act on behalf of the holder of the original note is/are as follows . . .]

[Alternatively: Plaintiff has been delegated the authority to institute a mortgage foreclosure action on behalf of . . . (*name of non-holder*) . . ., who is not the holder but is entitled to enforce the note under section 673.3011(2), Florida Statutes, because . . . (*allege specific facts*) . . . The document(s) that grant(s) plaintiff the authority to act on behalf of the person entitled to enforce the note is are as follows . . .]

5. Defendants JOE BORROWER and BARBARA BORROWER are the owners of the property subject to the Note and Mortgage.

6. Defendant JOE BORROWER has defaulted under the terms of the Note and Mortgage by failing to make the regular installment payment due on _____, 20[___], and all subsequent regular installment payments . . . (*provide any relevant facts*).

7. The Plaintiff declares the full amount under the Loan Documents to be due and payable.

8. There is now due, owing, and unpaid to the Plaintiff from Defendant JOE BORROWER $[_____] in principal under the Loan Documents and interest as provided therein from [_____], including title search expense for ascertaining necessary parties to this action.

9. The Plaintiff has satisfied any and all conditions precedent to the acceleration of the sums due under the Loan Documents and to the commencement of this foreclosure action.

10. The Defendant, DEL BOCA VISTA HOMEOWNERS' ASSOCIATION, may claim some interest in the subject property by virtue of certain restrictions or covenants of record as recorded in the Public Record of [_____] County, Florida, or that certain lien, filed in Official Records Book [_____], Page [_____] of the Public Records of [_____]

County, Florida. However, the Plaintiff's interest is either superior to any lien created thereby, or said lien is limited by the effect of Florida Statutes Section 720.3085.

11. The Defendant, SECOND MORTGAGEE, BANK N.A., claims or may claim an interest in the subject property by virtue of a final judgment recorded in the Official Records Book [_____], Page [_____] of the Public Records of [_____] County, Florida. However, the Plaintiff's interest is superior and the interest of the Defendant, if any, is inferior to the lien of the Plaintiff's Loan Documents.

12. Upon information and belief, the property may be in possession of UNKNOWN TENANT IN POSSESSION #1, the name of whom is unknown to the Plaintiff and whose interest in the property is inferior to the Plaintiff's.

13. Any and all unknown parties claiming by, through, under, and against the herein named individual defendant(s) who are not known to be dead or alive, whether said unknown parties may claim an interest as spouses, heirs, devisees, grantees, or other claimants are joined as defendants herein. The claims of said defendants are subordinate, junior, and inferior to the interest of the Plaintiff.

14. In order to protect its security, the Plaintiff may have to advance and pay Ad Valorum taxes, premiums required by the Loan Documents, and necessary costs during the pendency of this action. Any such sum so paid will be due and owing to the Plaintiff.

15. The Plaintiff has obligated itself to pay the undersigned attorneys a reasonable fee for their services in this action (*allege statutory and/or contractual bases, as applicable*).

WHEREFORE, the Plaintiff requests that the Court enter a final judgment, ascertain the sums due to the Plaintiff under the Loan Documents in principal, interest, late charges, advances for taxes and insurance, expenses and costs, including attorney's fees, and that if the same are not paid within the time set by this Court, said property be sold in accordance with the provisions of Florida Statute §45.031, to satisfy the Plaintiff's mortgage lien, and, that if the proceeds of such sale are insufficient to pay the Plaintiff's claim, that a deficiency decree be entered for the sums remaining unpaid against the Defendant liable therefore; and that the right, title, interest and estate of Defendants and all persons claiming by, through, or under each Defendant named herein since the filing of the lis pendens herein to be foreclosed and barred.

Verification of Complaint

Under penalty of perjury, the undersigned declares that I have read the foregoing, and the facts alleged therein are true and correct to the best of my knowledge and belief.

ANY BANK, N.A.

_____

By: _____

Printed Name: _____

State of [_____]
County of [_____]

The foregoing was acknowledged before me this _____ day of _____, 20[__], by _____ as _____ for [plaintiff or plaintiff's agent], who is personally known to me or who did produce identification.

My commission expires: _____

Notary Public

Certification of Original Promissory Note

The undersigned hereby certifies:

1. That the Plaintiff is in possession of the original promissory note upon which this action is brought.

2. The location of the original promissory note is: (*identify location*).

3. The name and title of the person giving the certification is: (*provide name and title*)

4. The name of the person who personally verified such possession is: (*provide name*).

5. The time and date on which possession was verified were: (*provide time and date*).

6. Correct copies of the note (and, if applicable, all endorsements, transfers, allonges, or assignments of the note) are attached to this certification.

7. I give this statement based on my personal knowledge.

Under penalties of perjury, I declare that I have read the foregoing Certification of Possession of Original Note and that the facts stated in it are true.

Executed on _____(date).

_____
(Person Signing Certification)

1-002 SAMPLE COMPLAINT LOST NOTE – PREPARED BY SARAH WEITZ

The following sample is for purposes of guidance only and care should be taken to check the case law for any decisions that may impact the claims, and to tailor the counts to the facts of the specific case.

IN THE CIRCUIT COURT OF THE [__]TH JUDICIAL CIRCUIT IN AND FOR [_____] COUNTY, FLORIDA

CASE NO.

ANY BANK, N.A.

    Plaintiff,

v.

JOE BORROWER, BARBARA BORROWER, SECOND MORTGAGEE, BANK N.A., DEL BOCA VISTA HOMEOWNER'S ASSOCIATION, UKNOWN TENANT IN POSSESSION #1, and ANY AND ALL UNKNOWN PARTIES CLAIMING BY, THROUGH, UNDER, AND AGAINST THE HEREIN NAMED INDIVIDUAL DEFENDANT(S) WHO ARE NOT KNOWN TO BE DEAD OR ALIVE, WHETHER SAID UNKNOWN PARTIES MAY CLAIM AN INTEREST AS SPOUSES, HEIRS, DEVISEES, GRANTEES, OR OTHER CLAIMANTS,
    Defendants.
_____/

VERIFIED COMPLAINT FOR MORTGAGE FORECLOSURE

Plaintiff, ANY BANK, N.A., sues Defendants, JOE BORROWER; BARBARA BORROWER; SECOND MORTGAGEE BANK, N.A.; DEL BOCA VISTA HOMEOWNER'S ASSOCIATION; UNKNOWN TENANT IN POSSESSION #1; and ANY AND ALL UNKNOWN PARTIES CLAIMING BY, THROUGH, UNDER, AND AGAINST THE HEREIN

NAMED INDIVIDUAL DEFENDANT(S) WHO ARE NOT KNOWN TO BE DEAD OR ALIVE, WHETHER SAID UNKNOWN PARTIES MAY CLAIM AN INTEREST AS SPOUSES, HEIRS, DEVISEES, GRANTEES, OR OTHER CLAIMANTS and alleges:

1. This is an action to foreclose a mortgage on real property located in [_____] County, Florida and venue is proper in this county and to reestablish a promissory note.

2. The Court has jurisdiction over this action.

3. On [_____], 20[___], JOE BORROWER executed and delivered a promissory note and he and BARBARA BORROWER executed and delivered a mortgage securing payment of the same to [original lender] which was recorded on [_____], 20[___] in official records book [____], page [____] of the Public Records of [_____] County, Florida, which mortgaged the property described therein, then owned by and in the possession of said Defendants. A copy of the mortgage and note are attached to the affidavit which is attached hereto as Composite Exhibit "B;" the contents of the affidavit are specifically incorporated by reference.

4. The Plaintiff is not in possession of the note but is entitled to enforce it.

5. The Plaintiff cannot reasonably obtain possession of the note because (select a, b, c, or d):

    (a) the note was destroyed.

    (b) the note is lost.

    (c) the note is in the wrongful possession of an unknown person.

    (d) the note is in the wrongful possession of a person that cannot be found or is not

APPENDIX A—FORMS AND SAMPLES 327

amenable to service of process.

6. (select a, b, c, d, e, or f):

(a) When loss of possession occurred, the Plaintiff was the holder of the original note secured by the mortgage.

(b) When loss of possession occurred, the Plaintiff was a person entitled to enforce the note under applicable law because . . . (*allege specific facts*) . . .

(c) The Plaintiff has directly or indirectly acquired ownership of the note from a person entitled to enforce the note when loss of possession occurred as follows: . . . (*allege facts as to transfer of ownership*) . . .

(d) The Plaintiff has been delegated the authority to institute a mortgage foreclosure action on behalf of the holder of the original note who lost possession of the note. The document(s) that grant(s) plaintiff the authority to act on behalf of the person entitled to enforce the note is/are as follows . . . (*attach documents if not already attached*).

(e) The Plaintiff has been delegated the authority to institute a mortgage foreclosure action on behalf of the person entitled to enforce the note when loss of possession occurred because . . . (*allege specific facts*) . . . The document(s) that grant(s) the Plaintiff the authority to act on behalf of the person entitled to enforce the note is/are as follows . . . (*attach documents if not already attached*).

(f) The Plaintiff has been delegated the authority to institute a mortgage foreclosure action on behalf of the person or entity who directly or indirectly acquired ownership of the note from a person entitled to enforce the note when loss of possession occurred, as follows:

... (*allege specific facts*) ... the document(s) that grant(s) the Plaintiff the authority to act on behalf of the person entitled to enforce the note is/are as follows .... (*attach documents if not already attached*).

7. The Plaintiff did not transfer the note or lose possession of it as the result of a lawful seizure.

8. The property is now owned by the Defendants, JOE BORROWER and BARBARA BORROWER, who hold possession.

9. The Defendant has defaulted under the note and mortgage by failing to pay the regular installment payment(s) due on [_____], and all subsequent payments (*include any relevant facts*).

10. The Plaintiff declares the full amount payable under the note and mortgage to be due.

11. The Defendant owes the Plaintiff $[_____] that is due on principal on the Note and Mortgage, interest from [_____(*date*)], and title search expense for ascertaining necessary parties to this action.

12. The Plaintiff has satisfied any and all conditions precedent to the acceleration of the sums due under the Loan Documents and to the commencement of this foreclosure action.

13. The Defendant, DEL BOCA VISTA HOMEOWNERS' ASSOCIATION, may claim some interest in the subject property by virtue of certain restrictions or covenants of record as recorded in the Public Record of [_____] County, Florida, or that certain lien, filed in Official Records Book [_____], Page [_____] of the Public Records of [_____]

APPENDIX A—FORMS AND SAMPLES

County, Florida. However, the Plaintiff's interest is either superior to any lien created thereby, or said lien is limited by the effect of Florida Statutes Section 720.3085.

14. The Defendant, SECOND MORTGAGEE, BANK N.A., claims or may claim an interest in the subject property by virtue of a final judgment recorded in the Official Records Book [_____], Page [_____] of the Public Records of [_____] County, Florida. However, the Plaintiff's interest is superior and the interest of the Defendant, if any, is inferior to the lien of the Plaintiff's Loan Documents.

15. Upon information and belief, the property may be in possession of UNKNOWN TENANT IN POSSESSION #1, the name of whom is unknown to the Plaintiff and whose interest in the property is inferior to the Plaintiff's.

16. Any and all unknown parties claiming by, through, under, and against the herein named individual defendant(s) who are not known to be dead or alive, whether said unknown parties may claim an interest as spouses, heirs, devisees, grantees, or other claimants are joined as defendants herein. The claims of said defendants are subordinate, junior, and inferior to the interest of the Plaintiff.

17. In order to protect its security, the Plaintiff may have to advance and pay Ad Valorum taxes, premiums required by the Loan Documents, and necessary costs during the pendency of this action. Any such sum so paid will be due and owing to the Plaintiff.

18. The Plaintiff is obligated to pay its attorneys a reasonable fee for their services. The Plaintiff is entitled to recover its attorneys' fees for prosecuting this claim pursuant to (*identify statutory and/or contractual bases, as applicable*).

WHEREFORE, the Plaintiff demands judgment re-establishing the promissory note, determining the amount and nature of adequate protection to be required by sections 673.3091(2) and 702.11, Florida Statutes, foreclosing the mortgage, for costs (and, where applicable, for attorneys' fees), and if the proceeds of the sale are insufficient to pay plaintiff's claim, a deficiency judgment.

Verification of Complaint

Under penalty of perjury, the undersigned declares that I have read the foregoing, and the facts alleged therein are true and correct to the best of my knowledge and belief.

ANY BANK, N.A.

_____

By: _____

Printed Name: _____

State of [_____]

County of [_____]

The foregoing was acknowledged before me this _____ day of _____, 20[__], by _____ as _____ for [plaintiff or plaintiff's agent], who is personally known to me or who did produce identification.

My commission expires: _____

Notary Public

Affidavit of Compliance

State of Florida
County of _____

BEFORE ME, the undersigned authority, personally appeared .....(*name*)....., who, after being first duly sworn, deposes and states, under penalty of perjury:

1. I am the plaintiff (or plaintiff's . . .) (*identify relationship to plaintiff*). I am executing this affidavit in support of plaintiff's Complaint against defendant and I have personal knowledge of the matters set forth herein.

2. On [_____(*date*)], the public records reflect that the Defendant executed and delivered a mortgage securing the payment of the note to [original lender]. The mortgage was recorded on [_____(*date*)], in Official Records Book [_____], page [_____] of the Public Records of [_____] County, Florida, and mortgaged the property described therein, which was then owned by and in possession of the mortgagor, a copy of the mortgage and the note being attached.

3. The Plaintiff is not in possession of the note but is entitled to enforce it.

4. The Plaintiff cannot reasonably obtain possession of the note because (*select a, b, c, or d*):

    (a) the note was destroyed.

    (b) the note is lost.

    (c) the note is in the wrongful possession of an unknown person.

    (d) the note is in the wrongful possession of a person who cannot be found or is not amenable to service of process.

5. (*select a, b, c, d, e, or f*):

(a) When loss of possession occurred, the Plaintiff was the holder of the original note secured by the mortgage.

(b) When loss of possession occurred, the Plaintiff was a person entitled to enforce the note under applicable law because . . . (*allege specific facts*)

(c) The Plaintiff has directly or indirectly acquired ownership of the note from a person entitled to enforce the note when loss of possession occurred as follows: . . . (*allege facts regarding transfer of ownership*)

(d) The Plaintiff has been delegated the authority to institute a mortgage foreclosure action on behalf of the holder of the original note who lost possession of the note. The document(s) that grant(s) the Plaintiff the authority to act on behalf of the person entitled to enforce the note is/are as follows . . . (*attach copy of document(s) or relevant portion(s) of the document(s)*).

(e) The Plaintiff has been delegated the authority to institute a mortgage foreclosure action on behalf of the person entitled to enforce the original note when loss of possession occurred, because . . . (*allege specific facts*). The document(s) that grant(s) the Plaintiff the authority to act on behalf of the person entitled to enforce the note is/are as follows . . . (*attach documents if not already attached*).

(f) The Plaintiff has been delegated the authority to institute a mortgage foreclosure action on behalf of the person or entity who directly or indirectly acquired ownership of the note from a person entitled to enforce the original note when loss of possession occurred, as follows . . . (*allege specific facts*). The document(s) that grant(s) the Plaintiff the authority to act on behalf of the person entitled to enforce the note is/are as follows . . . (*attach documents if not already attached*).

6. Below is the clear chain of the endorsements, transfers, allonges or assignments of the note and all documents that evidence same as are available to the Plaintiff: . . . (*identify in chronological order all endorsements, transfers, assignments of, allonges to, the note or other evidence of the acquisition, ownership and possession of the note*) . . . Correct copies of the foregoing documents are attached to this affidavit.

7. The Plaintiff did not transfer the note or lose possession of it as the result of a lawful seizure.

FURTHER, AFFIANT SAYETH NAUGHT.

_____
[Signature of Affiant]

[typed or printed name of affiant]

STATE OF FLORIDA
COUNTY OF [_____]

BEFORE ME, the undersigned authority appeared _____ (name of Affiant), who _____ is personally known to me or _____ produced identification _____ and acknowledged that he/she executed the foregoing instrument for the purposes expressed therein and who did take an oath.

WITNESS my hand and seal in the State and County aforesaid, this _____ (*date*).

NOTARY PUBLIC, State of Florida
Print Name: _____
Commission Expires: _____

1-003 SAMPLE ADDITIONAL CLAIMS – PREPARED BY SARAH WEITZ

The following sample is for purposes of guidance only and care should be taken to check the case law for any decisions that may impact the claims, and to tailor the counts to the facts of the specific case.

<u>Count for Equitable Lien Foreclosure</u>

1. This is an action to establish and foreclose an equitable lien on real property located in [_____] County, Florida in an amount in excess of $15,000 exclusive of interest, costs, and attorney's fees.

2. The Plaintiff realleges and reasserts the allegations contained in paragraphs [identify the paragraphs containing general allegations and standing allegations] as if set forth fully herein.

3. The Plaintiff's predecessor in interest loaned JOE BORROWER $[_____] ("the Mortgage loan") for the refinance of the following described real property:

[*Legal description of the property*] ("the Property")

4. At the closing of the Mortgage loan refinance, the Plaintiff's predecessor issued funds to protect its own interest and not as a volunteer and, the sum of $[_____] was paid from the proceeds in full satisfaction of . . . (description of the costs paid, such as real estate taxes or a mortgage executed by JOE BORROWER and BARBARA BORROWER, in favor of [*name of bank*], recorded on [_____], 20[___] in Official Records Book [_____], page [_____] of the Public Records of [_____] County, Florida ("the [*name of bank*] Mortgage"). A copy of the [name of bank] Mortgage is attached as Exhibit "B").

APPENDIX A—FORMS AND SAMPLES 335

5. The [*description of the costs paid*] provided for interest and the Plaintiff is entitled to recovery of interest herein.

6. The sums advanced at the closing were made by the Plaintiff's predecessor and on behalf of JOE BORROWER and BARBARA BORROWER in full satisfaction of the [description of the costs paid], a debt that the Plaintiff's predecessor was not primarily or otherwise liable for, and so that the Plaintiff's predecessor would be the first mortgage holder on the aforementioned Property at the conclusion of the transaction.

7. The Defendants, JOE BORROWER and BARBARA BORROWER, have and may claim that the Plaintiff's mortgage is not a valid lien on the Property.

8. Under the circumstances, it would be inequitable for the Defendants' interest to be superior to or free and clear of, the interest of the Plaintiff where there is an unjust enrichment as the Plaintiff seeks to recover money which paid off [description of the costs paid], which was a valid lien on the Property, and the Defendants have benefitted from the paying off of [*description of costs paid*], which were valid liens on the Property and but for the said payoff of these lien interests, would still encumber the Property.

9. The Defendant, JOE BORROWER and BARBARA BORROWER, had knowledge of this benefit conferred by the Plaintiff's predecessor and they accepted and retained that benefit.

10. The Plaintiff has no adequate remedy at law against the Defendants to compensate it for the Defendants' unjust enrichment should their, or any one of their, interests be deemed superior to that of the Plaintiff or should it be determined that they or any of them, should take the Property free and clear of the Plaintiff's claims.

11. The Plaintiff is entitled to the imposition of an equitable lien.

WHEREFORE, the Plaintiff respectfully requests that the Court enter a final judgment decreeing that the Plaintiff has an equitable lien on the Property, the amount thereof, including interest, fees and costs, declaring its lien on the Property to be superior to any interest of Defendants or anyone claiming by or through said party since the filing of the lis pendens herein, the sale of the Property to the highest bidder at a judicial sale pursuant to applicable law, and for such other and further relief as the Court deems just and proper.

<u>Count for Equitable Subrogation</u>

1. This is an action to establish and foreclose a subrogation (equitable or conventional) lien on real property located in [_____] County, Florida, in an amount in excess of $15,000 exclusive of interest, attorney's fees, and costs.

2. The Plaintiff realleges and reasserts the allegations contained in paragraphs [identify the paragraphs containing general allegations and standing allegations] as if set forth fully herein.

3. The Plaintiff's predecessor in interest loaned JOE BORROWER $[_____] ("the Mortgage loan") for the refinance of the following described real property:

[*Legal description of the property*] ("the Property")

4. At the closing of the Mortgage loan refinance, the Plaintiff's predecessor issued funds to protect its own interest and not as a volunteer and, the sum of $[_____] was paid from the proceeds in full satisfaction of . . . (*description of the costs paid, such as real estate taxes or a mortgage*) executed by JOE BORROWER and BARBARA BORROWER, in favor of [*name of bank*], recorded on [_____], 20[__] in Official Records Book [_____],

APPENDIX A—FORMS AND SAMPLES

page [_____] of the Public Records of [_____] County, Florida ("the [name of bank] Mortgage"). A copy of the [name of bank] Mortgage is attached as Exhibit "B").

5. The [description of the costs paid] provided for interest and the Plaintiff is entitled to recovery of interest herein pursuant to principles of subrogation.

6. The sums advanced at the closing were made by the Plaintiff's predecessor and on behalf of JOE BORROWER and BARBARA BORROWER in full satisfaction of the [description of the costs paid], a debt that the Plaintiff's predecessor was not primarily or otherwise liable for, and so that the Plaintiff's predecessor would be the first mortgage holder on the aforementioned Property at the conclusion of the transaction.

7. By virtue of the refinance of the Property, the proceeds of which went to pay off the [*name of bank*] Mortgage executed by JOE BORROWER and BARBARA BORROWER and the [*description of the costs paid by Plaintiff's predecessor*], both of which were valid, enforceable liens on the Defendants' interest in the Property, the Plaintiff is entitled to subrogation of all rights, interests and benefits possessed by the parties paid.

WHEREFORE, the Plaintiff respectfully requests that the Court enter a final judgment decreeing that it is subrogated to all of the rights, interests, and benefits possessed by the lienors described in paragraphs [_____] and [_____], the amount of the subrogation lien including interest, fees, and costs, declaring its lien on the Property to be superior to any interest of the Defendants, or anyone claiming by or through them since the filing of the lis pendens, the sale of the Property to the highest bidder at a judicial sale pursuant to applicable law, and for such other and further relief as the Court deems just and proper.

Reformation of the Mortgage

1. This is an equitable action to reform a mortgage given against real property in [_____] County, Florida.

2. The Plaintiff realleges and reasserts the allegations contained in paragraphs [identify the paragraphs containing general allegations and standing allegations as if set forth fully herein..

3. The true intention and agreement of JOE BORROWER and BARBARA BORROWER and [*original lender*] was for the Mortgage to encumber the Property as a first lien superior to all others.

4. The Mortgage does not accurately reflect the true intention and agreement of the parties because the legal description attached to the Mortgage reflects the following legal description which is incorrect:

(*provide the legal description in the mortgage*)

5. Instead, the following legal description should have been attached to the Mortgage:

(*provide the corrected legal description*)

6. JOE BORROWER and BARBARA BORROWER have never held an interest in the property legally described in the Mortgage.

7. JOE BORROWER and BARBARA BORROWER applied and were approved for the Mortgage loan with the understanding and intention of all parties that it would be secured by a lien against the Property, which is legally described in paragraph [____] above.

8. The attachment of an erroneous legal description was the result of a scrivener's error and the mutual mistake of [*original lender*] and JOE BORROWER and BARBARA BORROWER.

9. The Plaintiff has no adequate remedy at law.

WHEREFORE, the Plaintiff demands judgment reforming the Mortgage to reflect the legal description of the Property as set forth in paragraph [____] in lieu of the legal description provided in the Mortgage such that it encumbers the entire fee simple title to the Property, *nunc pro tunc*, relating back and taking effect from the date of the original execution of the Mortgage, and for such other relief as the Court deems proper.

1-004 SAMPLE LIS PENDENS

IN THE CIRCUIT COURT OF THE [_____]
JUDICIAL CIRCUIT IN AND FOR [_____]
COUNTY, FLORIDA

GENERAL JURISDICTION DIVISION
CASE NO. [_____]

PLAINTIFF A.B.,

    Plaintiff,

vs.

DEFENDANTS, C.D.;

    Defendants.

_____/

NOTICE OF LIS PENDENS

TO: THE DEFENDANTS NAMED ABOVE AND ALL OTHERS TO WHOM IT MAY CONCERN:

1. YOU ARE HEREBY NOTIFIED of the institution of this action by Plaintiff against you seeking to foreclose a note and mortgage encumbering the following described real property in [_____] County, Florida, at Instrument Number [_____]:

[INSERT LEGAL DESCRIPTION]

Including the buildings and appurtenances located thereon.

Dated this ____ day of _____, 2015.

                                       Attorney for Plaintiff

                                       By: _____
                                              Attorney Signature Block

1-005 SAMPLE ANSWER AND AFFIRMATIVE DEFENSES

IN THE CIRCUIT COURT OF THE [_____]
JUDICIAL CIRCUIT IN AND FOR [_____]
COUNTY, FLORIDA

GENERAL JURISDICTION DIVISION
CASE NO. [_____]

PLAINTIFF A.B.,

    Plaintiff,

vs.

DEFENDANTS, C.D.;

    Defendants.

_____/

ANSWER AND AFFIRMATIVE DEFENSES

Defendant, C.D., hereby responds to the allegations contained in Plaintiff, A.B.'s Complaint, and alleges:

> [For each numbered paragraph included in the Complaint, admit or deny the factual allegations contained within said paragraph. If the truth of the statement is unknown, the defendant should state that he/she is without knowledge, but must do so in compliance with Florida Rule of Civil Procedure 1.110(c).

AFFIRMATIVE DEFENSES

[The following constitutes examples of defenses contained within the forms following Florida Rule of Civil Procedure 1.900. Defenses should be pled according to the specifics facts of each case and should be specifically pled with particularity where appropriate or required by the Rules of Civil Procedure.]

1. Statute of Limitations: Each cause of action, claim, and item of damages did not accrue within the time prescribed by law for them before this action was brought.

2. Payment: Before commencement of this action Defendant discharged Plaintiff's claim and each item of it by payment.

3. Accord and Satisfaction: On [date], Defendant delivered to Plaintiff and Plaintiff accepted from Defendant [specify consideration] in full satisfaction of Plaintiff's claim.

4. Failure of Consideration: The sole consideration for the execution and delivery of the Note described in paragraph [___] of the Complaint was Plaintiff's promise to lend Defendant [$]; Plaintiff failed to lend the sum to Defendant.

5. Release: On [date], and after Plaintiff's claim in this action accrued, Plaintiff released Defendant from it, a copy of the release being attached.

[The following constitutes examples of additional defenses which may apply to mortgage foreclosure actions. Defenses should be pled according to the specifics facts of each case and should be specifically pled where appropriate or required by the Rules of Civil Procedure.]

6. Standing: Plaintiff was not the holder of the original Note, nor did Plaintiff have the right to enforce the original Note (on its own behalf or on behalf of another entity) as of the date of filing the instant lawsuit. [Provide factual basis for defense].

7. Condition Precedent: Plaintiff failed to fulfill a condition precedent to foreclosure prior to filing the instant lawsuit. [Provide factual basis for defense and identify condition precedent which was not fulfilled]

8. Fraud: Defendant did not execute the Note and Mortgage, and believes an unauthorized third party fraudulently executed the Note and Mortgage on his/her behalf. [Provide factual basis for defense, noting that Florida Rule of Civil Procedure 1.120(b) requires that fraud must be pled with particularity.]

WHEREFORE, Defendant requests that Plaintiff take nothing by this action and that the Court enter judgment in Defendant's favor, awarding attorneys' fees and costs to Defendant, and for any such further relief as the Court deems just and proper.

Attorney for Defendant

By: _____
Attorney Signature Block

1-006 SAMPLE REQUEST FOR PRODUCTION FROM DEFENDANT TO PLAINTIFF

The following sample is for purposes of guidance only and care should be taken to check the case law for any decisions that may impact the claims, and to tailor the discovery to the facts of the specific case.

FIRST REQUEST FOR PRODUCTION OF DOCUMENTS TO PLAINTIFF

Defendant, _____, by and through undersigned counsel and pursuant to Rule 1.350 of the Florida Rules of Civil Procedure, hereby requests that Plaintiff produce the following documents at (NAME AND ADDRESS) within thirty (30) days (or such shorter time as ordered by Court) from the date of service hereof.

I. DEFINITIONS

The following definitions apply for purposes of responding to these requests:

1. The "Plaintiff" means the foreclosing lender, its officers, directors, agents, employees, subsidiaries, parents, attorneys, accountants and representatives and its predecessors in interest and their officers, directors, agents, employees, subsidiaries, parents, attorneys, accountants and representatives.

2. The "Defendant" means any named Defendant to this action.

3. The "Loan" means the indebtedness that the Plaintiff seeks to foreclose in this lawsuit.

4. The "Property" means the property that is subject to the foreclosure action asserted by Plaintiff against the Defendant.

5. "Document" or "documents" as used herein shall mean the following:

APPENDIX A—FORMS AND SAMPLES

The original and any copy, regardless of its origin and location, of all writings of any kind whatsoever including, but not limited to, all abstracts, accounting journals, accounting ledgers, advertisements, affidavits, agendas, agreements or proposed agreements, analyses, appointment books, appraisals, articles of incorporation, balance sheets, bank checks, bank deposit or withdrawal slips, bank credit or debit memoranda, bank statements, blue prints, books, books of account, budgets, bulletins, bylaws, canceled checks, charts, checks, codes, communications, communications with government bodies, computer data or printouts, conferences, contracts, correspondence, data processing cards, data sheets, desk calendars, details, diagrams, diaries, disks or data compilations from which information can be obtained or translated, drafts, drawings, electromagnetic tapes, files, films, financial calculations., financial projections, financial statements, graphs, handwritten notes or comments however produced or reproduced, indexes, insertions, instructions, internal accounting records, interoffice communications, invoices, ledgers, letters, lists, logbooks, manuals, memoranda, microfilm, minutes of meetings, motion pictures, newspaper or magazine articles, networks, nonconforming copies which contain deletions, notations on records of meetings, notes, notices of wire transfer of funds, outlines, pamphlets, papers, passbooks, periodicals, photocopies, photographs, pictures, plans, preliminary drafts, press releases, proposals, publications, punch cards, raw and refined data, receipts, recommendations records, records of conferences or conversations or meetings, records of payment, reports, resolutions, results of investigations, schedules, schematics, sepia, shipping papers, slides, specifications, speeches, statements of account, studies, summaries, surveys, tape recordings, tax returns, telegrams, telephone logs and records, telephone and other conversations or communications, teletypes, telexes, transcripts, transcripts of tape recordings, video tapes, voice records, vouchers, work papers, worksheets, written notations, and any and all other papers similar to any of the foregoing. Any document containing thereon or attached thereto any alterations, comments, notes or other material not included in the copies or originals or referred to in the preceding definition shall be deemed a separate document within said definition. Any document shall include all exhibits, schedules or other writings affected by or referenced in any such document or other writings necessary to complete the information contained therein or make it not misleading.

II. INSTRUCTIONS

The following instructions apply in responding to this request for production of documents:

1. Plaintiff is hereby notified that the duty to respond includes the duty to supply all documents and materials in Plaintiff's physical possession, as well as those that which can be obtained from additional sources pursuant to Rule 1.350 of the Florida Rules of Civil Procedure.

2. In the event that any document called for by a request is withheld on the basis of a claim of privilege, please identify that document by stating: (a) any addressor or addressee, (b) matter, number of pages, and attachments or appendices, (c) all persons to whom the document was distributed shown or explained, (d) its present custodian, and (e) the nature of the privilege asserted.

APPENDIX A—FORMS AND SAMPLES

3. In the event that any document requested herein is not presently in your possession or subject to your control, please identify each person you have reason to believe had or has knowledge of its contents.

4. In the event that any document called for by a request has been destroyed or discarded, please identify that document by stating: (a) any addresser and addressee, (b) any indicated or blind copies, (c) the document's date, subject matter, number of pages, and attachments or appendices; (d) all persons to whom the document was distributed, shown or explained, (e) its date and destruction or discard, manner of destruction or discard, and reason for destruction or discard, and (f) the persons authorizing or carrying out such destruction or discard.

III. REQUEST TO PRODUCE

The Defendant requests that the Plaintiff produce the following documents.

1. All documents that the Plaintiff will introduce at trial or at a hearing on a motion for summary judgment, including impeachment or rebuttal documents.

2. All documents that reflect or demonstrate Defendants are indebted to the Plaintiff.

3. All documents that Plaintiff and/or its predecessor (the original lender) relied upon in extending credit to Defendant.

4. All correspondence between any debt collector acting on behalf of the Plaintiff to the Defendant. This includes the law firm representing the Plaintiff in this action.

5. All correspondence between Plaintiff and Defendant from the inception of the loan to the present.

6. All documents related to the procurement of any type of insurance by the Plaintiff for the Defendant or the Property.

7. A payment history for the Loan from inception of the loan to the present.

8. An escrow reconciliation for the Loan from inception of the loan to the present.

9. A copy of any and all monthly statements for the Loan account from the date of its inception to the date of this request to produce.

10. Any and all documents evidencing or related to any telephone or other oral communications between Plaintiff and Defendant regarding the Loan from the date of its inception to the date of this request to produce.

11. Any and all servicing and sub-servicing agreements which control, affect, or govern the servicing of the Loan.

12. Any and all pooling and servicing agreements, together with the relevant mortgage loan schedule, which control, affect, or govern the servicing of the Loan.

1-007 SAMPLE REQUEST FOR ADMISSIONS FROM DEFENDANT TO PLAINTIFF

The following sample is for purposes of guidance only and care should be taken to check the case law for any decisions that may impact the claims, and to tailor the discovery to the facts of the specific case.

REQUEST FOR ADMISSIONS TO PLAINTIFF

COMES NOW Defendant, _____, by and through undersigned counsel, pursuant to Rules 1.280 and 1.370 of the Florida Rules of Civil Procedure, and hereby requests Plaintiff to respond to the statements that follow within 30 days after service, or such shorter time as ordered by the Court and thereafter serve a copy of such answers on the attorney for Defendant, (NAME AND ADDRESS).

The Defendant requests that the Plaintiff *ADMIT OR DENY* the following.

1. Plaintiff is not the owner of the note and mortgage it seeks to foreclose.
2. Plaintiff is not the holder of the note and mortgage it seeks to foreclose.
3. Plaintiff does not have physical possession of the original note and mortgage.
4. Plaintiff did not have physical possession of the original note and mortgage prior to filing the Complaint in this action.
5. Plaintiff has not given Defendant(s) credit for all of the payments made on the Note and Mortgage.
6. The Plaintiff has refused, after demand, to give Defendant credit for the payments made to Plaintiff by Defendant.
7. Defendant has the right to reinstate the Note and Mortgage.

8. Defendant offered to reinstate the Note and Mortgage before the Plaintiff instituted this litigation.

9. The Plaintiff refused to accept reinstatement of the Note and Mortgage when offered by Defendant.

10. Plaintiff accepted late payments made by Defendant before Plaintiff filed this lawsuit.

11. Plaintiff knowingly waived the right to timely payments on the Note and Mortgage.

12. Defendant tendered all sums due under the Note and Mortgage before Plaintiff sent to Defendant the required notice of acceleration of sums due under the Note and Mortgage.

13. Defendant and Plaintiff agreed to payment arrangements on the Note and Mortgage before Plaintiff instituted this action.

14. Defendant paid the agreed-upon amounts to Plaintiff.

15. Defendant is entitled to an award of attorney's fees and costs if he successfully defends this action.

16. Plaintiff failed to comply or meet all of the conditions precedent to bringing this action.

17. Plaintiff charged Defendant(s) late fees and other charges within 60 days of the assignment of the Note and Mortgage.

18. Plaintiff and/or Plaintiff's agents have on previous occasions physically visited non-commercial real property for which it held a mortgage for the purpose of discussing defaulted loans and payment.

19. Plaintiff and/or Plaintiff's agents have on prior occasions assessed the costs of visiting non-commercial real property for which it held a mortgage to the borrower.

20. Plaintiff intended to visit the subject real property for the purpose of discussing the default and payment.

1-008 SAMPLE INTERROGATORIES FROM DEFENDANT TO PLAINTIFF

The following sample is for purposes of guidance only and care should be taken to check the case law for any decisions that may impact the claims, and to tailor the discovery to the facts of the specific case.

DEFENDANT'S FIRST SET OF INTERROGATORIES TO PLAINTIFF

Defendant, _____, by and through his undersigned counsel, pursuant to Rule 1.340 of the Florida Rules of Civil Procedure, hereby requests Plaintiff answer the following interrogatories under oath and return them to _____ (NAME AND ADDRESS) within 30 days of the date of service (or such shorter time as ordered by the court):

I. DEFINITIONS

The following definitions apply for purposes of responding to these interrogatories:

1. The "Plaintiff" means the foreclosing lender, its officers, directors, agents, employees, subsidiaries, parents, attorneys, accountants and representatives and its predecessors in interest and their officers, directors, agents, employees, subsidiaries, parents, attorneys, accountants and representatives.

2. The "Defendant" means any named Defendant to this action.

3. The "Loan" means the indebtedness that the Plaintiff seeks to foreclose in this lawsuit.

4. The "Property" means the property that is subject to the foreclosure action asserted by Plaintiff against the Defendant.

5. "Document" or "documents" as used herein shall mean the following:

The original and any copy, regardless of its origin and location, of all writings of any kind whatsoever including, but not limited to, all abstracts, accounting journals, accounting ledgers, advertisements, affidavits, agendas, agreements or proposed agreements, analyses, appointment books, appraisals, articles of incorporation, balance sheets, bank checks, bank deposit or withdrawal slips, bank credit or debit memoranda, bank statements, blue prints, books, books of account, budgets, bulletins, bylaws, canceled checks, charts, checks, codes, communications, communications with government bodies, computer data or printouts, conferences, contracts, correspondence, data processing cards, data sheets, desk calendars, details, diagrams, diaries, disks or data compilations from which information can be obtained or translated, drafts, drawings, electromagnetic tapes, files, films, financial calculations., financial projections, financial statements, graphs, handwritten notes or comments however produced or reproduced, indexes, insertions, instructions, internal accounting records, interoffice communications, invoices, ledgers, letters, lists, logbooks, manuals, memoranda, microfilm, minutes of meetings, motion pictures, newspaper or magazine articles, networks, nonconforming copies which contain deletions, notations on records of meetings, notes, notices of wire transfer of funds, outlines, pamphlets, papers, passbooks, periodicals, photocopies, photographs, pictures, plans, preliminary drafts, press releases, proposals, publications, punch cards, raw and refined data, receipts, recommendations records, records of conferences or conversations or meetings, records of payment, reports, resolutions, results of investigations, schedules, schematics, sepia, shipping papers, slides, specifications, speeches, statements of account, studies, summaries, surveys, tape recordings, tax returns,

APPENDIX A—FORMS AND SAMPLES

telegrams, telephone logs and records, telephone and other conversations or communications, teletypes, telexes, transcripts, transcripts of tape recordings, video tapes, voice records, vouchers, work papers, worksheets, written notations, and any and all other papers similar to any of the foregoing. Any document containing thereon or attached thereto any alterations, comments, notes or other material not included in the copies or originals or referred to in the preceding definition shall be deemed a separate document within said definition. Any document shall include all exhibits, schedules or other writings affected by or referenced in any such document or other writings necessary to complete the information contained therein or make it not misleading.

6. "And" and "or" as used herein are terms of inclusion and not of exclusion, and shall be construed either disjunctively or conjunctively as necessary to bring within the scope of the request for production of documents any document or information that might otherwise be construed to be outside its scope.

INTERROGATORIES

1. Identify all files and records you or your related companies have, keep or maintain, including, but not limited to printouts, ledgers or other files records, interoffice memoranda or books of accounts referencing or concerning the Note and Mortgage, and describe how you became the person or entity entitled to reestablish and or foreclose the Note and Mortgage.

2. Please identify all persons known to you who have personal knowledge of any servicing agreements concerning the Note and Mortgage.

3. State the total amount of dollars that the Defendant has paid in connection with the Note and Mortgage from its inception. Identify each payment individually and state the date of payment, and the components of each payment, i.e. what portion of the payment was interest, principal, late charges, and other charges.

4. Identify each telephone contact made to the Defendant, by you or your agent(s) with regard to this transaction or any subsequent default. Identify the date and time of each telephone contact and describe the substance of each conversation.

5. Describe in detail your policies and procedures pertaining to your solicitation and evaluation of short sale offers.

6. State whether you claim to be the holder of the note or mortgage or both, and if so, explain why you so claim, identifying any document(s) and clauses therein which gives you the interest(s) you. If you do not claim to be the holder of the note or mortgage, describe the basis for your claim that you have standing to foreclose.

7. State from what person or entity ("assignor") you took transfer or assignment of the note and/or mortgage, specifying the contact name, full legal name, address, and phone number of the assignor together with the date you took assignment, and state the same information for any person or entity to which the Loan was ever assigned.

8. State the date, amount and nature of and fully describe the consideration or value given in exchange for each and every assignment of the note and/or mortgage and identify from and to what person or entity such consideration or value was given providing the contact name, full legal name, address, and phone number of each such person or entity.

9. State all parties that took assignment of the note and/or mortgage between the making of same and your taking assignment of same and provide the contact name, full legal name, address, and phone number of each such party.

10. State whether between the time of making the Loan and the time of your assignment of the note and/or mortgage the original lender maintained ownership of the Loan.

11. State on what date you acquired the interest which you claim gives you standing to foreclose.

12. Please state, for the note and mortgage, whether and as of what date you secured the originals thereof and from whom providing the contact name, full legal name, address, and phone number of each such party.

13. List all servicers who have serviced the Loan from inception, including the dates of servicing of each servicer, whether that servicer is still doing business, and the last known address and phone number for each servicer.

14. Describe the Loan boarding process employed by each servicer identified in Interrogatory 13.

15. Identify your procedures for communicating with borrowers after they have missed at least one payment on their loan, including, but not limited to the manner and timing of phone calls, correspondence, and physical visits to the property.

1-009 SAMPLE REQUEST FOR PRODUCTION FROM PLAINTIFF TO DEFENDANT

PLAINTIFF'S REQUEST TO PRODUCE TO DEFENDANTS

Plaintiff, _____, by and through its undersigned counsel, propounds the following Request to Produce pursuant to Rule 1.350, Florida Rules of Civil Procedure, and requests that Defendant, _____, produce for inspection and copying within 30 days, the documents described below to _____ (*Name and Address*):

DEFINITIONS

1." Plaintiff" shall mean _____ and its/his officers, directors, agents, servants, employees and attorneys.

2. "You" shall mean Defendant, _____, including any person or entity answering on Defendant's behalf.

3. "Communications" shall mean all oral or written exchanges of words, thoughts or ideas to another person(s), whether person-to-person, in a group, by telephone, by letter, by telex or by any other process, electric, electronic or otherwise. All such communications in writing shall include, without limitation, printed, typed, handwritten or other readable documents, correspondence, memos, reports, contracts, drafts, both initial and subsequent, diaries, logbooks, minutes, notes, studies, surveys and forecasts.

4. "Document" has the broadest meaning accorded to it and includes without limitation all written, typed, printed, reproduced, filmed, electronically or computer-stored, or recorded material or information of any kind, in the possession, custody, or control of you or any of your past or present agents, employees, consultants, attorneys or other persons acting on your behalf, including but not

limited to any of the following: correspondence; letters; memoranda; interoffice memoranda; writings; notes; notebooks; maps; sketches; charts; films and microfilm; studies; plans; analyses; work papers; statistical records; bills and other billing records; receipts; books; press releases; reports; contracts and agreements; records; summaries; memorializations; minutes; agendas or notes of meetings; conferences; telephone calls or other conversations; calendars and diaries; appointment books and message pads; photographs; tape recordings or other audio or video records; handwritten notes or notations in any form; computer tapes, disks, and other data compilations from which information can be obtained and any printouts thereof, including internet postings and email; attachments and enclosures; drafts of any of the foregoing; and all non-identical copies or duplicates of any of the foregoing. For purposes of the foregoing, the term "draft" means any earlier, preliminary, preparatory, or tentative version of all or part of a "document," whether or not such draft was superseded by a later draft and whether or not the terms of the draft are the same as or different from the terms of the final document. The term shall also include any computers or their hard drives that contain or contained any "documents".

3. "Property" refers to the property which is the subject of this lawsuit located at (Property address).

4. "Note" means the Note dated _____, in the amount of $_____ executed by you.

5. "Mortgage" means the Mortgage on the Property dated _____, executed by you.

6. "Loan" means the debt evidenced by the Note and Mortgage.

7. "Identify" means:

    (a) When used with reference to a document state:

(i) The type of document (i.e., letter, memorandum, report, tape, printout, etc.);

(ii) The name of the individual who drafted or prepared the document;

(iii) The present or last known location of the document or other identity of the individual who has custody of the document; and

(iv) Such other information sufficient to enable Plaintiff to identify the document, such as the addressee(s), the approximate length in pages, persons who received copies, and a synopsis of its contents.

(b) When used with reference to a person, state its:

(i) Name;

(ii) Organizational status (i.e., corporation, partnership, etc.);

(iii) Other similar identifying information, with the exception that if the person to be identified is an individual then identify as in subparagraph (c).

(c) When used with reference to an individual, state his or her:

(i) Name;

(ii) Last known residence address;

(iii) Business address;

(iv) Job title or position; and

(v) Other similar identifying information.

(d) When used with reference to a communication:

(i) If written, identify the document as in subparagraph (a); and

APPENDIX A—FORMS AND SAMPLES

(ii) If oral, state the date of the communication and the individuals who sent, received and otherwise had knowledge of the communication, and state the substance thereof.

8. Wherever appropriate in these requests, the singular form of a word shall be interpreted as plural.

9. Wherever appropriate in these requests, the masculine form of a word shall be interpreted as feminine.

10. "And" as well as "or" shall be construed either disjunctively or conjunctively as necessary to bring within the scope of these requests any information which might otherwise be construed to be outside their scope.

11. The terms "concern," "concerning," "relate to," "relates to," "relating to," and "relation to" means consist of, refer to, reflect, or be in any way legally, logically, or factually connected with the matter discussed.

12. With respect to any document for which a privilege is being asserted, identify such document by stating:

(a) The name, title and job or position of document's author;

(b) The name, title and job or position of document's sender;

(c) The name, title and job or position of every person who received or saw the document or any of its copies;

(d) The date of the document;

(e) The physical description of the document, including size, length, typed or handwritten, etc.;

(f) A brief description of the document's subject matter;

(g) The basis for the privilege asserted; and

(h) The name, title and job or position of all persons on behalf of whom the privilege is asserted.

13. With respect to any conversation for which a privilege is being asserted, identify by stating:

(a) When the conversation occurred;

(b) Where the conversation occurred;

(c) The name, title and job or position of each person who was present at or during the conversation whether or not such conversation was in person or by telephone;

(d) A brief description of the conversation's subject matter; and

(e) The name, title and job or position of all persons on behalf of whom the privilege is asserted.

The Defendant is requested to produce at the time and place set forth above the following:

<u>DOCUMENTS REQUESTED</u>

1. Any contracts or other written agreements between you and _____ [*defense counsel*] showing or reflecting the retention or retainer agreement by which _____ was hired to represent you.

2. Any and all documents evidencing proof of payments you have made on the loan that is subject of this action from _____ [*DATE*] through the present date, including, but not limited to, bank statements, cancelled checks, receipts, account ledgers, mortgage coupons, etc.

3. Any documents evidencing your employment for the past ten (10) years.

APPENDIX A—FORMS AND SAMPLES

4. Any documents evidencing your sources of income for the past ten (10) years.

5. All documents, including but not limited to statements, notices, demand letters, correspondence and/or other documentation received by you from the Plaintiff regarding the loan subject of this action and/or foreclosure.

6. All documents, including but not limited to statements, notices, demand letters, correspondence and/or other documentation received by you from any and all entities who have serviced the loan that is the subject of this action.

7. Any and all documents provided to you from any individual and/or entity regarding the loan closing.

8. Any forbearance or loan modification agreements between you and any lenders related to the Property and/or Loan, including but not limited to Plaintiff (and/or its servicers or agents).

9. Any documents memorializing, referencing or describing any oral or written communications, specifically including telephone calls, between you and Plaintiff (and/or its servicers or agents).

10. All documents reflecting any real property tax and/or insurance escrow account payments concerning the Property or Loan made by you from the closing of the Loan to the present.

11. Copies of all cancelled checks, bank statements, financial institution statements, receipts of other documents that evidence or reflect payments or Property taxes, hazard insurance or flood insurance for the Property or Loan made by you or any other person from the date of closing on the Loan to the present.

12. Copies of all insurance policies pertaining to the Property.

13. Notwithstanding the foregoing, all documents supporting or contradicting the allegations in your papers and pleadings filed in this Lawsuit.

14. All documents you intend to introduce at trial.

15. Any and all documents showing proof of income received from any tenants residing in the subject property.

16. Any and all payment histories you have in your possession pertaining to the subject loan.

1-010 SAMPLE REQUEST FOR ADMISSIONS FROM PLAINTIFF TO DEFENDANT

The following sample is for purposes of guidance only and care should be taken to check the case law for any decisions that may impact the claims, and to tailor the discovery to the facts of the specific case.

PLAINTIFF'S REQUEST FOR ADMISSIONS UPON DEFENDANT

Plaintiff, _____, hereby serves its Request for Admissions on Defendant, _____ ("Borrower" or "Defendant") pursuant to Rules 1.280 and 1.370 of the Florida Rules of Civil Procedure, and requests that within thirty (30) days hereof, Defendant admits or denies the following:

DEFINITIONS

For purposes of this Request for Admissions, the following definitions apply and are incorporated into each Request as though fully stated therein:

1. "You" (including "your" and "yours") and "Defendant" and the "Borrower" shall refer to Defendant, _____.

2. "Plaintiff" means _____, as well as all of its successors and assigns, and their counsel and any of their officers, directors, affiliates, shareholders, attorneys, consultants, experts, investigators, agents or other persons acting on their behalf.

3. "Property" refers to the property which is the subject of this lawsuit located at _____.

4. "Note" means the Note dated _____, in the amount of $_____ executed by you.

5. "Mortgage" means the Mortgage on the Property dated _____, executed by you.

6. "Loan" means the debt evidenced by the Note and Mortgage.

STATEMENTS TO BE ADMITTED OR DENIED

1. Admit that you signed the promissory note, a copy of which is attached hereto as Exhibit A.

2. Admit that you signed the mortgage, a copy of which is attached hereto as Exhibit B.

3. Admit that you did not pay the monthly payment for the loan which was due on _____.

4. Admit that you have not paid any of the monthly payments for the loan which have come due since _____.

5. Admit that you are in default on your loan.

6. Admit that you received notice of your default of the Loan.

7. Admit that you received the [Notice of Intent to Accelerate], a copy of which is attached hereto as Exhibit C.

8. Admit that you failed to cure the default after receiving notice.

9. Admit that Plaintiff is entitled to enforce the terms of the Note and Mortgage.

10. Admit that, at the time you purchased the Property, you could comprehend the fact that you were signing a Note and Mortgage related to the purchase or financing of the property.

11. Admit that you were not incompetent at the time you signed the Note and Mortgage.

12. Admit that at the time you signed the Mortgage, you understood the effect and significance of the transaction.

13. Admit that the loan was not originated as a result of fraud.

1-011 SAMPLE INTERROGATORIES FROM PLAINTIFF TO DEFENDANT

The following sample is for purposes of guidance only and care should be taken to check the case law for any decisions that may impact the claims, and to tailor the discovery to the facts of the specific case.

PLAINTIFF'S INTERROGATORIES TO DEFENDANT

Pursuant to Florida Rule of Civil Procedure 1.340, Plaintiff, _____, by and through its undersigned attorneys, propounds the following Interrogatories to be answered by Defendant, _____, in writing and under oath within thirty (30) days from the date of service.

DEFINITIONS

1. "Communications" means any oral or written statement, dialogue, colloquialism, discussion, conversation or agreement.

2. "Document" means any written, recorded, imaged or graphic matter or other means of preserving thought or expression, and all tangible things from which information can be processed or transcribed, including the originals and all non-identical copies, whether different from the original by reason of any notation made on such copy or otherwise, including, but not limited to correspondence, memoranda, notes, messages, letters, telegrams, teletype, telefax, bulletins, meetings, or other communications, interoffice and intraoffice telephone calls, diaries, chronological data, minutes, books, reports, charts, ledgers, invoices, worksheets, receipts, returns, computer printouts, prospectuses, financial statements, schedules, affidavits, contracts, canceled checks, transcripts, statistics, surveys, magazine or newspaper articles, releases (and any and all drafts, alterations and modifications, changes and amendments of any of the foregoing), graphs or aural records or representations of any kind, including without limitation, photographs, charts,

graphs, microfiche, microfilm, videotape, recordings, motion pictures and electronic, mechanical or electric recordings, or representations of any kind (including without limitation, tapes, cassettes, discs and recordings), and including the file and file cover.

3. "You" (including "your" and "yours") and "Defendant" and the "Borrower" shall refer to Defendant, _____.

4. "Plaintiff" means _____, as well as all of its successors and assigns, and their counsel and any of their officers, directors, affiliates, shareholders, attorneys, consultants, experts, investigators, agents or other persons acting on their behalf.

5. "Property" refers to the property which is the subject of this lawsuit located at _____.

6. "Note" means the Note dated _____, in the amount of $_____ executed by you.

7. "Mortgage" means the Mortgage on the Property dated _____, executed by you.

8. "Loan" means the debt evidenced by the Note and Mortgage.

9. "Identify" means:

(a) When used with reference to a document state:

(i) The type of document (i.e., letter, memorandum, report, tape, printout, etc.);

(ii) The name of the individual who drafted or prepared the document;

(iii) The present or last known location of the document or other identity of the individual who has custody of the document; and

(iv) Such other information sufficient to enable Plaintiff to identify the document, such as the addressee(s), the approximate length in pages, persons who received copies, and a synopsis of its contents.

(b) When used with reference to an entity or business, state its:

    (i) Name;

    (ii) Organizational status (i.e., corporation, partnership, etc.);

    (iii) Business address; and

    (iv) Other similar identifying information, with the exception that if the person to be identified is an individual then identify as in subparagraph (c).

(c) When used with reference to an individual, state his or her:

    (i) Name;

    (ii) Last known residence address;

    (iii) Business address;

    (iv) Job title or position; and

    (v) Other similar identifying information.

(d) When used with reference to a communication:

    (i) If written, identify the document as in subparagraph (a); and

    (ii) If oral, state the date of the communication and the individuals who sent, received and otherwise had knowledge of the communication, and state the substance thereof.

10. Wherever appropriate in these requests, the singular form of a word shall be interpreted as plural.

11. Wherever appropriate in these requests, the masculine form of a word shall be interpreted as feminine.

12. The terms "concern," "concerning," "relate to," "relates to," "relating to," and "relation to" means consist of, refer to, reflect, or be in any way legally, logically, or factually connected with the matter discussed.

APPENDIX A—FORMS AND SAMPLES

13. With respect to any document for which a privilege is being asserted, identify such document by stating:

   (a) The name, title and job or position of document's author;

   (b) The name, title and job or position of document's sender;

   (c) The name, title and job or position of every person who received or saw the document or any of its copies;

   (d) The date of the document;

   (e) The physical description of the document, including size, length, typed or handwritten, etc.;

   (f) A brief description of the document's subject matter;

   (g) The basis for the privilege asserted; and

   (h) The name, title and job or position of all persons on behalf of whom the privilege is asserted.

14. With respect to any conversation for which a privilege is being asserted, identify by stating:

   (a) When the conversation occurred;

   (b) Where the conversation occurred;

   (c) The name, title and job or position of each person who was present at or during the conversation whether or not such conversation was in person or by telephone;

   (d) A brief description of the conversation's subject matter; and

   (e) The name, title and job or position of all persons on behalf of whom the privilege is asserted.

INSTRUCTIONS

1. If all of the information furnished in answer to all or part of an interrogatory is not within your personal knowledge, identify each person to whom all or part of the information furnished is a matter of personal knowledge and each person who communicated to you any part of the information furnished.

2. Instead of identifying any document, you may attach a copy of such document or communication as an exhibit to your answer to these interrogatories and specify to which interrogatory the document applies.

3. If you object to any interrogatory, in whole or in part, on the ground that it requests privileged information within the work-product doctrine:

> (a) Identify the document, the date and subject matter of the document, the name of the addressee, and all parties who have seen the document;
>
> (b) If your objection refers to an oral communication, identify who made the communication and all parties who heard it, the date the communication was made, and the subject matter of it.

INTERROGATORIES

1. What is the name and address of the person answering these interrogatories, and, if applicable, the person's official position or relationship with the party to whom the interrogatories are directed?

2. Do you contend that on or after _____, 20___ any payment was made on the promissory note and mortgage subject of this action? If your answer is yes, state the date of each payment, the amount of each payment, and the full name of the person who made the payment.

3. State the following information for each payment you made on the loan:

a. Date;

b. Amount;

c. Method;

d. Name and address of person or entity to whom payment was sent.

4. State the facts upon which you rely for each affirmative defense in your answer.

5. Do you deny that you signed the promissory note or mortgage which are the subject of this action? If the answer is yes, state which document (the promissory note or mortgage) was not signed, and state how to your knowledge your name came to appear to be signed on the document.

6. List the names and addresses of all persons who are believed or known by you, your agents, or your attorneys to have any knowledge concerning any of the issues in this lawsuit; and specify the subject matter about which the witness has knowledge.

7. Do you intend to call any expert witnesses at the trial of this case? If so, state as to each such witness the name and business address of the witness, the witness's qualifications as an expert, the subject matter upon which the witness is expected to testify, the substance of the facts and opinions to which the witness is expected to testify, and a summary of the grounds for each opinion.

1-012 SAMPLE REFERENCE CHART: EVIDENTIARY BASIS FOR INTRODUCTION OF TRIAL EXHIBITS – PREPARED BY RICHARD BASSETT

This is a quick reference guide which may be used at trial while considering the statutory basis for entry of certain exhibits into evidence. While this guide has proven helpful in many successful trials, some lawyers make different arguments for the same documents. Every trial lawyer should carefully consider alternate bases for the entry of exhibits (for example, statements of independent legal significance).

EVIDENTIARY BASIS FOR INTRODUCTION OF TRIAL EXHIBITS

- **POWER OF ATTORNEY**
    - If recorded
        - Fla. Stat § 90.803(8): public record
    - If not recorded
        - Fla. Stat § 90.803(6): business record exception to hearsay.
- **NOTE**
    - Original note filed at trial
        - Fla. Stat. § 90.902(8): self-authenticating commercial paper
    - Original note filed before trial
        - Fla. Stat. § 90.902(8): self-authenticating commercial paper
        - Fla. Stat. §90.202(6): court can take judicial notice of court record
- **MORTGAGE**
    - Original/copy of original mortgage filed at trial
        - Fla. Stat. § 90.803(14): record affecting an interest in property
    - Original/copy of original mortgage filed before trial
        - Fla. Stat. § 90.803(14): record affecting an interest in property
        - Fla. Stat. § 90.202(6): court can take judicial notice of court record
    - Certified copy of original mortgage
        - Fla. Stat. § 90.902(4): self-authenticating copy of document authorized to be recorded and actually recorded
- **DEMAND LETTER/RETURN RECIPT CARD/COLLECTION NOTES**
    - Fla. Stat. § 90.803(6): business record exception to hearsay
- **LOAN PAYMENT HISTORY**
    - Fla. Stat. § 90.803(6): business record exception to hearsay
- **POOLING AND SERVICING AGREEMENT (PSA)**
    - Fla. Stat. § 90.803(17) Exception to Hearsay – Market Reports, Commercial Publication.

APPENDIX A—FORMS AND SAMPLES

- o Certified copy of Pooling and Servicing Agreement
  - Fla. Stat. § 90.902(1): self-authenticating copy of document containing the seal of a government agency and signature of custodian (Securities and Exchange Commission)
- **MORTGAGE LOAN SCHEDULE** (typically part of PSA although not published with PSA due to confidential information – file as composite with PSA)
  - o Fla. Stat. § 90.803(17) Exception to Hearsay – Market Reports, Commercial Publication
- **CERTIFIED AOM**
  - o Fla. Stat § 90.803(8): public record
- **HELLO-GOODBYE LETTER**
  - o Fla. Stat. § 90.803(6): business record exception to hearsay
- **SEC DOCUMENT**
  - o Fla. Stat. § 90.803(17) Exception to Hearsay – Market Reports, Commercial Publication
  - o Fla. Stat. § 90.202(12): court can take judicial notice of the document and facts contained therein because from a source whose accuracy cannot be questioned.
- **DOCUMENT CONTAINING A SEAL**
  - o Fla. Stat. § 90.202(13): court can judicial notice of document containing official seal of government agency or department or of any state
- **JUDGMENT FIGURES**
  - o Fla. Stat. § 90.956: summaries (but note that timely written notice of intent to use summary must be provided, proof of which shall be filed with the court)

1-013 SAMPLE FINAL JUDGMENT

IN THE CIRCUIT COURT OF THE [   ]
JUDICIAL CIRCUIT IN AND FOR [   ]
COUNTY, FLORIDA

GENERAL JURISDICTION DIVISION
CASE NO. [   ]

PLAINTIFF A.B.,

    Plaintiff,

vs.

DEFENDANTS, C.D.;

    Defendants.

_____/

FINAL JUDGMENT OF FORECLOSURE
AND RE-ESTABLISHMENT OF LOST NOTE

This action was tried before the court. On the evidence presented, IT IS ADJUDGED that:

1. Plaintiff, [_____], whose address is [_____], is due:

    Principal: _____
    Interest to Date
    of This Judgment: _____
    Title Search Expenses: _____
    Taxes: _____
    Attorneys' Fees Total: _____
    Court costs, now taxed: _____
    Other: _____

    Subtotal: _____
    LESS Escrow Balance: _____
    LESS Other: _____

    TOTAL: _____

That shall bear interest at a rate of 7% per year.

2. **Lien on Property.** Plaintiff holds a lien for the total sum superior to all claims or estates of Defendant(s), on the following described property in [_____] County, Florida:

    Include Property Legal Description

APPENDIX A—FORMS AND SAMPLES 375

3. **Sale of Property.** If the total sum with interest at the rate described in paragraph 1 and all costs accrued subsequent to this judgment are not paid, the clerk of this court shall sell the property at public sale on [__date__], to the highest bidder for cash, except as prescribed in paragraph 4, at the courthouse located at [__street address of courthouse__] in [_____] County in [_____], Florida, in accordance with section 45.031, Florida Statutes (2013), using the following method (CHECK ONE):

-At [__location of sale at courthouse__], beginning at [_time_] on the prescribed date.
-By electronic sale beginning at [_time_] on the prescribed date at [website]

4. **Costs.** Plaintiff shall advance all subsequent costs of this action and shall be reimbursed for them by the clerk if Plaintiff is not the purchaser of the property for sale, provided, however, that the purchaser of the property for sale shall be responsible for the documentary stamps payable on the certificate of title. If Plaintiff is the purchaser, the clerk shall credit Plaintiff's bid with the total sum with interest and costs accruing subsequent to this judgment, or such part of it as is necessary to pay the bid in full.

5. **Distribution of Proceeds.** On filing the Certificate of Title, the clerk shall distribute the proceeds of the sale, so far as they are sufficient, by paying: first, all of Plaintiff's costs; second, documentary stamps affixed to the certificate; third, Plaintiff's attorneys' fees; fourth, the total sum due to Plaintiff, less the items paid, plus interest at the rate prescribed in paragraph 1 from this date to the date of the sale; and by retaining any remaining amount pending further order of this court.

6. **Right of Redemption/Right of Possession.** On filing the certificate of sale, Defendant(s) and all persons claiming under or against Defendant(s) since the filing of the notice of lis pendens shall be foreclosed of all estate or claim in the property and Defendant's right of redemption as prescribed by section 45.0315, Florida Statutes (2013) shall be terminated, except as to claims or rights under chapter 718 or chapter 720, Florida Statutes, if any. Upon the filing of the certificate of title, the person named on the certificate of title shall be let into possession of the property.

7. **Attorneys' Fees.**

[If a default judgment has been entered against the mortgagor]

Because a default judgment has been entered against the mortgagor and because the fees requested do not exceed 3% of the principal amount owed at the time the complaint was filed, it is not necessary for the court to hold a hearing or adjudge the requested attorneys' fees to be reasonable.

[If no default judgment has been entered against the mortgagor]

The court finds, based upon the affidavits/testimony presented and upon inquiry of counsel for the Plaintiff that ___ hours were reasonably expended by Plaintiff's counsel and that an hourly rate of $_____ is appropriate. Plaintiff's counsel represents that the attorneys' fees awarded does not exceed its contractual fee with Plaintiff. The court finds that there is/are no reduction or enhancement factors for consideration by the court pursuant to *Florida Patients Compensation*

Fund v. Rowe, 472 So. 2d 1145 (Fla. 1985). (If the court has found that there are reduction or enhancement factors to be applied, then such factors must be identified and explained herein).

[If the fees to be awarded are a flat fee]

The requested attorneys' fees are a flat rate fee that the firm's client has agreed to pay in this matter. Given the amount of the fee requested and the labor expended, the court finds that a lodestar analysis is not necessary and that the flat fee is reasonable.

8. Re-establishment of Lost Note. The court finds that Plaintiff has re-established the terms of the lost note and its right to enforce the instrument as required by applicable law. Plaintiff shall hold Defendant(s) maker of the note harmless and shall indemnify Defendant(s) for any loss Defendant(s) may incur by reason of a claim by any other person to enforce the lost note. Adequate protection has been provided as required by law by the following means:

[identify means of security under applicable law: a written indemnification agreement, a surety bond, include specific detail]

Judgment is hereby entered in favor of Plaintiff as to its request to enforce the lost note.

9. Jurisdiction Retained. Jurisdiction of this action is retained to enter further orders that are proper including, without limitation, a deficiency judgment.

IF THIS PROPERTY IS SOLD AT PUBLIC AUCTION, THERE MAY BE ADDITIONAL MONEY FROM THE SALE AFTER PAYMENT OF PERSONS WHO ARE ENTITLED TO BE PAID FROM THE SALE PROCEEDS PURSUANT TO THE FINAL JUDGMENT.

IF YOU ARE A SUBORDINATE LIENHOLDER CLAIMING A RIGHT TO FUNDS REMAINING AFTER THE SALE, YOU MUST FILE A CLAIM WITH THE CLERK NO LATER THAN 60 DAYS AFTER THE SALE. IF YOU FAIL TO FILE A CLAIM, YOU WILL NOT BE ENTITLED TO ANY REMAINING FUNDS.

[If the property being foreclosed on has qualified for the homestead tax exemption in the most recent approved tax roll, the final judgment shall additionally contain the following statement in conspicuous type:]

IF YOU ARE THE PROPERTY OWNER, YOU MAY CLAIM THESE FUNDS YOURSELF. YOU ARE NOT REQUIRED TO HAVE A LAWYER OR ANY OTHER REPRESENTATION AND YOU DO NOT HAVE TO ASSIGN YOUR RIGHTS TO ANYONE ELSE IN ORDER FOR YOU TO CLAIM ANY MONEY TO WHICH YOU ARE ENTITLED. PLEASE CONTACT THE CLERK OF THE COURT, [INSERT INFORMATION FOR APPLICABLE COURT] WITHIN 10 DAYS AFTER THE SALE TO SEE IF THERE IS ADDITIONAL MONEY FROM THE FORECLOSURE SALE THAT THE CLERK HAS IN THE REGISTRY OF THE COURT.

IF YOU DECIDE TO SELL YOUR HOME OR HIRE SOMEONE TO HELP YOU CLAIM THE ADDITIONAL MONEY, YOU SHOULD READ VERY CAREFULLY ALL PAPERS YOU ARE REQUIRED TO SIGN, ASK SOMEONE ELSE, PREFERABLY AN ATTORNEY WHO IS NOT RELATED TO THE PERSON OFFERING TO HELP YOU, TO MAKE SURE THAT YOU UNDERSTAND WHAT YOU ARE SIGNING AND THAT YOU ARE NOT TRANSFERRING YOUR PROPERTY OR THE EQUITY IN YOUR PROPERTY WITHOUT THE PROPER INFORMATION. IF YOU CANNOT AFFORD TO PAY AN ATTORNEY, YOU MAY CONTACT [INSERT LOCAL OR NEAREST LEGAL AID OFFICE AND TELEPHONE NUMBER] **TO SEE IF YOU QUALIFY FINANCIALLY FOR THEIR SERVICES. IF THEY CANNOT ASSIST YOU, THEY MAY BE ABLE TO REFER YOU TO A LOCAL BAR REFERRAL AGENCY OR SUGGEST OTHER OPTIONS. IF YOU CHOOSE TO CONTACT** [NAME OF LOCAL OR NEAREST LEGAL AID OFFICE AND TELEPHONE NUMBER] **FOR ASSISTANCE, YOU SHOULD DO SO AS SOON AS POSSIBLE AFTER RECEIPT OF THIS NOTICE.**

ORDERED at [City], [County], Florida, on _____, 20__.

  [Judge's Name], Circuit Judge

NOTE (as provided by Florida Rules of Civil Procedure Form 1.996(b)): Paragraph 1 must be varied in accordance with the items unpaid, claimed, and proven. The form does not provide for an adjudication of junior lienors' claims nor for redemption by the United States of America if it is a defendant. The address of the person who claims a lien as a result of the judgment must be included in the judgment in order for the judgment to become a lien on real estate when a certified copy of the judgment is recorded. Alternatively, an affidavit with this information may be simultaneously recorded. For the specific requirements, see section 55.10(1), Florida Statutes; *Hott Interiors, Inc. v. Fostock*, 721 So.2d 1236 (Fla. 4th DCA 1998).

1-014 SAMPLE FINAL JUDGMENT WITH RE-ESTABLISHMENT OF NOTE

IN THE CIRCUIT COURT OF THE [____] JUDICIAL CIRCUIT IN AND FOR [____] COUNTY, FLORIDA

GENERAL JURISDICTION DIVISION
CASE NO. [_____]

PLAINTIFF A.B.,

    Plaintiff,

vs.

DEFENDANTS, C.D.;

    Defendants.
_____/

FINAL JUDGMENT OF FORECLOSURE

This action was tried before the court. On the evidence presented, IT IS ADJUDGED that:

1. Plaintiff, [_____], whose address is [_____], is due:
   - Principal: _____
   - Interest to Date of This Judgment: _____
   - Title Search Expenses: _____
   - Taxes: _____
   - Attorneys' Fees Total: _____
   - Court costs, now taxed: _____
   - Other: _____

   Subtotal: _____
   - LESS Escrow Balance: _____
   - LESS Other: _____

   TOTAL: _____

That shall bear interest at a rate of 7% per year.

2. **Lien on Property.** Plaintiff holds a lien for the total sum superior to all claims or estates of Defendant(s), on the following described property in [_____] County, Florida:

Include Property Legal Description

3. **Sale of Property.** If the total sum with interest at the rate described in paragraph 1 and all costs accrued subsequent to this judgment are not paid, the clerk of this court shall sell the property at public sale on [__date__], to the highest bidder for cash, except as prescribed in paragraph 4, at the courthouse located at [__street address of courthouse__] in [_____] County in [_____], Florida, in accordance with section 45.031, Florida Statutes (2013), using the following method (CHECK ONE):

-At [__location of sale at courthouse__], beginning at [__time__] on the prescribed date.
-By electronic sale beginning at [__time__] on the prescribed date at [website]

4. **Costs.** Plaintiff shall advance all subsequent costs of this action and shall be reimbursed for them by the clerk if Plaintiff is not the purchaser of the property for sale, provided, however, that the purchaser of the property for sale shall be responsible for the documentary stamps payable on the certificate of title. If Plaintiff is the purchaser, the clerk shall credit Plaintiff's bid with the total sum with interest and costs accruing subsequent to this judgment, or such part of it as is necessary to pay the bid in full.

5. **Distribution of Proceeds.** On filing the Certificate of Title, the clerk shall distribute the proceeds of the sale, so far as they are sufficient, by paying: first, all of Plaintiff's costs; second, documentary stamps affixed to the certificate; third, Plaintiff's attorneys' fees; fourth, the total sum due to Plaintiff, less the items paid, plus interest at the rate prescribed in paragraph 1 from this date to the date of the sale; and by retaining any remaining amount pending further order of this court.

6. **Right of Redemption/Right of Possession.** On filing the certificate of sale, Defendant(s) and all persons claiming under or against Defendant(s) since the filing of the notice of lis pendens shall be foreclosed of all estate or claim in the property and Defendant's right of redemption as prescribed by section 45.0315, Florida Statutes (2013) shall be terminated, except as to claims or rights under chapter 718 or chapter 720, Florida Statutes, if any. Upon the filing of the certificate of title, the person named on the certificate of title shall be let into possession of the property.

7. **Attorneys' Fees.**

[If a default judgment has been entered against the mortgagor]

Because a default judgment has been entered against the mortgagor and because the fees requested do not exceed 3% of the principal amount owed at the time the complaint was filed, it is not necessary for the court to hold a hearing or adjudge the requested attorneys' fees to be reasonable.

[If no default judgment has been entered against the mortgagor]

The court finds, based upon the affidavits/testimony presented and upon inquiry of counsel for the Plaintiff that ___ hours were reasonably expended by Plaintiff's counsel and that an hourly rate of $_____ is appropriate. Plaintiff's counsel represents that the attorneys' fees awarded does not exceed its contractual fee with Plaintiff. The court finds that there is/are no reduction or enhancement factors for consideration by the court pursuant to *Florida Patients Compensation*

Fund v. Rowe, 472 So. 2d 1145 (Fla. 1985). (If the court has found that there are reduction or enhancement factors to be applied, then such factors must be identified and explained herein).

[If the fees to be awarded are a flat fee]

The requested attorneys' fees are a flat rate fee that the firm's client has agreed to pay in this matter. Given the amount of the fee requested and the labor expended, the court finds that a lodestar analysis is not necessary and that the flat fee is reasonable.

8. **Jurisdiction Retained.** Jurisdiction of this action is retained to enter further orders that are proper including, without limitation, a deficiency judgment.

IF THIS PROPERTY IS SOLD AT PUBLIC AUCTION, THERE MAY BE ADDITIONAL MONEY FROM THE SALE AFTER PAYMENT OF PERSONS WHO ARE ENTITLED TO BE PAID FROM THE SALE PROCEEDS PURSUANT TO THE FINAL JUDGMENT.

IF YOU ARE A SUBORDINATE LIENHOLDER CLAIMING A RIGHT TO FUNDS REMAINING AFTER THE SALE, YOU MUST FILE A CLAIM WITH THE CLERK NO LATER THAN 60 DAYS AFTER THE SALE. IF YOU FAIL TO FILE A CLAIM, YOU WILL NOT BE ENTITLED TO ANY REMAINING FUNDS.

[If the property being foreclosed on has qualified for the homestead tax exemption in the most recent approved tax roll, the final judgment shall additionally contain the following statement in conspicuous type:]

IF YOU ARE THE PROPERTY OWNER, YOU MAY CLAIM THESE FUNDS YOURSELF. YOU ARE NOT REQUIRED TO HAVE A LAWYER OR ANY OTHER REPRESENTATION AND YOU DO NOT HAVE TO ASSIGN YOUR RIGHTS TO ANYONE ELSE IN ORDER FOR YOU TO CLAIM ANY MONEY TO WHICH YOU ARE ENTITLED. PLEASE CONTACT THE CLERK OF THE COURT, [INSERT INFORMATION FOR APPLICABLE COURT] **WITHIN 10 DAYS AFTER THE SALE TO SEE IF THERE IS ADDITIONAL MONEY FROM THE FORECLOSURE SALE THAT THE CLERK HAS IN THE REGISTRY OF THE COURT.**

IF YOU DECIDE TO SELL YOUR HOME OR HIRE SOMEONE TO HELP YOU CLAIM THE ADDITIONAL MONEY, YOU SHOULD READ VERY CAREFULLY ALL PAPERS YOU ARE REQUIRED TO SIGN, ASK SOMEONE ELSE, PREFERABLY AN ATTORNEY WHO IS NOT RELATED TO THE PERSON OFFERING TO HELP YOU, TO MAKE SURE THAT YOU UNDERSTAND WHAT YOU ARE SIGNING AND THAT YOU ARE NOT TRANSFERRING YOUR PROPERTY OR THE EQUITY IN YOUR PROPERTY WITHOUT THE PROPER INFORMATION. IF YOU CANNOT AFFORD TO PAY AN ATTORNEY, YOU MAY CONTACT [INSERT LOCAL OR NEAREST LEGAL AID OFFICE AND TELEPHONE NUMBER] **TO SEE IF YOU QUALIFY FINANCIALLY FOR THEIR SERVICES. IF THEY CANNOT ASSIST YOU, THEY MAY BE ABLE TO REFER YOU TO A LOCAL BAR REFERRAL AGENCY OR**

SUGGEST OTHER OPTIONS. IF YOU CHOOSE TO CONTACT [NAME OF LOCAL OR NEAREST LEGAL AID OFFICE AND TELEPHONE NUMBER] **FOR ASSISTANCE, YOU SHOULD DO SO AS SOON AS POSSIBLE AFTER RECEIPT OF THIS NOTICE.**

ORDERED at [City], [County], Florida, on _____, 20__.

[Judge's Name], Circuit Judge

NOTE (as provided by Florida Rules of Civil Procedure 1.996(a)): Paragraph 1 must be varied in accordance with the items unpaid, claimed, and proven. The form does not provide for an adjudication of junior lienors' claims nor for redemption by the United States of America if it is a defendant. The address of the person who claims a lien as a result of the judgment must be included in the judgment in order for the judgment to become a lien on real estate when a certified copy of the judgment is recorded. Alternatively, an affidavit with this information may be simultaneously recorded. For the specific requirements, see section 55.10(1), Florida Statutes; *Hott Interiors, Inc. v. Fostock*, 721 So.2d 1236 (Fla. 4th DCA 1998).

1-015 SAMPLE AFFIDAVIT OF COMPLIANCE

IN THE CIRCUIT COURT OF THE [____]
JUDICIAL CIRCUIT IN AND FOR [____]
COUNTY, FLORIDA

GENERAL JURISDICTION DIVISION
CASE NO. [_____]

PLAINTIFF A.B.,

    Plaintiff,

vs.

DEFENDANTS, C.D.;

    Defendants.

_____/

AFFIDAVIT OF COMPLIANCE

STATE OF FLORIDA
COUNTY OF [_____]

BEFORE ME, the undersigned authority, personally appeared [_____] who, after being first duly sworn, deposes and states, under penalty of perjury:

1. I am the plaintiff [or Plaintiff's _____] (identify relationship to Plaintiff).

2. I am executing this affidavit in support of Plaintiff's Complaint against Defendants and I have personal knowledge of the matters set forth herein.

3. On [date], the public records reflect that Defendant executed and delivered a mortgage securing the payment of the Note to [_____]. The mortgage was recorded on [date

APPENDIX A—FORMS AND SAMPLES

], in Official Records Book [___] at page [___] of the public records of [_____] County, Florida, and mortgaged the property described therein, which was then owned by and in possession of the mortgagor, a copy of the Mortgage and the Note being attached.

4. (select a, b, c, or d) Plaintiff cannot reasonably obtain possession of the Note because

    (a) the Note was destroyed.

    (b) the Note is lost.

    (c) the Note is in the wrongful possession of an unknown person.

    (d) the Note is in the wrongful possession of a person who cannot be found or is not amenable to service of process.

5. (select a, b, c, or d)

    (a) At the time the original Note was lost, Plaintiff was the holder of the original Note secured by the Mortgage.

    (b) At the time the original Note was lost, Plaintiff was a person entitled to enforce the Note under applicable law because [allege specific facts].

    (c) Plaintiff has directly or indirectly acquired ownership of the Note from a person who was entitled to enforce the Note when loss of possession occurred as follows: [allege specific facts].

    (d) Plaintiff has been delegated the authority to institute a mortgage foreclosure action on behalf of the person entitled to enforce the Note, and the document(s) that grant(s) plaintiff the authority to act on behalf of the person entitled to enforce the Note is/are as follows [_____].

    (attach copy of document(s) or relevant portion(s) of the document(s)).

6. Below is the clear chain of the endorsements, transfers, allonges or assignments of the note and all documents that evidence same as are available to Plaintiff: [identify in chronological order all endorsements, transfers, assignments of, allonges to, the note or other evidence of the acquisition, ownership and possession of the note]. Correct copies of the foregoing documents are attached to this affidavit.

7. Plaintiff did not transfer the Note or lose possession of it as the result of a lawful seizure.

FURTHER, AFFIANT SAYETH NAUGHT.

_____
[signature]

_____
[typed or printed name of affiant]

STATE OF FLORIDA
COUNTY OF [_____]

BEFORE ME, the undersigned authority appeared _____, who [is personally known to me] or [produced identification] and acknowledged that he/she executed the foregoing instrument for the purposes expressed therein and who did take an oath.

WITNESS my hand and seal in the State and County aforesaid, this ____date of _____, 20__.

_____
NOTARY PUBLIC, State of Florida

Print Name: _____

Commission Expires: _____

1-016 FORM: FLORIDA STANDARD ADJUSTABLE RATE NOTE

ADJUSTABLE RATE NOTE
(1 Year Treasury Index -- Rate Caps)

THIS NOTE CONTAINS PROVISIONS ALLOWING FOR CHANGES IN MY INTEREST RATE AND MY MONTHLY PAYMENT. THIS NOTE LIMITS THE AMOUNT MY INTEREST RATE CAN CHANGE AT ANY ONE TIME AND THE MAXIMUM RATE I MUST PAY.

_____, _____   _____, _____
[Date]   [City]   [State]

_____
[Property Address]

1. BORROWER'S PROMISE TO PAY
In return for a loan that I have received, I promise to pay U.S. $_____ (this amount is called "Principal"), plus interest, to the order of the Lender. The Lender is _____
_____. I will make all payments under this Note in the form of cash, check or money order.
I understand that the Lender may transfer this Note. The Lender or anyone who takes this Note by transfer and who is entitled to receive payments under this Note is called the "Note Holder."

2. INTEREST
Interest will be charged on unpaid principal until the full amount of Principal has been paid. I will pay interest at a yearly rate of _____ %. The interest rate I will pay will change in accordance with Section 4 of this Note.
The interest rate required by this Section 2 and Section 4 of this Note is the rate I will pay both before and after any default described in Section 7(B) of this Note.

3. PAYMENTS
  (A) Time and Place of Payments
I will pay principal and interest by making a payment every month.
I will make my monthly payment on the first day of each month beginning on _____, _____. I will make these payments every month until I have paid all of the principal and interest and any other charges described below that I may owe under this Note. Each monthly payment will be applied as of its scheduled due date and will be applied to interest before Principal. If, on _____, 20____, I still owe amounts under this Note, I will pay those amounts in full on that date, which is called the "Maturity Date."
I will make my monthly payments at _____
_____ or at a different place if required by the Note Holder.
  (B) Amount of My Initial Monthly Payments
Each of my initial monthly payments will be in the amount of U.S. $_____. This amount may change.
  (C) Monthly Payment Changes
Changes in my monthly payment will reflect changes in the unpaid principal of my loan and in the interest rate that I must pay. The Note Holder will determine my new interest rate and the changed amount of my monthly payment in accordance with Section 4 of this Note.

4. INTEREST RATE AND MONTHLY PAYMENT CHANGES
  (A) Change Dates
The interest rate I will pay may change on the first day of _____, _____, and on that day every 12th month thereafter. Each date on which my interest rate could change is called a "Change Date."
  (B) The Index
Beginning with the first Change Date, my interest rate will be based on an Index. The "Index" is the weekly average yield on United States Treasury securities adjusted to a constant maturity of one year, as made available by the Federal Reserve Board. The most recent Index figure available as of the date 45 days before each Change Date is called the "Current Index."
If the Index is no longer available, the Note Holder will choose a new index which is based upon comparable information. The Note Holder will give me notice of this choice.

(C) Calculation of Changes

Before each Change Date, the Note Holder will calculate my new interest rate by adding _____ percentage points (_____%) to the Current Index. The Note Holder will then round the result of this addition to the nearest one-eighth of one percentage point (0.125%). Subject to the limits stated in Section 4(D) below, this rounded amount will be my new interest rate until the next Change Date.

The Note Holder will then determine the amount of the monthly payment that would be sufficient to repay the unpaid principal that I am expected to owe at the Change Date in full on the Maturity Date at my new interest rate in substantially equal payments. The result of this calculation will be the new amount of my monthly payment.

(D) Limits on Interest Rate Changes

The interest rate I am required to pay at the first Change Date will not be greater than _____% or less than _____%. Thereafter, my interest rate will never be increased or decreased on any single Change Date by more than one percentage point (1.0%) from the rate of interest I have been paying for the preceding 12 months. My interest rate will never be greater than _____%.

(E) Effective Date of Changes

My new interest rate will become effective on each Change Date. I will pay the amount of my new monthly payment beginning on the first monthly payment date after the Change Date until the amount of my monthly payment changes again.

(F) Notice of Changes

The Note Holder will deliver or mail to me a notice of any changes in my interest rate and the amount of my monthly payment before the effective date of any change. The notice will include information required by law to be given to me and also the title and telephone number of a person who will answer any question I may have regarding the notice.

5. BORROWER'S RIGHT TO PREPAY

I have the right to make payments of Principal at any time before they are due. A payment of Principal only is known as a "Prepayment." When I make a Prepayment, I will tell the Note Holder in writing that I am doing so. I may not designate a payment as a Prepayment if I have not made all the monthly payments due under the Note.

I may make a full Prepayment or partial Prepayments without paying a Prepayment charge. The Note Holder will use my Prepayments to reduce the amount of Principal that I owe under this Note. However, the Note Holder may apply my Prepayment to the accrued and unpaid interest on the Prepayment amount, before applying my Prepayment to reduce the Principal amount of the Note. If I make a partial Prepayment, there will be no changes in the due dates of my monthly payment unless the Note Holder agrees in writing to those changes. My partial Prepayment may reduce the amount of my monthly payments after the first Change Date following my partial Prepayment. However, any reduction due to my partial Prepayment may be offset by an interest rate increase.

6. LOAN CHARGES

If a law, which applies to this loan and which sets maximum loan charges, is finally interpreted so that the interest or other loan charges collected or to be collected in connection with this loan exceed the permitted limits, then: (a) any such loan charge shall be reduced by the amount necessary to reduce the charge to the permitted limit; and (b) any sums already collected from me which exceeded permitted limits will be refunded to me. The Note Holder may choose to make this refund by reducing the Principal I owe under this Note or by making a direct payment to me. If a refund reduces Principal, the reduction will be treated as a partial Prepayment.

7. BORROWER'S FAILURE TO PAY AS REQUIRED

(A) Late Charges for Overdue Payments

If the Note Holder has not received the full amount of any monthly payment by the end of _____ calendar days after the date it is due, I will pay a late charge to the Note Holder. The amount of the charge will be _____% of my overdue payment of principal and interest. I will pay this late charge promptly but only once on each late payment.

(B) Default

If I do not pay the full amount of each monthly payment on the date it is due, I will be in default.

(C) Notice of Default

If I am in default, the Note Holder may send me a written notice telling me that if I do not pay the overdue amount by a certain date, the Note Holder may require me to pay immediately the full amount of Principal which has not been paid and all the interest that I owe on that amount. That date must be at least 30 days after the date on which the notice is mailed to me or delivered by other means.

(D) No Waiver By Note Holder

Even if, at a time when I am in default, the Note Holder does not require me to pay immediately in full as described above, the Note Holder will still have the right to do so if I am in default at a later time.

(E) Payment of Note Holder's Costs and Expenses

If the Note Holder has required me to pay immediately in full as described above, the Note Holder will have the right

APPENDIX A—FORMS AND SAMPLES

to be paid back by me for all of its costs and expenses in enforcing this Note to the extent not prohibited by applicable law. Those expenses include, for example, reasonable attorneys' fees.

8. GIVING OF NOTICES

Unless applicable law requires a different method, any notice that must be given to me under this Note will be given by delivering it or by mailing it by first class mail to me at the Property Address above or a different address if I give the Note Holder a notice of my different address.

Any notice that must be given to the Note Holder under this Note will be given by delivering it or by mailing it by first class mail to the Note Holder at the address stated in Section 3(A) above or at a different address if I am given a notice of that different address.

9. OBLIGATIONS OF PERSONS UNDER THIS NOTE

If more than one person signs this Note, each person is fully and personally obligated to keep all of the promises made in this Note, including the promise to pay the full amount owed. Any person who is a guarantor, surety or endorser of this Note is also obligated to do these things. Any person who takes over these obligations, including the obligations of a guarantor, surety or endorser of this Note, is also obligated to keep all of the promises made in this Note. The Note Holder may enforce its rights under this Note against each person individually or against all of us together. This means that any one of us may be required to pay all of the amounts owed under this Note.

10. WAIVERS

I and any other person who has obligations under this Note waive the rights of Presentment and Notice of Dishonor. "Presentment" means the right to require the Note Holder to demand payment of amounts due. "Notice of Dishonor" means the right to require the Note Holder to give notice to other persons that amounts due have not been paid.

11. UNIFORM SECURED NOTE

This Note is a uniform instrument with limited variations in some jurisdictions. In addition to the protections given to the Note Holder under this Note, a Mortgage, Deed of Trust, or Security Deed (the "Security Instrument"), dated the same date as this Note, protects the Note Holder from possible losses which might result if I do not keep the promises which I make in this Note. That Security Instrument describes how and under what conditions I may be required to make immediate payment in full of all amounts I owe under this Note. Some of those conditions are described as follows:

If all or any part of the Property or any Interest in the Property is sold or transferred (or if Borrower is not a natural person and a beneficial interest in Borrower is sold or transferred) without Lender's prior written consent, Lender may require immediate payment in full of all sums secured by this Security Instrument. However, this option shall not be exercised by Lender if such exercise is prohibited by Applicable Law. Lender also shall not exercise this option if: (a) Borrower causes to be submitted to Lender information required by Lender to evaluate the intended transferee as if a new loan were being made to the transferee; and (b) Lender reasonably determines that Lender's security will not be impaired by the loan assumption and that the risk of a breach of any covenant or agreement in this Security Instrument is acceptable to Lender.

To the extent permitted by Applicable Law, Lender may charge a reasonable fee as a condition to Lender's consent to the loan assumption. Lender may also require the transferee to sign an assumption agreement that is acceptable to Lender and that obligates the transferee to keep all the promises and agreements made in the Note and in this Security Instrument. Borrower will continue to be obligated under the Note and this Security Instrument unless Lender releases Borrower in writing.

If Lender exercises the option to require immediate payment in full, Lender shall give Borrower notice of acceleration. The notice shall provide a period of not less than 30 days from the date the notice is given in accordance with Section 15 within which Borrower must pay all sums secured by this Security Instrument. If Borrower fails to pay these sums prior to the expiration of this period, Lender may invoke any remedies permitted by this Security Instrument without further notice or demand on Borrower.

12. DOCUMENTARY TAX

The state documentary tax due on this Note has been paid on the mortgage securing this indebtedness.

WITNESS THE HAND(S) AND SEAL(S) OF THE UNDERSIGNED.

_____(Seal)
-Borrower

_____(Seal)
-Borrower

_____(Seal)
-Borrower

[Sign Original Only]

1-017 FORM: FLORIDA STANDARD FIXED RATE NOTE

NOTE

_____, _____   _____, _____
[Date]   [City]   [State]

_____
                        [Property Address]

1. BORROWER'S PROMISE TO PAY

In return for a loan that I have received, I promise to pay U.S. $_____ (this amount is called "Principal"), plus interest, to the order of the Lender. The Lender is _____ _____. I will make all payments under this Note in the form of cash, check or money order.

I understand that the Lender may transfer this Note. The Lender or anyone who takes this Note by transfer and who is entitled to receive payments under this Note is called the "Note Holder."

2. INTEREST

Interest will be charged on unpaid principal until the full amount of Principal has been paid. I will pay interest at a yearly rate of _____%.

The interest rate required by this Section 2 is the rate I will pay both before and after any default described in Section 6(B) of this Note.

3. PAYMENTS

(A) **Time and Place of Payments**

I will pay principal and interest by making a payment every month.

I will make my monthly payment on the _____ day of each month beginning on _____, _____, I will make these payments every month until I have paid all of the principal and interest and any other charges described below that I may owe under this Note. Each monthly payment will be applied as of its scheduled due date and will be applied to interest before Principal. If, on _____, 20___, I still owe amounts under this Note, I will pay those amounts in full on that date, which is called the "Maturity Date."

I will make my monthly payments at _____
_____ or at a different place if required by the Note Holder.

(B) **Amount of Monthly Payments**

My monthly payment will be in the amount of U.S. $_____.

4. BORROWER'S RIGHT TO PREPAY

I have the right to make payments of Principal at any time before they are due. A payment of Principal only is known as a "Prepayment." When I make a Prepayment, I will tell the Note Holder in writing that I am doing so. I may not designate a payment as a Prepayment if I have not made all the monthly payments due under the Note.

I may make a full Prepayment or partial Prepayments without paying a Prepayment charge. The Note Holder will use my Prepayments to reduce the amount of Principal that I owe under this Note. However, the Note Holder may apply my Prepayment to the accrued and unpaid interest on the Prepayment amount, before applying my Prepayment to reduce the Principal amount of the Note. If I make a partial Prepayment, there will be no changes in the due date or in the amount of my monthly payment unless the Note Holder agrees in writing to those changes.

5. LOAN CHARGES

If a law, which applies to this loan and which sets maximum loan charges, is finally interpreted so that the interest or other loan charges collected or to be collected in connection with this loan exceed the permitted limits, then: (a) any such loan charge shall be reduced by the amount necessary to reduce the charge to the permitted limit; and (b) any sums already collected from me which exceeded permitted limits will be refunded to me. The Note Holder may choose to make this refund by reducing the Principal I owe under this Note or by making a direct payment to me. If a refund reduces Principal, the reduction will be treated as a partial Prepayment.

6. BORROWER'S FAILURE TO PAY AS REQUIRED

(A) **Late Charge for Overdue Payments**

If the Note Holder has not received the full amount of any monthly payment by the end of _____ calendar days after the date it is due, I will pay a late charge to the Note Holder. The amount of the charge will be _____% of my overdue

FLORIDA FIXED RATE NOTE--Single Family--Fannie Mae/Freddie Mac UNIFORM INSTRUMENT   Form 3210 1/01 *(page 1 of 3 pages)*

payment of principal and interest. I will pay this late charge promptly but only once on each late payment.

(B) Default

If I do not pay the full amount of each monthly payment on the date it is due, I will be in default.

(C) Notice of Default

If I am in default, the Note Holder may send me a written notice telling me that if I do not pay the overdue amount by a certain date, the Note Holder may require me to pay immediately the full amount of Principal which has not been paid and all the interest that I owe on that amount. That date must be at least 30 days after the date on which the notice is mailed to me or delivered by other means.

(D) No Waiver By Note Holder

Even if, at a time when I am in default, the Note Holder does not require me to pay immediately in full as described above, the Note Holder will still have the right to do so if I am in default at a later time.

(E) Payment of Note Holder's Costs and Expenses

If the Note Holder has required me to pay immediately in full as described above, the Note Holder will have the right to be paid back by me for all of its costs and expenses in enforcing this Note to the extent not prohibited by applicable law. Those expenses include, for example, reasonable attorneys' fees.

7. GIVING OF NOTICES

Unless applicable law requires a different method, any notice that must be given to me under this Note will be given by delivering it or by mailing it by first class mail to me at the Property Address above or at a different address if I give the Note Holder a notice of my different address.

Any notice that must be given to the Note Holder under this Note will be given by delivering it or by mailing it by first class mail to the Note Holder at the address stated in Section 3(A) above or at a different address if I am given a notice of that different address.

8. OBLIGATIONS OF PERSONS UNDER THIS NOTE

If more than one person signs this Note, each person is fully and personally obligated to keep all of the promises made in this Note, including the promise to pay the full amount owed. Any person who is a guarantor, surety or endorser of this Note is also obligated to do these things. Any person who takes over these obligations, including the obligations of a guarantor, surety or endorser of this Note, is also obligated to keep all of the promises made in this Note. The Note Holder may enforce its rights under this Note against each person individually or against all of us together. This means that any one of us may be required to pay all of the amounts owed under this Note.

9. WAIVERS

I and any other person who has obligations under this Note waive the rights of Presentment and Notice of Dishonor. "Presentment" means the right to require the Note Holder to demand payment of amounts due. "Notice of Dishonor" means the right to require the Note Holder to give notice to other persons that amounts due have not been paid.

10. UNIFORM SECURED NOTE

This Note is a uniform instrument with limited variations in some jurisdictions. In addition to the protections given to the Note Holder under this Note, a Mortgage, Deed of Trust, or Security Deed (the "Security Instrument"), dated the same date as this Note, protects the Note Holder from possible losses which might result if I do not keep the promises which I make in this Note. That Security Instrument describes how and under what conditions I may be required to make immediate payment in full of all amounts I owe under this Note. Some of those conditions are described as follows:

If all or any part of the Property or any Interest in the Property is sold or transferred (or if Borrower is not a natural person and a beneficial interest in Borrower is sold or transferred) without Lender's prior written consent, Lender may require immediate payment in full of all sums secured by this Security Instrument. However, this option shall not be exercised by Lender if such exercise is prohibited by Applicable Law.

If Lender exercises this option, Lender shall give Borrower notice of acceleration. The notice shall provide a period of not less than 30 days from the date the notice is given in accordance with Section 15 within which Borrower must pay all sums secured by this Security Instrument. If Borrower fails to pay these sums prior to the expiration of this period, Lender may invoke any remedies permitted by this Security Instrument without further notice or demand on Borrower.

11. DOCUMENTARY TAX

The state documentary tax due on this Note has been paid on the mortgage securing this indebtedness.

WITNESS THE HAND(S) AND SEAL(S) OF THE UNDERSIGNED

_____(Seal)
-Borrower

_____(Seal)
-Borrower

_____(Seal)
-Borrower

[Sign Original Only]

1-018 FORM: STANDARD FANNIE MAE-FREDDIE MAC MORTGAGE

After Recording Return To:
_____
_____
_____

_____ [Space Above This Line for Recording Data] _____

MORTGAGE

DEFINITIONS

Words used in multiple sections of this document are defined below and other words are defined in Sections 3, 11, 13, 18, 20 and 21. Certain rules regarding the usage of words used in this document are also provided in Section 16.

(A) "**Security Instrument**" means this document, which is dated _____,
_____, together with all Riders to this document.
(B) "**Borrower**" is _____. Borrower is the mortgagor under this Security Instrument.
(C) "**Lender**" is _____. Lender is a _____ organized and existing under the laws of _____. Lender's address is _____. Lender is the mortgagee under this Security Instrument.
(D) "**Note**" means the promissory note signed by Borrower and dated _____,
_____. The Note states that Borrower owes Lender _____ Dollars (U.S. $_____) plus interest. Borrower has promised to pay this debt in regular Periodic Payments and to pay the debt in full not later than _____.
(E) "**Property**" means the property that is described below under the heading "Transfer of Rights in the Property."
(F) "**Loan**" means the debt evidenced by the Note, plus interest, any prepayment charges and late charges due under the Note, and all sums due under this Security Instrument, plus interest.
(G) "**Riders**" means all Riders to this Security Instrument that are executed by Borrower. The following Riders are to be executed by Borrower [check box as applicable]:

☐ Adjustable Rate Rider ☐ Condominium Rider ☐ Second Home Rider
☐ Balloon Rider ☐ Planned Unit Development Rider ☐ Other(s) [specify] _____
☐ 1-4 Family Rider ☐ Biweekly Payment Rider

FLORIDA--Single Family--**Fannie Mae/Freddie Mac UNIFORM INSTRUMENT**   Form 3010 1/01 *(page 1 of 16 pages)*

APPENDIX A—FORMS AND SAMPLES

(H) **"Applicable Law"** means all controlling applicable federal, state and local statutes, regulations, ordinances and administrative rules and orders (that have the effect of law) as well as all applicable final, non-appealable judicial opinions.

(I) **"Community Association Dues, Fees, and Assessments"** means all dues, fees, assessments and other charges that are imposed on Borrower or the Property by a condominium association, homeowners association or similar organization.

(J) **"Electronic Funds Transfer"** means any transfer of funds, other than a transaction originated by check, draft, or similar paper instrument, which is initiated through an electronic terminal, telephonic instrument, computer, or magnetic tape so as to order, instruct, or authorize a financial institution to debit or credit an account. Such term includes, but is not limited to, point-of-sale transfers, automated teller machine transactions, transfers initiated by telephone, wire transfers, and automated clearinghouse transfers.

(K) **"Escrow Items"** means those items that are described in Section 3.

(L) **"Miscellaneous Proceeds"** means any compensation, settlement, award of damages, or proceeds paid by any third party (other than insurance proceeds paid under the coverages described in Section 5) for: (i) damage to, or destruction of, the Property; (ii) condemnation or other taking of all or any part of the Property; (iii) conveyance in lieu of condemnation; or (iv) misrepresentations of, or omissions as to, the value and/or condition of the Property.

(M) **"Mortgage Insurance"** means insurance protecting Lender against the nonpayment of, or default on, the Loan.

(N) **"Periodic Payment"** means the regularly scheduled amount due for (i) principal and interest under the Note, plus (ii) any amounts under Section 3 of this Security Instrument.

(O) **"RESPA"** means the Real Estate Settlement Procedures Act (12 U.S.C. §2601 et seq.) and its implementing regulation, Regulation X (24 C.F.R. Part 3500), as they might be amended from time to time, or any additional or successor legislation or regulation that governs the same subject matter. As used in this Security Instrument, "RESPA" refers to all requirements and restrictions that are imposed in regard to a "federally related mortgage loan" even if the Loan does not qualify as a "federally related mortgage loan" under RESPA.

(P) **"Successor in Interest of Borrower"** means any party that has taken title to the Property, whether or not that party has assumed Borrower's obligations under the Note and/or this Security Instrument.

TRANSFER OF RIGHTS IN THE PROPERTY

This Security Instrument secures to Lender: (i) the repayment of the Loan, and all renewals, extensions and modifications of the Note; and (ii) the performance of Borrower's covenants and agreements under this Security Instrument and the Note. For this purpose, Borrower does hereby

mortgage, grant and convey to Lender, the following described property located in the _____ of _____:
[Type of Recording Jurisdiction]   [Name of Recording Jurisdiction]

which currently has the address of _____
                                                    [Street]
_____, Florida _____ ("Property Address"):
         [City]   [Zip Code]

TOGETHER WITH all the improvements now or hereafter erected on the property, and all easements, appurtenances, and fixtures now or hereafter a part of the property. All replacements and additions shall also be covered by this Security Instrument. All of the foregoing is referred to in this Security Instrument as the "Property."

BORROWER COVENANTS that Borrower is lawfully seised of the estate hereby conveyed and has the right to mortgage, grant and convey the Property and that the Property is unencumbered, except for encumbrances of record. Borrower warrants and will defend generally the title to the Property against all claims and demands, subject to any encumbrances of record.

THIS SECURITY INSTRUMENT combines uniform covenants for national use and non-uniform covenants with limited variations by jurisdiction to constitute a uniform security instrument covering real property.

UNIFORM COVENANTS. Borrower and Lender covenant and agree as follows:
1. Payment of Principal, Interest, Escrow Items, Prepayment Charges, and Late Charges. Borrower shall pay when due the principal of, and interest on, the debt evidenced by the Note and any prepayment charges and late charges due under the Note. Borrower shall also pay funds for Escrow Items pursuant to Section 3. Payments due under the Note and this Security Instrument shall be made in U.S. currency. However, if any check or other instrument received by Lender as payment under the Note or this Security Instrument is returned to Lender unpaid, Lender may require that any or all subsequent payments due under the Note and this Security Instrument be made in one or more of the following forms, as selected by Lender: (a) cash; (b) money order; (c) certified check, bank check, treasurer's check or cashier's check, provided any such check is drawn upon an institution whose deposits are insured by a federal agency, instrumentality, or entity; or (d) Electronic Funds Transfer.

Payments are deemed received by Lender when received at the location designated in the Note or at such other location as may be designated by Lender in accordance with the notice provisions in Section 15. Lender may return any payment or partial payment if the payment or partial payments are insufficient to bring the Loan current. Lender may accept any payment or partial payment insufficient to bring the Loan current, without waiver of any rights hereunder or prejudice to its rights to refuse such payment or partial payments in the future, but Lender is not obligated to apply such payments at the time such payments are accepted. If each Periodic Payment is applied as of its scheduled due date, then Lender need not pay interest on unapplied funds. Lender may hold such unapplied funds until Borrower makes payment to bring the Loan current. If Borrower does not do so within a reasonable period of time, Lender shall either apply such funds or return them to Borrower. If not applied earlier, such funds will be applied to the outstanding principal balance under the Note immediately prior to foreclosure. No offset or claim which Borrower might have now or in the future against Lender shall relieve Borrower from making payments due under the Note and this Security Instrument or performing the covenants and agreements secured by this Security Instrument.

2. Application of Payments or Proceeds. Except as otherwise described in this Section 2, all payments accepted and applied by Lender shall be applied in the following order of priority: (a) interest due under the Note; (b) principal due under the Note; (c) amounts due under Section 3. Such payments shall be applied to each Periodic Payment in the order in which it became due. Any remaining amounts shall be applied first to late charges, second to any other amounts due under this Security Instrument, and then to reduce the principal balance of the Note.

If Lender receives a payment from Borrower for a delinquent Periodic Payment which includes a sufficient amount to pay any late charge due, the payment may be applied to the delinquent payment and the late charge. If more than one Periodic Payment is outstanding, Lender may apply any payment received from Borrower to the repayment of the Periodic Payments if, and to the extent that, each payment can be paid in full. To the extent that any excess exists after the payment is applied to the full payment of one or more Periodic Payments, such excess may be applied to any late charges due. Voluntary prepayments shall be applied first to any prepayment charges and then as described in the Note.

Any application of payments, insurance proceeds, or Miscellaneous Proceeds to principal due under the Note shall not extend or postpone the due date, or change the amount, of the Periodic Payments.

3. Funds for Escrow Items. Borrower shall pay to Lender on the day Periodic Payments are due under the Note, until the Note is paid in full, a sum (the "Funds") to provide for payment of amounts due for: (a) taxes and assessments and other items which can attain priority over this Security Instrument as a lien or encumbrance on the Property; (b) leasehold payments or ground rents on the Property, if any; (c) premiums for any and all insurance required by Lender under Section 5; and (d) Mortgage Insurance premiums, if any, or any sums payable by Borrower to Lender in lieu of the payment of Mortgage Insurance premiums in accordance with the provisions of Section 10. These items are called "Escrow Items." At origination or at any time during the term of the Loan, Lender may require that Community Association Dues, Fees, and Assessments, if any, be escrowed by Borrower, and such dues, fees and assessments shall be an Escrow Item. Borrower shall promptly furnish to Lender all notices of amounts to be paid under this Section. Borrower shall pay Lender the Funds for Escrow Items unless Lender waives Borrower's obligation to pay the Funds for any or all Escrow Items. Lender may waive Borrower's obligation to pay to Lender Funds for any or all Escrow Items at any time. Any such waiver may only be in writing. In the event of such waiver, Borrower shall pay directly, when and where payable, the amounts due for any Escrow Items for which payment of Funds has been waived by Lender and, if Lender requires, shall furnish to Lender receipts evidencing such payment within such time period as Lender may require. Borrower's obligation to make such payments and to provide receipts shall for all purposes be deemed to be a covenant and agreement contained in this Security Instrument, as the phrase "covenant and agreement" is used in Section 9. If Borrower is obligated to pay Escrow Items directly, pursuant to a waiver, and Borrower fails to pay the amount due for an Escrow Item, Lender may exercise its rights under Section 9 and pay such amount and Borrower shall then be obligated under Section 9 to repay to Lender any such amount. Lender may revoke the waiver as to any or all Escrow Items at any time by a notice given in accordance with Section 15 and, upon such revocation, Borrower shall pay to Lender all Funds, and in such amounts, that are then required under this Section 3.

Lender may, at any time, collect and hold Funds in an amount (a) sufficient to permit Lender to apply the Funds at the time specified under RESPA, and (b) not to exceed the maximum amount a lender can require under RESPA. Lender shall estimate the amount of Funds due on the basis of current data and reasonable estimates of expenditures of future Escrow Items or otherwise in accordance with Applicable Law.

The Funds shall be held in an institution whose deposits are insured by a federal agency, instrumentality, or entity (including Lender, if Lender is an institution whose deposits are so insured) or in any Federal Home Loan Bank. Lender shall apply the Funds to pay the Escrow Items no later than the time specified under RESPA. Lender shall not charge Borrower for holding and applying the Funds, annually analyzing the escrow account, or verifying the Escrow Items, unless Lender pays Borrower interest on the Funds and Applicable Law permits Lender to make such a charge. Unless an agreement is made in writing or Applicable Law requires interest to be paid on the Funds, Lender shall not be required to pay Borrower any interest or earnings on the Funds. Borrower and Lender can agree in writing, however, that interest shall be paid on the Funds. Lender shall give to Borrower, without charge, an annual accounting of the Funds as required by RESPA.

If there is a surplus of Funds held in escrow, as defined under RESPA, Lender shall account to Borrower for the excess funds in accordance with RESPA. If there is a shortage of Funds held in escrow, as defined under RESPA, Lender shall notify Borrower as required by RESPA, and Borrower shall pay to Lender the amount necessary to make up the shortage in accordance with RESPA, but in no more than 12 monthly payments. If there is a deficiency of Funds held in escrow, as defined under RESPA, Lender shall notify Borrower as required by RESPA, and Borrower shall pay to Lender the amount necessary to make up the deficiency in accordance with RESPA, but in no more than 12 monthly payments.

Upon payment in full of all sums secured by this Security Instrument, Lender shall promptly refund to Borrower any Funds held by Lender.

4. Charges; Liens. Borrower shall pay all taxes, assessments, charges, fines, and impositions attributable to the Property which can attain priority over this Security Instrument, leasehold payments or ground rents on the Property, if any, and Community Association Dues, Fees, and Assessments, if any. To the extent that these items are Escrow Items, Borrower shall pay them in the manner provided in Section 3.

FLORIDA--Single Family--**Fannie Mae/Freddie Mac UNIFORM INSTRUMENT** Form 3010 1/01 *(page 5 of 16 pages)*

Borrower shall promptly discharge any lien which has priority over this Security Instrument unless Borrower: (a) agrees in writing to the payment of the obligation secured by the lien in a manner acceptable to Lender, but only so long as Borrower is performing such agreement; (b) contests the lien in good faith by, or defends against enforcement of the lien in, legal proceedings which in Lender's opinion operate to prevent the enforcement of the lien while those proceedings are pending, but only until such proceedings are concluded; or (c) secures from the holder of the lien an agreement satisfactory to Lender subordinating the lien to this Security Instrument. If Lender determines that any part of the Property is subject to a lien which can attain priority over this Security Instrument, Lender may give Borrower a notice identifying the lien. Within 10 days of the date on which that notice is given, Borrower shall satisfy the lien or take one or more of the actions set forth above in this Section 4.

Lender may require Borrower to pay a one-time charge for a real estate tax verification and/or reporting service used by Lender in connection with this Loan.

5. Property Insurance. Borrower shall keep the improvements now existing or hereafter erected on the Property insured against loss by fire, hazards included within the term "extended coverage," and any other hazards including, but not limited to, earthquakes and floods, for which Lender requires insurance. This insurance shall be maintained in the amounts (including deductible levels) and for the periods that Lender requires. What Lender requires pursuant to the preceding sentences can change during the term of the Loan. The insurance carrier providing the insurance shall be chosen by Borrower subject to Lender's right to disapprove Borrower's choice, which right shall not be exercised unreasonably. Lender may require Borrower to pay, in connection with this Loan, either: (a) a one-time charge for flood zone determination, certification and tracking services; or (b) a one-time charge for flood zone determination and certification services and subsequent charges each time remappings or similar changes occur which reasonably might affect such determination or certification. Borrower shall also be responsible for the payment of any fees imposed by the Federal Emergency Management Agency in connection with the review of any flood zone determination resulting from an objection by Borrower.

If Borrower fails to maintain any of the coverages described above, Lender may obtain insurance coverage, at Lender's option and Borrower's expense. Lender is under no obligation to purchase any particular type or amount of coverage. Therefore, such coverage shall cover Lender, but might or might not protect Borrower, Borrower's equity in the Property, or the contents of the Property, against any risk, hazard or liability and might provide greater or lesser coverage than was previously in effect. Borrower acknowledges that the cost of the insurance coverage so obtained might significantly exceed the cost of insurance that Borrower could have obtained. Any amounts disbursed by Lender under this Section 5 shall become additional debt of Borrower secured by this Security Instrument. These amounts shall bear interest at the Note rate from the date of disbursement and shall be payable, with such interest, upon notice from Lender to Borrower requesting payment.

All insurance policies required by Lender and renewals of such policies shall be subject to Lender's right to disapprove such policies, shall include a standard mortgage clause, and shall name Lender as mortgagee and/or as an additional loss payee. Lender shall have the right to hold the policies and renewal certificates. If Lender requires, Borrower shall promptly give to Lender all receipts of paid premiums and renewal notices. If Borrower obtains any form of insurance coverage, not otherwise required by Lender, for damage to, or destruction of, the Property, such policy shall include a standard mortgage clause and shall name Lender as mortgagee and/or as an additional loss payee.

In the event of loss, Borrower shall give prompt notice to the insurance carrier and Lender. Lender may make proof of loss if not made promptly by Borrower. Unless Lender and Borrower otherwise agree in writing, any insurance proceeds, whether or not the underlying insurance was required by Lender, shall be applied to restoration or repair of the Property, if the restoration or repair is economically feasible and Lender's security is not lessened. During such repair and restoration period, Lender shall have the right to hold such insurance proceeds until Lender has had an opportunity to inspect such Property to ensure the work has been completed to Lender's satisfaction, provided that such inspection shall be undertaken promptly. Lender may disburse proceeds for the repairs and restoration in a single payment or in a series of progress payments as the work is completed. Unless an agreement is made in writing or Applicable Law requires interest to be paid on such insurance proceeds, Lender shall not be required to pay Borrower any interest or earnings on such proceeds. Fees for public adjusters, or other third parties, retained by Borrower shall not be paid out of the insurance proceeds and shall be the sole obligation of Borrower. If the restoration or repair is not economically feasible or Lender's security would be lessened, the insurance proceeds shall be applied to the sums secured by this Security Instrument, whether or not then due, with the excess, if any, paid to Borrower. Such insurance proceeds shall be applied in the order provided for in Section 2.

If Borrower abandons the Property, Lender may file, negotiate and settle any available insurance claim and related matters. If Borrower does not respond within 30 days to a notice from Lender that the insurance carrier has offered to settle a claim, then Lender may negotiate and settle the claim. The 30-day period will begin when the notice is given. In either event, or if Lender acquires the Property under Section 22 or otherwise, Borrower hereby assigns to Lender (a) Borrower's rights to any insurance proceeds in an amount not to exceed the amounts unpaid under the Note or this Security Instrument, and (b) any other of Borrower's rights (other than the right to any refund of unearned premiums paid by Borrower) under all insurance policies covering the Property, insofar as such rights are applicable to the coverage of the Property. Lender may use the insurance proceeds either to repair or restore the Property or to pay amounts unpaid under the Note or this Security Instrument, whether or not then due.

6. Occupancy. Borrower shall occupy, establish, and use the Property as Borrower's principal residence within 60 days after the execution of this Security Instrument and shall continue to occupy the Property as Borrower's principal residence for at least one year after the date of occupancy, unless Lender otherwise agrees in writing, which consent shall not be unreasonably withheld, or unless extenuating circumstances exist which are beyond Borrower's control.

7. Preservation, Maintenance and Protection of the Property; Inspections. Borrower shall not destroy, damage or impair the Property, allow the Property to deteriorate or commit waste on the Property. Whether or not Borrower is residing in the Property, Borrower shall maintain the Property in order to prevent the Property from deteriorating or decreasing in value due to its condition. Unless it is determined pursuant to Section 5 that repair or restoration is not economically feasible, Borrower shall promptly repair the Property if damaged to avoid further deterioration or damage. If insurance or condemnation proceeds are paid in connection with damage to, or the taking of, the Property, Borrower shall be responsible for repairing or restoring the Property only if Lender has released proceeds for such purposes. Lender may disburse proceeds for the repairs and restoration in a single payment or in a series of progress payments as the work is completed. If the insurance or condemnation proceeds are not sufficient to repair or restore the Property, Borrower is not relieved of Borrower's obligation for the completion of such repair or restoration.

Lender or its agent may make reasonable entries upon and inspections of the Property. If it has reasonable cause, Lender may inspect the interior of the improvements on the Property. Lender shall give Borrower notice at the time of or prior to such an interior inspection specifying such reasonable cause.

8. Borrower's Loan Application. Borrower shall be in default if, during the Loan application process, Borrower or any persons or entities acting at the direction of Borrower or with Borrower's knowledge or consent gave materially false, misleading, or inaccurate information or statements to Lender (or failed to provide Lender with material information) in connection with the Loan. Material representations include, but are not limited to, representations concerning Borrower's occupancy of the Property as Borrower's principal residence.

9. Protection of Lender's Interest in the Property and Rights Under this Security Instrument. If (a) Borrower fails to perform the covenants and agreements contained in this Security Instrument, (b) there is a legal proceeding that might significantly affect Lender's interest in the Property and/or rights under this Security Instrument (such as a proceeding in bankruptcy, probate, for condemnation or forfeiture, for enforcement of a lien which may attain priority over this Security Instrument or to enforce laws or regulations), or (c) Borrower has abandoned the Property, then Lender may do and pay for whatever is reasonable or appropriate to protect Lender's interest in the Property and rights under this Security Instrument, including protecting and/or assessing the value of the Property, and securing and/or repairing the Property. Lender's actions can include, but are not limited to: (a) paying any sums secured by a lien which has priority over this Security Instrument; (b) appearing in court; and (c) paying reasonable attorneys' fees to protect its interest in the Property and/or rights under this Security Instrument, including its secured position in a bankruptcy proceeding. Securing the Property includes, but is not limited to, entering the Property to make repairs, change locks, replace or board up doors and windows, drain water from pipes, eliminate building or other code violations or dangerous conditions, and have utilities turned on or off. Although Lender may take action under this Section 9, Lender does not have to do so and is not under any duty or obligation to do so. It is agreed that Lender incurs no liability for not taking any or all actions authorized under this Section 9.

Any amounts disbursed by Lender under this Section 9 shall become additional debt of Borrower secured by this Security Instrument. These amounts shall bear interest at the Note rate from the date of disbursement and shall be payable, with such interest, upon notice from Lender to Borrower requesting payment.

If this Security Instrument is on a leasehold, Borrower shall comply with all the provisions of the lease. If Borrower acquires fee title to the Property, the leasehold and the fee title shall not merge unless Lender agrees to the merger in writing.

10. Mortgage Insurance. If Lender required Mortgage Insurance as a condition of making the Loan, Borrower shall pay the premiums required to maintain the Mortgage Insurance in effect. If, for any reason, the Mortgage Insurance coverage required by Lender ceases to be available from the mortgage insurer that previously provided such insurance and Borrower was required to make separately designated payments toward the premiums for Mortgage Insurance, Borrower shall pay the premiums required to obtain coverage substantially equivalent to the Mortgage Insurance previously in effect, at a cost substantially equivalent to the cost to Borrower of the Mortgage Insurance previously in effect, from an alternate mortgage insurer selected by Lender. If substantially equivalent Mortgage Insurance coverage is not available, Borrower shall continue to pay to Lender the amount of the separately designated payments that were due when the insurance coverage ceased to be in effect. Lender will accept, use and retain these payments as a non-refundable loss reserve in lieu of Mortgage Insurance. Such loss reserve shall be non-refundable, notwithstanding the fact that the Loan is ultimately paid in full, and Lender shall not be required to pay Borrower any interest or earnings on such loss reserve. Lender can no longer require loss reserve payments if Mortgage Insurance coverage (in the amount and for the period that Lender requires) provided by an insurer selected by Lender again becomes available, is obtained, and Lender requires separately designated payments toward the premiums for Mortgage Insurance. If Lender required Mortgage Insurance as a condition of making the Loan and Borrower was required to make separately designated payments toward the premiums for Mortgage Insurance, Borrower shall pay the premiums required to maintain Mortgage Insurance in effect, or to provide a non-refundable loss reserve, until Lender's requirement for Mortgage Insurance ends in accordance with any written agreement between Borrower and Lender providing for such termination or until termination is required by Applicable Law. Nothing in this Section 10 affects Borrower's obligation to pay interest at the rate provided in the Note.

Mortgage Insurance reimburses Lender (or any entity that purchases the Note) for certain losses it may incur if Borrower does not repay the Loan as agreed. Borrower is not a party to the Mortgage Insurance.

Mortgage insurers evaluate their total risk on all such insurance in force from time to time, and may enter into agreements with other parties that share or modify their risk, or reduce losses. These agreements are on terms and conditions that are satisfactory to the mortgage insurer and the other party (or parties) to these agreements. These agreements may require the mortgage insurer to make payments using any source of funds that the mortgage insurer may have available (which may include funds obtained from Mortgage Insurance premiums).

As a result of these agreements, Lender, any purchaser of the Note, another insurer, any reinsurer, any other entity, or any affiliate of any of the foregoing, may receive (directly or indirectly) amounts that derive from (or might be characterized as) a portion of Borrower's payments for Mortgage Insurance, in exchange for sharing or modifying the mortgage insurer's risk, or reducing losses. If such agreement provides that an affiliate of Lender takes a share of the insurer's risk in exchange for a share of the premiums paid to the insurer, the arrangement is often termed "captive reinsurance." Further:

(a) Any such agreements will not affect the amounts that Borrower has agreed to pay for Mortgage Insurance, or any other terms of the Loan. Such agreements will not increase the amount Borrower will owe for Mortgage Insurance, and they will not entitle Borrower to any refund.

(b) Any such agreements will not affect the rights Borrower has – if any – with respect to the Mortgage Insurance under the Homeowners Protection Act of 1998 or any other law. These rights may include the right to receive certain disclosures, to request and obtain cancellation of the Mortgage Insurance, to have the Mortgage Insurance terminated

automatically, and/or to receive a refund of any Mortgage Insurance premiums that were unearned at the time of such cancellation or termination.

11. Assignment of Miscellaneous Proceeds; Forfeiture. All Miscellaneous Proceeds are hereby assigned to and shall be paid to Lender.

If the Property is damaged, such Miscellaneous Proceeds shall be applied to restoration or repair of the Property, if the restoration or repair is economically feasible and Lender's security is not lessened. During such repair and restoration period, Lender shall have the right to hold such Miscellaneous Proceeds until Lender has had an opportunity to inspect such Property to ensure the work has been completed to Lender's satisfaction, provided that such inspection shall be undertaken promptly. Lender may pay for the repairs and restoration in a single disbursement or in a series of progress payments as the work is completed. Unless an agreement is made in writing or Applicable Law requires interest to be paid on such Miscellaneous Proceeds, Lender shall not be required to pay Borrower any interest or earnings on such Miscellaneous Proceeds. If the restoration or repair is not economically feasible or Lender's security would be lessened, the Miscellaneous Proceeds shall be applied to the sums secured by this Security Instrument, whether or not then due, with the excess, if any, paid to Borrower. Such Miscellaneous Proceeds shall be applied in the order provided for in Section 2.

In the event of a total taking, destruction, or loss in value of the Property, the Miscellaneous Proceeds shall be applied to the sums secured by this Security Instrument, whether or not then due, with the excess, if any, paid to Borrower.

In the event of a partial taking, destruction, or loss in value of the Property in which the fair market value of the Property immediately before the partial taking, destruction, or loss in value is equal to or greater than the amount of the sums secured by this Security Instrument immediately before the partial taking, destruction, or loss in value, unless Borrower and Lender otherwise agree in writing, the sums secured by this Security Instrument shall be reduced by the amount of the Miscellaneous Proceeds multiplied by the following fraction: (a) the total amount of the sums secured immediately before the partial taking, destruction, or loss in value divided by (b) the fair market value of the Property immediately before the partial taking, destruction, or loss in value. Any balance shall be paid to Borrower.

In the event of a partial taking, destruction, or loss in value of the Property in which the fair market value of the Property immediately before the partial taking, destruction, or loss in value is less than the amount of the sums secured immediately before the partial taking, destruction, or loss in value, unless Borrower and Lender otherwise agree in writing, the Miscellaneous Proceeds shall be applied to the sums secured by this Security Instrument whether or not the sums are then due.

If the Property is abandoned by Borrower, or if, after notice by Lender to Borrower that the Opposing Party (as defined in the next sentence) offers to make an award to settle a claim for damages, Borrower fails to respond to Lender within 30 days after the date the notice is given, Lender is authorized to collect and apply the Miscellaneous Proceeds either to restoration or repair of the Property or to the sums secured by this Security Instrument, whether or not then due. "Opposing Party" means the third party that owes Borrower Miscellaneous Proceeds or the party against whom Borrower has a right of action in regard to Miscellaneous Proceeds.

Borrower shall be in default if any action or proceeding, whether civil or criminal, is begun that, in Lender's judgment, could result in forfeiture of the Property or other material impairment of Lender's interest in the Property or rights under this Security Instrument. Borrower can cure such a default and, if acceleration has occurred, reinstate as provided in Section 19, by causing the action or proceeding to be dismissed with a ruling that, in Lender's judgment, precludes forfeiture of the Property or other material impairment of Lender's interest in the Property or rights under this Security Instrument. The proceeds of any award or claim for damages that are attributable to the impairment of Lender's interest in the Property are hereby assigned and shall be paid to Lender.

All Miscellaneous Proceeds that are not applied to restoration or repair of the Property shall be applied in the order provided for in Section 2.

12. Borrower Not Released; Forbearance By Lender Not a Waiver. Extension of the time for payment or modification of amortization of the sums secured by this Security Instrument granted by Lender to Borrower or any Successor in Interest of Borrower shall not operate to release the liability of Borrower or any Successors in Interest of Borrower. Lender shall not be required to commence proceedings against any Successor in Interest of Borrower or to refuse to extend time for payment or otherwise modify amortization of the sums secured by this Security Instrument by reason of any demand made by the original Borrower or any Successors in Interest of Borrower. Any forbearance by Lender in exercising any right or remedy including, without limitation, Lender's acceptance of payments from third persons, entities or Successors in Interest of Borrower or in amounts less than the amount then due, shall not be a waiver of or preclude the exercise of any right or remedy.

13. Joint and Several Liability; Co-signers; Successors and Assigns Bound. Borrower covenants and agrees that Borrower's obligations and liability shall be joint and several. However, any Borrower who co-signs this Security Instrument but does not execute the Note (a "co-signer"): (a) is co-signing this Security Instrument only to mortgage, grant and convey the co-signer's interest in the Property under the terms of this Security Instrument; (b) is not personally obligated to pay the sums secured by this Security Instrument; and (c) agrees that Lender and any other Borrower can agree to extend, modify, forbear or make any accommodations with regard to the terms of this Security Instrument or the Note without the co-signer's consent.

Subject to the provisions of Section 18, any Successor in Interest of Borrower who assumes Borrower's obligations under this Security Instrument in writing, and is approved by Lender, shall obtain all of Borrower's rights and benefits under this Security Instrument. Borrower shall not be released from Borrower's obligations and liability under this Security Instrument unless Lender agrees to such release in writing. The covenants and agreements of this Security Instrument shall bind (except as provided in Section 20) and benefit the successors and assigns of Lender.

14. Loan Charges. Lender may charge Borrower fees for services performed in connection with Borrower's default, for the purpose of protecting Lender's interest in the Property and rights under this Security Instrument, including, but not limited to, attorneys' fees, property inspection and valuation fees. In regard to any other fees, the absence of express authority in this Security Instrument to charge a specific fee to Borrower shall not be construed as a prohibition on the charging of such fee. Lender may not charge fees that are expressly prohibited by this Security Instrument or by Applicable Law.

If the Loan is subject to a law which sets maximum loan charges, and that law is finally interpreted so that the interest or other loan charges collected or to be collected in connection with

APPENDIX A—FORMS AND SAMPLES

the Loan exceed the permitted limits, then: (a) any such loan charge shall be reduced by the amount necessary to reduce the charge to the permitted limit; and (b) any sums already collected from Borrower which exceeded permitted limits will be refunded to Borrower. Lender may choose to make this refund by reducing the principal owed under the Note or by making a direct payment to Borrower. If a refund reduces principal, the reduction will be treated as a partial prepayment without any prepayment charge (whether or not a prepayment charge is provided for under the Note). Borrower's acceptance of any such refund made by direct payment to Borrower will constitute a waiver of any right of action Borrower might have arising out of such overcharge.

15. Notices. All notices given by Borrower or Lender in connection with this Security Instrument must be in writing. Any notice to Borrower in connection with this Security Instrument shall be deemed to have been given to Borrower when mailed by first class mail or when actually delivered to Borrower's notice address if sent by other means. Notice to any one Borrower shall constitute notice to all Borrowers unless Applicable Law expressly requires otherwise. The notice address shall be the Property Address unless Borrower has designated a substitute notice address by notice to Lender. Borrower shall promptly notify Lender of Borrower's change of address. If Lender specifies a procedure for reporting Borrower's change of address, then Borrower shall only report a change of address through that specified procedure. There may be only one designated notice address under this Security Instrument at any one time. Any notice to Lender shall be given by delivering it or by mailing it by first class mail to Lender's address stated herein unless Lender has designated another address by notice to Borrower. Any notice in connection with this Security Instrument shall not be deemed to have been given to Lender until actually received by Lender. If any notice required by this Security Instrument is also required under Applicable Law, the Applicable Law requirement will satisfy the corresponding requirement under this Security Instrument.

16. Governing Law; Severability; Rules of Construction. This Security Instrument shall be governed by federal law and the law of the jurisdiction in which the Property is located. All rights and obligations contained in this Security Instrument are subject to any requirements and limitations of Applicable Law. Applicable Law might explicitly or implicitly allow the parties to agree by contract or it might be silent, but such silence shall not be construed as a prohibition against agreement by contract. In the event that any provision or clause of this Security Instrument or the Note conflicts with Applicable Law, such conflict shall not affect other provisions of this Security Instrument or the Note which can be given effect without the conflicting provision.

As used in this Security Instrument: (a) words of the masculine gender shall mean and include corresponding neuter words or words of the feminine gender; (b) words in the singular shall mean and include the plural and vice versa; and (c) the word "may" gives sole discretion without any obligation to take any action.

17. Borrower's Copy. Borrower shall be given one copy of the Note and of this Security Instrument.

18. Transfer of the Property or a Beneficial Interest in Borrower. As used in this Section 18, "Interest in the Property" means any legal or beneficial interest in the Property, including, but not limited to, those beneficial interests transferred in a bond for deed, contract for deed, installment sales contract or escrow agreement, the intent of which is the transfer of title by Borrower at a future date to a purchaser.

FLORIDA--Single Family--Fannie Mae/Freddie Mac UNIFORM INSTRUMENT   Form 3010 1/01

If all or any part of the Property or any Interest in the Property is sold or transferred (or if Borrower is not a natural person and a beneficial interest in Borrower is sold or transferred) without Lender's prior written consent, Lender may require immediate payment in full of all sums secured by this Security Instrument. However, this option shall not be exercised by Lender if such exercise is prohibited by Applicable Law.

If Lender exercises this option, Lender shall give Borrower notice of acceleration. The notice shall provide a period of not less than 30 days from the date the notice is given in accordance with Section 15 within which Borrower must pay all sums secured by this Security Instrument. If Borrower fails to pay these sums prior to the expiration of this period, Lender may invoke any remedies permitted by this Security Instrument without further notice or demand on Borrower.

19. Borrower's Right to Reinstate After Acceleration. If Borrower meets certain conditions, Borrower shall have the right to have enforcement of this Security Instrument discontinued at any time prior to the earliest of: (a) five days before sale of the Property pursuant to any power of sale contained in this Security Instrument; (b) such other period as Applicable Law might specify for the termination of Borrower's right to reinstate; or (c) entry of a judgment enforcing this Security Instrument. Those conditions are that Borrower: (a) pays Lender all sums which then would be due under this Security Instrument and the Note as if no acceleration had occurred; (b) cures any default of any other covenants or agreements; (c) pays all expenses incurred in enforcing this Security Instrument, including, but not limited to, reasonable attorneys' fees, property inspection and valuation fees, and other fees incurred for the purpose of protecting Lender's interest in the Property and rights under this Security Instrument; and (d) takes such action as Lender may reasonably require to assure that Lender's interest in the Property and rights under this Security Instrument, and Borrower's obligation to pay the sums secured by this Security Instrument, shall continue unchanged. Lender may require that Borrower pay such reinstatement sums and expenses in one or more of the following forms, as selected by Lender: (a) cash; (b) money order; (c) certified check, bank check, treasurer's check or cashier's check, provided any such check is drawn upon an institution whose deposits are insured by a federal agency, instrumentality or entity; or (d) Electronic Funds Transfer. Upon reinstatement by Borrower, this Security Instrument and obligations secured hereby shall remain fully effective as if no acceleration had occurred. However, this right to reinstate shall not apply in the case of acceleration under Section 18.

20. Sale of Note; Change of Loan Servicer; Notice of Grievance. The Note or a partial interest in the Note (together with this Security Instrument) can be sold one or more times without prior notice to Borrower. A sale might result in a change in the entity (known as the "Loan Servicer") that collects Periodic Payments due under the Note and this Security Instrument and performs other mortgage loan servicing obligations under the Note, this Security Instrument, and Applicable Law. There also might be one or more changes of the Loan Servicer unrelated to a sale of the Note. If there is a change of the Loan Servicer, Borrower will be given written notice of the change which will state the name and address of the new Loan Servicer, the address to which payments should be made and any other information RESPA requires in connection with a notice of transfer of servicing. If the Note is sold and thereafter the Loan is serviced by a Loan Servicer other than the purchaser of the Note, the mortgage loan servicing obligations to Borrower will remain with the Loan Servicer or be transferred to a successor Loan Servicer and are not assumed by the Note purchaser unless otherwise provided by the Note purchaser.

Neither Borrower nor Lender may commence, join, or be joined to any judicial action (as either an individual litigant or the member of a class) that arises from the other party's actions pursuant to this Security Instrument or that alleges that the other party has breached any provision of, or any duty owed by reason of, this Security Instrument, until such Borrower or Lender has notified the other party (with such notice given in compliance with the requirements of Section 15) of such alleged breach and afforded the other party hereto a reasonable period after the giving of such notice to take corrective action. If Applicable Law provides a time period which must elapse before certain action can be taken, that time period will be deemed to be reasonable for purposes of this paragraph. The notice of acceleration and opportunity to cure given to Borrower pursuant to Section 22 and the notice of acceleration given to Borrower pursuant to Section 18 shall be deemed to satisfy the notice and opportunity to take corrective action provisions of this Section 20.

21. Hazardous Substances. As used in this Section 21: (a) "Hazardous Substances" are those substances defined as toxic or hazardous substances, pollutants, or wastes by Environmental Law and the following substances: gasoline, kerosene, other flammable or toxic petroleum products, toxic pesticides and herbicides, volatile solvents, materials containing asbestos or formaldehyde, and radioactive materials; (b) "Environmental Law" means federal laws and laws of the jurisdiction where the Property is located that relate to health, safety or environmental protection; (c) "Environmental Cleanup" includes any response action, remedial action, or removal action, as defined in Environmental Law; and (d) an "Environmental Condition" means a condition that can cause, contribute to, or otherwise trigger an Environmental Cleanup.

Borrower shall not cause or permit the presence, use, disposal, storage, or release of any Hazardous Substances, or threaten to release any Hazardous Substances, on or in the Property. Borrower shall not do, nor allow anyone else to do, anything affecting the Property (a) that is in violation of any Environmental Law, (b) which creates an Environmental Condition, or (c) which, due to the presence, use, or release of a Hazardous Substance, creates a condition that adversely affects the value of the Property. The preceding two sentences shall not apply to the presence, use, or storage on the Property of small quantities of Hazardous Substances that are generally recognized to be appropriate to normal residential uses and to maintenance of the Property (including, but not limited to, hazardous substances in consumer products).

Borrower shall promptly give Lender written notice of (a) any investigation, claim, demand, lawsuit or other action by any governmental or regulatory agency or private party involving the Property and any Hazardous Substance or Environmental Law of which Borrower has actual knowledge, (b) any Environmental Condition, including but not limited to, any spilling, leaking, discharge, release or threat of release of any Hazardous Substance, and (c) any condition caused by the presence, use or release of a Hazardous Substance which adversely affects the value of the Property. If Borrower learns, or is notified by any governmental or regulatory authority, or any private party, that any removal or other remediation of any Hazardous Substance affecting the Property is necessary, Borrower shall promptly take all necessary remedial actions in accordance with Environmental Law. Nothing herein shall create any obligation on Lender for an Environmental Cleanup.

NON-UNIFORM COVENANTS. Borrower and Lender further covenant and agree as follows:

22. Acceleration; Remedies. Lender shall give notice to Borrower prior to acceleration following Borrower's breach of any covenant or agreement in this Security Instrument (but not prior to acceleration under Section 18 unless Applicable Law provides otherwise). The notice shall specify: (a) the default; (b) the action required to cure the default; (c) a date, not less than 30 days from the date the notice is given to Borrower, by which the default must be cured; and (d) that failure to cure the default on or before the date specified in the notice may result in acceleration of the sums secured by this Security Instrument, foreclosure by judicial proceeding and sale of the Property. The notice shall further inform Borrower of the right to reinstate after acceleration and the right to assert in the foreclosure proceeding the non-existence of a default or any other defense of Borrower to acceleration and foreclosure. If the default is not cured on or before the date specified in the notice, Lender at its option may require immediate payment in full of all sums secured by this Security Instrument without further demand and may foreclose this Security Instrument by judicial proceeding. Lender shall be entitled to collect all expenses incurred in pursuing the remedies provided in this Section 22, including, but not limited to, reasonable attorneys' fees and costs of title evidence.

23. Release. Upon payment of all sums secured by this Security Instrument, Lender shall release this Security Instrument. Borrower shall pay any recordation costs. Lender may charge Borrower a fee for releasing this Security Instrument, but only if the fee is paid to a third party for services rendered and the charging of the fee is permitted under Applicable Law.

24. Attorneys' Fees. As used in this Security Instrument and the Note, attorneys' fees shall include those awarded by an appellate court and any attorneys' fees incurred in a bankruptcy proceeding.

25. Jury Trial Waiver. The Borrower hereby waives any right to a trial by jury in any action, proceeding, claim, or counterclaim, whether in contract or tort, at law or in equity, arising out of or in any way related to this Security Instrument or the Note.

APPENDIX A—FORMS AND SAMPLES

BY SIGNING BELOW, Borrower accepts and agrees to the terms and covenants contained in this Security Instrument and in any Rider executed by Borrower and recorded with it.

Signed, sealed and delivered in the presence of:

_____   _____(Seal)
                                                                                  - Borrower

_____   _____(Seal)
                                                                                  - Borrower

_____ **[Space Below This Line for Acknowledgment]** _____

FLORIDA--Single Family--**Fannie Mae/Freddie Mac UNIFORM INSTRUMENT**   **Form 3010** **1/01** *(page 16 of 16 pages)*

Table of Cases

3709 N. Flagler Drive Prodigy Land Trust v. Bank of America, N.A., 226 So. 3d 1040 (Fla. 4th DCA 2017), 9-3, 10-2:4

40 N.E. Plantation Rd. #306, LLC v. PNC Bank, Nat'l Ass'n, No. SC17-65, 2017 WL 1279793 (Fla. Apr. 6, 2017), 9-3

743 Mahoney, LLC v. MDC 5, LLC, 204 So. 3d 116 (Fla. 2d DCA 2016), 19-3:3

944 CWELT-2007 LLC v. Bank of America, N.A., 194 So. 3d 470 (Fla. 3d DCA 2016), 14-2:2

A

A & B Discount Lumber & Supply, Inc. v. Mitchell, 799 So. 2d 301 (Fla. 5th DCA 2001), 11-9:2

Abdoney v. York, 903 So. 2d 981 (Fla. 2d DCA 2005), 1-1:2, 5-3, 6-1:2, 6-3:2, 6-3:4, 10-2:3

Abraham v. S.N.W. Corp., 549 So. 2d 776 (Fla. 4th DCA 1989), 16-3:9

Accurate Metal Finishing Corp. v. Carmel, 254 So. 2d 556 (Fla. 3d DCA 1971), 12-1:4

Achva Vahava, LLC v. Anglo Irish Bank Corp. PLC, 10-80649-CIV, 2011 WL 4389912 (S.D. Fla. 2011), 2-1:3.2

Acosta v. James A. Gustino, P.A., No. 6:11-cv-1266-Orl-31GHK (GAP), 2012 U.S. Dist. LEXIS 130656, 2012 WL 4052245 (M.D. Fla. Sept.13, 2012), 8-6

Adhin v. First Horizon Home Loans, 44 So. 3d 1245 (Fla. 5th DCA 2010), 5-5, 6-1:4, 10-1:1

Advanced Chiropractic & Rehab. Ctr., Corp. v. United Auto. Ins. Co., 140 So. 3d 529 (Fla. 2014), 16-3:9

Aegis Props. of S. Fla., LLC v. Avalon Master Homeowner Ass'n, Inc., 37 So. 3d 960 (Fla. 4th DCA 2010), 14-4

Aetna Casualty & Surety Co. v. Protective Nat'l Ins. Co., 631 So. 2d 305 (Fla. 3d DCA 1994), 9-4:5

AG Group Investments, LLC v. All Realty Alliance Corp., 106 So. 3d 950 (Fla. 3d DCA 2013), 6-3:4, 10-2:2, 10-2:3

AGM Inv'rs, LLC v. Bus. Law Grp., P.A., 219 So. 3d 920 (Fla. 2d DCA 2017), 9-1

Ahmad v. Cobb Corner, Inc., 762 So. 2d 944 (Fla. 4th DCA 2000), 19-2:2

AIB Mortgage Co. v. Sweeney, 687 So. 2d 68 (Fla. 3d DCA 1997), 1-1:1

Aills v. Boemi, 29 So. 3d 1105-108 (Fla. 2010), 18-3

Akin v. City of Miami, 65 So. 2d 54 (Fla. 1953), 9-3

Aldama v. JPMorgan Chase Bank, N.A., 194 So. 3d 543 (Fla. 3d DCA 2016), 16-3:5

Alejandre v. Deutsche Bank Trust Co. Ams., 44 So. 3d 1288 (Fla. 4th DCA 2010), 8-1, 12-1:3.2

Alexdex Corp. v. Nachon Enterprises, Inc., 641 So. 2d 858 (Fla. 1994), 6-1:3

Alfonso v. Dep't of Envtl. Regulation, 616 So. 2d 44 (Fla. 1993), 18-2

Alger v. Peters, 88 So. 2d 903, 908 (Fla. 1956); *Abdoney v. York,* 903 So. 2d 981 (Fla. 2d DCA 2005), 10-1

All-Brite Aluminum, Inc. v. Desrosiers, 626 So. 2d 1020 (Fla. 2d DCA 1993), 9-4:5

Allen v. McCurry, 449 U.S. 90 (1980), 3-2:2.1

Allen v. Shows, 532 So. 2d 1304 (Fla. 2d DCA 1988), 12-1:8

Allen v. Willmington Trust, 216 So. 3d 685 (Fla. 2d DCA 2017), 13-4:3

Allie v. Ionata, 503 So. 2d 1237 (Fla. 1987), 3-1:1, 3-2, 3-2:3.1, 3-2:6

Allstate Floridian Ins. Co. v. Farmer, 104 So. 3d 1242 (Fla. 5th DCA 2012), 2-2:2, 7-3:3

Allstate Floridian Ins. Co. v. Ronco Inventions, LLC, 890 So. 2d 300 (Fla. 2d DCA 2004), 1-4:4.3

Allstate Indemnity Co. v. Hicks, 880 So. 2d 772 (Fla. 5th DCA 2004), 16-3:6

Allstate Ins. Co. v. Gulisano, 722 So. 2d 216 (Fla. 2d DCA 1998), 14-3:3

Allstate Ins. Co. v. Langston, 655 So. 2d 91 (Fla. 1995), 11-1, 18-4:3.1

Allstate Ins. Co. v. Pinder, 746 So. 2d 1255 (Fla. 5th DCA 1999), 11-3:2.1

Aloff v. Neff-Harmon, Inc., 463 So. 2d 291 (Fla. 1st DCA 1984), 12-1:3

ALS-RVC, LLC v. Garvin, 201 So. 3d 687 (Fla. 4th DCA 2016), 4-7, 9-4:4, 12-1:10.1.b, 13-4:1.2

Alston v. Fla. Ins. Guar. Ass'n, 842 So. 2d 842 (Fla. 2003), 7-2:2

Altamonte Hitch and Trailor Services v. U-Haul Co. of Eastern Florida, 498 So. 2d 1346 (Fla. 5th DCA 1986), 6-3

Alvarez v. Florida Ins. Guar. Ass'n, 661 So. 2d 1230 (Fla. 3d DCA 1995), 12-1:3, 12-1:5

Alvarez v. Rendon, 953 So. 2d 702 (Fla. 5th DCA 2007), 7-3:3

Alvis v. Alvis, 95 So. 3d 910 (Fla. 1st DCA 2012), 14-2:2, 16-3:6

Alyeska Pipeline Serv. Co. v. Wilderness Society, 421 U.S. 240 (1975), 16-1:1

Am. Bankers Life Assur. Co. of Florida v. 2275 W. Corp., 905 So. 2d 189 (Fla. 3d DCA 2005), 3-1:2, 3-3:1

Am. Home Mortg. Servicing, Inc. v. Bednarek, 132 So. 3d 1222 (Fla. 2d DCA 2014), 6-4:3

Am. Legion Cmty. Club v. Diamond, 561 So. 2d 268 (Fla. 1990), 10-1:1

Amelio v. Marilyn Pines Unit II Condo. Ass'n, Inc., 173 So. 3d 1037 (Fla. 2d DCA 2015), 9-4:5

Amente v. Newman, 653 So. 2d 1030 (Fla. 1995), 11-1

TABLE OF CASES

American Bankers Life Assur. Co. of Florida v. 2275 W. Corp., 905 So. 2d 189 (Fla. 3d DCA 2005), 3-3:2.1, 3-3:2.5

American Express Travel Related Services, Co. v. Marrod, Inc., 637 So. 2d 4 (Fla. 3d DCA 1994), 14-3:8

American Funding, Ltd. v. Hill, 402 So. 2d 1369 (Fla. 1st DCA 1981), 11-7:3

American Network Transp. Mgmt. v. A Super-Limo Co., 857 So. 2d 313 (Fla. 2d DCA 2003), 14-3:4

American Process Co. v. Fla. White Pressed Brick Co., 56 Fla. 116, 47 So. 942 (1908), 9-3, 9-4:4

Ameriseal of North East Florida v. Leiffer, 738 So. 2d 993 (Fla. 5th DCA 1999), 12-1:7

Amey, Inc. v. Gulf Abstract & Title, Inc., 758 F.2d 1486 (11th Cir. 1985), 12-1:8

Amiker v. Mid-Century Ins. Co., 398 So. 2d 974 (Fla. 1st DCA 1981), 6-2:4

Amstone v. Bank of New York Mellon, 182 So. 3d 804 (Fla. 2d DCA 2016), 4-7

Anchor Towing, Inc. v. Florida Dep't. of Transp., 10 So. 3d 670 (Fla. 3d DCA 2009), 16-4:3

Anderson v. Burson, 424 Md. 232, 35 A.3d 452 (Md. 2011), 4-7

Anderson v. Liberty Lobby, Inc., 477 U.S. 242 (1986), 12-1:1

Anderson v. Maddox, 65 So. 2d 299 (Fla. 1953), 12-1:1

Andresix Corp. v. Peoples Downtown Nat. Bank, 419 So. 2d 1107 (Fla. 3d DCA 1982), 10-2:1, 10-2:2

Andrews v. Bayview Loan Servicing, LLC, 175 So. 3d 316 (Fla. 5th DCA 2015), 9-3

Anfriany v. Deutsche Bank Nat'l Tr. Co. for Registered Holders of Argent Secs., Inc., Asset-Backed Pass-Through Certificates, Series 2005-W4, 232 So. 3d 425 (Fla. 4th DCA 2017), 9-3, 9-4:4

Angelini v. HSBC Bank USA, N.A., 189 So. 3d 202 (Fla. 4th DCA 2016), 7-2:2, 7-3:2

Angora Enters., Inc. v. Cole, 439 So. 2d 832 (Fla.1983), 9-4:3

Aparicio v. Deutsche Bank Nat'l Tr. Co., 278 So. 3d 814 (Fla. 3d DCA 2019), 14-4

Applegate v. Barnett Bank of Tallahassee, 377 So. 2d 1150 (Fla. 1979), 18-3

Aquarian Foundation, Inc. v. Sholom House, Inc., 448 So. 2d 1166 (Fla. 3d DCA 1984), 9-4:3

Aquasol Condo. Ass'n v. HSBC Bank USA, N.A., No. 3D17-352, 2018 Fla. App. LEXIS 11414 (Fla. 3d DCA Aug. 15, 2018), 7-2:2

Aquasol Condo. Ass'n v. HSBC Bank USA, Nat'l Ass'n, 2018 Fla. App. LEXIS 14313 (Fla. 3d DCA Sept. 26, 2018), 15-1

Aquasol Condo. Ass'n v. HSBC Bank USA, Nat'l Ass'n, 2018 Fla. App. LEXIS 17361 (Fla. 3d DCA Dec. 5, 2018), 15-1

Arey v. Williams, 81 So. 2d 525 (Fla. 1955), 9-4:4

Argent Mortg. Co., LLC v. Wachovia Bank N.A., 52 So. 3d 796 (Fla. 5th DCA 2010), 6-5:4, 10-2:1, 10-4:1

Arguelles v. City of Orlando, 855 So. 2d 1202 (Fla. 5th DCA 2003), 12-1:8

Armstrong v. Harris, 773 So. 2d 7 (Fla. 2000), 18-6:1

Arsali v. Chase Home Finance LLC, 121 So. 3d 511 (Fla. 2013), 14-4, 18-10

Artime v. Brotman, 838 So. 2d 691 (Fla. 3d DCA 2003), 6-2

Ashear v. Sklarey, 239 So. 3d 786 (Fla. 3d DCA 2018), 16-3:9

Ashley v. Lamar, 468 So. 2d 433 (Fla. 5th DCA 1985), 7-2:2

Asian Imports, Inc. v. Pepe, 633 So. 2d 551 (Fla. 1st DCA 1994), 1-4:3

As Lily, LLC v. Brisell Vazquez, Blue Bay Tower Condo. Assoc., Inc., et al., 2013 WL 4519352 (Fla. Cir. Ct. Miami-Dade 2013), 9-4:5

AS Lily, LLC v. Morgan, 164 So. 3d 124 (Fla. 2d DCA 2015), 4-1, 7-3:2, 13-3:1

Aspen Shackleton II LLC v. Graham, 2013 WL 1874305 (Fla. Cir. Ct. Brevard Apr. 25, 2013), 9-4:5

Assil v. Aurora Loan Servs., LLC, 171 So. 3d 226 (Fla. 4th DCA 2015), 6-3:1

Ass'n of Poinciana Villages v. Avatar Props., Inc., 724 So. 2d 585 (Fla. 5th DCA 1998), 9-4:3

Astoria Fed. Sav. & Loan Ass'n v. Kaufman, 158 So. 3d 675 (Fla. 5th DCA 2015), 2-2:3.1

Astoria v. Kafuman, 2013 WL 10054283 (Fla. Cir. Ct Aug. 6, 2013), 2-2:3.1

Attorney Gen. v. Nationwide Pools, Inc., 270 So. 3d 406 (Fla. 4th DCA 2019), 14-3:7

Augustin v. Blount, 573 So. 2d 104 (Fla. 1st DCA 1991), 18-4:1

Aurora Loan Services, LLC v. Bravo, 2011 WL 10959417 (Fla. Cir. Ct. Palm Beach Cnty. 2011), 9-4:1

Aurora Loan Services LLC v. Senchuk, 36 So. 3d 716 (Fla. 1st DCA 2010), 5-4:2, 5-4:2.1, 6-5:4

Austin v. Barnett Bank of South Florida, N.A., 472 So. 2d 830 (Fla. 4th DCA 1985), 11-7:3

Austin v. Papol, 464 So. 2d 1338 (Fla. 2d DCA 1985), 14-3:7

Auto-Owners Ins. Co. v. Hooks, 463 So. 2d 468 (Fla. 1st DCA 1985), 16-6:1

Avalon Associates of Delaware, Ltd. v. Avalon Park Associates, Inc., 760 So. 2d 1132 (Fla. 5th DCA 2000), 5-5, 10-1:1

Avelo Mortg., LLC v. Vero Ventures, LLC, 254 So. 3d 439 (Fla. 4th DCA 2018), 3-4

Aventura Management, LLC v. Spiaggia Ocean Condominium Association, Inc., 105 So. 3d 637 (Fla. 3d DCA 2013), 9-4:1

Aventura Management, LLC v. Spiaggia Ocean Condominium Association, Inc., 149 So. 3d 690 (Fla. 3d DCA, 2014), 9-4:1

Avi-Isaac v. Wells Fargo Bank, N.A., 59 So. 3d 174 (Fla. 2d DCA 2011), 14-4

Ayala v. Pacific Coast Nat'l Bank, No. 5:16-cv- 00723, 2016 WL 1700376 (C.D. Cal. April 27, 2016), 14-4

Azalea Park Utilities, Inc. v. Knox-Florida Dev. Corp., 127 So. 2d 121, 123 (Fla. 2d DCA 1961), 2-1:1

B

Baader v. Walker, 153 So. 2d 51 (Fla. 2d DCA 1963), 2-3:1, 2-3:2

BAC Home Loans Servicing, Inc. v. Headley, 130 So. 3d 703 (Fla. 3d DCA 2013), 14-3:7

BAC Home Loans Servicing, L.P. v. The Plaza Condo. Assoc., Inc., 2012 WL 8015571 (Fla. Cir. Ct. Orange 2012), 9-4:5

Baez v. Perez, 201 So. 3d 692 (Fla. 4th DCA 2016), 14-3:3

Bags by Ande, Inc. v. Schilling, 406 So. 2d 536 (Fla. 4th DCA 1981), 14-3:4

Bahia at Delray Homeowners' Ass'n Inc. v. U.S. Bank National Association as Trustee for the Holders of Mastr Adjustable Rate Mortgages Trust 2006-OA1, et al., 2014 WL 4411579 (Fla. Cir. Ct. Palm Beach June 23, 2014), 9-4:6

Baker v. Baker, 920 So. 2d 689 (Fla. 2d DCA 2006), 5-6, 14-3:8

Baker v. Stearns Bank, N.A., 84 So. 3d 1122 (Fla. 2d DCA 2012), 1-3

Ballantrae Homeowners Ass'n, Inc. v. Fed. Nat. Mortg. Ass'n, 203 So. 3d 938 (Fla. 2d DCA 2016), 9-2, 9-4:3

Ballinger v. Bay Gulf Credit Union, 51 So. 3d 528 (Fla. 2d DCA 2010), 12-1:10.1.b

Balmaseda v. Okay Ins. Exch. of Am., LLC, 240 So. 3d 146 (Fla. 3d DCA 2018), 16-3:9

Banderas v. Advance Petroleum, Inc., 716 So. 2d 876 (Fla. 3d DCA 1998), 14-2:2

Bane v. Bane, 775 So. 2d 938 (Fla. 2000), 6-4:9, 14-3:5, 14-3:8, 15-1, 15-2:1

BankAtlantic v. Estate of Glatzer, 61 So. 3d 1222 (Fla. 3d DCA 2011), 2-1:3.2

Bankers Trust Co. of California, N.A. v. Weidner, 688 So. 2d 453 (Fla. 5th DCA 1997), 14-3:8

Bankers Trust Co. v. Edwards, 849 So. 2d 1160 (Fla. 1st DCA 2003), 1-9, 14-3:8

Bank of Am., N.A. v. Asbury, 165 So. 3d 808, 809 (Fla. 2d DCA 2015), 12-1:10.1.e

Bank of Am., N.A. v. Atkin, 43 Fla. L. Weekly D2799 (Fla. 3d DCA Dec. 14, 2018), 15-1

Bank of Am., N.A. v. Atkin, 271 So. 3d 145, 147 (Fla. 3d DCA 2019), 15-1

Bank of Am., N.A. v. Delgado, 166 So. 3d 857 (Fla. 3d DCA 2015), 1-1:1, 2-1, 3-2:1.2, 12-1:10.1, 13-3:1, 13-4:2, 13-4:4

Bank of Am., N.A. v. Graybush, 253 So. 3d 1188 (Fla. 4th DCA 2018), 3-2:1.2, 3-2:3.2

Bank of Am., N.A. v. Kipps Colony II Condo. Ass'n, Inc., 201 So. 3d 670 (Fla. 2d DCA 2016), 5-3, 9-4:6, 14-3:7

Bank of Am., N.A. v. Mirabella Owners' Ass'n, Inc., 238 So. 3d 405 (Fla. 1st DCA 2018), 6-3:8, 10-2:1, 10-2:2

Bank of Am., N.A. v. Ribaudo, 199 So. 3d 407, 409 (Fla. 4th DCA 2016), 14-2:2, 15-3:3

Bank of Am., N.A. v. Siefker, 201 So. 3d 811, 818 (Fla. 4th DCA 2016), 8-5

Bank of Am., Nat. Ass'n v. Asbury, 165 So. 3d 808 (Fla. 2d DCA 2015), 2-2:2

Bank of Am., Nat. Ass'n v. Enclave at Richmond Place Condo. Ass'n, 173 So. 3d 1095 (Fla. 2d DCA 2015), 9-3, 9-4:4

Bank of America, N.A. v. King-Fenn, 2011 WL 3515682 (Fla. Cir. Ct. Aug. 10, 2011), 15-2:3

Bank of America, N.A. v. Kipps Colony II Condominium Ass'n, Inc., 201 So. 3d 670 (Fla. 2d DCA 2016), 6-3:1

Bank of America, N.A. v. Lane, 76 So. 3d 1007 (Fla. 1st DCA 2014), 14-3:1

Bank of America, N.A. v. Leonard, 212 So. 3d 417 (Fla. 1st DCA 2016), 6-2:3

Bank of America, N.A. v. Mirabella Owners' Ass'n, Inc., 238 So. 3d 405 (Fla. 1st DCA 2018), 6-3:5

Bank of America, N.A., Successor by Merger to BAC Home Loans Servicing, LP v. Colonnade at the Forum Homeowners Assoc., Inc., 2012 WL 8015567 (Fla. Cir. Ct. Lee 2012), 9-4:5

Bank of America v. Cadet, 183 So. 3d 477 (Fla. 3d DCA 2016), 12-1:10.1.e

Bank of America v. Delgado, 166 So. 3d 857 (Fla. 3d DCA 2015), 3-2:1.2, 13-4:2, 13-4:4

Bank of America v. Ruiz, 2016 WL 6726326 (Fla. Cir. Ct. 6th Jud. Cir. Oct. 27, 2016), 16-3:7

Bank of New York Mellon Trust Co. v. Ginsberg, 221 So. 3d 1196 (Fla. 4th DCA 2017), 4-4

Bank of New York Mellon Trust Co., N.A. v. Conley, 188 So. 3d 884 (Fla. 4th DCA 2016), 4-7

Bank of New York Mellon Trust Company, N.A. v. Fitzgerald, 215 So. 3d 116 (Fla. 3d DCA 2017), 16-2:3

Bank of New York Mellon Trust Company, National Association v. Ginsberg, 221 So. 3d 1196, (Fla. 4th DCA 2017), 6-4:4

Bank of New York Mellon v. Atkin, 2019 WL 3820572 (Fla. Cir. Ct. July 31, 2019), 15-1

Bank of New York Mellon v. Clark, Sanctuary at Redfish Condo. Ass'n, Inc., et al., 183 So. 3d 1271 (Fla. 1st DCA 2016), 9-3

Bank of New York Mellon v. Condo. Ass'n of La Mer Estates, Inc., 175 So. 3d 282 (Fla. 2015), 5-3, 18-10

Bank of New York Mellon v. Glenville, 252 So. 3d 1120 (Fla. 2018), 14-4, 14-5

Bank of New York Mellon v. Heath, 219 So. 3d 104 (Fla. 4th DCA 2017), 4-4, 4-6

Bank of New York Mellon v. Johnson, 185 So. 3d 594, 597 (Fla. 5th DCA 2016), 7-3:3

TABLE OF CASES 417

Bank of New York Mellon v. Johnson, 270 So. 3d 1269, 1272 (Fla. 1st DCA 2019), 11-3:2.1

Bank of New York Mellon v. Mestre, 159 So. 3d 953 (Fla. 5th DCA 2015), 16-2:3

Bank of New York Mellon v. Pearson, 212 So. 3d 1071 (Fla. 3d DCA 2017), 15-3:3

Bank of New York Mellon v. Sandhill, 202 So. 3d 944 (Fla. 5th DCA 2016), 15-3:3

Bank of New York v. Calloway, 157 So. 3d 1064 (Fla. 4th DCA 2015), 13-3:1

Bank of New York v. Mieses, 187 So. 3d 919 (Fla. 3d DCA 2016), 2-2:3.1

Bank of New York v. Mirador 1200 Condo. Assoc., Inc., 2012 WL 6916808 (Fla. Cir. Ct. Miami-Dade 2012), 9-4:5

Bank of New York v. Williams, 979 So. 2d 347 (Fla. 1st DCA 2008), 16-3:2

Bank of N.Y. Mellon for Bear Stearns Arm Tr., Mortg. Pass-Through Certificates, Series 2003-7 v. Thompson, 230 So. 3d 638 (Fla. 5th DCA 2017), 6-4:5

Bank of N.Y. Mellon for Certificateholders CWALT, Inc. v. HOA Rescue Fund, LLC, 249 So. 3d 731, 734 (Fla. 2d DCA 2018), 10-2:1, 10-2:2

Bank of N.Y. Mellon v. Bloedel, 236 So. 3d 1164 (Fla. 2d DCA 2018), 2-1:1, 13-4:4

Bank of N.Y. Mellon v. Burgiel, 248 So. 3d 237 (Fla. 5th DCA 2018), 10-2:1, 13-3:1

Bank of N.Y. Mellon v. Diaz, 232 So. 3d 435 (Fla. 4th DCA 2017), 15-3:3

Bank of N.Y. Mellon v. Estate of Peterson, 208 So. 3d 1218 (Fla. 2d DCA 2017), 14-3:6, 14-3:8

Bank of N.Y. Mellon v. Fla. Kalanit 770 LLC, 269 So. 3d 571 (Fla. 4th DCA 2019), 4-3

Bank of N.Y. Mellon v. Ginsberg, 221 So. 3d 1196 (Fla. 4th DCA 2017), 12-1:10.1.b

Bank of N.Y. Mellon v. Heath, 219 So. 3d 104 (Fla. 4th DCA 2017), 4-6

Bank of N.Y. Mellon v. Johnson, 185 So. 3d 594 (Fla. 5th DCA 2016), 12-1:10.1.e

Bank of N.Y. Mellon v. Johnson, 270 So. 3d 1269 (Fla. 1st DCA 2019), 15-3:3

Bank of N.Y. Mellon v. Milford, 206 So. 3d 137 (Fla. 4th DCA 2016), 12-1:10.1.b

Bank of N.Y. Mellon v. Nunez, 180 So. 3d 160 (Fla. 3d DCA 2015), 12-1:10.1.e

Bank of N.Y. Mellon v. Sandhill, 202 So. 3d 944 (Fla. 5th DCA 2016), 14-2:2

Bank of N.Y. Mellon v. Welker, 194 So. 3d 1078 (Fla. 2d DCA 2016), 8-5

Bank of N.Y. v. Calloway, 157 So. 3d 1064 (Fla. 4th DCA 2015), 12-1:10.1.a

Bank of N.Y. v. Mieses, 187 So. 3d 919 (Fla. 3d DCA 2016), 12-1:10.1.e

Bank of N.Y. v. Obermeyer, 260 So. 3d 1155, 1156 (Fla. 3d DCA 2018), 15-4:1

Bank One, Nat'l Ass'n v. Batronie, 884 So. 2d 346, 349 (Fla. 2d DCA 2004), 14-3:1, 14-3:3, 14-3:6

Bank of New York Trust Co. v. Rodgers, 79 So. 3d 108 (Fla. 3d DCA 2012), 7-3:2

Banksville, N.V. v. McNeill, 529 So. 2d 828 (Fla. 5th DCA 1988), 2-1:4

BankUnited, N.A. v. Ajabshir, 207 So. 3d 354 (Fla. 3d DCA 2016), 16-3:1

Baptist Medical Center of Beaches, Inc. v. Rhodin, 40 So. 3d 112 (Fla. 1st DCA 2010), 18-4:3

Barbe v. Villeneuve, 505 So. 2d 1331 (Fla. 1987), 9-3, 9-4:4

Barco Holdings, LLC v. Terminal Inv. Corp., 967 So. 2d 281 (Fla. 3d DCA 2007), 12-1:8

Barco v. School Board of Pinellas County, 975 So. 2d 1116 (Fla. 2008), 16-3:3

Bardill v. Holcomb, 215 So. 2d 64 (Fla. 4th DCA 1968), 2-3:1

Barnes v. Escambia Cnty. Employees Credit Union, 488 So. 2d 879 (Fla. 1st DCA 1986), 3-2:7

Baron v. Aiello, 319 So. 2d 198 (Fla. 3d DCA 1975), 9-4:6, 14-3:7

Baron v. Baron, 941 So. 2d 1233 (Fla. 2d DCA 2006), 12-1:8, 14-3:7

Barton-Malow Co. v. Gorman Co. of Ocala, Inc., 558 So. 2d 519 (Fla. 5th DCA 1990), 17-3:1

Barton v. MetroJax Property Holdings, LLC, 207 So. 3d 304, 306 (Fla. 3d DCA 2016), 6-3:9, 10-4:1

Bartram v. U.S. Bank, Nat'l Ass'n, 211 So. 3d 1009 (Fla. 2016), 2-3:2, 2-3:4, 2-3:5.3, 3-2:1, 3-2:1.1, 3-2:1.1a, 3-2:1.2, 3-2:2, 3-2:2.1, 3-2:3.1, 6-4:7

Bates v. JPMorgan Chase, 768 F.3d 1126 (11th Cir. 2014), 8-4

Bay Holdings, Inc. v. 2000 Island Blvd. Condo. Ass'n, 895 So. 2d 1197 (Fla. 3d DCA 2005), 9-4:1, 9-4:2

Bayview Loan Servicing, LLC v. Heefner, 198 So. 3d 918, 919 (Fla. 5th DCA 2016), 2-2:2, 2-2:3.1, 12-1:10.1.e

Bazzichelli v. Deutsche Bank Tr. Co. Americas, 44 Fla. L. Weekly D860 (Fla. 3d DCA Apr. 3, 2019), 14-3:9

B.B.S. v. R.C.B., 252 So. 2d 837 (Fla. 2d DCA 1971), 12-1:4

BCML Holding LLC v. U.S. Bank Nat'l Ass'n (In re BCML Holding LLC), No. 18-11600-E PK, 2018 WL 2386814, 2018 Bankr. LEXIS 1530 (Bankr. S.D. Fla. May 24, 2018), 3-2:3.1

Beacham v. Bank of America, N.A., No. 3:12-CV-00801-G, 2012 U.S. Dist. LEXIS 86106, 2012 WL 2358299 (N.D. Tex. May 25, 2012), 8-3

Beach Cmty. Bank v. First Brownsville Co., 85 So. 3d 1119 (Fla. 1st DCA 2012), 19-3:3

Beach Cmty. Bank v. Spellman, 206 So. 3d 843 (Fla. 1st DCA 2016), 2-1:1, 3-2:1.1

Beach Higher Power Corp. v. Granados, 717 So. 2d 563 (Fla. 3d DCA 1998), 12-1:3.1

Beach v. Great Western Bank, 692 So. 2d 146, *passim* (Fla. 1997), 7-3:6

Beach v. Ocwen F.S.B., 523 U.S. 410 (1998), 8-2:2

Beacon Hill Homeowners Ass'n, Inc. v. Colfin Ah-Florida 7, LLC, 221 So. 3d 710 (Fla. 3d DCA 2017), 7-3:3, 9-4:3

TABLE OF CASES

Beacon Place of Coral Springs Condo. Ass'n, Inc. v. Nationstar Mortg., LLC, 182 So. 3d 834 (Fla. 4th DCA 2016), 9-3

Beauchamp v. The Bank of N.Y., Tr. Co., N.A., 150 So. 3d 827 (Fla. 4th DCA 2014), 1-10:3, 9-3, 10-2:4

Beaulieu v. JP Morgan Chase Bank, N.A., 80 So. 3d 365 (Fla. 4th DCA 2012), 14-3:3

Beaumont v. Bank of New York Mellon, 81 So. 3d 553 (Fla. 5th DCA 2012), 13-4:1.1

Begelfer v. Najarian, 381 Mass. 177, 409 N.E.2d 167 (1980), 8-6

Belcher Center, LLC v. Belcher Center, Inc., 883 So. 2d 338 (Fla. 2d DCA 2004), 18-6:1

Belflower v. Cushman & Wakefield of Fla., Inc., 510 So. 2d 1130 (Fla. 2d DCA 1987), 14-3:7

2017 Bell Ranch Residential Land Tr. v. Burrill, 264 So. 3d 295 (Fla. 2d DCA 2019), 14-5

Beltway Capital, LLC v. Greens COA, Inc., 153 So. 3d 330 (Fla. 5th DCA 2014), 7-2:2, 9-4:2, 9-4:4

Beltway Capital, LLC v. Lucombe, 211 So. 3d 328 (Fla. 2d DCA 2017), 6-2:2

Benjamin v. CitiMortgage, Inc., No. 12-62291-CIV, 2013 U.S. Dist. LEXIS 64515, 2013 WL 1891284 (S.D. Fla. May 6, 2013), 8-6

Bennett v. Berges, 50 So. 3d 1154 (Fla. 4th DCA 2010), 16-4:1

Bensman v. DeLuca, 498 So. 2d 645 (Fla. 4th DCA 1986), 2-1, 2-1:3.1

Benton v. Moore, 655 So. 2d 1272 (Fla. 1st DCA 1995), 7-2:2

Benzrent 1, LLC v. Wilmington Sav. Fund Soc'y, FSB, 273 So. 3d 107 (Fla. 3d DCA 2019), 9-3, 10-2:4

Berneike v. CitiMortgage, Inc., 708 F.3d 1141 (10th Cir. 2013), 8-2:1

Beseau v. Bhalani, 904 So. 2d 641 (Fla. 5th DCA 2005), 6-3

BiFulco v. State Farm Mut. Auto. Ins. Co., 693 So. 2d 707 (Fla. 4th DCA 1997), 12-1:5

Binger v. King Pest Control, 401 So. 2d 1310 (Fla. 1981), 13-3

Bionetics Corp. v. Kenniasty, 69 So. 3d 943 (Fla. 2011), 15-4:1, 16-4:2

Bitterman v. Bitterman, 714 So. 2d 356 (Fla. 1998), 16-4:1

Blackburn v. Boulis, 184 So. 3d 565 (Fla. 4th DCA 2016), 18-4:1

Black Diamond Properties, Inc. v. Haines, 69 So. 3d 1090 (Fla. 5th DCA 2011), 3-2:5.3

Black Point Assets, Inc. v. Federal National Mortgage Association (Fannie Mae), 220 So. 3d 566 (Fla. 5th DCA 2017), 3-2:1.2, 6-4:5, 9-2, 12-1:10.1, 13-4

Blanchard v. Continental Mortg. Investors, 217 So. 2d 586 (Fla. 1st DCA 1969), 5-3

Blatch v. Wesley, 238 So. 2d 308 (Fla. 3d DCA 1970), 12-1:7

Bliss v. Carmona, 418 So. 2d 1017 (Fla. 3d DCA 1982), 7-3:1, 7-3:7, 12-1:3.2

Block v. Orlando-Orange Cnty. Expressway Authority, 313 So. 2d 75 (Fla. 4th DCA 1975), 7-3:6

Blue Supply v. Novos, 990 So. 2d 1157 (Fla. 3d DCA 2008), 7-2:1

Blumberg v. USAA Cas. Ins., 790 So. 2d 1061 (Fla. 2001), 9-3, 9-4:4

Blum v. Deutsche Bank Trust Co., 159 So. 3d 920 (Fla. 4th DCA 2015), 2-2:3

BMG Realty Grp., LLC v. U.S. Bank Nat'l Ass'n, 45 Fla. D298 (Fla. 2d DCA February 7, 2020), 3-2:1.3d

BMR Funding, LLC v. DDR. Corp., 67 So. 3d 1137 (Fla. 2d DCA 2011), 16-3:1

Boca Stel 2, LLC v. Christiana Tr., 186 So. 3d 1117 (Fla. 4th DCA 2016), 1-3

Boettcher v. IMC Mortg. Co., 871 So. 2d 1047 (Fla. 2d DCA 2004), 12-1:10.1.b

Bollettieri Resort Villas Condo. Ass'n, Inc. v. Bank of N.Y. Mellon, 198 So. 3d 1140 (Fla. 2d DCA 2016), 3-2:1.1, 3-2:1.1c, 3-2:3.2, 6-4:7, 9-3

Bollettieri Resort Villas Condo. Ass'n, Inc. v. Bank of N.Y. Mellon, 228 So. 3d 72, 73 (Fla. 2017), 3-2:1.2

Bolous v. U.S. Bank Nat'l Ass'n, 210 So. 3d 691 (Fla. 4th DCA 2016), 4-4, 13-4:1.3

Bonafide Properties, As Trustee Only Under 14329 Village View Dr Land trust v. Wells Fargo Bank, N.A., as Trustee for the Certificate-holders of Banc of America Alternative Loan Trust 2006-5, Mortgage Pass-Through Certificates, Series 2006-5, 198 So. 3d 694 (Fla. 2d DCA 2016), 9-4:6

Bonafide Properties v. Wells Fargo Bank, N.A., 198 So. 3d 694 (Fla. 2d DCA 2016), 10-2:1, 10-2:2

Bonafide Props., LLC v. E-Trade Bank, 208 So. 3d 1279 (Fla. 5th DCA 2017), 4-7

Bona Vista Condominium Association, Inc. v. FNS6, LLC, 194 So. 3d 490 (Fla. 3d DCA 2016), 9-4:1

Bonfiglio v. EMC Mortgage Corporation, 935 So. 2d 561 (Fla. 4th DCA 2006), 16-3:2

Booker v. Sarasota, Inc., 707 So. 2d 886 (Fla. 1st DCA 1998), 4-3

Boosinger v. Davis, 46 So. 3d 152 (Fla. 2d DCA 2010), 9-4:6, 14-3:3

Booth v. Bd. of Pub. Instruction of Dade County, 67 So. 2d 690 (Fla. 1953), 12-1:10.1.b

Borden v. Guardianship of Borden-Moore, 818 So. 2d 604 (Fla. 5th DCA 2002), 12-1:4

Borg-Warner Acceptance Corp. v. Hall, 685 F.2d 1306 (11th Cir. 1982), 17-3:1

Bottalico v. Antonelli, 695 So. 2d 363 (Fla. 4th DCA 1997), 13-6

Boumarate v. HSBC Bank USA, N.A., 172 So. 3d 535 (Fla. 5th DCA 2015), 4-2, 4-8

Bowen v. Bowen, 471 So. 2d 1274 (Fla. 1985), 15-2:2

Bowe v. US Bank Nat'l Ass'n, 260 So. 3d 1189 (Fla. 5th DCA 2019), 9-4:5

Bowman v. Barker, 172 So. 3d 1013 (Fla. 1st DCA 2015), 12-1:2

Bowman v. Kingsland Development, Inc., 432 So. 2d 660 (Fla. 5th DCA 1983), 1-4:3, 16-3:4

Boxer Max Corporation v. Cane A. Sucre, Inc., 905 So. 2d 916 (Fla. 3d DCA 2005), 16-3:2

TABLE OF CASES

Boyd v. Wells Fargo Bank, N.A., 143 So. 3d 1128 (Fla. 4th DCA 2014), 18-6:1

Boyette v. BAC Home Loans Servicing, LP, 164 So. 3d 9 (Fla. 2d DCA 2015), 13-4:4

Braddy v. State, 111 So. 3d 810 (Fla. 2012), 18-4:1.1

Brakefield v. CIT Group/Consumer Fin., Inc., 787 So. 2d 115 (Fla. 2d DCA 2001), 12-1:3.1

Brake v. Wells Fargo, 2011 U.S. Dist. LEXIS 146875, 2011 WL 6719215 (M.D. Fla. Dec. 5, 2011), 8-4

Branch Banking & Tr. Co. v. Park Circle, LLC, No. 2:13-cv- 25-FtM- 38CM, 2014 WL 1870606 (M.D. Fla. May 8, 2014), 19-3:1

Brandenburg v. Residential Credit Solutions, Inc., 137 So. 3d 604 (Fla. 4th DCA 2014), 4-9, 12-1:10.1.b

Brevard Community College v. Barber, 488 So. 2d 93 (Fla. 1st DCA 1986), 16-3:5

Brickell Place Condo Association, Inc. v. Ganguzza & Associates, P.A., 31 So. 3d 287 (Fla. 3d DCA 2010), 16-3:7

Brindise v. U.S. Bank Nat. Ass'n, 183 So. 3d 1215 (Fla. 2d DCA 2016), 8-5

Brinkley v. County of Flagler, 769 So. 2d 468 (Fla. 5th DCA 2000), 14-3:7

Brinson v. Creative Aluminum Products, Inc., 519 So. 2d 59 (Fla. 2d DCA 1988), 16-4:2

Bristol v. Wells Fargo Bank, N.A., 137 So. 3d 1130, 1132 (Fla. 4th DCA 2014), 4-7, 7-3:2

Brittany's Place Condo. Ass'n, Inc. v. U.S. Bank, N.A., 205 So. 3d 794 (Fla. 2d DCA 2016), 9-4:2, 9-4:4

Broward County v. 8705 Hampshire Drive Condo., Inc., 127 So. 3d 853 (Fla. 4th DCA 2013), 2-1:3.1, 2-3:2, 3-2:1.3c, 3-2:2.1

Broward County v. Perdue, 432 So. 2d 742 (Fla. 4th DCA 1983), 1-4:4.3

Broward County v. Recupero, 949 So. 2d 274 (Fla. 4th DCA 2007), 10-4:1

Brown v. BNB Inv. Holdings, LLC, No. 3D-17-1993, 2018 Fla. App. LEXIS 10273 (Fla. 3d DCA July 25, 2018), 7-2:1

Brown v. Giffen Indust., Inc., 281 So. 2d 897 (Fla. 1973), 2-2:3

Brown v. McMillian, 737 So. 2d 570 (Fla. 1st DCA 1999), 14-3:5

Brown v. U.S. Bank Nat'l Assn., 117 So. 3d 823 (Fla. 4th DCA 2013), 1-3:2

Bryson v. Branch Banking & Tr. Co., 75 So. 3d 783 (Fla. 2d DCA 2011), 2-2:2

Buchanan & Crowder, Inc. v. Kreamer, 162 So. 500 (Fla. 1935), 16-3:2

Buckingham v. Bank of Am., N.A., 230 So. 3d 923 (Fla. 2d DCA 2017), 4-4

Bueno v. Workman, 20 So. 3d 993 (Fla. 4th DCA 2009), 7-3:5

Building Educ. Corp. v. Ocean Bank, 982 So. 2d 37 (Fla. 3d DCA 2008), 12-1:8

Burgos v. Burgos, 948 So. 2d 918 (Fla. 4th DCA 2007), 16-4:3

Burns v. Bankamerica Nat'l Trust Co., 719 So. 2d 999 (Fla. 5th DCA 1998), 1-10:3, 10-2:3

Burns v. Equilease Corp., 357 So. 2d 786 (Fla. 3d DCA 1978), 7-3:7

Burton Family Partnership v. Luani Plaza, Inc., 2019 WL 2844271 (Fla. 3d DCA 2019), 16-3:6

Busbee-Bailey Tomato Co. v. Bailey, 463 So. 2d 1255 (Fla. 1st DCA 1985), 12-1:7

Bush v. Belenke, 381 So. 2d 315 (Fla. 3d DCA 1980), 12-1:10.1.b

Bush v. Holmes, 919 So. 2d 392 (Fla. 2006), 18-6:1

Bush v. Whitney Bank, 219 So. 3d 257 (Fla. 5th DCA 2017), 19-4

Butler v. Harter, 152 So. 3d 705 (Fla. 1st DCA 2014), 11-1

Butner v. U.S., 440 U.S. 48, 99 S. Ct. 914 (1979), 17-2

Buzzi v. Quality Serv. Station, Inc., 921 So. 2d 14 (Fla. 3d DCA 2006), 12-1:5

Byers v. Callahan, 848 So. 2d 1180 (Fla. 2d DCA 2003), 14-3:9

Bymel v. Bank of America, N.A., 159 So. 3d 345 (Fla. 3d DCA 2015), 10-2:1, 10-2:2, 10-3:2

Byrd v. Leach, 226 So. 2d 866 (Fla. 4th DCA 1969), 12-1:3

C

Caballero v. U.S. Bank Nat'l Ass'n, 189 So. 3d 1044 (Fla. 2d DCA 2016), 4-3, 13-4:1.3

Cacho v. Bank of New York Mellon, 124 So. 3d 943 (Fla. 3d DCA 2013), 16-3:2

Cadle Co. v. McCartha, 920 So. 2d 144 (Fla. 5th DCA 2006), 3-2:5.1

Caduceus Props., LLC v. Graney, 137 So. 3d 987 (Fla. 2014), 6-4:7

Cady v. Chevy Chase Sav. & Loan, Inc., 528 So. 2d 136 (Fla. 4th DCA 1988), 7-3:1, 7-3:7, 12-1:3.2

Caggins v. Bank of N.Y. Mellon, No. 1511124, 2015 WL 4041350 (E.D. Mich. July 1, 2015), 14-4

Calendar v. Stonebridge Gardens Section III Condo. Ass'n, Inc., 234 So. 3d 18 (Fla. 4th DCA 2017), 9-4:1, 14-5

Campbell-Settle Pressure Grouting v. David M. Abel Constr. Co., 395 So. 2d 247 (Fla. 3d DCA 1981), 12-1:3

Campbell v. Goldman, 959 So. 2d 223 (Fla. 2007), 16-1:1, 16-5.2

Campbell v. Wells Fargo Bank, N.A., 204 So. 3d 476 (Fla. 4th DCA 2016), 6-2:3

Campbell v. Werner, 232 So. 2d 252, 254 (Fla. 3d DCA 1970), 2-3:2, 2-3:3, 14-3:8

Can Fin., LLC v. Krazmien, 253 So. 3d 8 (Fla. 4th DCA 2018), 3-2:1.3d

Cape Royal Realty, Inc. v. Kroll, 804 So. 2d 605 (Fla. 5th DCA 2002), 14-2:1

Capital Bank v. Needle, 596 So. 2d 1134 (Fla. 4th DCA 1992), 2-3:5.1

Captains Table, Inc. v. Khouri, 208 So. 2d 677 (Fla. 4th DCA 1968), 13-5

Caraccia v. U.S. Bank, N.A., 185 So. 3d 1277, 1279 (Fla. 4th DCA 2016), 4-6, 7-3:2, 12-1:10.1.b, 12-1:10.1.e, 13-4:1.3

Carbonell v. BellSouth Telcoms., 675 So. 2d 705 (Fla. 3d DCA 1996), 12-1:8

Carlisle v. U.S. Bank, Nat'l Ass'n, as Tr. for the Benefit of Harborview 2005-10 Tr. Fund, 225 So. 3d 893 (Fla. 3d DCA 2017), 10-2:1, 10-2:2, 14-2:2

Carlton v. Wal-Mart Stores, 621 So. 2d 451 (Fla. 1st DCA 1993), 18-4:1

Carpenter v. Super Pools, Inc., 534 So. 2d 426 (Fla. 5th DCA 1988), 12-1:9

Carriage Hills Condominium, Inc. v. JBH Roofing & Constructors, Inc., 109 So. 3d 329 (Fla. 4th DCA 2013), 11-6:1.1, 13-3:1

Carter v. Kingsley Bank, 587 So. 2d 567 (Fla. 1st DCA 1991), 14-3:7

Casa Inv. Co. v. Nestor, 8 So. 3d 1219 (Fla. 3d DCA 2009), 12-1:4

Castelo Development, LLC v. Aurora Loan Services LLC, 85 So. 3d 515 (Fla. 4th DCA 2012), 1-10:2

Castillo v. Deutsche Bank Nat'l Trust Co., 89 So. 3d 1069 (Fla. 3d DCA 2012), 9-3, 12-1:10.1.h

Castro v. Brazeau, 873 So. 2d 516 (Fla. 4th DCA 2004), 12-1:3

Catalina West Homeowners Ass'n v. Federal National Mortg. Ass'n, 188 So. 3d 76 (Fla. 3d DCA 2016), 9-4:3, 9-4:4

Caulfield v. Cantele, 837 So. 2d 371 (Fla. 2002), 16-3:1

Cayea v. Citimortgage, Inc., 138 So. 3d 1214 (Fla. 4th DCA 2014), 12-1:10.1.a

CCM Pathfinder Palm Harbor Mgmt., LLC v. Unknown Heirs of Gendron, 198 So. 3d 3 (Fla. 2d DCA 2015), 3-3:2.2, 10-2:1, 10-2:4

Cedar Mountain Estates, LLC v. Loan One, LLC, 4 So. 3d 15 (Fla. 5th DCA 2009), 1-4:4.3

Cellular Warehouse, Inc. v. GH Cellular, LLC, 957 So. 2d 662 (Fla. 3d DCA 2007), 13-2:2

Centerstate Bank Cent. Fla., N.A. v. Krause, 87 So. 3d 25 (Fla. 5th DCA 2012), 10-2:2

Central Home Trust Co. of Elizabeth v. Lippincott, 392 So. 2d 931 (Fla. 5th DCA 1980), 2-3:2, 3-2:1.1b

Central Mortgage Co. v. Callahan, 155 So. 3d 373 (Fla. 3d DCA 2014), 9-4:5

Central Park A Metrowest Condominium Assoc., Inc. v. Amtrust REO I, LLC, 169 So. 3d 1223 (Fla. 5th DCA 2015), 9-3, 9-4:4, 9-4:5

Certo v. Bank of N.Y. Mellon, 268 So. 3d 901 (Fla. 1st DCA 2019), 4-7

Cesaire v. State, 811 So. 2d 816 (Fla. 4th DCA 2002), 14-3:7

CGI Fin., Inc. v. C & V Sportfishing, LLC, 12-60857-CIV, 2012 WL 5077139 (S.D. Fla. Sept. 21, 2012), 2-1:3.2

Chandris, S.A. v. Yanakakis, 668 So. 2d 180 (Fla. 1995), 16-3:7

Channell v. Deutsche Bank Nat'l Trust Co., 173 So. 3d 1017 (Fla. 2d DCA 2015), 11-9:3

Chaphe v. Chaphe, 19 So. 3d 1019 (Fla. 1st DCA. 2009), 14-2:2

Chaplin v. Cooke's Estate, 432 So. 2d 778 (Fla. 1st DCA 1983), 3-2:5.1

Charles E. Burkett & Associates, Inc. v. Vick, 546 So. 2d 1190 (Fla. 5th DCA 1989), 12-1:3

Charter Review Comm'n of Orange County v. Scott, 627 So. 2d 520 (Fla. 5th DCA 1993), 13-2:1

Chase Financial Services, LLC. v. Edelsberg, 129 So. 3d 1139 (Fla. 3d DCA 2013), 14-4

Chase Home Finance LLC v. Guerrero, 2015 WL 10945252 (Fla. Cir. Ct. Miami-Dade June 15, 2015), 16-3:7

Chaudhry v. Pedersen, No. 5D18-709, 44 Fla. L. Weekly D405 (Fla. 5th DCA Feb. 8, 2019), 6-3:6

Chestnut v. Nationstar Mortg., LLC, No. 3D17-1752, 2018 Fla. App. LEXIS 11406 (Fla. 3d DCA Aug. 15, 2018), 7-2:2

Chetu, Inc. v. Franklin First Fin., Ltd., 4D18-2428, 2019 Fla. App. LEXIS 11309 (Fla. 4th DCA July 17, 2019), 1-4:4

Chidnese v. McCollem, 695 So. 2d 936 (Fla. 4th DCA 1997), 19-3:2

Chiusolo v. Kennedy, 614 So. 2d 491 (Fla. 1993), 10-1:1

Chmura v. Sam Rodgers Props., 2 So. 3d 984 (Fla. 2d DCA 2008), 15-3:3

Chrestensen v. Eurogest, Inc., 906 So. 2d 343 (Fla. 4th DCA 2005), 3-2:7, 14-3:8

Chris Craft Ind. v. Van Valkenberg, 267 So. 2d 642 (Fla. 1972), 12-1:3.2

Chrzuszcz v. Wells Fargo Bank, N.A., 250 So. 3d 766 (Fla. 1st DCA 2018), 2-2:2, 2-2:6, 8-4

Chuchian v. Situs Invs., LLC, 219 So. 3d 992 (Fla. 5th DCA 2017), 4-10

Church of Christ Written in Heaven of Georgia, Inc. v. Church of Christ Written in Heaven of Miami, Inc., 947 So. 2d 557 (Fla. 3d DCA 2006), 1-4:4.2

Ciolli v. City of Palm Bay, 59 So. 3d 295 (Fla. 5th DCA 2011), 12-1:3

Citation Way Condominium Association, Inc. v. Wells Fargo Bank, N.A., 172 So. 3d 558 (Fla. 4th DCA 2015), 9-4:2, 9-4:4, 9-4:5

CitiBank, N.A. v. Manning, 221 So. 3d 677 (Fla. 4th DCA 2017), 4-4

Citibank, N.A. v. Villanueva, 174 So. 3d 612 (Fla. 4th DCA 2015), 6-1:2, 6-3:5, 10-2:1, 14-3:7

Citigroup Mortg. Loan Tr. Inc. v. Scialabba, 238 So. 3d 317 (Fla. 4th DCA 2018), 2-2:2

CitiMortgage, Inc. v. Flowers, 41 Fla. L. Weekly D916 (Fla. 4th DCA Apr. 13, 2016), 5-5

CitiMortgage, Inc. v. Flowers, 189 So. 3d 1032 (Fla. 4th DCA 2016), 9-4:6, 14-3:7

TABLE OF CASES

CitiMortgage, Inc. v. Hoskinson, 200 So. 3d 191 (Fla. 5th DCA 2016), 2-2:3, 12-1:10.1.a

Citi-Mortgage, Inc. v. Wachovia Bank, 24 So. 3d 641 (Fla. 2d DCA 2009), 9-4:6, 14-3:7

Citing Harrell v. State, 894 So. 2d 935 (Fla. 2005), 18-3

Citizens Property Insurance Corp. v. River Oaks Condo. II Ass'n, Inc., 190 So. 3d 1110 (Fla. 2d DCA 2016), 16-3:7

City of Cooper City v. Sunshine Wireless Co., 654 So. 2d 283 (Fla. 4th DCA 1995), 12-1:4

City of Miami v. Dade County, 321 So. 2d 140 (Fla. 3d DCA 1975), 13-2:2

City of North Miami Beach v. Berrio, 64 So. 3d 713 (Fla. 3d DCA 2011), 16-4:3

City of Palm Bay v. Wells Fargo Bank, N.A., 114 So. 3d 924 (Fla. 2013), 6-3:9, 10-4:1

City of Riviera Beach v. J & B Motel Corp., 213 So. 3d 1102 (Fla. 4th DCA 2017), 10-4:1

City of Riviera Beach v. Reed, 987 So. 2d 168 (Fla. 4th DCA 2008), 3-1:2

City of Tallahassee v. Big Bend PBA, 703 So. 2d 1066 (Fla. 1st DCA 1997), 18-4:1

City of Tallahassee v. Blankenship & Lee, 736 So. 2d 29 (Fla. 1st DCA 1999), 16-6:1

So. -*Clark v. Ocwen Loan Servicing, LLC,* No. 1:15-cv- 659, 2015 WL 6159447 (W.D. Mich. Oct. 20, 2015), 14-4

Clay Cty. Land Tr. No. 08-04-25-0078-014-27, Orange Park Tr. Servs., LLC v. JP Morgan Chase Bank, Nat'l Ass'n, 152 So. 3d 83 (Fla. 1st DCA 2014), 2-2:2, 4-5, 6-4:3, 7-3:2, 9-3, 10-2:4, 12-1:10.1.b, 12-1:10.1.h

Cleveland v. Crown Fin., LLC, 212 So. 3d 1065 (Fla. 1st DCA 2017), 14-3:5

Coastal Creek Condo. Ass'n, Inc. v. Fla Tr. Services LLC, 275 So. 3d 836 (Fla. 1st DCA 2019), 9-4:1

Coconut Key Homeowner's Ass'n, Inc. v. Gonzalez, 246 So. 3d 428 (Fla. 4th DCA 2018), 9-4:5

Cocoves v. Campbell, 819 So. 2d 910 (Fla. 4th DCA 2002), 12-1:3.2

Coe v. Finlayson, 41 Fla. 169 (Fla. 1899), 9-3

Cohen v. Arvin, 878 So. 2d 403 (Fla. 4th DCA 2004), 12-1:2

Cohen v. Cohen, 158 Fla. 802 (1947), 18-3

Cohn v. Grand Condo. Ass'n, Inc., 62 So. 3d 1120 (Fla. 2011), 9-4:3

Colby v. Ellis, 562 So. 2d 356 (Fla. 2d DCA 1990), 12-1:8

Coleman (Parent) Holdings, Inc. v. Morgan Stanley & Co., Inc., 20 So. 3d 952 (Fla. 4th DCA 2009), 14-3:2, 14-3:6

Coley v. Accredited Home Lenders, 2011 U.S. Dist. LEXIS 38294, 2011 WL 1193072 (E.D. Ark. 2011), 8-4

Collazo v. HSBC Bank USA, N.A., 213 So. 3d 1012 (Fla. 3d DCA 2016), 2-3:5.2, 6-4:7

Collazo v. Hupert, 693 So. 2d 631 (Fla. 3d DCA 1997), 11-9:2

Collins Asset Grp., LLC v. Prop. Asset Mgmt., Inc., 197 So. 3d 87 (Fla. 1st DCA 2016), 19-2:2

Collins v. Holland, 409 So. 2d 1097 (Fla. 3d DCA 1982), 11-3:1

Colon v. JP Morgan Chase Bank, N.A., 162 So. 3d 195 (Fla. 5th DCA 2015), 12-1:10.1.f

Columbia Bank v. Turbeville, 143 So. 3d 964 (Fla. 1st DCA 2014), 6-5:4

Commercial Bank of Kendall v. Heiman, 322 So. 2d 564 (Fla. 3d DCA 1975), 12-1:8

Commercial Laundries, Inc. v. Golf Course Towers Associates, 568 So. 2d 501 (Fla. 3d DCA 1990), 6-3:7, 10-3:1

Commercial Laundries of W. Florida, Inc. v. Tiffany Square Inv'rs Ltd. P'ship, 605 So. 2d 116 (Fla. 5th DCA 1992), 5-8

Commonwealth Land Title Ins. Co. v. Freeman, 884 So. 2d 164 (Fla. 2d DCA 2004), 14-3:3

Components Corp. v. Florida Dep't of Trans., 14 So. 3d 967 (Fla 2009), 18-1

Concrete & Lumber Enterprises Corp. v. Guaranty Business Credit Corp., 829 So. 2d 247 (Fla. 3d DCA 2002), 16-3:1

Condominium Ass'n of La Mer Estates, Inc. v. Bank of New York Mellon Corp., 137 So. 3d 396, 400-01 (Fla. 4th DCA 2014), 9-4:6, 14-2:1, 14-3:1, 14-3:7

Cone Bros. Constr. Co. v. Moore, 141 Fla. 420 (1940), 9-4:6, 14-3:7

Congress Park Office Condos II, LLC v. First-Citizens Bank & Trust Co., 105 So. 3d 602 (Fla. 4th DCA 2013), 1-6, 7-3:6, 12-1:3.2

Conner v. Coggins, 349 So. 2d 780 (Fla. 1st DCA 1977), 3-2:1.2

Cooke v. Ins. Co. of N. Am., 652 So. 2d 1154 (Fla. 2d DCA 1995), 12-1:10.1.e

Coral Lakes Community Ass'n, Inc. v. Busey Bank, N.A., 30 So. 3d 579 (Fla. 2d DCA 2010), 9-4:3

Cornelius v. Bank of Am., N.A., 2012 U.S. Dist. LEXIS 139173, 2012 WL 4468746 (N.D. Ga. Sept. 27, 2012), 8-4

Cornelius v. Holzman, 193 So. 3d 1029 (Fla. 4th DCA 2016), 5-9, 14-3:1, 14-3:3, 14-3:7

Corrigan v. Bank of Am., N.A., 189 So. 3d 187 (Fla. 2d DCA 2016), 4-1, 12-1:3.2

Couchman v. Goodbody & Co., 231 So. 2d 842 (Fla. 4th DCA 1970), 12-1:4

Country Place Community Ass'n, Inc. v. J.P. Morgan Mortg. Acquisition Corp., 51 So. 3d 1176 (Fla. 2d DCA 2010), 9-3

Countrywide Home Loans, Inc. v. Burnette, 177 So. 3d 1032 (Fla. 1st DCA 2015), 3-1:1

County of Pasco v. Riehl, 635 So. 2d 17 (Fla.1994), 14-3:7

Courtney v. Catalina, Ltd., 130 So. 3d 739 (Fla. 3d DCA 2014), 9-4:6, 14-3:3

Cox v. CSX Intermodal, Inc., 732 So. 2d 1092, 1095 (Fla. 1st DCA 1999), 12-1:3

Creadon v. U.S. Bank, N.A., 166 So. 3d 952 (Fla. 2nd DCA 2015), 4-9, 13-4:1.2

Creative Choice Homes, II, Ltd. v. Keystone Guard Servs., 137 So. 3d 1144 (Fla. 3d DCA 2014), 15-2:3

Crespo v. Florida Entm't Direct Support Org., Inc., 674 So. 2d 154 (Fla. 3d DCA 1996), 11-9:2

Cromer v. Mullally, 861 So. 2d 523 (Fla. 3d DCA 2003), 7-3:7

Cronkhite v. Kemp, 741 F. Supp. 822 (E.D. Wash. 1989), 8-4:1

Crowley v. Crowley, 678 So. 2d 435 (Fla. 4th DCA 1996), 14-3:1, 14-3:6

Crystal River Lumber Co. v. Knight Turpentine Co., 67 So. 974 (Fla. 1915), 5-8

CSI Servs., Ltd. v. Hawkins Concrete Constr. Co., 516 So. 2d 337 (Fla. 1st DCA 1987), 19-3

Cuillo v. McCoy, 810 So. 2d 1061 (Fla. 4th DCA 2002), 3-2:5.1

Curbelo v. Ullman, 571 So. 2d 443 (Fla. 1990), 14-3:3

Custer Med. Ctr. v. United Auto. Ins. Co., 62 So. 3d 1086 (Fla. 2010), 7-2:2, 7-3:3, 12-1:10.1.e

Cutler v. U.S. Bank Nat'l Ass'n, 109 So. 3d 224 (Fla. 2d DCA 2012), 12-1:10.1.b

D

Dabas v. Boston Inv'r Grp., Inc., 231 So. 3d 542 (Fla. 3d DCA 2017), 14-3:7

Dade County v. Pena, 664 So. 2d 959 (Fla. 1995), 16-1:1

Dage v. Deutsche Bank Nat'l Trust Co., 95 So. 3d 1021 (Fla. 2d DCA 2012), 14-2:1, 14-3:1, 14-3:7

Dailey v. Leshin, 792 So. 2d 527 (Fla. 4th DCA 2001), 3-2:4, 8-1

Danford v. Rockledge, 387 So. 2d 968 (Fla. 5th DCA 1980), 12-1:4

Dan Galasso Waste Serv., Inc. v. Hemery, 528 So. 2d 1356 (Fla. 3d DCA 1988), 16-3:4

D'Angelo v. Fitzmaurice, 863 So. 2d 311 (Fla. 2003), 18-6:1

David v. City of Jacksonville, 534 So. 2d 784 (Fla. 1st DCA 1988), 11-6:3

David v. Sun Federal Savings & Loan Ass'n, 461 So. 2d 93 (Fla. 1984), 1-1:1, 3-2:3.1, 13-4:3, 14-3:8

Daw v. Peoples Bank & Trust Co., 5 Fed. Appx. 504 (7th Cir. 2001), 8-3

Days Inns Acquisition Corp. v. Hutchinson, 707 So. 2d 747 (Fla. 4th 1997), 1-4

Day v. Amini, 550 So. 2d 169 (Fla. 2d DCA 1989), 13-6

Deakter v. Menendez, 830 So. 2d 124 (Fla. 3d DCA 2002), 4-8, 12-1:10.1.b, 13-4:1.3

De Ardila v. Chase Manhattan Mortg. Corp., 826 So. 2d 419 (Fla. 3d DCA 2002), 14-4

DeBartolo-Aventura, Inc. v. Hernandez, 638 So. 2d 988 (Fla. 3rd DCA 1994), 11-3:2.1

Debolt v. Debolt, 90 So. 3d 374 (Fla. 1st DCA 2012), 14-2:2, 16-3:6

DeClaire v. Yohanan, 453 So. 2d 375 (Fla.1984), 14-3:6

Decosmo v. Fisher, 683 So. 2d 659 (Fla. 5th DCA 1996), 12-1:4

Deemer v. Hallett Pontiac, Inc., 288 So. 2d 526 (Fla. 3d DCA), 14-2:2

DeGuzman v. Balsini, 930 So. 2d 752 (Fla. 5th DCA 2006), 5-5

De La Osa v. Wells Fargo Bank, N.A., 208 So. 3d 259 (Fla. 3d DCA 2016), 9-4:6, 14-3:3

Delcher Bros. Storage Co. v. Carter, 132 So. 2d 593 (Fla. 1965), 9-4:4

Delgado v. Strong, 360 So. 2d 73 (Fla. 1978), 2-1:3.1

Della Ratta v. Della Ratta, 927 So. 2d 1055 (Fla. 4th DCA 2006), 6-5:4

Delno v. Market Ry. Co., 124 F.2d 965 (9th Cir. 1942), 18-6:2

DeLong v. Lakeview Loan Servicing, LLC, 222 So. 3d 662 (Fla. 5th DCA 2017), 7-3:3

Del Rio v. Brandon, 696 So. 2d 1197 (Fla. 3d DCA 1997), 12-1:9

Deluxe Motel, Inc. v. Patel, 727 So. 2d 299 (Fla. 5th DCA 1999), 12-1:4

Deluxe Motel, Inc. v. Patel, 770 So. 2d 283 (Fla. 5th DCA 2000), 10-2:3

Dema Invs., LLC v. Wells Fargo Bank, N.A., 207 So. 3d 977 (Fla. 5th DCA 2016), 10-2:1, 10-2:2

De Mesme v. Stephenson, 498 So. 2d 673 (Fla. 1st DCA 1986), 12-1:3, 12-1:8

Demetree v. Stae, 89 So. 2d 498 (Fla. 1956), 13-3:3

Dempsey v. Law Firm of Cauthen & Odham, P.A., 781 So. 2d 1141 (Fla 5th DCA 2001), 12-1:3

Denino v. Abbate, 247 So. 3d 48 (Fla. 2d DCA 2018), 15-4:2

Denton v. HSBC Bank USA, N.A., 45 Fla. L. Weekly D270 (Fla. 4th DCA February 5, 2020), 2-2:2

De Pass v. Chitty, 90 Fla. 77, 105 So. 148 (Fla. 1925), 5-5, 6-1:4, 10-1:1

Depicciotto v. Nationstar Mortgage, LLC, 225 So. 3d 390 (Fla. 4th DCA 2017), 3-2:1.1c

Dep't of Rev. ex rel. Smith v. Selles, 47 So. 3d 916 (Fla. 1st DCA 2010), 18-3

Dep't of Revenue ex rel. Stephens v. Boswell, 915 So. 2d 717 (Fla. 5th DCA 2005), 5-6

Derouin v. Universal Am. Mortg. Co., Ltd. Liab. Co., 254 So. 3d 595 (Fla. 2d DCA 2018), No. 2D17-1002, LEXIS 11800, 2018 WL 3999415, *passim*, 2-2:2, 2-2:6, 8-4, 7-3:3, 13-4:3

Desai v. Bank of N.Y. Mellon Tr. Co., 240 So. 3d 729 (Fla. 4th DCA 2018), 3-2:2.1

De Sousa v. JP Morgan Chase, N.A., 170 So. 3d 928 (Fla. 4th DCA 2015), 10-2:1, 10-2:2, 10-2:3, 10-2:4

Destin Pointe Owners' Ass'n v. Destin Parcel 160, Ltd., 44 Fla. L. Weekly D1869, 2019 WL 3282621, 2019 Fla. App. LEXIS 11460 (Fla. 1st DCA July 22, 2019), 12-1:6

Desylvester v. Bank of New York, 219 So. 3d 1016 (Fla. 2d DCA 2017), 6-4:7

Deubert v. Gulf Fed. Sav. Bank, 820 F.2d 754 (5th Cir. 1987), 8-4

Deutsche Bank, Nat'l Tr. Co. as Tr. for Holders of the BCAP LLC Tr. 2007-AA1 v. Quintela, 268 So. 3d 156 (Fla. 4th DCA 2019), 16-3:2

Deutsche Bank Nat. Tr. Co. v. Hagstrom, 203 So. 3d 918 (Fla. 2d DCA 2016), 8-5

Deutsche Bank Nat. Trust Co. v. Basanta, 88 So. 3d 216 (Fla. 3d DCA 2011), 9-4:6, 14-3:3

Deutsche Bank Nat. Trust Co. v. Patino, 192 So. 3d 637 (Fla. 1st DCA 2016), 14-3:7

Deutsche Bank National Trust Co. v. LGC, 107 So. 3d 486 (Fla. 2d DCA 2013), 11-7:3

Deutsche Bank National Trust Company, as Trustee for the Registered Holders of Morgan Stanley ABS Capital I Inc. Trust 2007-NC3 Mortgage Pass-Through Certificates, Series 2007-NC3 v. Jill S. Nickens, 2014 WL 519354 (Fla. 9th Jud. Cir. Orange Feb. 6, 2014), 9-4:5

Deutsche Bank Nat'l Tr. Co. for Certificateholders of Morgan Stanley ABS Capital 1 Inc. Tr. 2003-NC10 v. Del Busto, 254 So. 3d 1050 (Fla. 3d DCA 2018), 14-1

Deutsche Bank Nat'l Tr. Co. v. Avila-Gonzalez, 164 So. 3d 90 (Fla. 3d DCA 2015), 11-3:2.1

Deutsche Bank Nat'l Tr. Co. v. Hagstrom, 203 So. 3d 918 (Fla. 2d DCA 2016), 12-1:3.2, 12-1:10.1.e

Deutsche Bank Nat'l Tr. Co. v. Sombrero Beach Rd., LLC, 260 So. 3d 424 (Fla. 3d DCA 2018), 11-3:2.1, 15-3:3

Deutsche Bank Nat'l Trust Co. v. Applewhite, 213 So. 3d 948 (Fla. 4th DCA 2017), 4-6, 6-2:3

Deutsche Bank Nat'l Trust Co. v. Avila-Gonzalez, 164 So. 3d 90 (Fla. 3d DCA 2015), 11-3:2.1

Deutsche Bank Nat'l Trust Co. v. Baker, 199 So. 3d 967 (Fla. 4th DCA 2016), 13-4:4

Deutsche Bank Nat'l Trust Co. v. Clarke, 87 So. 3d 58 (Fla. 4th DCA 2012), 4-2, 7-3:2, 12-1:10.1.b

Deutsche Bank Nat'l Trust Co. v. Coral Key Condo. Ass'n, 32 So. 3d 195 (Fla. 4th DCA 2010), 9-3

Deutsche Bank Nat'l Trust Co. v. Huber, 137 So. 3d 562 (Fla 4th DCA 2014), 13-4:1.1

Deutsche Bank Nat'l Trust Co. v. Marciano, 190 So. 3d 166 (Fla. 5th DCA 2016), 4-4, 13-4:1.3

Deutsche Bank Nat'l Trust Co. v. Noll, 261 So. 3d 656 (Fla. 2d DCA 2018), 4-6

Deutsche Bank Nat'l Trust Co. v. Perez, 180 So. 3d 1186 (Fla. 3d DCA 2015), 13-3

Deutsche Bank Nat'l Trust Co. v. Plageman, 133 So. 3d 1199, 1202 (Fla. 2d DCA 2014), 6-2:2, 7-2:2

Deutsche Bank Nat'l Trust Co. v. Prevratil, 120 So. 3d 573, 575 (Fla. 2d DCA 2013), 6-2:2, 7-2:2

Deutsche Bank Nat'l Trust Co. v. Quinion, 198 So. 3d 701 (Fla. 2d DCA 2016), 2-2:2, 7-3:3, 12-1:10.1.e

Deutsche Bank Nat'l Trust Co. v. Smith, 2019 Fla. App. LEXIS 11298, No. 4D18-2265 (Fla. 4th DCA July 17, 2019), 7-3:2

Deutsche Bank Nat'l Trust Co. v. Viteri, 264 So. 3d 963 (Fla. 4th DCA 2019), 4-4

Deutsche Bank Nat'l Trust Co., as Trustee of the Indymac Indx Mortgage Loan Trust 2006-AR15, Mortgage Pass-Through Certificates, Series 2006-AR15 Under the Pooling and Servicing Agreement Dated May 1, 2006 v. Labarile, 2014 WL 624401 (Fla. Cir. Ct. Pinellas January 16, 2014), 9-4:5

Deutsche Bank Nat'l Trust Co., as Trustee Under the Pooling and Servicing Agreement Relating to Impac Secured Assets Corp., Mortgage Pass Through Certificates, Series 2007-3 v. Tuscany No. 3 Condo. Assoc., Inc., 2012 WL 8255399 (Fla. Cir. Ct. Broward 2012), 9-4:5

Deutsche Bank Nat'l Trust Co., Etc. v. Alaqua Prop., Etc., 190 So. 3d 662 (Fla. 5th DCA 2016), 12-1:10.1.a, 12-1:10.1.b, 12-1:10.1.c, 13-4:1

Deutsche Bank Tr. Co. Ams. v. Beauvais, 188 So. 3d 938 (Fla. 3d DCA 2016), 1-1, 2-3:4, 6-4:7

Deutsche Bank Tr. Co. Ams. v. Frias, 178 So. 3d 505 (Fla. 4th DCA 2015), 12-1:10.1.a

Deutsche Bank Trust Co. Americas v. Nash, 136 So. 3d 1267 (Fla. 2d DCA 2014), 17-7

Deutsche Bank Trust Co. Ams. v. Beauvais, 188 So. 3d 938 (Fla. 3d DCA 2016), 3-2:1.1, 3-2:1.1a

Deutsche Bank Trust Co. Ams. v. Harris, 264 So. 3d 186 (Fla. 4th DCA 2019), 7-3:2

Deutsche Bank Trust Co. Ams. v. Merced, 238 So. 3d 438 (Fla. 5th DCA 2018), 13-3, 13-4

Deutsche Bank Trust Company Americas v. Page, 274 So. 3d 1116 (Fla. 4th DCA 2019), 16-2:3

Deutsche Bank v. Dofflevisnd, 2009 WL 8626512 (Fla. Cir. Ct. Palm Beach Cnty. 2009), 9-4:1

Dewsnup v. Timm, 502 U.S. 410 (1992), 17-6:1

Dhanasar v. JP Morgan Chase Bank, N.A., 201 So. 3d 825 (Fla. 3d DCA 2016), 3-2:1.1c

Diaz v. Diaz, 826 So. 2d 229, 232 (Fla. 2002), 15-2:3

Dimitri v. Commercial Ctr. of Miami Master Ass'n, Inc., 253 So. 3d 715 (Fla. 3d DCA 2018), 9-4:3

DiPiazza v. Palm Beach Mall, Inc., 722 So. 2d 831 (Fla. 2d DCA 1998), 14-3:9

Diquollo v. TD Bank, N.A., 224 So. 3d 341 (Fla. 5th DCA 2017), 14-3:1, 14-3:4

DiSalvo v. SunTrust Mortgage, Inc., 115 So. 3d 438 (Fla. 2d DCA 2013), 1-1:1, 12-1:10.1.f

Dish Network Service LLC v. Myers, 87 So. 3d 72 (Fla. 2d DCA 2012), 16-3:7

Ditech Fin. LLC v. White, 222 So. 3d 603 (Fla. 4th DCA 2017), 9-4:6

Dixon v. Wells Fargo Bank, N.A., 207 So. 3d 899 (Fla. 4th DCA 2017), 2-2:5, 3-2:1.1a

TABLE OF CASES 431

DK Arena, Inc. v. EB Acquisitions I, LLC, 112 So. 3d 85 (Fla. 2013), 9-3, 9-4:4

DLJ Mortg. Capital, Inc. v. Fox, 112 So. 3d 644 (Fla. 4th DCA 2013), 11-3:2.2

Dobrick v. Discovery Cruises, Inc., 581 So. 2d 645 (Fla. 4th DCA 1991), 18-4:1

Doe v. Hillsborough County Hosp. Auth., 816 So. 2d 262 (Fla. 2d DCA 2002), 3-1

Dominguez v. Barakat, 609 So. 2d 664 (Fla. 3d DCA 1992), 14-2:1

Donaldson Engineering, Inc. v. City of Plantation, 326 So. 2d 209 (Fla. 4th DCA 1976), 9-4:4

Donato v. PennyMac Corp., 174 So. 3d 1041 (Fla. 4th DCA 2015), 6-2:2

Dorta v. Wilmington Trust Nat'l Assoc., 13-cv-185-OC-10PRL, 2014 WL 1152917 (M. D. Fla. Mar. 24, 2014), 3-2:2.1

Douglas v. Johnson, 65 So. 3d 605 (Fla. 2d DCA 2011), 14-3:7

Downing v. First Nat'l Bank of Lake City, 81 So. 2d 486 (Fla. 1955), 12-1:10.1.b, 13-4:1.1

Doyle v. CitiMortgage, Inc., 162 So. 3d 340 (Fla. 2d DCA 2015), 13-4:4

Dukes v. Suncoast Credit Union (In re Dukes), 909 F.3d 1306 (11th Cir. 2018), 17-7

Duncan Properties, Inc. v. Key Largo Ocean View, Inc., 360 So. 2d 471 (Fla. 3d DCA 1978), 7-3:6

Dundee Naval Stores Co. v. McDowell, 65 Fla. 15, 61 So. 108 (Fla. 1913), 1-10:3, 1-11, 10-3:1

Durie v. State, 69 So. 3d 274 (Fla. 2011), 15-2:1, 15-2:3

Dvorak v. First Family Bank, 639 So. 2d 1076 (Fla. 5th DCA 1994), 16-3:8

Dyck-O'Neal, Inc. v. Lanham, 257 So. 3d 1 (Fla. 2018), 6-5:7, 19-2:2

Dyck-O'neal, Inc. v. Lanham, 264 So. 3d 1115 (Fla. 1st DCA, 2019), 19-3:4

Dyck-O'Neal, Inc. v. Norton, 267 So. 3d 478 (Fla. 2d DCA 2019), 19-3:4, 19-4

Dyck-O'Neal v. Lanham, 257 So. 3d 1 (Fla. 2018), 19-2:3

Dykes v. Trustbank Sav., F.S.B., 567 So. 2d 958 (Fla. 2d DCA 1990), 12-1:9

E

Eaddy v. Bank of America, N.A., 197 So. 3d 1278 (Fla. 2d DCA 2016), 13-4:1.3

Eagle's Crest LLC v. Republic Bank, 42 So. 3d 848 (Fla. 2d DCA 2010), 19-3:3, 19-3:4

Easterly v. Wildman, 99 So. 359 (Fla. 1924), 7-3:7

Echeverria v. BAC Home Loans, 2012 U.S. Dist. LEXIS 44487, 2012 WL 1081176 (M.D. Fla. Mar. 30, 2012), 8-4

Economakis v. Butler & Hosch, P.A., No. 2:13-CV-832-FTM-38DN, 2014 U.S. Dist. LEXIS 26779, 2014 WL 820623 (M.D. Fla. Mar. 3, 2014), 8-6

Ecoventure WGV, Ltd. v. Saint Johns Northwest Residential Ass'n, Inc., 56 So. 3d 126 (Fla. 5th DCA 2011), 9-4:3

Edason v. Central Farmers' Trust Co., 100 Fla. 348, 129 So. 698 (1930), 5-8

Edelman v. Breed, 836 So. 2d 1092 (Fla. 5th DCA 2003), 14-3:7

Edenfield v. Wingard, 89 So. 2d 776 (Fla. 1956), 5-4:1

Edrisi v. Sarnoff, 715 So. 2d 1124 (Fla. 3d DCA 1998), 16-2:1

Eduartez v. Fed. Nat'l Mortgage Ass'n, 251 So. 3d 227 (Fla. 3d DCA 2018), 14-3:7

Eduartez v. Fed. Nat'l Mortgage Ass'n, SC18-1436, 2018 WL 6434740 (Fla. Dec. 7, 2018), 14-3:7, 14-5

EGF Tampa Associates v. Edgar V. Bohlen, G.F.G.M.A.G., 532 So. 2d 1318 (Fla. 2d DCA 1988), 1-4:2

E.I. DuPont De Nemours & Co. v. Lambert, 654 So. 2d 226 (Fla. 2d DCA 1995), 14-3:7

E & I, Inc. v. Excavators, Inc., 697 So. 2d 545 (Fla. 4th DCA 1997), 12-1:7

Elliott v. Aurora Loan Services, LLC, 31 So. 3d 304 (Fla. 4th DCA 2010), 1-4:4, 18-6:2

Elliott v. Elliott, 648 So. 2d 135 (Fla. 4th DCA 1994), 14-2:2, 18-9

Ellison v. City of Fort Lauderdale, 175 So. 2d 198 (Fla. 1965), 7-3:1, 7-3:7

Elsman v. HSBC Bank USA, 182 So. 3d 770 (Fla. 5th DCA 2015), 6-4:3

Elston/Leetsdale, LLC v. CW Capital Asset Management, LLC, 87 So. 3d 14 (Fla. 4th DCA 2012), 6-3:1, 7-3:2

Emerald Coast Utils. Auth. v. Bear Marcus Pointe, LLC, 227 So. 3d 752 (Fla. 1st DCA 2017), 14-3:1, 14-3:4

Emerald Estates Cmty. Ass'n v. U.S. Bank Nat'l Ass'n, 242 So. 3d 429 (Fla. 4th DCA 2018), 9-4:4

EMM Enters. Two, LLC v. Fromberg, Perlow & Kornik, P.A., 202 So. 3d 932 (Fla. 4th DCA 2016), 15-3:2, 15-3:3

English v. Bankers Trust Co. of California, 895 So. 2d 1120 (Fla. 4th DCA 2005), 10-1, 10-2:1

Ennis v. Finanz und Kommerz-Union Establ., 565 So. 2d 374 (Fla. 2d DCA 1990), 5-2:1.3

Ensler v. Aurora Loan Servs., LLC, 178 So. 3d 95 (Fla. 4th DCA 2015), 2-2:3

Epstein v. Bank of Am., Nat'l Ass'n, 162 So. 3d 159 (Fla. 4th DCA 2015), 5-9, 14-3:3, 14-3:7

Ernest v. Carter, 368 So. 2d 428 (Fla. 2d DCA 1979), 12-1:10.1

Ero Properties, Inc. v. Cone, 418 So. 2d 434 (Fla. 3d DCA 1982), 9-4:3

Estate of Herrera v. Berlo Indus., Inc., 840 So. 2d 272 (Fla. 3d DCA 2003), 11-9:2, 12-1:8

Eurovest, Ltd. v. Segall, 528 So. 2d 482 (Fla. 3d DCA 1988), 10-2:4, 12-1:10.1.h

Evergrene Partners, Inc. v. Citibank, N.A., 143 So. 3d 954 (Fla. 4th DCA 2014), 3-2:1.1

Everhome Mortg. Co. v. Janssen, 100 So. 3d 1239 (Fla. 2d DCA 2012), 9-4:4

TABLE OF CASES 433

Executive Square, Ltd. v. Delray Executive Square, Ltd., 553 So. 2d 803 (Fla. 4th DCA 1989), 16-3:5

Ezem v. Fed. Nat. Mort., 153 So. 3d 341 (Fla. 1st DCA 2014), 6-3:2

F

Fa. Bar. v. Forrester, 916 So. 2d 647 (Fla. 2005), 15-2:2

Fannie Mae v. Hawthorne, 197 So. 3d 1237 (Fla. 4th DCA 2016), 12-1:10.1.e

Fannie Mae v. Rafaeli, 225 So. 3d 264 (Fla. 4th DCA 2017), 4-6

Fara Manufacturing Co., Inc. v. First Federal Savings and Loan Association of Miami, 366 So. 2d 164 (Fla. 3d DCA 1979), 19-3:1, 19-3:2

Farrey v. Bettendorf, 96 So. 2d 889 (Fla. 1957), 12-1:3

Fassy v. Bank of New York Mellon, 273 So. 3d 52 (Fla. 4th DCA 2019), 16-2:3

F.D. Rich Co. v. United States ex rel. Industrial Lumber Co., 417 U.S. 116 (1974), 16-4:1

Fed. Nat. Mort. Ass'n v. Linner, 193 So. 3d 1010 (Fla. 2d DCA 2016), 14-3:7

Fed. Nat. Mortg. Ass'n v. Hawthorne, 197 So. 3d 1237 (Fla. 4th DCA 2016), 2-2:2, 3-2:1.1a

Fed. Nat. Mortg. Ass'n v. Legacy Parc Condo. Ass'n, Inc., 177 So. 3d 92 (Fla. 5th DCA 2015), 9-4:5

Fed. Nat. Mortg. Ass'n v. Linares, 202 So. 3d 886 (Fla. 3d DCA 2016), 2-2:2

Fed. Nat'l Mortg. Ass'n v. Karastamatis, 52 Misc. 3d 1007, 36 N.Y.S.3d 360 (N.Y. Sup. Ct. 2016), 14-4

Fed. Nat'l Mortg. Assoc. v. Mirabella At World Gateway Condo. Assoc., Inc., 2012 WL 8015568 (Fla. Cir. Ct. Orange 2012), 9-4:5

Fed. Nat'l Mortgage Ass'n v. JKM Services, LLC for Cedar Woods Homes Condo. Ass'n, Inc., 256 So. 3d 961, 967 (Fla. 3d DCA 2018), 9-1

Fed. Nat'l Mortgage Assoc. v. Cordoba at Beach Park Condo. Assoc., Inc., 2012 WL 6916814 (Fla. Cir. Ct. Hillsborough 2012), 9-4:5

Fed. Nat'l Mortgage Assoc. v. Countryside Master Assoc., Inc., 2012 WL 6916812 (Fla. Cir. Ct. Collier 2012), 9-4:5

Fed. Nat'l Mortgage Assoc. v. The Cove at Pearl Lake Condo. Assoc., Inc., 2013 WL 1889432 (Fla. Cir. Ct. Seminole March 11, 2013), 9-4:5

Fed. Nat'l Mortgage Assoc. v. The Quarter at Ybor Condo. Assoc., Inc., 2013 WL 1889465 (Fla. Cir. Ct. Hillsborough March 5, 2013), 9-4:5

Federal Deposit Ins. Corp. v. Morley, 915 F.2d 1517 (11th Cir. 1990), 19-3:2

Federal Home Loan Mortg. Corp. v. Taylor, 318 So. 2d 203 (Fla. 1st DCA 1975), 13-4:2

Federal Land Bank of Columbia v. Godwin, 107 Fla. 537 (1933), 5-4:2, 5-4:2.1

Federal Nat. Mortg. Ass'n v. Mirabella at Mirasol Homeowners' Ass'n, Inc., 204 So. 3d 164 (Fla. 4th DCA 2016), 9-2

Federal Nat'l Mortg. Ass'n v. Sanchez, 187 So. 3d 341 (Fla. 4th DCA 2016), 5-9

Fidelity & Cas. Co. of New York v. Tiedtke, 207 So. 2d 40 (Fla. 4th DCA 1968), 12-1:10.1.e

Fielder v. Weinstein Design Group, Inc., 842 So. 2d 879 (Fla. 4th DCA 2003), 16-2:3

Fielding v. PNC Bank Nat'l Ass'n, 239 So. 3d 140 (Fla. 5th DCA 2018), 4-7

Fields v. Beneficial Florida, Inc., 208 So. 3d 278 (Fla. 5th DCA 2016), 14-3:4

Fiera .com, Inc. v. DigiCast New Media Group, Inc., 837 So. 2d 451 (Fla. 3d DCA 2002), 1-4

Fifth Third Bank v. ACA Plus, Inc., 73 So. 3d 850 (Fla. 5th DCA 2011), 11-3:2.2

FIGA v. R. V.M.P. Corp., 681 F.Supp. 806 (S.D. Fla. 1988), 16-3:7

Figueroa v. Federal Nat'l Mortg. Ass'n, 180 So. 3d 1110 (Fla. 5th DCA 2015), 4-7, 13-4

Fiorito v. JP Morgan Chase Bank, Nat'l Ass'n, 174 So. 3d 519 (Fla. 4th DCA 2015), 4-7

First Equitable Realty III, Ltd. v. Grandview Palace Condo. Ass'n, Inc., 246 So. 3d 445, 446-47 (Fla. 3d DCA 2018), 9-4:4

First Nat'l Bank v. Braun, 474 So. 2d 386 (Fla. 2d DCA 1985), 7-3:4

Fish Carburetor Corp. v. Great American Insurance Company, 125 So. 2d 889 (Fla. 1st DCA 1961), 12-1:7

Fish Tale Sales & Serv., Inc. v. Nice, 106 So. 3d 57 (Fla. 2d DCA 2013), 18-3

Fla. Bar v. Kivisto, 62 So. 3d 1137, 1139-40 (Fla. 2011), 15-2:3

Fla. Bar v. Palmer 149 So. 3d 1118, 1120 (Fla. 2013), 15-2:1

Fla. Cmty. Bank, N.A. v. Red Rd. Residential, LLC, 197 So. 3d 1112 (Fla. 3d DCA 2016), 10-2:4

Fla. Holding 4800, LLC v. Lauderhill Lending, LLC, 275 So. 3d 183 (Fla. 4th DCA 2019), 12-1:4.1

Flagship State Bank of Jacksonville v. Drew Equip. Co., 392 So. 2d 609 (Fla. 5th DCA 1981), 19-3, 19-3:1

Flagstar Bank, F.S.B. v. Cleveland, 87 So. 3d 63 (Fla. 4th DCA 2012), 14-4

Flemenbaum v. Flemenbaum, 636 So. 2d 579 (Fla. 4th DCA 1994), 14-3:2, 14-3:6

FL Homes 1 LLC v. Kokolis Trustee of Toula Kokolis Revocable Trust, 271 So. 3d 6 (Fla. 4th DCA 2019), 6-3:5, 10-2:1, 14-3:7

Floorcraft Distributors v. Horne-Wilson, Inc., 251 So. 2d 138 (Fla. 1st DCA 1971), 5-2:1.3

Flores v. Riscomp Indus., Inc., 35 So. 3d 146 (Fla. 3d DCA 2010), 3-2:4

Florida Atl. Univ. Bd. of Trs. v. Lindsey, 50 So. 3d 1205 (Fla. 4th DCA 2010), 12-1:3

Florida Community Bank, N.A. v. Red Road Residential, LLC, 197 So. 3d 1112 (Fla. 3d DCA 2016), 16-2:3

Florida Dep't of Agric. v. Go Bungee, 678 So. 2d 920, 921 (Fla. 5th DCA 1996), 12-1:6

TABLE OF CASES 435

Florida Dep't of Fin. Servs. v. Associated Indus. Ins. Co., 868 So. 2d 600 (Fla. 1st DCA 2004), 12-1:5

Florida Dep't of Revenue v. Pough, 723 So. 2d 303 (Fla. 2d DCA 1998), 14-3:3, 14-3:4, 14-3:5

Florida Fed. Sav. & Loan Ass'n v. Sanchez, 553 So. 2d 1254 (Fla. 3d DCA 1989), 16-3:8

Florida Gamco, Inc. v. Fontaine, 68 So. 3d 923 (Fla. 4th DCA 2011), 6-1:3

Florida Marine Enterprises v. Bailey, 632 So. 2d 649 (Fla. 4th DCA 1994), 13-3

Florida Patient's Comp. Fund v. Rowe, 472 So. 2d 1145 (Fla. 1985), 16-1:1, 16-3:5, 16-3:7, 16-4:1

Florida Patient's Compensation Fund v. Rowe, 472 So. 2d 1145 (Fla. 1985), 16-3:5

Florida Peninsula Ins. Co. v. Wagner, 196 So. 3d 419 (Fla. 2d DCA 2016), 16-3:7

Foche Mortg., LLC v. CitiMortgage, Inc., 163 So. 3d 525 (Fla. 3d DCA 2015), 18-6:2

Focht v. Wells Fargo Bank, N.A., 124 So. 3d 308 (Fla. 2d DCA 2013), 4-1, 12-1:3.2, 13-4:1.2

Fogarty v. Nationstar Mortgage, LLC, 224 So. 3d 313 (Fla. 5th DCA 2017), 9-3, 9-4:4

Foodtown Inc. of Jacksonville v. Argonaut Ins. Co., 102 F. 3d 483 (11th Cir.1996), 16-3:7

Forero v. Green Tree Servicing, LLC, 223 So. 3d 440 (Fla. 1st DCA 2017), 2-3:5.1, 2-3:5.2, 3-2:1.1, 3-2:1.1c, 6-4:7

Fore v. State, 201 So. 3d 839 (Fla. 4th DCA 2016), 15-2:2

Fort Plantation Investments, LLC v. Ironstone Bank, 85 So. 3d 1169 (Fla. 5th DCA 2012), 6-5:1

Fortune Insurance Co. v. Sanchez, 490 So. 2d 249 (Fla. 3d DCA 1996), 1-4:4.2

Foster v. Foster, 703 So. 2d 1107 (Fla. 2d DCA 1997), 5-8

Foster v. Tourtellotte, 704 F.2d 1109 (9th Cir. 1983), 16-4:1

Fountainspring II Homeowners Ass'n, Inc. v. Veliz, 212 So. 3d 1049 (Fla. 4th DCA 2017), 14-3:7

Fowler v. First Fed. Sav. & Loan Ass'n of Defuniak Springs, 643 So. 2d 30 (Fla. 1st DCA 1994), 2-3:2, 12-1:10.1

Franklin v. Regions Bank, 25 So. 3d 621 (Fla. 4th DCA 2009), 19-2:2

Frank v. Levine, 159 So. 2d 665 (Fla. 3d DCA 1964), 19-3:4

Fraser v. Security and Inv. Corp., 615 So. 2d 841 (Fla. 4th DCA 1993), 16-3:5

Fremont Investment and Loan v. Earl Winston Roache, et al., 2009 WL 8626511 (Fla. Cir. Ct. Miami-Dade 2009), 9-4:5

Fremont Reorganizing Corp. v. The Grand Condo. Ass'n, Inc., No. 11-15916 CC 05, 2017 WL 3317502 (Fla. Cir. Ct. 2017), 14-3:7

Friedle v. Bank of New York Mellon, 226 So. 3d 976 (Fla. 4th DCA 2017), 4-5, 6-4:3, 7-3:2

Friedman v. Heart Institute of Port St. Lucie, Inc., 863 So. 2d 189 (Fla. 2003), 11-7:2

Frumkes v. The Mortg. Guarantee Corp., 173 So. 2d 738 (Fla. 3d DCA 1965), 19-3:4

Frym v. Flagship Community Bank, 96 So. 3d 452 (Fla. 2d DCA 2012), 6-1:3

Fuller v. General Motors Corp., 353 So. 2d 1236 (Fla. 3d DCA 1978), 12-1:8

G

Gables Club Marina, LLC v. Gables Condo & Club Ass'n, Inc., 948 So. 2d 21 (Fla. 3d DCA 2006), 1-4:4.1

Gans v. Heathgate-Sunflower Homeowners Ass'n, Inc., 593 So. 2d 549 (Fla. 4th DCA 1992), 5-2:1.1

Garcia v. Lincare, Inc., 906 So. 2d 1268 (Fla. 5th DCA 2005), 13-2:1

Garcia v. Stewart, 906 So. 2d 1117 (Fla. 4th DCA 2005), 9-4:6, 14-3:7

Gardner v. Broward Cnty., 631 So. 2d 319 (Fla. 4th DCA 1994), 7-2:2

Geer v. Jacobsen, 880 So. 2d 717 (Fla. 2d DCA 2004), 1-4:4.1, 14-3:4

Gee v. U.S. Bank Nat'l Ass'n, 72 So. 3d 211 (Fla. 5th DCA 2011), 12-1:4

Genesis Re Holdings, LLC v, Woodside Estates Homeowners Association, Inc., 2015 WL 5511558 (Fla. Cir. Ct. Broward May 8, 2015), 9-4:3

Genvest Gen. Investments v. Lake Nona Corp., 594 So. 2d 787 (Fla. 5th DCA 1992), 2-1:4

George v. Radcliffe, 753 So. 2d 573 (Fla. 4th DCA 1999), 1-4:4

Georgia Cas. Co. v. O'Donnell, 147 So. 267 Fla. 290 (1933), 1-2, 6-1:3

Getman v. Tracey Constr., Inc., 62 So. 3d 1289 (Fla. 2d DCA 2011), 12-1:3.1

Geweye v. Ventures Trust 2013-I-H-R, 189 So. 3d 231 (Fla. 2d DCA 2016), 4-9

Gibson Trust, Inc. v. Office of the Attorney General, 883 So. 2d 379 (Fla. 4th DCA 2004), 1-4:4.1

Ginn v. Weiss, 183 So. 2d 6 (Fla. 1st DCA 1966), 1-1:1

Ginsberg and *Deutsche Bank Tr. Co. Ams. v. Harris*, 264 So. 3d 186 (Fla. 4th DCA 2019), 4-4

Ginsberg v. Lennar Florida Holdings, Inc., 645 So. 2d 490 (Fla. 3d DCA 1994), 6-5:6

Giroux v. Ronald W. Williams Constr. Co., 705 So. 2d 663 (Fla. 1st DCA 1998), 12-1:8

Glace & Radcliffe, Inc. v. City of Live Oak, 471 So. 2d 144 (Fla. 1st DCA 1985), 16-6:1

Glarum v. La Salle Bank, 83 So. 3d 780 (Fla. 4th DCA 2011), 12-1:10.1.a

Glen Garron, LLC v. Buchwald, 210 So. 3d 229 (Fla. 5th DCA 2017), 2-1:1, 6-2:4, 7-2:2

Godsell v. United Guar. Residential Ins., 923 So. 2d 1209 (Fla. 5th DCA 2006), 5-2:1.1, 5-7

Godshalk v. Countrywide Home Loans Servicing, L.P., 81 So. 3d 626 (Fla. 5th DCA 2012), 12-1:10.1.f

TABLE OF CASES

Goersch v. City of Satellite Beach, 252 So. 3d 309 (Fla. 5th DCA 2018), 15-4:2

Goldfarb v. Daitch, 696 So. 2d 1199 (Fla. 3d DCA 1997), 16-4:1

Gomez v. Household Fin. Corp., III, 688 Fed. Appx. 680, 684 (11th Cir. 2017), 2-3:4

Goncharuk v. HSBC Mortg. Servs., Inc., 62 So. 3d 680 (Fla. 2d DCA 2011), 12-1:3.1, 12-1:3.2

Gonzalez v. Chase Home Fin. LLC, 37 So. 3d 955 (Fla. 3d DCA 2010), 12-1:3

Gonzalez v. Deutsche Bank Nat'l Trust Co., 95 So. 3d 251 (Fla. 2d DCA 2012), 18-6:1

Gonzalez v. Fed. Nat'l Mortgage Ass'n, 276 So. 3d 332 (Fla. 3d DCA 2018), 3-2:3.2

Gonzalez v. Totalbank, 472 So. 2d 861 (Fla. 3d DCA 1985), 1-3:2

Good v. Deutsche Bank Nat'l Trust Co., 98 So. 3d 1255 (Fla. 4th DCA 2012), 7-3:6

Goodwin v. State, 751 So. 2d 537 (Fla. 1999), 18-3

Gorel v. Bank of New York Mellon, 165 So. 3d 44 (Fla. 5th DCA 2015), 2-2:2, 2-2:5, 3-2:1.1a, 7-3:3, 8-4, 12-1:10.1.e, 13-4

Goter v. Brown, 682 So. 2d 155 (Fla. 4th DCA 1996), 14-2:2

Gourley v. Wollam, 348 So. 2d 1218 (Fla. 4th DCA 1977), 5-2:1.3

Gozzo Dev., Inc. v. Prof'l Roofing Contractors, Inc., 211 So. 3d 145 (Fla. 4th DCA 2017), 14-2:2

Grand Cent. at Kennedy Condo. Ass'n, Inc. v. Space Coast Credit Union, 173 So. 3d 1089 (Fla. 2d DCA 2015), 9-3, 9-4:4, 9-4:5

Grant v. Citizens Bank, N.A., 263 So. 3d 156 (Fla. 5th DCA 2018), 3-2:1.2, 3-2:3.2

Green Emerald Homes, LLC v. Bank of N.Y. Mellon, 204 So. 3d 512 (Fla. 4th DCA 2016), 5-2:1.1

Green Emerald Homes, LLC v. Residential Credit Opportunities Tr., 256 So. 3d 211 (Fla. 2d DCA 2018), 6-5:6

Green Emerald Homes, LLC v. 21st Mortgage Corp., 2D17-2192, 44 Fla. L. Weekly D1449, 2019 WL 2398015 (Fla. 2d DCA June 7, 2019), 9-3, 10-2:4

Greene v. Bursey, 733 So. 2d 1111 (Fla. 4th DCA 1999), 3-2:1.2, 3-2:3.1, 12-1:10.1

Greene v. Lifestyle Builders, 985 So. 2d 588 (Fla. 5th DCA 2008), 12-1:3.1

Greene v. Seigle, 745 So. 2d 411 (Fla. 4th DCA 1999), 14-3:7

Green Tree Servicing, LLC v. Milam, 177 So. 3d 7 (Fla. 2d DCA 2015), 2-2:2, 2-2:4, 7-3:3, 12-1:10.1.e

Green v. Green Tree Servicing, LLC, 230 So. 3d 989 (Fla. 5th DCA 2017), 4-7

Green v. Sun Harbor Homeowners' Ass'n, Inc., 730 So. 2d 1261 (Fla. 1998), 16-3:1

Greenwald v. Graham, 100 Fla. 818, 130 So. 608 (1930), 1-2, 6-3:5

Gregory v. Rice, 727 So. 2d 251 (Fla. 1999), 15-2:2

Griffin v. Am. Gen. Life & Accident Ins. Co., 752 So. 2d 621 (Fla. 2d DCA 1999), 12-1:10.1.e

Grimaldi v. U.S. Bank Nat'l Ass'n, Civ. A. No. 16-519 WES, 2018 U.S. Dist. LEXIS 70927, 2018 WL 1997277 (D.R.I. Apr. 27, 2018), 8-4

Grimsley v. Moody, Jones, Ingino & Morehead, P.A., 70 So. 3d 761 (Fla. 4th DCA 2011), 12-1:3

Grosso v. HSBC Bank USA, N.A., as Trustee on Behalf of Ace Securities Corp., 275 So. 3d 642 (Fla. 4th DCA 2019), 16-3:2

Grove Isle Ass'n, Inc. v. Grove Isle Assocs., LLLP, 137 So. 3d 1081 (Fla. 3d DCA 2014), 9-4:3

Gulf Insurance Co. v. Stofman, 664 So. 2d 1083 (Fla. 4th DCA 1995), 12-1:4

Gunderson v. Sch. Dist. of Hillsborough Cnty., 937 So. 2d 777 (Fla. 1st DCA 2006), 12-1:3.2

Gus' Baths v. Lightbown, 101 Fla. 1211 (Fla. 1931), 2-3:2

Gutierrez v. Bermudez, 540 So. 2d 888 (Fla. 5th DCA 1989), 12-1:7

Gutierrez v. Vargas, 239 So. 3d 615 (Fla. Mar. 2018), 13-3

H

Haberl v. 21st Mortg. Corp., 138 So. 3d 1192 (Fla. 5th DCA 2014), 2-2:3.2

Habib v. Maison Du Vin Francais, Inc., 528 So. 2d 553 (Fla. 4th DCA 1988), 11-4:2

Haines City Community Development v. Heggs, 658 So. 2d 523 (Fla. 1995), 11-8

Hall v. BAC Home Loans, 2013 U.S. Dist. LEXIS 71645, 2013 WL 2248253 (N.D. Ala. May 21, 2013), 8-4

Halpern v. Houser, 949 So. 2d 1155 (Fla. 4th DCA 2007), 14-3:1, 14-3:4

Hamilton v. Bank of Palm Beach & Trust Co., 348 So. 2d 1190 (Fla. 4th DCA 1977), 12-1:3

Ham v. Dunmire, 891 So. 2d 492 (Fla. 2004), 15-3:3

Ham v. Nationstar Mortg., LLC, 164 So. 3d 714 (Fla. 1st DCA 2015), 4-7, 7-3:2

Hanft v. Phelan, 488 So. 2d 531 (Fla. 1986), 7-2:1

Hankey v. Yarian, 755 So. 2d 93 (Fla. 2000), 3-2:5.1

Hanna v. Beverly Enterprises-Florida, 738 So. 2d 424 (Fla. 4th DCA 1999), 16-2:3

Hannett v. Bryan, 640 So. 2d 203 (Fla. 4th DCA 1994), 3-2:1.1b

Hann v. Balogh, 920 So. 2d 1250 (Fla. 2d DCA 2006), 13-3:2

Harley Shipbuilding Corp. v. Fast Cats Ferry Service, LLC, 820 So. 2d 445 (Fla. 2nd DCA 2002), 11-7:3

Harper v. Chase Manhattan Bank, 138 F. App'x 130 (11th Cir. 2005), 8-1

Harper v. HSBC Bank USA, Nat. Ass'n, 148 So. 3d 1285 (Fla. 1st DCA 2014), 2-2:3.2, 2-2:5, 3-2:1.1a

Harris v. Bank of New York Mellon, 2018 WL 6816177 (Fla. 2nd DCA 2018), 16-2:3

Harris v. Lewis State Bank, 436 So. 2d 338 (Fla. 1st DCA 1983), 12-1:3

Harris v. U.S. Bank Nat'l Ass'n, 223 So. 3d 1030 (Fla. 1st DCA 2017), 2-2:6, 7-2:2

Harrod v. Union Fin. Co., 420 So. 2d 108 (Fla. 3d DCA 1982), 10-2:1, 10-2:2

Hart Properties, Inc. v. Slack, 159 So. 2d 236 (Fla. 1963), 12-1:4

Harvey Bldg., Inc. v. Haley, 175 So. 2d 780 (Fla. 1965), 12-1:3

Harvey v. Deutsche Bank Nat'l Trust Co., 69 So. 3d 300 (Fla. 4th DCA 2011), 7-2:2

Hastings v. State, 79 So. 3d 739 (Fla. 2011), 15-2:1

Hatadis v. Achieva Credit Union, 159 So. 3d 256 (Fla. 2d DCA 2015), 2-2:2

Haven Federal Savings & Loan Ass'n v. Kirian, 579 So. 2d 730 (Fla. 1991), 1-1:1, 12-1:3.2

Hayslip v. Douglaw, 400 So. 2d 553 (Fla. 4th DCA 1981), 18-4:3.3

H.B. Adams Distribs., Inc. v. Admiral Air of Sarasota Cty., Inc., 805 So. 2d 852 (Fla. 2d DCA 2001), 12-1:4

Heartwood 2, LLC v. Dori, 208 So. 3d 817 (Fla. 3d DCA 2017), 6-5:3

Heath v. State, 532 So. 2d 9 (Fla. 1st DCA 1988), 9-4:1

Heekin v. Del Col, 60 So. 3d 437 (Fla. 1st DCA 2011), 11-8

Heimer v. Albion Realty & Mortg. Inc., 300 So. 2d 31 (Fla. 3d DCA 1974), 2-1:3.1

Heldt-Pope v. Thibault, 198 So. 3d 650 (Fla. 2d DCA 2015), 15-4:1

Heller v. Bank of Am., N.A., 209 So. 3d 641 (Fla. 2d DCA 2017), 4-2

Hembd v. Dauria, 859 So. 2d 1238 (Fla. 4th DCA 2003), 14-3:2, 14-3:6

Hemingway Villa Condo. Owners Ass'n, Inc. v. Wells Fargo Bank, N.A., 240 So. 3d 104 (Fla. 3d DCA 2018), 9-4:2, 9-4:4, 9-4:5

Henderson v. Deutsche Bank Nat'l Tr. Co., 158 So. 3d 705 (Fla. 4th DCA 2015), 8-2

Henderson v. Reyes, 702 So. 2d 616 (Fla. 3d DCA 1997), 11-9:2

Henry v. Guaranteed Rates, Inc., 415 F. App'x 985 (11th Cir. 2011), 9-3

Hensley v. Eckerhart, 461 U.S. 424, 103 S. Ct. 1933, 76 L. Ed.2d 40 (1983), 16-3:2

Hepburn v. All American General Const. Corp., 954 So. 2d 1250 (Fla. 4th DCA 2007), 1-4:4.3

Heritage Circle Condo. Ass'n, Inc. v. State of Florida, 121 So. 3d 1141 (Fla. 4th DCA 2013), 14-3:7

Hernandez v. United Auto. Ins. Co., 730 So. 2d 344 (Fla. 3d DCA 1999), 12-1:3

Herranz v. Siam, 2 So. 3d 1105 (Fla. 3d DCA 2009), 14-3:7

Hervey v. Alfonso, 650 So. 2d 644 (Fla. 2d DCA 1995), 12-1:3

Hess v. Philip Morris USA, Inc., 175 So. 3d 687 (Fla. 2015), 3-1, 3-1:2, 3-2, 3-2:1

HFC Collection Center, Inc. v. Alexander, 190 So. 3d 1114 (Fla. 5th DCA 2016), 15-4:2, 16-2:3

HHA Borrower, LLC. v. W.G. Yates & Sons Constr. Co., 266 So. 3d 1267 (Fla. 5th DCA 2019), 16-3:2

Hicks v. Wells Fargo Bank, N.A., 178 So. 3d 957 (Fla. 5th DCA 2015), 3-2:1.1, 3-2:1.2, 6-4:7

Hidden Ridge Condo. Homeowners Ass'n, Inc. v. OneWest Bank, N.A., 183 So. 3d 1266 (Fla. 5th DCA 2016), 9-3, 9-4:4

Hidden Ridge Condo. Homeowners v. Greentree Servicing, LLC, 167 So. 3d 483 (Fla. 5th DCA 2015), 9-3, 9-4:4

Hightower v. Bigoney, 156 So. 2d 501 (Fla. 1963), 13-2

Hlad v. State, 565 So. 2d 762 (Fla. 5th DCA 1990), 12-1:3

Hobbs v. Weinkauf, 940 So. 2d 1151 (Fla. 2d DCA 2006), 9-4:5

Hodkin v. Ledbetter, 487 So. 2d 1214 (Fla. 4th DCA 1986), 12-1:3.1

Hoffman v. BankUnited, N.A., 137 So. 3d 1039 (Fla. 2d DCA 2014), 14-2:2, 14-4

Hoffman v. Hall, 817 So. 2d 1057 (Fla. 1st DCA 2002), 18-4:1

Hoffman v. Wells Fargo Bank Minnesota, 987 So. 2d 206 (Fla. 5th DCA 2008), 16-3:8

Hojan v. State, 212 So. 3d 982 (Fla. 2017), 3-2

Holcomb v. Hardeman (In re Holcomb), 380 B.R. 813 (10th Cir. B.A.P. 2008), 17-3:3

Hollifield v. Renew & Co., 18 So. 3d 616 (Fla. 1st DCA 2009), 14-2:2

Holl v. Talcott, 191 So. 2d 40 (Fla. 1966), 12-1:3

Holly Lakes Ass'n v. Fed. Nat'l Mortgage Ass'n, 660 So. 2d 266 (Fla.1995), 9-4:3

Hollywood Towers Condo. Ass'n, Inc. v. Hampton, 40 So. 3d 784 (Fla. 4th DCA 2010), 9-4:5

Holt v. Calchas, LLC, 155 So. 3d 499 (Fla. 4th DCA 2015), 2-2:2, 3-2:1.1a, 12-1:10.1.a

Home Dev. Co. of St. Petersburg v. Bursani, 178 So. 2d 113 (Fla. 1965), 2-1:1

Homestead Ins. Co. v. Poole, Masters & Goldstein, C.P.A., P.A., 604 So. 2d 825 (Fla. 4th DCA 1991), 16-3:9

Hopson v. Deutsche Bank, 278 So. 3d 306 (Fla. 2nd DCA 2019), 16-2:3

Hosp. Constructors Ltd. ex rel. Lifemark Hospitals of Florida, Inc. v. Lefor, 749 So. 2d 546 (Fla. 2d DCA 2000), 3-2:5.1

Houck Corp. v. New River, Ltd., Pasco, 900 So. 2d 601 (Fla. 2d DCA 2005), 3-1, 3-1:1, 3-1:2, 3-2:1.3b, 3-3:1, 3-3:2.2, 3-3:2.4

Hough v. Menses, 95 So. 2d 410 (Fla. 1957), 12-1:3.2

Houle v. Green Tree Servicing, LLC, No. 14-CV- 14654, 2015 WL 1867526 (E.D. Mich. Apr. 23, 2015), 14-4

TABLE OF CASES 441

Household Fin. Corp., III v. Mitchell, 51 So. 3d 1238 (Fla. 1st DCA 2011), 14-3:4

House of Lyons v. Marcus, 72 So. 2d 34 (Fla. 1954), 5-4:1

Hovercraft of South Florida, LLC v. Reynolds, 211 So. 3d 1073 (Fla. 5th DCA 2017), 16-3:3

Howard Cole & Co. v. Williams, 27 So. 2d 352 (Fla. 1946), 10-2:1, 10-3:2

Howard v. Gualt, 259 So. 3d 119 (Fla. 4th DCA 2018), 5-2:1.1

Howard v. Shirmer, 334 So. 2d 103 (Fla. 3d DCA 1976), 12-1:8

Howarth Trust v. Howarth, 310 So. 2d 57 (Fla. 1st DCA 1975), 12-1:7

Howell v. Miller, 638 So. 2d 544 (Fla. 2d DCA 1994), 12-1:9

Hoyt v. Commonwealth Land Title Ins. Co., 532 So. 2d 72 (Fla. 2d DCA 1988), 11-1, 11-8

Hoyt v. State, 810 So. 2d 1007 (Fla. 4th DCA 2002), 18-4:2

HSBC Bank USA, N.A. v. Alejandre, 219 So. 3d 831 (Fla. 4th DCA 2017), 4-4, 13-4:1.3

HSBC Bank USA, N.A. v. Angelini, 2016 WL 3547023 (Fla. Cir. Ct. June 29, 2016), 14-3:8

HSBC Bank USA, N.A. v. Angelini, 2016 WL 4702598 (Fla. Cir. Ct. Broward Aug. 31, 2016), 16-3:7

HSBC Bank USA, N.A. v. Biscayne Point Condo. Ass'n, 184 So. 3d 606 (Fla. 3d DCA 2016), 9-4:6

HSBC Bank USA, N.A. v. Buset, 241 So. 3d 882, 889 (Fla. 3d DCA 2018), 4-10

HSBC Bank USA, N.A. v. Frenkel, 208 So. 3d 156 (Fla. 3d DCA 2016), 16-2:3

HSBC Bank USA, N.A. v. Sanchez, 245 So. 3d 784 (Fla. 4th DCA 2018), 6-4:7

HSBC Bank USA, N.A., as Trustee on Behalf of Ace Securities Corp. Home Equity Loan Trust and for the Registered Holders of Ace Securities Corp. Home Equity Loan Trust, Series 2006-ASAP5, Asset Backed Pass-Through Certificates v. Miguel Abreu, 2014 WL 708904 (Fla. Cir. Ct. Duval Feb. 24, 2014), 9-4:5

HSBC Bank USA, Nat. Ass'n v. Karzen, 157 So. 3d 1089 (Fla. 1st DCA 2015), 6-3:6, 6-4:7

HSBC Bank USA, National Association v. Centre Court Ridge Condominium Association, Inc., 147 So. 3d 593 (Fla. 5th DCA 2014), 9-4:6, 14-3:7

HSBC Bank USA, Nat'l Ass'n v. Buset, 241 So. 3d 882 (Fla. 3d DCA 2018), 4-4

HSBC Bank USA, Nat'l Assoc., as Trustee for Nomura Asset Acceptance Corp. Mortgage Pass-Through Certificates, Series 2006-AR4 v. The Villas Condo. Assoc., Inc., 2011 WL 9919180 (Fla. Cir. Ct. Hillsborough 2011), 9-4:5

HSBC Bank USA, NA v. Perez, 165 So. 3d 696 (Fla. 4th DCA 2015), 9-4:4

HSBC Bank U.S.A, N.A. v. Buset, 241 So. 3d 882 (Fla. 3d DCA 2018), 13-4:1.2

HSBC Mortg. Corp. v. Mullan, 159 So. 3d 250 (Fla. 2d DCA 2015), 12-1:4

Hudlett v. Sanderson, 715 So. 2d 1050 (Fla. 4th DCA 1998), 1-2, 6-1:3

Hudson v. U.S. Bank Nat'l Ass'n, 240 So. 3d 34 (Fla. 4th DCA 2018), 19-3:4

Hughes v. Home Savings of America, F.S.B., 675 So. 2d 649 (Fla. 2d DCA 1996), 6-2:4

Hulley v. Cape Kennedy Leasing Corp., 376 So. 2d 884 (Fla. 5th DCA 1979), 7-3:7

Humphrys v. Jarrell, 104 So. 2d 404, 410 (Fla. 2d DCA 1958), 12-1:3

Hunter v. Aurora Loan Services, LLC, 137 So. 3d 570 (Fla. 1st DCA 2014), 12-1:10.1.a

I

Iannucci v. Bank of Am., NA, No. 2:14-cv-106-FtM-38DNF, 2014 U.S. Dist. LEXIS 74699, 2014 WL 2462978 (M.D. Fla. June 2, 2014), 8-1

Igbinadolor v. Deutsche Bank Nat'l Trust Co., 215 So. 3d 192 (Fla. 3d DCA 2017), 10-3:1, 10-3:2

Indymac Federal Bank FSB v. Machado, 2010 WL 8250945 (Fla. Cir. Ct. Palm Beach July 1, 2010), 16-3:7

In re Albany Partners, Ltd., 749 F.2d 670 (11th Cir. 1984), 17-3:2, 17-9

In re Aldrovandi, 568 B.R. 154 (Bankr. M.D. Fla. 2017), 16-3:8

In re Amend. Fla. Rules Civ. Pro., 131 So. 3d 643 (Fla. 2013), 14-2:1

In re Amendments to Florida Rules of Appellate Procedure, 183 So. 3d 245 (Fla. 2014), 14-2:1, 16-3:9

In re Amendments to Florida Rules of Civil Procedure, 190 So. 3d 999 (Fla. 2016), 6-2:2

In re Amendments to the Fla. Rules of Civ. Procedure, 153 So. 3d 258 (Fla. 2014), 12-1:10.1.b

In re Amends. to Fla. Rules of Civ. Pro., 257 So. 3d 66 (Fla. 2018), 12-1:7

In re Atkins, 176 B.R. 998, 1008 (Bankr. D. Minn. 1994), 17-4

In re Ayala, No. 6:11-BK- 15964-RAC, 2017 WL 2874499 (Bankr. M.D. Fla. Apr. 17, 2017), 17-8

In re Barr, 318 B.R. 592 (Bankr. M.D. Fla. 2004), 17-3:2, 17-4

In re Barrera, 2016 WL 6990876 (Bankr. M.D. Fla. Nov. 29, 2016), 17-5

In re BCML Holding LLC, 65 Bankr. Ct. Dec. 193 (Bankr. S.D. Fla. May 24, 2018), 3-2:3.2

In re Bertolami, 235 B.R. 493 (Bankr. S.D. Fla. 1999), 17-3:1

In re Brooks, 407 B.R. 429 (Bankr. M.D. Fla. 2009), 17-2

In re Citadel Properties, Inc., 86 B.R. 275 (Bankr. M.D. Fla. 1988), 17-3:2

In re Clark, 107 B.R. 376 (S.D. Fla. 1988), 17-9

In re Clarke, 373 B.R. 769 (Bankr. S.D. Fla. 2006), 17-4

In re Colbourne, 550 Fed. Appx. 687 (11th Cir. 2013), 17-6:2

TABLE OF CASES

In re Crispell, 73 B.R. 375 (Bankr. E.D. Mo. 1987), 17-4

In re Doyle, 63 Bankr. Ct. Dec. 114 (Bankr. M.D. Fla. 2016), 17-6:2

In re Duvar Apt. Inc., 205 B.R. 196 (9th Cir. BAP 1996), 17-9

In re Estate of Rifkin, 359 So. 2d 1197 (Fla. 3d DCA 1978), 9-3

In re Estate of Smith, 685 So. 2d 1206, 1209 (Fla. 1996), 3-2

In re Failla, 838 F.3d 1170 (11th Cir. 2016), 17-8

In re Haas, 31 F.3d 1081 (11th Cir. 1994), 10-4:2

In re Hamrick, 175 B.R. 890 (W.D.N.C. 1994), 17-4

In re Henry, 200 B.R. 59 (Bankr. M.D. Fla. 1996), 5-4:1

In re Hill, 305 B.R. 100 (Bankr. M.D. Fla. 2003), 17-9

In re Jackson, 482 B.R. 659 (Bankr. S.D. Fla. 2012), 17-2, 17-5

In re Janet Deloris Keddo, Case No. 14-28640-JKO, Bankr. Southern District of Florida, ECF No. 36, 17-8

In re Karim Craig Thomas, and Kelly Mitchell Thomas, Case No. 12-38513-E PK, Bankr. Southern District of Florida ECF No.66, 17-8

In re Keen, 301 B.R. 749 (2003), 17-3:1

In re Laurent, 193 Fed. Appx. 831 (11th Cir. 2006), 17-3:2

In re Macaluso, 254 B.R. 799 (Bankr. W.D.N.Y. 2000), 17-6:2

In re Mead, 374 B.R. 296 (Bankr. M.D. Fla. 2007), 5-4:1

In re Menasche, 301 B.R. 757 (Bankr. S.D. Fla. 2003), 17-8

In re Miller, 124 Fed. Appx. 152 (4th Cir. 2005), 8-4

In re O'Quinn, 98 B.R. 86 (Bankr. M.D. Fla. 1989), 17-3:2

In re Phoenix Piccadilly, Ltd., 849 F.2d 1393 (11th Cir. 1988), 17-3:2

In re Piazza, 719 F.3d 1253 (11th Cir. 2013), 17-9

In re Pierre, 468 B.R. 419 (Bankr. M.D. Fla. 2012), 17-6:1

In re Plummer, 484 B.R. 882 (M.D. Fla. Bankr. Jan. 14, 2013), 9-4:1, 9-4:3

In re Plummer, 513 B.R. 135 (Bankr. M.D. Fla. 2014), 17-8

In re Price, 42 F.3d 1068 (7th Cir. 1994), 17-4

In re Record, 347 B.R. 450 (M.D. Fla. 2006), 17-8

In re Richard Kurzban and Dalain Kurzban, Case No. 09-30656-LMI, Bankr. Southern District of Florida, ECF No. 39, 17-8

In re S. White Transp., Inc., 725 F.3d 494 (5th Cir. 2013), 17-2

In re Sagamore Partners, Ltd, No. 11-3122, 2012 Bankr. LEXIS 3800 (Bankr. S.D. Fla. Aug. 15, 2012), 12-1:10.1.a

In re Salvador, 456 B.R. 610 (Bankr. M.D. Ga. 2011), 8-3

In re Scantling, 754 F.3d 1323 (11th Cir. 2014), 17-6:2

In re Scott, 567 B.R. 847 (Bankr. S.D. Fla. 2017), 17-8

In re Senior Care Properties, Inc., 137 B.R. 527 (Bankr. N.D. Fla. 1992), 17-3:2

In re Silva, 63 Collier Bankr. Cas. 2d 400 (Bankr. S.D. Fla. 2010), 17-6:2

In re SR Real Estate Holdings, LLC, 506 B.R. 121 (Bankr. S.D. Cal. 2014), 17-9

In re Std. Jury Instructions-Contract & Bus. Cases, 116 So. 3d 284 (Fla. 2013), 12-1:10.1.e

In re Steinmetz Group, Ltd., 85 B.R. 633 (S.D. Fla. 1988), 17-9

In re Sunbeam Sec. Litig., 261 B.R. 534 (S.D. Fla. 2001), 17-3:1

In re Taylor, 3 F.3d 1512 (11th Cir. 1993), 17-8

In re Tomasevic, 275 B.R. 86 (Bankr. M.D. Fla. 2001), 8-1

In re Weinstein, 234 B.R. 862 (Bankr. E.D.N.Y. 1999), 17-7

In re Williford, 294 Fed. Appx. 518 (11th Cir. 2008), 17-3:2

In re Wright, 486 B.R. 491 (Bankr. D. Ariz. 2012), 17-5

In re Yukon Enters., Inc., 39 B.R. 919 (Bankr. C.D. Cal. 1984), 17-9

In re Zaldivar, 441 B.R. 389 (Bankr. S.D. Fla. 2011), 17-6:2

Intermediary Fin. Corp. v. McKay, 111 So. 531 (Fla. 1927), 6-3:5, 10-2:1, 10-2:2

Intermediary Finance Corporation v. McKay, 93 Fla. 101, 111 So. 531 (Fla. 1927), 10-2:1

International Union, United Mine Workers v. Bagwell, 512 U.S. 821 (1994), 15-2:1, 15-2:2, 15-2:3

Investor Tr. Servs., LLC v. DLJ Mortg. Capital, Inc., 225 So. 3d 833 (Fla. 5th DCA 2017), 9-4:6, 10-2:1, 10-2:2

Irwin v. Grogan-Cole, 590 So. 2d 1102 (Fla. 5th DCA 1991), 3-3:2.1, 9-3, 10-2:4, 12-1:10.1.h

Isaac v. Deutsche Bank Nat'l Trust Co., 74 So. 3d 495 (Fla. 4th DCA 2011), 4-3, 7-3:2

Isaacs v. Deutsch, 80 So. 2d 657 (Fla. 1955), 3-2:1.1b, 3-2:3.3

Isla Blue Devel., LLC v. Moore, 223 So. 3d 1097 (Fla. 2d DCA 2017), 15-4:2

J

Jackson v. Relf, 26 Fla. 465 (1890), 5-2:1.3

Jaffer v. Chase Home Fin., LLC, 155 So. 3d 1199 (Fla. 4th DCA 2015), 12-1:10.1

Jagodinski v. Washington Mut. Bank, 63 So. 3d 791 (Fla. 1st DCA 2011), 10-2:4

Jallali v. Knightsbridge Village Homeowners Ass'n, Inc., 211 So. 3d 216 (Fla. 4th DCA 2017), 6-3:8, 9-4:6, 14-3:7

Jarvis v. Deutsche Bank Nat'l Trust Co., 169 So. 3d 194 (Fla. 4th DCA 2015), 4-4

Jaudon v. Equitable Life Assur. Soc. of United States, 102 Fla. 782, 136 So. 517 (Fla. 1931), 12-1:10.1

Jaye v. Royal Saxon, Inc., 720 So. 2d 214 (Fla. 1998), 18-4:3.1

Jelic v. Citimortgage, Inc., 150 So. 3d 1223 (Fla. 4th DCA 2014), 12-1:3.2

Jenkins v. W.L. Roberts, Inc., 851 So. 2d 781 (Fla. 1st DCA 2003), 12-1:3

J.J. Gumberg Co. v. Janis Services, Inc., 847 So. 2d 1048 (Fla. 4th DCA 2003), 13-4

J.J.K. Int'l, Inc. v. Shivbaran, 985 So. 2d 66 (Fla. 4th DCA 2008), 14-3:1

Joe-Lin, Inc. v. LRG Restaurant Grp., Inc., 696 So. 2d 539, 541 (Fla. 5th DCA 1997), 1-4:4.1

Johns v. Gillian, 134 Fla. 575 (Fla. 1938), 4-2, 6-4:3, 12-1:10.1.b

Johns v. Gillian, 184 So. 140 (Fla. 1938), 7-3:2

Johnson v. Home State Bank, 501 U.S. 78 (1991), 3-2:1.3d, 17-2, 19-5:2

Johnson v. Maroone Ford, LLC, 944 So. 2d 1059 (Fla. 4th DCA 2006), 16-3:9

Johnston v. Hudlett, 32 So. 3d 700 (Fla. 4th DCA 2010), 3-1, 12-1:10.1.b, 13-4:1.1, 14-3:8

Jones-Bishop v. Estate of Sweeney, 27 So. 3d 176 (Fla. 5th DCA 2010), 14-2:1, 14-3:1, 14-3:7

Jones v. Carpenter, 106 So. 127 (1925), 6-5:4

Jones v. Florida Ins. Guar. Ass'n, Inc., 908 So. 2d 435 (Fla. 2005), 16-3:9

Jones v. Peninsula Motor Club, Inc., 558 So. 2d 517 (Fla. 1st DCA 1990), 18-2

Jones v. Stoutenburgh, 91 So. 2d 299 (Fla. 1956), 12-1:1

Joseph v. BAC Home Loans Servicing, LP, 155 So. 3d 444, *passim* (Fla. 4th DCA Jan. 7, 2015), 7-2:2

Joseph v. State, 103 So. 3d 227 (Fla. 4th DCA 2012), 18-4:3

Jove Engineering, Inc v. IRS, 92 F.3d 1539 (11th Cir. 1996), 17-3:1, 17-3:2

Joyce v. Federated National Insurance Co., 228 So. 3d 1122 (Fla. 2017), 16-3:7

J.P. Morgan Acquisition Corporation v. Golden, 98 So. 3d 220 (Fla. 2d DCA 2015), 16-3:7

JP Morgan Chase Bank, N.A. v. Hernandez, 99 So. 3d 508 (Fla. 3d DCA 2011), 14-3:8, 16-4:2

JP Morgan Chase Bank, N.A. v. Ostrander, 201 So. 3d 1281 (Fla. 2d DCA 2016), 2-2:3, 12-1:10.1.f

JP Morgan Chase Bank Nat'l Ass'n v. Pierre, 215 So. 3d 633 (Fla. 4th DCA 2017), 4-4

JRBL Dev., Inc. v. Maiello, 872 So. 2d 362 (Fla. 2d DCA 2004), 14-4

Juliano v. Juliano, 687 So. 2d 910 (Fla. 3d DCA 1997), 14-3:7

Jumpp v. Chase Home Fin., LLC (In re Jumpp), 356 B.R. 789 (1st Cir. B.A.P. 2006), 17-3:3

K

Kaan v. Wells Fargo Bank, N.A., 981 F. Supp. 2d 1271 (S.D. Fla. 2013), 2-1:3.1

Kass Shuler, P.A. v. Barchard, 120 So. 3d 165 (Fla. 2d DCA 2013), 7-3:6

Katline Realty Corp. v. Avedon, 183 So. 3d 415 (Fla. 3d DCA 2014), 8-1, 8-2:1

Katz Deli of Aventura, Inc. v. Waterways Plaza, LLC, 183 So. 3d 374 (Fla. 3d DCA 2013), 16-3:7

Kaufman v. Shere, 347 So. 2d 627 (Fla. 3d DCA 1977), 9-4:3

Kebreau v. Bayview Loan Servicing, LLC, 225 So. 3d 255 (Fla. 4th DCA 2017), 6-4:7

Keller v. Belcher, 256 So. 2d 561 (Fla. 3d DCA 1971), 14-3:9

Kelly v. BankUnited, FSB, 159 So. 3d 403 (Fla. 4th DCA 2015), 16-3:2

Kelsey v. SunTrust Mortgage, Inc., 131 So. 3d 825 (Fla. 3d DCA 2014), 12-1:10.1, 13-4

Kersey v. City of Riviera Beach, 337 So. 2d 995 (Fla. 4th DCA 1976), 12-1:3.2

Keys Citizens for Responsible Gov't v. Fla. Keys Aqueduct Auth., 795 So. 2d 940, 948 (Fla. 2001), 12-1:4

Keys Country Resort v. 1733 Overseas High., LLC, 272 So. 3d 500 (Fla. 3d DCA 2019), 12-1:1

Key West Wharf & Coal Co. v. Porter, 63 Fla. 448, 58 So. 599 (Fla. 1912), 10-2:1, 14-3:7

Khleif v. Bankers Trust Co. of California, 215 So. 3d 619 (Fla. 2d DCA 2017), 6-2:4, 7-2:2

Kiefert v. Nationstar Mortgage, LLC, 153 So. 3d 351 (Fla. 1st DCA 2014), 4-1, 12-1:3.2, 12-1:10.1.b

Kimmick v. United States Bank Nat'l Ass'n, 83 So. 3d 877, *passim* (Fla. 4th DCA 2012), 7-3:5

King v. Harrington, 411 So. 2d 912 (Fla. 2d DCA 1982), 14-3:5

Kinney v. Countrywide Home Loans Servicing, L.P., 165 So. 3d 691 (Fla. 4th DCA 2015), 13-2

Klebanoff v. Bank of New York Mellon, No. 5D16-1637, 2017 WL 2818078 (Fla. 5th DCA June 30, 2017), 3-2:1.1c

Klebanoff v. Bank of New York Mellon, 228 So. 3d 167 (Fla. 5th DCA 2017), 6-4:7

Knight Energy Servs., Inc. v. Amoco Oil Co., 660 So. 2d 786 (Fla. 4th DCA 1995), 7-3:6, 12-1:3.2

Knowles v. C.I.T. Corp., 346 So. 2d 1042 (Fla. 1st DCA 1977), 13-5

Koch v. Koch, 47 So. 3d 320 (Fla. 2d DCA 2010), 16-4:1

Konsulian v. Busey Bank, N.A., 61 So. 3d 1283 (Fla. 2d DCA 2011), 12-1:3.2

Kontrick v. Ryan, 540 U.S. 443 (2004), 17-7

Kopel v. Kopel, 229 So. 3d 812 (Fla. 2017), 3-2:4

TABLE OF CASES

Koresko v. Coe, 683 So. 2d 602 (Fla. 2d DCA 1996), 12-1:3

Korte v. U.S. Bank Nat. Ass'n., 64 So. 3d 134 (Fla. 4th DCA 2011), 16-4:2

Koster v. Sullivan, 103 So. 3d 882 (Fla. 2d DCA 2012), 1-3:2

Kotlyar v. Metropolitan Cas. Ins. Co., 192 So. 3d 562 (Fla. 4th DCA 2016), 6-4:8

Kozel v. Ostendorf, 629 So. 2d 817 (Fla. 1994), 9-3, 11-3:2.1, 11-7:3, 14-3:7, 15-1, 15-3:3

KRC Enters., Inc. v. Soderquist, 553 So. 2d 760 (Fla. 2d DCA 1989), 2-3:2

Kreiss Potassium Phosphate Co. v. Knight, 124 So. 751 (Fla. 1929), 2-3:3

Krell v. National Mortg. Corp., 214 Ga. App. 503, 448 S.E. 2d 248 (1994), 8-4

Kresmer v. Tonokaboni, 356 So. 2d 1331 (Fla. 3d DCA 1978), 7-3:6

Krivanek v. Take Back Tampa Political Comm., 625 So. 2d 840 (Fla. 1993), 7-2:2, 7-3:2

Kronen v. Deutsche Bank Nat'l Trust Co., 267 So. 3d 447 (Fla. 4th DCA 2019), 4-4, 4-5, 6-2:5, 6-4:3

Kuehlman v. Bank of Am., N.A., 177 So. 3d 1282 (Fla. 5th DCA 2015), 2-1:1

Kumar Corp. v. Nopal Lines, Ltd., 462 So. 2d 1178 (Fla. 3d DCA 1985), 6-3:1

Kurian v. Wells Fargo Bank, Nat. Ass'n, 114 So. 3d 1052 (Fla. 4th DCA 2013), 2-2:3.2

Kush v. Lloyd, 616 So. 2d 415, 421 (Fla. 1992), 3-3:2.4

L

L.A.D. Prop. Ventures v. First Bank, 19 So. 3d 1126 (Fla. 2d DCA 2009), 19-2:1

LaFaille v. Nationstar Mortg., LLC, 197 So. 3d 1246 (Fla. 3d DCA 2016), 2-2:2, 9-3, 10-2:4, 12-1:10.1.h

Lago v. Kame, 120 So. 3d 73 (Fla. 4th DCA 2013), 15-4:2

Lake Towers, Inc. v. Axelrod, 216 So. 2d 86 (Fla. 4th DCA 1968), 1-5

Lambert v. Dracos, 403 So. 2d 481 (Fla. 1st DCA 1981), 6-3:3, 7-3:6

Lamb v. Nationstar Mortg., LLC, 174 So. 3d 1039 (Fla. 4th DCA 2015), 9-4:4

Lamoise Grp., LLC v. Edgewater S. Beach Condo. Ass'n, 278 So. 3d 796 (Fla. 3d DCA 2019), 14-3:7

Land Dev. Servs., Inc. v. Gulf View Townhomes, LLC, 75 So. 3d 865 (Fla. 2d DCA 2011), 12-1:3, 12-1:5

Landers v. Milton, 370 So. 2d 368 (Fla. 1979), 12-1:3

Larson & Larson, P.A. v. TSE Indus., Inc., 22 So. 3d 36 (Fla. 2009), 3-2:5.1

Lasala v. Nationstar Mortg., LLC, 197 So. 3d 1228 (Fla. 4th DCA 2016), 13-4:4

Lassiter v. Curtiss-Bright Co., 129 Fla. 728 (Fla.1937), 5-4:1

Lauxmont Farms, Inc. v. Flavin, 514 So. 2d 1133 (Fla. 3d DCA 1987), 1-4:3

Law Offices of Fred Cohen, P.A. v. H.E.C. Cleaning, LLC, 2020 WL 559240 (Fla. 4th DCA 2020), 16-4:3

Law Offices of David J. Stern, P.A. v. Sec. Nat'l Servicing Corp., 969 So. 2d 962 (Fla. 2007), 7-2:2

Laws v. Wells Fargo Bank, N.A., 159 So. 3d 918 (Fla. 1st DCA 2015), 8-4

Layton v. Bay Lake Ltd. P'ship, 818 So. 2d 552 (Fla. 2d DCA 2002), 3-3:2, 3-3:2.2

Lazcar Int'l, Inc. v. Caraballo, 957 So. 2d 1191 (Fla. 3d DCA 2007), 1-4:4.3, 14-3:4

Lazuran v. Citimortgage, Inc., 35 So. 3d 189 (Fla. 4th DCA 2010), 12-1:3.2

L.B.T. Corp. v. Camacho, 429 So. 2d 88 (Fla. 5th DCA 1983), 14-3:4

Leach v. Salehpour, 19 So. 3d 342 (Fla. 2d DCA 2009), 14-2:1, 14-3:1

Ledo v. Seavie Resources, LLC, 149 So. 3d 707 (Fla. 3d DCA 2014), 11-3:2.1

Lee-Booth, Inc. v. Fid. & Deposit Co. of Md., 399 So. 2d 531 (Fla. 2d DCA 1981), 12-1:5

Lee County v. Barnett Banks, Inc., 711 So. 2d 34 (Fla. 2d DCA 1999), 13-3:2

Leeds v. C.C. Chemical Corp., 280 So. 2d 718 (Fla. 3d DCA 1973), 13-2:1

Lefler v. Lefler, 776 So. 2d 319 (Fla. 4th DCA 2001), 14-3:6

Lennar Homes, Inc. v. Gabb Constr. Services, 654 So. 2d 649, 651 (Fla. 3d 1995), 1-3:2

Leonard v. Cook & Pruitt Masonry, Inc., 126 So. 2d 136, 139 (Fla. 1960), 16-3:4

Les Chateaux at Int'l Gardens Condo. Ass'n v. Cuevas & Assocs., P.A., 219 So. 3d 106 (Fla. 3d DCA 2017), 12-1:7

Lesnoff v. Becker, 135 So. 146, 147 (Fla. 1931), 10-2:1

Le v. U.S. Bank, 165 So. 3d 776, 778 (Fla. 5th DCA 2015), 12-1:10.1.a

Levine v. Fieni McFarlane, Inc., 690 So. 2d 712 (Fla. 4th DCA 1997), 9-4:4

Leviton v. Philly Steak-Out, Inc., 533 So. 2d 905, 906 (Fla. 3d DCA 1988), 12-1:8

Lewis v. Barnett Bank of South Florida, N.A., 604 So. 2d 937, 938 (Fla. 3d DCA 1992), 7-2:1

Lewis v. Fifth Third Mortg. Co., 38 So. 3d 157 (Fla. 3d DCA 2010), 5-7

Lewis v. U.S. Bank Nat'l Ass'n, 188 So. 3d 46 (Fla. 4th DCA 2016), 4-4

Lezcano v. Estate of Hidalgo, 88 So. 3d 306 (Fla. 3d DCA 2012), 14-3:7

Liberty Bus. Credit Corp. v. Schaffer/Dunadry, 589 So. 2d 451 (Fla. 2d DCA 1991), 19-3

Liberty Home Equity Solutions, Inc. v. Raulston, 206 So. 3d 58, 60 (Fla. 4th DCA 2016), 3-2:1.2, 6-4:1

Linares v. Bank of Am., N.A., 278 So. 3d 330 (Fla. 3d DCA 2019), 14-3:1, 14-3:3, 14-3:6

Lindgren v. Deutsche Bank, 115 So. 3d 1076 (Fla. 4th DCA 2013), 12-1:10.1.b

Lindsey v. H.M. Raulerson, Jr., Memorial Hosp., 452 So. 2d 1087 (Fla. 4th DCA 1984), 9-3

Liukkonen v. Bayview Loan Servicing, 243 So. 3d 981 (Fla. 4th DCA 2018), 13-4:4

TABLE OF CASES

Local No. 666, Concrete Products and Material Yard Workers, Laborers Int'l Union of North America, AFL-CIO v. Dennis, 453 So. 2d 1138 (Fla. 4th DCA 1984), 18-4:2

Locke v. State Farm Fire and Casualty Co., 509 So. 2d 1375 (Fla. 1st DCA 1987), 3-2:1.2, 6-4:7, 12-1:10.1

Lomas Mtg., Inc. v. Louis, 82 F.3d 1 (1st Cir. 1996), 17-6:2

Lopez v. JP Morgan Chase Bank, 187 So. 3d 343 (Fla. 4th DCA 2016), 12-1:10.1.e

Lopez v. U.S. Bank, 116 So. 3d 640 (Fla. 3d DCA 2013), 13-2

Losner v. HSBC Bank USA, N.A., 190 So. 3d 160 (Fla. 4th DCA 2016), 6-5:3

Lovett v. Nat'l Collegiate Student Loan Trust 2004-1, 149 So. 3d 735 (Fla. 5th DCA 2014), 14-3:3

LR5A-JV v. Little House, LLC, 50 So. 3d 691 (Fla. 5th DCA 2010), 14-3:8

Lucas v. Barnett Bank of Lee Cty., 705 So. 2d 115 (Fla. 2d DCA 1998), 14-3:3, 14-3:7

Lunn Woods v. Lowery, 577 So. 2d 705 (Fla. 2d DCA 1991), 2-1:3.1, 7-3:4

Lutsch v. Smith, 397 So. 2d 337 (Fla. 1st DCA 1981), 11-4:2.2

M

Mac-Gray Serv., Inc. v. DeGeorge, 913 So. 2d 630 (Fla. 4th DCA 2005), 8-6

Machules v. Department of Admin., 523 So. 2d 1132 (Fla. 1988), 3-2:5.2

Madl v. Wells Fargo Bank, N.A., 244 So. 3d 1134 (Fla. 5th DCA 2017), 16-2:3

Mahmoud v. King, 824 So. 2d 248 (Fla. 4th DCA 2002), 12-1:5

Major League Baseball v. Morsani, 790 So. 2d 1071 (Fla. 2001), 3-2:2.1, 3-2:5.1, 3-2:5.2

Manatee County v. Harbor Ventures, Inc., 305 So. 2d 299 (Fla. 2d DCA 1974), 16-3:5

Manning v. Clark, 71 So. 2d 508 (Fla. 1954), 12-1:3

Manzaro v. D'Alessandro, 229 So. 3d 843 (Fla. 4th DCA 2017), 14-3:6

Mariner Health Care of Metrowest, Inc. v. Best, 879 So. 2d 65 (Fla. 5th DCA 2004), 11-7:3

Market Tampa Investments, LLC v. Stobaugh, 177 So. 3d 31 (Fla. 2d DCA 2015), 10-2:1, 10-2:2

Marsh v. Marsh, 72 Fla. 142, 72 So. 638 (1916), 14-4

Martinec v. Early Bird Int'l, Inc., 126 So. 3d 1115 (Fla. 4th DCA 2012), 8-2:1

Martinec v. Early Bird Int'l, Inc., 262 So. 3d 205 (Fla. 4th DCA 2018), 19-3

Martin-Johnson, Inc. v. Savage, 509 So. 2d 1097 (Fla. 1987), 11-8, 18-4:3.1

Martins v. PNC Bank, N.A., 170 So. 3d 932 (Fla. 5th DCA 2015), 11-9:2

Martorano v. Spicola, 148 So. 585 (1933), 10-3:3

Martyn v. First Federal Savings & Loan Ass'n, 257 So. 2d 576 (Fla. 4th DCA 1971), 1-10

Maslak v. Wells Fargo Bank, N.A., 190 So. 3d 656 (Fla. 4th DCA 2016), 11-9:3

Mason v. Flowers, 91 Fla. 224, 107 So. 334 (Fla. 1926), 4-10

Mathis v. Nationstar Mortg., LLC, 42 Fla. L. Weekly D 1190 (Fla. 4th DCA 2017), 4-3

Matter of Crum, 55 B.R. 455 (Bankr. M.D. Fla. 1985), 17-4

Matte v. Caplan, 140 So. 3d 686 (Fla. 4th DCA 2014), 15-4:2

Maw v. Abinales, 463 So. 2d 1245 (Fla. 2d DCA 1985), 16-2:1

Mayfield v. First City Bank of Florida, 95 So. 3d 398 (Fla. 1st DCA 2012), 5-4

Maynard v. Household Fin. Corp. III, 861 So. 2d 1204 (Fla. 2d DCA 2003), 3-2:6

Mazine v. M & I Bank, 67 So. 3d 1129 (Fla. 1st DCA 2011), 12-1:10.1.a

McCabe v. Howard, 281 So. 2d 362 (Fla. 2d DCA 1973), 4-6

McCall v. HSBC Bank USA, N.A., 186 So. 3d 1134 (Fla. 1st DCA 2016), 8-5

McClean v. JP Morgan Chase Bank N.A., 79 So. 3d 170 (Fla. 4th DCA 2012), 4-4

McClung v. Posey, 514 So. 2d 1139 (Fla. 5th DCA 1987), 16-3:2

McIntosh v. Wells Fargo Bank, N.A., 226 So. 3d 377 (Fla. 5th DCA 2017), 2-2:2

McLean v. JP Morgan Chase Bank, Nat'l Ass'n., 79 So. 3d 170 (Fla. 4th DCA 2012), 1-1:1, 4-4, 6-4:3, 7-3:2, 13-4:1.2

McNutt v. Sherrill, 141 So. 2d 309 (Fla. 3d DCA 1962), 12-1:8

Meadows on the Green Condo. Ass'n, Inc. v. Nationstar Mortg., LLC, 188 So. 3d 883 (Mem), 2016 WL 72585 (Fla. 4th DCA 2016), 9-3, 9-4:4, 9-4:5

Mederos v. Selph (L.T.), Inc., 625 So. 2d 894 (Fla. 5th DCA 1993), 5-3

Mediplex Construction of Fla., Inc. v. Schaub, 856 So. 2d 13 (Fla. 4th DCA 2003), 16-3:6

Meilleur v. HSBC Bank USA, N.A., 194 So. 3d 512 (Fla. 4th DCA 2016), 12-1:10.1.b

Melody Tours, Inc. v. Granville Market Letter, Inc., 413 So. 2d 450 (Fla. 5th DCA 1982), 11-4:2

Mendelson v. Great Western Bank, F.S.B., 712 So. 2d 1194 (Fla. 2d DCA 1998), 6-5:3

Mendez v. W. Flagler Family As'n. Inc., 303 So. 2d 1 (Fla. 1974), 18-4:1

Merritt v. Unkefer, 223 So. 2d 723 (Fla. 1969), 6-5:4

MERS v. Azize, 965 So. 2d 151 (Fla. 2d DCA 2007), 7-2:2

Messer v. E.G. Pump Controls, Inc., 667 So. 2d 321 (Fla. 1st DCA 1995), 11-3:2.1

Meyerson v. Boyce, 97 So. 2d 488 (Fla. 3d DCA 1957), 7-3:6

Miami Airlines v. Webb, 114 So. 2d 361 (Fla. 3d DCA 1959), 4-9

Miami-Dade Cty. Lansdowne Mortg., LLC, 235 So. 3d 960 (Fla. 3d DCA 2017), 6-3:9, 10-4:1

TABLE OF CASES

Miami-Dade Water & Sewer Auth. v. Metro. Dade Cty., 469 So. 2d 813 (Fla. 3d DCA 1985), 18-4:1

Michel v. Bank of N.Y. Mellon, 191 So. 3d 981 (Fla. 2d DCA 2016), 12-1:10.1.a

Michnal v. Palm Coast Development, Inc., 842 So. 2d 927 (Fla. 4th DCA 2003), 16-3:7

Midland Funding, LLC v. Johnson, 137 S. Ct. 1407 (2017), 17-5

Mielke v. Deutsche Bank Nat'l Trust Co., 264 So. 3d 249 (Fla. 1st DCA 2019), 6-5:2

Mihalyi v. LaSalle Bank, N.A, 162 So. 3d 113 (Fla. 4th DCA 2014), 16-2:2

Miles v. Robinson, 803 So. 2d 864 (Fla. 4th DCA 2002), 12-1:3.1

Millennium Group I, L.L.C. v. Attorneys Title Ins. Fund, Inc., 847 So. 2d 1115 (Fla. 1st DCA 2003), 12-1:9

Miller v. Balcanoff, 566 So. 2d 1340 (Fla. 1st DCA 1990), 2-3:1

Miller v. Bank of New York Mellon, 149 So. 3d 1198 (Fla. 4th DCA 2014), 16-3:5

Miller v. Estate of Baer, 837 So. 2d 448 (Fla. 4th DCA 2002), 2-1:3.2

Miller v. Miller, 801 So. 2d 1056 (Fla. 1st DCA 2001), 14-2:2, 16-3:6

Miller v. Nifakos, 655 So. 2d 192 (Fla. 4th DCA 1995), 1-1:1

Miller v. Washington Mut. Bank, 184 So. 3d 558 (Fla. 4th DCA 2016), 6-3:6

Millett v. Perez, 418 So. 2d 1067 (Fla. 3d DCA 1982), 2-2:1, 2-2:4

Mills v. Avon Park Motor Co., 223 So. 2d 802 (Fla. 2d DCA 1969), 18-2

Miranda v. RBS Citizens, N.A., 2018 WL 3862706 (Fla. 3d DCA Aug. 15, 2018), 18-3

Mitchell v. Beach Club of Hallandale Condo. Ass'n, Inc., 17 So. 3d 1265 (Fla. 4th DCA 2009), 9-4:5

Mitchell v. Chase Home Fin. LLC, 2008 U.S. Dist. LEXIS 17040, 2008 WL 623395 (N.D. Tex. 2008), 8-4

Mitchell v. DiMare, 936 So. 2d 1178 (Fla. 5th DCA 2006), 12-1:3.2

Mitchell v. Federal Nat. Mortg. Ass'n, 763 So. 2d 358 (Fla. 4th DCA 2005), 6-3:3

MML Development Corp. v. Eagle Nat. Bank of Miami, 603 So. 2d 646 (Fla. 3d DCA 1992), 6-1:3

Moakley v. Smallwood, 826 So. 2d 221 (Fla. 2002), 15-1, 15-2:1, 15-2:2, 15-2:3, 16-4:1

Moforis v. Moforis, 977 So. 2d 786 (Fla. 4th DCA 2008), 14-3:9

Moise v. JP Morgan Chase Bank Nat'l Ass'n, 137 So. 3d 1192 (Fla. 3d DCA 2014), 13-2

Monnot v. U.S. Bank, Nat'l Ass'n, 188 So. 3d 896 (Fla. 4th DCA 2016), 8-2

Monte v. Tipton, 612 So. 2d 714 (5th DCA 1993), 3-2:1.2

Montreux at Deerwood Lake Condominium Association, Inc. v. Citibank, N.A., 153 So. 3d 961 (Fla. 1st DCA 2014), 9-3, 9-4:4, 9-4:5

Moore v. Morris, 475 So. 2d 666 (Fla. 1985), 12-1:2, 12-1:3

Morales v. Fifth Third Bank, 275 So. 3d 197 (Fla. 4th DCA 2019), 2-1:1, 6-2:4, 6-4:2

Morgan v. Kelly, 642 So. 2d 1117 (Fla. 3d DCA 1994), 19-3, 19-3:2

Moritz v. Hoyt Enterprises, Inc., 604 So. 2d 807 (Fla. 1992), 16-3:2

Morris v. Osteen, 948 So. 2d 821 (Fla. 5th DCA 2007), 1-9

Mortgage Electronic Registration Sys., Inc. v. Badra, 991 So. 2d 1037 (Fla. 4th DCA 2008), 4-8

Mortgage Electronic Registration Sys., Inc. v. Azize, 965 So. 2d 151 (Fla. 2d DCA 2007), 9-4:4

Morton v. Ansin, 129 So. 2d 177 (Fla. 3d DCA 1961), 9-4:5

MR&F Enterprises v. Citicorp Savings of Florida, 764 So. 2d 783 (Fla. 3d DCA 2000), 19-3

Mullane v. Central Hanover Bank & Trust Co., 339 U.S. 306 (1950), 14-3:7

Mullins v. Tompkins, 15 So. 3d 798 (Fla. 1st DCA 2009), 11-3:3

Murray v. HSBC Bank USA, 157 So. 3d 355 (Fla. 4th DCA 2015), 4-7, 13-4:1.2

Muss v. Lennar Fla. Partners, 673 So. 2d 84 (Fla. 4th DCA 1996), 12-1:10.1.b

Myers v. Siegel, 920 So. 2d 1241 (Fla. 5th DCA 2006), 12-1:8

N

Nack Holdings, LLC v. Kalb, 13 So. 3d 92 (Fla. 3d DCA 2009), 5-6

Nathan v. Bates, 998 So. 2d 1178 (Fla. 3d DCA 2008), 16-4:3

National Collegiate Student Loan Tr. 2007-1 v. Lipari, 224 So. 3d 309 (Fla. 5th DCA 2017), 8-5

National Collegiate Student Loan Trust 2006-4 v. Meyer, 265 So. 3d 715 (Fla. 2d DCA 2019), 6-2:4

National Portland Cement Co. v. Goudie, 718 So. 2d 274 (Fla. 2d DCA 1998), 16-3:6

National Union Fire Ins. Co. of Pittsburgh, Pa. v. KPMG Peat Marwick, 742 So. 2d 328 (Fla. 3d DCA 1999), 5-4:2.1

Nationstar Mortgage, LLC v. Bo Chan, 226 So. 3d 330 (Fla. 5th DCA 2017), 4-9

Nationstar Mortgage, LLC v. Johnson, 2018 Fla. App. LEXIS 9266 (Fla. 2d DCA, June 29, 2018), 4-9

Nationstar Mortgage, LLC v. Kelly, 199 So. 3d 1051 (Fla. 5th DCA 2016), 4-7

Nationstar Mortgage, LLC v. Marquez, 180 So. 3d 219 (Fla. 3d DCA 2015), 6-4:3

Nationstar Mortgage, LLC v. Berdecia, 169 So. 3d 209 (Fla. 5th DCA 2015), 12-1:10.1.a

Nationstar Mortgage, LLC v. Faramarz, 275 So. 3d 668 (4th DCA 2019), 16-2:3

Nationstar Mortgage LLC v. Glass, 219 So. 3d 896 (Fla. 4th DCA 2017), 16-2:3

Nat'l Educ. Centers, Inc. v. Kirkland, 635 So. 2d 33 (Fla. 4th DCA 1993), 2-3:1

TABLE OF CASES 453

NCR Corp. v. Cannon & Wolfe Lumber Co., Inc., 501 So. 2d 157 (Fla. 1st DCA 1987), 1-4:1

Nedd v. Gary, 35 So. 3d 1028 (Fla. 3d DCA 2010), 16-4:3

Nelson v. Balkany, 620 So. 2d 1138 (Fla. 3d DCA 1993), 12-1:7

Nemeth v. Shore, 511 So. 2d 1118 (Fla. 2d DCA 1987), 1-4:1

Nesbitt v. Citicorp Savings of Fla., 514 So. 2d 371 (Fla. 3d DCA 1987), 10-2:4, 12-1:10.1.h

Neuschatz v. Rabin, 760 So. 2d 1018 (Fla. 4th DCA 2000), 10-3:3

New York Life Ins. and Annuity Corp. v. Hammocks Community Ass'n, Inc., 622 So. 2d 1369 (Fla. 3d DCA 1993), 5-3

Nikooie v. JP Morgan Chase Bank, N.A., 183 So. 3d 424 (Fla. 3d DCA 2014), 5-5, 7-3:6

Nobani v. Barcelona Dev. Corp., 655 So. 2d 250 (Fla. 5 DCA 1995), 5-8

Nobelman v. Am. Sav. Bank, 508 U.S. 324 (1993), 17-6:2

Nogales v. Countrywide Home Loans, Inc., 100 So. 3d 1161 (Fla. 2d DCA 2012), 14-2:1

Norris v. Paps, 615 So. 2d 735 (Fla. 2d DCA 1993), 13-2

Northamerican Van Lines, Inc. v. Roper, 429 So. 2d 750 (Fla. 1st DCA 1983), 16-6:1

North Brevard County Hospital Dist., Inc. v. Florida Public Employees Relations Commission, 392 So. 2d 556 (Fla. 1st DCA 1980), 14-2:2

North Shore Hospital, Inc. v. Barber, 143 So. 2d 849 (Fla. 1962), 14-2:2

Northwestern Nat'l Life Ins. Co. v. Riggs, 203 U.S. 243 (1906), 2-1:2, 2-1:3.1

Norwest Bank Owatonna, N.A. v. Millard, 522 So. 2d 546 (Fla. 4th DCA 1988), 19-3

Nour v. All State Pipe Supply Co., 487 So. 2d 1204 (Fla. 1st DCA 1986), 12-1:5

Novastar Mortgage, Inc. v. Strassburger, 855 So. 2d 130 (Fla. 4th DCA 2003), 10-2:4, 16-2:3, 16-5.1

Nowlin v. Nationstar Mortg., LLC, 193 So. 3d 1043 (Fla. 2d DCA 2016), 2-1:1, 6-4:2

Nucci v. Target Corp., 162 So. 3d 146 (Fla. 4th DCA 2015), 11-1, 11-8

Nudel v. Flagstar Bank, FSB, 60 So. 3d 1163 (Fla. 4th DCA 2011), 16-3:1, 16-3:2, 18-8

Nunez v. Allen, 2019 WL 5089715 (Fla. 5th DCA 2019), 16-3:2

O

Oakland Properties Corp. v. Hogan, 117 So. 846 (Fla. 1928), 6-3:2, 6-3:5, 10-2:1, 14-3:7

Oasis Builders, LLC v. McHugh, 138 So. 3d 1218 (Fla. 4th DCA 2014), 15-2:3

Obermeyer v. Bank of New York, 272 So. 3d 430 (Mem.) (Fla. 3d DCA 2019), 16-3:6

Ober v. Town of Lauderdale-by-the-Sea, 218 So. 3d 952 (Fla. 4th 2017), 9-4:1

Ocean Bank v. Caribbean Towers Condo. Assoc., Inc., 121 So. 3d 1087 (Fla. 3d DCA 2013), 9-4:5

Ocwen Loan Servicing, LLC v. Gundersen, 204 So. 3d 530 (Fla. 4th DCA 2016), 12-1:10.1.a

Okeechobee Resorts, L.L.C. v. E Z Cash Pawn, Inc., 145 So. 3d 989 (Fla. 4th DCA 2014), 2-1:2, 2-1:3.1

Old Republic Ins. Co. v. Lee, 507 So. 2d 754 (Fla. 5th DCA 1987), 2-3:4

Olivera v. Bank of Am., N.A., 141 So. 3d 770 (Fla. 2d DCA 2014), 4-9, 7-3:2, 12-1:3.2

Olympia Mortgage Corp. v. Pugh, 774 So. 2d 863 (Fla. 4th DCA 2000), 2-3:5, 2-3:5.1, 2-3:5.2

One 79th Street Estates, Inc. v. American Investment Services, 47 So. 3d 886 (Fla. 3d DCA 2010), 5-6, 14-3:8

One West Bank, F.S.B. v. Bauer, 159 So. 3d 843 (Fla. 2d DCA 2014), 4-4, 9-4:4

OneWest Bank, FSB v. Jasinski, 173 So. 3d 1009 (Fla. 2d DCA 2015), 1-7, 12-1:3, 12-1:10.1.a

Opportunity Funding I, LLC v. Otetchestvennyi, 909 So. 2d 361 (Fla. 4th DCA 2005), 14-4

Orange Park Tr. Servs. v. JP Morgan Chase Bank, Nat'l Ass'n, 152 So. 3d 83 (Fla. 1st DCA 2014), 1-10:3

Orsonio v. Fuller, Maliah & Assocs., 857 So. 2d 973 (Fla. 3d DCA 2003), 18-4:1

Ortiz v. PNC Bank, Nat'l Ass'n, 188 So. 3d 923 (Fla. 4th DCA 2016), 2-2:2, 2-2:3.1, 4-5, 6-4:3, 7-3:2, 7-3:3, 8-4, 12-1:10.1.b, 13-4:1.2

Osorio v. State Farm Bank, F.S.B., 746 F.3d 1242 (11th Cir. 2014), 16-6:1

Osorto v. Deutsche Bank Nat'l Trust Co., 88 So. 3d 261 (Fla. 4th DCA 2012), 11-9:2, 12-1:8

P

Pabian v. Pabian, 469 So. 2d 189 (Fla. 4th DCA 1985), 18-5

Padgett v. Kessinger, 190 So. 3d 105 (Fla. 4th DCA 2015), 16-3:2

Padow v. Knollwood Club Association, Inc., 839 So. 2d 744 (Fla. 4th DCA 2003), 16-3:2

Paladyne Corp. v. Weindruch, 867 So. 2d 630 (Fla. 5th DCA 2004), 16-3:6

Palma v. JPMorgan Chase Bank, NA, 208 So. 3d 771 (Fla. 5th DCA 2016), 2-2:2, 2-2:6, 7-3:3, 8-4, 12-1:10.1.e

Palmetto Federal Savings and Loan Ass'n v. Day, 512 So. 2d 332 (Fla. 3d DCA 1987), 16-3:5

Palm v. Taylor, 929 So. 2d 566 (Fla. 2d DCA 2006), 6-5:3

Pan Am. Bank of Miami v. City of Miami Beach, 198 So. 2d 45 (Fla. 3d DCA 1967), 10-2:1, 14-3:7

Paneson v. Paneson, 825 So. 2d 523 (Fla. 2d DCA 2002), 7-3:4

Panzera v. O'Neal, 198 So. 3d 663 (Fla. 2d DCA 2015), 12-1:3

TABLE OF CASES

Pardo v. State, 596 So. 2d 665 (Fla. 1992), 9-3

Parisi v. Broward County, 769 So. 2d 359 (Fla. 2000), 15-2:1, 15-2:2, 15-2:3

Paris v. Paris, 427 So. 2d 1080 (Fla. 1st DCA 1983), 13-3:3

Parker v. Dinsmore Co., 443 So. 2d 356 (Fla. 1st DCA 1983), 7-3:6

Parker v. Parker, 950 So. 2d 388 (Fla.2007), 14-3:6

Park West Professional Center Condominium Association, Inc. v. Londono, 130 So. 3d 711 (Fla. 3d DCA 2013), 9-4:1

Partridge v. Nationstar Mortg., LLC, 224 So. 3d 839 (Fla. 2d DCA 2017), 4-6

Pastore-Borroto Dev., Inc. v. Marevista Apartments, M.B., Inc., 596 So. 2d 526 (Fla. 3d DCA 1992), 16-3:8

Paton v. GEICO General Ins. Co., 190 So. 3d 1047 (Fla. 2016), 16-3:5

Pawlik v. Barnett Bank, 528 So. 2d 965 (Fla. 1st DCA 1988), 12-1:3

Paxton v. Williams Scotsman, Inc., 924 So. 2d 37 (Fla. 5th DCA 2006), 14-3:7

PB Surf, LTD v. Beach Community Bank, RFP, LLC, 139 So. 3d 463 (Fla. 1st DCA 2014), 19-3:3

Pealer v. Wilmington Tr. Nat'l Ass'n for MFRA Tr., 212 So. 3d 1137 (Fla. 2d DCA 2017), 3-2:1.2, 9-3, 10-2:4, 12-1:10.1, 12-1:10.1.h

Pearce v. Sandler, 219 So. 3d 961 (Fla. 3d DCA 2017), 14-3:6

Pearlman v. Pearlman, 405 So. 2d 764 (Fla. 3d DCA 1981), 14-2:2

Pelycado Onroerend Goed B.V. v. Ruthenberg, 635 So. 2d 1001 (Fla. 5th DCA 1994), 9-4:6, 14-3:7

Pemco, Inc. v. American Gen. Home Equity, 629 So. 2d 307 (Fla. 2d DCA 1993), 7-3:4

Peninsular Naval Stores Company v. Cox, 49 So. 191 (Fla. 1909), 10-2:2

PennyMac Corp. v. Frost, 214 So. 3d 686 (Fla. 4th DCA 2017), 4-4, 4-7

Penton v. Intercredit Bank, N.A., 943 So. 2d 863 (Fla. 3d DCA 2006), 6-1:3

Penzer v. Transp. Ins. Co., 29 So. 3d 1000 (Fla. 2010), 3-3:2

Peoples v. Sami II Trust 2006-AR6, 178 So. 3d 67 (Fla. 4th DCA 2015), 12-1:3.2

Perez v. Deutsche Bank Nat'l Trust Co., 174 So. 3d 489 (Fla. 4th DCA 2015), 4-4

Perez v. Perez, 973 So. 2d 1227 (Fla. 4th DCA 2008), 13-6

Perry v. Fairbanks Capital Corp., 888 So. 2d 725 (Fla. 5th DCA 2004), 4-2

Personalized Air Conditioning, Inc. v. C.M. Sys. of Pinellas Cty., Inc., 522 So. 2d 465, 466 (Fla. 4th DCA 1988), 17-3:1

Peters v. Bank of New York Mellon, 227 So. 3d 175 (Fla. 2d DCA 2017), 6-4:3

Petsoules v. State, 140 So. 3d 1284 (Fla. 5th DCA 2013), 15-2:1

Peuguero v. Bank of Am., N.A., 169 So. 3d 1198 (Fla. 4th DCA 2015), 4-4, 7-3:2, 13-4:4

Pezzimenti v. Cirou, 466 So. 2d 274 (Fla. 2d DCA 1985), 2-1:3.1

Phadael v. Deutsche Bank Tr. Co. Ams., 83 So. 3d 893 (Fla. 4th DCA 2012), 12-1:3.2

Phan v. Deutsche Bank Nat'l Trust Co., 198 So. 3d 744 (Fla. 2d DCA 2016), 4-1, 4-6, 6-3:1, 12-1:10.1.b

PHH Mortg. Corp. v. Parish, 244 So. 3d 338 (Fla. 2d DCA 2018), 6-4:7

Philippe v. Weiner, 143 So. 3d 1086 (Fla. 3d DCA 2014), 5-2:1.3

Phillips v. Green Tree Servicing LLC, No. 15-13582, 2016 WL 627903 (E.D. Mich. Feb. 17, 2016), 14-4

Phillips v. State, 69 So. 3d 951 (Fla. 2d DCA 2010), 18-4:3.3

Pierce v. Anglin, 721 So. 2d 781 (Fla. 1st DCA 1998), 1-4:3

Pijuan v. Bank of Am., N.A., 253 So. 3d 112 (Fla. 3d DCA 2018), 2-1:1

Pino v. Bank of N.Y., 121 So. 3d 23 (Fla. 2013), 15-2:3, 15-4:1, 15-4:2

Pitts v. Pastore, 561 So. 2d 297 (Fla. 2d DCA 1990), 2-1:1, 3-2:1.1, 3-3:2.2, 6-1:1, 6-3:6

Plapinger v. E. States Properties Realty Corp., 716 So. 2d 315 (Fla. 5th DCA 1998), 16-3:4

PLCA Condominium Association v. Amtrust-NP SFR Venture, LLC, 182 So. 3d 668 (Fla. 4th DCA 2015), 9-4:5

PMI Mortg. Ins. Co. v. Cavendar, 615 So. 2d 710 (Fla. 3d DCA 1993), 19-3:4

PMT NPL Fin. 2015-1 v. Centurion Sys., LLC, 2018 Fla. App. LEXIS 11956 (Fla. 5th DCA 2018), 4-4, 4-9

PNC Bank, N.A. v. Monument Ctr., LLC, No: 6:15-cv- 859-Orl- 40DAB, 2016 WL 4435698 (M.D. Fla. July 27, 2016), 19-3:1

PNC Bank, Nat'l Ass'n v. Inlet Vill. Condo. Ass'n, Inc., 204 So. 3d 97 (Fla. 4th DCA 2016), 9-3

PNC Bank, Nat'l Ass'n v. MDTR, LLC, 243 So. 3d 456 (Fla. 5th DCA 2018), 10-2:4

PNC Bank, NA v. Duque, 137 So. 3d 476 (Fla. 4th DCA 2014), 15-3:3

PNC Mortg. v. Garland, 7th Dist. Mahoning No. 12 MA 222, 2014-Ohio-1173 (7th Dist. Ohio Mar. 20, 2014), 8-4

Poinciana Hotel of Miami Beach, Inc. v. Kasden, 370 So. 2d 399 (Fla. 3d DCA 1979), 5-3

Pompano Ledger v. Greater Pompano Beach Chamber of Commerce, 802 So. 2d 438 (Fla. 4th DCA 2001), 16-3:7

Pomponio v. Claridge of Pompano Condo., Inc., 378 So. 2d 774 (Fla.1979), 9-4:3

Popescu v. Laguna Master Ass'n, Inc., 126 So. 3d 449 (Fla. 4th DCA 2013), 14-2:2

Porras v. Wachovia Bank NA, 3D18-1382, 2019 WL 3309190 (Fla. 3d DCA July 24, 2019), 14-2:2

Portfolio Investments Corp. v. Deutsche Bank Nat. Trust Co., 81 So. 3d 534 (Fla. 3d DCA 2012), 10-2:4

TABLE OF CASES 457

Posnansky v. Breckenridge Estates Corp., 621 So. 2d 736 (Fla. 4th DCA 1993), 5-3

Powers v. HSBC Bank USA, N.A., 202 So. 3d 121 (Fla. 2d DCA 2016), 13-4:1.2

Precision Constructors, Inc. v. Valtec Construction Corp., 825 So. 2d 1062 (Fla. 3d DCA 2002), 13-2:2

Premier Holdings, Inc. v. Federal Nation Mortg. Ass'n, 2015 WL 4276169 (D. Nev. July 13, 2015), 9-4:5

Prigal v. Kearn, 557 So. 2d 647 (Fla. 4th DCA 1990), 5-2:1.3

Procacci v. Solomon, 317 So. 2d 467 (Fla. 4th DCA 1975), 18-6:3

Progressive Exp. Ins. Co. v. Schultz, 948 So. 2d 1027 (Fla. 5th DCA 2007), 16-3:5, 16-3:7

Prosperi v. Code, Inc., 626 So. 2d 1360 (Fla. 1993), 16-3:2

Providence Square Ass'n, Inc. v. Biancardi, 507 So. 2d 1366 (Fla. 1987), 6-5:3

Pudlit 2 Joint Venture, LLP v. Westwood Gardens Homeowners Association, Inc., 169 So. 3d 145 (Fla. 4th DCA 2015), 9-4:3

Pugliese v. Pugliese, 347 So. 2d 422 (Fla. 1977), 13-3:3

Purdue v. R.J. Reynolds Tobacco Co., 259 So. 3d 918 (Fla. 2d DCA 2018), 14-3:9

Pure H2O Biotechnologies, Inc. v. Mazziotti, 937 So. 2d 242 (Fla. 4th DCA 2006), 5-6, 14-3:8

Purificato v. Nationstar Mortg., LLC, 182 So. 3d 821 (Fla. 4th DCA 2016), 4-3

Puryear v. State, 810 So. 2d 901 (Fla. 2002), 9-4:6, 14-3:7

Q

QBE Ins. Corp. v. Jorda Enters., Inc., 277 F.R.D. 676 (S.D. Fla. 2012), 11-6:1.1

Quay Dev., Inc. v. Elegante Bldg. Corp., 392 So. 2d 901 (Fla.1981), 14-3:7

Quinn Plumbing Co. v. New Miami Shores Corp., 129 So. 690 (1930), 5-3

R

Racetrac Petroleum, Inc. v. Sewell, 150 So. 2d 1247 (Fla. 3d DCA 2014), 11-1, 11-8

Radison Properties v. Flamingo Groves, 767 So. 2d 587 (Fla. 4th DCA 2000), 5-4:2.1

Raissi v. Valente, 247 So. 3d 629 (Fla. 2d DCA 2018), 12-1:3

Rambo v. Dickenson, 110 So. 352 (Fla. 1926), 10-2:1

Ramos v. Growing Together, Inc., 672 So. 2d 103 (Fla. 4th DCA 1996), 11-4:2

Ramos v. Sabadell United Bank, N.A., 137 So. 3d 557 (Fla. 4th DCA 2014), 3-2:1.1a

Raven v. Roosevelt Reo US LLC, 44 Fla. L. Weekly D2096, 2019 WL 3807022, 2019 Fla. App. LEXIS 12464 (Fla. 3d DCA Aug. 14, 2019), 12-1:3.1

Raymond James & Assocs., Inc. v. Godshall, 851 So. 2d 879 (Fla. 1st DCA 2003), 18-4:1

Raymond James Fin. Servs., Inc. v. Saldukas, 896 So. 2d 707 (Fla. 2005), 7-3:5

Ray v. Hocker, 65 Fla. 265, 61 So. 500 (1913), 1-11

Ray v. TCF Nat'l Bank, No. 1-15-0001, 2015 WL 9590282 (Ill. App. Ct. Dec. 31, 2015), 14-4

RBS Citizens N.A. v. Reynolds, 231 So. 3d 591 (Fla. 2d DCA 2017), 6-2:3

Redding v. Stockton, Whatley, Davin & Co., 488 So. 2d 548 (Fla. 5th DCA 1986), 1-11, 6-3:7, 10-3:1, 10-3:3

Reddish v. Ritchie, 17 Fla. 867 (Fla. 1880), 4-10

Redd v. Justice Admin. Comm'n, 140 So. 3d 1085 (Fla. 2d DCA 2014), 14-2:1

Reed v. Fain, 145 So. 2d 858 (Fla.1961), 5-4:1

Reed v. Lincoln, 731 So. 2d 104 (Fla. 5th DCA 1999), 2-1, 2-3:1, 3-2:1.2

Re-Employment Services, Ltd. v. National Loan Acquisitions Co., 969 So. 2d 467 (Fla. 5th DCA 2007), 1-3:2

Regions Bank v. Cuny, 118 So. 3d 329 (Fla. 1st DCA 2013), 3-2:6

Regner v. Amtrust Bank, 71 So. 3d 907 (Fla. 4th DCA 2011), 14-4

Reina v. Barnett Bank, N.A., 766 So. 2d 290 (Fla. 4th DCA 2000), 1-3:2

Reiterer v. Monteil, 98 So. 3d 586 (Fla. 2d DCA 2012), 16-6:1

Rennick v. Wilmington Savings Fund Society, FSB, 276 So. 3d 29 (Fla. 4th DCA 2019), 16-2:3

REO Properties Corp. v. Binder, 946 So. 2d 572 (Fla. 2d DCA 2006), 10-2:4

Republic Fed. Bank, N.A. v. Doyle, 19 So. 3d 1053 (Fla. 3d DCA 2009), 14-3:8

Residential Funding Co., LLC v. Lincoln Place Residences Condo. Assoc., Inc., 2012 WL 8015558 (Fla. Cir. Ct. Miami-Dade 2012), 9-4:5

Residential Funding Co., LLC v. Lincoln Place Residences Condo. Assoc., Inc., 2013 WL 1889386 (Fla. Cir. Ct. Miami-Dade Feb. 27, 2013), 9-4:5

Reswick v. Reswick (In re Reswick), 446 B.R. 362 (9th Cir. B.A.P. 2011), 17-3:3

Reverse Mortg. Sols., Inc. v. Unknown Heirs, 207 So. 3d 917 (Fla. 1st DCA 2016), 3-1:1

Reyes v. Roush, 99 So. 3d 586 (Fla. 2d DCA 2012), 7-3:7

Reznek v. Chase Home Finance, LLC, 152 So. 3d 793 (Fla. 3d DCA 2014), 16-4:3

Rice v. James, 740 So. 2d 7 (Fla. 1st DCA 1999), 14-3:4

Rigby v. Wells Fargo Bank, N.A., 84 So. 3d 1195 (Fla. 4th DCA 2012), 12-1:10.1.b

Riggs v. Aurora Loan Services, LLC, 36 So. 3d 932 (Fla. 4th DCA 2010), 7-3:2, 13-4:1.1

Riley v. Grissett, 556 So. 2d 473 (Fla. 1st DCA 1990), 10-2:3

Rinzler v. Carson, 262 So. 2d 661 (Fla. 1972), 12-1:10.1.b

Rissman on Behalf of Rissman Inv. Co. v. Kilbourne, 643 So. 2d 1136 (Fla. 1st DCA1994), 9-4:5

TABLE OF CASES

Rivera v. Bank of Am., N.A. ex rel. BAC Home Loans Servicing, L.P., 190 So. 3d 267 (Fla. 5th DCA 2016), 17-8

Rivera v. Bank of N.Y. Mellon, 276 So. 3d 979 (Fla. 2d DCA 2019), 2-2:3

Rivera v. Deauville Hotel, Employers Service Corp., 277 So. 2d 265 (Fla. 1973), 16-1:1

R.K. Cooper Constr. Co. v. Fulton, 216 So. 2d 11 (Fla. 1968), 19-3

Robbie v. City of Miami, 469 So. 2d 1384 (Fla. 1985), 14-3:8

Robbins v. McGrath, 955 So. 2d 633 (Fla. 1st DCA 2007), 16-6:1

Roberts v. Cameron-Brown Co., 556 F.2d 356 (5th Cir. 1977), 8-4

Robinson v. State, 84 So. 3d 1130 (Fla. 5th DCA 2012), 15-2:1

Rocketrider Pictures, LLC v. BankUnited, 138 So. 3d 1223 (Fla. 3d DCA 2014), 6-3:6

Rockwood v. DeRosa, 279 So. 2d 54 (Fla. 4th DCA 1973), 16-2:1

Rodriguez v. Banco Industrial de Venezuela, C.A., 576 So. 2d 870 (Fla. 3d DCA 1991), 5-5

Rodriguez v. Tri-Square Constr., Inc., 635 So. 2d 125 (Fla. 3d DCA 1994), 12-1:7

Rodriguez v. Wells Fargo Bank, 178 So. 3d 62 (Fla. 4th DCA Oct. 14, 2015), 9-4:4

Rojo v. Rojo, 84 So. 3d 1259 (Fla. 3d DCA 2012), 15-2:3

Rolle v. Birken, 994 So. 2d 1129 (Fla. 3d DCA 2008), 13-2:2

Rollet v. de Bizemont, 159 So. 3d 351 (Fla. 3d DCA 2015), 18-3

Romeo v. U.S. Bank Nat'l Assn., 144 So. 3d 585 (Fla. 4th DCA 2014), 1-3:2

Rooney v. Wells Fargo Bank, N.A., 102 So. 3d 734 (Fla. 4th DCA 2012), 14-3:2

Roosevelt Cayman Asset Co. II v. Mercado, No. 15-2314 (BJM), 2016 WL 3976627 (D.P.R. July 22, 2016), 14-4

Rosenwater v. Deutsche Bank Nat'l Trust Co., 220 So. 3d 1204 (Fla. 4th DCA 2017), 15-2:2

Ross v. City of Tarpon Springs, 802 So. 2d 473 (Fla. 2d DCA 2001), 14-3:7

Ross Dress for Less Va., Inc. v. Castro, 134 So. 3d 511 (Fla. 3d DCA 2014), 15-2:2

Ross v. Wells Fargo Bank, 114 So. 3d 256 (Fla. 3d DCA 2013), 5-8

Rouffe v. CitiMortgage, Inc., 241 So. 3d 870 (Fla. 4th DCA 2018), 2-1:1, 10-2:1, 10-2:2, 10-2:3

Roussell v. Bank of N.Y. Mellon, 263 So. 3d 100 (Fla. 4th DCA 2019), 2-2:2

Rozanski v. Wells Fargo Bank, Nat'l Ass'n, 250 So. 3d 747 (Fla. 2d DCA 2018), 2-1, 6-5:4

Russell v. Aurora Loan Servs., LLC, 163 So. 3d 639 (Fla. 2d DCA 2015), 6-4:3, 12-1:10.1.b

Russell v. Bac Home Loans Servicing, 239 So. 3d 98 (Fla. 4th DCA 2018), 7-3:2

Ruwitch v. First National Bank of Miami, 327 So. 2d 833 (Fla. 3d DCA 1976), 16-3:5

RV-7 Prop. v. Stefani De La O, Inc., 187 So. 3d 915 (Fla. 3d DCA 2016), 12-1:2

R.W. Holding Corp. v. R.I.W. Waterproofing & Decorating Co., Inc., 131 Fla. 424, 179 So. 753 (Fla. 1938), 10-2:1, 14-3:7

Ryan v. Countrywide Home Loans, Inc., 743 So. 2d 36 (Fla. 2d DCA 1999), 14-4

Rybovich Boat Works, Inc. v. Atkins, 585 So. 2d 270 (Fla. 1991), 3-2:6

S

Sabina v. Dahlia Corporation, 678 So. 2d 822 (Fla. 2nd DCA 1996), 16-3:9

SADCO, Inc. v. Countrywide Funding, Inc., 680 So. 2d 1072 (Fla. 3d DCA 1996), 10-2:1, 10-2:2

Saidi v. Wasko, 687 So. 2d 10 (Fla. 5th DCA 1996), 10-2:3

Salam v. U.S. Bank, Nat'l Ass'n, 233 So. 3d 473 (Fla. 4th DCA 2017), 6-5:3

Salauddin v. Bank of Am., N.A., 150 So. 3d 1189 (Fla. 4th DCA 2014), 12-1:10.1.g

Salazar v. HSBC Bank, USA, NA, 158 So. 3d 699 (Fla. 3d DCA 2015), 14-4

Samaroo v. Wells Fargo Bank, 137 So. 3d 1127 (Fla. 5th DCA 2014), 2-2:2, 2-2:3.2, 3-2:1.1a, 7-3:3

Sample v. Wells Fargo Bank, N.A., 150 So. 3d 1191 (Fla. 4th DCA 2014), 12-1:3.2

Samuels v. King Motor Co., 782 So. 2d 489 (Fla. 4th DCA 2001), 7-2:2

Sanchez v. OneWest Bank, FSB, No. 11CV 6820, 2013 U.S. Dist. LEXIS 3861, 2013 WL 139870 (N.D. Ill. Jan. 10, 2013), 8-3

Sanchez v. State, 909 So. 2d 981, 984 (Fla. 5th DCA 2005), 18-3

Sanderson v. Hudlett, 832 So. 2d 845 (Fla. 4th DCA 2002), 5-2:1.3

Sanger v. Nightingale, 122 U.S. 176, 7 S. Ct. 1109 (1887), 9-3

San Matera the Gardens Condo. Ass'n, Inc. v. Fed. Home Loan Mortg. Corp., 207 So. 3d 1017 (Fla. 4th DCA 2017), 9-4:2, 9-4:4

Sans Souci v. Div. of Florida Land Sales & Condominiums, Dep't of Bus. Regulation, 421 So. 2d 623 (Fla. 1st DCA 1982), 9-4:3

Sardon Found. v. New Horizons Serv. Dogs, Inc., 852 So. 2d 416 (Fla. 5th DCA 2003), 2-1:1, 2-1:3.1, 3-2:1.1

Sas v. Federal Nat. Mortg. Ass'n, 112 So. 3d 778 (Fla. 2d DCA 2013), 1-1:1, 11-9:3

Sas v. Federal Nat'l Mortg. Ass'n, 165 So. 3d 849 (Fla. 2d DCA 2015), 13-3:1, 13-4:2

Saticoy Bay, LLC, Series 2714 Snapdragon v. Flagstar Bank, FSB, 2016 WL 1064463 (D. Nev. Mar. 17, 2016), 9-4:5

Savarese v. Schoner, 464 So. 2d 695 (Fla. 2d DCA 1985), 16-2:1

Sayles v. Nationstar Mortg., LLC, 268 So. 3d 723 (Fla. 4th DCA 2018), 7-3:7

Scarborough Assocs. v. Financial Federal Savings & Loan Ass'n of Dade Cnty., 647 So. 2d 1001 (Fla. 3d DCA 1994), 12-1:10.1.e

TABLE OF CASES

461

Scarborough v. Chase Manhattan Mortg. Corp., 461 F.3d 406 (3d Cir. 2006), 17-6:2

Schere v. Z.F., Inc., 578 So. 2d 739 (Fla. 3d DCA 1991), 16-3:9

Schiderman v. Fitness Innovations & Technology, Inc., 994 So. 2d 508 (Fla. 4th DCA 2008), 16-4:1

Schmidt v. Schmidt, 997 So. 2d 2d 451 (Fla. 2d DCA 2008), 18-4:1.1

Schroeder v. MTGLQ Investors, L.P., 4D18-3177 (Fla. 4th DCA 2019), 7-3:6

Schwartz v. Bank of Am., N.A., 267 So. 3d 414 (Fla. 4th DCA 2019), 11-9:2, 12-1:8

Schwartz v. Business Cards Tomorrow, Inc., 644 So. 2d 611 (Fla. 4th DCA 1994), 14-3:4

S/D Enterprises v. Chase Manhattan Bank, 374 So. 2d 1121 (Fla. 3d DCA 1979), 19-3:1

Se. & Associates, Inc. v. Fox Run Homeowners Ass'n, Inc., 704 So. 2d 694 (Fla. 4th DCA 1997), 5-2:1.1

Searle v. Fortune Federal Sav. and Loan Ass'n, 480 So. 2d 187 (Fla. 2d DCA 1985), 6-1:3

Seaside Cmty. Dev. Corp. v. Edward, 573 So. 2d 142 (Fla. 1st DCA 1991), 7-3:3

Sedra Family Ltd. Partnership v. 4750, LLC, 124 So. 3d 935 (Fla. 4th DCA 2012), 6-3:7, 10-2:3, 10-3:1

Seffar v. Residential Credit Solutions, Inc., 160 So. 3d 122 (Fla. 4th DCA 2015), 13-4:1.2

Seidler v. Wells Fargo Bank, N.A., 179 So. 3d 416 (Fla. 1st DCA 2015), 6-4:3

Seligman v. Bisz, 123 Fla. 493, 167 So. 38 (Fla. 1936), 12-1:10.1

Shahar v. Green Tree Serv. LLC, 125 So. 3d 251 (Fla. 4th DCA 2013), 18-3

Shamrock Jewelers, Inc. v. Schillaci, 126 So. 3d 1073 (Fla. 4th DCA 2011), 18-4:1

Shelby Mut. Ins. Co. of Shelby, Ohio v. Pearson, 236 So. 2d 1 (Fla. 1970), 14-1

Shelswell v. Bourdeau, 239 So. 3d 707 (Fla. 4th DCA 2018), 14-2:2

Shepheard v. Deutsche Bank Trust Co. Americas, 922 So. 2d 340 (Fla. 5th DCA 2006), 1-3:2, 5-2:1.1

Sheriff of Orange County v. Boultbee, 595 So. 2d 985 (Fla. 5th DCA 1992), 12-1:10.1.e

Sherman v. Deutsche Bank Nat'l Trust Co., 100 So. 3d 95 (Fla. 3d DCA 2012), 5-4:2.1, 6-5:4

Sher v. Liberty Mutual Insur. Co., 557 So. 2d 638 (Fla. 3d DCA 1990), 11-4:2, 12-1:5

Siahpoosh v. Nor Properties, Inc., 666 So. 2d 988 (Fla. 4th DCA 1996), 2-1:3.1

Siegel v. Husak, 943 So. 2d 209 (Fla. 3d DCA 2006), 13-3:2

Siemer v. Geringer, 617 So. 2d 1155 (Fla. 4th DCA 1993), 16-2:1

Singleton v. Greymar Associates, 840 So. 2d 356 (Fla. 4th DCA 2003), 2-3:5.1

Singleton v. Greymar Associates, 882 So. 2d 1004 (Fla. 2004), 2-3:5, 2-3:5.1, 3-2:1.2, 6-1:1

Skydive Space Ctr., Inc. v. Pohjolainen, 275 So. 3d 825 (Fla. 5th DCA 2019), 12-1:8

Skylights LLC v. Fannie Mae, 2015 WL 3887061 (D. Nev. June 24, 2015), 9-4:5

Smiley v. Manufactured Hous. Assocs. III Ltd. P'ship, 679 So. 2d 1229 (Fla. 2d DCA 1996), 2-1:2

Smith v. Branch, 391 So. 2d 797 (Fla. 2d DCA 1980), 3-2:1.3a

Smith v. Smith, 734 So. 2d 1142 (Fla. 5th DCA 1999), 12-1:8

Smith v. Weede, 433 So. 2d 992 (Fla. 5th DCA 1983), 18-4:1

Smulders for 129-31 Harrison St., LLC v. Thirty-Three Sixty Condo. Ass'n, Inc., 245 So. 3d 802, 805 (Fla. 4th DCA 2018), 9-4:4

Snell v. State, 522 So. 2d 407 (Fla. 5th DCA 1988), 14-2:2

Solonenko v. Georgia Notes 18, LLC, 182 So. 3d 876 (Fla. 4th DCA 2016), 3-2:1.1, 3-2:1.1a

Somero v. Hendry Gen. Hosp., 467 So. 2d 1103 (Fla. 4th DCA 1985), 1-4:4.1

Sottilaro v. Figueroa, 86 So. 3d 505 (Fla. 2d DCA), review denied, 103 So. 3d 139 (Fla. 2012), 18-6:2

Soule v. U.S. Bank Nat'l Ass'n, 253 So. 3d 679 (Fla. 2d DCA 2018), 2-2:3

SourceTrack, LLC v. Ariba, Inc., 958 So. 2d 523 (Fla. 2d DCA 2007), 9-3, 9-4:4

Southeast. & Assocs., Inc. v. Fox Run Homeowners Ass'n, Inc., 704 So. 2d 694 (Fla. 4th DCA 1997), 5-2:1.1

Southern California Funding, Inc. v. Hutto, 438 So. 2d 426 (Fla. 1st DCA 1983), 12-1:8

Southern Waste Sys., LLC v. J & A Transfer, Inc., 879 So. 2d 86 (Fla. 4th DCA 2004), 12-1:3.2

Space Coast Credit Union v. Goldman, 262 So. 3d 836 (Fla. 3d DCA 2018), 10-2:2

Spartan Holdco, LLC v. Cheeburger Cheeburger Restaurants, 2011 WL 6024487 (M.D. Fla. Nov. 18, 2011), 16-2:2

Spicer v. Ocwen Loan Servicing, LLC, 238 So. 3d 275 (Fla. 4th DCA 2018), 4-9, 6-3:1, 7-3:2

Spinney v. Winter Park Bldg. & Loan Ass'n, 120 Fla. 453, 162 So. 899 (Fla. 1935), 10-2:1, 10-2:4, 12-1:10.1.h

Square D Co. v. State Farm Fire & Cas. Co., 610 So. 2d 522 (Fla. 3d DCA 1992), 3-1

SR Acquisitions-Fla. City, LLC v. San Remo Homes at Fla. City, LLC, 78 So. 3d 636 (Fla. 3d DCA 2011), 18-4:3.2

St. Clair v. U.S. Bank Nat'l Ass'n, 173 So. 3d 1045 (Fla 2d DCA 2015), 13-4:1.2

St. Paul Mercury Ins. Co. v. Coucher, 837 So. 2d 483 (Fla. 5th DCA 2002), 7-3:1, 7-3:7, 8-1, 12-1:3.2

Stacknik v. U.S. Bank Nat'l Ass'n, 283 So. 3d 981 (Fla. 2d DCA 2019), 2-2:3

Standard Guaranty Insurance Co. v. Quanstrom, 555 So. 2d 828 (Fla. 1990), 16-3:5, 16-3:7

State, DOT v. Bailey, 603 So. 2d 1384 (Fla. 1st DCA 1992), 14-3:6

State Department of Revenue v. Haughton, 188 So. 3d 32 (Fla. 3d DCA 2016), 9-4:6, 14-3:3

State ex rel. Buchwalter v. City of Lakeland, 150 S. 508 (Fla. 1933), 18-4:3.2

State Farm Fire & Cas. Co. v. Palma, 629 So. 2d 830 (Fla. 1993), 16-1:1, 16-3:6

State Farm Fire & Cas. Co. v. Pritcher, 546 So. 2d 1060 (Fla. 3d DCA 1989), 16-6:1

State Farm Mut. Auto. Ins. Co. v. Curran, 135 So. 3d 1071 (Fla. 2014), 7-3:1, 7-3:7

State Farm Mut. Auto. Ins. Co. v. Horkheimer, 814 So. 2d 1069 (Fla. 4th DCA 2001), 1-4

State Farm Mut. Auto. Ins. Co. v. Lee, 678 So. 2d 818 (Fla. 1996), 3-2:1, 3-2:1.1a

State of Florida, Department of Transportation v. SouthTrust Bank, 886 So. 2d 393 (Fla. 1st DCA 2004), 16-3:3

State of Wis. on Behalf of N. v. Martorella, 670 So. 2d 1161 (Fla. 4th DCA 1996), 2-3:5.1

State Road Dept. v. Florida East Coast Ry. Co., 212 So. 2d 315 (Fla. 3rd DCA 1968), 11-5:2

State St. Bank & Tr. Co. v. Badra, 765 So. 2d 251 (Fla. 4th DCA 2000), 2-3:5.1

State Trust Realty, LLC v. Deutsche Bank Nat. Trust Co. Americas, 207 So. 3d 923 (Fla. 4th DCA 2016), 9-4:6, 10-1:1

State v. Rolack, 104 So. 3d 1286 (Fla. 5th DCA 2013), 13-3

State v. Speights, 864 So. 2d 73 (Fla. 1st DCA 2003), 14-3:6

S & T Builders v. Globe Props., Inc., 944 So. 2d 302 (Fla. 2006), 10-1:1

Steeprow Enters., Inc. v. Lennar Homes, Inc., 590 So. 2d 21 (Fla. 4th DCA 1991), 14-4

Steinhardt v. Intercondominium Group, Inc., 771 So. 2d 614 (Fla. 4th DCA 2000), 14-3:4

Sterling Factors Corp. v. U.S. Bank Nat. Ass'n, 968 So. 2d 658 (Fla. 2d DCA 2007), 5-2:1.1, 9-4:6, 14-2:1, 14-3:1, 14-3:7

Sterling v. City of West Palm Beach, 595 So. 2d 284 (Fla. 4th DCA 1992), 11-4:2

Stewart v. Tasnet, Inc., 718 So. 2d 820 (Fla. 2d DCA 1998), 16-2:3

Stockman v. Downs, 573 So. 2d 835 (Fla. 1991), 16-3:1

Stoner v. W. G., Inc., 300 So. 2d 268 (Fla. 2d DCA 1973), 14-2:2

Stone v. BankUnited, 115 So. 3d 411 (Fla. 2d DCA 2013), 4-1, 4-7, 7-3:2

Stratton v. 6000 Indian Creek, LLC, 95 So. 3d 334 (Fla. 3d DCA 2012), 7-3:2

Student Loan Mktg. Ass'n v. Morris, 662 So. 2d 990 (Fla. 2d DCA 1995), 6-2:4

Suchman Corp. Park, Inc. v. Greenstein, 600 So. 2d 532 (Fla. 3d DCA 1992), 16-2:3

Sudhoff v. Fed. Nat. Mortg. Ass'n., 942 So. 2d 425 (Fla. 5th DCA 2005), 6-3:6, 10-1, 10-2:1, 10-2:3, 14-3:7

Sun Mircosystems of California, Inc. v. Engineering and Manufacturing. Systems, C.A., 682 So. 2d 219 (Fla. 3d DCA 1996), 5-6, 14-3:8

Sunseeker Int'l Ltd. v. Devers, 50 So. 3d 715 (Fla. 4th DCA 2010), 1-3:2

Suntrust Bank v. Riverside Nat. Bank of Florida, 792 So. 2d 1222 (Fla. 4th DCA 2001), 5-4:2, 5-4:2.1, 6-5:4

Suntrust Mortg., Inc. v. Garcia, 186 So. 3d 1036 (Fla. 3d DCA 2016), 12-1:10.1.e

Surratt v. Fleming, 309 So. 2d 614 (Fla. 1st DCA 1975), 14-4

Szucs v. Qualico Development, Inc., 893 So. 2d 708 (Fla. 2d DCA 2005), 1-4:4.1, 14-3:4

T

Tampa Properties, Inc. v. Great American Mortg. Investors, 333 So. 2d 480 (Fla. 2d DCA 1976), 6-4:4

Tank Tech, Inc. v. Valley Tank Testing, LLC, 244 So. 3d 383 (Fla. 2d DCA 2018), 6-5:4

Tara Woods SPE, LLC v. Cashin, 116 So. 3d 492 (Fla. 2d DCA 2013), 9-3, 9-4:4

Taufer v. Wells Fargo Bank, N.A., 278 So. 3d 335 (Fla. 3d DCA 2019), 14-3:1

Taufer v. Wells Fargo Bank, N.A., No. 3D18-2004, 2019 WL 3209962 (Fla. 3d DCA July 17, 2019), 14-2:2

Tavernier Towne Associates v. Eagle Nat'l Bank of Miami, 593 So. 2d 306 (Fla. 3d DCA 1992), 6-1:3

Taylor v. AGE Fed. Credit Union (In re Taylor), 3 F.3d 1512 (11th Cir. 1993), 17-8

Taylor v. Bayview Loan Servicing, LLC, 74 So. 3d 1115 (Fla. 2d DCA 2011), 12-1:3.2

Taylor v. Deutsche Bank Nat'l Trust Co., 44 So. 3d 618 (Fla. 5th DCA 2010), 4-7, 7-3:2

Taylor v. Steckel, 944 So. 2d 494 (Fla. 3d DCA 2006), 5-5, 10-1:1

TD Bank, N.A. v. Graubard, 172 So. 3d 550 (Fla. 5th DCA 2015), 19-2:1, 19-3:1

Techvend, Inc. v. Phoenix Network, Inc., 564 So. 2d 1145 (Fla. 3d DCA 1990), 1-4:4.3

Terra Firma Holdings v. Fairwinds Credit Union, 15 So. 3d 885 (Fla. 2d DCA 2009), 1-1:1

Tetrault v. Calkins, 79 So. 3d 213 (Fla. 2d DCA 2012), 5-5

The Bank of New York, as Tr. for the Benefit of the Certificate-Holders CWALT, Inc., Alternative Loan Trust 2007-OA10,Mortgage Pass-Through Certificates, Series 2007-OA10 v. The Sterling Villages of Palm Beach Lakes Condo. Assoc., Inc., 2012 WL 8015574 (Fla. Cir. Ct. Palm Beach 2012), 9-4:5

The Bank of New York, as Tr. for the Certificate Holders CWALT, Inc., Alternative Loan Trust 2006-19CB, Mortgage Pass-Through Certificates, Series 2006-19CB v.

TABLE OF CASES 465

River Walk Townhomes Assoc., Inc., 2012 WL 8015562 (Fla. Cir. Ct. Hillsborough 2012), 9-4:5

The Bank of New York as Tr. for the Benefit of the Certificate Holders, CWALT, Inc., Alternative Loan Trust 2007-OA8 Mortgage Pass-Through Certificates v. The Greens COA, Inc., 2013 WL 1889448 (Fla. Cir. Ct. Orange March 11, 2013), 9-4:5

The Bank of New York as Tr. for the Certificate Holders CWABS, Inc. Asset-Backed Certificates, Series 2006-23 v. Colombine, 2011 WL 10725888 (Fla. Cir. Ct. Palm Beach 2011), 9-4:5

The Bank of New York as Tr. for the Certificate Holders CWALT, Inc., Alternative Loan Trust 2005-62 Mortgage Pass Through Certificates, Series 2005-62 v. Serenade on Palmer Ranch Condo. Assoc., Inc., 2013 WL 1889451 (Fla. Cir. Ct. Sarasota Feb. 19, 2013), 9-4:5

The Bank of New York for the Benefit of the CWABS, Inc. v. The Sterling Villages of Palm Beach Lakes Condo. Assoc., Inc., 2012 WL 8255393 (Fla. Cir. Ct. Palm Beach 2012), 9-4:5

The Bank of New York Mellon Trust Company, N.A., F/K/A/ The Bank of New York Trust Company, N.A., Successors To JP Morgan Chase Bank, N.A.,RAMP 2006-RS3, v. Palmy Del Rosario, Merrill Pines Condo. Ass'n, et al., 2014 WL 1052431 (Fla. Cir. Ct. Duval March 5, 2014), 9-4:5

The Bank of New York Mellon v. Horton, 2017 WL 538317 (Fla. Cir. Ct. Broward Feb. 9, 2017), 16-3:7

The Bank of New York Mellon v. Mestre, 159 So. 3d 953 (Fla. 5th DCA 2015), 16-2:1

The Bank of New York Mellon v. Midport Place II Condo. Ass'n, Inc., 2012 WL 12869502 (Fla. Cir. Ct. St. Lucie Cnty. 2012), 9-4:1

The Bank of New York Mellon v. The Plaza Condo. Assoc., Inc., 2013 WL 1889419 (Fla. Cir. Ct. Orange February 7, 2013), 9-4:5

The Bank of New York v. Condominium Association of La Mer Estates, Inc., 175 So. 3d 282 (Fla. 2015), 9-4:6, 14-2:1, 14-3:1, 14-3:7

The Florida Bar v. Mogil, 763 So. 2d 303 (Fla. 2000), 12-1:3

The Florida Bar v. Woods, 131 So. 3d 791 (Fla. 2013), 16-4:2

The Law Offices of Lynn W. Martin, P.A. v. Madson, 144 So. 3d 707 (Fla. 1st DCA 2014), 16-4:2

The Plantation at Ponte Vedra, Inc. v. U.S. Bank, N.A., No. CA13-1072, 2014 WL 786346 (Fla. Cir. Ct. St. Johns Feb. 5, 2014), 9-4:3

The Plantation at Ponte Vedra, Inc. v. Wells Fargo Bank, N.A., 2016 WL 6127570 (Fla. Cir. Ct. St. Johns Feb. 25, 2016), 9-4:3

Thigpen v. United Parcel Services, Inc., 990 So. 2d 639 (Fla. 4th DCA 2008), 13-4

Third Fed. Sav. & Loan Ass'n v. Koulouvaris, 2018 Fla. App. LEXIS 6941 (Fla. 2d DCA 2018), 4-10

Thomas v. Premier Capital, Inc., 906 So. 2d 1139 (Fla. 3d DCA 2005), 19-2:2, 19-3:1

Thompson v. Bank of N.Y., 862 So. 2d 768 (Fla. 4th DCA 2003), 12-1:3.2

Thornton v. Jabeen, 683 So. 2d 150 (Fla. 3d DCA 1996), 14-2:2

Thurner v. Thurner, 584 So. 2d 150 (Fla. 2d DCA 1991), 14-3:7

Ticktin v. Kearin, 807 So. 2d 659 (Fla. 3d DCA 2001), 3-4

TICO Ins. Co. v. Schonning, 960 So. 2d 6 (Fla. 3d DCA 2005), 14-3:7

Tieche v. Florida Physicians Ins. Reciprocal, 431 So. 2d 287 (Fla. 5th DCA 1983), 14-2:2

TIG Ins. Corp. of America v. Johnson, 799 So. 2d 399 (Fla. 4th DCA 2001), 11-3:2.2

Tikhomirov v. Bank of N.Y. Mellon, 223 So. 3d 1112 (Fla. 3d DCA 2017), 9-4:6, 10-2:1, 10-2:2, 14-3:2, 14-3:6

Tillman v. Baskin, 260 So. 2d 509 (Fla. 1972), 13-6

Tilus v. AS Michai, LLC, 161 So. 3d 1284 (Fla. 4th DCA 2015), 4-4, 9-4:4

Timmers v. Harbor Fed. Sav. & Loan Ass'n, 548 So. 2d 282 (Fla. 1st DCA 1989), 19-2:1

Timucuan Props. v. Bank of New York Mellon, 135 So. 3d 524 (Fla. 5th DCA 2014), 10-2:1, 10-2:2

Titusville Assoc. v. Barnett Banks Trust Co., 591 So. 2d 609 (Fla. 1991), 12-1:8

Tolin v. Doudov, 626 So. 2d 1054, 1056 (Fla. 4th DCA 1993), 12-1:9

Tompkins v. Jim Walter Homes, Inc., 656 So. 2d 963 (Fla. 5th DCA 1995), 2-3:3

Tooltrend, Inc. v. C.M.T. Utensili, 707 So. 2d 1162 (Fla. 2d DCA 1998), 12-1:9

Toscana at Vasari Village Association, Inc., v. Deutsche Bank National Trust Company as Indentured Trustee for American Home Mortgage Investment Trust 2005-2, et al., 2014 WL 1102739 (Fla. Cir. Ct. Lee Marcht 14, 2014), 9-4:6

Toscione v. Wells Fargo, No. 8:13-CV-02065-T-27AEP, 2013 U.S. Dist. LEXIS 189690 (M.D. Fla. Sept. 17, 2013), 8-3

Townsend v. Lane, 659 So. 2d 720 (Fla. 5th DCA 1995), 14-3:6

Tracey v. Wells Fargo, Nat'l Ass'n, 264 So. 3d 1152 (Fla. 2d DCA 2019), 6-2:4, 6-4:2

Tradewinds of Pompano Ass'n, Inc. v. Rosenthal, 407 So. 2d 976 (Fla. 4th DCA 1981), 9-4:3

Travelers Indem. Co. v. Hutchins, 489 So. 2d 208 (Fla. 2d DCA 1986), 18-5

Travis Co. v. Mayes, 36 So. 2d 264 (Fla. 1948), 2-3:2, 3-4

Tremblay v. U.S. Bank, N.A., 164 So. 3d 85 (Fla. 4th DCA 2015), 4-6

Trent v. Mortgage Electronic Registration Systems, Inc., 618 F.Supp.2d 1356 (M.D. Fla. 2007), 8-6

Trial Practices, Inc. v. Hahn Loeser & Parks, LLP for Antaramian, 228 So. 3d 1184 (Fla. 2d DCA 2017), 16-3:6

Tribeca Lending Corp. v. Real Estate Depot, Inc., 42 So. 3d 258 (Fla. 4th DCA 2010), 6-5:4

TABLE OF CASES 467

Tropicana Condo. Ass'n, Inc. v. Tropical Condo., LLC, 208 So. 3d 755 (Fla. 3d DCA 2016), 9-4:3

Trucap Grantor Trust 2010-1 v. Pelt, 84 So. 3d 369 (Fla. 2nd DCA 2012), 7-2:2, 11-8

Trueman Fertilizer Co. v. Lester, 155 Fla. 338, 20 So. 2d 349 (1944), 5-8

Trupei v. City of Lighthouse Point, 506 So. 2d 19 (Fla. 4th DCA 1987), 13-3:3

Trust No. 602W0 Dated 7/16/15, Dema Investments, LLC v. Wells Fargo Bank, N.A., 207 So. 3d 977 (Fla. 5th DCA 2016), 6-3:5, 10-3:2

Trust Real Estate Ventures v. Desnick, 44 Fla. L. Weekly D2016, 2019 WL 3675266, 2019 Fla. App. LEXIS 12199 (Fla. 3d DCA Aug. 7, 2019), 12-1:8

Trytek v. Gale Industries, Inc., 3 So. 3d 1194 (Fla. 2009), 16-1:1, 16-3:2

Tubbs v. Mechanik Nuccio Hearne & Webster, P.A., 125 So. 3d 1034 (Fla. 2d DCA 2013), 16-3:2

Tumelaire v. Naples Estates Homeowners Ass'n, Inc., 137 So. 3d 596 598 (Fla. 2nd DCA 2014), 11-1

Turf Express, Inc. v. Palmer, 209 So. 2d 461 (Fla. 3d DCA 1968), 12-1:4

Turkell-White v. Wells Fargo Bank, N.A., 273 So. 3d 1021 (Fla. 4th DCA 2019), 6-3:5, 7-2:2

U

Ultimate Corp. v. CG Data Corp., 575 So. 2d 1338 (Fla. 3d DCA 1991), 12-1:7

Underwriters at Lloyd's London v. Rolly Marine Service, Inc., 475 So. 2d 265 (Fla. 4th DCA 1985), 14-3:9

Union Cent. Life Ins. Co. v. Carlisle, 593 So. 2d 505 (Fla. 1992), 10-2:2

United Services Auto. Ass'n v. Phillips, 775 So. 2d 921 (Fla. 2000), 16-3:9

United States v. Bridgewater Community Ass'n, Inc., 2013 WL 3285399 (M.D. Fla. 2013), 9-4:4

United States v. Forest Hill Gardens East Condo. Ass'n, Inc., 2014 WK 28723 (S.D. Fla. Jan. 3, 2014), 990 F.Supp.2d 1344 (S.D. Fla. 2014), 9-4:3, 9-4:4, 9-4:5

United States v. Int'l Horizons, Inc. (In re Int'l Horizons, Inc.), 751 F.2d 1213 (11th Cir.1985), 17-5

United States v. Parker, 749 F.2d 628 (11th Cir. 1984), 13-3:1

United States v. Pfeiffer, 539 F.2d 668 (8th Cir. 1976), 13-3:1

United States Bank N.A. v. Adams, 219 So. 3d 211 (Fla. 2d DCA 2017), 8-5

United States Bank v. Holbrook, 226 So. 3d 363 (Fla. 2d DCA 2017), 12-1:7, 12-1:8

U.S. Bank v. Becker, 211 So. 3d 142 (Fla. 4th DCA 2017), 4-4

U.S. Bank v. Glicken, 228 So. 3d 1194 (Fla. 5th DCA 2017), 4-7

U.S. Bank v. King-Fenn, 2012 WL 4983784 (Fla. Cir. Ct. Oct. 17, 2012), 15-2:3

U.S. Bank v. Mateiola and Summit Place, 2010 WL 8742249 (Fla. Cir. Ct. Palm Beach 2010), 9-4:5

U.S. Bank, N.A. v. Angeloni, 199 So. 3d 492 (Fla. 4th DCA 2016), 4-6, 12-1:10.1.b

U.S. Bank, N.A. v. Glicken, 228 So. 3d 1194 (Fla. 5th DCA 2017), 6-3:1

U.S. Bank, N.A. v. Vogel, 137 So. 3d 491 (Fla. 4th DCA 2014), 5-7, 18-6:2

U.S. Bank, N.A. v. Wanio-Moore, 111 So. 3d 941 (Fla. 5th DCA 2013), 6-2:2

U.S. Bank Nat. Ass'n v. Anthony-Irish, 204 So. 3d 57 (Fla. 5th DCA 2016), 14-3:7

U.S. Bank Nat. Ass'n v. Farhood, 153 So. 3d 955 (Fla. 1st DCA 2014), 9-3

U.S. Bank Nat. Ass'n v. Grant, 180 So. 3d 1092 (Fla. 4th DCA 2015), 9-4:3

U.S. Bank Nat. Ass'n v. Quadomain Condo. Ass'n, Inc., 103 So. 3d 977 (Fla. 4th DCA 2012), 1-2, 5-5, 9-4:6, 10-2:1, 14-3:7

U.S. Bank Nat. Ass'n v. Sturm, 280 So. 3d 1124 (Fla. 2d DCA 2019), 2-2:3.1

U.S. Bank Nat. Ass'n v. Tadmore, 23 So. 3d 822 (Fla. 3d DCA 2009), 9-3

U.S. Bank Nat. Ass'n v. The Stratford Winter Park Condo. Ass'n, Inc., 2012 WL 12869501 (Fla. Cir. Ct. Seminole Cnty. 2012), 9-4:1

U.S. Bank National Association as Trustee for Ramp 2005-EFC2 v. Pine Rush Villas Condo. Ass'n, Inc., 2013 WL 6991983 (Fla. Cir. Ct. Pinellas Aug. 27, 2013), 9-4:5

U.S. Bank Nat'l Ass'n v. Bartram, 140 So. 3d 1007 (Fla. 5th DCA 2014), 3-2:1, 3-2:1.2, 3-2:2.1, 3-2:3.1

U.S. Bank Nat'l Ass'n v. Bevans, 138 So. 3d 1185 (Fla. 3d DCA 2014), 6-1:4, 6-3:1, 6-4:5, 9-4:6, 10-1:1, 10-2:1, 14-3:7

U.S. Bank Nat'l Ass'n v. Bjeljac, 43 So. 3d 851 (Fla. 5th DCA 2010), 14-4

U.S. Bank Nat'l Ass'n v. Busquets, 135 So. 3d 488 (Fla. 2d DCA 2014), 2-2:1, 2-2:2, 2-2:3.1, 3-2:1.1a, 7-3:3

U.S. Bank Nat'l Ass'n v. Clarke, 192 So. 3d 620 (Fla. 4th DCA 2016), 7-2.2, 12-1:10.1, 12-1:10.1.b, 13-3:1

U.S. Bank Nat'l Ass'n v. Cook, 2019 Fla. App. LEXIS 11282 (Fla. 2d DCA 2019), 276 So. 3d 472, 474 (Fla. 2d DCA 2019), 4-6, 6-4:3

U.S. Bank Nat'l Ass'n v. Kachik, 222 So. 3d 592 (Fla. 4th DCA 2017), 4-3

US Bank Nat'l Ass'n v. Laird, 200 So. 3d 176 (Fla. 5th DCA 2016), 12-1:10.1.b

U.S. Bank Nat'l Ass'n v. McMullin, 55 Misc. 3d 1053, 47 N.Y.S.3d 882, 889 (N.Y. Sup. Ct. 2017), 8-4

U.S. Bank Nat'l Ass'n v. Valdes, 2011 WL 10725878 (Fla. Cir. Ct. Palm Beach Cnty. 2011), 9-4:1

U.S. Bank Nat'l Ass'n as Tr. for Certificateholders of Structured Asset Mortgage Investments II, Inc., Bear Stearns Arm Tr., Mortgage Pass-Through Certificates, Series 2006-2 v. Williamson, 273 So. 3d 190, 192 (Fla. 5th DCA 2019), 11-6:1.1

U.S. Bank Nat'l Assoc., as Tr. for the BNC Mortgage Loan Trust 2006-1 v. Valdes, 2011 WL 10725878 (Fla. Cir. Ct. Palm Beach 2011), 9-4:5

United States Sav. Bank v. Pittman, 86 So. 567 (Fla. 1920), 15-1, 15-2:1, 16-4:1

USA Residential Properties, LLC v. Ventzlislav Slavov, Ocean Grande Condo. Ass'n, Inc., 2013 WL 5462324 (Fla. Cir. Ct. St. Johns Sept. 26, 2013), 9-4:5

UV Cite III, LLC v. Deutsche Bank National Trust Co., 215 So. 3d 1280 (Fla. 3d DCA 2017), 6-5:6

V

Valcarcel v. Chase Bank USA, N.A., 54 So. 3d 989 (Fla. 4th DCA 2010), 16-3:2

Valderrama v. Portfolio Recovery Assocs., LLC, 972 So. 2d 239 (Fla. 3d DCA 2007), 12-1:3

Van Egmond v. Wells Fargo Home Mortg., No. SACV 12-0112, 2012 U.S. Dist. LEXIS 42061, 2012 WL 1033281 (C.D. Cal. Mar. 21, 2012), 8-3

Vantium Capital, Inc. v. Hobson, 137 So. 3d 497 (Fla. 4th DCA 2014), 19-3:1, 19-3:2

Vargas v. Deutsche Bank Nat'l Trust Co., 104 So. 3d 1156 (Fla. 3d DCA 2012), 7-3:4

Vasilevskiy v. Wachovia Bank, Nat. Ass'n, 171 So. 3d 192 (Fla. 5th DCA 2015), 2-2:5, 12-1:10.1.e

Velazquez v. Serrano, 43 So. 3d 82 (Fla. 3d DCA 2010), 5-4:2.1

Venezia v. JP Morgan Mortgage Acquisition Corp., 279 So. 3d 145 (Fla. 4th DCA 2019), 16-3:2

Venture Holdings & Acquisitions Grp., LLC v. A.I.M Funding Grp., LLC, 75 So. 3d 773 (Fla. 4th DCA 2011), 13-4:1.2

Ventures Trust 2013-I-H-R v. Asset Acquisitions & Holdings Trust, 202 So. 3d 939 (Fla. 2d DCA 2016), 4-9

Vercosa v. Fields, 174 So. 3d 550 (Fla. 4th DCA 2015), 13-4:4

Verizzo v. Bank of N.Y. Mellon, 220 So. 3d 1262 (Fla. 2d DCA 2017), 13-4:1.3

Vidal v. Liquidation Props., 104 So. 3d 1274 (Fla. 4th DCA 2013), 8-1

Viking Gen. Corp. v. Diversified Mortgage Investors, 387 So. 2d 983 (Fla. 2d DCA 1980), 14-3:3

Vill. Square Condo. v. U.S. Bank Nat. Ass'n, 206 So. 3d 806, (Mem)-807 (Fla. 5th DCA 2016), 9-4:2, 9-4:4

Village 45 Partners, LLC v. Racetrac Petroleum Inc., 831 So. 2d 758 (Fla. 4th DCA 2002), 16-3:4

Villages at Mango Key Home Owners Assoc., Inc. v. Hunter Development, Inc., 699 So. 2d 337 (Fla. 5th DCA 1997), 12-1:8

Villagio at Estero Condominium Ass'n, Inc. v. Deutsche Bank Nat. Trust Co., 2016 WL 4580146 (Fla. Cir. Ct. Lee Cnty. 2016), 9-4:1

Villareal v. Eres, 128 So. 3d 93 (Fla. 2d DCA 2013), 12-1:6

Villas of Windmill Point II Prop. Owners' Ass'n, Inc. v. Bank of N.Y. Mellon, 197 So. 3d 1288,(Fla. 4th DCA 2016), 9-4:5

Villas of Windmill Point II Prop. Owners' Ass'n, Inc. v. Nationstar Mortg., LLC, 229 So. 3d 822,(Fla. 4th DCA 2017), 9-4:1, 9-4:2

Visoly v. Security Pac. Credit Corp., 768 So. 2d 482 (Fla. 3d DCA 2000), 16-4:2

Vives v. Wells Fargo Bank, N.A., 128 So. 3d 9 (Fla. 3d DCA 2012), 1-3:2

Vivona v. Colony Point 5 Condo. Ass'n, 706 So. 2d 391 (Fla. 4th DCA 1998), 12-1:7

Voce v. Wachovia Mortgage, FSB, 174 So. 3d 545 (Fla. 4th DCA 2015), 14-3:3

Vogel v. Wells Fargo Bank, N.A., 192 So. 3d 714 (Fla. 4th DCA 2016), 4-7

Vorbeck v. Betancourt, 107 So. 3d 1142 (Fla. 3d DCA 2012), 14-2:2

VOSR Indus. v. Martin Props., 919 So. 2d 554 (Fla. 4th DCA 2005), 10-2:3

W

Wagner v. Bank of America, N.A., 143 So. 3d 447 (Fla. 2d DCA 2014), 13-4:4

Walker v. Cash Register Auto Ins. of Leon County, Inc., 946 So. 2d 66 (Fla. 1st DCA 2006), 15-4:2

Walker v. City of Bartow Police Dep't (In re Forfeiture of 1982 Ford Mustang), 725 So. 2d 382,(Fla. 2d DCA 1998), 12-1:5

Walsh v. Bank of New York Mellon Trust, 219 So. 3d 929 (Fla. 5th DCA 2017), 13-4:1.2

Walter E. Heller & Co. Southeast, Inc. v. Williams, 450 So. 2d 521 (Fla. 3d DCA 1984), 6-3:9

Walton v. Walton, 181 So. 2d 715 (Fla. 2d DCA 1966), 1-3

WAMCO XXVIII, Ltd. v. Integrated Electronic Environments, Inc., 903 So. 2d 230 (Fla. 2d DCA 2005), 12-1:10.1.a, 13-3:1

Warfield v. Stewart, 434 Fed. Appx. 777 (11th Cir. 2011), 16-2:3

Washington Mutual Bank, F.A. v. Shelton, 892 So. 2d 547 (Fla. 2d DCA 2005), 7-3:4, 16-3:2

Waters v. Wilmington Trust, N.A., 268 So. 3d 722 (Fla. 4th DCA 2018), 6-3:1

Waverly at Las Olas Condo. Ass'n, Inc. v. Waverly Las Olas, LLC, 88 So. 2d 386 (2012), 16-3:6

Weisenberg v. Deutsche Bank Nat'l Trust Co., 89 So. 3d 1111 (Fla. 4th DCA 2012), 12-1:10.1.a

Weisser Realty Group, Inc. v. Porto Vita Prop. Owners Ass'n, Inc., 44 Fla. L. Weekly D1904 (Fla. 3d DCA July 24, 2019), 11-9:2

Wells Fargo Bank, N.A. v. Bilecki, 192 So. 3d 559 (Fla. 4th DCA 2016), 12-1:3, 12-1:5, 12-1:7

Wells Fargo Bank, N.A. v. Bohatka, 112 So. 3d 596 (Fla. 1st DCA 2013), 4-3

Wells Fargo Bank, N.A. v. Cook (Fla. 2d DCA 2019), No. 2D17-3913, 2019 Fla. App. LEXIS 11785, 2019 WL 3367299, 4-4, 4-7, 7-3:2, 13-4:3

Wells Fargo Bank N.A. v. Diz, 253 So. 3d 705 (Fla. 3d DCA 2018), 6-2:3

Wells Fargo Bank, N.A. v. Donaldson, 165 So. 3d 40 (Fla. 3d DCA 2015), 12-1:5

Wells Fargo Bank, N.A. v. Giesel, 155 So. 3d 411 (Fla. 1st DCA 2014), 5-9

Wells Fargo Bank, N.A. v. Lupica, 36 So. 3d 875 (Fla. 5th DCA 2010), 5-6, 14-3:8

Wells Fargo Bank, N.A. v. Morcom, 125 So. 3d 320 (Fla. 5th DCA 2013), 4-1, 4-4, 7-3:2, 9-4:4

Wells Fargo Bank, N.A. v. Russell, 194 So. 3d 1094 (Fla. 3d DCA 2016), 9-4:4

Wells Fargo Bank, N.A. v. Rutledge, 148 So. 3d 533 (Fla. 2d DCA 2014), 9-4:6, 14-3:7

Wells Fargo Bank, N.A. v. Rutledge, 230 So. 3d 550 (Fla. 2d DCA 2017), 9-3, 10-2:4

Wells Fargo Bank, N.A. v. Uribe, No. 2012-CA-5930, 2018 WL 1936303, (Fla. Cir. Ct. Orange 2018), 15-2:3

Wells Fargo Bank, N.A v. Uribe, 2018 WL 3635764 (Fla. Cir. Ct. July 24, 2018), 15-2:3

Wells Fargo Bank, N.A., As Trustee for Carrington Mortgage Loan Trust, Series 2006-RFC1, Asset Backed Passed Through Certificates v. Debesa, 2011 WL 8151877 (Fla. Cir. Ct. Miami-Dade 2011), 9-4:5

Wells Fargo Bank, NA v. BH-NV Invs. 1, LLC, 230 So. 3d 60 (Fla. 3d DCA 2017), 3-2:2.1

Wells Fargo Bank, NA v. Giglio, 123 So. 3d 60, 60-61 (Fla. 4th DCA 2013), 5-6, 14-3:8

Wells Fargo Bank, NA v. The Plaza Condo. Ass'n at Berkman Plaza, 2013 WL 12096560 (Fla. Cir. Ct. Duval Cnty. 2013), 9-4:1

Wells Fargo Bank v. Ousley, 201 So. 3d 1056 (Fla. 1st DCA 2016), 13-4:1

Wells Fargo Del. Tr. Co., N.A. for Vericrest Opportunity Loan Tr. 201-NPL1 v. Petrov, 230 So. 3d 575 (Fla. 2d DCA 2017), 6-2:2, 9-3, 10-2:4

Westburne Supply, Inc. v. Cmty. Villas Partners, Ltd., 508 So. 2d 431 (Fla. 1st DCA 1987), 10-1:1

Westbury Properties, Inc. v. Cardillo, 638 So. 2d 519 (Fla. 2d DCA 1994), 5-2:1.3

Westco, Inc. v. Scott Lewis' Gardening & Trimming, Inc., 26 So. 3d 620 (Fla. 4th DCA 2009), 11-8

601 West 26 Corp. v. Equity Capital Co., 178 So. 2d 894 (Fla. 3d DCA 1965), 9-4:4

West Edge II v. Kunderas, 910 So. 2d 953 (Fla. 2d DCA 2005), 12-1:3.2

West Fla. Cmty. Builders v. Mitchell, 528 So. 2d 979 (Fla. 1988), 12-1:3.1

Westinghouse Elevator Co. v. DFS Constr. Co., 438 So. 2d 125 (Fla. 2d DCA 1983), 14-3:4

Weston Orlando Park, Inc. v. Fairwinds Credit Union, 86 So. 3d 1186 (Fla. 5th DCA 2012), 5-6

Wharton v. Dubose, 458 So. 2d 411 (Fla. 4th DCA 1984), 14-2:1

Wheaton v. Wheaton, 261 So. 3d 1236 (Fla. 2019), 14-4, 15-4:2, 16-4:3

Whipple v. State, 431 So. 2d 1011 (Fla. 2d DCA 1983), 14-2:2

Whitburn, LLC v. Wells Fargo Bank, N.A., 190 So. 3d 1087 (Fla. 2d DCA 2015), 6-3:5, 10-1:1, 10-2:1, 10-2:2, 10-2:4, 12-1:10.1.h

Whitehurst v. Camp, 699 So. 2d 679 (Fla.1997), 5-6

White v. Fletcher, 90 So. 2d 129 (Fla. 1956), 12-1:4

White v. Mid-State Federal Savings & Loan Ass'n, 530 So. 2d 959 (Fla. 5th DCA 1988), 5-3

White v. Ocwen Loan Servicing, 159 So. 3d 1009 (Fla. 3d DCA 2015), 12-1:7

White v. Planet Home Lending, LLC, 234 So. 3d 802 (Fla. 4th DCA 2018), 8-4

Whitney Bank v. Grant, 223 So. 3d 476 (Fla. 1st DCA 2017), 19-4

Wiggins v. Portmay Corp., 430 So. 2d 541 (Fla. 1st DCA 1983), 8-1, 12-1:3.2

Wiley v. Roof, 641 So. 2d 66 (Fla. 1994), 3-2

Williams v. Bank of Am. Corp., 927 So. 2d 1091 (Fla. 4th DCA 2006), 12-1:4

Williams v. City of Lake City, 62 So. 2d 732 (Fla. 1953), 12-1:3

Williams v. Nuno, 239 So. 3d 153 (Fla. 3d DCA 2018), 1-3:2

Williams v. Oken, 62 So. 3d 1129 (Fla. 2011), 7-2:2

Williams v. Wells Fargo Bank, N.A., Inc., No. C 10-00399, 2010 U.S. Dist. LEXIS 36247, 2010 WL 1463521 (N.D. Cal. Apr. 13, 2010), 8-3

Willis v. Gami Golden Glades, LLC, 967 So. 2d 846 (Fla. 2007), 12-1:2

Willoughby Estates v. BankUnited, 2015 WL 5472506 (Fla. Cir. Ct. Palm Beach June 23, 2015), 9-2, 9-4:3

Wilmington Bank v. Garcia, 2015 WL 11022890 (Fla. Cir. Ct. Broward Nov. 20, 2015), 16-3:7

Wilmington Savings Fund Society, FSB v. Contreras, 278 So. 3d 744 (Fla. 5th DCA 2019), 44 Fla. L. Weekly D1925, 2019 Fla. App. LEXIS 11698, 2019 WL 3366143, 4-9, 6-4:4, 6-4:6, 7-2:1, 7-2:2, 7-3:6

Wilmington Savings Fund Society, FSB v. Louissaint, 212 So. 3d 473 (Fla. 5th DCA 2017), 4-8, 6-4:3

Wilmington Savings Society v. Steele, 2017 WL 2870985 (Fla. Cir. Ct.), 17-8

Wilmington Trust, N.A. v. Alvarez, 239 So. 3d 1265 (Fla. 3d DCA 2018), 9-3, 10-2:4

Wilmington Trust, Nat'l Ass'n v. Moon, 238 So. 3d 425 (Fla. 5th DCA 2018), 4-9, 6-3:1

Wilmington Trust Co. v. Hines, 2016 WL 3356996 (Fla. Cir. Ct. Bay Mar. 9, 2016), 16-3:7

Wilmott v. Equitable Building & Loan Ass'n., 44 Fla. 815, 33 So. 447 (1903), 1-11

Wilson v. Salamon, 923 So. 2d 363, 367 (Fla. 2006), 15-2:2

TABLE OF CASES 473

Winchel v. PennyMac Corp., 222 So. 3d 639 (Fla. 2d DCA 2017), 12-1:3.2

Windsor Falls Condominium Association, Inc. v. Davis, 265 So. 3d 709 (Fla. 1st DCA 2019), 16-3:6

Winston Park, Ltd. v. City of Coconut Creek, 872 So. 2d 415 (Fla. 4th DCA 2004), 12-1:3

Wisman v. Nationstar Mortg., LLC, 239 So. 3d 726 (Fla. 5th DCA 2017), 4-8

Withers v. Blomberg, 41 So. 3d 398 (Fla. 3d DCA 2010), 18-3

Witkowski v. Knight (In re Witkowski), 523 B.R. 291 (1st Cir. B.A.P. 2014), 17-3:3

WM Specialty Mortgage, LLC v. Salomon, 874 So. 2d 680 (Fla. 4th DCA 2004), 1-1:1, 4-2, 4-7, 7-3:2, 12-1:10.1.b

Wolfe v. Nazaire, 758 So. 2d 730 (Fla. 4th DCA 2000), 16-3:7

Wollman v. Levy, 489 So. 2d 1239 (Fla. 3d DCA 1986), 14-2:2, 14-4

Worley v. Sheffield, 538 So. 2d 91 (Fla. 1st DCA 1989), 12-1:4

Y

Yacenda Hudson & Amina McNeil & DItech Fin., LLC v. Marin, So. 3d 148 (Fla. 3d DCA 2018), 15-2:3

Yakowicz v. BAC Home Loans Servicing, LP, No. 12-1180, 2013 U.S. Dist. LEXIS 20586, 2013 WL 593902 (D. Minn. Feb. 15, 2013), 8-3

Yelen v. Bankers Trust Co., 476 So. 2d 767 (Fla. 3d DCA 1985), 2-1, 2-1:3.1

YEMC Const. & Dev., Inc. v. Inter Ser, U.S.A., Inc., 884 So. 2d 446 (Fla. 3d DCA 2004), 10-2:3

YHT & Assocs., Inc. v. Nationstar Mortg. LLC, 177 So. 3d 641 (Fla. 2d DCA 2015), 10-2:1, 10-2:4

Yisrael v. State, 993 So. 2d 952 (Fla. 2008), 12-1:10.1.a

Young v. Taubman, 855 So. 2d 184 (Fla. 4th DCA 2003), 16-3:5

Yoxsimer v. Yoxsimer, 918 So. 2d 997 (Fla. 2d DCA 2006), 14-3:7

Z

Zanathy v. Beach Harbor Club Ass'n, Inc., 343 So. 2d 625 (Fla. 2d DCA 1977), 12-1:9

Zieman v. Cosio, 578 So. 2d 332 (Fla. 3d DCA 1991), 19-2:1

Zimmerman v. Hill, 100 So. 2d 432 (Fla. 3d DCA 1958), 10-2:4

Zimmerman v. Olympus Fidelity Trust, LLC, 936 So. 2d 652 (Fla. 4th DCA 2006), 1-10:3

Zito v. Washington Federal Sav. & Loan Assoc., 318 So. 2d 175 (Fla. 3rd DCA 1975), 12-1:3.2

Zlinkoff v. Von Aldenbruck, 765 So. 2d 840 (Fla. 4th DCA 2000), 3-3:2.3

Zoda v. Hedden, 596 So. 2d 1225 (Fla. 2d DCA 1992), 12-1:5

Index

A

ACCELERATION CLAUSES, 2-3. *See also* **STATUTES OF LIMITATION**
- automatic *vs.* optional, 2-3:2
- contractual nature of, 2-3:1
- post-acceleration foreclosure/dismissal/new foreclosure, 2-3:5
  - res judicata, 2-3:5.1
  - statute of limitations, 2-3:5.3
  - two-dismissal rule, 2-3:5.2
- pre-acceleration payments, effects of, 2-3:3
- standard residential mortgage, 2-3:4

ACCRUAL, STATUTE OF LIMITATIONS, 3-2:1
- acceleration theory of accrual, 3-2:1.2
- default theory of accrual, 3-2:1.1
  - continuing state of default, 3-2:1.1c
  - effect of conditions precedent on accrual, 3-2:1.1a
  - successive accruals, 3-2:1.1b
- examples, 3-2:1.3
  - bankruptcy discharge, 3-2:1.3d
  - lacking payment date but maturity date specified, 3-2:1.3b
  - lacking payment/maturity dates, 3-2:1.3a
  - lender's demand, 3-2:1.3c

APPEALS
- attorneys' fees on appeal, 18-8
- error preservation, 18-3
- final appeal, 18-4:1
  - record on, 18-4:1.1
  - supplementation of record, 18-4:1.2
  - timing of briefs, 18-4:1.3
- generally, 18-1
- initiating, 18-2
- interlocutory appeals and writs, 18-4:3
  - certiorari, 18-4:3.1
  - mandamus, 18-4:3.2
  - prohibition, 18-4:3.3
- non-final appeals, 18-4:2
  - record on, 18-4:2.1
  - timing of briefs, 18-4:2.2
- oral argument, 18-7
- rehearing and clarification, 18-9
- standards of review, 18-6
  - abuse of discretion, 18-6:2
  - competent, substantial evidence, 18-6:3
  - de novo, 18-6:1
- stay of action pending appeal, 18-5
- Supreme Court jurisdiction, 18-10
- types of, 18-4

ATTORNEY'S FEES IN FORECLOSURE ACTIONS
- attorney's fees as a sanction, 16-4
  - attorney's fees for raising unsupported claim, 16-4:2
  - court's authority to assess, 16-4:1
  - procedure to obtain attorney's fees, 16-4:3
- introduction, 16-1
  - "American Rule" on Attorney's Fees, 16-1:1
- note and mortgage contracts, 16-2
  - no contract, no fees, 16-2:3
  - note and mortgage control, 16-2:1
  - reciprocal provisions of Fla. Stat. § 57.105(7), 16-2:2
- offers of judgment, 16-5
  - demand for judgment—Fla. Stat. § 768.79, 16-5:1
  - procedural rule governing offers of judgment—Rule 1.442, 16-5:2
- procedures to recover, 16-3
  - burden of proof and evidence required, 16-3:4
  - contingency fee multipliers, 16-3:7
  - fees to determine party's entitlement, 16-3:6
  - must prove fees, 16-3:5
  - pleading requirement, 16-3:1
  - prevailing party, 16-3:2
  - recovery incurred in bankruptcy, 16-3:8
  - recovery on appeal, 16-3:9
  - time for filing of motion, 16-3:3
- wrongful act doctrine, 16-6
  - doctrine, 16-6:1

B

BANKRUPTCY
- automatic stay, 17-3
  - effect of, 17-3:1
  - repeat filers, 17-3:3
  - termination of, 17-3:2
  - violations of, 17-4
- discharge and dischargeability, 17-7
- dismissal, 17-9
- generally, under Chapters, 7, 11, and 13, 17-1
- mortgagee's interest in proceedings, 17-2
- proofs of claim, 17-5
- statement of intentions and surrender, 17-8
- strip offs and strip downs, 17-6

BANKRUPTCY (*cont.*)
    matter of equity, 17-6:1
    principal residences, 17-6:2
BREACH OF CONTRACT, 13-4:2. *See also* ACCELERATION CLAUSES; DEFAULTS, ON COMPLAINTS
BURDEN OF PROOF, 13-5

C

CERTIORARI REVIEW, IN DISCOVERY OF PRIVILEGED INFORMATION, 11-8
CLERICAL ERRORS, RULE 1.540(a) TO CORRECT, 14-3:9
COMPLAINTS (FORECLOSURE)
    appropriate venue and forum for action, 6-1:3
    causes of action and allegations, 6-4
        agreement between the parties, 6-4:2
        amount due to plaintiff resulting from borrower's default, 6-4:8
        attorney's fees, 6-4:9
        borrower's default, 6-4:7
        claim against a guarantor, 6-5:1
        claim for mortgage foreclosure, 6-4:1
        equitable subrogation and equitable liens, 6-5:4
        injunctive relief and assignments of rent riders, 6-5:6
        plaintiff's capacity to sue, 6-4:4
        plaintiff's standing, 6-4:3
        plea for deficiency judgment, 6-5:7
        reestablishment: when the note has been lost, 6-5:2
        reformation: when the mortgage or deed contains mistake, 6-5:3
        satisfaction of conditions precedent, 6-4:6
        seeking show cause order under Section 702.10, 6-5:5
        superiority of plaintiff's interest to other defendants, 6-4:5
    commencement of foreclosure action, 6-1:1
    filing and recording of lis pendens, 6-1:4
    form of complaint, 6-2
        attachments to complaint, 6-2:4
        caption, 6-2:1
        certification of possession of promissory note, 6-2:3
        electronic filing required, 6-2:6
        minimizing filing of sensitive information in exhibits, 6-2:5
        verification, 6-2:2
    parties, 6-3
        borrowers, 6-3:3
        condominiums and homeowners' associations, 6-3:8
        defendants, 6-3:2
        junior lienholders, 6-3:4
        lessees in possession, 6-3:7
        municipal, state, and federal lienholders, 6-3:9
        owners of property, 6-3:5
        plaintiff, 6-3:1
        tenants by entirety, 6-3:6
    responses to. *See* **RESPONSES TO COMPLAINTS**
    review of title, 6-1:2
CONDITIONS PRECEDENT (FLA. R. CIV. P. 1.120(C))
    failure of, as affirmative defense, 7-3:3
    proof of elements at trial, 13-4:3

D

DEFAULTS, ON COMPLAINTS
    acceleration, 2-3
        automatic *vs.* optional, 2-3:2
        contractual nature of, 2-3:1
        post-acceleration foreclosure/dismissal/new foreclosure, 2-3:5
            res judicata, 2-3:5.1
            statute of limitations, 2-3:5.3
            two-dismissal rule, 2-3:5.2
        pre-acceleration payments, effects of, 2-3:3
        standard residential mortgage, 2-3:4
    default judgments, 1-4:3
    defined, 2-1, 2-1:1
    generally, 1-4
        by clerks, 1-4:1
        by judges, 1-4:2
    grace periods, 2-1:4
    monetary, 2-1:2
    non-monetary, 2-1:3
        by act or omission, 2-1:3.1
        due to existence of condition, 2-1:3.2
    notice of, 2-2
        compliant, example of, 2-2:3.1
        as condition precedent, 2-2:2
        face-to-face interview requirement in FHA mortgage, 2-2:6
        as matter of contract, 2-2:1
        non-compliant, example of, 2-2:3.2
        in standard residential mortgage, 2-2:3
    opportunity to cure
        as matter of contract, 2-2:4
        in standard residential mortgage, 2-2:5
    vacating default, 1-4:4
        due diligence, 1-4:4.3
        excusable neglect, 1-4:4.1
        meritorious defenses, 1-4:4.2
DEFENSES, TO FORECLOSURES
    affirmative defenses, 7-3
        failure of conditions precedent (Fla. R. Civ. P. 1.120(c)), 7-3:3
        lack of standing, 7-3:2
        motions to strike, 7-3:7
        payments, 7-3:4
        waiver, 7-3:5
    other defenses, 7-3:6
    statutory defenses, 8-1
        FCCPA, 8-5
        FDUTPA, 8-6

INDEX

FHA Home Loan Defenses, 8-4
  HUD Counseling, 8-4:1
RESPA, 8-3
  claims, 8-3:1
TILA, 8-2
  damages, 8-2:3
  HOEPA, 8-2:1
  rescission, 8-2:2

DEFICIENCY JUDGMENTS
calculation of deficiency amount, 19-3
  burden of proof, 19-3:1
  defenses, 19-3:4
  judge's discretion, 19-3:2
  timing of appraisals, 19-3:3
generally (Fla. Stat. § 702.06), 19-1
jurisdiction, 19-2
  in personam, 19-2:1
  recover deficiency, 19-2:3
  rights of assignees, 19-2:2
statute of limitations, 19-4
unavailability of deficiency judgements, 19-5
  waiver of deficiency–settlement, 19-5:1

DEPOSITIONS, 11-6
defending deposition of party-deponent, 11-6:3
preparing deponent for, 11-6:1
  non-party deponent, 11-6:1.2
  party deponent, 11-6:1.1
taking, 11-6:2

DISCOVERY, IN FORECLOSURE
certiorari review, 11-8
continuances/pending discovery issues, in summary judgments, 12-1:8
depositions, 11-6
  defending deposition of party-deponent, 11-6:3
  preparing deponent for, 11-6:1
    non-party deponent, 11-6:1.2
    party deponent, 11-6:1.1
  taking, 11-6:2
generally, 1-6, 11-1
interrogatories, 11-5
  propounding, 11-5:1
  responding to, 11-5:2
    answering, as individual *vs.* corporation, 11-5:2.2
    objections, 11-5:2.1
    option to produce records, 11-5:2.3
judicial resolution, 11-7
  failure to produce discovery; sanctions, 11-7:3
  motions for protective orders, 11-7:2
  motions to compel, 11-7:1
methods, 11-2
RFAs, 11-4
  propounding, 11-4:1
  responding to, 11-4:2
    admitting, 11-4:2.2
    denying, 11-4:2.3
    objections, 11-4:2.1

RTPs, 11-3
  inadvertent production of privileged materials, 11-3:3
  no duty to supplement responses, 11-3:4
  propounding, 11-3:1
  responding to, 11-3:2
    objections, 11-3:2.1
    production, 11-3:2.2
unique considerations for foreclosures, 11-9
  discovery and final judgment, 11-9:2
  foreclosure plaintiff's witness, 11-9:3
  local rules, 11-9:1

DISCOVERY/CONTINUANCE, IN SUMMARY JUDGMENTS (FLA. R. CIV. P. 1.510(F)), 12-1:8

E

EVIDENCE, IN FORECLOSURE TRIALS
"newly discovered evidence" (Fla. R. Civ. P. 1.540(b)(2)), 14-3:5

EVIDENCE, IN SUMMARY JUDGMENTS, 12-1:5
identification in motion, 12-1:4.1
partial summary judgment, 12-1:6
timing of service, 12-1:7

EXCUSABLE NEGLECT (FLA. R. CIV. P. 1.540(B)(1)), 14-3:4

F

FCCPA (FLORIDA CONSUMER COLLECTION PRACTICES ACT), 7-3:6, 8-5

FDCPA (FAIR DEBT COLLECTION PRACTICES ACT OF 1977), 7-3:6

FDUTPA (FLORIDA DECEPTIVE AND UNFAIR TRADE PRACTICES ACT), 8-6

FHA (Federal Housing Administration) Home Loan Defenses, 8-4
HUD Counseling, 8-4:1

FORECLOSURE CLAIMS, 12-1:10.1
amounts due and owing, 12-1:10.1g
business records, 12-1:10.1a
conditions precedent, 12-1:10.1e
default, 12-1:10.1d
loan agreement, 12-1:10.1c
non-borrower defendants' affirmative defenses, 12-1:10.1h
pre-acceleration default notice, 12-1:10.1f
standing, 12-1:10.1b

FORECLOSURE LAWSUITS, SUMMARY JUDGMENT IN, 12-1:10

FORECLOSURE TRIALS
burden of proof, 13-5
generally, 1-8, 13-1
motions for involuntary dismissal, 13-6
proof of elements, 13-4
  breach of contract, 13-4:2
  conditions precedent, 13-4:3

FORECLOSURE TRIALS (*cont.*)
   contract: mortgage and note, 13-4:1
      lost note, 13-4:1.1
      right to enforce contract, 13-4:1.2
   damages, 13-4:4
   setting trials, Rule 1.440, 13-2
      readiness for trial, 13-2:1
      timing and notice requirements, 13-2:2
   witnesses, 13-3
      expert witnesses (Fla. E.C. § 90.702), 13-3:2
      fact witnesses, 13-3:1
      subpoenas for testimony, 13-3:3
FRAUD ALLEGATIONS (FLA. R. CIV. P. 1.540(B)(3)), 14-3:6

H

HOEPA (HOME OWNERSHIP AND EQUITY PROTECTION ACT OF 1994), 8-2:1
HUD (Housing and Urban Development), 8-4:1

I

INTERROGATORIES, 11-5
   propounding, 11-5:1
   responding to, 11-5:2
      answering, as individual *vs.* corporation, 11-5:2.2
      objections, 11-5:2.1
      option to produce records, 11-5:2.3

J

JUDICIAL RESOLUTION, OF DISCOVERY DISPUTES, 11-7
   failure to produce discovery; sanctions, 11-7:3
   motions for protective orders, 11-7:2
   motions to compel, 11-7:1

L

LACHES, 3-4
LITIGATING WITH ASSOCIATIONS IN THE FORECLOSURE CONTEXT
   during foreclosure, 9-3
   introduction, 9-1
   post-foreclosure, 9-4
      anatomy of estoppel dispute, 9-4:1
      declaration trumps the safe harbor statute, 9-4:3
      foreclosing first mortgagees get safe harbor from associations that are properly named in the foreclosure as defendants, 9-4:2
      remedies where association denies safe harbor or otherwise demands improper amounts, 9-4:5
      Rule 1.540(b)(4) in the context of association litigation, 9-4:6
      various arguments put forth by associations seeking to deny safe harbor, 9-4:4
   pre-foreclosure, 9-2
LITIGATING WITH OTHER INTERESTS IN THE FORECLOSURE CONTEXT
   governmental entities, 10-4
      internal revenue service, 10-4:2
      local government liens, 10-4:1
   necessary and indispensable parties, 10-1
      lis pendens, 10-1:1
   tenants, 10-3
      lessee pendente lite, 10-3:2
      tenancies established prior to foreclosure, 10-3:1
      writ of possession, 10-3:3
   third-party purchasers, 10-2
      interest subordinate to prior mortgage and lis pendens, 10-2:1
      intervention, 10-2:2
      right of redemption, 10-2:3
      standing to raise defenses/otherwise participate, 10-2:4

M

MODIFICATION OF LOAN, POST-JUDGMENT (FLA. R. CIV. P. 1.540(B)(5)), 14-3:8
MORTGAGE FORECLOSURES, 1-1. *See also* **MOTIONS/PLEADING PRACTICE**
   complaints. *See* **COMPLAINTS (FORECLOSURE)**
   defaults, 1-4
      by clerks, 1-4:1
      default judgments, 1-4:3
      defined, 2-1, 2-1:1
      by judges, 1-4:2
      monetary, 2-1:2
      non-monetary, 2-1:3
      vacating default, 1-4:4
   discovery, 1-6
   elements of, 1-1:1
   final judgment, 1-9
   foreclosure action, initiation of, 1-2
   sale, 1-10. *See also* **DEFICIENCY JUDGMENTS**
      auction/bidding, 1-10:4
      objections to, 1-10:5
      publication of scheduled, 1-10:2
      redemption/reinstatement, 1-10:3
      scheduling sale, 1-10:1
   service of process, 1-3
      methods of service, 1-3:1
      motions to quash, 1-3:2
   summary judgment, 1-7. *See also* **SUMMARY JUDGMENT MOTIONS**
   title and possession, 1-11
   title reports/junior liens, 1-1:2
   trial, 1-8

INDEX

MOTIONS/PLEADING PRACTICE. *See also* **POST-JUDGMENT MOTION PRACTICE; SUMMARY JUDGMENT MOTIONS**
affirmative defenses, 7-3
  failure of conditions precedent (Fla. R. Civ. P. 1.120(c)), 7-3:3
  lack of standing, 7-3:2
  motions to strike, 7-3:7
  related to payment, 7-3:4
  waiver, 7-3:5
default, responding to, 1-5. *See also* **RESPONSES TO COMPLAINTS**
estoppel, 7-3:6
generally, 7-1:1
judicial resolution, of discovery disputes
  motions for protective orders, 11-7:2
  motions to compel, 11-7:1
motions to dismiss, 7-2
  common grounds for, 7-2:2
  introduction, 7-2:1
to quash service of process, 1-3:2
unclean hands, 7-3:6

N

NOTICE OF DEFAULT
failure of conditions precedent (Fla. R. Civ. P. 1.120(c)), 7-3:3

P

PAYMENTS, DEFENSES RELATED TO, 7-3:4
POST-JUDGMENT MOTION PRACTICE
claims for surplus funds (Fla. Stat. § 45.031), 14-5
generally, Fla. R. Civ. P. 1.530 and 1.540, 14-1
objections to sale, 14-4
Rule 1.540, relief from judgment, decrees, or orders, 14-3
  appellate considerations (Fla. R. Civ. P. 1.540(b)(4)), 14-3:1
  evidentiary hearing, 14-3:2
  one-year limitation (Fla. R. Civ. P. 1.540(b)(1)-(3)), 14-3:3
  procedure (Fla. R. Civ. P. 1.540(b)(1)), 14-3:4
  procedure (Fla. R. Civ. P. 1.540(b)(2)), 14-3:5
  procedure (Fla. R. Civ. P. 1.540(b)(3)), 14-3:6
  procedure (Fla. R. Civ. P. 1.540(b)(4)), 14-3:7
  procedure (Fla. R. Civ. P. 1.540(b)(5)), 14-3:8
  Rule 1.540(a) to correct clerical errors, 14-3:9
Rule 1.530, motions for new trial/rehearing, 14-2
  appellate considerations (Fla. R. App. P. 9.020(i)), 14-2:1
  general considerations, 14-2:2
PROOF OF ELEMENTS AT TRAIL, 13-4
breach of contract, 13-4:2
conditions precedent, 13-4:3
contract: mortgage and note, 13-4:1
  lost note, 13-4:1.1
  right to enforce contract, 13-4:1.2
damages, 13-4:4

R

RESPA (REAL ESTATE PRACTICES ACT OF 1974), 7-3:6, 8-3
claims, 8-3:1
RESPONSES TO COMPLAINTS
affirmative defenses, 7-3
  failure of conditions precedent (Fla. R. Civ. P. 1.120(c)), 7-3:3
  lack of standing, 7-3:2
  payments, 7-3:4
motions and pleadings, generally, 1-5, 7-1:1
motions to dismiss, 7-2
  common grounds for, 7-2:2
  introduction, 7-2:1
motions to strike affirmative defenses, 7-3:7
other defenses, 7-3:6
RFAs (REQUESTS FOR ADMISSION), 11-4
propounding, 11-4:1
responding to, 11-4:2
  admitting, 11-4:2.2
  denying, 11-4:2.3
  objections, 11-4:2.1
RTPs (REQUESTS TO PRODUCE), 11-3
inadvertent production of privileged materials, 11-3:3
no duty to supplement responses, 11-3:4
propounding, 11-3:1
responding to, 11-3:2
  objections, 11-3:2.1
  production, 11-3:2.2

S

SALE, IN FORECLOSURE, 1-10. *See also* **DEFICIENCY JUDGMENTS**
auction/bidding, 1-10:4
objections to, 1-10:5
publication of scheduled, 1-10:2
redemption/reinstatement, 1-10:3
scheduling sale, 1-10:1
title/possession following sale, 1-11
SANCTIONS
court's inherent authority, 15-2
  contempt *vs.* sanctions, 15-2:2
  limitations, 15-2:3
generally, 15-1
pursuant to rule (Fla. R. Civ. P. 1.380), 15-3
  discovery violations, 15-3:2
  generally, 15-3:1
  limitations on sanctions for discovery violations, 15-3:3
statutes, 15-4
  frivolous claims/defenses (Fla. Stat. § 57.105), 15-4:1
  safe harbor provision (Fla. Stat. § 57.105(4)), 15-4:2
SERVICE OF PROCESS, 1-3
methods of service, 1-3:1
motions to quash, 1-3:2
timing, 12-1:7

STANDING TO FORECLOSE
   additional evidence of, 13-4:1.3
   constructive possession of note, 4-6
   foreclose line of credit, 4-10
   lack of, as affirmative defense, 7-3:2
   overview, 4-1
   prima facie evidence, 4-5
   promissory notes, allonges to, 4-3
   right to enforce contract, 13-4:1.2
   standing as non-holder in possession, 4-7
   standing through indorsement, 4-4
   standing to enforce lost note, 4-8
   substitution of plaintiff, 4-9
   surrender of original note, 4-2

STATUTES OF LIMITATION, 3-2
   acceleration, effect of, 2-3:5.3
   accrual, 3-2:1
     acceleration theory of accrual, 3-2:1.2
     default theory of accrual, 3-2:1.1
       continuing state of default, 3-2:1.1c
       effect of conditions precedent on accrual, 3-2:1.1a
       successive accruals, 3-2:1.1b
     examples, 3-2:1.3
       bankruptcy discharge, 3-2:1.3d
       lacking payment date but maturity date specified, 3-2:1.3b
       lacking payment/maturity dates, 3-2:1.3a
       lender's demand, 3-2:1.3c
   deficiency actions, 3-2:7
   recoupment, counterclaim in, 3-2:6
   relation back doctrine, 3-2:3.4
   repose *vs.*, 3-1
     comparison table, 3-1:3
     statute of limitations, generally, 3-1:1
     statute of repose, generally, 3-1:2
   successive foreclosures, 3-2:2
     Bartram v. U.S. Bank, N.A., 3-2:2.1
   time bar on debt, effect of, 3-2:3
     on foreclosure of standard residential mortgage, 3-2:3.2
     on no separate obligation to pay full debt, 3-2:3.3
     on past due installment payments, 3-2:3.1
   tolling, 3-2:5
     equitable estoppel, 3-2:5.3
     equitable tolling, 3-2:5.2
     statutory tolling, 3-2:5.1

STATUTES OF REPOSE, 3-3
   limitations *vs.*, 3-1
     comparison table, 3-1:3
     statute of limitations, generally, 3-1:1
     statute of repose, generally, 3-1:2
   mortgage liens, effect on, 3-3:1
   time periods, 3-3:2
     extension agreements, 3-3:2.3
     five years after maturity, 3-3:2.1
     no tolling, 3-3:2.5
     for railroads/public utilities/construction liens, 3-3:2.6
     repose *vs.* limitations, 3-3:2.4
     obligations paid by mortgagee, 3-3:2.4b
     savings clause for mortgages with no ascertainable maturity, 3-3:2.4a
     twenty years post-maturity date, 3-3:2.2

SUMMARY JUDGMENT MOTIONS
   burden of proof, 12-1:3
     motions before answer is filed, 12-1:3.1
     as plaintiff facing affirmative defenses, 12-1:3.2
   continuances/pending discovery issues (Fla. R. Civ. P. 1.510(f)), 12-1:8
   foreclosure claims, 12-1:10.1
     amounts due and owing, 12-1:10.1g
     business records, 12-1:10.1a
     conditions precedent, 12-1:10.1e
     default, 12-1:10.1d
     loan agreement, 12-1:10.1c
     non-borrower defendants' affirmative defenses, 12-1:10.1h
     pre-acceleration default notice, 12-1:10.1f
     standing, 12-1:10.1b
   foreclosure lawsuits, 12-1:10
   generally, 1-7, 12-1
     legal standard, 12-1:2
     overview, in Florida, 12-1:1
   motion
     contents of, 12-1:4
     evidence forms, 12-1:5
     identification of evidence in, 12-1:4.1
   partial summary judgment, 12-1:6
   pending counterclaims, 12-1:9

T

TILA (TRUTH IN LENDING ACT OF 1968), 7-3:6, 8-2
   damages, 8-2:3
   HOEPA, 8-2:1
   rescission, 8-2:2

TITLE/POSSESSION FOLLOWING SALE, 1-11

TITLE TRANSFER. *See* **TYPICAL TITLE TRANSFERS IN FORECLOSURE LITIGATION**

TYPICAL TITLE TRANSFERS IN FORECLOSURE LITIGATION, 5-2
   certificate of title following a foreclosure sale, 5-2:1
     deeds in lieu of foreclosure, 5-2:1.2
     merger of lien and title, 5-2:1.3
     void *versus* voidable certificates of title, 5-2:1.1
   final judgment and merger, 5-6
   jurisdiction and necessary parties, 5-3
   lis pendens tool, 5-5
   overview, 5-1
   priority of interests and Florida's Recording Act, 5-4
     equitable subrogation, 5-4:2
       prejudice to prior lienholder, 5-4:2.1
     recording errors and notice, 5-4:1

INDEX

reforeclosure, 5-8
reformation, 5-9
risks for purchasers at foreclosure sales, 5-7
short-sales and short-payoffs, 5-2:2

V

VOIDABLE JUDGMENT (FLA. R. CIV. P. 1.540(B)(4)), 14-3:7

W

WAIVERS, AS DEFENSE TO FORECLOSURE, 7-3:5
WITNESSES, IN FORECLOSURE TRIALS, 13-3
expert witnesses (Fla. E.C. § 90.702), 13-3:2
fact witnesses, 13-3:1
subpoenas for testimony, 13-3:3